MEDIUM ÆVUM MONOGRAPHS

MEDIUM ÆVUM
MONOGRAPHS XLIV

RUSHWORTH ONE

AN EDITION OF FARMAN'S OLD ENGLISH INTERLINEAR GLOSS TO THE RUSHWORTH GOSPELS (OXFORD, BODLEIAN LIBRARY, MS AUCT. D. 2.19)

EDITED BY
TADASHI KOTAKE

THE SOCIETY FOR THE STUDY OF MEDIEVAL LANGUAGES AND LITERATURE

OXFORD · MMXXIII

The Society for the Study of Medieval Languages and Literature
Oxford, 2023

http://aevum.space/monographs

ISBN:
978-1-911694-15-1 (pb)
978-1-911694-16-8 (hb)
978-1-911694-17-5 (pdf)

British Library Cataloguing in Publication Data
A catalogue record for this book is available
from the British Library

In memoriam
Shoichi Oguro

CONTENTS

ACKNOWLEDGEMENTS

The core of this book began as my PhD thesis submitted to Keio University. I would like to express my sincere thanks to John Scahill, my supervisor, not only for his guidance during my days at Keio but for his continuing friendship and advice even after he left the university.

I was fortunate to have had the opportunity of studying at King's College London as an exchange student from Keio under the supervision of David Ganz, who introduced me to the depth of palaeographical studies and encouraged me to examine the Rushworth Gospels at the Bodleian Library. It was still the days when we read manuscripts in Duke Humfrey's Library and I remember the excitement of finding all those minute things lost in black and white reproduction, an experience that became the springboard for this project. I am thankful to the Bodleian Library and especially Martin Kauffmann for sustained support and understanding ever since the first time I used the manuscript.

The bulk of the edition was prepared during my postdoctoral research fellowship at the Institute of English Studies, School of Advanced Study, University of London, whose welcoming atmosphere fostered academic exchanges that have meant a lot to me. I am grateful to the Institute and the then Director Warwick Gould. I should also like to thank Pamela Robinson for her suggestion of adopting a desk-less visiting fellow into the office she shares in the Institute. It was immensely valuable to have an anchor point in Senate House from which I could simply go upstairs to the Palaeography Room in the library. The stays were made possible by two successive grants by the Japan Society for the Promotion of Science, for which I express my sincere gratitude.

I met lots of friends and colleagues in the UK. My thanks go especially to, and purely in alphabetical order, Stewart Brookes, Michelle Brown, Julia Crick, Elizabeth Danbury, Richard Dance, Carol Farr and Sara Pons-Sanz. In Japan, I am indebted to Michiko Ogura for her unfailing help in the early years of my research career. I would also like to thank Taro Ishiguro, Kousuke Kaita and Tomonori Yamamoto for their help and friendship. I am immensely grateful to Nicholas Sparks, my good friend, for his encouragement and friendship; his acute interest in related topics never ceases to inspire me. This book could not have completed without the constant encouragement of Jane Roberts, who read my notes and drafts at various points of preparation of the monograph and who became my advisor once the proposal was accepted by the Society for the

Study of Medieval Languages and Literature. To the external reader I owe thanks for helpful comments and suggestions; and I am deeply grateful to the Society, especially Stephen Pink and Anthony Lappin, for their patience and assistance.

I am very much indebted to my parents for their support. My thanks also go to the Shaddad family, with whom I lodged in London for many years. Last but not least, I must thank Misato, my wife, for all her support and encouragement.

ABBREVIATIONS

BT	Joseph Bosworth and T. N. Toller, *An Anglo-Saxon Dictionary* (Oxford: Oxford University Press, 1898)
BTS	T. N. Toller, *An Anglo-Saxon Dictionary: Supplement* (Oxford: Oxford University Press, 1921)
Campbell *Addenda*	A. Campbell, *An Anglo-Saxon Dictionary: Enlarged Addenda and Corrigenda* (Oxford: Clarendon Press, 1972)
Campbell OEG	A. Campbell, *Old English Grammar* (Oxford: Clarendon Press, 1959; repr. with corrections, 1968)
CH	J. R. Clark Hall, *A Concise Anglo-Saxon Dictionary*, 4th edn with a Supplement by Herbert D. Meritt (Toronto, University of Toronto Press, 1960)
Cod. Lind.	Kendrick, T. D., T. J. Brown, R.L.S. Bruce-Mitford, H. Roosen-Runge, A. S. C. Ross, E. G. Stanley, and A. E. A. Werner. *Evangelium Quattuor Codex Lindisfarnensis*, 2 vols (Olten and Lausanne: Urs Graf, 1956–60)
DOE	*Dictionary of Old English: A to I online*, ed. by Angus Cameron, Ashley Crandell Amos, Antonette diPaolo Healey *et al.* (Toronto: Dictionary of Old English Project, 2018)
DOE Corpus	*Dictionary of Old English Web Corpus*, compiled by Antonette diPaolo Healey with John Price Wilkin and Xin Xiang (Toronto: Dictionary of Old English Project 2009)
Holthausen	F. Holthausen, *Altenglisches etymologisches Wörterbuch* (Heidelberg: C. Winter, 1934)
Itala	Adolf Jülicher, Walter Matzkow, and Kurt Aland. (eds) *Itala: Das Neue Testament in altlateinische Überlieferung*, 1. Matthäus-Evangelium, 2nd edn (Berlin: De Gruyter, 1972)

Li	Aldred's gloss to the Lindisfarne Gospels
McAllister	Douglas H. McAllister, 'An Edition of the "Mercian" Portions of the Rushworth Manuscript' (Unpublished B.Litt. thesis, University of Oxford, 1952)
MED	*Middle English Dictionary*. Ed. Robert E. Lewis, et al. Ann Arbor: University of Michigan Press, 1952–2001. Online edition in Middle English Compendium. Ed. Frances McSparran, *et al.* Ann Arbor: University of Michigan Library, 2000–2018.
Mitchell OES	Bruce Mitchell, *Old English Syntax*, 2 vols (Oxford: Clarendon Press, 1985)
OED2/3	*OED Online* (Oxford: Oxford University Press)
R	The Latin text of the Rushworth Gospels
Ru1	Rushworth One, i.e., Farman's gloss to the Rushworth Gospels
Ru2	Rushworth Two, i.e., Owun's gloss to the Rushworth Gospels
Schulte	Ernst Schulte, *Glossar zu Farmans Anteil an der Rushworth-Glosse (Rushworth I)* (Bonn: Carl Georgi, 1904)
Skeat	Walter W. Skeat, (ed.) *The Holy Gospels in Anglo-Saxon, Northumbrian, and Old Mercian Versions* (Cambridge: The University Press, 1871–87; see the bibliography for full bibliographical information)
Tamoto	Kenichi Tamoto, *The Macregol Gospels or The Rushworth Gospels: Edition of the Latin text with the Old English Interlinear Gloss Transcribed from Oxford Bodleian Library, MS Auctarium D. 2. 19* (Amsterdam: John Benjamins, 2013)
TOE	*A Thesaurus of Old English* (Glasgow: University of Glasgow, 2017; http://oldenglishthesaurus.arts.gla.ac.uk/)
WSCp	The West Saxon Gospels based on Cambridge, Corpus Christi College 140 (Citations from WSCp are taken from Skeat)

WW John Wordsworth and H. I. White. (eds) *Nouum testamentum domini nostri Iesu Christi Latine: secundum editionem Sancti Hieronymi. Pars Prior: Quattuor Euangelia* (Oxford: Clarendon Press, 1889–98)

Xz R. Weber, R. Gryson et al. (eds) *Biblia Sacra iuxta Vulgatam versionem*, 5th edn (Stuttgart: Deutsche Bibelgesellschaft, 2007)

Y The Latin text of the Lindisfarne Gospels

INTRODUCTION

I. General introduction

1. The editorial history of the Old English glosses in the Rushworth Gospels

The Old English glosses to the Rushworth Gospels have been edited in their entirety three times in modern scholarship, apart from a partial edition in an unpublished thesis and some excerpts included in other publications.[1] Being one of the two manuscripts containing continuous Old English glosses to the Gospels, the Rushworth glosses were first edited in relation to those in the other, the Lindisfarne Gospels (London, British Library, Cotton MS Nero D. iv). This is obvious from the titles of the two nineteenth-century editions: the earlier, published in four volumes as part of the publications of the Surtees Society (Stevenson and Waring 1854–65), has the simple title *The Lindisfarne and Rushworth Gospels: Now First Printed from the Original Manuscripts in the British Museum and the Bodleian Library*; a more extensive scope is indicated by the title of the Cambridge edition, originally planned by John M. Kemble and completed by Walter W. Skeat (1871–87), *The Holy Gospels in Anglo-Saxon, Northumbrian, and Old Mercian Versions, Synoptically Arranged, with Collations Exhibiting All the Readings of All the MSS.; together with the Early Latin Version as Contained in the Lindisfarne MS., Collated with the Latin Version in the Rushworth MS.*[2] It was not until Kenichi Tamoto published *The Macregol Gospels or The Rushworth Gospels: Edition of the Latin Text with the Old English Interlinear Gloss Transcribed from Oxford Bodleian Library, MS Auctarium D. 2. 19* in 2013 that the Rushworth Gospels became the central text in an edition.

1 An unpublished Oxford B.Litt. thesis by Douglas H. McAllister (1952) presents an edition of Ru1, along with detailed introductory materials, commentary and a glossary. Bouterwek (1858: 31–65) edited Mark alone from the Rushworth Gospels in a supplementary volume to his edition of the Lindisfarne Gospels (Bouterwek 1857), printing the Rushworth gloss interlinearly with its own Latin text. Hoad (1978: 142–71) anthologizes Matthew Chapters 6–8, with the Rushworth Latin reduced to textual variants to the Lindisfarne Gospels.

2 The circumstances concerning the early phase of the publication are stated by Charles Hardwick in the original edition of Matthew published in 1858 (reprinted in full in the preface to Skeat's new edition of Matthew in 1887). See also Wiley (1979: 250–51).

Despite the attention paid to the Rushworth manuscript and its Old English glosses, their editorial history is not a happy one. The two nineteenth-century editions print the Rushworth glosses at the bottom of the pages containing the Lindisfarne Latin and glosses. The Latin text of the Rushworth manuscript was omitted from the text pages. Skeat, as shown in his title, collated it with that of the Lindisfarne Gospels, but the presentation of the results in the form of appendices at the end of each volume is cumbersome at best, and does not encourage full use of the materials. Nevertheless, Skeat's edition, presenting in parallel columns the two manuscript versions of the prose translation called the West-Saxon Gospels and the two interlinear glosses, proves to be useful and is still the standard edition, even after the publication of the EETS edition of the West-Saxon (or 'Old English' according to the title of the edition) Gospels by Roy M. Liuzza (1994–2000). The layout and arrangement adopted by Skeat takes the Rushworth glosses from their manuscript context and implicitly makes them secondary to the Lindisfarne Gospels. This tendency seems corroborated by the fact that the latter has, on two occasions, been published in printed facsimiles, while the Rushworth Gospels has never been published in a printed facsimile.[3]

Tamoto's edition, published in 2013, distinguishes itself from earlier editions by presenting both the Latin text and Old English glosses from the Rushworth Gospels manuscript, with the glosses positioned between the lines of the Latin text. This publication has improved the editorial situation of the Rushworth glosses, although Houghton, in his review of the edition, notes some errors in the text and also points out that Tamoto's introduction 'consists of the quotation of information from earlier sources with little in the way of editorial comment or adjudication between differing scholarly positions' (Houghton 2015: 96). Tamoto's edition would have benefited from additional care to facilitate the understanding of the Rushworth Latin, whose importance will be

[3] Facsimiles of the Lindisfarne Gospels have been published by Kendrick *et al.* (1956–60, abbreviated as *Cod. Lind.* in this book), including a very substantial commentary volume with contributions by leading scholars of the time, and by Glauser and Brown (2002–3), a full-colour facsimile accompanied by a bilingual (English-German) commentary by Michelle P. Brown, which was later built upon in an independent monograph (Brown 2003). Both Lindisfarne and Rushworth are published in black and white microfiche facsimiles as part of Volume 3 of the Anglo-Saxon Manuscripts in Microfiche Facsimile series with brief commentary by Liuzza and Doane (1995). The Lindisfarne Gospels is now fully available at the British Library's 'Digitised Manuscripts' (http://www.bl.uk/manuscripts/FullDisplay.aspx?ref=Cotton_MS_Nero_D_IV) and the Rushworth Gospels at the Digital Bodleian (https://digital.bodleian.ox.ac.uk/objects/b708f563-b804-42b5-bd0f-2826dfaeb5cc/).

discussed below. It seems that he was regrettably unable to consult some works crucial to philological analysis of the Rushworth glosses, notably papers by Alan S. C. Ross. In short, Tamoto's edition leaves gaps to be filled on various topics related to the Old English glosses to the Rushworth Gospels.

2. Scope and aims of the edition

The aim of this edition is to give an accurate text of a significant part of the Rushworth Gospels in its manuscript context, to facilitate use of the digital surrogate (see footnote 3 above). It will build on the advances made by Tamoto, by providing more systematic introductory materials, a full commentary and a glossary. The text is accompanied by a critical apparatus which presents collations of the Latin text with standard editions of the Vulgate Gospels and with the Lindisfarne Gospels in order to further the understanding of the Old English gloss. Given the very different nature of the two parts of the Rushworth glosses, Rushworth One (Ru1) written by Farman and Rushworth Two (Ru2) by Owun, the present volume focuses on the former. Nevertheless, some parts of the Introduction will necessarily deal with the manuscript as a whole, including its physical description, provenance, and, though only in general terms, its place in the tradition of the Latin Vulgate Gospel manuscripts.

II. The manuscript: description and historical provenance

1. Introduction

The manuscript, Oxford, Bodleian Library, MS Auct. D. 2.19 (SC 3946), is dated to around 800AD and is thought to have been written in Ireland. Both the dating and the localization, as will be discussed shortly, are based mostly on a Latin colophon and its historical implications, and the internal evidence available does not contradict them.

The manuscript, known as the MacRegol Gospels after the name of the scribe who was an abbot at Birr, Co. Offaly (hence also referred to as the Birr Gospels) as recorded in the Latin colophon, or the Rushworth Gospels after its seventeen-century donor to the Bodleian Library, has been described in various contexts in modern scholarship. E. A. Lowe presents an exemplary description of the manuscript in his *Codices latini antiquiores* (1935: no. 231); no revision to the MacRegol entry is signalled in the second edition published in 1972. Lowe's description can be supplemented from Patrick McGurk's seminal catalogue of Latin Gospel books written before 800 (1961: no. 33), especially on matters related to the manuscript's specific features as a Latin Gospel book.[4] A

[4] See also Houghton (2016: 275–76).

comprehensive art-historical description by Jonathan Alexander can be found in the first volume of the *Survey of Manuscripts Illuminated in the British Isles* series (Alexander 1978: no. 54). Andrew Watson's *Catalogue of Dated and Datable Manuscripts* (1984: no. 43, 'before 822' and 'Birr, Ireland') also presents useful insights, especially, into the identification of the scribes who wrote the Latin text of the manuscript. In addition to identifying two hands as have been agreed generally, he presents a detailed analysis of their distribution, as will be reviewed below. Tamoto's unconventional discussion of the same topic (2013: xlv–lxxv) would have been more meaningful had he not overlooked Watson's suggestions. The Old English glosses are described in his monumental *Catalogue of Manuscripts Containing Anglo-Saxon* by Neil Ker (1957: no. 292). A. N. Doane also provides a description in the volume accompanying the Anglo-Saxon Manuscripts in Microfiche Facsimile series with a short bibliography (Liuzza and Doane 1995: 20–25). Gneuss and Lapidge's *Handlist* (2014: no. 531) provides an extensive bibliography. The catalogue of the British Library's grand exhibition of Anglo-Saxon manuscripts (Breay and Story 2018: no. 75) has an entry by Bernard Meehan, one of the most recent, albeit necessarily brief, descriptions of the manuscript.

The description of the manuscript presented below naturally relies heavily on these works, with their information checked against the manuscript. The content and the script of the Latin Gospels will be described below only in general terms, while palaeographical notes on Farman's Old English gloss will be presented separately in the section on the gloss (III.3). The last part of this section will discuss the manuscript's provenance, especially in the early modern period, and will re-examine several points that have tended to be overlooked in previous scholarship. Given the nature of the present edition's focus on the Old English glosses, it is beyond the scope, and indeed the ability of the editor, to present an art-historical description, but efforts are made to refer to some specific discussions and desiderata at relevant points (e.g., the two Incipit and the Mark portrait pages) in the commentary to the edition.

2. Physical descriptions and contents

The manuscript consists of 168 parchment folios, now foliated as ff. 1–169, skipping 133, where there is no text missing (f. 132 is noted as '132–3' in pencil). Two flyleaves and two endleaves (the latter foliated as 170–1) are contemporary with the nineteenth-century binding.[5] Nothing

[5] For modern additions in pencil on f. 170r, which are a transcription of parts of the Latin colophon on f. 169v and its correction, see Tamoto (2010: 39), who attributes, probably rightly, the transcription to John Obadiah

is known about earlier bindings. The page size is *c.* 350×270mm and the written space *c.* 270×210mm, mostly in 22 long lines, though the number of lines varies from 19 or 20 when the page has a border surrounding the text (e.g., ff. 1v–3r, 50v, 52v–3r) to 24 (not found in the section dealt with in this edition; cf. ff. 101–2). The manuscript is made up of sixteen quires, normally of ten folios, but there are some irregular quires. A full collation is available in Liuzza and Doane (1995: 22); loss of leaves or quires, while frequent in Luke, does not occur in the section that the present edition deals with.[6] Prickings are in both inner and outer margin.

The manuscript contains the four Gospels in Latin, and the text has been aligned by previous scholarship to the so-called mixed-Irish family of the Vulgate, which contains a substantial number of Old Latin readings. Accordingly, it contains a great number of variant readings when compared with modern standard editions of the Vulgate.[7] No prefatory or accessory texts are included, nor are there canon tables. The text is not marked with either the Eusebian numbers or any other chapter numbers, though decorated capitals often, but not systematically, agree with the Eusebian sections.[8] Each Gospel is preceded by its evangelist portrait (Matthew missing) and a full-page Incipit page.[9] There is a full-page colophon on f. 169v, as will be discussed shortly.

Additions other than the Old English glosses are rare in the manuscript. An important exception is what is usually called the 'liturgical signs', added, most likely before the Old English glosses, to the passion narratives in Matthew and Luke. These signs, as Karl Young notes (1933: 100–101), appear to have indicated changes in tone and pitch when the passion texts were read aloud in liturgical contexts. The types of signs and exact deployment of each sign vary from one manuscript to another, and

---

Westwood and the correction to W. W. Skeat, based on examination of their signatures.

6 On the question about the possible loss of a quire at the beginning of the manuscript as noted by Doane and other scholars, see note to f. 1r in the commentary.

7 In a list presented in a posthumous publication of Fischer (2010: 132–36) that examines the degree to which each manuscript agrees with the Stuttgart Vulgate, the Rushworth Gospels is listed as the 415th of the 462 manuscripts surveyed. The history of the text of the Vulgate is too complicated a topic to be discussed within the scope of an edition of Old English glosses. See Kotake (2016: 379, esp. n. 7) for fundamental references, to which Houghton (2016) is now a substantial and indispensable addition.

8 See McGurk (1987: 172); see also III.1.3.3 below about the use of enlarged letters in the Old English gloss that apparently emphasize textual division not indicated in the Latin text.

9 On the added evangelist portrait on f. 51r, see the commentary to the folio.

this is certainly a topic that awaits further systematic investigation.[10] In our manuscript, two signs are used along with additional punctuation: a sign of the cross to indicate the words of Christ and a long horizontal line given at the beginning of narrative passages.[11] The words by the Jews are not marked. In the Luke passion (22:1–23:53), the end of the passion narrative (f. 123v, 16) is marked with 'hic finit', written in Insular script and with the apparently same ink as the one used for the signs. In Matthew (26:2–27:66), the end of the section is not marked, while the beginning is marked with a dry-point cross added in the outer margin on f. 43v.

There are very occasional dry-point additions in the manuscript, for which see note to 26:55 in the commentary.[12]

3. The script and the scribes of the Latin text

The script of the Latin text is described as 'Irish majuscule' by Lowe (1935: no. 231), for which more recent scholarship tends to prefer the term 'Insular Half-Uncial', or more specifically Julian Brown's 'Phase II Insular Half-Uncial' (cf. Brown 1993: 209–10).[13] Lowe's 'SAEC. VIII–IX' is generally agreed as a reasonable palaeographical dating. It is usually assumed that two hands are distinguishable for the Latin text. A sceptical opinion about making such a distinction is voiced by a calligrapher, Timothy O'Neill (2014: 24), who states: 'some palaeographers claim to distinguish the hands of two scribes [...] The distinction is unclear in the strong horizontal flow of the script in long lines'. Lowe's simple statement that the manuscript was '[w]ritten by two scribes' is certainly tantalizing, especially given the differing opinions of later scholars on where division(s) occur. The simplest division so far suggested is that of Doane (Liuzza and Doane 1995: 21), who states that the 'first writes Matthew and Mark [i.e., up to f. 84r], second, with a squarer and more open ductus, Luke and John'. Yet, his division is over-simplistic, because the

10 Young (1910) records the signs used in a number of manuscripts, but there are very many yet to be recorded just within Anglo-Saxon manuscripts.

11 Young (1910: 328) notes that the sign resembling a cross used as part of liturgical signs originates in the letter of *t*, which stands for either *trahere* or *tenere*, indicating retardation.

12 Throughout this monograph, given its focus on Farman's gloss which occurs mostly in Matthew, references to verses in Matthew will be made simply by chapter and verse as above, while those in other Gospels will be preceded by Mk, Lk and Jn.

13 See also Michelle Brown's extended comparison (2012: 151): 'The Lichfield, MacRegol and Rawlinson Gospels, the Lincoln College Luke fragment, one of the scribes of the Cambridge-London Gospels and two of the scribes of the Barberini Gospels all favour a broad, regular Half-Uncial of mature "Phase II" character'.

first hand reappears on the last page of Luke (f. 126r), the first folio of Quire XIII, where the concluding verses of the final chapter of Luke are followed by the Luke explicit and the incipit of John. It is also probable that the first hand reappears towards the end of John. Tamoto (2013: xlv) believes that this change occurs at f. 148r, after which the first scribe wrote to the very end, including the colophon. Meehan's description in the BL exhibition catalogue (Breay and Story 2018: no. 75) is similar, but his precise intention is not clear when he writes the 'second scribe copied Luke's Gospel, apart from a single page, and the first two quires of John' without presenting the collation. The third quire of John begins at f. 149 according to Doane's collation, thus disagreeing with Tamoto on the exact point of scribal change. A further complication must be introduced, because Watson (1984: no. 43) considers that the second scribe wrote all of Luke except for f. 126r, but only ff. 127v and 147v in John. His suggestion that the second scribe also wrote several lines on two pages in Mark (f. 58v, 15–22 and f. 75r, 19–22) may hardly be tenable, but certainly indicates the difficulty of distinguishing the two hands.

Despite these differing opinions, the first scribe, who also wrote the colophon, appears to be responsible for all the text dealt with in this edition. The colophon, on the verso of the final folio (f. 169v), is divided into six compartments, grouped as three rows of two columns. The four compartments of the top two rows each contain a verse for one evangelist. The verses are transmitted with Juvencus's *Libri Evangeliorum Quattuor*.[14] In biblical contexts, Dom De Bruyne (1912: 195) records that the text appears in the Cadmug and MacDurnan Gospels, both omitting one for John.[15] As noted by Nees (2003: 365–67, esp. 365, n. 121), the verses present a late instance of identifying Mark with the eagle and John with the lion, at odds with the identifications expressed in the manuscript's own portraits (Mark with the lion on f. 51v; John with the eagle on f. 126v). The bottom two compartments contain the colophon proper, reading 'Macregol dipincxit hoc euangelium Quicumque legerit | Et intellegerit istam narrationem orat pro macreguil scriptori'. This colophon is generally taken to indicate the origin of the manuscript in Ireland, because the name MacRegol has been identified with the 'scribe,

[14] For a full transcription of the version in the Rushworth manuscript, see McGurk (1961: no. 33). For an edition of the versions transmitted with Juvencus, see Huemer (1891: not paginated, facing p. 1). On the use of Juvencus's *Libri Evangeliorum Quattuor* in Anglo-Saxon England, especially in glossing contexts, see Lapidge (1982: 108–13).

[15] The former is Fulda, Landesbibliothek Bonif. 3, f. 51r; see McGurk (1961: no. 68). The version in the latter, London, Lambeth Palace Library, MS 1370, f. 1r, is likely to be a later addition to the manuscript; see Farr (2011: 93–94).

bishop, and abbot' of Birr who died in 822, according to the *Annals of Ulster*.[16] Although slight doubt as to this identification has been raised on linguistic grounds, the assumption that the manuscript was made *c.* 800 in Ireland is compatible with its other features, including text, script, and illumination.[17]

4. The medieval and early modern provenance of the manuscript

It is not known when and how the manuscript travelled from Ireland to Anglo-Saxon England, where the two glossators, Farman and Owun, whose names are recorded in their colophons, added their Old English glosses. Farman's colophon as edited in the present edition occurs on f. 50v. Owun wrote his colophon on ff. 168v–9r: 'ðe min bruche gibidde fore owun ðe ðas boc gloesde. færmen ðæm preoste æt harawuda. | hæfe nu boc awritne bruca mið willa symle mið soðum gileofa sibb is eghwæm leofost:·' ('Let him who uses me pray for Owun, who glossed this book for Farman the priest at *harawuda*; take now the book written [or 'glossed'?]; use [it] with joy, always with true belief; peace is dearest to everyone'; the translation is from Kotake [2016: 377, n. 2]). The scripts used for Old English are datable only broadly to the tenth century; the dialects of Farman and Owun are generally regarded as Mercian and Northumbrian, respectively. Because there is no reliable evidence to date and localize the Old English glosses, scholars often differ with one another in interpreting the patchy evidence. The name Owun, for example, is taken as Welsh by Helen McKee (2012: 343), whereas this interpretation is ruled out by Paul Bibire and Alan S. C. Ross (1981: 98, n. 2), who argue that Owun is not identical with the Welsh name Owen. The only other internal evidence of potential significance is the place name *harawuda*, given in Owun's colophon. However, it, too, presents difficulties. Amongst many possible modern reflexes of Old English *harawuda*, two have received special attention: Harewood near Leeds and Harewood near Ross-on-Wye. Andrew Breeze (1996) attempts to rule out the latter, first suggested by Max Förster as reported by Ker (1957: no. 292), because the region is considered to have had a strongly Welsh character during the Anglo-Saxon period. Whereas Harewood near Leeds may account for the Anglian dialect of the Old English glosses, there is no

16 First identified by O'Conor (1814: ccxxix–ccxxxvii). The entry of 822 in the *Annals of Ulster* reads in the translation of Mac Airt and Mac Niocaill (1983: 276–77): 'Mac Riaguil grandson of Magléne, scribe, bishop and abbot of Biror, died'.

17 Kenney (1968: 641–42) notes that the change from *ē* to *ia* is likely to have completed at the time of MacRegol's writing, though he does not consider this evidence strong enough to reject the identification.

firm evidence to support the identification. Richard Coates (1997), from the perspective of Brittonic-Anglo-Saxon bilingualism, also proposes as a candidate 'a "hoar wood" in the vicinity of Lichfield' in a paper filled with informed, yet hard-to-prove, speculation. It is probably wise not to draw any conclusion as to the identification of *harawuda*, or more broadly as to the place where the two glossators added their glosses, unless further evidence becomes available.

There is no record of the manuscript's whereabouts later in the medieval period,[18] and it is next traced with a reasonable degree of certainty in the middle of the seventeenth century, when it is associated with John Rushworth. Two pieces of evidence have been proposed as a record of the manuscript at an earlier date, though with questionable reliability. The earlier of the two involves the sixteenth-century lexicographer Laurence Nowell (1530–*c.* 1570). M. S. Hetherington (1980: 13) regards the Rushworth Gospels as one of the manuscripts that might have been used by Nowell for his *Vocabularium saxonicum*. Her evidence is, however, slender: an entry in Nowell's *Vocabularium* 'Nic. No, nay, not. Not I. Properly, Nicc ic. Not I' (printed by Marckwardt 1952: 128) is taken as confirming Nowell's use of the Rushworth Gospels, because, Hetherington (1980: 13) argues, the form *nic* is found only in the Rushworth gloss (Matthew 25:9). The form is, however, found also in the Corpus manuscript of the West Saxon Gospels (CCCC 140, John 1:21), another manuscript which Hetherington thinks Nowell used for his *Vocabularium*.

The other possible evidence for an earlier provenance of the manuscript relates to Sir Robert Cotton (1571–1631). Colin Tite (1997), in his interesting discussion of a note written by Cotton, argues for the possibility that the Gospel book mentioned in the note may have been the Rushworth Gospels. The note on f. 84r of London, BL, Harley MS 6849, a collection of miscellaneous papers, is a letter, or more likely a draft for a letter to be sent to an unnamed intermediary, listing eight items that Sir Robert Cotton wishes to acquire from a certain Sir Thomas Tempest, whom Tite identifies as Sir Thomas Tempest of Stella, Co. Durham. Though the note itself is undated, Tite proposes a date between 1626–31. The item in question reads 'Quatuor Evangelia Saxonica Charactere et Saxonica Interpretatione in Foll', a description which Tite believes applicable to 'only two known manuscripts of the Gospels': the Lindisfarne Gospels and the Rushworth Gospels, i.e., the two Latin

[18] There is no reference to the Rushworth Gospels in Ker's *Medieval Libraries of Great Britain* (Ker 1964), including the online MLGB3 (http://mlgb3.bodleian.ox.ac.uk/).

gospel books containing continuous Old English glosses. Because the provenance of the Lindisfarne Gospels is at that time traceable, he then argues that the Gospel book in the Tempest list is likely to have been the Rushworth Gospels, and he considers possible links between the Tempest family and John Rushworth. Thus, we may be able to trace the whereabouts of the Rushworth Gospels to a few decades earlier than previously identified. The links suggested may prompt further speculation about the earlier provenance of the Rushworth Gospels, because much of the Tempest collection derives from the library of Durham Cathedral Priory.[19]

Nevertheless, it is difficult to accept Tite's account without reservations. First and foremost, there is his interpretation of the wording of the note. It is not entirely clear why Tite limits the candidates to manuscripts containing interlinear glosses, and why he excludes other kinds of *interpretatio*. An interlinear format is not specified, but could have been – the Cottonian catalogue (Harley MS 6018, f. 119v) describes the Lindisfarne Gospels as 'Saxonica Lingua per Aldredum presbiterum interlineatus'.[20] In contrast, this same catalogue describes a copy of the West Saxon Gospels (now BL, Cotton MS Otho C. i, vol. 1) as 'A Book of Saxon toung and letters of sum part of the new testament', a phrasing, though in English, somewhat comparable with the entry in the Tempest list.[21] It is also important to note that there is no indication of Tempest's ownership in the Rushworth Gospels, unlike the many other Tempest books, which generally contain ownership inscriptions; but it is possible that such indications were lost later, especially given its much later, nineteenth-century binding. It appears that we lack decisive evidence for or against Tite's identification of the Gospel book in the Tempest list with the Rushworth Gospels.

From the middle of the seventeenth century, the manuscript becomes associated with John Rushworth (*c.* 1612–1690), who donated the book to the Bodleian Library in *c.* 1681.[22] Tite (1997: 434) states that the manuscript 'came into the hands of John Rushworth [...] in 1650', but as far as I am aware, there is no evidence that Rushworth *acquired* the manuscript in that year, while it is probable that he came to possess it by

19 The fullest account of the collection is found in Doyle (1984).

20 '323. Textus Evangeliorum pulcherimus ab Eadfrido postea Lindisfarnensis Episcopo circa annum Christi 660 scriptus et Saxonica Lingua per Aldredum presbiterum interlineatus. De istius libri amissione in mare et miraculosa inuentione extat narration in historia Dunelmensi. Capite 32.' See Brown (2003: 136).

21 See Ker (1957: no. 181).

22 See the *Summary Catalogue* (Madan et al. 1895–1953: i, 120).

or in that year. Though associated with Rushworth, the manuscript apparently had been lodged with Sir Simonds D'Ewes (1602–1650) for some time. In an undated letter, evidently written in March 1650, Roger Dodsworth (bap. 1585, d. 1654) wrote to William Dugdale (1605–1686):

> I know no more of the Saxon Gra. then what the beast averreth, and believe hee will not ly, viz. that itt is ready. My cosen Rushworth hath taken his Saxon Testament from him, and doth much distaste his prittle prattle; he hath a desire to p'cure some helps to p'fect your Saxon Dictionary, wch the Beast undervalued to my Cosen (when [we] were wth him and saw it in his study window) in regard what Hee had done to that purpose wch is finished by Mr. Sumners hand, and would have you put out the Dictionary by such helpes &c.[23]

The 'beast' mentioned in the letter is D'Ewes, a noteworthy antiquary whose collections were to form an important part of the future Harley collection, and he is known to have been working on an edition of Ælfric's grammar and an Anglo-Saxon dictionary. The 'Saxon Testament' is probably the Rushworth Gospels, though 'Testament' is not a particularly precise description, and the letter seems to indicate that the manuscript had been on loan to D'Ewes for some time. D'Ewes died on 18 April, 1650 without publishing the planned grammar and dictionary. His working papers are now in Harley MSS 8 and 9,[24] and D'Ewes's dictionary is sometimes seen by modern scholars as hardly any more than a mere transcript of John Joscelyn's dictionary.[25] Hetherington's (1975: 83) study of D'Ewes's dictionary is unable to confirm his use of the Rushworth Gospels, listing it only as a 'possible source'.

Francis Junius, one of the greatest philologists of the seventeenth century, is known to have stayed at D'Ewes's house for some months in 1648–49.[26] He is probably the first person who made substantial use of

[23] Edited by Hamper (1827: 226–27). See also Watson (1966: 11).

[24] Harley MSS 8 and 9 apparently belonged to Rushworth for some time after D'Ewes's death, though they later entered the Harley collection as part of D'Ewes's collection. The name of John Rushworth is not listed as an owner of these manuscripts in Wright's *Fontes Harleiani* (Wright 1972; but see Watson 1966: 54–55). As noted by Watson (1966: 154, A433), there is a strip stuck on f. 1 of Harley MS 8, on which is written 'This booke with another volume of the same matter & forme was lent me by my most assured loveing friend Mr John Rushworth. October 25 1653. Ita testor Ger*ard* Langbaine', with a similar note also in MS 9.

[25] See Lutz (2000: 35 and n. 91).

[26] See Timmer (1957: 143).

the Rushworth Gospels. Whereas it is not clear whether he used the manuscript while D'Ewes was still alive, he did borrow it from John Rushworth soon after D'Ewes's death. He wrote from London to his nephew (Francis Junius F.N.) that

> Even very recently indeed, the excellent gentleman John Rushworth most kindly lent me the Vulgate version of the four Gospels interlineated with Anglo-Saxon by a glossator eight or nine hundred years ago, I believe… I have inserted much information from this most friendly gentleman's treasure, hitherto unknown and especially useful for my purpose, in my etymological work.[27]

The records of Junius's use of the Rushworth Gospels are found in Oxford, Bodleian Library, MS Junius 76, which contains excerpts from both the Lindisfarne and Rushworth Gospels.[28] As discussed by Kees Dekker (2008), Junius also noted variant readings from the Rushworth Gospels in his copy of the edition of the Old English gospels printed by John Foxe in 1571 (the copy is now Oxford, Lincoln College Library, MS N. 1. 7), which was then used by Thomas Marshall in preparing for their edition of the Gospels published in 1665.

Eric Stanley (1998: 171) points out that Junius was the first person to scrutinize the glosses in the Rushworth and Lindisfarne Gospels for dialectal comparison. It is this dialect perspective that made the Rushworth Gospels a focus of the philological studies in the following decades. George Hickes lists the Rushworth Gospels in his brief *Catalogus veterum librorum septentrionalium* printed in his *Institutiones grammaticae Anglo-Saxonicae, et Moeso-Gothicae* (1689). As Richard L. Harris (1992: 71–74) reconstructs in detail from Hickes's correspondence, the publication of the *Institutiones* invited responses from William Nicolson (1655–1727), who suggested further possibilities for a chapter on dialect variations of the Anglo-Saxon language. This eventually led to the addition of Chapter 20 ('*De dialecto* Dano-Saxonica, *in soluta oratione*') to his grammar published as part of *Linguarum veterum septentrionalium thesaurus grammatico-criticus et archaeologicus* (1703–5), in which the Lindisfarne and Rushworth glosses are used as the main source for what

[27] 'Quinetiam nuperrime adhuc Quatuor Evangelia vulgatae versionis a glossatore quodam ante annos, credo, octingentos nongentosve Anglo-Saxonice interlineata humanissime suppeditavit mihi vir optimus Io. Rushworth … ex hoc amicissimi viri thesauro multa recondita et proposito meo apprime utilia operi etymologico inserui'. The translation is by van Romburgh (2001: 24, and n. 98); the letter, noting that D'Ewes died about twenty or more days ago, is edited in van Romburgh (2004: no. 168).

[28] See Stanley (1998: 171).

he called Dano-Saxon. BL, Harley MS 3449 contains a transcript of the Rushworth Gospels, along with a transcript of a late copy of the West Saxon Gospels (Oxford, Bodleian Library, MS Hatton 38), made for Hickes by Edward Thwaites and Joseph Todhunter.[29]

The Rushworth Gospels was catalogued a few times after it was donated to the Bodleian Library, culminating in the entry in the magnificent catalogue by Humfrey Wanley.[30] It may be pointed out that in these early catalogues the Rushworth Gospels is associated with the Venerable Bede, while the descriptions usually report the Latin colophon containing the name MacRegol. This Bedan connection is, of course, to be rejected (e.g., see the *Summary Catalogue* entry), but the same view is repeated in some letters of Wanley. Unfortunately, we do not know whether the prevalence of this account is based on any tradition known to the scholars of the period.

III. Old English glosses

1. Introduction: Farman's gloss and its background

1.1 Two glossators in the Rushworth Gospels: date and provenance

The Rushworth Gospels was glossed by two glossators whose hands are distinguishable from each other on palaeographical grounds. Farman wrote all of Matthew, Mark 1–2:15 (f. 55r, 12, up to 'ł hleonadun') and John 18:1–3 (Rushworth One, hereafter Ru1), and Owun the remainder (Rushworth Two, Ru2).[31] Their names, recorded in the two colophons as seen above, have not been identified with names in any other records from Anglo-Saxon England.[32] The date and provenance of the glosses must therefore be inferred from internal evidence: as to dating, there is little evidence other than their scripts, which Ker (1957: no. 292) dates

29 They were apparently working on the transcriptions in Harley MS 3449 in 1696 and the manuscript was sent to Hickes in 1698. See Thwaites's letters to Hickes (Harris 1992: Letters nos. 41 and 62).

30 In Hickes (1703–5: ii, 81–82). In addition to the entry in Hickes's *Catalogus* mentioned above, it is described in the 1697 Bodleian catalogue (*Catalogi librorum manuscriptorum Angliae et Hiberniae in unum collecti*, vol.1, 181). Kenneth Sisam (1953: 266) notes the existence of Wanley's elaborate notes on the Rushworth Gospels in Harley MS 5911, which is probably an error for '7055' and a leaf prepared for a printer dealing with the same manuscript (Bodl. L. MS Rawlinson D. 377). J. A. W. Bennett (1938: 147, and n. 2) also points out that there are some differences in Wanley's versions of the description of the Rushworth manuscript, noting that 'Folios 121–3 of MS Harley 7055 form a last recension of' his draft.

31 In the section in John, Owun's hand also appears, as noted by Ker (1957: no. 292). See note to f. 162r in the commentary.

32 See 'Farmon 1' and 'Owun 1', Prosopography of Anglo-Saxon England, http://www.pase.ac.uk, accessed 24 March 2021.

broadly to the tenth century; no decisive evidence to identify the location of *harawuda* is available as seen above.

To make the identification of the place name even harder, the dialects of the two glossators are distinct from each other. Owun's dialect is Northumbrian, regarded as one of the important texts of the dialect along with the language of Aldred, who glossed the Lindisfarne Gospels and the Durham Ritual.[33] Traditional views, based on Lindelöf (1901), have further distinguished Owun's dialect from Aldred's, regarding the former as South Northumbrian and the latter North Northumbrian, but Hogg (2004) points out that their linguistic differences are not likely to reflect the geographic difference between the two glossators. Farman's dialect, on the other hand, is regarded as Mercian. His gloss also contains a substantial number of linguistic features unexpected in a Mercian text, many of which have been deemed due to West Saxon influence. Before this apparent dialectal mixture is discussed, it is necessary to introduce two contrasting theories about how such a mixture could have arisen. Menner (1934), for instance, tries to show that this allegedly mixed dialect is in fact the dialect of Farman himself. In contrast, non-Mercian features have been explained by the external influence of West Saxon features: Schulte (1903), notably, argues that such West Saxon features came into Farman's gloss through an exemplar, which he hypothesizes from his textual analysis of Farman's gloss.[34]

Thus, whether Farman used an exemplar or not is a key question that underlies various other issues concerning his gloss. As will be shown below, the scrutiny of this key question will eventually enable us to gain a better understanding of the context in which Farman was writing his gloss to the Rushworth Gospels.

1.2 The relationship between Ru1/Ru2 and Li

To address the question of Farman's use of external sources, it is first necessary to consider the relationship between the two Rushworth glosses

[33] Campbell (OEG §6).

[34] The traditional division of Old English into the four distinct dialects, West Saxon, Kentish, Mercian and Northumbrian, may be criticized as a 'rather essentialist view of dialects', overlooking the development in dialectology, as the anonymous peer-reviewer has rightly pointed out (the quotation is from his/her report). Throughout this monograph, especially in the discussion of dialect *mixture*, a term clearly reflecting the essentialist view (see III.2 below), I employ the four-fold division, in order to consider various possible, but impossible-to-prove, hypotheses concerning Farman's linguistic backgrounds. I do not mean to disregard the development in the field of dialectology, but it seems that the traditional approach is fitting to the purpose of the discussion.

(Ru1 and Ru2) and the other substantial extant Old English interlinear gloss to the Gospels, that is, Aldred's gloss to the Lindisfarne Gospels (Li).

The Lindisfarne Gospels (London, BL, Cotton MS, Nero D. iv) is a Latin Gospel manuscript produced at around the beginning of the eighth century.[35] Aldred added his Old English interlinear glosses to the entire text of the four Gospels around the middle of the tenth century, or more precisely, some time before 970, probably around 950.[36] Owun's gloss, and part of Farman's as well, are often considered to have been copied from Aldred's gloss.

1.2.1 The relationship between Li and Ru2

One of the grounds for postulating so direct a relationship is the close similarity between Aldred's gloss (Li) and Owun's (Ru2). They agree with one another so closely that Ru2 has been seen as a copy of Li. Yet, one should not accept too readily the widespread notion that Ru2 is a simple copy of Li. The notion appears to stem from Sir James Murray (1875: 452), who, reviewing the first volume of Skeat's Cambridge edition of the Old English Gospels, wrote that Skeat 'is the first to point out with regard to (a great part of) the Rushworth gloss, that it is simply a copy of that of the Lindisfarne'. Murray's note was then incorporated into Skeat's edition of John's Gospel (Skeat 1878: xii–xv). These circular assessments, as it were, appear to have reinforced the notion of simple copying, but differences between the two glosses are much more significant than the phrase 'simple copy' would suggest.[37]

Close examinations have, in fact, revealed that there are substantial disagreements between Li and Ru2. Bibire and Ross (1981) present a long list of differences between the two glosses. I have shown in a syntactic

35 As to the dating, see Brown (2003: 10). See also Lowe (1935: no. 187), *Cod. Lind.*, and Liuzza and Doane (1995: 1–12). For recent publications on the manuscript, see the two collections of papers edited by Fernández Cuesta and Pons-Sanz (2016) and Gameson (2017), and Gameson's monograph (2013).

36 This dating is based on the colophons he wrote in the Lindisfarne Gospels and in another manuscript called the Durham Ritual (Durham, Cathedral Library, MS A.IV.19). In his colophon to the latter manuscript, Aldred called himself 'provost'. The Lindisfarne Gospels must have been glossed earlier than the Durham Ritual, because according to the colophon to the Lindisfarne Gospels he described himself as a 'presbyter' when he glossed that manuscript. The Durham Ritual colophon is datable to 970 from his account that he wrote it on a certain Wednesday, which was the Feast of St Lawrence (10 August), and that the moon was five nights old on the day. For a detailed analysis, see Julian Brown's introduction to the facsimile of the manuscript (1969: 24).

37 For details about these mutually reinforcing correspondences, see Kotake (2016: 378, n. 4).

analysis of the two glosses (Kotake 2008) that disagreements are frequent especially in John's Gospel, and furthermore that they are likely to have been caused by changes in Aldred's glossing practice, whereas Owun keeps his practice consistent throughout his portion.[38] I also have pointed out in the paper entitled 'Did Owun Really Copy from the Lindisfarne Gospels?' (Kotake 2016) that Owun's corrections to the Latin text – and to some extent his glosses themselves – betray the influence of Latin variant readings that are not recorded in either the Rushworth or the Lindisfarne Gospels. My tentative answer to the question raised in the paper's title was 'No', and I think it still holds.

1.2.2 The relationship between Li and Ru1 (Mt 26–28 and Mark)

Farman's gloss (Ru1) in Mark, too, bears similarities to that of Aldred, and the similarities have been interpreted as evidence for his use of Aldred's gloss as an exemplar, by extending the theory that Owun copied from Li.[39] As in the case of Ru2, the evidence is not conclusive, however. Menner (1934: 7–8), though his argument is based on the hypothesis that Ru1 is copied from Li in Mark, notes the sheer fact that Ru1 more often differs from Li than they agree exactly with each other. Farman's corrections to the Latin text of the Rushworth Gospels, too, often disagree with the readings of the Lindisfarne Gospels in this section, as will be seen below (see §1.3.2). Of course, linguistic features of Farman's gloss in Mark are clearly different from those in Matthew and resulting similarities to Li are obvious, but these similarities do not assert Farman's use of the Lindisfarne Gospels itself as an exemplar, given their differences and also given that the evidence for Owun's copying from Li is in serious doubt.

Alan S. C. Ross (1979a) further argues that Farman also copied from Li in Matthew Chapters 26–28. However, as I have shown in a paper re-examining his argument (Kotake 2012b), while his argument is sound in so far as it points out similarities between the two glosses in these particular chapters, his theory of Farman's copying from the Lindisfarne Gospels is problematic. If we accept the assumption that Farman used a newly gained exemplar for the section, regardless of whether it was the Lindisfarne Gospels itself or not, it must have been Farman who changed the linguistic nature of the gloss there (as he did in Mark), reflecting the features found in his new exemplar. However, the linguistic evidence

38 On changing linguistic features of the Lindisfarne gloss, see also Cole's studies on verbal morphosyntax and the Northern Subject Rule (Cole 2014, esp. §4.2.4 and Cole 2016) and van Bergen (2008: esp. 291–93) on negative contraction.

39 Murray (1874) and (1875), Lindelöf (1901: 2–6) and Menner (1934: 4–19).

examined indicates that it was Aldred who changed his glossing practice in Matthew 26–28.[40] Therefore, if we accept the notion of direct copying, then the conclusion must be that Aldred copied from the Rushworth Gospels, that is, the reverse direction of influence to the one Ross envisages.

There is no evidence for direct copying. As an alternative interpretation of the similarities occurring in the specific chapters, I have called attention to the fact that these chapters comprise a Passion narrative, whose significance as a textual unit is obvious in various respects.[41] There are, for instance, two distinct Old English texts that are virtually independent translations of Matthew Chapters 26–27, both usually labelled as homilies.[42] The similarities between Li and Ru1 in this particular section could have resulted from their sharing a widespread tradition of glossing and translating the Passion text independently from the other parts of the Gospels.

So, as to the relationship between the Rushworth glosses (Ru1 and Ru2) and Li, the fact that the two extant glosses resemble each other does not necessarily lead to the conclusion that one of them was copied from the other. To understand the significance of the similarities found between the two glosses, it is essential that we pay due attention to the wider context rather than argue for direct copying between the two extant manuscripts.

1.3 Farman's use of external sources

It is generally agreed that Farman's gloss up to the end of Matthew Chapter 25 does not show any special resemblance to Aldred's gloss. It

40 Cole reports that the data gained in her studies mentioned above (Cole 2014 and 2016) corroborate this conclusion.

41 Whether we should include Chapter 28, dealing with the Resurrection, in this unit is difficult to determine, because the linguistic evidence examined is equivocal as regards this matter. In Chapter 28, Aldred goes back to his earlier practices as to some features, and for others he continues to use the practices he started to employ in Chapters 26–27.

42 For these texts, see Kotake (2012b: 18–19) and references cited there. As regards the importance of Matthew Chapter 26–27 as a Passion text and its influence on Old English writings, see also a group of dry-point glosses occurring in the section in London, BL, Add. MS 40000 (Kotake 2013) and a fragment of a passion narrative homily now in Oxford. On the fragment (Oxford, Bodleian Library, MS Broxbourne 90.28), see Kotake (2021). It may be relevant to the current discussion that even in the tradition of the Old Latin text of Matthew, Burton (2000: 36–44) has suggested the possibility that the Matthew Passion narrative in the Old Latin Gospels may have been 'based on an older, liturgical translation', giving a possible parallel case of using a distinct source for the Passion narrative section.

does not follow that Farman's gloss was original, not least because of the implication of the foregoing discussion that we need to consider a wider context of glossing the Gospels in Old English than the two extant manuscripts. In fact, whether Farman used a pre-existing but now-lost source or not is a question that divides scholarly opinions. Besides, if he did, another question comes into play about the nature of the exemplar(s), especially of the texts available. The following sections will examine Farman's Old English gloss and his corrections to the Latin text in order to consider if he had access to external sources, whether written in Latin or Old English, or both. Because Farman's gloss in Matthew does not change its nature after the end of Chapter 25, as noted above, the following discussion will consider his Matthew gloss in its entirety.

1.3.1 Old English glosses reflecting Latin variant readings

Schulte (1903), following an earlier suggestion by Förster (1900: 428–29), argues that Farman's gloss is based not on the Latin text of the Rushworth Gospels (R), which contains a number of non-Vulgate readings, but on a purer Vulgate text. Using the Oxford edition of the Vulgate by Wordsworth and White (WW) for comparison, Schulte (1903: 15) identifies 215 instances where Farman's gloss agrees with the readings recorded in WW rather than with R's non-Vulgate readings. Although the exact number could vary depending on how to interpret individual instances and therefore statistical data may be of less significance than it may appear, these instances cumulatively speak for Farman's knowledge of a purer Vulgate text. Yet, the data alone cannot be decisive about the availability of an Old English exemplar, because Farman might have carefully collated the Rushworth Latin with another Latin manuscript in making his Old English gloss. Thus, Menner (1934: esp. 19–27; the citation below is from p. 27) argues against Schulte's assumption that Farman's exemplar was an older interlinear gloss, and thinks it 'most probable' that 'Farman's translation is independent of an older gloss', though not without some concessions. This question will be addressed in analyzing the data gathered below.

While Farman's knowledge of a purer Vulgate text is clearly noticeable, it is also important to emphasize that Farman's gloss follows R in many instances, even when it disagrees with WW. Furthermore, because our use of WW for textual comparison is a conventional choice, it is necessary to consider, where possible, the textual nature of the Latin readings by which Farman's gloss is likely to have been influenced. The following sections examine Farman's Old English glosses that betray the influence of Latin variant readings, citing several examples according to the patterns of disagreement between R and WW.

(a) Extra word(s)/phrase(s) in R

When R has words or phrases that are not in WW, Farman in some cases leaves them unglossed. In (1) below, *triclinio*, presumably an Old Latin reading and accordingly not adopted in WW, receives no gloss.

(1) 14:6 (f. 23v, 3–4)
on dæg þa gebyrde herode pleagade dohter
Die autem natalis herodis saltauit filia
þara herodiade in midle ⁊ licade herodes
herodiadis in medio triclinio· et placuit herodi·
triclinio] *om.* Y WW

While one might argue that such an unglossed word may have been due to Farman's unfamiliarity with the Latin word, the following verse in (2) contains two instances of the adverb *iam*, which would have caused no difficulty, being left unglossed. WW wants the two instances of *iam*.

(2) 19:9 (f. 30v, 16–19)
ic sæcge þanne eow
dico autem uobis
ꝥ swa hwa swa forleteþ his wif nymðe fore
quia quicumq(ue) diserit uxorem suam sine causa
forlegernisse ⁊ him oþer lædeþ he forlegenisse fremmaþ
fornicationis et aliam duxerit iam mechatur
⁊ se þe forletnisse lædaþ forlægnisse fremmaþ
et qui demisam duxerit iam mechatur·
sine causa fornicationis] nisi ob fornicationem Y WW iam (*bis*)] *om.* Y WW

Whereas Farman often corrects the Latin text in the Rushworth manuscript as will be examined shortly (see III.1.3.2 below), there is no trace of cancelling the unglossed Latin words in these instances. Such resulting discrepancy between the Latin text and its corresponding gloss appears to suggest that Farman copied his gloss from an Old English exemplar which was based on a purer Vulgate text, without taking care to match the copied glosses with his own Latin text.

In contrast, there are instances where Farman translates words that are not in WW, indicating that he was translating the Latin text in front of him. In (3) below, *populi* is unique amongst the manuscripts recorded in WW's critical apparatus, but Farman neatly glosses it with *þæs folces*.

(3) 27:3 (f. 46v, 22–f. 47r, 3)
þa geseah iudas se þe hine salde
tunc uidens iudas qui eum tradidit
ꝥ he niðrad wæs mid hreownisse lædde ⁊ brohte
quia dampnatus est penetentia ductus re(-)
eft ðritig scyllinga aldursacerdum
tullit xxx· argenteos principibus sacerdotu(m)

⁊ þa eldran þæs folces
et seniorib(us) populi

quia] quod Y WW est] esset Y WW populi] *om.* Y WW

This type of evidence should not be overlooked, as a caution against the risk of overgeneralizing the observation made in the previous paragraph. In many instances, Farman's gloss reflects non-Vulgate readings of the Rushworth manuscript, suggesting that his main aim was doubtless to provide Old English glosses that match his own Latin text.

In the next two instances, the situation appears similar to (3) above, i.e., Farman translating his own Latin text. However, as noted above, our comparison with WW is conventional, and therefore more complications must be introduced. In (4) below, *inmundos* is not in WW, and it is tempting to suppose that Farman translated his own Latin text with *únklene* rather than copying it from his exemplar(s).

(4) 8:16 (f. 12r, 20–f. 12v, 1)

efen þonne
Uespere autem
hit þa wæs þa brohtun him monige deofulseoke hæbbende ⁊
facto obtulerunt ei multos demonia habentes et
ut awearp þurh h'i's worde þa gastas únklene ⁊ alle yfle
ieciebat uerbo sp(iritu)s inmundos et omnes male
hæbbende gehælde
habentes curauit

ieciebat uerbo spiritus inmundos] eiciebat spiritus uerbo Y WW

Yet, it is impossible to rule out the possibility that *unklene* was found in Farman's exemplar, especially when the verse in WSCp is examined:[43]

(5) WSCp 8:16
Soþlice þa hyt æfen wæs hig brohton him manege defolseoce; ⁊ he utadræfde þa unclænan gastas mid hys worde ⁊ he ealle gehælde þa yfelhæbbendan.

Similarly, in (6) below, *candita*, a reading found in some Irish and Old Latin manuscripts (with spelling variations), is glossed with *hwit* by Farman.

(6) 28:3 (f. 50r, 3–4)

wæs þa his onseone swa leget ⁊ wæda ł rægl
erat autem aspectus eius sicut fulgor· et ues⟨-⟩

[43] For Latin manuscripts with 'inmundos', see Fischer (1988–91: i, 177).

his hwit swa snau
timenta eius candita sicut nix·
uestimenta] uestimentum Y WW candita] *om.* Y WW

Yet again, Farman's gloss is comparable with WSCp:[44]

(7) WSCp 28:3
Hys ansyn wæs swylce ligyt ⁊ hys reaf swa hwite swa snaw.

In the instances like (4) and (6), it is simply impossible to decide whether Farman's gloss to R's non-Vulgate reading was copied from his exemplar or was his spontaneous reaction to his own Latin text, confirming the difficulty of using statistical data as evidence for or against his use of external sources as Schulte attempts.

Furthermore, in the following instance (8), Farman apparently fails to provide an equivalent to *autem*, which agrees with the text in WW.

(8) 14:25 (f. 24r, 16–17)
feorðe þære wacone næhtes cuom to heom
quarta autem uigilia noctis uenit ad eos
se helend gangende ofer þone sǽe
ie(su)s ambulans supra maræ

This example may easily be dismissed as an accidental omission, but WW's critical apparatus records that the Lichfield Gospels wants *autem* here. Whether any textual variant underlies the unglossed *autem* is an insoluble question, but this instance certainly exemplifies the complexity of the topic we are now looking into.

(b) Missing word(s)/phrase(s) in R

Similarly, R often wants words that occur in WW. In many such instances, Farman follows R, leaving no traces of variant readings. His gloss, however, sometimes appears to reflect Latin words missing in R.

(9) 22:23 (f. 36v, 17–18)
on þæ(m) dæge him eodun to saduceas þa þe cwædun þæt
In illa die accesserunt saducei qui dicunt non
seo æriste ł uparisnisse ⁊ frugnon .ł axsadun hine
esse resurrectionem· interrogauerunt eum
illa] illo Y WW accesserunt] + ad eum Y WW resurrectionem] + et Y WW

[44] Liuzza (1994–2000: ii, 38) lists this instance as one of about 140 readings in WSCp that can be influenced by non-Vulgate readings.

Farman's *him eodun to* appears to translate WW *accesserunt ad eum*. Many examples of this type involve conjunctions (as in the case of ⁊ for missing Latin *et* above) and adverbs (e.g., *enim*, *autem*), which may have been inserted by Farman even without the support of Latin variants, making it difficult to evaluate them as evidence for his use of external sources. One exception is his glosses to *enim* and *autem*: due to the high frequency of occurrence, it is possible to gather statistical data, which show that Farman often inserts an Old English adverb corresponding to the Latin adverb in WW, even when R lacks an adverb. Details can be discussed more effectively in relation to lexical variants; see below (c) and especially Table 1.

The following citation (10) contains an example of Farman's gloss that may reflect a reading not agreeing with R or WW.

(10) 24:1 (f. 39v, 2–4)

⁊ ut gangande
Et egres⟨-⟩
hælend of temple eode ⁊ him eodun to leorneras his
sus de templo· ibat et accesserunt discipuli eius·
ꝥ eawden him getimbru þæs temples
ut ostenderent ei aedificationem templi·
egressus] + iesus R[Fa] Y WW

Whereas Farman's insertion of Latin *iesus*, which appears to have been added with his gloss *hælend* judging from the layout, follows the Vulgate reading, his gloss *him eodun to* appears to reflect *accesserunt ad eum*, a variant reading found in some manuscripts but not adopted by WW.

Another intriguing instance is found in the following verse:

(11) 8:17 (f.12v, 1–3)

ꝥte gefylled wę̨re ꝥ gecwæden wæs
ut adinpleretur quod dictum (est)
þurh esaiam þe witgu cweþende he wiotudlice untrymnissu(m)
per iesaiam profetam dicentem ipse infirmitates
urum onfeng ⁊ metrymnisse ure he bær
nostras accipit et egritudines nostras portauit·
accipit] accepit YWW egritudines nostras] aegrotationes Y WW

wiotudlice in this verse has no corresponding word in R, and even the extensive collations by Fischer (1988–91: i, 181) record no reading with a Latin adverb which may have prompted Farman's gloss. However, the Old Testament source alluded to here is comparable (cited from the Stuttgart Vulgate): Is 53:4 *vere languores nostros ipse tulit et dolores nostros ipse portavit*. Its Latin *vere* could lie behind the inclusion of an Old English adverb; Ælfric in his homily for the third Sunday after Epiphany (ÆCHom I, 8), discussing Christ's healing of a leper (8:1–4), translates this Isaiah passage by *Soðlice he sylf ætbræd ure adlunga. ⁊ ure sarnyssa he sylf bær.*[45] Although it is impossible to know exactly how Farman's gloss came to reflect the Old Testament reading, it certainly reveals greater complexity behind the extant glosses than one may suppose.

(c) Lexical variants in R

It is often difficult to discuss which Latin lexical variant a particular Old English gloss translates, because such lexical variants tend to reflect Latin synonyms. There are relatively straightforward instances such as (12) below, where it is reasonable to attribute Farman's *ingaa* to WW *ingredi* rather than R *uenire*, which Farman would have glossed more naturally with a form of *cuman*.

(12) 19:17 (f. 31r, 12–14)

he cwæþ
qui dixit
him to hwæt ðu mec geaxast ɫ frægnast be góde an is gód
ei quid me interrogas de bono unus (est) bonus
god gif ðu þonne wilt innga to life hald bebodu
d(eu)s· si autem uís uenire ad uitam serua mandata
uenire ad uitam] ad uitam ingredi Y WW

There are also many instances where he sticks to his own Latin text, as can be observed by comparing his glosses to *consilium fecerunt* (for WW *consilium inierunt*) in the next two instances.

(13) 22:15 (f. 36v, 3–5)

þa awæg gangænde þa fariseas
Tunc abeuntes faris(-)
geþæhtungę dydun ꝥ gefenge hinæ in worde
sæi consilium fecerunt ut caperent eum in sermo(-)
ne fecerunt] inierunt Y WW

(14) 27:1 (f. 46v, 17–20)

þa hit þa morgen
mane
wæs in þæhtunge eodun ealle aldur(-)
iam facto consilium fecerunt omnes principes
sacerdæs ⁊ ældre þæs folces wið þæ(m) hælend
sacerdotum et seniores populi aduersus ie(su)m
ꝥ hine to deaþe salden
ut eum morti traderent·
iam] autem Y WW fecerunt] inierunt Y WW

[45] Ælfric's source here is identified as Haymo's *Homiliae*; see Godden (2000: 62).

In (13), Farman's gloss is a straightforward translation of his own Latin text, glossing *fecerunt* with *dydun*, wheareas *in … eodun* in (14) clearly points to the influence of Vulgate *inierunt.*

It is possible to take a statistical approach to this issue for *autem* and *enim* due to the high frequency of occurrence (see Table 1 below). First of all, it must be noted that Farman does not make a clear distinction between *autem* and *enim* in the first three chapters, using *soþlice* almost exclusively for both *autem* and *enim.*[46] Later on, he differentiates the two words by using *þa* or *þonne* for *autem* and *forþon (þe)* for *enim.* It is remarkable, therefore, that *forþon (þe)* is used three times when WW has *enim* in place of R's *autem* and also that, when R's *enim* corresponds with *autem* in WW, Farman tends to use *þonne.* As discussed in the previous section, the table also shows that, even when there is no adverb in R, Farman often uses an Old English adverb that reflects the one found in WW. Furthermore, there are cases in which Farman left a Latin adverb unglossed when it is missing in WW. The data confirm that Farman's gloss often, though not always, translates the text of the purer Vulgate when there is a difference between the two versions.

Table 1: Counterparts of *autem* and *enim* in Ru1 (Matthew only)

Latin		OE Ru1						
R	WW	*forþon (þe)*	*soþlice*	*þa*	*þonne*	*wiotudlice*	[others]	[unglossed]
autem	*autem*	0	13	118	158	5	1	7
	enim	3	0	0	2	0	0	0
	[others]	0	0	2	3	0	0	0
	[zero]	0	1	5	2	1	0	4
enim	*enim*	76	9	0	2	3	5	2
	autem	1	0	0	6	0	0	0
	[others]	1	0	0	0	0	0	0
	[zero]	3	2	0	2	1	1	2
[zero]	*autem*	0	0	2	5	0	0	3
	enim	4	0	0	0	0	0	6

46 The section may be narrowed down more precisely to 1:1–3:10. Although *þonne* and *forþon (þe)* are used in this section, the frequency is very low. Among 13 instances of *soþlice* glossing *autem* (R=WW), 11 are in the section. The other two are in 13:25 and 13:26. Another instance of *soþlice* is found also in the section (Mt 2:21), translating R's *autem*, whose corresponding adverb is wanting in WW. Seven instances of *soþlice* glossing *enim* (R=WW) are in 1:1–3:10. The other two are in 7:25 and 23:19. The two instances that are used for R's *enim* with its counterpart lacking in WW are in 4:7 and 18:7.

(d) Double glosses reflecting variant readings

It is a common practice for Old English interlinear glossators to give double, or even multiple, glosses to a single Latin word or phrase.[47] Some of Farman's double glosses betray his attempt to translate two Latin variant readings side by side. In (15) below, the second gloss *ꝉ se þe*, added above the line, appears to translate WW *qui*, whereas the first gloss *all* reflects R *omni*. The rest of the gloss is, in fact, closer to the Vulgate reading, as suggested by the finite form of *bidde*, corresponding to WW *petit*, not R *petenti*.

(15) 5:42 (f. 8v, 1–2)

all ˋꝉ se þeˊ bidde
omni petenti
þe sele him ⁊ þæ(m) ˋðeˊ wille on borg nioma æt þe ne beo ungeþwære
té tribue ei et uolenti mutari a té né auertaris
omni petenti te tribue ei] qui petit a te da ei Y WW

The double gloss in (16) also reflects two Latin variant readings.

(16) 21:38 (f. 35v, 4–7)

þa begengu
agri⟨-⟩
þa geségun þone sunu cwedun in innan heom
culae autem uidentes filium dixerunt intra sé
þis is se erfeweard cymeþ wutu ofslan þane ⁊ uru ˋꝉ ⁊ habbe we usˊ bið
hic est heres uenite occidamus eum· Et nostra erit
erfe his
hereditas eius
nostra erit hereditas eius] habebimus hereditatem eius Y WW

The first gloss, which should be read as *⁊ uru bið erfe his*, corresponds closely with R, whereas the inserted second gloss *⁊ habbe we us [erfe his]* clearly reflects the Vulgate reading. As I have discussed elsewhere (Kotake 2017: 88), some less obvious cases may also be comparable.

(17) 14:11 (f. 23v, 10–12)

⁊ broht wæs
et allatum est ca⟨-⟩
heafud his on disce ⁊ sald wæs þæ(m) mægden ⁊ ꝥ mægden ber ꝉ salde
pud eius in disco et datum est puellae et puella dedit
moder hire
matri suae
puella] *om.* Y WW dedit] tulit Y WW

[47] See, for instance, Ross and Squires (1980) and Kotake (2017).

At first glance, Farman's double gloss *bęr ł salde* appears to be a pair of synonyms to translate R's *dedit*, for which Vulgate reads *tulit*. In fact, Farman's usual lexical choice suggests that the first gloss appears to reflect the Vulgate reading, while the second his own Latin text, because he never uses *beran* for Latin *dare* elsewhere, which is usually glossed with *sellan*.

So far, we have examined evidence for Farman's knowledge of another Latin text by examining his Old English glosses. His gloss certainly reflects a purer Vulgate text in many cases. It is important to emphasize that, in such cases, Farman often leaves the Latin text of his own manuscript uncorrected, suggesting the possibility that he was copying from an Old English gloss or translation based on a purer Vulgate text. There is also a small number of instances where his gloss reflects Latin readings different from the standard Vulgate text, though the number of instances is too small to deduce the textual nature of the non-Vulgate readings. Furthermore, although his knowledge of a purer Vulgate text is discernible, Farman was also keen to provide Old English glosses matching his own Latin text, as exemplified by several instances. His use of double glosses to reflect Latin variant readings may also have been a result of deliberate attempts to introduce an Old English gloss reflecting a variant reading alongside the gloss matching to his own Latin text.

1.3.2 Corrections to the Latin text

Whereas the evidence examined in the previous sections suggests the availability of an Old English exemplar, it is equally possible that Farman had access to another Latin text, whether in a bilingual manuscript or in a separate manuscript from his Old English exemplar. There are, in fact, numerous corrections to the Latin text in the section Farman glossed. By examining the corrections attributable to Farman, it is possible to scrutinize his use of a Latin exemplar, and to speculate on the textual nature of the Latin text(s) he is likely to have had access to. When corrections involve writing of letters rather than cancelling by erasing, expuncting or crossing out, it is usually possible to decide whether they were added by Farman, on the basis of handwriting, colour of ink and their relative position to the Old English gloss. One exception is the Passion text in Matthew (Chapters 26–27), where a hand possibly different from his is active, which may be identical with the one that added liturgical signs and extra punctuation in the section (for the signs and punctuation, see II.2 above). The script used is still a type of Anglo-Saxon minuscule similar to Farman's (for Farman's handwriting, see III.3 below). The ink is black, and it becomes prominent especially when compared with Farman's browner ink used for Old English glosses in the section. It cannot be denied that they might indeed have been added by Farman on a different occasion. For the sake of uncertainty of identification, I will deal with them separately below under (b).

(a) Latin corrections attributable to Farman

The corrections to the Latin text I have attributed to Farman in the edition are presented in Appendix 1.[48] His corrections generally alter either defective or non-Vulgate readings to Vulgate ones, confirming his knowledge of a purer Vulgate text. At the same time, however, several instances betray the influence of non-Vulgate readings. When those corrections are compared with the critical apparatus of the Oxford Vulgate, the agreement may be summarized as in Table 2 below. The table shows, as might be expected, that no single manuscript can account for all of Farman's corrections. One thing that must be stressed is that the six corrections listed as nos. 117, 118, 124, 126, 127 and 128 occur in Mark, where Farman is often considered to be copying from the Lindisfarne Gospels (Y). No instances other than no. 124 can be accounted for by Farman's reliance on Y as an exemplar.

Table 2: List of manuscripts that have Farman's corrected readings

	A	B	C	D	E	EP	EPm	F	G	H	Θ	J	K	L	M	MT	O	Q	T	V	W	X	Y	Z
12				+		+						+		+				+						
15	+	+						+		+					+			+				+	+	
49																								+
70					+					+											+	+		
74		+		+	+		+						+		+	+				+				
96				+										+			+	+						
98				+	+					+	+		+	+				+	+	+	+	+		+
103		+				+				+		+	+			+	+	+		+		+		+
117				+	+		+		+							+	+	+						
118										C+	+						+							+
124	+	+				+				+							+					+	+	
126		+		+	+				+					+			+							
127									+															
128		+	+						+												+	+		

NB: The numbers in the leftmost column agree with the item numbers in Appendix 1. '+' indicates that the manuscript shares Farman's correction. 'c' indicates the reading is found as a correction in the manuscript. For the manuscripts and sigla, with up-to-date information, most conveniently, see Houghton (2016: Chapter 10 'Catalogue of Latin New Testament Manuscripts' and Appendix I 'Concordances of Manuscript Sigla').

48 In the edition, I have noted as 'R^{Fa}' the corrections attributable to Farman on the basis of the criteria mentioned above.

Another interesting result of this comparison is that the manuscripts showing a high rate of agreement, especially B and O, are also the ones that often share the non-Vulgate readings added by Owun in the Rushworth Gospels.[49] While their Old English glosses are markedly different from each other, Farman and Owun might have shared a Latin text of the Gospels available for consultation. It is tantalizingly interesting that O, one of the so-called Gospels of St Augustine (Oxford, Bodleian Library, Auct. D. 2.14), is reported by Ganz (2001: 36) to 'have been heavily corrected' in 'the gospel text of Matthew and the first two chapters of Mark', a curious correspondence to the division between Ru1 and Ru2, and that corrections added to O by an Insular scribe 'bring the text closer to the Irish gospel text found in the Book of Kells and the MacRegol Gospels'. Although the possible Lichfield provenance for the Oxford Gospels of St Augustine, a suggestion based on its inscription referring to St Chad, may invite further speculations, we have currently no evidence to prove any direct relationship between the Oxford St Augustine's Gospels and the Rushworth Gospels.[50]

Whereas Farman's corrections to the Latin text, whether they bring the text closer to Vulgate or non-Vulgate, point to the availability of other Latin texts for his use, his corrections sometimes result in Latin readings not recorded elsewhere. Although it cannot be denied that such Latin readings are to be found in the manuscripts not examined by WW, actual examples speak against the possibility:

(18) 5:15 (f. 7r, 5–7)

ne menn blæcern inbeornað
neq(ue) accendunt lucer⟨-⟩
⁊ settaþ hine under mytte ah on candel⟨-⟩
nam et ponunt eam sub modio sed supra can⟨-⟩
treow ꝥ he gelihte allum þe in husae sindun
dillabrum ut luceant omnibus qui in domu sunt
neq(ue)] + homines R^{Fa} supra] super Y WW ut luceant] et luceat Y ut luceat WW

Here, Farman's addition of *homines* after *neque* results in a unique Latin reading. His Old English gloss, in contrast, gives a smooth reading, perhaps comparable to the prose translation of the verse in King Alfred's *Pastoral Care* (CP [0116 (5.43.1)]): *ne scyle nan mon blæcern ælan under mittan*. This instance raises the suspicion that the addition of *homines* could possibly result from back-translation from his Old English gloss.

The suspicion may be strengthened by introducing another instance:

49 See Kotake (2016: esp. Table 3).

50 For the Oxford St Augustine Gospels, see also Marsden (1999), in addition to Ganz (2001) cited above.

(19) 14:16 (f. 23v, 22–f. 24r, 1)

se helend þa cwæþ to heom nabbaþ hię
ie(su)s autem dixit illis non habent
þearfe sella heom ge etan
necessire date illis uos manducare

illis] eis Y WW necessire] + adeuntes (*in the upper margin with the gloss,* to gangenne) R^{Fa} necesse ire Y WW

R's reading in its original state was defective: the expected reading *necesse ire* was written *necessire* without space. Farman's gloss *to gangenne*, added in the upper margin of f. 24r, properly translates the correct reading. In contrast, his Latin addition *adeuntes* cannot be explained by Latin grammar and is not found in the critical apparatus of WW. The only feasible explanation is that Farman, failing to see the infinitive 'ire' fused into *necesse*, tried to add an equivalent of *to gangenne* to the Latin text. The use of *adeuntes*, apparently the present participle plural form of *adire*, may have been intended as *ad eundum*, given that Farman uses '*to* + inflected infinitive' to translate Latin '*ad* + gerundium', as in 2:13 *herodes soecaþ þone cneht to ofslæanne hine* as a gloss to *herodes quaerat puerum ad perdendum eum*.

In (20) below, there is a more substantial addition to supply a defective reading in R, originally caused by homeoteleuton:

(20) 16:9 (f. 26v, 10–12)

ne ge cuþlice ne ongetaþ ne ge ne myngað
nondum enim intellegitis neq(ue) meministis
þara fif hlafa fif þusenda monna ⁊ hu monige monde
de quinq(ue) panibus ·u· milia hominum quot coffinos
genoman
sumpsistis

16:10 (f. 26v, addition in left-hand margin)

ni þara siofun hlafas
et de uii panes
feower þusenda
iiii milia ho⟨-⟩
monna ⁊ hu monige
minum ⁊ q(uo)t
sperta ge geno⟨-⟩
sporte acci⟨-⟩
man
pistis

[WW (16:10): neque septem panum quattuor milium hominum et quot sportas sumsistis]

Fischer's collation (Fischer 1988–91: i, 262–64) is available for the verse and enables an extensive comparison with extant variant readings. *et* instead of *neque* is rare (found in only two Old Latin manuscripts), and so is the use of *de*, which would require an ablative form instead of *panes*, as in 16:9. Farman's *sporte* is unique in not having the *-as* ending. The use of *accipistis* (for *accepistis*) is also rare, found in two Old Latin manuscripts with spelling variation. It is unlikely that all these rare readings occur in a single manuscript. In contrast, Farman's gloss gives a smooth reading apart from the unexpected nominative/accusative plural *hlafas* for the genitive plural. *ni* is probably a variant spelling of *ne* meaning 'nor', perhaps reminding us of the repeated use of the *ni* spelling in this specific sense in the Leiden Riddle.[51] This instance appears to reinforce the suspicion that Farman occasionally relied on Old English glosses to correct defective Latin readings.

(b) Latin corrections by an Anglo-Saxon hand in Matthew 26–27

Before considering the significance of the evidence presented above, we turn our attention to a group of Latin corrections found in the Passion section in Matthew. As in the case corrections attributable to Farman, many of the corrections bring the text of the Rushworth Gospels closer to a purer Vulgate, as presented in Appendix 2. While there is no hint of back-translation from Old English glosses, several corrections result in non-Vulgate readings, as summarized in Table 3 below:

Table 3: List of manuscripts that share corrections by an Anglo-Saxon hand in Matthew 26–27

	A	B	C	D	E	EP	EPm	F	G	H	Θ	J	K	L	M	MT	O	Q	T	V	W	X	Y	Z
7		+			+					c+	+		+			+	gl+			+	+			3+
8																				+				3+
19																		+						
22												+					+							
24		+										+					+					+		+
26								+											+					
35					+					+					+									
40					+									+			gl+				+			

NB: The numbers in the leftmost column agree with the item numbers in Appendix 2. '+' indicates that the manuscript shares Farman's correction. 'c', 'gl', '3' indicate the reading is a later addition in the manuscript, as identified by WW.

Four corrections are shared by O, two of which WW identifies as being added by a glossator, a fact that would perhaps add to the oddity noted above. The following instance (21) contains the corrections listed as nos. 7 and 8 in the table above.

[51] See, for instance, the text edited by Smith (1933).

(21) 26:10 (f. 43v, 19–20)

witende þa se hæl(end) cwæþ heo(m) to
sciens autem ie(su)s ait illis·
†for'h'won sindun ge swæncende þæm wife werc þon(ne) god hio worhte in mec
quid molesti estis mulieri bonum operata est in me,
estis] + huic R^c Y WW=R* mulieri] + opus enim R^c + opus Y WW

huic and *opus enim* are added in the Rushworth Gospels by the hand in question, and *huic* (no. 7) and *enim* (no. 8) are not in WW.[52] In O, too, *huic* is added to the main text by an Insular hand, which is shown in the plate in *Codices latini antiquiores* (Lowe 1935: no. 230). However, Farman's gloss *þæm*, neatly placed above the inserted *huic*, may be deemed not to reflect exactly the corrected reading, because a form of *þes* would provide a closer rendering of *huic*. Farman may have been copying here an Old English exemplar which was based on a Latin text without *huic*. In this sense, Li *forhuon erfeðo sindon gie ðæm wife* (for *quid molesti estis mulieri*) is comparable (note, however, the different lexical choices in translating *molesti*). This slight discrepancy between the Latin correction and its Old English gloss may support the possibility that the Latin corrections in this section may have been added by a hand different from Farman's, or if by Farman, on a different occasion. It may be possible to detect a similar discrepancy in (22) below:

(22) 27:52 (f. 49r, 10–11)

⁊ byrgenne ontynde werun ⁊ monig lic
et monumenta aperta sunt et multa corpora
haligra þære ðe ær sleptun arisen
s(an)c(t)orum· dormientium surrexerunt·,
dormientium] qui dormierunt R^c qui dormierant Y WW

þære ðe clearly follows *qui* in the corrected reading, but *ær sleptun* raises the question whether Farman's gloss follows R^c *domierunt* (perfect) or WW *dormierant* (pluperfect). Farman uses *ær* to express temporal relationship in nine other instances, seven of which translate the Latin pluperfect, whereas the other two the perfect.[53] Tempting though it is to attribute Farman's use of the *ær* in (22) to the influence of the Vulgate

[52] Note, however, both *huic* and *enim* are adopted in the Sixtine (1590) and the Clementine Vulgates (1592). In fact, it is likely that the reading with *huic* was current in Anglo-Saxon England, given that three Old English translations of the verse have forms of *þes*: WSCp 'hwi synt ge grame þysum wife'; HomS18 'To hwan yrsige ge wið þis wif'; HomS19 'Hwæt is eow uneaðe æt þissum wife'.

[53] Pluperfect 2:9, 2:16, 8:33, 18:11, 27:55, 27:60, 28:16; perfect 14:33, 26:57. For this use of *ær*, see DOE s.v. *ær* I.A.7 and Mitchell OES §§637–38.

reading, the variation between the Latin readings is too slight to draw any decisive conclusion.

The evidence concerning Latin corrections suggests that one or more Latin texts must have been available for Farman's – and another corrector's – consultation. Of course, some of those corrections could have been made even from memory, but the extent of the corrections makes it unlikely that all the corrections were made from memory. The nature of corrections can be summarized as bringing the text of the Rushworth manuscript closer to the Vulgate text, but there are also corrections that appear to reflect non-Vulgate readings. Given the high rate of agreement with O, the purer Vulgate text used by Farman might have had closer affinity to what modern scholars term as the mixed Italian family than to the Italo-Northumbrian, the latter of which the Lindisfarne Gospels is a fine example. Of course, it is not wise to press this conclusion too hard given the small amount of evidence available, but it certainly reminds us that we have to deal with a much broader context than the two extant Latin gospel manuscripts with Old English interlinear glosses.

The several instances of potential back-translation from Old English to Latin by Farman pose a question about the format in which Latin gospel texts were available for him to consult. Given the likelihood that Farman also used an Old English exemplar, as discussed above (III.1.3.1), it may be reasonable to assume that his exemplar was a Latin manuscript with corresponding Old English glosses, similar to what he eventually produced. Yet, the examples of potential back-translation strongly suggest that he occasionally did not or could not consult another Latin text, implying in turn the possibility that his Latin source may have been separate from his Old English exemplar. This is only a speculation based on limited evidence and cannot be proven. Nevertheless, the possibility that his Old English exemplar may have been written independently from Latin (hence excluding the format of interlinear gloss) will be important when linguistic features of his gloss are examined.

1.3.3 Other evidence for Farman's use of external sources

One further slender but intriguing piece of evidence about Farman's use of external sources may be discussed here. As described above (II.1.2), the Rushworth manuscript itself is void of any signs of liturgical use, apart from the later addition of liturgical signs and punctuation in the Matthew and Luke passion narratives. In contrast, Farman occasionally appears to indicate liturgical textual units by using enlarged letters. In 4:18 (f. 6r, 6), the verse begins with an enlarged *h*, whereas the Latin text receives no emphasis. His use of the enlarged letter is unlikely to be accidental, given that the verse opens a new chapter in some medieval chapter divisions (see De Bruyne 1914: 500), and also that it coincides with the beginning of the pericope assigned to the feast of St Andrew, as marked, for instance, in MS A of the West Saxon Gospels.[54] Because the Latin text itself does not receive any emphasis here, the enlarged letter seems to reflect either Farman's awareness of the textual unit, or possibly the layout of his exemplar that reflects such a unit.

Similarly, another enlarged *h* in 5:1 (f. 6v, 7) coincides not only with the modern chapter division, but with the beginning of the pericope assigned to the feast of All Saints (1 November), as noted in MS A of the West Saxon Gospels. Ælfric also cites the Beatitudes (5:1–12) in his homily for the occasion (ÆCHom I, 36), which ends in the middle of verse 12 (up to *in caelis*). The same point is also marked in the Rushworth manuscript by a dry-point cross (f. 6v, 22), though it cannot be known whether it was written by Farman or not.

Two instances of enlarged *g* mark two successive pericopes in 5:31 (f. 8r, 2) and 5:43 (f. 8v, 3), whereas the Latin text receives no emphasis in either case. The former is marked as an opening of the pericope for Wednesday of the sixteenth week after Pentecost in MS A of the West Saxon Gospels and the latter with *Đis sceal on wodnesdæg on þære systeoðan wucan ofer pentecosten. and on frigedæg innan þære cyswucan* in the same manuscript.[55]

There are no other similar instances and these enlarged letters occur in a relatively short section near the beginning of Matthew. It is possible that Farman may have introduced the capitalization or paragraph division of his exemplar by copying it very faithfully, a practice which he soon abandoned. It is perhaps worth noting that, although I have referred to MS A of the West Saxon Gospels for its liturgical notes, even the Corpus manuscript (CCCC 140), which does not have these notes, starts these textual units with a new paragraph. It is impossible to deduce in what kind of exemplar these divisions are likely to be found, but the potential value of these enlarged letters as a sign of Farman's use of external sources must be emphasized.

1.3.4 Farman's use of external sources: conclusions and their implications about the date and provenance of Ru1

The conclusions drawn from the foregoing discussion are: (1) Farman is likely to have used an Old English exemplar which was based on a purer Vulgate text (with some non-Vulgate readings); (2) he also had access to

[54] Cambridge, University Library, MS Ii 2.11, f. 6r; see Lenker (1997: 372–73) for details.

[55] See DOE s.v. *cyswucu* for 'the week following Quinquagesima Sunday'.

another Latin source – or possibly multiple sources – which had also a purer Vulgate text, containing some non-Vulgate readings, a relatively high proportion of which is shared by mixed Italian family texts; (3) he seems occasionally to have back-translated from Old English to correct or supply the Latin text of the Rushworth manuscript, suggesting that his Latin exemplar may have been in a different source from the Old English exemplar; and (4) there is a slight indication in his gloss that his Old English exemplar might have been divided or marked in a way similar to the West Saxon Gospels.

The implication of these conclusions about the date and provenance of Farman's gloss cannot be definitive, given that all these conclusions, it must be stressed, involve varying degrees of speculation. However, the foregoing discussion certainly shows that we should exclude the simple picture of Farman and Owun copying from the Lindisfarne Gospels. Accordingly, the relative dating of the Rushworth glosses to Aldred's gloss, which is more narrowly datable as seen above, must be discarded. So, rather frustratingly, we are taken back to Ker's dating of the glosses broadly to the tenth century and the unlocalized *harawuda*, until linguistic and palaeographical evidence is scrutinized below.

2. Language of Farman's gloss: introduction

The language of Farman's gloss has received much scholarly attention, especially because of its status as a rare sample of the Mercian dialect of the tenth century.[56] Brown's two-volume study (1891 and 1892) describes the phonology and morphology of Ru1, providing useful materials that formed the basis of further discussion by major Old English grammarians such as Luick (1914–40), Campbell (OEG), Brunner (1965), Hogg (1992) and Hogg and Fulk (2012).[57] As to vocabulary, Schulte's glossary (1904) laid the foundation, and its Anglian nature is considered by Jordan (1906), a topic which, later in the century, was to attract further attention in a series of studies of dialect vocabulary, notably those focusing on what is termed the Winchester group vocabulary.[58] Much less attention has been paid to the syntax of Ru1, with the significant exception of Crowley's survey (2000) on the word order of noun phrases, in which Ru1 stands out as being less dependent on the Latin word order than most of the other interlinear glosses

56 See, for example, Campbell (OEG §11), Hogg (1992: §1.8).

57 Brown (1891) and (1892) are now in the public domain and accordingly freely available online.

58 See, among others, Schabram (1965), Gneuss (1972), Wenisch (1979), and Hofstetter (1987). For a useful summary of the discipline, see Hofstetter (1988).

examined. In addition, linguistic studies focused on particular interlinear glosses make reference to Ru1. Ross's extensive work on Aldred's gloss often deals with Ru1 for comparison, and one of his numerous contributions (Ross 1976) is entirely devoted to the accidence of Ru1 and another (Ross 1979b) to its rare words.

Thanks to these scholarly works devoted to Ru1, there is little need of repeating descriptive overviews for phonology and morphology, as they are available in the works of Brown and Ross, supplemented by modern Old English grammars. Farman's syntax, in contrast, requires a fuller treatment, which will be presented below (2.4). His vocabulary is certainly of great interest, but will be discussed more conveniently in the commentary, requiring only a summary here (2.3).

However, there is one specific – and indeed controversial – topic, related to both phonology and orthography, and to a certain degree morphology and vocabulary, which needs to be fully considered in the sections that follow. That is Farman's dialect and its implications. As mentioned above, the dialect of Ru1 has been classified as Mercian, or more broadly Anglian, but a number of non-Anglian – mostly explicable as West Saxon – features are also evident, and Campbell (OEG §263 n. 1) helpfully makes us 'recall how many striking non-Angl[ian] features invade' Ru1. While such a mixed state is an accurate description of the language of Ru1, its interpretation cannot be straightforward.[59]

Because our knowledge of the Mercian dialect depends on a very small number of texts, notably the Old English gloss to the Vespasian Psalter, some scholars, such as Luick (1914–40: i, 165) and Menner (1934), regard the language of Ru1 as a type of Mercian distinct from that of the Vespasian Psalter gloss ('Unterdialekt' in Luick's term). One clear shortcoming of this 'subdialect' argument is that it does not take account of the fact that, as Campbell's use of the verb 'invade' implies, non-Anglian features are found alongside the corresponding Anglian forms that are usually more predominant in Ru1.[60] Kuhn (1945: 665), while conceding that he cannot 'determin[e] whether the inconsistencies of [Farman's] spelling reflect a mixed type of speech or merely a mixed orthography', postulates that Farman is likely to have been 'imitating the official West Saxon of the tenth century'; but there is little evidence about

[59] On potential difficulties concerning dialectological studies, see footnote 34 above.

[60] Of course, sound changes may have happened gradually, as Toon (1992) emphasizes with various examples, and the apparently mixed state may reflect a certain point in such gradual development. It is nevertheless difficult to regard, for example, the co-occurrences of *eall-* and *all-* (see below) as a pure reflection of how Farman pronounced the word.

Farman's scribal or personal background from which to argue for or against such a historical interpretation. A more concrete suggestion is made by Schulte (1903: 30), that the West Saxon features in Ru1 were introduced by Farman's copying from an exemplar which, he hypothesizes, was a Latin Gospel manuscript with an interlinear Old English gloss in the West Saxon dialect. His argument has been criticized, notably by Menner and Kuhn, but the results of the foregoing discussion about Farman's use of pre-existing sources clearly suggest the need for reconsideration. Hogg (1992) also repeatedly resorts to 'WS scribal influence' (or uses similar wording) to account for the many non-Anglian features found in Ru1.

Kuhn, Schulte and Hogg all implicitly accept that Farman's own dialect was Mercian, or Anglian, and that non-Anglian features were introduced into his gloss because of some kind of external influence. It would be a subtle question to ask whether we can completely rule out the possibility, say, that Farman was a West Saxon scribe who faithfully copied from an Anglian exemplar, yet occasionally introduced non-Anglian features that were more familiar to him. In fact, amongst Old English manuscripts, there are West-Saxonized copies of works considered to have been composed in Anglian; in such copies, non-Anglian, and perhaps late Old English as well, linguistic features can appear alongside Anglian ones in varying degrees.[61] There is, if we think of an extreme example, even a text copied in the twelfth century, in which Anglian features are predominant to the extent that scholars are able to argue that the text was originally composed in Anglian.[62]

One potential piece of evidence against the possibility that Farman was a West Saxon scribe copying a Mercian exemplar can be found in Kuhn's analysis. Discussing Farman's notorious use of <e> and <æ>, he notes that, while Ru1 often has <æ> as expected in West Saxon (as against <e> in Mercian), <æ> also appears where <e> is expected in both Mercian and West Saxon (i.e., from West Germanic /e/).[63] Kuhn (1945: 642) considers these unexpected instances of <æ> as resulting from 'carr[ying] the imitation [of West Saxon] too far' – a West Saxon scribe would have had no reason to use <æ> for West Germanic /e/. The argument for

[61] See Bately (1988: 98ff.), who carefully reviews scholarly opinions concerning a group of texts that are often cited as works originally composed in Anglian, but 'preserved in late-tenth-, or eleventh- or even twelfth-century copies, with a West Saxon veneer'.

[62] An Old English homily on St Chad, preserved in Oxford, Bodleian Library, Hatton MS 116. See Vleeskruyer (1953).

[63] In this section, Hogg's conventions (see Hogg 1992: §2.8 n.1) are followed: angled brackets (< >) indicate graphic sequences; slant brackets (/ /) phonemic transcriptions; and square brackets ([ ]) phonetic transcriptions.

hypercorrection – Kuhn himself did not use the terminology but Smith (1996: 20–21) employs it to refer to Kuhn's findings – may appear convincing, especially seen in isolation, but it should also be remembered that, as I have shown elsewhere (2012a), Farman's preference for <æ> as against <e> is found regardless of its etymological value, sometimes even for unaccented vowels, and that his preference for <æ> becomes more prominent towards the end of Matthew. It is not particularly convincing to argue that forms like *hiæ/hię* (third person plural pronoun) or *siæ/się* (subjunctive present of *beon*) are a result of over-imitating West Saxon forms. Such an extensive use of <æ> instead of <e> seems to suggest Farman's personal – and indeed idiosyncratic in some cases – preference, perhaps in orthography rather than reflecting his pronunciations, and such a personal preference may be found whether he was a Mercian or West Saxon scribe.

If Farman was indeed a Mercian scribe, as usually assumed, what kind of scenario would lead to the mixed state of his language? If a West Saxon exemplar was available to Farman, a Mercian scribe, as Schulte supposed, then he was either 'translating' it into Mercian while copying, or using it only sporadically, perhaps for reference. The latter is less likely, because, as Hogg observes (1992: §1.8 n. 3), the West Saxon features in Ru1 'have a tendency to be restricted to more common words'. This tendency will be confirmed below, and in some cases, the number of non-Anglian features often increases as Farman moves on through Matthew. If Farman was using a West Saxon exemplar for reference, West Saxon features are more likely to have occurred also in rarer words. Under the hypothesis of a Mercian scribe copying a West Saxon exemplar, then, it is more likely that he was translating the exemplar into Mercian with effort, while admitting some West Saxon forms that became familiar to him in the course of copying. This interpretation can be supported further by Menner's observation that even in the Mark portion, where Farman is thought to have been using an exemplar that is closely related to Li, his spelling shows tendencies similar to those in Matthew. If Farman's gloss ended up being something like a mixture of Mercian and West Saxon even when he was copying a Northumbrian exemplar, then, Menner concluded, the apparently mixed state of dialects indeed reflects Farman's own dialect. Yet, it is equally possible that the mixed state was established only during his long labour of translating a West Saxon exemplar into Mercian.

If Farman was a Mercian scribe and his exemplar was also written in a dialect similar to or the same as his own, it is not easy to imagine that Farman was deliberately, yet very incompletely, introducing dialect features not native to him. Hogg (1992: §1.8 n. 3) interprets the tendency that non-Anglian features are 'restricted to more common words' as 'suggest[ing] that they were learned by Farman at a WS(-influenced) scriptorium', somehow echoing Kuhn's suggestion that Farman was 'imitating the official West Saxon'. Such an interpretation is tempting as a possible cause of the sporadic appearance of West Saxon features in a copy made from a Mercian exemplar by a Mercian scribe, but, as noted above, we know nothing about Farman's background. It is impossible, for instance, even to confirm that Ru1 post-dated the Benedictine Reform of the late tenth century; and if it did, we know little about the kind of influence the West Saxon dialect could have exerted upon scribes who were not under direct influence of the reform.[64]

All these seemingly nonsensical hypotheses are mentioned to emphasize the danger of accepting too hastily the widespread notion that Farman was a Mercian scribe influenced by West Saxon. It seems impossible to draw a secure conclusion about whether Farman was a Mercian scribe affected by West Saxon, or vice versa; or whether he may have been someone who had not yet established his own orthographical practices in writing Old English. In the latter case, his spelling could have been unstable regardless of his own dialect. His handwriting, as will be seen below (III.3), suggests a scribe with some formal training, but that does not necessarily mean that he had worked on vernacular works previously. In any case, as we have seen above, we do not have any internal or external evidence about the exact dating and location of his glossing. Neither will linguistic data present us with any secure evidence on this matter. Disappointing though it may sound, it is with this acknowledgement that I embark on the following sections, in the hopes of prompting further discussion of Farman's language and its interpretation.

The sections below are subdivided into conventional categories: orthography and phonology (2.1), morphology (2.2), vocabulary (2.3) and syntax (2.4). The section on syntax will also consider methods of translation from Latin.

2.1 Orthography and phonology

2.1.1 Introduction

Farman's orthography conforms, in general, to Old English practice, using <p> (*wynn*), which is transcribed as <w> here and in the edited text, both <þ> and <ð> for the dental spirants, and <æ> alongside *e*-caudata

64 See, for instance, Gneuss (1972) on issues relating to 'Standard Old English'. Smith (1996: 19–21), based on Menner (1934) and Kuhn (1945), presents a similar conclusion, that 'Farman was not a West Saxon, but aspired to West Saxonism'.

<ę>. The use of the runes is confined to the single instance in his colophon (f. 50v), spelling out his own name as *Farᛗ*.[65]

The following discussion starts with relatively straightforward orthographical features and then moves to phonology, mostly focusing on the discussion of dialectal mixtures as noted above. The distinction between orthography and phonology, however, is necessarily obscure in historical studies. Whereas the general assumption, as, for instance, put forward by Samuels (1952: 20), that the orthography adopted by the scribes writing Old English would be 'roughly phonetic, bore some relation to the spoken sounds, and – excepting OE of the eleventh century – was not bound by meaningless traditional conventions', is valid, it should also be remembered that orthographic conventions do play a role in Old English even before the eleventh century, leading Stanley (1988: 328) in a paper addressing Luick's notion of 'man schrieb wie man sprach' to the conclusion that English scribes 'never wrote as they spoke'. Given this difficulty, the divisions between orthography and phonology are conventional, and some of the variations dealt with as orthographic may indeed represent underlying phonetic or phonological variations.[66]

2.1.2 Orthographic variations

Spelling variations of presumably purely orthographic nature in Ru1 include (1) the use of <th>[67], <d>[68], <t>[69] for <þ>/<ð> in Old English words (cf. Campbell OEG §57 (5)–(7) and Hogg 1992: §2.59); (2) <qu>

[65] This may be contrasted with Aldred's more frequent use of runes in the Lindisfarne Gospels; he uses the 'dæg' rune (ᛞ) in addition to the 'mann' rune. See *Cod. Lind.* (Book ii, 16–17) and Brookes (2016: 111).

[66] This is especially true about the variation between <t>, <d> and <þ>/<ð>, which may involve dental instability as observed in Middle English; see Lass and Laing (2009). I am grateful to the anonymous reviewer for the critical comments on my treatment. I have kept the general outline of these sections, but this does not mean ruling out the phonetic or even phonological significance of the spelling variations.

[67] <th> initial *thæm* (7:9), *the* (5:17, 23:17), *thi* (21:42), *thuað* (15:2, preceded by an erased *þ*); <th> final *biddeth* (7:10), *ripath* (6:26).

[68] <d> initial *dægne* (5:25), *de* (11:25); <d> medial *eordan* (18:18), *eordu* (23:15), *nider* (11:23); <d> final: *cræd* (26:34, 26:75), *cwæþad* (23:16), *cymid* (24:42), forms of *deaþ* (5x), *habbad* (26:11), *geweorðæd* (13:22). There are a smaller number of instances of <þ> or<ð> appearing where <d> is expected: *nemneþ* (pt.part., 5:19), *genægeþ* (pt.part., 23:12), *þusenð* 14:21, and probably *þune* (4:8, where *dune* is expected; see the commentary to the verse).

[69] All relevant instances occur in the present endings *-eþ*, *-aþ* of weak verbs; for Campbell (OEG §735(b)) the *-t* ending 'suggests a genuine phonetic variant': *adwæscet* (12:20), *gehnyscet* (21:44), *neolicet* (4:17), *ræccet* (2:6), *scyldigat* (6:12), *soecet* (12:39), *swerat* (23:22).

for <cw>;[70] and (3) <u> and <uu> for <w>.[71] These features appear to be mostly due to remnants of early orthographical practices and, while their implications about Farman's scribal background and orthographic features of his exemplar(s) are tantalizing, the alternative spellings are unlikely to differentiate their pronunciation.

2.1.3 Instable graphs for consonants: orthographical or phonological?

The <k> graph occurs in relatively large numbers in Ru1, with resulting orthographic variations between <c> and <k> for the phoneme /k/.[72] As has been pointed out, the variation is not random. There appears to have been some attempt to disambiguate two allophones, the velar [k] and the palatal [c]; Hogg (1992: §2.50) observes that '<k> predominates over <c> when a front vowel follows', and he also suggests that the choice may have been 'on a lexeme-by-lexeme basis'.[73] Yet, as can be seen from the relevant entries in the glossary, many of the words that are spelled with <k> also occur elsewhere with <c> instead and the attempt to disambiguate the two allophones was not complete.

70 *quartern* (25:39), *quom* (28:9), *quomon* (2:1). Hogg (1992: §2.45 n. 1) notes that 'some early texts have <qu> for initial /kw/', citing one instance from the Épinal Glossary.

71 See Campbell (OEG §60), who sees *u* and *uu* as older spelling that remained longer in Northumbrian texts. See also Hogg (1992: §2.77). <u> *andsuari* (2:12), preterite forms of *cuman* (<cu-> spellings are more frequent in the earlier portion of Matthew, with the instance of *cuom* in 21:19 being the last occurrence, except for *quom* in 28:9; <cw-> spellings occur throughout Ru1; see the glossary for details under *cuman* and *forecuman*), *fulluihte* (3:7), *huat* (16:13), *sua* (5:16), *thuað* (15:2), *uitgana* (23:30), *uulfum* (10:16); <uu> *uuiltu* (26:17). To these, *winduiscoful* (3:12) may be added, depending on the interpretation of its etymology. See the commentary to the verse.

72 <k> initial (of a word or an element) *kaseres* (22:21), *kasere* (22:17, 22:21 *bis*); *kægen* (16:19); *kælic* (20:22, 20:23); *kęmpe* (27:27), *kempum* (28:12); *kende* (1:2, 1:16), *kenneþ* (1:21, 1:23); *kennisse* (1:1, 1:18); forms of *acennan* (9x); *æftakennisse* 19:28; *frumkendu* 1:25; forms of *cyning* (7x); medial *arkę* (24:38); *ascakeþ* (10:14); *akcras* (12:1); *bilketto* (13:35); *besenked* (18:6); forms of *bocere* (20x); *gebroken* (21:44); *carkærn* (25:36), *calkern* (25:43); *ceke* (5:39); *ciken* (23:37); *deofulseoke* (8:16, 8:33, 12:22), *deofulseoka* (8:28); *ek* (x32); *eknum* (24:19); *eknisse* (21:19); *folkes* (2:4, 13:15, 26:3); *lokende* (19:26), *lokigæþ* (27:24); *gemerkade* (27:66); *monsek* (17:15), *monsekae* (4:24); *onsaekeþ* (10:33); *roketto* (13:35); *smikende* (12:20); *sukendra* (21:16); *taken* (12:39, 16:1); *toekan* (15:38); *toeke* (25:20); *wolken* (17:5); in cluster with another consonant: *kneorisse* (1:17 *bis*), *kneo* (1:17), *kneorissum* (1:17); *kneu* (27:29); *krist* (1:16, 2:4), *kristes* (Mt INCIPIT, 1:18, 11:2), *kriste* (1:17); *tungulkræftgu* (2:1), *tungulkræftgum* (2:7, 2:16), *tungulkreftgum* (2:16); *unklene* (8:16, 12:43).

73 Hogg (1992: §2.50, n.1). See also Campbell (OEG §427, n.1) and Kuhn (1970: 25–26).

Similarly, <i> occasionally occurs instead of <g> for the palatal spirant, another possible instance of disambiguating allophones, although it is equally possible that <i> spellings are due to the influence of an earlier orthographical practice (cf. Campbell OEG §58).[74] Many of the words spelled with <i> are also found with <g> as in *gearu*, *(ge)gearwian* and *geomonn*, and there are words in which the palatal spirant is always spelled with *g-*. These seem to point to, as in the case of <c> and <k>, the likelihood that the distinction is not complete. *iarward* (20:23, f. 33r, 8) is preceded by an erased *ge-*, possibly suggesting Farman's uncertainty.

Another feature of Farman's spelling is the instability of <h>, which can either be inserted without historical grounds or omitted where expected.[75] This involves both <h> followed by a vowel and <h> in the consonant groups, <hl, hn, hr, hw>, as summarized in Table 4 below. Scragg (1970: 194) in his extensive study of initial <h> followed by a vowel states that 'evidence from Ru1 for instability of the aspirate, as opposed to the symbol, is not strong'. The same may be true for <h> in the consonant groups, especially <hr>, for which both inorganic <h> and omitted <h> occur at similar rates. It appears, however, difficult to conclude that the instability as to the use of <h> is purely graphic,[76] as most of the cases involving <hn> and <hw> omit <h>, which may point to the loss of /h/ in these clusters.[77] The overall data appear to suggest a situation in which Farman occasionally pronounced words with inorganic /h/ or by omitting /h/, perhaps depending on the phonological environment. This does not mean, however, that his spelling in each occurrence necessarily reflects exactly how he pronounced the specific

[74] <i> for <g> *iara* (11:21) for adverb *geara*; *iare* (22:8), *iara* (22:4) for adjective *gearu*; forms of *(ge)gearwian* (3x); *ioc* (11:29, 11:30) for *geoc*; *iuguðe* (19:20) for *geogup*; *iumonnum* (5:21) for *geomonn*; *iungæ* (19:20), *iunge* (19:22); *ierde* (10:10) for *gyrd*.

[75] Scragg (2012: 222) notes that 'unstable *h* is particularly prevalent in the work of writers working in the middle of the [eleventh] century' and the manuscripts written before the year 1000 contain 'very few instances of omitted *h-* and even fewer of unhistoric *h-*'. See also Johannesson (2000).

[76] As to one of possible causes of the graphic instability of <h>, one may suggest Aldred's use of suprascript <h>, described as having 'the form of the left half of the modern letter H, by origin an imitation of one of the earliest forms of rough breathing used in Greek manuscripts' (*Cod. Lind*, Book ii, 14). Farman himself did not use the form, but such a letter form, if found in his exemplar(s), could have confused him in copying.

[77] For a summary of two contrasting views about the phonological value of the graph <h> in these consonant groups, see Hogg (1992: §2.72). See also Toon (1992: 437–38), who sees these spellings as evidence of gradual sound changes of /h/, but his discussion focuses on the loss of /h/ in the consonant groups and does not deal with the instances of inorganic <h>, making it difficult to assess his argument.

instance, because orthographical practices must also have played a role in deciding the spelling.

Table 4: Inorganic <h> and omitted <h>

	inorganic <h>	**omitted <h>**
+ vowel	*haþas* (5:33) *hað* (5:34) *hehtende* (5:11, 10:23) *hoehtende* (5:12) *hefalsaþ* (9:3) *heofolsaþ* (Mk2:7) *hefalsadun* (27:39) *hefalsunge* (15:19) *his* (for *is*) (3:3, 3:10, 5:3, 5:41, 17:4, 22:20, 23:18, 26:66) (*aþ* 5:36, f. 8r, 14, *unc* 9:27, f. 14v, 5, *eodun* 24:3, f. 39v, 8 and *æfenne* 27:57, f. 49r, 21 are preceded by an erased <h>)	*æfð* (13:12) *æfdon* (8:33) *eard* (25:24) *eora* (6:15, 7:16, 7:20, 8:34, 9:30, 10:18, 15:8, 23:30, 24:31) *is* (for *his*) (7:24, 22:24, 24:46, 25:33) *eo* (16:18) *eorta* (6:21) *eortum* (18:35) *us* (17:25) *yngrade* (25:35) *geyrdon* (from *gehyran*) (19:25)
hl	*hlafe* (14:20) (for *lafe*) *forehlutende* (Mk1:7)	
hn		*genægeþ* (23:12, *bis*) *næscum* (11:8, *bis*) *nyte* (7:16)
hr	*gæfelhroefe* (9:10) *gæfelgehrefum* (9:11) *hræfneð* (6:24) *gehreofa* (27:11) *hreordeþ* (12:3) *hreordun* (22:31) *gehreorde* (15:33) *hriopan* (12:1) *hryft* (5:40) *hripes* (9:38)	*ræþe* (14:31, 24:29, Mk1:28, Mk1:30) *rægl* (28:3) *read* (11:7) *reuwe* (18:10) *ruxlende* (9:23) *ridesohte* (Mk 1:31)[78]
hw-[79]	*hwute* (27:49)	*ægwilc* (7:17, 12:36)

78 For the possible interpretations of the word, see the commentary to the verse.

79 <hw> is written twice with <h> added as a suprascript: *ge\h/werfad* (16:23), *for\h/won* (26:10). There is also an instance of *hw-* preceded by an erased wynn; see note to 13:26. To the examples of the lack of *h* in the <hw> cluster, *wite* (11:21) might be included, depending on how to read the word. See

wa (22:24)
wær (8:20)
welpas (15:27)
werfde (9:22)
weorfe (10:13)
wẹrfende (21:18)
weorfaþ (6:1)
gewyrfeþ (6:19)
gewyrfeð (6:20)
gewerfe (18:3)
wilce (21:24)
wilen (13:21)
miswerfde (17:17)

Farman's spelling also betrays, though much less frequently, instability as regards <r>, which is occasionally omitted or inserted. The examples of omitted <r> include: *boþer* (5:23), *dyste* (for *dyrste*, 22:46), *foletend* (4:20), *foleteþ* (6:14, omission is marked by a caret-like sign), *ðefra* (26:17, genitive plural of *þeorf*), and possibly *oferswiðiaþ*, if taken as a form of *oferswiðrian* (16:18). The inorganic <r> is found in *fringre* (23:4), *iarward* (20:23), *geiarward* (25:41), and *geþriostra* (27:45).[80] The examples of the inorganic <r> may be due to the influence of another <r> in proximity. The omission of <r>, on the other hand, is harder to account for, but the two instances of *forletan* may be compared with similar instances from the Hatton manuscript of the Old English Pastoral Care as reported by Cosijn (1883–86: §143), who lists several examples of the omission of <r> in the *for-* prefix, often followed by an <l>. Besides, there are two other instances of *forletan* in Ru1, which have <r> written *in rasura*: *forleteþ* (5:32, f. 8r, 5) and *forletne* (9:2, f. 13r, 18). Similarly, there are instances of the same verb where an apparently abandoned stroke is visible above <r> in the manuscript, which might have started an <l>, in 9:6 (f. 13v, 3), 11:24 (f. 18r, 4), 15:39 (f. 26r, 16). Given that the high proportion of Farman's uncertainty about <r> involves the word *forletan*, the omission of <r> may have been related to dissimulation, which can also be detected in *bloeþrẹ* (1:2), a curious accusative plural form of *broþer*, as discussed by Brown (1892: §10). In addition to the influence of dissimulation, the *br-* cluster itself appears to have caused some confusion to Farman, as <r> is written *in rasura* also in the following instances: forms of *brengan* (*brohtun* [8:16, f. 12r, 21], *brohtun* [9:2, 13r, 16], *brohte* [17:16, f. 28r, 13], *brohte* [25:20, f. 42r, 15]), and *bry(m)stream* (8:18, f. 13r, 5). While the exact nature of Farman's pronunciation of /r/ and /l/

note to the verse.

80 Similarly, the inorganic <l> is found in *fluglas* (13:32).

cannot be retrieved, these spelling features suggest that the two liquids could have affected one another in Farman's language and that <r> tends to be lost under certain phonological environment. In other words, the inconsistency between <r> and <l> is likely to have been related more closely to phonological causes than orthographical. Yet, with few comparable instances reported in other Old English texts,[81] it has to be admitted that the implications of Farman's uncertainty about <r>, whether phonological or orthographical, are almost impossible to assess.[82]

2.1.4 Vowels in stressed syllables: dialect features

Thus, our discussion has moved gradually into the field of phonology, as anticipated. The phonological examination proper mostly focuses on the vowels in accented syllables, but it must be emphasized that even here orthographical factors cannot be ignored. I have shown elsewhere (Kotake 2012a) that some of the variations between <e> and <æ> in Ru1, which have been variously interpreted in phonological studies, notably by Kuhn (1945), may have been, at least partially, due to orthographical factors. Not only does the variation between <e> and <æ> occur irrespective of the expected phonological values represented by those graphs, but <æ> becomes more frequent towards the end of Matthew, suggesting that there may have been some change in Farman's orthographical preference. As a result, it is difficult to take his spellings as phonological evidence at face value, especially where the <e>–<æ> variation is involved. In fact, Kuhn (1945: 665) begins the conclusion of his extensive study of <e> and <æ> in Ru1 by conceding that 'at present I see no way of determining whether the inconsistencies of his spelling reflect a mixed type of speech or merely a mixed orthography'.

The following analysis focuses on dialectal features found in accented vowels in Ru1, guided mainly by Campbell (OEG §§256–64). As noted earlier, because Brown's works (1891 and 1892) are still serviceable as a descriptive study of Farman's phonology especially when supplemented by more recent publications on Old English grammar, the sections focus on considering how Anglian and non-Anglian features occur side by side in Ru1.

[81] It is not certain whether these examples can be seen as relevant, if remotely, to the late Old English loss of <r> in *sprecan* and similar instances; cf. Campbell (OEG §475) and Hogg (1992: §7.86 n. 3).

[82] There are also some signs of confusion between <c> – <g>: *galdes* (10:42; see note to the verse for details), *cnidan* (21:35), forms of *þonc-*. See also note to 24:49 where *drinceþ* for *bibit* is corrected from *drigð*.

2.1.4.1 <o>/<a> before nasal

Prim. Gmc. /ā/, from /a/ before nasal consonants, came to be spelled in Old English as both <a> and <o>. Eventually, this sound is spelled with <a> in most of later Old English texts,[83] suggesting that the nasal /ā/ became identical with /a/. In Anglian texts, <o> spellings are frequently found, in accordance with Middle English evidence that shows the distinction was kept still in the West Midland areas.[84] In Ru1, <o> predominates, while <a> spellings are also found, which Hogg (1992: §5.5) regards as either 'a feature imported from WS [...] or a characteristic of' Farman's dialect. The predominance of <o> can be confirmed by looking at the entries in the glossary for such high frequency words as *from*, *hond*, *lichoma*, *lond*, *monn* (also as the second element of the compounds *ealdormonn*, *geomonn*, *hyrmonn*), *noma*, *(ge)somnian* and *(ge)somnung*, which are always spelled with <o>.

In contrast, <a> spellings occur when the conjunction *and* and the *and*-prefix are spelled out (as against the use of the Tironian note).[85] Both *þonne* and *þanne* occur, though the former is much more frequent.[86] Besides, the preterite singular forms of strong class III verbs have a relatively large number of <a> spellings.[87] In fact, amongst the class III verbs for which preterite singular forms are recorded, *gebindan* is the only verb that does not show <a> spelling (*gebond* 14:3).[88] Another instance where <a> before nasal is more frequent than <o> is the forms of *gangan* (including prefixed ones), for which *gong-* spellings occur only twice (*gongende* 15:21, *gongen* 15:22).[89] It can be safely concluded that the use

83 Hence, the <o> spelling is not an exclusively Anglian feature, as it is also the case in early West Saxon texts. See, for instance, Bately (1986; cxxxiii–cxxxiv) for <o> spellings in the Parker Chronicle manuscript.

84 See Campbell (OEG §130), Hogg (1992: §§5.3–5.5), and for Middle English examples, see Luick (1914–40: §367).

85 *and* (1:17, elsewhere the conjunction is always spelled with the Tironian note), *andswarade* (16:2, 17:11, 19:27, 25:40, 28:5), *andswaredun* (14:17, 25:9), *andsuari* (2:12), *andwyrde* (verb, 15:15, 15:28, 27:14), *geandwyrdan* (22:46), *andwyrde* (noun, 2:12); *andwlitu* (6:17, 18:10), *andwliotu* (6:16); three instances of *onfon* (*andfoað* 17:25, *andfoa* 11:14, *andfoeþ* 18:5).

86 *þanne* is once altered to *þonne* by writing <o> above <a> in 9:15 (f. 14r, 2).

87 *bewand* (27:59), *blan* (14:32), *ingann* (4:17, but also *ingon* [2x], *ingonn* [3x]), *gelamp* (11:1, 13:53, 19:1), *ongan* (26:74, but also *ongon* [3x]), *sprang* (Mk1:28); with metathesis, *arn* (27:48).

88 Both Hogg (1992: §5.4) and Toon (1992: 439) note that the late Northumbrian texts, Li, Ru2 and DurRit, always have <a> in the preterite singular forms of strong class III verbs. Hogg considers such forms 'analogically reformed', while Toon regards them as 'an important example of constrained lexical diffusion', where 'a single grammatical class counts for the entire residue of an otherwise completed sound change'.

89 See Toon (1983: 115–18), who points out that <o> is by far more frequent

of <a> spelling before nasal consonants in Ru1 is limited to several lexical items and one specific grammatical form, apart from some sporadic instances in other words.[90]

2.1.4.2 <e>/<æ> for Prim. Gmc. /ǣ/

Prim. Gmc. /ǣ/, when not followed by nasal consonants, becomes /ǣ/ in West Saxon, but /ē/ in the other Old English dialects.[91] Farman uses both <æ> and <e>, and, according to Kuhn (1945: 653), they occur in the proportion 7:10. Although this proportion is cited repeatedly in subsequent studies (e.g., Campbell OEG §128 n. 2 and Hogg 1992: §3.25 n. 1), Kuhn's list (1945: 653–54) of the <æ> spellings is worth revisiting, as the 165 <æ> spellings he counted include 62 instances of *þær* (including variants spelled with *ð*-, -*ę*-), significantly reducing the number of types against tokens. In fact, if we take a close look at, for example, the preterite plural forms of strong class V verbs,[92] <æ> spellings occur only for *cweþan*, *fretan*, *geseon*, and *wesan*,[93] whereas <e> is consistently used for the other ten verbs for which preterite plural forms are recorded.[94] The fact that the <æ> spelling appears to be confined to specific lexical items, some of which are of high frequency, rather than being found universally in the text, appears to have prompted Hogg (1992: §3.25 n. 1) to state that it is 'doubtless' that Farman's <æ> spelling 'is merely one sign of WS influence on' him.

2.1.4.3 <a>/<ea> before <l> + consonant

Retraction of the front vowel /æ/ to /a/ before /l/ followed by a consonant is an Anglian feature, though also found in early West Saxon and early Kentish, as against breaking to /ea/ in the other dialects. Besides the predominant <a> spellings, Farman also uses <ea> spellings, which both Campbell (1959: §258) and Hogg (1992: §5.15) attribute to the

---

when followed by /ŋ/.

90 *lange* (17:17 *bis*), *standende* (20:3, 20:6).

91 See Campbell (OEG §128) and Hogg (1992: §§3.22–3.25). The present discussion does not enter into details of the Gmc. development, especially whether Prim. Gmc. /ǣ/ became /ā/ or was retained in West Gmc. Note, however, Kuhn (1945: 653–57) takes the former view, discussing relevant instances under 'Isolative development of West Germanic *ā*'. For the two contrasting views, see Campbell (OEG §129) and Hogg (1992: §3.23 n. 2).

92 As to strong class IV verbs, only *beran* presents relevant instances, for which the past plural form is recorded only once, spelled with <e> (*beron*, 20:12).

93 For why *wesan* is included here, see Hogg and Fulk (2011: §6.61).

94 I count *ge*- prefixed forms separately: *biddan*, *gebiddan*, *gefeon*, *gefetan*, *ongietan*, *seon*, *sittan*, *gesittan*, *sprecan*. For *gefetan*, which occurs only in Ru1, see the commentary to 13:7.

influence of the West Saxon orthographical practice. Ru1's <ea> spellings are confined to several lexical items, notably *eall* instead of *all.* Svensson (1883: 23) notes that the <ea> spellings become more frequent in the latter half of Matthew, as can be confirmed from Table 5 below on the distribution of *eall-* and *all-* (reproduced from Kotake 2012a: 29, Table 1).

Table 5: Distribution of *eall-/all-* forms

	Matthew			Mark	Total
Chap	1–10	11–20	21–28	1–2:15	
eall-	12	19	37	2	70
all-	24	13	15	9	61

Svensson suggests that the increasing use of <ea> is due to 'a lessening accuracy on the part of the scribe' (cited in McAllister's translation [1952: Part 1, 119] of 'minskad noggrannhet hos afskrifvaren'). While the increase of <ea> can also be observed in other words than *eall/all,*[95] it is hardly possible to determine just what made Farman use the non-Anglian spellings more frequently as he progressed in Matthew.[96] What should be emphasized as to <a>/<ea> before <l> + consonant is that the Anglian <a> is predominant in Ru1 and the use of <ea> spellings is confined to some specific lexical items and becomes more frequent in the latter half of Matthew.

2.1.4.4 Palatal diphthongization

Extensive diphthongization of front vowels by the influence of preceding palatal consonants is a feature of West Saxon and Northumbrian, but lacking in Mercian.[97] Ru1 is seen as an exception to the general tendency, as it contains several instances of /æ/ > /ea/; Hogg (1992: §5.52) suggests that it may have been due to the West Saxon influence. The <ea> spelling is not predominant and its distribution is uneven.[98] If we take a closer

95 *behealdene* (16:12), *behealdeþ* (16:6), *ealde* (9:17), *ealdormen* (Jn18:3), *feallep* (12:11), *feallan* (15:30), *healdene* (28:20), *healfe* (20:21 [2x], 25:33 [2x], 25:34), *healte* (15:31, 21:14), *healt* (18:8), *scealt* (18:28).

96 It could indeed have been caused by his increasing familiarity with West Saxon orthographical practice, if we assume Farman was a Mercian scribe, as Stanley (1969: 38–39) posited in discussing 'the *waldend* group': 'Anglian scribes [...] substituted the West Saxon spelling sequence *eal* + consonant for the own *al* + consonant. We may presume that they were taught to write that way; at least initially the process of converting *al* to *eal* was a conscious effort, though it may have become automatic'.

97 Campbell (OEG §§185–87).

98 *ceaf* (3:12; preceded by erasure, possibly of *s*); *ceastre* (21:10, 21:18, 23:34 [2x], Mk1:45), *ceastræ* (21:17); *geatt* (7:13); *geate* (7:13, 7:14), *geat* (Mk1:33); *sceal* (3:14, 26:54), *scealt* (18:28); *sceat* (1:18).

look at the distribution of *ceaster/cæster*, which occurs most frequently amongst the words subject to this sound change, it is easily recognizable that the <æ> spelling is predominant (23 occ., against six <ea> examples) and that the <ea> spelling occurs only later in Farman's gloss, with the first instance occurring in 21:10.[99]

2.1.4.5 Forms lacking Anglian smoothing

The monophthongizations of /ĕ̄a (ǣ̆a)/, /ĕ̄o/, /ĭ̄o/ to /ǣ̆/, /ĕ̄/, /ĭ̄/ respectively before the back consonants /c/ /ʒ/ /χ/ with or without intervening liquids /r/ or /l/ are termed as smoothing and it is a characteristic feature of the Anglian dialects. Ru1, however, is noted as 'the only noteworthy exception' by Campbell (OEG §263 n.1), containing forms without smoothing, and he attributes them to the influence of West Saxon spellings.

As a result, the short diphthong /ea (æa)/ is smoothed to /æ/, or /e/ when /r/ intervenes.[100] This general rule is kept in Ru1, though there are instances of <e> spellings where <æ> is expected, thus bringing about another case of the confusion between <æ> and <e>.[101] These <e> spellings are deemed as inexplicable in previous studies, and Hogg suggests that 'scribal error is most probable', a reasonable deduction given the general confusion about the two graphs in Ru1.[102] Forms lacking smoothing are confined to *geseah*, found six times (2:16, 4:16, 9:22, 9:36, 14:30, 27:3) alongside more frequent *gesæh*.[103]

The smoothing of the long diphthong /ēa (ǣa)/ is spelled with <e>, and sometimes <æ>.[104] Ru1's spellings that show the lack of smoothing are

[99] It may also be noted that *scepa* 'sheep' (gen. pl., 7:15) may have been altered from *sceapa*; there is an erased letter between <e> and <p> (f. 11r, 6), though the erasure is not clearly legible. Ru1 also has *scipa* (gen. pl., 18:12), which can be compared with spellings found in Northumbrian; cf. Campbell (OEG §186) and Hogg (1992: §5.54).

[100] Campbell (OEG §223) and Hogg (1992: §5.98).

[101] In addition to the references cited in the previous note, see Kuhn (1945: 651–52).

[102] Campbell (OEG §223) and Hogg (1992: §5.98 n. 2). The <e> spellings include: *ehtu* (11:16), *exlan* (23:4), *geþehtunge* (12:14, but elsewhere <æ> is used), *wexan* (*inf.*, 13:30), *wexeþ* (13:32, possibly due to *i*-umlaut).

[103] In 21:33, Farman spelled *heage* for the expected *hege*, with the <a> added as suprascript. This instance is not relevant to the discussion of smoothing, because the first <e> in *hege* is developed from /æ/ by *i*-umlaut of an *i*-stem noun. Yet, it may be noted here because such a hypercorrection may have been caused by his knowledge of the contrast between forms with smoothing and those without.

[104] Campbell (OEG §225), Hogg (1992: §5.99) and Kuhn (1945: 661), who provides a full list. <æ> spellings occur frequently again in the latter half of Matthew: *þæh* (15:20, 21:21, 24:26, 26:33, 26:35); *æc* (24:27); *bæg* (27:29).

confined to two lexical items: *þeah* (24:23), *ðeah* (16:26); *eagan* (18:9 *bis*), *eagun* (26:43); elsewhere <e> or <æ> is used. The regularity of the operation of this smoothing can be observed from *ec*/*ek* and *heh* (including *heh-* compounds), all of which are spelled with <e>; <ea> spellings occur only when /χ/ stands between the diphthong and a nasal in *heanes* (5x) and when the back consonant is lost in declension (*hea*, fem. dat. sg. 17:1).[105]

Similarly, /eo/ is smoothed to /e/ in Anglian, and it is spelled with <e>, again alongside some instances of <æ>. Whereas spellings with smoothing are the norm in Ru1,[106] Hogg (1992: §5.96) observes that it also contains 'a large number of unsmoothed forms' and considers that they 'may show no more than the WS influence'. The unsmoothed forms are, in fact, confined to three lexical items: *feoh* (10:9, 25:18, 25:27, 28:12); *feorh* (16:25 *bis*, 16:26); *weorc* (5:16, <o> is written as a suprascript), *weorcæ* (instr. sg., 16:27).

The situation involving the smoothing of /ēo/ is also similar; it undergoes smoothing to /ē/ in Anglian, as in *flege* ('fly, gnat', 23:24). As to *leht*/*leoht* (also as the first element of *leohtfæt*), forms both with and without smoothing are found; once they occur side by side even within a single verse (4:16).[107] In contrast, *seoc* as part of *deofulseoc* is consistently spelled with <eo>: *deofulseoke* 8:16, 8:33, 12:22, *deofulseoka* 8:28.[108]

Ru1 shows the smoothing /io/ to /i/ as expected in Anglian (cf. Campbell OEG §229). The long diphthong /īo/ is also smoothed to /ī/ in Ru1, with some forms without smoothing. Two words clearly show that forms both with and without smoothing occur in Ru1. For *betweonan*, forms with smoothing occur when the back consonant following the vowel is still present in the spelling: *betwig* (24:10), *betwih* (18:15, 26:58, Mk2:8), *betwihc* (20:26, Mk1:27), *betwihs* (21:25), *betwix* (20:26, 20:27, 27:56). In contrast, when the consonant is not present in the spelling, unsmoothed <eo> and <io> occur: *betweon* (3:9, 11:11) and *betwion* (16:7, 16:8, 23:35). Similarly, Farman uses the double glosses *weofud ł wibede* (5:23, see the commentary to the verse), pairing the forms with and without smoothing.

105 See Hogg (1992: §5.100(2)) for the exception of smoothing, and Hogg and Fulk (2011: §4.27) for the paradigm of *heah*. Another instance of fem. dat. sg. is spelled as *heh* in 4:8, which may be an undeclined form.

106 <æ> spellings occur again mostly in the latter half of Matthew: *cnæhte* (18:5), *cnæhtas* (18:2, 21:15), *cnęhte* (2:8); *gefæht* (24:6), *gefæhta* (24:6); *wærc* (23:5), *wærcum* (23:3).

107 The examples without showing the smoothing include *leoht* (4:16, 5:14, 24:29) and *leohtfatu* 25:1, 25:3, 25:7 (*o* written suprascript).

108 Once it is spelled with <oe> instead of <eo>: *deofulsoece* (10:8).

As Campbell noted, the lack of Anglian smoothing is a feature of Farman's language, but the overall data suggest that forms without smoothing are limited.

2.1.5 The vowels in unstressed syllables

The state of Farman's vowels in unstressed syllables is succinctly described by Ross (1976: 493–94). One feature relevant to the foregoing discussion is that even in unstressed syllables, <æ> occurs instead of <e>, another indication of the possibility that the interchange between <æ> and <e> in Ru1 may be largely due to orthographical causes rather than phonological.

2.1.6 Consonants

Most of the features of Farman's consonants that require comments have been dealt with in the orthography sections above. One further feature to be noted is the loss of final /n/, especially frequent in weak nouns, a feature generally restricted to Northumbrian (cf. Brown 1892: §12, Campbell OEG §473 and Hogg 1992: §7.100). In contrast, the inorganic <n> occurs in the nominative singular forms of weak nouns, as noted by Brown (1892: § 12) and Ross (1976: 497).

2.2 Morphology

2.2.1 Introduction

As noted earlier, we have two important studies on the morphology of Ru1 by Brown (1891 and 1892) and Ross (1976) available for consultation. Instead of adopting a descriptive approach, the sections that follow will reconsider two of Ross's remarks made in his paper.[109] The first is that 'the gender-conditions of Anglo-Saxon are preserved in Rushworth[1] (and Rushworth[2])' (Ross 1976: 492–93). Of course, Ross undoubtedly had in mind, when making the statement, the much more disrupted conditions in Aldred's language; we therefore should understand it in relative terms.[110] There are, in fact, some signs of disruption of Old English historical gender distinctions in Farman's gloss,

[109] As a result, this section deals only with part of nominal morphology. Due to the limited treatment presented here within the scope of an introduction to an edition, I admit that there are lacunae to be filled in this section by specialized studies, as suggested especially by such recent works on nominal and verbal morphology and morphosyntax of Aldred glosses as Cole (2014) and (2016), Fernández Cuesta and Langmuir (2019) and Rodríguez Ledesma (2022).

[110] For the situations in Aldred's glosses, see especially Ross (1936) and Jones (1967) and (1988). Millar (2016) is also an important survey on Aldred's noun phrase morphology, to which reference is frequently made in relevant sections below, along with his earlier monograph (Millar 2000).

a point which has not been discussed fully in previous studies. The first part of this morphology section (2.2.2) addresses the statement.

Ross also points out that the 'nominative-accusative singular can be used for the dative' in Ru1 (1976: 499), noting at the same time that such instances are 'much rarer' than in Li. The second part (2.2.3) will consider the possible weakening of case distinctions in Farman's language.

In both sections, the main purpose is to cast light upon some of the instances in Farman's gloss that deserve close attention from specialists working on relevant topics in Old and later English. Identifying a particular instance of the two phenomena is not without problems, partly because of the format of interlinear glossing. Glossators may not have followed strict Old English syntax, and thus it becomes more difficult to decide on the expected grammatical form in a particular instance. The influence of the Latin source cannot be ignored, either. The sections that follow do not purport to be exhaustive in terms of the collection of examples. Various issues related to the following sections are also discussed individually in the commentary to the texts.

2.2.2 Weakening gender distinctions in Ru1

2.2.2.1 *þæm*/*ðæm* + feminine dative singular

The first instances to be considered here are those in which historically feminine nouns are used with masculine or neuter forms of the demonstrative. Millar (2016: 154–56) notes that some feminine nouns in the dative singular are often used with *þæm*/*ðæm* in Li. Ru1 has similar instances, as in (23) below:[111]

(23) 15:28[112]
R: et sana facta est filia illius ex illa hora
Ru1: ⁊ gehæled wæs dohter hire of **ðæm hwile**
Li: ⁊ gehæled wæs dohter ðæs ł hire of ðæm tid
WSCp: ⁊ þa of þære tide wæs hyre dohtor hal ge-worden;

[111] It must be kept in mind that Farman and Aldred may have shared their sources – not by direct copying from one another but via common textual tradition –, almost certainly in the Mark portion of Ru1 and probably in Matthew 26–27, as noted above (III.1.2.2). However, the majority of the instances examined here are found outside these particular sections, making it hardly possible to attribute the disruption of gender distinctions entirely to the influence of shared sources.

[112] Citations in the morphology and syntax sections are, unless otherwise noted, presented in a simplified format to facilitate comparison with Li and WSCp. Latin citations are taken from R in the corrected state. Unless otherwise noted, textual variants are noted only when relevant to the discussion, and abbreviations and contractions are expanded silently in both Latin and Old English except for Old English ⁊ and ꝥ. Li and WSCp are cited from Skeat.

The historically feminine *hwil* occurs with *ðæm* in (23) above, while the same noun is paired with another feminine noun *tid* as a double gloss in (24) below, preceded by two instances of *þæm*. In fact, *tid* is one of the 'two nouns [that] dominate' this type of evidence in Li, as found in (23) above, according to Millar (2016: 154; cf. the other, *byrgen* 'tomb').

(24) 20:5
R: Iterum exiit circa sextam et nonam horam et fecit similiter
Ru1: eft ut eode æt **þæm** sextan ⁊ **þæm** nigoþan **tide ł hwile** ⁊ dyde gelice
Li: eftsona soðlice ge-eode ymb ða seista ⁊ non tid ⁊ dyde gelic
WSCp: Eft he ut-eode embe þa sixtan ⁊ nigoþan tide. ⁊ dyde þam swa gelice;

Old English *healf* is historically feminine when used as a noun (see DOE s.v. *healf*, n.), but it is used with *þæm* in (25) below:[113]

(25) 25:41
R: Tunc dicet rex hiis qui a sinistris eius (*eius* om. in WW) erunt
Ru1: þonne cwæþ se cyning ec to þæm þa þe on **þæm winstran halfe**
Li: ða coeðes ⁊ ðæm ða ðe to winstrum biðon
WSCp: Þonne segþ he þam þe beoð on hys wynstran healfe;

One may argue that *þæm*/*ðæm* is on the way to becoming a marker of the dative case, irrespective of gender, in Ru1; however, it should also be noted that the number of relevant instances is small.

2.2.2.2 Feminine nouns in congruence with non-historical gender attributes

There is another type of unhistorical gender congruence involving historically feminine nouns in Ru1. In (26) below, feminine *eorþe* is used with an adjective with the strong masculine accusative singular ending *-ne*.

(26) 13:23
R: qui uero in terram bonam seminatus est
Ru1: se þe þonne in **eorðe godne** gesauwen wæs
Li: seðe uutedlice in eorðo godo (altered from *goda*) sawende wæs
WSCp: Soþlice ꝥ þe asawen wæs on þæt gode land

[113] *healf* is also used with the masculine/neuter dative singular *æghwilcum* in Mk 1:45 (*æghwonan from æghwilcum halfe* for *undique*; cf. Li *eghuona ł from halfe gehuelc*, WSCp *æghwanon*).

In (27) below, a mixture of different gender forms is observed. The weak feminine[114] *heorte* is used with a feminine form of an adjective (*alre*), but also followed by the masculine/neuter genitive singular *þines*.

(27) 22:37
R: dileges dominum deum tuum in toto corde tuo et in tota anima tua et in tota mente tua
Ru1: lufa dryhten god þinne of **alre heortan þines** ⁊ of alra saule þinre ⁊ of alra mode þinum
Li: lufa drihten god ðinne of alle hearte ðine ⁊ of alle sauele ðine ⁊ in alle ðoht ðinne
WSCp: lufa drihten þinne god on ealre þinre heortan. ⁊ on ealre þinre sawle. ⁊ on eallum þinum mode.

The use of *-ne* or *-re* where not historically expected occurs in Ru1 so haphazardly that one might attribute these instances to error. While they are not frequent enough to suggest that the endings *-ne* and *-re* have gained new functions as case marker irrespective of gender in Ru1, their potential significance as a sign of weakening gender distinctions should not be overlooked.

2.2.2.3 Analogical *-es* genitives of feminine nouns

The instances examined above, potentially indicating weakening gender distinctions, would naturally raise the question whether Ru1 has the analogical *-es* genitive forms of feminine nouns, for which Li provides ample examples.[115] There are three instances in Ru1: *weoruldes* for *saeculi* in 13:49 (where Li also has the *-es* ending) and 24:14 (where Y does not have *saeculi*) and *helles* for *gehenae* (Li *cursunges*) in 23:14.[116] In terms of frequency, Farman's use of the analogical *-es* genitive of feminine nouns may not be significant, especially in comparison with Li, but, again, the forms may in fact be a harbinger of weakening gender distinctions.

[114] On the possibility that the noun could be used as masculine/neuter in Northumbrian, see the commentary to the verse.

[115] See Ross (1937: 99). See also Rodríguez Ledesma (2022) for an extensive survey of the analogical *-s* ending as genitive and plural marker in Aldred's gloss in the Lindisfarne Gospels and the Durham Collectar.

[116] Ross (1976: 498) further includes *næhtes* from 14:25, but, though corresponding to the genitive *noctis* in the Latin text, it may be regarded as a variant spelling of the adverb *nihtes* 'at night' (in CH's spelling) in the context: *feorðe þære wacone næhtes* for *quarta autem uigilia noctis*. The adverb form is widespread in Old English and therefore may be less relevant here.

2.2.2.4 The demonstrative *se* used with feminine nouns

Having identified these examples, it becomes difficult simply to dismiss the instances of the *se* spelling used with feminine nouns in the nominative singular either as error or as a variant spelling of the demonstrative *seo*.[117]

(28) 6:3
R: te autem faciente elimoysinam nesciat sinistra quid faciat dextera tua
Ru1: ðe þonne wircendum ælmesse nyte **se winstrae hond þin** hwat þin sio swiþre doa
Li: ðu ł ðeh uutedlice wyrcende ða ællmissa nyta winstra ðin huæt wyrcas ł doas suiðra ðin
WSCp: Soþlice þonne þu þine ælmessan do nyte þin wynstre hwæt do þin swyþre

In (28) above, the historically feminine *hond*, occurs with *se*. In (29) below, the historically feminine *duru* is also used with *se*. Conversely, DOE (s.v. *duru*, n.) suggests that the noun *dure* is masculine in Ru1.

(29) 25:10
R: dum autem irent emere uenit sponsus et quae parate erant intrauerunt cum eo ad nuptias et clausa est ianua
Ru1: ðenden hiæ þa eodun bycgan com se brydguma ⁊ þa þe gearwe wæron ineodun mid hine to gemungæ ⁊ belocen wæs **se dure**
Li: miððy uutedlice geeodon to bycganne cuom ðe brydguma ⁊ ða ðe weron innfoerdon mið him to brydloppum ⁊ getyned wæs ðe dura
WSCp: Witodlice þa hig ferdun ⁊ woldon bycgean þa com se brydguma ⁊ þa ðe gearwe wærun eodun in mid him to þam gyftum. ⁊ seo duru wæs belocyn

The *se* spelling is once used for a female referent as in (30) below:

(30) 27:61
R: Erat autem ibi maria magdalena et altera maria sedentes contra sepulchrum
Ru1: wæs þa þær maria **se magdalenisca** ⁊ oþer maria sittende togægnes þara byrgenne
Li: wæs ðonne ðer ðiu magdalenisca ⁊ oðero sittendo wið ðæt byrgenn
WSCp: Ðær wæs soðlice seo magdalenisce maria ⁊ seo oðer maria sittende æt þære byrgene;

[117] McAllister (1952: Part1, 196) attributes the feminine nominative singular *se* to error. For a similar instance in Li, see Millar (2016: 159, citation 14).

The possible influence of the Latin gender is not relevant to any of these *se* instances. Whether these instances should be seen as evidence reinforcing weakening gender distinctions in Ru1 or as a variant spelling of *seo* seems to be an unanswerable question.

2.2.2.5 The expanded use of *þæt* with non-neuter

The use of *þæt* with non-neuter also involves feminine nouns.[118] In (31) below, the historically feminine *tid* is used with *þæt*.

(31) 21:34
R: cum autem tempus adpropinquasset fructum uiniae missit seruos tuos ad agriculas ut acciperent fructum eius
Ru1: þa **þæt tid** tonealehte wæstma þæs wintreowes sende esnas his to þæm begængum ꝥ hi onfengon þæm wæstmum
Li: mið ðy uutedlice tid ðæra wæstma geneolecde sende ðegnas his ⁊ ða lond-buend suæ ꝥ onfengon wæstm his
WSCp: Þa ðara weastma tid ge-nealæhte þa sende he hys þeowas to þam eorðtylion. ꝥ hig onfengon his wæstmas;

In the manuscript (f. 35v, 19), the *þæt* in (31) is written as if a gloss to Latin *autem*; but given that *autem* is never glossed with the conjunction *þæt* elsewhere in Ru1,[119] it appears wise not to rule out the possibility that the *þæt* is the demonstrative in congruence with a feminine noun.[120]

Apart from the instance cited above (31), the use of *þæt* for non-neuter is rare in Ru1, but the following instance deserves attention, not only because of its congruence with a masculine noun, but also because it accompanies a noun with the dative case inflection *-um*.

(32) 15:20
R: haec sunt quae quoinquinant hominem non lotis autem manibus manducare non quoinquinat hominem
Ru1: þis sindon þa þe besmitaþ monnum þæh unðwegenum þonne hondum ete ne besmitaþ **ꝥ monnum**
Li: ðas aron ða widlas ðone monno unðuenum uutedlice hondum eatta ne widlas ðone monno
WSCp: Þis synt þa ðing þe þone mann besmitað; Ne besmit þone mann þeah he unþwogenum handum ete

118 For comparable examples in Li, see Millar (2016: 158, citations 11–12).

119 There is another instance of *þæt* written above *autem* in 19:22, which is also unlikely to translate the Latin as in the instance in (31); see the commentary to the verse.

120 For a possibly comparable instance of *þæt þeostre*, see commentary to 6:23.

In fact, this instance presents several difficulties: the verb *besmitan* is usually used with an accusative object, but the spelling *monnum* suggests the dative plural. Even if *monnum* is taken as a variant spelling of the accusative singular of the weak masculine noun *manna*, the historically wrong gender congruence must be noted as the use of the abbreviation for *þæt*.[121]

2.2.2.6 Masculine nouns in congruence with other gender forms

The following instance of a masculine noun in historically aberrant gender congruence is from the Mark portion of Ru1, where it is not shared by Li.

(33) Mk 1:2
R: qui praeparabit uiam tuam
Ru1: se þe foregearwað **weg þinre**
Li: seðe foregearuas wege ðin
WSCp: Se ge-gearwað þinne weg be-foran ðe

One could perhaps dismiss the use of *þinre* as a miscopying of the expected masculine accusative singular *þinne*, not least because there are some instances of palaeographical confusion that apparently suggest Farman's difficulty in distinguishing between **n** and **r** in his exemplar.[122] However, the use of the *-re* ending with masculine/neuter nouns in the Prose Guthlac in London, British Library, Cotton MS Vespasian, D. xxi (s. xi^2, according to Ker no. 344) is comparable, presumably functioning as a dative marker.[123] In (33), the expected case is the accusative, and we cannot make direct comparison with the dative usage in the Guthlac examples, but they seem to point to the risk of dismissing too readily the Rushworth example as copying error.[124]

There is a further instance in which a mixture of different gender forms is observed as in (34) below:

[121] In 13:47, *congreganti* is glossed with *þ somnendum*, similarly presenting various difficulties. See the commentary to the verse.

[122] See note to 10:15 in the Commentary.

[123] See Roberts (1970: 32–33).

[124] Note also that the same noun is referred back to by the double gloss *þære ł þæne*, glossing Latin *eam*, in 7:13. It is, of course, possible that the first gloss reflects the gender of *eam* and the second Old English *weg*, but the double gloss may indeed be another indication of weakening gender distinctions.

(34) 9:26
R: et exit fama haec in uniuersam terram illam
Ru1: ⁊ eode **se hlisa þis** in all ꝥ lond
Li: ⁊ ge-eade ł spranc mersung ðas ł ðius (altered from *ðys*) in alle eorðo ða ilco
WSCp: ⁊ þes hlisa sprang ofer eall þæt land

While the historically masculine *hlisa* is preceded by the masculine *se*, it is also followed by the neuter *þis*, written above *haec*.

Like the *se* spelling used with feminine nouns, there is a question as to whether *þios* and *þeos* used with masculine nouns are variant spellings of the expected *þes* or examples of historically wrong gender congruence. In (35) below, the historically masculine *cælic* is used with *þeos*.

(35) 26:42
R: pater mi si non potest hic calix transire a me nisi ut illum bibam fiat uoluntas tua
Ru1: fæder min gif ne mæge **þeos cælic** leoran from me nymþe þæt ic of him drince beo hit þin willæ
Li: fader min gif ne mæge ðes cælc oferliora nymðe ic drinca hine ł ðene sie willo ðin
WSCp: Min fæder gyf þes calic ne mæge gewitan buton ic hyne drince gewurþe þin willa;

Similarly, in (36), the masculine *cneht* is used with *þios*, which is followed by the non-gender sensitive relative pronoun *þe*, while glossing the Latin *iste hic*.

(36) 18:4
R: Quicumque humiliauerit se sicut paruulus iste hic est maior in regno caelorum
Ru1: forþon swa hwa eadmedaþ hine swa **cneht þios** þe is mare in rice heofunas
Li: swæ huælc forðon eðmodiges ł beges hine suæ lytel cnæht ðes ðis is maast in ric heofna
WSCp: Swa hwylc swa hyne ge-eaþmet swa þes lytling. se ys mara on heofena rice

In (37) below, *ðeos* is used as a pronoun referring to Christ.

(37) 27:47
R: quidam autem illic stantes et audientes dicebant heliam uocat iste
Ru1: sume þa þær stondende ⁊ þa geherende cwedun eliam cleopaþ **ðeos**
Li: sume ðonne ðer stondende ⁊ geherende hia cuoedon ceigas ðes
WSCp: Soþlice sume þa ðe þær stodon ⁊ þis gehyrdon cwædon; Nu he clypað heliam;

In (38) below, *þios* is used not only in congruence with the historically masculine noun *middangeard* but also in a syntactic environment where the dative is required (the noun is written as *middang* with a suspension stroke, making it impossible to know the exact case ending of the word).

(38) 18:7
R: uae enim mundo huic a scandalis
Ru1: wa soþlice **middang(earde) þios** from fælnissum
Li: wæ middangeard from ðæm ondspyrnisum
WSCP: Wa þysum middangearde þurh swicdomas

It is again difficult to decide if these instances are due to weakening gender distinctions or if we should regard *þeos/þios* as variant spellings of *þes* in Ru1.

2.2.2.7 Neuter nouns in congruence with other gender forms

The following instance contains a possible instance of a historically neuter noun used in unhistorical gender congruence:

(39) 26:61
R: et dixerunt hic dixit possum distruere hoc templum dei et post triduum ædificabo illud
Ru1: ⁊ cwædun þes cwæþ ic mæg toweorpan **þas tempel** godes ⁊ æfter ðrim dagum getimbre þæt
Li: ⁊ cuoedon ðes cuoeð ic mæge toslita ł toworpa tempel godes ⁊ æfter ðrim dagum getimbra ꝥ
WSCp: Ðes sæde ic mæg towurpan godes templ. ⁊ æfter þrym dagum hyt eft getimbrigean.

While the historically neuter noun *tempel* is referred to by *þæt* at the end of the verse, the Latin *hoc templum dei* is glossed with *þas tempel godes* by Farman. While *þas* may be regarded as the plural form disagreeing with the Latin, it cannot be ruled out that *þas* is a feminine form in unhistorical gender congruence with the neuter noun.[125]

2.2.2.8 Unhistorical gender congruence in Ru1: summary

The examples discussed above, taken together, suggest weakening gender distinctions in Ru1, although it is difficult to determine exactly how advanced such weakening was. They clearly point to the need for investigation that would relate the conditions of Farman's language to synchronic and diachronic examination of the changes concerning grammatical gender in English.

2.2.3 Possible signs of the weakening case system

Ross points to the nominative/accusative-dative syncretism in Ru1 (1976: 499), as seen above. Similarly, Clark (1970: liii) states that the abandonment of the dative case observed in the first continuation of the Peterborough Chronicle is 'foreshadowed' in Ru1 (and Li). In making these statements, both scholars refer to the examples collected by Brown (1892: 71, 73), who lists relevant instances as dative singular forms '[w]ithout ending, disregarding syntax' (p. 71) or '[e]nding wanting' (p. 73). It should be carefully considered whether those endingless forms are actually the result of gradual loss of the dative case in particular in Farman's language, as implied by Ross and Clark, or whether they are not restricted to the dative, suggesting wider effect of the weakening case system. It is also necessary to take into consideration the common glossing practice to give only a lexical equivalent, 'disregarding syntax' if we adopt Brown's wording. As noted above, the examples shown below should not be regarded as a complete set of data, because, where case endings are absent, the collection of examples must rely partly on Old English syntax and partly on the Latin equivalent, involving subjective judgements at various levels.[126]

There are instances of dative singular forms without the *-e* ending for various strong nouns. For example, there are case-endingless nouns with a dative attribute, which are relatively straightforward to identify, as in (40) and (41) below:[127]

[125] See also the commentary to 17:18 for another possible instance (*of ðære yfle*), though involving some uncertainties.

[126] As to the loss of the case marking in Old and later English, see, for instance Allen (1995), though Ru1 is not examined in the study. On Aldred's gloss in the Lindisfarne Gospels, see Fernández Cuesta and Rodríguez Ledesma (2020).

[127] Similar examples are found in 20:3 (*þære ðridda tid*), 21:28 (*wingeard minum*), 25:6 (*middere niht*), 26:71 (*þæm hælend*), 27:1 (*þæm hælend*), Mk1:44 (*ðæm aldorsacerd*).

(40) 14:11
R: et allatum est capud eius in disco et datum est puellae et puella dedit matri suae
Ru1: ⁊ broht wæs heafud his on disce ⁊ sald wæs **þæm mægden** ⁊ þæt mægden bęr ł salde moder hire
Li: ⁊ gebroht ł gefered wæs heafud (altered from *heofod*) his in disc ⁊ gesald wæs ðær mædne ⁊ brohte moder hire
WSCp: ⁊ man brohte þa his heafod on anum disce. ⁊ sealde þam mædene ⁊ ꝥ mæden hyre meder;

(41) 18:33
R: nonne ergo oportuerat et te misereri conseruo tuo tui sicut et tui misertus sum
Ru1: ah þe ne gedæfnade ek ꝥte ðu miltsade **ęfnðeuw þinum** swa ic ðe miltsade
Li: ah ne[128] ne forðon reht were ⁊ ðeh milsades efneesne ðin suæ ⁊ ic ðe ł ðines milsande am
WSCp: hu ne gebyrede þe gemiltsian þinum efen-ðeowan swa swa ic þe gemiltsode

While the dative case is expressed by the forms of the attributes in (40) and (41), case-endingless forms are also found by themselves in the syntactic environment that clearly requires the dative case, of which most frequent is their use after prepositions, as in (42) and (43):

(42) 12:33
R: Aut facite arborem bonam et fructum eius bonum aut facite arborem malam et fructum eius malum siquidem ex fructu arbor agnoscetur
Ru1: oþþe wyrceþ treow god ⁊ westem his godne oþþe wyrceþ treuw yfel ⁊ westem his yfelne forþon þe **of westem** bið treow ongeten
Li: ł doæð tre god ⁊ wæstm his god ł doæð ðæt tre yfel ⁊ wæstm his yfel gif ec soðlic from wæstm treo oncnaua eaða mæg
WSCp: Oþþe wyrceað god treow ⁊ hys weastm godne. oððe wyrceað yfel treow ⁊ hys wæstm yfelne. Witodlice be þam wæstmme byð ꝥ treow oncnawen;

[128] Skeat, followed by DOE, transcribes the repetition of *ne* as part of the Old English gloss. The layout in the manuscript (f. 64v, 7a), however, clearly suggests that the first *ne*, written closer to the Latin text, is a correction to the Latin text by Aldred, altering *non* in his Latin text to *nonne*.

(43) 18:1
R: In illa hora accesserunt discipuli ad iesum dicentes quis putas maior est in regno caelorum
Ru1: on þære hwile eodun þa leorneras **to hælend** cwęþende hwa wenest nu mare sie in heofuna rice
Li: in ðæm tid geneolecdon ða ðegnas to ðæm hælend hia cueðende huelc wenes ðu maast is in ric heofna
WSCp: On þære tide genealæhton hys leorningcnihtas to þam hælende ⁊ cwædon; Hwa wenst þu ys yldra on heofena rice.

In (44) below, *drihten* is an indirect object of *agiefan*, but lacks the dative ending.

(44) 5:33
R: iterum audistis quia dictum est antiquis non periurabis reddes autem domino iuramenta tua
Ru1: eft ge geherdun þætte cwęden wæs gumonnum ne swer þu man agef þonne **drihten** þine haþas
Li: eft sona herde ge forðon acueden is ðæm aldum ne ðerh-suere ðu to suiðe ðu forgeldes soðlice drihtne gihata aðas ðine
WSCp: Eft ge gehyrdon ꝥ gecweden wæs on ealdum cwydum. ne forswere þu; Soðlice drihtne þu agylst þine aðas

These instances certainly give the impression that endingless forms can be used for the dative. While both Ross and Clark focus on the eventual loss of the dative case, however, it must be emphasized that case-endingless forms are not restricted to the dative in Ru1. For instance, both *hælend* and *drihten*, seen above in (43) and (44) respectively, are used without a case ending where the genitive is expected as in (45) and (46):

(45) 27:57
R: cum autem sero factum esset uenit quidam homo diues ab arimathia nomine ioseph qui et ipse discipulus erat iesu
Ru1: æt æfenne geworden wæs cwom sum monn wælig from arimaðia se wæs haten ioseph se ec wæs leornere **þæs hælend**
Li: mið ðy efern uutedlice geworden were cuom summ monn wlong from ðæs wæs noma se ðe ⁊ ðe discipul wæs ðæs hælendes
WSCp: Soðlice þa hyt æfen wæs com sum weli mann of arimathia þæs nama wæs iosep. se sylfa wæs þæs hælyndes leorningcniht.

(46) 25:18
R: qui uero acciperat unum abiens fodit in terra et abscondit pecuniam domini sui
Ru1: se þe þonne onfeng anum eode bedælf in eorþe ⁊ ahydde feoh **dryhten** his
Li: seðe uutedlice an ł enne onfeng geeade gedalf in eorðo ⁊ gehydde feh ł strion hlaferdes his
WSCp: Witodlice seþe ꝥ an underfeng ferde ⁊ bedelf hyt on eorðan ⁊ behydde hys hlafurdes feoh;

As to (46), one may argue that *dryhten* is a case-endingless dative, instead genitive, used as the possessive dative, but the use of the demonstrative *þæs* in (45) clearly shows that *hælend* is an example of the case-endingless genitive.[129]

Another reason for difficulty in identifying case-endingless forms must be considered.

(47) 13:4
R: et dum seminat quaedam ciciderunt secus uiam et uenerunt uolucres caeli (*caeli* om. in Y WW) et comederunt ea
Ru1: ⁊ þa he seow sume gefeollun bi wæge ⁊ cuomun fuglas **heofun** ⁊ frætun
Li: ⁊ mið ðy ł ða huile saues ðorlease ł sum oðer gefeollon neh ł æt stræt ł woeg ⁊ cuomun ða flegendo (altered from *flegende*) ⁊ gebrecon ł eton ł freton ða ilco
WSCp: ⁊ þa þa he seow. sume hig feollon wiþ weg. ⁊ fuglas comun ⁊ æton þa;

Here (and similarly in 13:32), the form *heofun*, glossing R's *caeli*, appears to be an instance of the case-endingless genitive, but, as discussed in detail in the commentary to the verse, there is illegible erasure immediately following *heofun*, which could have been the *-es* ending. Furthermore, Farman's use of the case-endingless form in this instance may in fact reflect the compound *heofonfugel* (Farman uses it in 6:26; cf. DOE s.v. *heofonfugel*), which was rearranged to give a word-for-word gloss to the Latin.

Despite difficulties in identifying relevant instances, it is important to emphasize that case-endingless forms are not restricted to the instances where the dative is expected. To reinforce this point, I cite some potential

[129] Similar examples are found in 9:20 (*hrægl*, glossing *uestimenti*) 10:30 (*heafod*, glossing *capitis*), 10:42 (*leornere*, glossing *discipuli*), 16:3 (*heofun*, glossing *caeli*).

instances of case-endingless forms for other cases below. In (48), the syntax in both the gloss and the Latin source requires the nominative plural, but Ru1 reads *lateuw*, which has no ending (cf. *latewas* 23:16 and *latuwas* 23:24).[130]

(48) 15:14
R: sinete illos caeci sunt duces cæcorum cæcus autem si caeco ducatum praestat ambo in foueam cadunt
Ru1: forleteð hiæ blinde sindon **lateuw** blindra blind þonne gif blindne lædeþ begen in seaþ fallen
Li: forletas ða ł hia blinde aron latuas blindra ungleu ł blind uutetlice gif blinde lat forelædas boege in seað fallas
WSCp: Lætað hi hig synt blinde ⁊ blindra latteowas; Se blinda gyf he blindne læt hig feallað begen on ænne pytt;

Similarly, in (49) below:

(49) 20:18
R: ecce ascendimus hierusolimam et filius hominis tradetur principibus sacerdotum et scribis et condempnabunt eum morte
Ru1: henu we astigað ⁊ sunu monnes bið sald **aldorsacerd** ⁊ bokerum ⁊ gedoemeþ hine to deade
Li: heonu we stiges ł we scilon stige ⁊ sunu monnes gesald bið forwuostum ł aldormonnum ðæra sacerda ⁊ wuðuutum ⁊ geniðredon ł geteldon hine to deaðe
WSCp: Nu we farað to hierusalem. ⁊ mannes sunu byþ ge-seald þæra sacerda ealdrum ⁊ bocerum. ⁊ hig genyþeriað hyne to deaþe.

While *bokerum* is inflected as the dative plural, *aldorsacerd* clearly lacks the expected *-um* ending.[131]

Another complication that may be mentioned here is the fact that some of the alternative glosses introduced by *ł* lack a case ending. The two instances of the feminine noun *bled* 'fruit' used as the second gloss in 5:17 (*westmas ł blęd*) and 5:18 (*wæstmas ł blęd*), both glossing the accusative plural *fructus*, lack a case ending. Similarly, the case-endingless *gedrif* is used as the second gloss in the syntactic environment where the dative (either singular or plural) is expected, as in (50) below:

[130] Similar examples are found in 6:20 (*þeof*, glossing *fures* and the verb forms suggest the plural reading) and, possibly, 8:27 (*wind*, glossing *uenti*, but the singular reading cannot be ruled out).

[131] See also *in gyrdels eowrum* for *in zonis uestris* in 10:9.

(50) Mk 1:31
R: et accedens leuauit eam adpræchensa manu eius et continuo dimisit eam febris et minisbat eis
Ru1: ⁊ com geneolacede ahof ða ilca ⁊ mið þy gegripen wæs hond his ⁊ ricenlice forlet hio hal from ridesohte ł **gedrif** ⁊ geþæignade heom.
Li: ⁊ cwom ł geneolecde ahof ða ilca ⁊ miððy ge-grippen wæs hond his ⁊ reconlice forleort hia hal from februm ⁊ ge-emb-ehtade him
WSCp: ⁊ ge-nealæcende he hi up ahof hyre handa ge-gripenre. ⁊ hrædlice se fefor hi forlet. ⁊ heo þenode him;

It is possible that in these instances Farman may give only lexical information, 'disregarding the syntax', and this possibility should be considered carefully when an exhaustive search for relevant instances is conducted.

In passing, we may briefly mention another type of evidence that may also indicate weakening case distinctions in Ru1. In (51) below, the accusative/dative form *hire* is apparently used as an accusative object.

(51) 1:25
R: et non cognoscebat eam donec peperit filium suum primogenitum et uocauit nomen eius iesum
Ru1: ⁊ ne groette **hire** oþ þæt hit gebær sunu his þone frumkendu ⁊ nemde noma his hælend
Li: ⁊ ne cuðe ł ne cunnade hea ł ða ilco wið ł ða huile gecende sunu hire frum-cende ⁊ ceigde noma his hælend
WSCp: ⁊ he ne grette hi; Heo cende hyre frum-cennedan sunu ⁊ nemde hys naman hælend;

The verb *gretan* is normally used with an accusative object, and indeed DOE (s.v. *gretan*[1]) lists this particular instance under '1.c. to have carnal relations or sexual intercourse with (**someone** ***acc.***)' (my emphasis) without further comment on the form *hire*. There is another possible case in 14:4, where *hire* is an object of *habban* (*nis alefed ðe to habbanne hire*), which can also take a genitive object, making the example equivocal, as noted in the commentary.

The instances presented so far appear to suggest that what has been often considered as loss of the dative case may in fact have been a sign of weakening case distinctions that involve more than just the dative, while some features specific to interlinear glossing add to further complication. This possibility may be reiterated by pointing out that adjectives and possessives, too, occasionally occur without case ending in Ru1, which is especially clear when the marked endings like *-ne*, *-es*, or *-um* are missing. In fact, these examples take us back to the discussion of weakening gender distinctions, because a particular example of case-endingless forms of adjectives and possessives may in fact be a result of being in unhistorical gender congruence. In (52) below, the adjectives *deaf* and *dumb* refer to *monnu*, apparently an accusative singular spelling of the weak masculine *manna*, with loss of the final *-n.*[132]

(52) 9:32
R: egressis autem illis ecce obtulerunt ei hominem mutum et surdum (*et surdum* om. in Y WW) demonium habentem
Ru1: ut gangende þa hie þa weron henu brohtun him monnu **dumb** ⁊ **deaf** deofulseocne hæbbende
Li: ða hia weron færend uutedlice ða ilco heonu gebrohtun him monno dumbne diwlas hæbbend
WSCp: Ða hig wæron soðlice ut agane hig brohton him dumbne man se wæs deofulseoc.

When the noun is treated as masculine as normally expected, these adjectives must be interpreted as examples of case-endingless forms. It must be remembered, however, that the same noun occurs with a *þ* in (32) above, making it difficult to evaluate the significance of the examples. Similarly, there are some instances in which possessives appear to lack the masculine accusative singular ending *-ne*. In 17:23, for instance, Latin *amum tuum* is glossed with *hoc ðin*. According to DOE (s.v. *hocc*), the noun is masculine. It is uncertain whether this instance should be regarded as an example of unhistorical gender congruence or of the case-endingless form of the possessive.

Another area in which the loss of case distinctions interrelates to that of gender distinctions relates to possible instances of the indeclinable *þe* as a demonstrative in Ru1. In Li, *þe/ðe* is a variant spelling of the masculine nominative singular *se*,[133] and this usage becomes frequent in Ru1 in the Mark portion.[134] But *þe* is occasionally used in Ru1 where forms other than the masculine nominative singular are expected. Indeed, OED3 lists the following instance as the first attestation of the 'Uninflected (generalized) forms' of the Modern English definite article *the* (OED3 s.v. *the*, adj., pron.2, and n.1).

[132] As noted in the commentary, both *dumb* and *deaf* are followed immediately by illegible erasure, which, however, is unlikely to have contained the *-ne* ending given the size of the erased spaces.

[133] See Campbell (OEG: §708). The use of *þe/ðe* for other gender/case is also attested as known from Cook's glossary (Cook 1894: s.v. *se*) or Millar's tables (Millar 2000: 77).

[134] *þe* Mk1:9, Mk1:42; *ðe* Mk1:12, Mk1:26; *ðæ* Mk1:24.

(53) 1:22
R: hoc autem totum factum est ut adinpleretur quod dictum est a domino per essaiam prophetam dicentem
Ru1: þas soþlice eall geworden is ł wæs ꝥte gefylled wære þæt acweden is ł wæs from drihtne þurh esaiam **þe** witgu cweþende
Li: ðis soðlice all geworden is ł geweard ꝥte sie gefylled ꝥ ðætte gecueden is from drihtne ðerh ðone witgo cuoeðende
WSCp: Soþlice eal þys wæs geworden. ꝥ gefylled wære ꝥ fram drihtne gecweden wæs. þurh þone witegan;

While this instance[135] may indeed be an example of the accusative use of the indeclinable *þe*, governed by *þurh*, it should also be noted that Farman's choice of grammatical cases for the noun in apposition with a proper noun shows some uncertainties, as in *þurh essaiam* ***se*** *witga cwæðende* for *per esseiam profetam dicentem* in 21:4 or *mid* ***þæm*** *hælend* ***þone*** *nazarenisco* for *cum iesu nazareno* in 26:71. Yet, the following instance in (54) may confirm the demonstrative use of *þe* in the accusative.

(54) 26:51
R: et ecce unus ex hiis qui erant cum iesu extendens manum exemit gladium suum et percussit seruum principis sacerdotum et abscidit auriculam eius dexteram (*dexteram* om. in Y WW)
Ru1: ⁊ henu an of þara þe werun mið þæm hælende aþenende honda gebrægd his sweord ⁊ slog esne þæs aldorsacerdos ⁊ heow eara his **þe** swiðræ
Li: ⁊ heono an of ðæm ða ðe weron mið ðone hælend aðenede hond ⁊ gebrægd suord his ⁊ slænde ł slog esne aldor-sacerdas aslog earo-liprice his
WSCp: Witudlice an þæra þe mid þam hælende wæs abræd hys swurd. ⁊ asloh of anys þæra sacerda ealdres þeowan eare;

Referring to the neuter accusative singular *eara*, the expected form of the demonstrative is *þæt*, a fact that may have contributed to the use of *þe*, possibly affected by the confusion about how to expand the crossed thorn. There is one more neuter usage – nominative singular, this time – of *þe*, as in (55) below:

(55) 8:24
R: et ecce tempestas magna facta est in mari erat autem illis uentus contrarius ita ut nauicula operetur fluctibus ipse uero dormiebat

[135] See also *þurh esaiam* ***þe*** *witgu* glossing the same Latin phrase in 8:17.

Ru1: ⁊ henu hreornis micel geworden wæs on þæm sæ wæs þonne heom wind wiðerweard swa ꝥte **þe** scip wæs urnen yðum he wiotudlice ł he soþ ł þonne slepte
Li: ⁊ heonu styrnise ł hroernis michelo geworden wæs in sae suæ ꝥ scipp ofer-wrigen wæs mið yðum he soðlice geslepde ł slepende wæs.
WSCp: Ða wearð mycel styrung geworden on þære sæ swa ꝥ ꝥ scyp wearð ofergoten mid yþum. witodlice he slep;

These sporadic instances interpretable as examples of indeclinable demonstrative *þe* seem to await further scrutiny, especially in conjunction with other signs of weakening gender and case distinctions.[136]

While the examples of potential case-endingless adjectives may allow alternative interpretations, it is clear that case-endingless forms are not restricted to instances where the dative case is expected. Of course, it is possible that statistical data would indeed reveal that the loss of the dative case account for the majority of case-endingless forms in Ru1. It is also important to emphasize the need to consider various causes of complication discussed above in conducting such statistical investigations.

2.2.4 Morphology: summary

It has become clear that Ross's two statements should not be regarded as definitive descriptions of the morphology of Farman's language, but, instead, they point to research desiderata that await close attention from specialists. His statements could be misleading, if one fails to take into consideration that he had in mind, when making those statements, the more disrupted conditions in Aldred's language. The sections above have identified some potential examples that may be interpreted as signs of weakening gender and case distinctions in Ru1, while pointing to various causes of complication in collecting and analyzing these examples. It is hoped that future studies will situate more accurately Farman's language in the history of the English language as regards disruptions in the case and gender systems.

2.3 Vocabulary

Since Jordan's seminal work on 'Wortgeographie' (Jordan 1906), there have been various attempts to assign certain Old English words to specific

[136] It should also be noted here that there are two instances of *þa*, the plural nominative/accusative form of the demonstrative *se*, used where the dative case is expected; see the commentary to 21:12. What may also have potential significance is the use of *þe* with superlative forms of adjectives: 12:45 (*þe ytmæste dæg* for *nouissima*), 22:27 (*þe lætest … ealra* for *nouissime …omnium*), 25:40 (*anum þe læsesta þara broþre* for *uni ex minimis his fratribus*).

dialects, while limitations of the methodology have also been noted. Vleeskruyer's highly influential 'list of dialectal, rare or archaic words' in his edition of the homily of St Chad (1953: 23–37) is, for instance, preceded by cautious remarks about 'reservations' that occupy more than two pages. While one may be tempted to use the results of such word geography studies as if a set of criteria upon which to decide the dialect of a given text, the present study deliberately avoids doing so.[137] It must be remembered that Ru1 is one of the texts that are examined to define the Anglian, or Mercian, vocabulary, hence a risk of circular argument. This does not entail ignoring the development of the discipline, especially the works of such scholars as Schabram, Gneuss, Wenisch and Hofstetter, and care is taken to refer to the works relevant to individual words in the commentary. The glossary, it is hoped, will prove useful to future lexical studies. The sections below, instead, will briefly consider one of the main issues in this linguistic introduction, i.e., the dialect mixture, by examining some cases in point.

In discussing various functions of Farman's double or multiple glosses, Kotake (2017: 89–91) has noted some double glosses in which a word with Anglian colouring is paired with a synonymous word with wider distribution in Old English. In glossing Latin *merces* 'reward', for instance, Farman uses both *lean* and *meord*, but the latter, which is considered as an Anglian word by Wenisch (1979: 183–84), occurs only as a second gloss, always paired with *lean* (5:12, 6:1, 10:41). In contrast, *lean* also occurs by itself as a gloss to the Latin word, as well as part of the phrasal rendering *mið leane gebohte* 'bought with remuneration, hired' of *conduxit* in 20:16. One may be tempted to suppose that, based on the hypothesis that he was a Mercian scribe, Farman may have added a synonym of his own preference to the word found in his exemplar written presumably in West Saxon. Yet, because the hypothesis itself cannot be taken for granted as we have seen above, the more frequent use of *lean* may instead reflect Farman's own preference, while the additions of *meord* may have been occasional notes recording his exemplar's reading.

The limited use of *meord* may give the impression that Anglian words tend to be secondary to and less frequent than more widely distributed alternatives, but such generalization is hardly possible. For instance, *(ge)leoran*, a verb of motion with Anglian colouring, is used by Farman, indeed sometimes paired with a synonymous verb of wider distribution,

[137] For example, Fulk (2008: 88), discussing Anglian features in anonymous Old English homilies, lists two groups of words amongst 'Anglian features surveyed': 'Anglian words not normally found in West Saxon' and 'Anglian words not normally found in Late West Saxon, though they occur in Early West Saxon'.

but unlike the case of *meord*, *(ge)leoran* occurs not only as an alternative gloss to another verb of motion (5 occ., of which four are used as a second gloss), but more frequently as a simple gloss (10 occ.). Similarly, the passage of 'love for enemies' (5:43–44) could suggest that *hatian* is the basic word for 'hate', while *feogan*, another word with Anglian colouring, is used only as a second gloss in 5:44. The latter verb, however, occurs elsewhere both as a first gloss paired with *hatian* (6:24) and by itself (24:10).

Apparent rivalries between words with different dialect colouring are not the only notable feature of Farman's gloss. As expected in a text generally categorized as Mercian, preferences for words identified as Anglian are also perceptible, though not without complication. The interjection *onu*, for example, is found in the Old English Bede and considered to be Anglian as discussed by Miller in the introduction to his edition (Miller 1890–98: xxix–xxxiii). Farman's relatively consistent translation of *ecce* into *henu*, a variant spelling of the interjection, then would appear to reinforce the likelihood that his dialect is Anglian. The Vespasian Psalter gloss, probably the most influential text in determining the Mercian dialect, however, uses *sehðe* for *ecce* (as against *efen nu* in the Royal Psalter, for instance), and Farman indeed uses the same interjection (spelled as *sihþe*) too, either by itself or occasionally paired with *henu* as a double gloss (2:9, 10:16, 24:26). We will not enter into the seemingly insolvable question whether or not the two interjections reflect regional differences within the Anglian dialect as Miller supposes; rather, they clearly point to the difficulty of employing lexical evidence to decide the dialect in which a particular text is written. It must be stressed that the presence of a certain lexical item identified as belonging to specific dialect vocabulary does not necessarily indicate the text's origin, any more than it is possible to argue from the absence of certain words.

Farman uses a number of words that are not recorded elsewhere. They are marked accordingly in the glossary and discussed in the commentary. A useful overview of rare words in Ru1 is available in Ross (1979b).

2.4 Syntax

More than a century before Crowley's survey (2000) on the word order of noun phrases finds that Ru1 is less dependent on Latin word order than most of the other interlinear glosses he examined, Sir James Murray had already noted Farman's syntactic independence from the Latin in his two short articles on the Rushworth Gospels, published in 1874 and 1875. In the earlier article (Murray 1874: 562), he characterizes Ru1 as 'not a word-for-word gloss but a readable idiomatic version'. Kotake (2010) considers what syntactic features could have made Farman's gloss 'idiomatic', finding that his syntactic features are not consistent through

Matthew and that there are sections in which he tends to choose word order less affected by the Latin source. The same study also points out that Farman sometimes cancelled his own gloss that deviates from Latin word order and then added a more word-for-word phrase. I have interpreted these erasures and corrections in the manuscript as evidence for the possibility that his exemplar could have contained a freer translation than a word-for-word interlinear version and accordingly that his faithful copying from such an exemplar made his gloss more idiomatic than one would expect to find in an interlinear gloss text. Farman's changing syntactic tendency, I have argued, reflects varying degrees of his reliance on his exemplar.

Instead of merely repeating what Kotake (2010) discusses, the following sections will examine several other syntactic features that may be considered as making Farman's gloss more idiomatic.[138] Because of its emphasis on recurrent syntactic patterns to illustrate how Farman's syntax was changing within the text, the paper did not fully discuss less frequent – and more dynamic in most cases – patterns.

One such dynamic syntactic deviation from the Latin can be observed in the ways of translating Latin infinitives. Latin infinitival constructions are often rendered into Old English clausal ones in Ru1. Although it is not a simple question whether a clausal construction is more 'idiomatic' than an infinitival one in Old English,[139] what should be emphasized is that the clausal construction naturally obscures word-for-word correspondence between the Latin source and its gloss, potentially reducing the usefulness of the gloss. The fact that a syntactic construction deviating markedly from the Latin is chosen despite potential disadvantages seems to indicate the glossator's deliberate decision. For instance, the *þæt*-clause in (56) translates the Latin infinitive *tenere*, which can be contrasted with the more straightforward gloss using the *to*-infinitive in Li.

[138] Syntactic features examined in Kotake (2010) include (1) Latin Noun + Possessive > OE Possessive + Noun; (2) the initial position of *forþon (þe)* translating Latin *enim* which occurs as a second element; and (3) other less frequent inversions of such Latin word order patterns as Participle + *esse*, Complement + Verb, Verb + Object, Verb + Subject. The results from the survey suggest that Farman tends to employ freer syntactic patterns in the first six chapters and from Chapter 22 onwards in Matthew.

[139] As part of a linguistic study on the development of the *to*-infinitive, Los (2005: 179–90) discusses this question, especially by comparing two versions of the Old English translation of Gregory's *Dialogues*.

(56) 21:46
et quaerentes eum tenere timuerunt turbas
Ru1: ⁊ soecende hiæ þ **hine genoman** ⁊ reordun him mængu
Li: ⁊ sohton hine to haldanne ondreardon ða menigo
WSCp: Hi sohton hyne ⁊ ondredon þ folc

The examples (57) and (58) below suggest that clausal constructions may have been employed to signal clearly the passive voice of Latin infinitives in Old English.[140]

(57) 19:7
quid ergo moyses mandauit dari libellum repudi et dimittere
Ru1: ah hwæt moyses bebead þ **monn salde boec aweorpnisse ⁊ forlete**
Li: huæt forðon bebead sella boc freodomas ⁊ forleta
WSCp: hwi het moyses syllan hiw-gedales boc; ⁊ hig forlæton;

(58) 20:28
sicut filius hominis non uenit ministrari sed ministrare et dare animam suam redemptionem pro multis
Ru1: swa sunu monnes ne cwom þ **him wære ðægnad ah he ðægnade ⁊ salde ferh his for mongum to alesnisse**
Li: sua sunu monnes ne cuom him to heranne ah he to embehtane oðrum ⁊ sella sawel his eft-lesing ł alesenis fore monigum
WSCp: Swa mannes sunu ne com þ **him man þenode ac þ he þenode ⁊ sealde his sawle lif to alysednesse for manegum;**

In (57), the passive infinitive *dari* is translated by a *þæt*-clause in which the indefinite pronoun subject *monn* is used with the active verb *salde*, effectively expressing the passive.[141] The same indefinite pronoun appears also in WSCp in translating *ministrari* in (58). In Ru1, the contrast between the passive *ministrari* and the active *ministrare* is clearly expressed in the *þæt*-clause by the contrasting verb forms, *wære ðægnad* and *ðægnade*, unlike in Li, where the contrast is not clear, either syntactically or lexically (both *hieran* and *embehtan* mean 'to serve').[142]

140 This does not mean that Ru1 does not have any passive infinitives; Kilpiö (1989: 92) counts ten instances in Ru1. The passive infinitive is yet to develop fully in Old English, as discussed by Mitchell (OES §922).

141 For a discussion of the use of the indefinite pronoun with an active verb as a 'periphrasis for the passive voice', see Mitchell (1988: 267–68).

142 Both verbs are placed in the same category in TOE: '12.01.01.08|12 (v.) Service :: To serve, wait upon.' A Thesaurus of Old English. Glasgow: University of Glasgow, 2021. Web. 16 September 2021. http://oldenglish

Another pattern is found when Latin *facere* is used as a causative verb with an infinitive; WSCp again chooses clausal constructions in (59) and (60).[143]

(59) 4:19
et ait illis iesus uenite post me et faciam uos fieri piscatores hominum
Ru1: ⁊ þa cwæþ to him cumaþ æfter me ⁊ ic gedom ꝥ **git beoþan monna fisceres**
Li: ⁊ cuoeð him cumas æfter mec ⁊ ic gedo iuih sie ł wosa fisceras monna
WSCp: ⁊ he sæde him; Cumað æfter me ⁊ ic do ꝥ **gyt beoð manna fisceras**;

(60) 5:32
quia omnis qui dimisserit uxorem suam excepta fornicationis causa facit eam mechari
Ru1: þætte æghwilc þara þe forleteþ his wif butan forlegennisse þinge ł intinga he doeþ ꝥ **hiu dernunge licgę**
Li: forðon eghuelc seðe forletes wif his buta unclænes lustas Inting gedoeð [ł] wircas ða ilca gesyngege
WSCp: ꝥ ælc þe his wif forlæt buton forlegennysse þingum. he deð ꝥ **heo unriht-hæmð**;

The use of *þæt*-clauses instead of direct translation by infinitives in these examples may not be surprising when seen in the context of translation in general, but, given the nature of the interlinear gloss format in which one would naturally expect word-for-word correspondences, the deviation from the Latin is clearly significant, making Ru1 appear more idiomatic than other interlinear glosses.[144]

Taking into consideration syntactic units larger than single words, there are further indications that Farman freely deviates from the practice of word-for-word glossing. In her recent study on Farman's use of *þa*, focusing on its use as a 'signal of idiomatic discourse structuring', Lenker (2018: 499–500) discusses a group of instances where *þa* is used 'without a Latin lemma' in Ru1. While the two citations discussed in the study exemplify the use of added *þa* as an adverb in line with her discussion

thesaurus.arts.gla.ac.uk/category/?id=17125.

143 On the syntactic patterns used with causative *(ge)don*, see Mitchell (OES §668) as well as DOE s.v. *don* III.A. (infinitive) and III.B. (*þæt*-clause) and *gedon* 2.a. (infinitive) and 2.b. (*þæt*-clause).

144 For further similar and comparable instances, see the glossary, s.v. '*þæt* conj.', where a group of instances is listed as having no corresponding Latin (NL).

about discourse markers, it is also interesting to consider the instances of *þa* without a corresponding Latin that can be interpreted as functioning as a conjunction, because they involve another type of dynamic syntactic deviation from the Latin. For example, Ru1 employs *þa* in translating the Latin ablative absolute construction in (61):

(61) 27:5
et proiectis argenteis in templo recessit et abiens laqueo se suspendit
Ru1: ⁊ **þa** wearp he þa scillingas in templ gewat ⁊ þonan gangende awyrgde hine
Li: ⁊ worpende ða scillingas in tempel[145] gewat ⁊ ðona eode ł ðona geongende mið sade hine awurigde
WSCp: ⁊ he awearp þa scyllingas inon ꝥ templ. ⁊ ferde ⁊ mid gryne hyne sylfne aheng;

It is, of course, possible to read the added *þa* at the beginning as an adverb, resulting in something similar to the paratactic structure found in WSCp (*he awearp ... ⁊ ferde...*); [146] however, the absence of the conjunction *and* connecting the two finite verbs, *wearp* and *gewat*, seems to suggest that the added *þa* functions more likely as a conjunction with the meaning 'when'. This use of *þa* may be compared with the following instance, where the correlation of *þa ... þa ...* is used without equivalent Latin lemmas, also translating the Latin ablative absolute.[147]

(62) 11:7
abeuntibus autem illis (illis autem abeuntibus Y) coepit iesus dicere ad turbas de iohanne baptiza
Ru1: **þa** eoden þonan hie **þa** ingon se hælend cweþan to þæm menigu bi iohanne se fullwihtere
Li: ðæm uutedlice fromgeongendum ongann ðe hælend gecuoeða to ðæm menigom from iohannæ
WSCp: Ða hi ut-eodon soþlice þa ongan se hælynd secgan be iohanne

In (62) above, Ru1 can be compared closely with WSCp and clearly contrasted with Li, which has a more literal rendering of the Latin

[145] Skeat's reading *temple* is an error.

[146] This is certainly not the place to discuss questions about the ambiguities between adverbs and conjunctions, for which see Mitchell (OES §§2536–60) and a variety of references cited there.

[147] The correlation of *þa ... þa...* is also used when translating a Latin temporal clause introduced by *cum*; e.g., 14:32, where the second *þa* is used without a Latin equivalent.

construction. Another conjunction, *þende*, is also employed in a similar manner as in (63) below, where it presumably emphasizes the sense of duration or co-occurrence.

(63) 26:26
coennantibus autem eis accipit iesus panem et benedixit ac fregit deditque discipulis suis
Ru1: **þende** hiæ þa æt þæm efenmete werun genom se hælend hlaf ⁊ bletsade ⁊ bræc ⁊ salde his discilum
Li: ⁊ efenmeti weron ðonne ł ða hia onfeng ðe hælend hlaf ł genom se hælend hlaf ⁊ gebloedsade ⁊ bræcg ⁊ salde ðegnum his
WSCp: Witodlice þa hig ætun se hælend nam hlaf ⁊ hyne gebletsode ⁊ bræc. ⁊ sealde hys leorningcnihtum

The examples so far examined underline two syntactic features of Ru1. First, when larger syntactic units such as phrases and clauses are taken into consideration, Farman freely adopts word order patterns deviating from the Latin rather than simple word-for-word agreement. Second, Old English words are often added without any equivalent lemmas in Latin.[148] As a result of these features, Ru1 often has syntactic structures closer to the prose version in WSCp than the interlinear gloss in Li. To conclude this section, we turn our attention to a rare piece of evidence of how such a syntactically free interlinear gloss could have been treated by a contemporary glossator. Farman's hand happens to reappear in John's Gospel, in Owun's section of the manuscript, in the first three verses of Chapter 18. Seemingly, Farman had already provided these verses with glosses, into which Owun's hand intrudes, as is shown for John 18:1–2 below (Owun's addition in verse 3 supplies a gloss to a Latin word that had been left unglossed by Farman).[149]

[148] Both points can also be exemplified by another type of evidence concerning the position of added subject pronouns when glossing Latin verbs, as discussed in Kotake (2022). Of course, it is not surprising for a glossator to add pronouns to clarify the meaning expressed by the personal endings of a Latin verb, but when a Latin verb occurs not in the position immediately following the conjunction in subordinate clauses, Ru1 tends to place a pronominal subject in the clause initial position rather than immediately preceding the verb. The comparable syntactic feature can be observed in other interlinear glosses, but the frequency is much higher in Ru1 than in Li, and the resulting word order in Ru1 very often agrees with that of WSCp in terms of the position of pronouns.

[149] For a brief discussion of possible reasons why Farman glossed only these three verses, see the note to this section in the Commentary.

(64) Jn 18:1–2 (f. 162r, 3–7)

þa mið ðy cwæþ se hæl(end) eode þa mid his þægnu(m)
<XVIII 1>Haec cum dixisset ie(su)s egressus est cum discipulís
his ofer þah hlynne þe mon cedron nemneþ þær wæs fæger gewyrtun in þæ(m)
suis trans torrentem cedron ubi erat hortus in que(m)
he eode sylf ⁊ his þægnas **his** þa wiste soþlice ⁊ iudas
introiit ipse et discipuli eius· <2>sciebat autem et iudas
þe hine to deaþe sellan walde **hine** þa stowe f(or)þon þider gelome se hæl(end) cwom
qui tradebat eum locum quia frequenter ie(su)s conue⟨-⟩
ðer mið his ðægnum **his**
nerat illuc cum discipulís suís:·

Here, Owun added five words; all five are redundant. Three instances of *his* are written neatly above *suis* or *eius*; however, these Latin possessives had already been translated by Farman, who placed the Old English possessives before the head nouns. Both *hine* and *ðer*, written by Owun above *eum* and *illluc* respectively, are also redundant; in these cases, Farman's dislocation of the glosses (*hine* and *þider*) from the Latin lemmas is more radical. Farman's freer syntax does indeed appear 'idiomatic' to the modern reader, but Owun's reaction reveals that such an approach was not necessarily satisfactory as interlinear glossing to his contemporary reader. Farman's syntax is unrestricted by the Latin to the extent that his contemporary glossator found the need to add more literal glosses, thereby suggesting the questionable utility of such an 'idiomatic' rendering in the context of interlinear glossing. This observation appears to reinforce the hypothesis advanced in Kotake (2010) introduced at the outset of this section. The dynamic patterns of syntactic deviation from the Latin as discussed here, along with more frequent patterns also examined in Kotake (2010), strongly suggest that Farman's gloss does not fit the picture of a glossator either translating the Latin text word by word or copying another word-for-word gloss into his manuscript. He is more likely to have had a free translation available for use. That his gloss can be sometimes more word-for-word and sometimes freer and more idiomatic seems to reflect varying degrees of his faithfulness to such an exemplar, because he, like Owun, would naturally have noticed that a freer translation might not necessarily be more useful than a literal one in the interlinear context.

3. Some palaeographical notes on Farman's gloss

Ker (1957: no. 292) dates the scripts of both Farman and Owun to the tenth century, characterizing the hand of Farman, who concerns us here, as 'upright and stiffly careful without ligatures, except **eg**, **et**, **st**, and with the letters often widely spaced from one another', while Owun's hand is 'more fluent and cursive'. That Ker dates them to 's. x' rather than to a shorter chronological range may reflect the difficulty of aligning either hand squarely with one of the three phases of Anglo-Saxon minuscule that are generally distinguished in the tenth century, i.e., pointed, square and round, albeit the first and the last standing at either end of the century.[150] Besides, scripts used for glosses are often set apart from book-hands, making it difficult for a glossing hand to be considered in the wider context of script history.[151] The following is an attempt to describe the distinctive features of Farman's script, which have not been discussed in detail except in Ker's *Catalogue.*[152]

It is useful to begin by examining Farman's brief colophon (f. 50v, reproduced on the back cover), because it is not interlinear and therefore gives some indications of his script when not constrained by an interlinear layout. The Old English part is written in the script he uses for glossing, though the ascenders and descenders appear slightly more pronounced than in the glosses because of the space available in the colophon. While Farman sometimes imitates the Insular Half-Uncial of the main text in adding corrections to the Latin text (such as the 'oc' **a** in *abscondito*, f. 9r, 2), the Latin part of the colophon is similar to the Old English, though the smaller number of ascenders and descenders due to the nature of the language gives a neater impression.[153] No clear sign of influence of Caroline minuscule is perceptible. In contrast, the partly abbreviated final

[150] For an excellent overview of scripts used in Anglo-Saxon vernacular manuscripts, see Ker (1957: xxv–xxxiii); see also Roberts (2005: esp. 38–41). For the pointed phase, it is always useful to refer to studies dealing with the hands in the Parker Chronicle, notably Parkes (1976) and Bately (1986). For the origin and development of Square minuscule, see Bishop (1964–68), Dumville (1987) and (1994), and Ganz (2012). In recent scholarship, the round phase is central to 'English Vernacular Minuscule', for which see Stokes (2014: see especially p. 8 for his terminology).

[151] The distinction is of course well founded and has its own merit. For the concept and terminology 'Glossenschrift', see Bischoff (1954: 8). Stokes (2014: 195–96) considers scripts used for glossing as one of the possible causes that eventually led to the creation of the elongated 'English Vernacular Minuscule'. He also presents a chapter (Chapter 5) on glossing hands, in which the Rushworth glosses are not included, as they stand outside the timeframe set for his study (*c.* 990 – *c.* 1035).

[152] The situation is markedly different for the literature available on Aldred's handwriting, which has been described and discussed repeatedly. Even the description of the Rushworth manuscript presented by Liuzza and Doane (1995) does not discuss the palaeography of the Old English glosses. Tamoto's section on 'letter form' [*sic*] (2013: cii–civ) is unconventional and takes little account of the discipline of Insular palaeography; for instance, the typical Insular form of **f** is described as '**f** is like "F", a capital letter in modern type, with a longer descender'.

[153] However, the square phase of the Anglo-Saxon minuscule can have the 'oc' **a**, making it impossible to attribute Farman's use of the form solely to the imitation of Insular Half-Uncial.

words, *si fieri po(test) ap(ud) d(eu)m*, indicates the scribe's ability to write a more cursive script, perhaps echoing a type of earlier Insular minuscule.[154] He was clearly capable of handling different grades of script, presumably choosing a cursive one as a space-saving measure at the end of the line in this colophon.

On the same folio (f. 50v), one can notice that Ker's statement about Farman's limited use of ligatures needs modification. Ligatures of **e** with a following letter are, in fact, more frequent, usually with tall **e**: **en** (*ineoden*, line 1), **eo** (*heo(m)*, line 12), **er** (*werun*, line 6, **e** not tall), **es** (*gastes*, line 15). Besides, we find on other folios **ec** (*ec*, f. 49v, line 1), **em** (*femnan*, f. 41v, 6), **er** with tall **e** (*hwæþer*, f. 49r, 3), **ex** (*exlan*, f. 37v, 16), along with **eg** and **et** as noted by Ker. The **ea** ligature has the square letter-form of **a**, whose first stroke descends vertically as in *eall* (f. 31r, 22) and *ealle* (f. 41v, 12). While the number of unambiguous examples of the **ea** ligature is small, the **e** ligatures in general are much more frequent than Ker's description implies and are clearly part of Farman's repertoire. The **st** ligature with the tall **s** connected with a loop to the vertical stroke of **t**, might well be regarded as an indication of his familiarity with Caroline minuscule; but if it was indeed due to Caroline influence, we should also note the permissive attitude to Insular elements standing alongside, as suggested by the **s** in the ligature usually having a descender well below the baseline.[155] Another ligature that should be noted is **or** in which **r** is a single angled stroke (there is no initial vertical stroke). Farman does not employ this ligature before *forðbereþ* (f. 21v, 5), after which it is used with a somewhat high frequency. Brookes (2016: 113–14) regards Aldred's use of similar forms as a sign of influence from Caroline minuscule, although the same ligature occurs in the first hand of the Parker Chronicle.[156] Farman's use of ligatures seems to fit the tenth-century context, when more complicated ones in Insular current minuscule had ceased to be in use but **e** ligatures were used with high frequency where possible. Caroline influence is not strong enough to change the overall Insular appearance of Farman's hand.

As to possible indications that Farman was to some extent familiar with the earlier tradition of Insular handwriting, as hinted by his cursive

[154] *potest* has *po* followed by the Insular *est* abbreviation (÷), i.e., *poest*; given that the usual method of abbreviating *potest* was to use the *est* abbreviation (*pot÷*) in the tenth century (Bains 1936: 31–32), Farman's form should probably be regarded as a variant (or maybe an error).

[155] Note the statement of Bishop (1971: 9) that Caroline *s* is 'normal in *st* in Insular script'. For English Caroline minuscule, see Bishop (1971), Dumville (1993) and Rushforth (2012). That Insular elements can occur alongside Caroline may be compared with 'Style II' English Caroline minuscule.

[156] See Roberts (2005: 48–50), to whom Brookes duly refers.

writing in the colophon – and by some features of orthography as discussed above (§2.1.2.) –, one may refer to space-saving vowels written below the baseline. Similar instances are found in Aldred's gloss, as noted by Roberts (2005: 18, 37), but Farman's use is very restricted: only the combinations of **hi**, **mi** and **ni** are found (e.g., *hie*, f. 24r, 1, f. 26v, 5; *hię*, f. 37v, 17, f. 44r, 11; *his*, f. 12r, 22; *mid*, f. 45r, 6; *nyhtsumigæ*, f. 41v, 19 ; *genimeþ*, f. 45v, 5). A similar degree of restriction is perceptible in his treatment of some of the **e** ligatures: for instance, the **eo** ligature in *neoliceþ* (f. 4v, 3), appears in its morphology to echo the so-called 'eight figure' **e**, which is likely to reflect Insular cursive practices, but its ductus does not give any impression of cursive features.[157]

The general proportion of Farman's hand may be described as square. The ascenders and descenders are usually long in relation to small letter sizes required by the interlinear format. The ascenders usually have a wedge or a more informal approach stroke at the top. As Ker notes, the letters are often separated from one another, especially when there is ample lateral space available to match the Latin equivalent. Yet, the degree of separation varies significantly throughout; when words need to be squeezed into a limited space, spacing adopted by Farman appears to give some hints about how he would have written without being constrained by the interlinear format (e.g., *forþon þe ge bioþ geherende*, f. 39v, 13).

The following points may be noted on individual letter-forms: **a** is normally pointed with the first stroke round and the second either jointed neatly at the top or slightly protruding. Very occasionally, it appears to be open at the top (e.g., *arþu*, f. 17r, 5), but it is still written with two strokes, unlike the open **a** found in earlier Insular minuscule. As noted on the **ea** ligature above, a form resembling square **a**, with both its first and top strokes straight, is found also as a simple letter, but only sporadically (e.g., *allunga* (first), f. 8r, 10; *naarwe* (second), f. 10v, 22; *alle*, f. 18r, 11; *þas*, f. 46r, 13). What is sometimes called the Caroline-like **a** also occurs, most frequently at the beginning of a word, but also medially and finally (e.g., *aris*, f. 3v, 16; *sald*, f. 35v, 15; *synna*, f. 52v, 7). Occasionally, a Caroline-like **a**, whether enlarged or not, appears to function as capitalization, for which see below on punctuation. The significance of this **a** form as an indication of the scribe's familiarity with Caroline minuscule must be treated with caution, as discussed in relation to Aldred's use by Roberts (2005: 36–37) and Brookes (2016: 112–13). In

[157] On this form of **e** in the Insular minuscule tradition, see Sparks (2013: 30, esp. n. 9). See also Brookes (2016: 108) for comparable examples in Aldred's gloss.

Farman's case, its infrequency appears to suggest that it cannot be regarded as indicating significant influence of Caroline minuscule.

æ, as noted on the **e** ligatures, is often written with the **e** portion being tall when connected to the next letter; the *e-caudata* is also used.

Both **c** and **e** (not tall **e**) are often written in the form described as 'horned', with the heavy first stroke protruding leftwards, as well as in round forms. The tongue of **e** is often elongated, sometimes with great exaggeration, at the end of a word.

d is round-backed and the length of the ascender is usually not differentiated from that of **ð**.

The insular form of **g** is consistently used, with the tail open. The top horizontal stroke is sometimes straight and sometimes wavy. Some examples (e.g., *gesomnade*, f. 3r, 14) of **g** with the wavy top stroke may be compared with the forms found in some plates of Bishop's *English Caroline Minuscule* (e.g., for items nos. 6, 8, 9), in which the wavy stroke is in fact a slightly incomplete circular top of the Caroline form and the downward stroke begins at the right side of the wavy stroke. In Farman's case, the downward stroke sometimes begins in the middle of the top stroke, whether straight or wavy, and sometimes towards very right, making the left side of the head look separate from the right. The Insular form is occasionally enlarged; for discussion, see above (§1.3.3.).

The second limb of **h** may be turned slightly outwards or almost perpendicular to the baseline. The enlarged **h** (for its function, see §1.3.3.) has the second limb turning inwards; the same form is used occasionally in the normal size (e.g., *heora*, f. 9r, 10).

The *i-longa* is used, in most cases not as capitalization but to differentiate successive minims (e.g., as often in *In*).

k, used frequently by Farman as discussed under Orthography, always has a descender.

There is no clear example of the low-slung **l**.

Both **m** and **n** usually appear to have been written with pen lifts, though there are instances in which each minim is written more cursively (e.g., **m** in *cwomun*, f. 50v, 3). Occasionally, the final minim of **m** turns inwards (e.g., *heom*, f. 10v, 21). The majuscule, or Uncial form, **n** occurs twice as *þonNe* (f. 4v, 9, f. 18v, 4), which may reflect the practice of using the form to fill up the space at a line-end in Anglo-Saxon manuscripts (cf. Ker 1957: p. xxx).

r is Insular throughout the gloss, apart from the **or** ligature mentioned above. The descender is almost always long and the second stroke appears to start with a pen lift in most cases. Cursive features are occasionally betrayed by the descender connected to the upper stroke with a loop (e.g., *bokerum* f. 32v, 18). There are also examples of **r** with a short descender (e.g., *sacerdos*, f. 3r, 12; *winstrae*, f. 9r, 1) which resembles Caroline **r**, but a similar form also occurs in the Vespasian Psalter gloss (cf. Roberts 2005: 22–25; see also the commentary to 10:15).

Both low and long **s** are used. Long **s** is frequent in the combinations **sp**, **ss** and **sw**, as well as the **st** ligature noted above. Long **s** also appears in word-final position, possibly as a space-saving measure (e.g., *his*, f. 3v, 20). Round **s** is found only very infrequently (e.g., *snytru*, f. 17v, 14). In the case of *Sume* (f. 20v, 17), round **s** is enlarged, corresponding to a Latin decorated letter, followed by another round **s**, not as tall as the one above, in the same word (line 18) in the passage.

v for **u** is rare (e.g., *vntrymum*, f. 13v, 15; *þv*, f. 53v, 9).

y is straight-limbed and undotted.

Both **þ** and **ð** are used with the former more frequent. As discussed under Orthography, **th** appears sporadically instead of these letters.

As seems usual in the other extant Old English interlinear glosses, there are few marks of punctuation in Farman's gloss. The *vel* abbreviation (*ł*) introducing alternative glosses may be either preceded or followed by a dot, which should probably be regarded as marking the abbreviation. What may be regarded as a punctus occurs twice, of which one (after *mægden*, f. 14v, 2) corresponds with the end of the modern verse division; the other (after *micel*, f. 4r, 9) is also at the end of a syntactic unit in the Latin text. Enlarged letters are also used occasionally, and these are discussed above in the context of textual units (§1.3.3.). Even when there is no clear textual division, as in the middle of a modern verse division (22:14, *ah*, f. 40r, 9), the Caroline-like **a** appears to indicate the syntactic division. All these instances are apparently *ad hoc* occurrences and can hardly be regarded as indicating the systematic use of punctuation or capitalization in Farman's gloss.

For the conjunction *and* the Tironian note is consistently used, apart from one spelled-out *and* (f. 2r, 16). Most of the other abbreviations in Farman's gloss are either those found universally in Anglo-Saxon manuscripts or those employed specifically in glossing contexts. The former include the crossed thorn for *þæt* and a suspension stroke for the nasal consonants (generally at the end of words). Other instances of the suspension stroke, especially frequent in glosses, include *f(or)-* prefix, *-(er)* (*æft(er)*, f. 27r, 10; *wæt(er)*, f. 47v, 21), and the more radically abbreviated *middang(earde)* (f. 44r, 3).

Farman uses the *xb* sign (with an abbreviation stroke through the ascender of *b*) in the margin, which first appears on f. 13r, and then on ff. 13v, 15v, 17v, 18r, 19v, 23r, 31v, 32v, 34r, 36r, 45r and 45v. The abbreviation is usually interpreted as *Christe, benedic* and found commonly in Insular manuscripts. Farman's use of the sign may have been somewhat reminiscent of 'the habit of beginning the day's task of transcription by a prayer recorded in the top-margin', as Lindsay (1923: 25) notes about the practice of Irish scribes.[158]

Instead of narrowing down Ker's 's. x' dating, the description here presented emphasizes the appropriateness of his wide chronological range for Farman's gloss. The script is clearly an example of tenth-century Anglo-Saxon minuscule, but we have seen that it also contains signs of Farman's understanding of the cursive scripts in the earlier period, possible indications of his awareness of the ongoing development of Square minuscule, and perhaps slight hints of influence from the gradual introduction of Caroline minuscule into Anglo-Saxon England.[159] Such a conclusion cannot add to our knowledge about the origin of Farman's gloss, but it certainly points to a research desideratum, i.e., to discuss glossing hands in a wider context. While isolating glossing hands from book-hands has its merits, that Farman's script, or the aspect of his script, can be called 'upright and stiffly careful' suggests that it may meaningfully be compared with Anglo-Saxon Square minuscule, whose general features are often described as 'upright', 'stately' or 'formalised'.[160] Whether or not comparison of Farman's script with Square minuscule is accepted as valid, we may be able to achieve a much fuller understanding of individual glossing hands by considering how each glossing hand relates to contemporary book-hands.

4. Conclusion

One significant feature of Farman's gloss that has recurred in the previous sections is 'mixture', or a variegated nature of his gloss. Textually speaking, while his gloss reflects a glossing tradition shared by Aldred in some portions, Farman is likely to have relied on another exemplar, presumably in a format other than the interlinear gloss. In fact, we also find at times similarities – in a broader sense – to the West Saxon Gospels, when discussing textual divisions or syntactic independence from the Latin source. Linguistically speaking, too, one of the important keys was a mixture of dialects. Besides, we find sometimes more conservative features (e.g., some of his orthographical features) and sometimes more progressive ones (e.g., weakening gender/case distinctions). His handwriting, too, shows some remnants of older Insular features, the

[158] See Gameson (2001: 21) for comparable instances and Jolly (2012: 80–81, especially fn. 37 for further references) for Aldred's use in the Durham Collectar.

[159] However, it must be stressed that such hints are so slight that it is impossible to decide whether Caroline influence, if any, was due to the adoption and adaption of the script in Anglo-Saxon England or imported manuscripts.

[160] The first two are quoted from the description of Square minuscule in Roberts (2005: 39) and the last from Ganz (2012: 188).

ongoing tenth-century characteristics, and possible Caroline influence. These mixtures clearly complicate the dating and localization of Farman's gloss, hindering us from advancing much from where we started.

Dissatisfactory though the results of the present study may seem, it is in fact these mixtures and complicated elements that it has intended to emphasize. Farman's gloss was not a copy of Aldred's, even when they show similarities to one another, and it is not necessarily an 'original' work of the glossator when we do not find any related gloss in the extant corpus. Undoubtedly, Farman's gloss stands upon a long tradition of reading, interpreting, glossing and translating the Latin Gospels in Anglo-Saxon England, thus containing a variety of features that trouble us who desire definitive answers to the questions we raise. We still do not know where the *harawuda* was, but it does not necessarily mean that he was working in a small obscure place we now do not know. The hints of his fluent Latin handwriting in his colophon, the availability of his exemplars in both Old English and Latin, and indeed even the mixture of two different dialects, may point to an important ecclesiastical centre. It is very tantalizing that, while we do know the names of the glossators, Farman and Owun, and the placename *harawuda*, we know virtually nothing about them. The introductory sections on Farman's gloss have endeavored not to hasten to draw conclusions about these unanswerable – at least at present – questions, but to describe and discuss various facts that can be observed in his gloss when examined in detail, which in turn will help solve such seemingly unanswerable questions in the future.

EDITORIAL PROCEDURES AND CONVENTION

The text in the edition is laid out to reproduce the manuscript layout. Although the printed layout should not be understood as an accurate reproduction of the manuscript, the aim of folio-by-folio presentation is to enable easy consultation alongside the manuscript or its digital images available online at the Digital Bodleian (see footnote 3 in the Introduction) and also to allow the reader to examine the glosses in relation to the Latin text, whereby the functions and meanings of the glosses will become clearer.

Several editorial conventions have been introduced: editorial additions, such as chapter/verse numbers and hyphens at the line break, are presented in < > (in the manuscript, modern verse divisions are marked with a sign resembling an asterisk; these are modern and accordingly not reproduced in the edition). Abbreviations, both in the Latin text and in the gloss, are expanded in round brackets. *Nomina sacra* are also expanded in the same manner. Exceptions are ꝥ (for *þæt*) and ⁊ (for *and/ond*) in the gloss, which are not expanded. Neither is ł (sometimes preceded and/or followed by a punctus) expanded, which introduces a double (or multiple) gloss. The ł abbreviation originally stands for Latin *uel*; see Robinson (1994: 163) for the possibility that it represented Old English *oþþe*.

Word divisions, too, are necessarily editorial. At times, the edition adopts word divisions different from earlier editions, and major departures from previous readings are discussed in the commentary. Rather than purporting to be definitive, these editorial interventions are intended to bring to attention those instances where multiple interpretations are possible.

The Old English gloss involves a great number of corrections by various modes of alterations, including simple erasure, additions *in rasura*, transformation of one or several letters. These alterations are not signalled in the text, as the text would be marked so heavily that one might find it hard to read through. Instead, they are reported, and discussed when appropriate, in the commentary.

The Latin text in the edition represents the original state of the manuscript as far as possible and later corrections and additions are reported in the textual apparatus. Latin corrections will be reported with R^{c} or R^{Fa}, the latter denoting that the corrections can be ascertained to have been added by Farman due to the presence of his handwriting. Many of the corrections by R^c may in fact be also by Farman, since it is impossible to attribute those corrections that involve little or no writing to him with any certainty. R^* denotes the original reading before correction.

The apparatus compares R with the standard editions of the Latin Gospels, i.e., the Oxford Vulgate by Wordsworth and White (WW) and the Stuttgart *Biblia Sacra* (Xz), and with the Lindisfarne Gospels (Y). The latter is included because it contains Aldred's Old English gloss. Although R contains various orthographical variants, the apparatus reports only major textual differences. As the readings of the two standard editions differ from one another only occasionally, WW is used as a representative, reporting Xz readings only when it differs from WW. Aldred's corrections in Y are reported as Y^{Ald}.

Textual variants other than those reported in the apparatus will be reported in the commentary only when they are relevant to discussion.

THE TEXT

her onginneþ godspell
incipit· euan⟨-⟩
to cyþenne æfter
gelium secun⟨-⟩
matheus tosagan
dum· matheum·

bóec sindun þare kennisse
<I 1>**Liber generationis**
hælendes kristes dauiðes sunu
ie(s)u cr(ist)i filii dauid
ðæs abrahames sune
fili abraham

soðlice kende
<2>Abraham (autem) genuit isac isac (autem) genuit
⁊ blo`e´þrę
iacob iacob autem genuit iudam et fra(-)
his
tres eius <3>iudas autem genuit fares et
of ðamar
zaram de thamar fares autem genuit
esrom esrom autem genuit aram <4>aram
autem genuit aminadap aminadap (autem)
genuit nasson nasson autem genuit
of rachab
salmon <5>salmon autem booz de racab
of ruð
boz autem genuit obed ex ruth obed aute(m)
genuit iesse <6>iesse autem genuit dauid
þone cyning
regem dauid autem rex genuit solamone(m)
of þære þe urias ahte
ex ea quae fuit uriae <7>salamon autem
rex genuit roboam roboas (autem) genuit
abiud abiud (autem) genuit assafath <8>assa(-)
fath (autem) genuit iosaphath iosaphath (autem)
genuit iuram iuras autem genuit ioziam
<9>iozias autem genuit iotham iothas (autem)
genuit achaz achaz autem genuit ezec(-)
hiam <10>ezechias autem genuit mannassen
mannasses autem genuit amos amos (autem)

1 (autem)[1]] *om.* Y WW 8 autem] + genuit Y WW 10 autem] *om.* Y WW=R 13 rex] *om.* Y WW

genuit iosiam <11>iosias (autem) genuit ioconiam
⁊ broeþre his in babilonia fære
et fratres eius in transmigratione
⁊ æfter babilonia fære
babilonis <12>et post transmigratione

babilonis iechonias (autem) genuit salathiel

salathiel (autem) genuit zorbabiel <13>sorbabiel

autem genuit abiud abiud (autem) genuit eli⟨-⟩

achim eliachim autem genuit azor <14>azor

autem genuit saddoc saddoc autem

genuit achim achim autem genuit eliud

<15>eliud autem geniut elizar elizar autem

genuit mathan mathan (autem) genuit iacob
kende iosepe maria wær
<16>iacob autem genuit ioseph uiru(m) mariæ
of þære akenned wæs hælend se þe is nemned krist
de qua natus est ie(su)s qui uocatur cr(istu)s
ealra cuþlice kneorissum from abrahame
<17>Omnes igitur generationes ab abra⟨-⟩
oþ to dauide feowertene kneorisse sint
ham usque ad dauid generationes
and from dauiðe oþþe to færennisse
sunt xiiii· et ad dauid usque ad transmigra⟨-⟩
babylonie feowertene kneo sint
tionem babilonis generationes sunt xiiii
⁊ from færennisse babilonie oþþe
et ad transmigratione babilonis usq(ue)
to kriste kneorisse sint feowertene
ad cr(istu)m generationes sunt xiiii:·

In the bottom margin, *cr(istu)m ad* is added, presumably as *probatio pennae.*

1 ioconiam] iochoniam R[c] iechoniam Y WW 2 transmigratione] transmigrationem Y WW=R 3 transmigratione] transmigrationem Y WW 4 (autem)] *om.* Y WW 14 igitur] ergo Y WW 16 sunt] *om.* Y WW | ad[1]] a Y WW | ad[2]] *om.* Y WW=R 17 sunt] *om.* Y WW 18 ad] a Y WW | transmigratione] transmigrationem Y WW=R 19 sunt] *om.* Y WW

kristes soþlice kennisse þus wæs
<18>Cr(ist)i autem generatio sic
þa þe hio wæs bewedded ł be⟨-⟩
erat cum esset dis⟨-⟩
fest ł in sceat alegd his moder
ponsata mater eius
maria iosefae ær þon
maria ioseph ante⟨-⟩
hiae tosomne cwoman hio wæs gemóeted in hire innoþe
quam conuenirent inuenta est in utero
hæbbende of þæ(m) halgan gaste ioseph soþlice hire wer
habens de sp(irit)u s(an)c(t)o:· <19>Ioseph autem uir ei(u)s
swa he wæs monn soþfæst ⁊ ne walde hie
cum esset homo iustus et nolet eam tradu⟨-⟩
wolde degullice forleten hio ðendi he þa ꝥ þohte 'ł þis'
cere uoluit occulte demitere eam <20>haec
soþlice he þohte henu engel drihtnes æt⟨-⟩
autem eo cogitante ecce angelus d(omi)ni ap⟨-⟩
eawde him in slepe cweþende iosep sunu
paruit ei in somnis dicens ioseph filii
dauiþes ne ondréd þu þe onfoh ł onfoiæ maria
dauid noli timere accipere mariam con⟨-⟩
wife þinum þætte soþlice in hire akenned is of þæm
iugem tuam quod enim in ea natum est de
halgan gaste is hio kenneþ ł bereþ soþlice sunu ⁊ þu nemnest
sp(irit)u s(an)c(t)o est <21>pariet autem filium et uocabis
his noma hælend he selfe soþlice he gehæleþ
nomen eius ie(su)m· Ipse enim saluum faciet
folc his from hiora synnum þas soþlice
populum suum a pecatis eorum <22>hoc aute(m)
eall geworden is ł wæs ꝥte gefylled wære þæt
totum factum est ut adinpleretur quod
acweden is ł wæs fro(m) drihtne þurh esaiam þe witgu
dictum est a d(omi)no per essaiam prophetam
cweþende henu ł her is 'ł sihþe' fæmne in innoþe ł in hrife hæfð ⁊ bereþ ł kenneþ
dicentem <23>ecce uirgo in utero habebit et pa⟨-⟩
sunu ⁊ hie nemnaþ noma his
riet filium et uocabunt nomen eius eman(u)el
ꝥ is gereht god mid usic
quod est interpraetatum nobiscum d(eu)s

7 homo] *om.* Y WW 9 apparuit ei in somnis] in somnis paruit Y^{*} in somnis apparuit Y^{c} WW 16 quod] id quod Y WW 17 essaiam] *om.* Y WW

þa arisende soþlice from slepe dyde
<24>exsurgens autem ioseph a somno fecit
swa him bebead se engel dryhtnes ⁊ feng
sicut praecipit ei angelus d(omi)ni et accipit
wiue his ⁊ ne groette hire oþ þæt
coiugem suam <25>et non cognoscebat eam do⟨-⟩
hit gebær sunu his þon(e) fru(m)kendu
nec peperit filium suum primogenitum
⁊ nemde noma his hælend þa soþlice
et uocauit nomen eius ie(su)m:· <II 1>Cum ergo
akenned wæs hælend iudeana in dagum
natus esset ie(su)s in bethlem iudae in dieb(us)
erodes þæs kyninges henu tungulkræftgu eastan quomon
erodis regis ecce magi ab oriente uenerunt
to h`i´erosolimam cweþende hwær is se þe akenned is
in hierusolimam <2>dicentes ubi est qui natus (est)
kining iudeana we gesegon soþlice steorra his
rex iudeorum uidimus enim stellam eius
in eastdæle ⁊ cuomon to gebiddenne to him
in oriente et uenimus adorare eum:·
ꝥ þa gehérde soþlice herodes king wæs gedróefed in mode
<3>Audiens autem herodis rex turbatus est
⁊ ealle hierosolima mid hine ⁊ gesomnade
et omnis hierusolima cum eo· <4>et congregans
ealle aldursacerdos ⁊ bokeras
omnes principes sacerdotum et scribas
þæs folkes ahsade fro(m) heom hwær krist wære akenned
populi sciscitabatur ab eis ubi cr(istu)s nasce⟨-⟩
hie þa cwædon in bethlem iudeana
retur· <5>at illi dixærunt in bethlem iudae
swa soþlice awriten is þurh witgu cwæþende
síc enim scriptum est per profetam dicen⟨-⟩
⁊ þu eorðu nænig þinga
tem <6>et tú bethlem terra iuda nequaquam
læsæst eart in aldurmonnum iuda of þe soþlice gæþ
minima es in principib(us) iuda ex té enim ex⟨-⟩
lat`t´euw se þe ræc`c´et folc min israhæl
eat dux qui regat populum meum israhel:·
þa herodes dernunga acægde tungulkræftgu(m) ⁊ georne
<7>Tunc herodis cla(m) uocatís magís diligenter

2 praecipit] praecepit Y(pre-) WW | accipit] accepit Y WW 3 coiugem] coniugem Y WW 8 in] *om.* Y WW 12 eo] illo Y WW 15 dixærunt] dixerunt ei Y WW 16 dicentem] *om.* Y WW 18 exeat] exiet Y WW 19 regat] reget Y WW

geliornade æt him þa tíd þæs æteawde him
dedicit ab eis tempus quae apparuit eis
steorra ⁊ sendende heom to bethlem cwæþ gæþ ⁊ ahsiað
stellae <8>et mittens eos in bethlem dixit ite inter⟨-⟩
georne bi ðem cnęhte ⁊ þanne ge gemoeteþ
rogate diligenter de puero et cum inueneretis
hine sæcgað eft me ꝥ ic swilce cymende gebidde
eum renuntiate mihi ut et ego ueniens adorem
to him þa hie þa geherdon `ðæs´ kyninges word eodun þonan ⁊ henu ł sihþe
eum <9>qui cum audissent regem abierunt· et ecce
steorra þe hiae ær gesægon in eastdæle foreeade
stella quam uiderant in oriente antecedebat
hię oþ þætti he cumende gestod bufan ðær se cneht wæs
eos usq(ue) dum ueniens staret supra ubi erat puer
hie geseænde soþlice steorran gefegon gefea miccle
<10>uidens autem stellam gauissi sunt gaudio magno
swiþe ⁊ ingangende ꝥ hus gemoettun þone cneht
ualde <11>et intrantes domum inuenerunt puerum
mid maria moder his ⁊ forþfallende gebedun to
cum maria matre eius et procedentes adoraue⟨-⟩
him ⁊ ontynden heora goldhord brohtun
runt eum et apertís thesaurís suís obtulerunt
him lac gold recils ⁊ murra `ꝥ is smerennis´ ⁊ andwyrde ł andsuari
ei munera aurum tus et mirram <12>et responso
onfengon in slepe ꝥ hię ne cerdun to herode
accepto in somnís né redirent ad herodem
þurh oþer wege gewendun to heora londe
per aliam uiam reuersi sunt in suam regionem
þa hie weron gewitenę henu engel drihtnes æteawde
<13>qui cum regressisent ecce angelus d(omi)ni appar(u)it
in swefne iosep cweþende aris ⁊ genim þone cneht
in somnís ioseph dicens surge et accipe pueru(m)
⁊ his moder ⁊ fleoh in ægypti ⁊ wæs þær
et matrem eius et fuge in aegiptum et esto ibi
oþ þæt ic sæcge ðe f(or)þon ðe toward is soþlice ꝥte
usq(ue) dum dicam tibi:· Futurum est enim ut he⟨-⟩
herodes soecaþ þone cneht to ofslæanne hine
rodis querat puerum ad perdendum eum·
he arisende genom þone cneht ⁊ his moder
<14>Qui consurgens accipit puerum et matrem
on niht ⁊ gewat in ægypti ⁊ wæs þær oþ
nocte et secessit in aegyptum <15>et erat ibi usq(ue)
herodes dead ꝥte gefylled wære ꝥte
ad obitum herodis ut adinpleretur quod

1 dedicit] didicit Y WW | quae apprauit eis stellae] stellae quae apprauit eis Y WW 2 eos] illos Y WW | ite] + et Y WW 4 eum] *om.* Y WW 8 uidens] uidentes R^{Fa} Y WW 10 procedentes] procidentes Y WW 13 somnís] somnis Y^{*} WW sompnis Y^{c} 14 suam regionem] regionem suam Y WW 15 regressisent] recessissent Y WW 16 somnis] somnio Y WW=R 20 accipit] accepit Y WW | matrem] + eius Y WW 21 secessit] recessit Y WW

acweden wæs fro(m) drihtne þurh witgu cweþende of
dictum est a d(omi)no per profetam dicentem ex ae⟨-⟩
ægypto ic acægde minum sunę þa herodes geseah
gypto uocaui filium meum <16>tunc herodis uidens
ꝥ he wæs awæged fro(m) þæ(m) tungulkræftgu(m) he wæs swiðe eorre
q(uonia)m inlussus esset a magis iratus est ualde
⁊ sendende ofslog ealle þa cnehtas þa þe werun
et mittens occidit omnes pueros qui erant
in bethlem ⁊ in allum heora gemoerum fro(m) twæm wintru(m)
in bethlem et in omnib(us) regionibus eius a bimatu
⁊ beniuþa æfter þære tide þe he ær asohte
et infra secundum tempus quod exquisierat
fro(m) þæ(m) tungulkreftgu(m) þa wæs gefylled þætte cweden wæs
a magis· <17>tunc adinpletum est quod dictum erat
þurh hieremiam þone witgu cweþende stefú in heanisse
per hirimiam profetam dicentem <18>uox in rama
gehered wæss wop ⁊ heaf micel. rachel
audita est ploratus et ululatus multus rachel
wepende hire bearn ⁊ ne walde beon afroefred forþon
plorans filios suos et noluit consulari quia
þe hie ne sendun þa herodes wæs soþlice dead henu drihtnes engel
non sunt:· <19>Defuncto autem herode ecce angelus
æteaude in slepe iosep in ægypto cweþende
d(omi)ni apparuit in somnís ioseph in aegypto <20>dicens
aris ⁊ genim þone cneht ⁊ his moder ⁊ fær
surge et accipe puerum et matrem eius et uade
to israheles eorþu f(or)þon þe deaðe sindun soþlice þe þe sohtun
in terram israhel defuncti sunt enim qui quere⟨-⟩
ferh þas cnehtes he arisende soþlice iosep
bant animam pueri <21>exsurgens autem ioseph
genom þone cneht ⁊ his moder ⁊ cuo(m) in israheles
accipit puerum et matrem eius et uenit in ter⟨-⟩
eorþu ⁊ geherdun soþlice ꝥte archelaus
ram israhel <22>audiens autem quod archilaus
ricsade in iudea for herodem his fæder ne durste
regnaret in iudea pro herode patre suo timuit
þider gangan ˋꝉ færanˊ ⁊ gemynga in slepe gecerde in galilea
illuc ire et admonitus in somnís secessit in par⟨-⟩
dęle ⁊ cumende ⁊ eardade in þęre cæstre
tes galileae <23>ueniens et habitauit in ciuitate
ðe hatte nazareþ ꝥte gefylled wære þæt
quae uocatur nazareth ut adinpleretur quod
acweden wæs þurh witgu ꝥte he bið nazarenisc
dictum est per profetas quoniam nazareus
nemned
uocabitur:·

4 erant] erat Y WW=R 5 regionibus] + ꝉ finibus R^{Fa} finibus Y WW 7 erat] est Y WW 11 angelus d(omi)ni apprauit] apprauit angelus domini Y WW 15 exsurgens autem ioseph accipit] qui surgens accepit Y WW 16 accipit] accepit Y WW 17 quod] quia Y WW Xz=R 20 ueniens et] et ueniens et R^{Fa} et ueniens Y WW

in þæm soþlice dagum cuom iohannes se bezera
<III 1>In illis autem diebus uenit iohannis baptista
bodende in iudea woestenne ⁊ cweþende dóeþ
praedicans in deserto iudeae:· <2>Et dicens peni(-)
hreunisse forþon þe neoliceþ soþlice heofuna
tentiam agite adpropinquauit enim regnum
rice þis his soþlice se þe cweden wæs þurh esaia(m)
caelorum <3>hic est enim qui dictus est per esaia(m)
witgu cweþende stemn cegende in westinne
profetam dicentem uox clamantis in deserto
gearwigað drihtnes wæg wircaþ rihte his stígas
parate uiam d(omi)ni rectas facite semitas eius:·
sylf þanne hæfde hrægl
<4>Ipse autem iohannis habebat uestimentum
of olbendena herum ⁊ fellen gyrdels ymb
de pillís camillorum et zonam pelliciam circa
his lendu his mete þanne wæs græshoppa
lumbos suos esca autem eius erat locustae
⁊ wudehuniges þa eode ut to him hieroso(-)
et mel siluestrae <5>tunc exiebat ad eum hieruso(-)
lima ⁊ ealle iudea ⁊ eall þæt lond ymb iordane
lima et omnis iudea et omnis regio circa iorda(-)
ondentende heora synne he þa gesæh þonne
nen <6>confitentes peccata sua:· <7>Uidens autem
monige farisea ⁊ saducea cumende
multas fariseorum et saduceorum uenientes
to his fulluihte cwæþ to him ge nedrana cynn
ad baptismum suum dixit eis progenies uipera(-)
hwa getahtæ eow ꝥ ge flugan fro(m) þæ(m) towardan
rum quis demonstrauit uobis fugere ab ira
eorre wyrceþ soþlice wyrþe westem hreunisse
futura <8>facite ergo dignum fructum penitentiæ
⁊ ne wellað cweþan betweon eow \ł in innan eow/ fæder we habbaþ
<9>et ne uellitis dicere inter uos patrem habemus
abraham soþ ic eow sæcge forþon ꝥ mæg god of þissu(m)
abraham dico enim uobis quia potest d(eu)s de la(-)
stanum awęccan bearn abrahame þe nu is
pidibus istís suscitare filios abrahae <10>iam
soþlice axe to wyrtruma treowes aseted his
enim securis ad radices arborum possita (est)
æghwilc treow þara þe ne bereþ godne woestim
omnis arbor quae non facit fructum bonum
bið acorfen ⁊ in fyre sended ic eowic depu ł dyppe
excidetur et in ignem mittetur:· <11>Ego quidem bab(-)
tiszo uos

1 illis autem diebus] diebus autem illis Y WW 9 suos] eius Y WW=R 11 circa] circum Y WW Xz=R | 12 R *om.* et baptizabantur in iordane ab eo (Y WW) *at the beginning of the verse 6, but the corresponding gloss is added to the left-hand margin,* [ ]run depte in ior | [ ]ne fro(m) him 13 multas] multos Y WW 15 ira futura] futura ira Y WW 16 fructum dignum] dignum fructum Y WW 17 inter] intra Y WW 18 quia] quoniam Y WW 19 abrahae] abraham Y WW=R 20 radices] radicem Y WW 21 omnis] + ergo Y WW 22 excidetur] exciditur Xz Y WW=R | ignem] igne Y WW | mittetur] mittitur Xz Y WW=R | babtiszo uos] uos baptizo WW Y(baptizo)=R

in wættre in hreunisse se þe þonne æft(er) me cymeð se is
in aqua in penitentiam qui autem uenturus est for(-)
me strængra þ ic næm wyrþe scoas
tior me est cuius non sum dignus calciamenta
to beranne se eowic depið ł dyppeþ in ðæ(m) halgan gaste ⁊ fyre
portare:· Ipse uos baptizabit in sp(irit)u s(an)c(t)o et igni
þæs winduiscoful in his honda ⁊ þurhclęnsaþ
<12>cuius uentilabrum in manu sua et permundabit
his bęreflor ⁊ gesomnaþ his hwæte in berern
aream suam et congregabit triticum suum in or(-)
þa ceaf þone forbęrneþ fyre unaduescendlice
reum paleas autem comburet igni inextinguibili:·
þa cuom fro(m) galilea in iordane to iohanne
<13>Tunc uenit ie(su)s a galilea in iordanen ad iohanne(m)
þte he wære depid from him iohannes þonne werede him cweþende
ut baptizaretur ab eo <14>prohibebat autem eum io(-)
ic sceal fro(m) þe beon ł wesa deped ł fullwihted ⁊ ðu cymest
hannis dicens ego a te debeo baptizari et tú uenis
to me þa ondswarende se hælend cwæþ to him lét þus nu forðon
ad me <15>respondens autem ie(su)s dixit ei sine modo síc
ðe þus we sculon gefyllan æghwilce soþfęstnisse þa
enim decet nos omnem inplere iustitiam:· Tunc
forlet hine he þa gedeped se hælend hræþe
dimissit eum <16>baptizatus est autem ie(su)s confestim
ástág of þæm wættre ⁊ henu him weron ontynde heofunas ⁊ he
ascendit de aqua et ecce aperti sunt ei caeli et
gesæg godes gast niþerstigend\`n´e swa culfre cumende
uidit sp(iritu)m d(e)i discendentem sicut columbam ueni(-)
ofer hine ⁊ henu stemn of heofune cweþende þis is
entem super sé <17>et ecce uox de caelís dicens hic est
min sune se leofa in ðæm me gelicade
filius meus dilectus in quo mihi conplacui:·
þa wæs hælend læded in woestenne from gaste þæt he wære
<IV 1>Tunc ie(su)s ductus est in desertum á sp(irit)u ut tempta(-)
costad fro(m) deofle ⁊ þa he fæstę feowertig daga
retur a diabulo <2>et cum ieiunasset xlta diebus
⁊ feowertig næhta æfter þon hine hyngrade ⁊ geneleccende
et xlta noctibus post ea esuriit <3>et accedens
to him se costere cwæþ to him gif þu godes sunu siæ gecwæþ
ad eum temptator dixit ei si filius d(e)i es dic
þæt þas stanes hlafes beon ł gewærþe se ⁊swara\`n´de
ut lapides isti panes fiant <4>qui respondens
cwęþ awriten is nalles in hlafe anum lifgaþ menn
dixit scriptum est non in pane solo uiuit homo

1 autem] + post me Y WW 4 permundabit] permundauit Y WW=R 8 prohibebat autem eum iohannis] iohannes autem prohibebat eum Y WW 11 omnem inplere] implere omnem Y WW 12 baptizatus est autem ie(su)s] baptizatus autem Y Xz baptizatus autem iesus WW 20 ad eum] *om.* Y WW 22 uiuit] uiuet Xz Y WW=R

ah in æghwelceu(m) worde þæ(m) þe forþgaeþ of godes muðe
sed in omni uerbo quod procedit de ore d(e)i
þa genom hine ꝥ deoful in þa halgan
<5>tunc adsumpsit eum zabulus in s(an)c(t)am ciui⟨-⟩
cæstre ⁊ sette hine on hehstowe
tatem et statuit eum supra pinnaculum
temples ⁊ cwæþ to him gif þu sie godes sunu send þec niþer
templi <6>et dixit ei si filius d(e)i es mitte té deorsu(m):·
forþon gewriten is þæt he his englum bebeodeþ
scriptum enim quia angelis suis mandauit
be þe ꝥte he þe gehalden in allum weogas þine ⁊ hie hondu(m)
de te ut custodiant té in omnib(us) uís tuis et in ma⟨-⟩
ahebbaþ þec þy les ðu ⁊spurne æt stane
nibus tollent té ne forte offendas ad lapide(m)
þinum fotum cwęþ ie(su)s to him æft awriten is
pedem tuum <7>ait illi ie(su)s rursum scriptum est
soþlice ne costa þu dryhtnes þines godes æft
enim non temptabis d(omi)n(u)m d(eu)m tuum <8>Iterum ad⟨-⟩
genom hine ꝥ deaful on þune heh swiþe
sumpsit eum zabulus in montem excelsum ualde
⁊ æteawde him eall rice middangeardes ⁊ wuldor
et ostendit ei omnia regna mundi et gloriam
þara ⁊ cwæþ to him þas ic þe eall selle gif þu fal⟨-⟩
eorum <9>et dixit illi haec omnia tibi dabo si ca⟨-⟩
lende to me gebiddes þa cwæþ to him hælend ga
dens adoraueris me:· <10>Tunc ait illi ie(su)s uade
onbæclinc þu wiþerwearde forþon awriten is to dryhtne þinu(m) gode
retro satanas scriptum est enim d(omi)n(u)m d(eu)m tuu(m)
ðu ł to gebidde ⁊ him anum ðewige þa hine forlet
adorabis et illi soli seruies <11>tunc reliquit eum
ꝥ deoful ⁊ henu englas cwoman ⁊ ðęgnadun
zabulus et ecce angeli accesserunt et ministra⟨-⟩
him þa he þa geherdę þæt iohannes
bant ei:· <12>Cum audisset autem ie(su)s quod iohannis
wæs afongen gewat in galilea ⁊ forlet
traditus esset secessit in galileam:· <13>Et relicta
nazaret caestrae cwom ⁊ geeardade in cafarnaum
ciuitate nazareth uenit et habitauit in cafar⟨-⟩
sæcaestrae in gemaerum zabulones ⁊ nepthales
nauum maritimam in finib(us) zabulon et neptalim
ꝥte gefylled wære þæt acwæden wæs þurh essaiam
<14>ut adinpleretur quod dictum est per essaiam
þone witgu cweþende zabulones eorðu ⁊ neptalimes
profetam dicentem <15>terra zabulon et terra

2 adsumpsit] assumsit Y^{*} assumpsit Y^{c} assumit WW 5 scriptum] + (est) R^{Fa} Y WW | mandauit] mandabit WW Y=R 6 ut custodiant te in omnib(us) uis tuis] *om.* Y WW 9 enim] *om.* Y WW 9 adsumpsit] assumit Y^{*} WW assumpsit Y^{c} 10 montem] monte Y WW=R 12 omnia tibi] tibi omnia Y WW 13 ait illi] dicit ei Y WW 14 retro] *om.* Y WW | enim] *om.* Y Xz WW=R 17 Cum audisset autem ie(su)s] Cum autem audisset Y WW 21 adinpleretur] impleretur Y WW adimpleretur Xz 22 dicentem] *om.* Y WW | terra neptalim] neptalim Y terra nepthalim WW

eorþe sáes weg ofer iordane þara þeoda
neptalim uia maris trans iordanen galileae
galilea folc þætte sætt in þiostre geseah
gentium <16>populus qui sedebat in tenebrís luce(m)
micel leoht ⁊ þæm sittendum in þeode londe ⁊ deade
uidit magnam et sedentibus in regione et um(-)
scade ł scua leht æteawde upp þæm seoðþan ingann
bre mortis lux orta est eis:· <17>Exinde coepit
læran ⁊ cweþan doaþ hrewnisse
ie(su)s praedicare et dicere penetentiam agite
forðon þe neolicet heofuna rice He þa
adpropinquauit enim regnum caelorum <18>am(-)
gangande bi galilea sáe gesæh
bulans autem ie(su)s iuxta mare galileae uidit
twegen gebroþer simon þane þe is nemned petrus
duos fratres simonem qui uocabatur petrus
⁊ andreas his broþer settende nett in sáe
et andream fratrem eius mittentes retia in ma(-)
forþon þe hię werun fisceras ⁊ þa cwæþ to him
re erant enim piscatores:· <19>Et ait illis ie(su)s
cumaþ æfter me ⁊ ic gedom ꝥ git beoþan monna
uenite post me et faciam uos fieri piscatores
fisceres ⁊ hie hræþe foletende ꝥ nett heora
hominum:· <20>At illi continuo relictis retibus suis
folgedun him ⁊ he forþgangande þonan gesægh oþre
secuti sunt eum:· <21>Et procedens inde uidit alios
twegen gebroþer Iacob zebed`e´aes sunu ⁊ iohannem his
duos fratres iacobum zebedei et iohannem fra(-)
broþer in scipe mid hiora fæder boeten(-)
trem eius in naui cum zebedeo patre eorum re(-)
de heora nett ⁊ gecægde ł cliopade him ⁊ hie þa
ficientes retia sua et uocauit eos <22>illi autem
sona forletun heora nett ⁊ fæder folgadun him
statim relictís retibus suís et patre secuti s(un)t eu(m):·
⁊ hælend geondeade alle galilea lærende
<23>Et circumibat ie(su)s totam galileam docens
in heora synagogu(m) `ł somnungum´ ⁊ bodende godspelles
in sinagogis eorum et praedicans euangeliu(m)
rice ⁊ hælde æghwilce adle ⁊ æghwilce
regni et sanans omnem langorem et omnem
untrymnisse in þæm folce ⁊ eode his hlisa
infirmitatem in populo:· <24>Et abít opinnio
in alle syria ⁊ him brohtun alle
eius in totam siriam et obtulerunt ei omnes

2 luce(m)] lumen Y WW=R **3** umbre] umbra Y WW **7** ie(su)s] *om.* Y WW **8** uocabatur] uocatur Y WW **9** retia] rete Y WW **10** ie(su)s] *om.* Y WW **12** suis] *om.* Y WW **15** naui] naue Y WW=R **17** suis] *om.* Y WW

yfel hæbende ⁊ missenlicu(m) adlum ⁊ tintre\`ter´gu(m)
male habentes uarís langoribus et tormentís
gefongnae ⁊ þa þe dioful hæfdun
conpraehensos et qui demonia habebant
⁊ monsekae ⁊ loman ⁊ he gehælde þa
et lunaticos et paraliticos et curauit eos
⁊ him fylgendun monige mængu of galilea
<25>et secuti sunt eum turbae multae a galilea
⁊ of decapoli ⁊ of hierosolimis ⁊ of iudea ⁊ of londe begeonda
et decapuli et de hierusolimís et de iudea trans
iordane He þa geseende þa menigu astahg
iordanen:· <V 1>Uidens autem ie(su)s turbas ascendit
on dune ⁊ þa he wæs gesett him eodun to his discipuli
in montem et cum sedisset accesserunt ad eum
ꝉ his þægnas ⁊ ontynde his muþ lærde hię cweþende
discipuli eius <2>et aperuit os suum docebat eos dicens:·
eadig þa þurfende in gaste forþon heora his heofuna rice
<3>Beati pauperes sp(irit)u q(uonia)m ipsoru(m) est regnu(m) cælorum:·
þa milde forþon þe hie gesittaþ eorðu
<4>Beati mites q(uonia)m ipsi possidebunt terram:·
þa wepende nu f(or)þon þe hię beoþ afróefrede
<5>Beati qui lugent nunc qu(onia)m ipsi consulabuntur:·
þa þe hie hyngriþ ⁊ ðyrsteþ soðfæstnisse f(or)þon þe hie fulle weorþaþ \`ꝉ beon´
<6>Beati qui esuriunt et sitiunt iustitia(m) q(uonia)m ipsi saturab(u)ntur:·
þa mildheortnisse f(or)þon þe hie mildheortnisse begetaþ
<7>Beati missericordes qu(onia)m ipsi misericordia(m) consequent(u)r
þa clæne heortan þe hie god gescawað ꝉ geseoþ
<8>Beati mundo corde quoniam ipsi d(eu)m uidebunt:·
þa sibsume \`ꝉ friðsume´ f(or)þon þe hie beoþ godes bearn genemde
<9>Beati pacifici quoniam filii d(e)i uocabuntur:·
þa þe hóehtnisse þrowiaþ fore
<10>Beati qui persecutionem patiuntur propter
soþfæstnisse f(or)þon þe heora is heofuna rice
iustitiam quoniam ipsoru(m) est regnu(m) cæloru(m):·
eadig ge beoþ þonne eowic wærgaþ mennisc
<11>Beati estis cum maledixerint uobis homines
⁊ eower hehtende beoþan ⁊ cwæþan æghwilc yfel
et persecuti uos fuerint et dixerint omne malu(m)
wið eow ligende for mec gefeaþ
aduersum uos mentientes propter me <12>gaudete
⁊ geblissiað f(or)þon lean \`ꝉ meard´ eowra is genihtsumað
et exsultate quoniam mercis uestra copiosa est
in heofunum f(or)þon þe hię swa hoehtende sint witgena þara þe
in caelís síc enim persecuti sunt prophetas qui
weron ær eow
fuerunt ante uos:·

4 secuti] secutae Y WW | a galilea] de galilaea Y WW 5 de hierusolimis] hierosolimis Y WW | de[2]] *om.* WW Y=R | trans iordanen] et de trans iordanen Y WW 6 ie(su)s] *om.* Y WW 8 aperuit] aperiens Y WW 11 lugent] lugunt Y WW=R | nunc] *om.* Y^{*} WW Y^{c}=R 13 qu(onia)m] quia Xz Y WW=R 15 quoniam] + ipsi Y WW Xz=R 18 homines] *om.* Y WW 19 et[1]] + cum Y WW=R 21 mercis] merces Y WW

ge sindun eorðu salt gif ꝥ salt þonne awerdað
<13>Uos estis sál terrae quod si sal euanuerit

in þæm þe hit bið salten to nohte mæg seoþþan nymþe þæt
in quo sallietur ad nihelum ualet ultra nisi ut

hit sie worpen út ⁊ tredan fro(m) monnum
mittatur foras et conculcetur ab hominibus:·

ge sindun leoht middangeardes ne mæg cæstra beon ahýded
<14>Uos estis lux mundi non potest ciuitas abscondi

on dun aseted ne menn blæcern inbeornað
supra montem possita <15>neq(ue) accendunt lucer⟨-⟩

⁊ settaþ hine under mytte ah on candel⟨-⟩
nam et ponunt eam sub modio sed supra can⟨-⟩

treow ꝥ he gelihte allum þe in husae sindun
dillabrum ut luceant omnibus qui in domu sunt

sua lihte liht eower fore monnum ꝥte hiae geseon
<16>síc luceat lux uestra coram hominib(us) ut uideant

eower god we\`o´rc ⁊ wuldrigen fæder eowru(m)
uestra bona opera et magnificent patrem ues⟨-⟩

ðe in heofunu(m) is ne wenaþ ge forþon the ic c\`u´ome
trum qui in caelis est:· <17>Nolite putare q(uonia)m ueni

to brecanne ae ł lare eþþa witga ne cuom ic to breccane
soluere legem aut profetas non ueni soluere

ah to gefyllenne soþ ic sæcge eow oþ þæt geleoreþ
sed adinplere:· <18>Amen dico uobis donec transeat

heofun ⁊ eorþe an í eþþa an hol stæfes ne gelioreþ
caelum et terra iota unum uel unus apex non præ⟨-⟩

fro(m) ae ær þon all þus geweorþe se þe forþon toleseþ
teribit a lege donec omnia fiant:· <19>Qui ergo solue⟨-⟩

an of þisse beboda læsest ⁊ swa læreþ
rit unum de mandatís istís minimis et sic docue⟨-⟩

menn he biþ se læsesta nemned in heofuna rice
rit homines minimus uocabitur in regno cælorum:·

se þe þonne wyrceþ ⁊ swa læreþ se bið micel
Qui autem fecerit et síc docuerit hic maximus

nemneþ in heofuna rice forþon ic sæcge eow
uocabitur in regno caelorum:· <20>Dico enim uobis

nymþe eower soþfæstnisse genihtsumige mæ þon(ne)
quia nisi habundauerit iustitia uestra plus qua(m)

bokere ⁊ farisea ne gaþ ge in heofuna
scribarum et fariseorum non intrabitis in regnu(m)

rice geherdun þætte cwæden wæs þæ(m) iumonnum
caelorum:· <21>Audistis quia dictum est antiquis

ne slag þu se þe þon(ne) slæþ scyldig he biþ dome \`he bið doma scyldig´
non occides qui (autem) occiderit reus erit iudicio:·

5 montem] monte Y WW=R | neq(ue)] + homines R^{Fa} 6 supra] super Y WW 7 ut luceant] et luceat Y ut luceat WW 9 magnificent] glorificent Y WW 10 qui in caelis est] qui est in caelis Y WW=R 12 Amen] + quippe Y WW 13 uel] aut Y WW 15 sic docuerit] docuerit sic Y WW 17 sic] *om.* Y WW | maximus] magnus Y WW

ic þonne sæcge eow þætte ˙ æghwilc þara eorsaþ
<22>Ego autem dico uobis quia omnis qui irascitur
his broþer he biþ doma scyldig se þe þonne cwaeþ
fratri suo reus erit iudicio qui autem dixerit
his broþer idla he biþ gemote scyldig se þe þanne
patri suo racha reus erit concilio qui autem
cwæþe dysig 'ł dole' he biþ scyldig hellefyres forþon gif þu brin⟨-⟩
dixerit fatuae reus erit gehenne ignis <23>si ergo of⟨-⟩
ga þin lac to weofud 'ł wibede' ⁊ ðęr gemyne
feris mun(u)s tum ad altare et ibi recordatus
bist þæt þin boþer hæbbe hwæthwugu wið ðe
fueris quia frater tuus habet aliquid aduer⟨-⟩
forlet þær þin lac beforan þæt weofud ł wibed
sus té <24>relinque ibi munus tuum ante altare
⁊ gae ærest geþinge wiþ ðinu(m) broþer ⁊ þanne cumest þu
et uade prius reconciliari fratri tuo et tunc ueni⟨-⟩
agefes þin lac wæs 'ł beo ðu' gemod 'þencende' þinu(m)
ens offeris munus tuum:· <25>Esto consentiens ad⟨-⟩
þæ(m) wiðerwearde hræþe þanne þu sie on wæge mid hine þy laes
uersario tuo cito dum es in uia cum eo ne forte
se wiðerwearde þec selle doeme ⁊ se doeme sellað
tradat te aduersarius iudici et iudex tradat
ðe his dægne ⁊ þu se in carcern sended soþ ic sæcga
te ministro et in carcerem mittaris:· <26>Amen dico
þe ne gæs þu ut þonan ær þon ðu agefe þon(e) næhstu
tibi non exies inde donec reddas nouissimum
feorþan dæl ge geherdun þte cwæden wæs þæ(m) gúmonnu(m)
quadrantem:· <27>Audistis quia dictum est antiq(u)is
ne lige dernunge ic þonne sæcge eow þæt æghwilc
non mechaberis:· <28>Ego autem dico uobis quia omnis
þara þe gesihþ wif to gitsanne .ł forlicgan hire 'þæs'
qui uiderit mulierem ad concupiscendam eam
gewemmed is wiþ þ in his heorte gif þanne þin ége
iam mechatus est eam in corde suo <29>quod si oculus
þ swiþre æswicað þe 'ł fælle þec' ahloca hit ⁊ awerp
tus dexter scandalizat té erue eum et proiece
fro(m) ðe forþon þe þe beþerfeð þ to lore weorðe an þine
abs te expedit enim tibi unum membrorum tuoru(m)
lioma þonne all þin lichoma się sended
ut pereat quam totum corpus tuum mittatur
in helle ⁊ gif seo swiþre hond þin fælle 'ł æswicað'
in gihennam <30>et si dextera manus tua scandali⟨-⟩
ðec aceorf hiae ⁊ aweorp fro(m) þe f(or)þon þe þe beðęrfeþ
zat té abscide eam et proiece abs te expedit enim

1 irascitur] irascetur Y WW=R **3** patri] fratri R^{Fa} Y WW **4** offeris] offeres Y WW **5** tum] tuum R^{Fa} Y WW **6** aduersus] aduersum Y WW **7** ante] ad Y WW=R **8** reconciliari] reconciliare Y WW **9** offeris] offeresY offers WW **15** quia] quoniam Y WW **16** milierem] miliem Y^{*} Y^{c} WW=R | concupiscendam] concupiscendum WW Y=R **18** tus] tuus Y WW **19** unum membrorum tuorum ut pereat] ut pereat unum membrorum tuorum Y WW **21** gihennam] gehenna Y gehennam WW **22** enim] + tibi Y WW *om.* Xz

þæt to lose wearþe ˋł lore beon′ an þine leoman þon(ne) eall
ut pereat unum membrorum tuorum quam totu(m)
þin lichoma gæþ in helle Gecwæden wæs þonne
corpus tuum eat in geghennam <31>dictum est aute(m)
swa hwa swa forletae his wif selle hi(m) boec
quicumq(ue) dimisserit uxorem suam det ei libel⟨-⟩
þare áweorpnisse ic þonne sæcge eow ˋł iu′ þætte æghwilc þara
lum repudi· <32>ego autem dico uobis quia omnis
þe forleteþ his wif butan forlegennisse
qui dimisserit uxorem suam excepta fornica⟨-⟩
þinge ˋł intinga′ he doeþ ꝥ hiu dernunge licgę ⁊ se þe ꝥ forletne
tionis causa facit eam mechari et qui dimissa(m)
hi(m) lædeþ he fæþ unrehthæmeþ eft ge geherdun
duxerit adulterium committit <33>iterum audistis
þætte cwęden wæs gúmonnum ne swer þu man
quia dictum est antiquis non periurabis
agef þonne drihten þine haþas ic þonne
reddes autem d(omi)no iuramenta tua <34>ego autem
cweþe to eow ꝥ ge ne sellaþ hað ˋł swerge′ allunga ˋł eower nan′ ne þurh heofun
dico uobis non iurare omnino neq(ue) per caelum
forþon ðe he is godes seþel ne þurh eorðæ forþon þi hio is fotscamel
quia tronus d(e)i est <35>neq(ue) per terram quia sca⟨-⟩
ł tæppelbred his fota ne þurh hierusalem forþon
billum peduum eius neq(ue) per hierusalem quia
þe hio is cæstra þæs micclan kyninges ne þurh þin heafud
ciuitas est magni regis <36>neq(ue) per capud tuum
aþ selle ˋł swerigę′ forþon þe þu ne mæht ænne loc hwitne
iuraueris quia non potes unum capillum album
gewirce oþþe blæcne sie þonne eower word ł is ł hit is
facere uel nigrum:· <37>Sit autem sermo uestro est
is ˋł hit is′ nis ˋł nis hit′ nis ˋł nis hit′ þætte þonne þæm wordu(m) genyhtsume is fro(m) yflę is
est non non· quod autem his amplius est a malo (est)
ge geherdun þætte cwæden wæs ege for ege toð
<38>audistis quia dictum est oculum pro oculo dente(m)
for tóþ ic þonne cwæþe to eow ꝥ ge ne wiðstonde yflæ
pro dente <39>ego autem dico uobis non resistere malo:·
ah gif hwa ðec sláe on ðæt swiðran wonge ł ceke
Sed si quis te percusserit in dexteram maxilla(m)
þin sel him ek þæt oþer ⁊ þæ(m) þe wille wið þe
tuam praebe illi et alteram <40>et qui ei uult tecu(m)
dom geflitan ⁊ þinne tonica genioman
iudicio contendere et tonicam tuam tollere
forlet him ˋł swilce′ ⁊ hryft ⁊ swa hwa swa ðe nede to lædenne ˋł to ferganne′
demitte ei et pallium:· <41>Et quicumq(ue) té angariza⟨-⟩ uerit

2 geghennam] gehenna Y gehennam WW **3** ei] illi Y WW **7** adulterium committit] adulterat Y WW **8** periurabis] peierabis WW Y=R **9** reddes] redens Y* reddens Y^{c} WW=R | d(omi)no] + uota Y WW=R **11** tronus] trhonus R^{c} thronus Y WW | scabillum] + est Y WW | peduum] pedum Y* WW Y^{c}=R **15** uel] aut Y WW | uestro] uester Y WW **16** amplius] habundantius Y abundantius WW **17** oculo] + et Y WW **19** dexteram maxilla(m) tuam] dextera maxilla tua Y WW **20** alteram] altera Y WW=R | qui ei] illi qui Y ei qui WW **22** demitte] remitte Y WW | ei] *om.* Y WW=R | angarizauerit] angariaberit Y angariauerit WW

þusend ˋþæt his an milˊ steppan ga mid hinę oþre twege all ˋł se þeˊ bidde
mile passus uade cum illo alia duo <42>omni petenti

þe sele him ⁊ þæ(m) ˋðeˊ wille on borg nioma æt þe ne beo ungeþwære
té tribue ei et uolenti mutari a té né auertaris

Ge geherdun þte cwęden wæs lufa þine þa nexstan
<43>audistis quia dictum est diligis proximum tuum

⁊ hate þine fiond ic þon(ne) cwæþe to eow
et odies inimicum tuum:· <44>Ego autem dico uobis

lufigaþ eowre fiondas ⁊ dóeþ wæl þæm þe eowic
diligite inimicos uestros et benefacite hís qui

hateþ ˋł fiegęˊ ⁊ gebiddaþ for hearmcuidele .ł oihtende eowic
oderunt uos et orate pro calumpnientib(us) uobis

⁊ for ehtendum ˋł hoelendeˊ eowic þæt ge sie bearn eowres fæder þe
et persequentib(us) uos <45>ut sitis filii patris uestri qui

in heofon(um) is se þe his sunne dóeþ upp gangan ofer gode
in caelís est qui solem suum orri facit super bonos

⁊ yfle ⁊ regneþ ofer soþfeste ⁊ unsoþfæste forþon gif ge
et malos et pluit super iustos et iniustos:· <46>Si enim

lufigaþ þa þe eow lufigaþ hwylce lean
diligatis eos qui uos diligunt quam mercidem

habbaþ ge ah gæfelgeróefe þæt ne doeþ ⁊ gif ge
habebitis nonne et puplicani hoc faciunt <47>et si

halettaþ eowre broþer æfne hwæt
salutaueritis fratres uestros tantum quid

doaþ ge marae ah hæðne ꝥ ne doaþ
amplius facietis nonne æthnici hoc faciunt:·

forþon beoþ ge gedˋoˊefe. swa swilce eower fæder
<48>Estote ergo uos perfecti sicut pater uester

se heofunlica gedoefe is behaldeþ ꝥ ge eowre soþfest(-)
caelestis perfectus est:· <VI 1>Adtendite né iustitia(m)

nisse ne doan fore monnum ꝥ ge sie geseˋaˊnę
uestram faciatis coram hominib(us) ut uidiamini

fro(m) heo(m) fro(m) him elles ł elcur ge ne habbaþ lean .ł mearde mid eower
ab eis alioquin mercidem non habebitis apud

fæder þæne þe in heofunu(m) is f(or)þon þon(ne) þu wirce
patrem uestrum qui in caelis est· <2>Cum ergo fa(-)

ælmisse ne blau þu beman for þe swa
cies elimoysinam noli tuba canere ante té sicut

liceteras doan in heora somnungu(m) ⁊ in tunum ꝥ hie
hyppochrite faciunt in synagogis et in uicis ut

sie weorþade fro(m) monnum soþ ic sæcge eow hie on(-)
honorificentur ab hominib(us) amen dico uobis reci(-)

fengun heora lean ðe þonne wircendum ælmesse
perunt mercidem suam <3>té autem faciente elimoysi(-)
nam

1 mile] mille R[c] Y WW | omni petenti te tribue ei] qui petit a te da ei Y WW 3 diligis] diliges Y WW 4 odies inimicum tuum] odio habebis inimicum tuum Y WW 5 et] *om.* Y WW 6 calumpnientib(us) uobis et persequentib(us) uos] persequentibus et calumniantibus uos Y WW 8 qui] quia Y WW=R | orri] oriri Y WW | bonos] bonus Y[*] Y[c] WW=R 13 facietis] facitis Y facitis et WW 14 sicut] + et Y WW 15 iustitia(m)] iustitam Y[*] Y[c] WW=R 19 elimoysinam] elemosyna Y elemosynam WW 21 reciperunt] receperunt Y WW 22 elimoysinam] aelemosyna Y elemosynam WW

nyte se winstrae hónd þin hwat þin sio swiþre doa þæt þin
nesciat sinistra quid faciat dextera tua <4>ut sit
ælmes sie in degulnisse ꝧ þin fæder se þe gesið in degulnisse
ælimosina tua et pater tuus qui uidit in absconso
geldeþ ðe ꝧ þonne ge bidde eow ne beoþ ge swa liceteras
reddet tibi <5>et cum oratis non eritis sicut hippochrite
þa þe lufigaþ stalle .ł stonde in gesomnungum ꝧ in hwommum worþana
qui amant stare in sinagogis et in angulis platearu(m)
stondende him gebidde ꝥ hie sie gesęnæ fro(m) monnum soþ
stantes orare· ut uideantur ab hominib(us)· Amen
ic sæcge eow hie onfengun heora lean ðu þonne
dico uobis recepierunt mercidem suam <6>tu autem
þonne þu gebidde ga in þine cofan ꝧ betun þine dure
cum orabis intra in cubiculum tuum et cluso hostio
bidde þin fæder in degulnisse geldeþ ðe
tuo ora patrem tuum in absconso reddet tibi:·
ꝧ þonne gebiddendae ne scule ge feola spreocan swa hæðene
<7>Orantes autem nolite multum loqui sicut æthnici
doan f(or)þon þe hiae w\`o´enaþ þæt him sie in heora feolasprece ge⟨-⟩
faciunt putant enim quod in multiloquio suo ex⟨-⟩
héred ne scule forþon gelice beon him forþon þe
audiantur <8>nolite ergo adsimilare eis scit enim
eower fæder hwæs eow ðærf sie ær þon ge hine bid⟨-⟩
pater uester quid uobis opus sit antequam petatis
dan þus ge þonne eow gebiddað fæder ure þu þe in heofu⟨-⟩
eum <9>sic ergo uos orabitis:· Pater noster qui es in
num earð beo gehalgad þin noma cume to þin rice
caelís s(an)c(t)ificetur nomen tuum <10>adueniat regnu(m) tuu(m)
weorþe þin willa swa swa on heofune swilce on eorþe hlaf userne
fiat uoluntas tua sicut in caelo et in terra <11>panem
ł ure dæghwæmlicu .ł instondenlice sel us todæge ꝧ forlet
nostrum substantialem da nobis hodie <12>et remitte
us ure scylde swa swa we éc forleten þæ(m) þe scyl⟨-⟩
nobis debita nostra sicut et nos remittimus debito⟨-⟩
digat wið us ꝧ ne gelaet us gelaede in constungae
ribus nostris <13>et ne patiaris nos induci in temptatio⟨-⟩
ah gelese us of yfle forþon þy gif ge forleteð
nem sed libera nos a malo:· <14>Si enim dimiseritis
monnum heora synna heow swilce fo·leteþ eower fæder
hominibus peccata eorum dimittet uobis pater uester
se heofunlica eowre scyldæ gif ge þonne ne forleteþ monnum
caelestis delicta uestra <15>si autem non demiseritis peccata
eora synne ne eower fæder se þe in heofunum is forleteð
hominibus eorum nec pater uester qui in caelis (est) dimittet
eow eowra synne
uobis peccata uestra:·

1 sinistra] + tua Y WW 2 tua] + in abscondito R^Fa Y WW | uidit] uidet Y WW | absconso] abscondito Y WW 4 stare] *om.* Y WW 6 recipierunt] receperunt R^c Y WW 7 cluso] clausso R^c clauso Y WW Xz=R* 8 tuum] + et pater tuus qui uidet R^Fa (*in margin with the gloss*, ꝧ þin fæder se þe gesihð) + in abscondito et pater tuus qui uidet Y WW | absconso] abscondito Y WW 10 faciunt] *om.* Y* WW Y^c=R | quod] qui Y quia WW 11 adsimilare] assimilari Y WW 12 quid uobis opus sit] quibus opus sit uobis Y WW 13 es in caelis] in caelis es Xz Y WW=R 14 adueniat] ueniat Xz Y WW=R (cont. on p. 104)

þonne ge þon(ne) faesten ne beoþ ge swa swa licetteras
<16>Cum autem ieiunatis nolite fieri sicut hyppochrite

unrote forþon þe hię weorfaþ heora andwliotu ꝥ hie sie geséanae
tristes demoliuntur enim facies suas ut pareant

monnu(m) fæstende soþ ic eow sæcge f(or) ꝥ hiæ
hominibus ieiunantes amen dico uobis quoniam re⟨-⟩

onfengun heora lean þu þonne þonne þu fæste sme⟨-⟩
ciperunt mercidem suam <17>tu autem cum ieiunas unge

re þin heafod ⁊ þine andwlitu þwah þy les þu sie gesene mon⟨-⟩
capud tuum et faciem tuam laua <18>ne hominibus ui⟨-⟩

num fæstende ah þinu(m) fæder ðæ(m) þe in degulnisse is
dearis ieiunans sed patri tuo qui est in absconso

⁊ þin fæder se þe geseoþ in degulnisse geldeþ ðe
et pater tuus qui uidit in absconso reddet tibi

ne hydeþ eow hord in eorþe
<19>nolite thesaurizate uobis thesauros in terra

þær om ⁊ mohþa gewyrfeþ ł etaþ ⁊ þær ðiofes adel⟨-⟩
ubi tinea et erugo demollitur et ubi fures effo⟨-⟩

faþ ⁊ forstelaþ hydeþ eow þonne
diunt et furantur:· <20>Tehsaurizate autem uobis

hord in heofunum þær ne om ne mohþa
tesauros in caelo ubi neq(ue) tinea neq(ue) erugo

gewyrfeð ⁊ þær þeof ne adelfaþ ne forstelaþ
demolitur et ubi fures non effudiunt nec furan⟨-⟩

forþon þær þin hord is þær is þin
tur <21>ubi enim est tesaurus tuus ibi erit et cór

eorta lichoma blæcern is þin ege
tuum:· <22>Lucerna corporis tui occulus tuus

gif þin ege biþ anfald all þin lichoma
si oculus tuus simplex est totum corpus tuu(m)

biþ liht gif þin ege þonne ne bið nan
lucidum erit:· <23>Si autem oculus tuus nequa(m)

eall þin lichoma beoþ ðeostru forþon
est totum corpus tuum tenebrosum erit si ergo

gif þæt leht þætte in ðe is þeostru sint þæt þeostre
lumen quod in té est tenebrae sunt tenebrae

hu micel biþ ne mæg ænig twæm
ipse quantae sunt:· <24>Nemo potest duobus

godum ðeowigan forþon þe he þa oþerne fiað. ł hateþ
dominis seruire aut enim unum odio habebit

⁊ oþerne lufað herweþ ne magun ge gode ðeowige
et alterum contempnet non potestis d(e)o seruire

⁊ dwale forþon ic cweþ`e´ to eow ꝥ ge sorgige
et mammone:· <25>Ideo dico uobis ne soliciti sitis

(f. 9r) 16 substantialem] supersubstantiale Y supersubstantialem WW | remitte] demitte Y dimitte WW **17** et] *om.* Y WW=R | remittimus] dimittimus Y WW dimisimus Xz **18** patiaris nos induci] inducas nos Y WW **20** dimittet] + et Y WW **21** peccata] *om.* Y WW **22** eorum] *om.* Y WW | qui in caelis (est)] *om.* Y WW **23** uobis] *om.* Y WW

(f. 9v) 2 demoliuntur] exterminant Y WW=R **3** quoniam] quia Y WW | reciperunt] receperunt Y WW **5** hominibus uidearis] uidearis hominibus Y WW **6** absconso] abscondito Y WW **7** uidit] uidet Y WW | absconso] abscondito Y WW **8** thesaurizate] thesaurizare Y WW **9** tinea et erugo] aerugo et tinea Y erugo et tinea WW | et[2]] *om.* Y Xz WW=R **10** furantur] furentur Y WW=R **(cont. on p. 105)**

eowru(m) fere hwæt ge etan ne eowrum
animae uestrae quid manducetis neq(ue) corpori
lichoma hu ge eowic gearwige ah nis mare ꝥ ferh
uestro quid induamini nonne plus est anima
þonne se mete ⁊ se lichoma þonne ꝥ hrægl geseoþ .ł behaldeþ
quam esca et corpus quam uestimentum <26>respici⟨-⟩
heofunfuglas ꝥ hię ne saweð ne ripath
té uolatilia caeli quoniam non serunt neq(ue) me⟨-⟩
ne somniaþ in berern ⁊ eower fæder
tunt neq(ue) congregant in horrea et pater uester
se heofunlica foedeþ þa ah ge ne sindun diorre þonne
caelestis pascet illa nonne uos magis plures istis
þa hwilc eower mæg þonne þencende ætece
illis <27>quis autem uestrum cogitans potest adicere
to his lengo ane elne ⁊ be hræglę
ad staturam suam cubitum unum <28>et de uestimento
forhwon sorgiaþ ge sceawigaþ lilia londes hu hie
quid soliciti estis considerate lilia agri quomodo
waexaþ ne winnaþ ne spinnaþ soþ ic eow
crescunt non laborant nec neunt:· <29>Amen dico
þonne sæcge ꝥ ne salomon in allum his
autem uobis quoniam non salamon in omni gloria
wuldre węs beþæht swa swa an þara nu nu þonne
sua coopertus est sicut unum ex istis <30>si autem
ꝥ londes hóeg þæt todæge is ⁊ to mærgen ˋł marneˊ bið in ofne sended
fenum agri quod hodie est et cras in clibanum mit⟨-⟩
god swa gearwæþ hu micele mae eowic þæs medmasta geleˋaˊfe menn
tur d(eu)s sic uestit quanto magis uos modice fidei:·
forþon ne sorgigaeþ ge cweþende hwæt geetaþ wæ
<31>Nolite ergo solliciti esse dicentes quid manducabi⟨-⟩
oþþe hwæt drincaþ wæ oþþe hu beoþ we gewrigene forþon þe þas
mus aut quid bibimus aut quo operiemur <32>haec enim
þeode all soeceþ forþon þe eower fæder wat ꝥ ge
omnia gentes inquirunt scit enim pater uester quid
þissa alra ðurfun soecaþ þonne ærest godes
horum omnium indigitis <33>querite ergo primum regnum
rice ⁊ his soþfæstnisse ⁊ all þas bioð geeced eow
d(e)i et iustitiam eius et haec omnia adicientur uobis:·
ne forþon sorgigaþ ge in morgen se morgen
<34>Nolite ergo solliciti esse in crastinum crastinus
forþon dæg sorgaþ beoþ selfa him genoh weotudlice
enim dies sollicitus erit ipse sibi suffecit enim
dæge wea his ne doemeþ ge þy les ge sien doemed
diei malitia sua:· <VII 1>Nolite iudicare ut non iudicemi⟨-⟩
ni

(f. 9v) 11 tesauros] tehsauros R^c thesauros Y WW | tinea neq(ue) erugo] erugo neque tinea Y WW **13** erit] est Y WW **14** tui] + (est) R^c est Y WW (*omitting* tui) | tuus] *om.* Y WW **15** oculus tuus simplex est] fuerit oculus tuus simplex Y WW **17** est] fuerit Y WW **19** ipse] *om.* Y WW | sunt] erunt Y WW **21** alterum] + diligit (*with further addition to the lower margin,* aut unu(m) sustinebit et alterum, *with gloss* eþa oþerne hræfneð ⁊ oþerne) R^Fa + diliget aut unum sustinebit et alterum Y WW
(f. 10r) 2 plus est anima] anima est plus Y WW **3** corpus] + plus est Y Xz WW=R **6** pascet] pascit Y WW | istis] estis R^c Y WW | plures] pluris WW Y=R **10** neunt] nent Y WW | Amen] *om.* Y WW **11** non] nec Y WW **(cont. on p. 106)**

on ðæm ˋin ðæmˊ wiotudlice dome þe ge doemeþ ge beoþ doemde ⁊ in ðæm
<2>in quo enim iudicio iudicaueritis iudicabemini et in
gemete þe ge metaþ bið eow meten
qua mensura mensi fueritis remittietur uobis:·
forhwon þonne gesihstu streu in ege broþer þine
<3>quid autem uidis fistucam in oculo fratris tui
⁊ beam in ege þinum ne geseẹṣ ˋł sisˊ oþþa hu cweþestu
et trabem in oculo tuo non uidis <4>aut quomodo dicis
broþer þinu(m) ⁊ sihþe beam in ege þinu(m) is þu licettere
fratri tuo:· Et ecce trabis in oculo tuo est <5>hyppoc⟨-⟩
geþo æræst þone beam of ege þinu(m) ⁊ þonne
hrite eice primum trabem de oculo tuo et tunc
gesihst þu awearpe ꝥ streu of þines broþer ege
uidebis eicere fistucam de oculo fratris tui:·
ne sellað ge halig hundum ne gewearpaþ ercnanstanas
<6>Nolite dare s(an)c(tu)m canibus neq(ue) mittatis margare⟨-⟩
eowre beforan swinum þy les hiæ tredan ða
tas uestras ante porcos ne forte conculcent eas
heora fotum ⁊ gehwerfeþ toslite eowic
pedibus suis et conuersi disrumpant uos:·
biddaþ ⁊ eow biþ sald soecaþ ⁊ ge gemoetaþ cnyssaþ
<7>Petite et dabitur uobis querite et inuenietis pul⟨-⟩
⁊ eow biþ ontyned æghwilc wiotudlice se þe bit he on⟨-⟩
sate et aperietur uobis <8>omnis enim qui petit acci⟨-⟩
foeþ ⁊ se þe soeceþ he findeð ⁊ cnyssande him bið ontyned
pit et qui querit inuenit et pulsanti aperietur:·
oþþa hwælc is eower monn þe hine bidde sunu
<9>Aut quis est ex uobis homo quem si petierit filius
his hlaf ah he stan ræceþ thæm oþþe gif
suus panem numquid lapidem porriget ei <10>aut
he fiscæs biddeth ah he nedra ræceþ
si piscem petierit numquid serpentem porriget
him nu nu þonne ge þe ge sindun yfle cunneþ gód sellan
ei <11>si ergo uos cum sitis mali nostis bona dare
beaearnu(m) eowrum hu miccle mae fæder ewer se þe
filis uestris quanto magis pater uester qui in
in heofunu(m) is selleþ gód þæm þe biddaþ hine all
caelis est dabit bona petentib(us) se:· <12>Omnia
forþon swa hwẹt swa ge willað þæt doá eow menn
ergo quaecumq(ue) uultis ut faciant uobis homi⟨-⟩
gód swa ⁊ ge doaþ heom þis is wiotudlice
nes bona ita et uos facite illis haec est enim
áe ⁊ witgu gaþ inn þurh naarwe geate
lex et profete:· <13>Intrate per angustam por⟨-⟩
tam

(f. 10r) 13 mittur] mittitur Y WW **14** modice] minimæ Y minimae WW **16** bibimus] bibemus Y WW **17** quid horum omnium] quia his omnibus Y WW **18** indigitis] indigetis Y WW | ergo] autem Y WW **19** d(e)i] *om.* Xz Y WW=R | haec omnia] omnia haec Xz Y WW=R **20** solliciti esse] esse solliciti Y WW **21** ipse sibi] sibi ipse Y WW | suffecit] sufficit Y WW | enim] *om.* Y WW
(f. 10v) 1 iudicaueritis] iudicaberitis Y WW=Y **2** remittietur] metietur Y WW **3, 4** uidis] uides Y WW **(cont. on p. 107)**

forþon wíd geatt ⁊ rúm weg þe lǽdeþ
quia lata porta et spatiosa uia quae ducit
to forwyrde ł forlore ⁊ monige sindun þa þe ingan þurh þære ł þæne
ad perditionem et multi sunt qui intrant per ea(m)
hu naru ˋł wiðerduneˊ geate ⁊ eorfeþe is se wég þe lædeþ
<14>quam angusta porta et arta est uia quae ducit
to life ⁊ feawe sindun þa þe gemoetaþ þane ˋł cymeð in þaraˊ
ad uitam et pauci sunt qui inueniunt eam:·
behaldeþ eow wið lyge ł lease witgu þa þe cumaþ
<15>Adtendite uobis a falsís profetís qui ueniunt
to eow in gewedum scépa in innan þanne
ad uos in uestimentís ouium intrinsecus autem
sindun wulfas risænde ł woedende fro(m) wæstmum eora ge ongetaþ heo
sunt lupi rapaces <16>á fructib(us) eorum cognoscetis eos:·
ah he somnigaþ of þornum winbegȩr oþþe of gorstum
Numquid colligunt de spinis uuas aut de tribulis
ficos ˋł nyteˊ swa ægwilc treow gód godne wȩstmas bereþ .ł wyrceþ
ficos:· <17>Síc omnis arbor bona bonos fructus facit
yfel þonne treow yfle westmas ˋł blȩdˊ bereþ
mala autem arbor malos fructus facit:·
ne mæg treow þæt góde yfle westmas beoran .ł wyrcende
<18>Non potest arbor bona malos fructus facere·
ne þ treow yfle góde wæstmas ˋł blȩdˊ beoran æghwilc
Neq(ue) arbor mala bonos fructus facere <19>omnis
þara treow þe ne bereþ westȩm gódne bið
ergo arbor quae non facit fructum bonum exci(-)
acorfen ⁊ in fyre sended forþon ˋł cuþliceˊ of wæstmum eora
detur et in ignem mittitur <20>igitur ex fructib(us) eorum
ge ongetaþ heo ˋł hiȩˊ ne ˋł nallæsˊ æghwilc þara þe cweþ to me dryhten
cognoscetis eos:· <21>Non omnis qui dicit mihi d(omi)ne
drihten gæþ in rice heofuna ah se þe wyrceþ
d(omi)ne intrabit in regnum caelorum sed qui facit
wille fæder mines þæs þe in heofunum is se ˋł heˊ gáeþ
uoluntatem patris mei qui in caelis est ipse intra(-)
in heofuna rice monige cweþað to me on ðæm
bit in regnum caelorum:· <22>Multi dicent mihi in illa
dæge dryht(en) dryhten ah ne in þinu(m) noma witgadun we
die d(omi)ne d(omi)ne nonne in tuo nomine profetauimus
⁊ in þinu(m) noma deoful ut wyrpon ⁊ in þinu(m) noman
et in tuo nomine demonia eicimus et in tuo nomine
mægen monige worhton ⁊ ic þonne ondetu heom
uirtutes multas fecimus <23>et tunc confitebor illis
þæt ic nǽfræ cuþe eow gewitaþ fro(m) me ge þe wyrcaþ
quia numqua(m) noui uos discidite a me qui opera(-)
unrihtnisse
mini iniquitatem:·

(f. 10v) 5 tuo[1]] + frat(er) sine eiciam festucam de oculo tuo R[Fa] (*in the left-hand margin with the gloss,* broþer abíd þ ic ofdo þ streu of ege þinum) + sine eiciam festucam de oculo tuo Y WW | trabis] trabes Y WW Xz=R | in oculo tuo est] est in oculo tuo Y WW **16** petierit] petet Y WW **21** bona ita] *om.* Y WW | illis] eis Y WW
(f. 11r) 3 arta] arcta R[c] Y WW=R[*] | est] *om.* Y WW **5** uobis] *om.* Y WW **9** ficos] ficus WW Y=R | bonos fructus] fructos bonos Y fructus bonos WW **10, 11** malos fructus] fructus molos Y[*] WW fructos malos Y[c] **12** bonos fructus] fructus bonos Y WW **13** ergo] *om.* Y WW | excidetur] exciditur Y WW **(cont. on p. 108)**

æghwilc þara þe gehéreð word min þas ⁊ fremmað hie
<24>Omnis ergo qui audit uerba mea haec et facit ea
he bið lic were þæ(m) snottra þe getimbrade hus
adsimilabitur uiro sapienti qui aedificauit do⟨-⟩
is on stane ⁊ astág niþer rægn
mum suam super petram <25>et discendit pluia
⁊ cuomun eáé ⁊ blewan windas ⁊ fellun
Et uenerunt flumina et flauerunt uenti et inrue⟨-⟩
on hus þæt ⁊ hit no gefeoll gestaþulad soþlice
runt in domum illam et non cicidit fundata enim
hit wæs on stáne ⁊ æghwilc þe gehéreþ word min
erat su petram:· <26>Et omnis qui audit uerba mea
þas ⁊ ne fremmaþ þa gelic bið were dysig ˋł dolumˊ þæ(m) þe tim⟨-⟩
haec et non facit ea similis erit uiro stulto qui ae⟨-⟩
brade hus his on sónde ⁊ astag
dificauit domum suam super harenam <27>et discen⟨-⟩
rægn niþer ⁊ cuomon eae ⁊ bleowen windas
dit pluia et uenerunt flumina et flauerunt uenti
⁊ feollun in hus þæt ⁊ hit gefeoll ⁊ wæs hryre
et inruerunt in domum illam et cicidit et fuit ruina
his micel ⁊ gewarð þa hæfde geendad
eius magna:· <28>Et factum est cum consummasset
hælend word þas þæt wundradun þa mengu be láre
ie(su)s uerba haec admirantur turbae super doc⟨-⟩
his he wæs forþon hˋiˊe lǽrde swa swa mæht
trinam eius <29>erat enim docens sicut potestatem
hæbbende nallas swa swa bocera heora ⁊ fariseas þa he
habens non sicut scribae eorum et farisei:· <VIII 1>Cum
þa wæs astigen of dune folgedun him menga
autem discendisset de monte secuti sunt eum tur⟨-⟩
monige ⁊ henu hreof sumne cumende to⟨-⟩
bae multae <2>Et ecce liprosus quidam ueniens ado⟨-⟩
gebędd him cweþende driht(en) gif þu wilt þu mæht mec geclęnsige
rabat eum dicens d(omi)ne si uis potis me mundare
⁊ aþenende hælend honda his ⁊ æthrán him cwæþende
<3>extendens ie(su)s manum suam et tetegit eum dicens
ic wille geclænsige ⁊ hrǽþe geclensad wæs hreoful
uolo mundare et confestim mundatus est lepra
his ⁊ cweþ to him hælend gesech ꝥ þu nængum sæcge ah gá
eius <4>et ait illi ie(su)s uide nemini dixeris sed uade
⁊ æteaw þe messepreoste ⁊ breng ꝥ lác þætte bebead
et ostende sacerdoti et offer munus quod prae⟨-⟩
moyses in cyþnisse heora æft(er) þas þa he þa
cipit moyses in testimonium illis:· <5>Post haec cu(m) (autem)

(f. 11r) 19 tuo nomine] nomine tuo Y Xz WW=R **20** tuo nomine[1, 2]] nomine tuo Y Xz WW=R | eicimus] eiecimus Y WW
(f .11v) 5 cicidit] cecidit R^{c} Y WW **6** su] super R^{Fa} Xz supra Y WW **8** super] supra Y WW **10** cicidit] cecidit R^{c} Y WW **12** admirantur] ammirabantur Y WW **13** docens] + eos Y WW **15** secuti] secutae Y WW **16** liprosus] leprosus R^{c} Y WW | quidam] *om.* Y WW **17** potis] potes Y WW **18** extendes] et extendes R^{Fa} Y WW | ie(su)s manum suam et tetegit eum] manum tetigit eum iesus Y WW **19** mandatus] mandata Y WW **21** et[1]] *om.* Y WW | ostende] + te Y WW | praecipit] praecepit Y WW **22** Post haec] *om.* Y WW

éode cafarnaum cuom to him
introisset cafarnaum accessit ad eum centorio
biddende hine ⁊ cweþende drihten cneht min ligeþ in
rogans eum <6>et dicens d(omi)ne puer meus iactet in do⟨-⟩
huse loma ⁊ is yfle wælid ⁊ cweþ to him se hælend
mu paraliticus et male torquetur <7>et ait illi ie(su)s
ic cume ⁊ gehæle hine ⁊ ondswarande centurio
ego ueniam et curabo eum <8>et respondens centorio:·
cweþ to him drihten nam ic wyrðe ꝥ ðu gá under þacu minne
Ait illi d(omi)ne non sum dignus ut intres sub tectu(m) meu(m)
ah efne gecweþ word ⁊ bið gehæled cneht min wiotudlice
sed tantum dic uerbo et sanabitur puer meus· <9>nam
⁊ ic monn eam under mæhti geseted hæbbende
et ego homo sum sub potestate constitutus habens
under me cempa ⁊ ic cweðe þissu(m) gá ⁊ he gæþ ⁊ to oþru(m) cyme
sub me milites et dico huic uade et uadit et alio ueni
⁊ he cymeþ ⁊ to esne ˋɫ ðeowˊ minum ⁊ ic cweþe do þis ⁊ he doeþ geherende
et uenit et seruo meo dico fac hoc et facit· <10>Audiens
he þa hælend wundriende wæs ⁊ fylgendun him to þæ(m) cwæþ soþ ic
autem ie(su)s miratus est et sequentib(us) sé dixit ámen
sæcge eow swa micel geleafa ne gemotte ic in israhęle
dico uobis tantum fidem non inueni in israhel:·
sæcge þonne eow þæt monige fro(m) eastan ⁊ wéstan
<11>Dico autem uobis quod multi ab oriente et occidente
cumaþ ⁊ hleonigaþ mid abraham ⁊ isaac ⁊ iacob
uenient et recumbent cum abraham et isác et iacob
in heofuna rice bearn þonne rice þeos bioþ aworpenne
in regno caelorum:· <12>Filii autem regni huius eicient(u)r
in þiostre þa ytmæste þær bið wóp ⁊ gristbatung tóþa
in tenebras exteriores ubi erit fletus et stridor dentiu(m):·
⁊ cwæþ ða se hælend to þæ(m) centurione gang ⁊ swa þu gelefdest geweorðe
<13>Et dixit ie(su)s centorioni uade et sicut credidisti fiat
ðe ⁊ gehæled wæs se cneht on þære hwile ˋɫ tideˊ ⁊ þa cuom se
tibi et sanatus est puer ex illa hora:· <14>Et cum uenisset
hælend in huse petrus gesæh swægre his licgende ⁊ bif⟨-⟩
ie(su)s in domum petri uidit socrum eius iacentem et feb⟨-⟩
gende ⁊ æthrán honda his ⁊ forlet hiae sio drif
ricantem <15>et tetigit manum eius et demisit eam febris
⁊ hiu áras ⁊ ðægnade heom efen þonne
et surrexit et ministrabat eis:· <16>Uespere autem
hit þa wæs þa brohtun him monige deofulseoke hæbbende ⁊
facto obtulerunt ei multos demonia habentes et
ut awearp þurh hˊiˋs worde þa gastas únklene ⁊ alle yfle
ieciebat uerbo sp(iritu)s inmundos et omnes male

2 iactet] iacet Y WW | domu] domo Y WW 3 et²] *om.* Y WW Xz=R 5 illi] *om.* Y WW 7 constitutus] *om.* Y WW 9 dico] *om.* Y WW 11 tantum fidem non inueni] non inueni tantam fidem Y WW 14 huius] *om.* Y WW 15 ubi] ibi Y WW 17 ex illa hora] in hora illa Y WW 18 febricantem] febricitantem Y WW 22 ieciebat uerbo spiritus inmundos] eiciebat spiritus uerbo Y WW

hæbbende gehælde þte gefylled wę̄re þ gecwæden wæs
habentes curauit <17>ut adinpleretur quod dictum (est)
þurh esaiam þe witgu cweþende he wiotudlice untrymnissu(m)
per iesaiam profetam dicentem ipse infirmitates
urum onfeng ⁊ metrymnisse ure he bær
nostras accipit et egritudines nostras portauit·
geseonde þa hælend mengu monige ymb hine heht
<18>Uidens autem ie(su)s turbas multas circum sé iusit
feran ofer sáé ˋł bry(m)streamˊ ⁊ cumende an bokera cweþ to him
ire trans fretum <19>et acedens unus scriba ait ei
laruw ic wille folgian þe hwider swa þu ganges ł gæst ⁊ cwæþ to him hælend
magister sequar te quocumq(ue) ieris <20>et dicit ei ie(su)s
foxes hole habbaþ ⁊ fuglas heofunas selescota
uulpes foueas habent et uolucres caeli taberna(-)
þer hie restaþ bearn ˋł sunuˊ þonne monnes næfð
cula ubi requiescant filius autem hominis non ha(-)
wær he heafud ahélde oþer þa of leornere
bet ubi capud reclinet <21>alius autem de discipulis
his cwæþ to him drihten læt me ærest gangan ⁊ be(-)
eius ait illi d(omi)ne permitte me primum ire et se(-)
byrgen fæder minu(m) hælend þanne cweþ to þę̄m fylge
pelire patrem meum <22>ie(su)s autem ait illi sequere
me ⁊ forlet deaða bebyrgen deada heora
me et dimitte mortuos sepelire mortuos suos:·
⁊ þa stag he on scipe folgadun him
<23>Et ascendente eo in nauicula secuti sunt eum
leorneras his ⁊ henu hreornis micel geworden wæs
discipuli eius <24>et ecce tempestas magna facta est
on þæ(m) sǽ wæs þonne heom wind wiðerweard swa þte
in mari· erat autem illis uentus contrarius ita ut
þe scip wæs urnen yðum he wiotudlice ˋł heˊ soþ ˋł þonneˊ slepte
nauicula operetur fluctibus ipse uero dormiebat
⁊ eodun to him discipulas his ⁊ wehton
<25>et accesserunt ad eum discipuli eius et suscitauer(u)nt
hine cweþende dryhten hǽl usic we forweorðað ⁊ cweþ to heom se hælend forhwon ˋł hwætˊ
eum dicentes d(omi)ne salua nos perimus <26>et dicit eis ie(su)s quid
gefrohte sindun medmiccles geleafa ⁊ þa arisende bebead wínd
timidi estis modice fidei tunc surgens imperauit uentis
⁊ sáé ⁊ geworden wæs smyltnisse micel þa menn
et mari et facta est tranquillitas magna <27>porro ho(-)
wundradun cwæþende hulic is þes þe wind
mines mirati sunt dicentes qualis est hic quia uenti
⁊ sáé gehę̄raþ him ⁊ þa he cuom ofer sáé
et mare oboediunt ei:· <28>Et cum uenisset trans fretum

3 accipit] accepit YWW | egritudines nostras] aegrotationes Y WW 5 acedens] accedens R[c] Y WW | ei] illi Y WW 7 tabernacula ubi requiescant] nidos Y tabernacula WW 13 nauicula] nauiculam WW Y Xz=R 14 tempestas magna facta] motus magnus factus Y WW 15 erat autem illis uentus contrarius] *om.* Y WW 16 operetur] opiriretur Y WW 17 ad eum discipuli eius] *om.* Y WW 18 ie(su)s] *om.* Y WW 19 imperauit uentis] increpauit uento Y WW Xz=R 21 quia] + et Y WW

in lond gerasinga urnon ongægn him twegen menn
in regionem gerasenorum occurrerunt ei duo homi(-)
deofulseoka hæbbende of byrgennum ut gangende grimme
nes demonia habentes de monumentís exeuntes seui
swiðe swa þætte nænig mæhte faran þyrh wæge þæm
nimis ita ut nemo posset transire per uiam illam
⁊ henu cegende cwæþende hwæt is us ⁊ ðe hælend
<29>et ecce clamauerunt dicentes quid nobis et tibi ie(s)u
sunu godes cwome hider ær tide tinterga usic wæs þa
filii d(e)i uenisti huc ante tempus torcere nos <30>erat (autem)
unfeor suner swina fro(m) heo(m) monegra etende
non longe grex porcorum ab eis multorum:· Pascens
þa deoful þonne bedun hinae cweþende gif ðu ut awearpa
<31>demones autem rogauerunt eum dicentes si iecis
usic send usic in þas sunrae swina ⁊ cweþ to heo(m) gaeð
nos mitte nos in gregem porcorum <32>et ait illis ite
⁊ hie ut gangende eodun in swinum ł in þassu(m) ⁊ henu ungerece ł ræsed
at illi exeuntes abierunt in porcos et ecce inpetu
eode all siu suner ˋł wræðˊ niðerweardes in sáé ⁊ deade wurdon
abít totus grex per praeceps in mare et mortui sunt
in wættrum hiordes þonne flugon ⁊ cumende
in aquís:· <33>Pastores autem fugerunt et uenientes
in cæstræ sægdun .ł cyðdon all ⁊ be þæm þe
in ciuitatem nuntiauerunt omnia et de hiis qui de(-)
deofulseoke werun ˋł æfdonˊ ær ⁊ henu all cæstra ut eode ongægn
monia abebant <34>et ecce tota ciuitas exit obuiam
hælend ⁊ geseende hine bedun hine ꝥ he ferde .ł liorde fro(m) gemeru(m)
ie(s)u et uiso eo rogabant eum ut transiret a finib(us)
eora ⁊ astigende on scipe oferlaþ þone sǽe
eorum:· <IX 1>Et ascendens in nauicula transfreta(-)
⁊ cwom in cæstre his ⁊ henu brohtun him
uit et uenit in ciuitatem suam <2>et ecce offerebant ei
loma licende in bedde ⁊ geseende hælend leafa
paraliticum iacentem in lecto et uidens ie(su)s fide(m)
hiora cwæþ to þæ(m) loma getreowe sunu þe sindun for(-)
illorum:· Dixit paralitico confide filí remiten(-)
letne synnae þine ⁊ henu sume þara bocera
tur tibi peccata tua <3>et ecce quidam de scribís
cwedun in innan heo(m) þes hefalsaþ ⁊ þa geseende
dixerunt intra sé híc blasfemat <4>et cum uidisset
ðohtas heora cwæþ to heo(m) forhwon þencaþ ge
ie(su)s cogitationes eorum dixit eis ut quid cogitatis
yfel in heortum eowrum hweþer is eþre to cweþane
mala in cordib(us) uestrís <5>quid est facilius dicere xƀ

1 regionem] regione Y WW=R | duo homines demonia habentes] duo habentes daemonia Y WW 4 ie(s)u] *om.* Y WW 5 torcere] torquere R^c (c *not cancelled*) Y WW 6 grex porcorum ab eis] ab illis grex porcorum Y WW 7 rogauerunt] rogabant Y WW 13 abebant] habuerunt Y habuerant WW 14 eum] *om.* Y WW 15 nauicula] nauiculam WW Y=R 18 remitentur] remittuntur Y WW 21 eis] *om.* Y WW

xƀ sindu`n′ forletnae þe synne þe to gecweþanne aris ⁊ gá
dimituntur tibi peccata aut dicere surge et ambula
þæt ge wite þonne þætte sunu monnes hæfeþ mæhte
<6>ut sciatis autem quoniam filius hominis habet potesta⟨-⟩
on eorðan to forletenne synne þa cwæþ to þæ(m) loman
tem in terra demittendi peccata· Tunc ait paralitico
aris ⁊ genim bedd þin ⁊ gá in hus þin ⁊
surge et tolle lectum tuum et uade in domum tuam <7>et
he aras ⁊ eode in hus his gesegon þa menigu
surrexit et habít in domum suam <8>uidentes turbae
⁊ dreordun heom ⁊ wuldradun god þe swilce mæhte
timuerunt et glorificauerunt d(eu)m qui talam potesta⟨-⟩
gesalde monnum ⁊ þa foérde þonan hælend gesæh
tem dedit hominibus:· <9>Et cum transire inde ie(su)s uidit
monnu sittende æt gæflaes monunge matheus haten
hominem sedentem in theloneo matheum nomine
⁊ cwæþ to him fylgæ me he aras ⁊ fylgænde wæs him
et ait illi sequere me surgens et secutus est eum:·
⁊ geworden wæs þær hlionede he in huse ⁊ henu monige
<10>Et factum est discumbente eo in domu et ecce multi
gæfelhróefe ⁊ synnfulle cwomon ⁊ hlionadun
puplicani et peccatores uenientes discumbebant
mið hælend ⁊ leorneras his ⁊ geségon farisei cwedun
cum ie(s)u et discipuli eius <11>et uidentes farisei dicebant
leornerum his forhwon lar`e′uw eower mið gæfelgehre⟨-⟩
Discipulis eius quare magister uester cum puplica⟨-⟩
fum ⁊ synnfullum eteþ ⁊ þa gehóerde se hælend
nis et peccatorib(us) manducat:· <12>At audiens ie(su)s
cwæþ nis þærf halum læces ah yfle `ł vntrymum′
ait non est opus ualentibus medicus sed male
hæbbende gǽþ þonne geleornigaþ hwæt ꝥ sie mild⟨-⟩
habentibus:· <13>Euntes autem discite quid est· mi⟨-⟩
heortnisse ic wille ⁊ nalles asægdnisse ne forþon
sericordiam uolo et non sacrificium non enim
ic cwom to ceganne soþfestum ah synfullum þa eodun
ueni uocare iustus sed peccatores:· <14>Tunc acces⟨-⟩
to him leorneras iohannes cwæþende for⟨-⟩
serunt ad eum discipuli iohannis dicentes qua⟨-⟩
hwon we ⁊ farisei fæstaþ gelóme leorneras
re nos et farisei ieiunamus frequenter· disci⟨-⟩
þonne þine ne fæstaþ ⁊ cwæþ to heo(m) hælend ah
puli autem tui non ieiunant:· <15>Et ait illis ie(su)s num⟨-⟩
ne magun bearn brydguma wépan þende
quid possunt filii sponsi lugere quamdiu

4 et[1]] *om.* Y WW 5 uidentes] + autem Y WW 6 talam potestatem dedit] dedit potestatem talem] Y WW | transire] transiret Y WW 9 surgens et] et surgens Y WW 10 domu] domo Y WW | et[2]] *om.* Y WW 12 discipuli] discipulis WW Y=R 13 magister uester cum puplicanis et peccatorib(us) manducat] cum publicanis et peccatoribus manducat magister uester Y WW | audiens ie(su)] iesus audiens Y WW 15 medicus] medico Y WW 18 iustus] iustos Y WW

mid heom is se brýdguma cumaþ þonne dagas þæt bið
cum illis est spoñsus uenient autem dies cum au⟨-⟩
afirred fro(m) heo(m) se brydguma ⁊ þonne fæsten nænig mon
feretur ab eis sponsus et tunc ieiunabunt <16>nemo
þonne setteþ claþ flyhti neowenne in hrægl
enim immittit commisuram panni rudis in uestimen⟨-⟩
ald he ahefeþ forþon fyllnisse his fro(m) þæ(m) hrægle
tum fetus tollit enim plenitudinem eius a uestimen⟨-⟩
⁊ wyrse slite werþeð ne menn geotaþ win niowe
to et peior scisura fit <17>neq(ue) mittunt uinum nouu(m)
in winbeligas alde elcur ˋł ellesˊ tobersteþ þa belgas ealde
in utres ueteres alioquin rumpentur utres ue⟨-⟩
⁊ ꝥ win bið agoten ⁊ þa beligas to lore weorðaþ ah
teres et uinum effunditur et utres peribunt sed
win neowe in belgas neowe geotaþ .ł gedoaþ ⁊ bu beoþ
uinum nouum in utres nouos ponunt et ambo
gehalden þa he þis spræc to heom henu
conseruantur:· <18>Haec illo loquente ad eos ecce
aldurmon an cwom ⁊ gebed to him cweþende
princeps unus accessit et adorabat eum dicens
drihten dohter min is nu aswolten is ah cym gesette
d(omi)ne filia mea modo defuncta est sed ueni inpone
hond þin ofer ˋł onˊ heo ⁊ heo leofaþ ⁊ he aras se hælend fol⟨-⟩
manum tuam super eam et uiuet <19>et surgens ie(su)s se⟨-⟩
gade him ⁊ his leorneras ⁊ henu wíf
quebatur eum et discipuli eius:· <20>Et ecce mulier
ꝥte blódes flownisse þrowade twelf winter geneolicte
quæ sanguinis fluxum patiebatur ·xii· annis acces⟨-⟩
behyndan ⁊ æthran fæss hrægl his heo cwæþ
sit retro et tetigit fimbriam uestimenti eius <21>dice⟨-⟩
forþon in innan hire gif ic gehrine efne ł swa micel hrægl
bat enim intra sé si tetigero tantum uestimentum
his hal ic eam ˋł ic beomˊ ⁊ hælend þa gecerde ˋł werfdeˊ ⁊ geseah heo
eius salua ero <22>at ie(su)s conuersus et uidens eam
⁊ cweþ getreuwe þu dohter geleafa þin þec halne dyde ⁊
dixit confide filia fides tua té saluam fecit et
warð ða hal ꝥ wif of þære hwile ˋł tideˊ ⁊ þa cwom
facta est salua mulier ex illa hora <23>et cum uenisset
se hælend in hus þas aldormonnes ⁊ þa gesæh piperas
ie(su)s in domum principes et cum uidiset tubicines
⁊ menigu ruxlende cwæþ gewitaþ heonan nis dead
et turbam túmultuantem <24>dicebat recedete non mor⟨-⟩
þæt mægden ah hio slepeþ ⁊ hię bismeradun hine
tua est puella sed dormit et diridebant eum

2 ieiunabunt] ieiunabant Y WW=R 3 enim] autem Y WW | rudis] rudi Y WW=R 6 rumpentur] rumpuntur Y WW | ueteres[2] *om.* Y WW 7 peribunt] pereunt Y WW 8 ponunt] mittunt Y WW 11 d(omi)ne] *om.* Y WW 12 tuam] *om.* Y WW 18 facta est salua] salua facta est Y WW 20 principes] principis Y WW | cum] *om.* Y WW tuuicines] tubicines R[c] tibicines Y WW 21 et turbam] *om.* Y R=WW 21 mortua est] est enim mortua Y WW

⁊ þa ut aworpen wæs siu mengu he eode in hus ⁊ genom
<25>et cum iecta esset turba intrauit in domum et tenuit

hond hire ⁊ aras ꝥ mægden. ⁊ eode se hlisa þis
manum eius et surrexit puella <26>et exít fama haec

in all ꝥ lónd ⁊ forþfo`e´rde `ł liorde´ þonan
in uniuersam terram illam:· <27>Et transeuntes inde

se hælend fylgdun him twa blinde cegende ⁊ cweþende
ie(su)s secuti sunt eum duo caeci clamantes et dicentes

miltsa unc þu sunu dauiðes þa he þa cwom in hus
miserere nostri filii dauid <28>cum autem ueniset domu(m)

eodun to him þa twa `tu´ blinde biddende ⁊ cwæþ to heo(m)
accesserunt ad eum duo caeci rogantes et dicit eis

se hælend gelefaþ git þe ic mæge þæt gedoa inc cwædon to him la
ie(su)s creditis quia possum hoc facere dicunt ei utiq(ue)

drihten þa he æthran egan heora cweþende æfter
d(omi)ne <29>tunc tetigit oculos eorum dicens secundum

geleafan incrum geweorðe inc ⁊ werun ontyned
fidem uestram fiat uobis <30>et statim aperti sunt

egan eora ⁊ forbead `ł biatadae´ heo(m) cwæþende geseáéþ
oculi eorum et comminatus est eis dicens uidete

ꝥ þis nænig mon wite hiae þa ut gangende gemérdon
ne quis sciat <31>illi autem exeuntes defamauerunt

hine geond all ꝥ lond ut gangende þa hie þa weron
eum in totam terram illam <32>egressis autem illis

henu brohtun him monnu dumb ⁊ deaf deoful⟨-⟩
ecce obtulerunt ei hominem mutum et surdum demo⟨-⟩

seocne hæbbende ⁊ ut wearp ꝥ deoful sprecende wæs se dumbe
nium habentem <33>et iecto demonio locutus est mutus

⁊ wundradun mengu cweþende næfre swa æt⟨-⟩
et miratæ sunt turbae dicentes nusquam síc ap⟨-⟩

eawde in israhel farisei þonne cwedun in aldre
paruit in israhel <34>farisei autem dicebant in prin⟨-⟩

deofla he ut weorpeð deoful ⁊ geond⟨-⟩
cipe demoniorum hic iecit demones:· <35>Et circum⟨-⟩

eode se hælend þa burgas alle ⁊ cæstras lǽrende in
ibat ie(su)s ciuitates omnes et castella docens in

gesomnungum heora ⁊ bodede godspelles rices
sinagogis eorum et praedicans euangelium reg⟨-⟩

⁊ hælende æghwilce adle ⁊ æghwilce untrymnis⟨-⟩
ni et curans omnem langorem et omnem infirmi⟨-⟩

se in folce geseah he þa se hælend þa mengu
tatem in populo:· <36>Uidens autem ie(su)s turbas

efnþrowade þæm þe hie weron gewælde ⁊ liccende
missertus est eis qui erant uexati et iacentes

1 in domum] *om.* Y WW 3 transeuntes] transeunte Y WW 4 ie(su)s] iesu Y WW 6 duo] *om.* Y WW | rogantes] *om.* Y WW 7 facere] + uos R^{Fa} + uobis Y WW 9 statim] *om.* Y WW 10 eorum] illorum Y WW | eis] illis iesus Y WW 12 totam terram illam] tota terra illa Y WW 13 et surdum] *om.* Y WW | demonium] dęmonia Y daemonium WW 14 demonio] daemone Y WW 15 nusquam] numquam Y WW | síc apparuit] apparuit sic Y WW paruit sic Xz 17 hic] *om.* Y WW 21 in populo] *om.* Y WW | ie(su)s] *om.* Y WW 22 qui] quia Y WW

swa scep heordeleas þa cwæþ to
sicut oues non habentes pastorem:· <37>Tunc dicit
leorneras his rip þis is micel ⁊ wyrhtu
discipulis suis mensis quidem multa operari
þonne feawe biddaþ þanne dryhten þæs hripęs þæt he sende
autem pauci <38>rogate ergo d(omi)n(u)m messis ut mittat
wyrhte in ripae his ⁊ þa tosomne cegende twælf
operarios in messem suam:· <X 1>Et cumuocatis ·xii·
his leorneras salde heom mæhtae gastas
discipulis suis dedit eis potestatem spirituu(m)
unclen\r/a þ ut awurpe þa ⁊ hælde æghwilce
inmundorum ut iecerent eos et curarent omnem
adle ⁊ æghwilce untrymnisse þara twelf apostola
langorem et omnem infirmitatem:· <2>Xii· autem apos⟨-⟩
noma þonne sindun þas ærest simon se þe is nemned
tolorum nomina sunt haec primus· simon· qui dicit(u)r
petrus ⁊ andreas his broþer iacobus zebedees sunu
petrus· et andreas· frater eius· iacobus· zebedei·
⁊ iohannes his broþer philippus ⁊ bartholomeus
et iohannis· frater eius· <3>philippus· et bartholome(u)s·
tomas ⁊ matheus se gæfelgeroefe ⁊ iacobus alfeęs sunu
thomas· et matheus· puplicanus· et iacobus· alfei·
⁊ taddeus ⁊ simon se cananisca ⁊ iudas
et thatheus· zelotis· <4>simon· channaneus· et iudas·
scariothes se þe salde hine þas twælfe sende
scariothes· qui tradidit eum:· <5>Hos duodecim misit
se hælend bebeodende heom ⁊ cweþende in wæg ðeode n gæþ
ie(su)s praecipiens eis et dicens in uiam gentium né abi⟨-⟩
ge ⁊ cæstra samaringa ne iongaþ
eretis et in ciuitates samaritanorum ne introieri⟨-⟩
ah mae gaþ to þæ(m) sciopum þe to lore wyrðon huses
tis <6>sed putius ite ad oues quae perierant domus
israhela ⁊ gangende þonne bodigað cwęþende
israhel:· <7>Euntes autem praedicate dicentes
þætte neoliceþ rice heofunas untry(m)nisse
quia adpropinquauit regnum caelorum <8>infimos
hæleþ deaðe wæcceþ hreofe clænsigæþ
curate mortuos suscitate leprosus mundate
deofulsoéce ut weorpaþ arwunga ge onfengon arwunge gesellaþ
demonia iecite gratis accipistis gratis date
ne sculon ge agan gold ne sylfur ne
<9>nolite possidere aurum neq(ue) argentum neque
feoh in gyrdels e\o/wrum ne bisæc on wæge ne
pecuniam in zonis uestris <10>non peram in uia neque

2 mensis] messis R^c Y WW 3 mittat] eiciat Y WW 5 eis] illis Y WW | spirituu(m)] spiritum Y WW=R 12 zelotis] *om.* Y WW 11 et²] *om.* WW Y Xz=R 13 tradidit] et tradidit Y WW 14 abieretis] abieritis Y WW 15 introieritis] intraueritis Y WW 16 peierant] perierunt Y WW 18 infimos] infirmos R^c Y WW 20 accipistis] accepistis WW Y=R

twa tunica ne scoas ne ierde in hondum
duas tonicas neq(ue) calciamenta neq(ue) uirgam in manib(us)
eowrum wyrðe is wyrhta mete his in swa hwilce
uestris dignus est operarius cibo suo:· <11>In quamcumq(ue)
burh oþþe cæstre swa ge ingæn ahsigaþ hwa
ciuitatem aut castellum intraueritis interrogate quis
in þære wyrþe sie ⁊ þær wynigaþ oþ þæt ge ut gæn ⁊ ge gangan
in ea dignus sit et ibi manete donec exiatis <12>intrantes
þonne in huse haleteþ þæt cwæþende sibb .ł frið þissu(m)
autem in domum salutate eam dicentes pax huic
huse ⁊ gif þæt siae hus wyrþe cyme sibb
domui <13>et si quidem fuerit domus digna ueniet pax
eowra on ł ofer hiæ gif þonne ne siae wyrðe frið eowra
uestra super eam si autem non fuerit digna pax uestra
xƀ to eow gecerre .ł weorfe ⁊ swa hwilce swa nyle onfo eow
ad uos reuertetur:· <14>Et quicumque non reciperit uos
ne heran wordum eowrum gáð ut of þæ(m)
neq(ue) audierit sermones uestros exeuntes foras de
huse oþþe þære cæstre ascákeþ dust of fotum
domu uel de ciuitate excutite puluerem de pedibus
eowrum soþ ic sæcge eow árefrendlicre bið eorðe
uestrís <15>amen dico uobis tollerabilius erit terrae
sodominga ⁊ gomorringa æt domesdæge þonne þære
sodomorum et gomorreorum in die iudici quam illi
cæstre henu ic sende eow swa swa scép in midde
ciuitati:· <16>Ecce ego mitto uos sicut oues in medio lu⟨-⟩
uulfum bioþ ł wesaþ forþon snottre swa swa nedra
porum estote ergo prudentes sicut serpentes
⁊ bilwite swa swa culfra beháldeþ þonne wið
et simplices sicut columbe:· <17>Cauete autem ab
monnum hie sellaþ forþon eowic on gemótum ⁊ in gesomnunge
hominib(us) tradent enim uos in concilís et in sinagogis
heora swingaþ eowic ⁊ to kyningum ⁊ geróefum
suis flagillabunt uos <18>et ad reges et praessides
ge bioþ gelædde for me in cyþnisse eora ⁊ þeodum
ducemini propter me in testimonium illis et gentib(us):·
þonne hie wiotudlice selleþ eowic ne þencaþ ge hu
<19>Cum autem tradent uos nolite cogitare quomodo
oþþe hwæt ge sprece biþ sald forþon eow in þære hwile
aut quid loquemini dabitur enim uobis in illa hora
hwæt ge sprecan ne forþon ge sindun ꝥte ge sprecaþ
quid loquemini <20>non enim uos estis qui loquemini:·
ah gast fæder eower se sprecaþ in eow sellaþ
sed sp(iritu)s patris uestri qui loquitur in uobís <21>tradet
þonne
autem

1 in manib(us) uestris] *om.* Y WW | dignus est] + enim Y dignus enim est WW 4 ea] eam Y WW=R | exiatis] exeatis Y WW 5 dicentes pax huic domui] *om.* WW Y=R 6 ueniet] ueniat Y WW 8 reuertetur] reuertatur Y WW | reciperit] receperit Y WW 9 domu] domo Y WW | audierit] audierint Y WW=R 11 uestris] + [ ]n testimoniu(m) [ ]llorum, R[Fa] (*in the margin with the gloss,* in cyþnisse heora) + in testimonium eorum Y WW=R[*] 12 illi] illa R[Fa] Y WW= R[*] 17 flagillabunt] flagellabunt R[c] Y WW | ad reges et praessides] ad praesides et ad reges Y WW 18 ducemini] ducimini Y WW=R 20 loquemini] loquimini R[c] loquamini Y WW **(cont. on p. 117)**

broþer oþerne in dead ⁊ fæder sunu ⁊ áriseþ
frater fratrem in mortem et pater filium et insur(-)
suna wið freondum ⁊ deaþe hiae cwelmaþ ⁊ ge beoþ
gent filium parentes et morte eos adficiant <22>et eri(-)
in fiunge allum monnum for noma minum se þe þon(ne)
tis odio omnib(us) hominib(us) propter nomen meum qui (autem)
þurhwunaþ oþ his ende se bið hal þon(ne) hiæ þon(ne)
perseuerauit usq(ue) in finem hic saluus erit:· <23>Cum ate(m)
ehtende eowic in cæstre þas fleoþ in oþre soþ ic
persecuntur uos in ciuitate ista fugite in aliam amen
sæcge eow ne geendigaþ ge cæstre israheles
dico uobis non consummabitis ciuitates israhel
ær þon cume sunu monnæs nis leornere
donec ueniat filius hominis:· <24>Non est discipulus
ofer laruw ne esne ofer laferd his
super magistrum nec seruus super dominum suum
genoh biþ leornere ꝥte he sie swa swa laruw his ⁊ esne
<25>suffecit discipulo ut sit sicut magister eius et seru(u)s
swa swa laford his nu hie fæder heora belzebub nemdun
sicut d(omi)n(u)s eius:· Si patrem familias belzebul uoca(-)
hu micle mæ hiwæ ł hine his ne forþon ondre(-)
uerunt quanto magis domisticos eius <26>non ergo timu(-)
daþ eow hiae þe nis forþon owiht bewrigenes þæt ne sie vnwrigan
eritis eos:· Nihil enim est opertum quod non reuela(-)
⁊ dégles þæt ne sie witen ꝥ ic sæcge
bitur et occultum quod non scietur:· <27>Quod dico
eow in þeostre cweþaþ in lihte ⁊ þætte ge in eare
uobis in tenebrís dicite in lumine et quod in aure
gehóerað bodigaþ on þacum ⁊ ne ondredaþ eow
auditís praedicate super tecta <28>et nolite timere
þa se þe slæhþ se lichoma saule þonne ne magun
eos qui occidunt corpus animam autem non pos(-)
ofsléan ah mae ł swiðor ondredaþ hine se þe mæg
sunt occidere:· Sed putius timete eum qui potest
ge lichoma ⁊ saule fordoan ł sla in helle
corpus et animam perdedere in gehennam:·
ah twegen spearwas to hi(m) cumende \`ne beoþ punde bohte´ ⁊ an þære
<29>Nonne duo passeres á se ueniunt Et unus ex eis
ne falleþ on eorþan butan fæder eower
non cadit super terram sine patre uestro <30>uestri
þonne loccas heafod sindun gerimde ealle ne
autem capilli capitis numerati sunt omnes <31>nolite
forþon f\`o´rhtigaþ mongu(m) ge sindun bettra þon(ne) þas spearwas
ergo timere multís uos meliores istis passeribus:·

(f. 15v) 21 loquemini] loquamini Y WW **22** patris] patres Y^c Y^* WW=R | qui] quid Y WW=R | loquemini] loquimini Y WW
(f. 16r) 2 filium] filii Y WW | adficiant] afficient Y WW **3** hominib(us)] *om.* Y WW **4** usq(ue)] *om.* Y WW | perseuerauit] perseuerauerit Y WW | ate(m)] autem Y WW **5** persecuntur] persequentur Y WW | amen] + enim Y WW **6** consummabitis] commabitis Y WW=R **9** suffecit] sufficit Y WW **11** non] ne Y WW **12** est] *om.* Y WW **13** scietur] sciatur Y WW=R **17** timete eum] eum timete Y WW **18** corpus et animan] et animam et corpus Y WW **18** perdedere] perdere R^c Y WW **19** á se] asse Y WW | ueniunt] ueneunt WW Y=R | eis] illis Y WW **20** cadit] cadet Y WW **(cont. on p. 118)**

æghwilc forþon þara þe ondeteþ mec for monnum
<32>Omnis ergo qui confitebitur me coram hominib(us)
ondeto ⁊ ic þone beforan fæder minu(m) ðe in heofunu(m) is
confitebor et ego eum coram patre meo qui in cælis est:·
se þe þonne me onsaekeþ beforan monnum onsaece
<33>Qui autem me necauerit coram hominib(us) negabo
ic swilce þone beforan faeder minum þæ(m) ðe in heofunum is ne
et ego eum coram patre meo qui in caelís est:· <34>Nolite
wenaþ ge þe ic cwome frið ł sibb to sendanne on eorðe
arbitrari quia uenirim pacem mittere in terram
ne cwom ic frið to sendanne ah sweord ic cwom forþon to
non ueni pacem mittere sed gladium:· <35>Ueni enim· se⟨-⟩
delanne ˋł sceadenneˊ monnu wið faeder his ⁊ dohter
parare hominem aduersus patrem suum et filia(m)
wið moder hire ⁊ snore wið swegre
aduersus matrem suam et nurum aduersus socru(m)
hire ⁊ fiondas monnes higu ł hine ˋhiwenˊ his se þe lufað
suam <36>et inimici hominis domistici eius:· <37>Qui amat
fæder oþþe moder swiðor þonne me nis he me wyrðe ˋł meodumaˊ
patrem aut matrem plus quam me non est me dig⟨-⟩
⁊ se þe lufiaþ sunu oþþe dohter ofer me
nus et qui amat filium aut filiam super me:·
nis he me wyrðe ⁊ se þe ne genimaþ rode his
Non est me dignus <38>et qui non accipit crucem sua(m)
⁊ fylgeþ me nis se me wyrðe se þe gemoete
et sequatur me non est me dignus:· <39>Qui inuenit
saule .ł ferh his forleose þæt ⁊ se þe forleoseð
animam suam perdet illam et qui perdiderit
ferh his for mec he gemoeteþ þæt se þe onfoeð
animam suam pro me inueniet eam:· <40>Qui recipit
eow me onfóeþ se þe me onfóeþ he onfóeð þæm se þe me
uos me recipit qui me recipit recipit eum qui me
sende se þe onfoeþ witgu in noman witgu
missit:· <41>Qui recipit profetam in nomine profetae
lean ł mearde witgu he onfóeþ ⁊ se þe onfóeþ soþfest in
mercidem profetae accipiet et qui recipit iustum in
noman soþfest lean soþfestes he onfóeþ ⁊ swa hwa swa
nomine iusti mercidem iusti accipiet:· <42>Et quicu(m)q(ue)
drync seleþ anum læsest þissę cælc fulne wættres
potum dederit uni ex minimis istis calicem aquae
galdes efne in noman leornere soþ ic sæcge eow
frigide tantum in nomine discipuli amen dico uobis
ne forleoseþ lean his ⁊ gelamp þa geendade
non perdet mercidem suam:· <XI 1>Et factum est cum con⟨-⟩
se hælend
summasset ie(su)s

(**f. 16r**) **21** autem] + et Y WW | numerati sunt omnes] omnes numerati sunt Y WW **22** uos meliores istis passeribus] passeribus meliores estis uos Y WW
(**f. 16v**) **1** confitebitur] confitetur Y WW=R **2** in cælis est] est in caelis Y WW **3** me necauerit] negauerit me Y WW **4** in caelís est] est in caelis Y WW **5** uenirim] uenerim Y WW | pacem mittere] mittere pacem Y WW **10** aut] et Y WW=R **13** sequatur] sequitur Y WW **15** pro] propter Y WW **16** recipit[1]] + et Y WW **19** et] *om.* Y[*] Y[c] WW=R

wórd þas bebeodende twelfe his leorneras
uerba haec praecipiens duodecim discipulis
leorde ðonan þæt he lærde ⁊ bodade in
suis transít inde ut doceret et praedicaret in
cæstrum heora iohannes þonne geherende
ciuitatibus eorum:· <2>Iohannis autem cum audisset
in bendum werc kristes gesende twægen leorneras his
in uinculis opera cr(ist)i mittens duos de discipulís suís
cwæþ to heo(m) fęreþ sęcgaþ arþu se þe cwome scalt þe we oþres
<3>ait illís euntes dicite tu és qui uenturus és an alium
bideþ ⁊ ondswarade cwęþ to heom se hælend gǽþ sæcgaþ
exspectamus <4>et respondens ait illís ie(su)s euntes re⟨-⟩
ł cyþaþ iohannes ꝥ ge geherdun ⁊ ꝥ ge segun blinde
nuntiate iohanni quae audistis et uidetis <5>caeci
geseeþ halte gangaþ hreofe sindun clænsade ⁊ deafe
uident cludi ambulant leprosi mundantur et surdi
geheraþ ⁊ deade arisaþ þorfende godspell secgaþ
audiunt et mortui resurgunt pauperes euangeliz`a´n⟨-⟩
⁊ eadig is se þe in me ne bið geincfullad
tur <6>et beatus est qui in me non fuerit scandalizat(u)s:·
þa eoden þonan hie þa ingon se hælend cweþan to þæ(m)
<7>Abeuntibus autem illis coepit ie(su)s dicere ad
menigu bi iohanne se fullwihtere forhwon eoden ge in wæs⟨-⟩
turbas de iohanne baptiza quid existis in de⟨-⟩
tenne to geseenne read wínd styred
sertum uidere arundinem uento agitatam
oþþe forhwon eodun to geseonne monnu næscum hræglum ge⟨-⟩
<8>sed quid existis uidere hominem mollibus uesti⟨-⟩
gearwæd henu þa þe næscum gegearwade in husum kyninga
tum ecce qui mollib(us) uestiuntur in domibus reguu(m)
sindun oþþe forhwon eoden ge to seenne witgu ic ek
sunt <9>sed quid existis uidere profetam etiam
eow sæcge ⁊ mare þonne witgu þis is forþon
uobis dico et plus quam profeta:· <10>Hic est enim
be þæm þe awriten is henu ic sende engel minne
de quo scriptum est ecce ego mitto angelum meu(m)
for þinu(m) ondwliota se foregearweþ weg þinne beforan þe
ante faciem tuam qui praeparabit uia(m) tua(m) ante té:·
soþ ic sæcge eow ne aras betweon wifa bearnum
<11>Amen dico uobís non surrexit inter natos mulieru(m)
maræ iohanne þæm bæzere se þe þonne lessa is
maior iohanne baptista qui autem minor est
in heofuna rice se is him mare
in regnum caelorum maior est illo:·

1 uerba haec] *om.* Y WW 5 illís] illi Y WW | euntes dicite] *om.* Y WW 6 ait illís ie(su)s] iesus ait illis Y WW 7 audistis et uidetis] audistis et uidistis Y WW auditis et videtis Xz 8 et] *om.* Y WW 9 et] *om.* Y WW 10 in me non fuerit scandalizat(u)s] non fuerit scandalizatus in me Y WW 11 Abeuntibus autem illis] illis autem abeuntibus Y WW 12 baptiza] *om.* Y WW 13 agitatam] agitatum Y WW=R 15 reguu(m)] regum Y^{*} WW Y^{c}=R 17 uobis dico] dico uobis Y WW | profeta] prophetam Y WW | est enim] enim est Y WW 22 regnum] regno Y WW

from dagum þonne iohannes se bęzeres oþ þis nú
<12>A diebus autem ihannis baptistae usq(ue) nunc
rice heofunas mægen þrowiaþ ℸ gerisaþ nedniomu
regnum caelorum uim patitur et uiuolenti rapi⟨-⟩
þæt þe alle forþon witgu ℸ áe oþ
unt illud:· <13>Omnes enim profetae et lex usque
iohannem witgadun ℸ gif ge willað andfoa
ad iohannem profetauerunt <14>et si uultis perci⟨-⟩
he is se elias se þe cume scal se þe hæbbe earan
pere ipse est helias qui uenturus est <15>qui habet au⟨-⟩
gehernisse gehere hwæ(m) þonne gelice ehtu
res audiendi audiat:· <16>Cui autem similem aesti⟨-⟩
ic cneorisse þas gelic is cnehtum sit⟨-⟩
mabo generationem istam similis est puerís seden⟨-⟩
tende on prodbore þæ(m) þe clipende to heora gemeccum cweþað
tibus in foro qui clamantes coecalibus <17>dicunt
we sungan eow ℸ ge ne weopun cuom forþon iohan(nes)
cæcinimus uobis et non plancxisti <18>uenit enim ·io⟨-⟩
ne etende ne drincende ℸ cwæþað
hannis· neq(ue) manducans neque bibens et dicunt
xƀ henu deoful he hæfæþ cuom ℸ sune monnes etende
demonium habet <19>uenit et filius hominis mandu⟨-⟩
ℸ drincende ℸ cwæþað henu monn glendrende .ł swelgande
cans et bibens et dicunt ecce homo deuorator
ℸ drincande wines gæfelgeroefena ℸ firenfullra
et potatur uini puplicanorum et peccatorum á⟨-⟩
freond ℸ gesoþfęsted wæs snytru fro(m) bearnu(m) heora
micus et iustificata est sapientia á filís suís:·
þa ingonn ætwitan cæstrum in ðæm ðe
<20>Tunc coepit exprobrare ciuitatibus in quibus
geworhte wærun þa mængistu mægen his þe hiæ ne dydon
factae sunt plurime uirtutes eius quia non egrese⟨-⟩
hreuwnissę wa þe chorazam ℸ wa þe bethsaidæ
rent penitentiam <21>ue tibi chorozain et bethsaida
forþon þe þær in tyro ℸ sidone geworht werun mægen
quia si in thiro et sidonæ factae fuissent uirtutes
þe worht werun in eow iara in wite ℸ ascan
quae factae sunt in uobis olim in cylicio et cynere
hreuwnisse dydun soþ ic sæcge eow tiro ℸ
penitentiam egissent <22>Ámen dico uobis thyro et
sidone forletendre bið in domdæge þonne eow ℸ ðu
sydoni remisius erit in die iudicí quam uobis <23>et tú
cafarnaum ah þu oð heofun bist áhæfen
cafarnauum numquid usq(ue) ad caelum exaltaberis
oð helle ðu nider astigest
usq(ue) in infernum discendes:·

1 ihannis] iohannis R^{c} Y WW 2 uiuolenti] uiolenti Y WW 4 et] *om.* Y WW=R | percipere] recipere Y WW 9 uobis] + et non saltastis lamentauimus Y WW *(the omission is marked by the glossator, but the Latin is not supplied, while the gloss to the missing portion,* ge ne plagadun cwiddun, *is added to the left-hand margin)* 10 dicunt] + ecce R^{Fa} Y WW=R* | et] *om.* Y WW 12 deuorator] uorax Y WW 16 egreserent] egissent Y WW 17 et] + ue tibi R^{Fa} uae tibi (*omitting* et) Y WW 18 fuissent] essent Y WW 20 Ámen] uerumtamen Y WW 22 ad] in Y WW

f(or)ðon þe þær in sodomingum worht were mægen þa
Quia si in sodomis factae fuissent uirtutes quæ
worht werun in ðe wén þe hiæ wunade oð þisne dæg
factae sunt in té forte mansissent usq(ue) in hunc die(m):·
hweðre þonne ic sæcge eow þæt eorðe sodominga
<24>Uerumtamen dico uobis quia terrae sodomoru(m)
forletendæ bið in domdæge þonne þe in þa tid
remissius erit in die iudicí quam tibi:· <25>In illo te(m)pore
ondwyrde se hælend ⁊ cweþ ic ondetu þe fæder dryhten
respondens ie(su)s dixit confiteor tibi pater d(omi)ne
heofunæs ⁊ eorðe forþon de þu ahyddest þas fro(m) snottrum
caeli et terrae quia abscondisti haec á sapientib(us)
⁊ forðonclum ⁊ onwrige hiae lytlum swa fæder
et prudentib(us) et reuelasti ea paruulís <26>ita pater
forþon ðe swa gelicade beforan ðe all me sald
quia síc fuit placitum ante té:· <27>Omnia mihi tradita
sindun fro(m) fæder minum ⁊ nænig con þone sunu nymþe fæder
sunt a patre meo et nemo nouit filium nisi pater
ne þone fæder hwa con nymþe se sunu ⁊ ðæm þe wile se sunu
neq(ue) patrem quis nouit nisi filius et cui uoluerit filius
onwrigan cumeþ to me alle ge þe winnaþ ⁊ gebyrde
reuelare:· <28>Uenite ad me omnes qui laboratis et hono⟨-⟩
sindun ⁊ ic gereorde eow habbaþ .ł nimaþ ioc min ofer
rati estis et ego reficiam uos <29>tollite iugum meum super
eowic ⁊ leorn`i´að æt me f(or)þon milde ic eam ⁊ eadmod heorte ⁊ ge
uos et discite a me quia mitis sum et humilis corde et in⟨-⟩
gemoeteþ ræste saulum eowrum ioc forþon min
uenietis requiem animabus uestrís <30>iugum enim meum
wynsum is ⁊ byrðen min liht is in þa tid eode
suaue est et honus meum leue:· <XII 1>In illo tempore abiit
se hęlend þurh ak`c´ras on ræstedæge leorneras þa his hyngrede xb̄
ie(su)s per sata sabbato discipuli autem eius essurien⟨-⟩
ongunnon hriopan æchir ⁊ éton farissæis
tes coeperunt uellere spicas et manducare <2>faris⟨-⟩
þa gesęgon cwedun to him henu discipulas þine doaþ
sei autem uidentes dixerunt ei ecce discipuli tui faci⟨-⟩
on restedagum þæt nis alefed heo(m) to doanne he þa
unt sabbatis quod non licet eis facere <3>ille autem
cweð to heo(m) ah ge hreordeþ hwæt dyde dauið þa hine hyngre⟨-⟩
dixit eis non legistis quid fecerit dauid quando esu⟨-⟩
de ⁊ þa þe mid him węron hu he eode in hus
rít et qui cum eo erant <4>quomodo intrauit in domu(m)
gode ⁊ hlaf forðsetennisse ét þa þe ne wæs gelæfed `ł ne byrede´
d(e)i et panes propossitionis comedit quos non licebat
him to etanne
ei comedere

1 si] *om.* Y WW=R 8 quia] quioniam Y WW 15 leue] + (est) R[Fa] Y WW 16 per sata sabbato] sabbato per sata Y WW 19 sabbatis quod non licet eis facere] quod non licet eis facere sabbatis Y WW | ille autem] at ille Y WW 23 comedere] edere Y WW

ne þæ(m) þe mid him wæron nymþe anum sacerdum
neq(ue) hís qui cum eo erant nisi solis sacerdotibus:·
oþþ ne reordaþ in áe þæt on restedægum sacerdes
<5>Aut non legistis in lege quia sabbatis sacerdotes
in templ þa ræstedæge wemmaþ ⁊ butan hehsynne syndon
in templo sabbatum uiolant et sine crimine sunt:·
ic sæcge þonne eow þæt templ mara is her þær ge þon(ne)
<6>Dico autem uobis quia templo maior est hic <7>si aute(m)
wiston hwæt þæt is mildheortnisse ic wille ⁊ no asægd⟨-⟩
scieritis quid est missericordiam uolo et non sacri⟨-⟩
nisse næfre ge niðrade þa unsceþðende driht(en) is
ficium numquam condemnasetis innocentes <8>d(omi)n(u)s est
forþon ge ec gerestedæges sunu monnes ⁊ þa he þonan geliorde
enim etiam sabbati filius hominis:· <9>Et cum inde transiset
cuom in somnunge heora ⁊ mon wæs ðær honda
uenit in sinagogam eorum <10>et homo erat ibi manum
xƀ hæbbende adrugade ⁊ hie frugan .ł ahsadun hine cweþende mot monn
habens aridam et interrogabant eum dicentes si liciet
on restedagum hælon þæt hie cwæmdon ˋł acusteˊ hine he þa cwæþ to
sabbatis curare ut accussarint eum <11>ipse autem dixit
heom hwilc bið eower monn se þe hæbbe scep an
illís quis erit ex uobis homo qui habeat ouem unam
⁊ gif fealleþ þæt in seaþ .ł pytt on restedægu(m) ah he ne genimeþ
et si ciciderit haec in foueam sabbatis nonne tenebit
hine ⁊ ahefeþ hu miccle mae ˋł swiðorˊ bettra is monn þon(ne) scep
eam et leuauit <12>quanto magis melior est homo oue
forþon is aléfed on restedagum god to doanne þa cwæþ he to þæ(m) menn
itaq(ue) licet sabbatis bene facere:· <13>Tunc ait homini
aþene hondæ þine ⁊ he aþenede honda his ⁊ age⟨-⟩
extende manum tuam et extendit manum suam et re⟨-⟩
fen wæs þęm hælo swa siu oþeru ⁊ ut gangende þa
stituta est ei sanitati sicut altera:· <14>Et euntes autem
fariseas geþehtunge dydun wið hine hu hie
farissei consilium faciebant aduersus eum quomo⟨-⟩
hine ofslean sculdon se hælend þa wiste gewat
do eum perderent:· <15>Ie(su)s autem sciens secessit
þonan ⁊ folgadun hine monige ⁊ he gehælde þa ealle
inde et sequti sunt eum multi et curabat eos om⟨-⟩
⁊ bebead heo(m) ꝥ hiæ ne gecuðne ˋł ewisadeˊ hine dydun
nes <16>et praecipit eis ne manifestum eum facerent
ꝥte gefylled wære ꝥ acwedan wæs þurh esaias þone wit⟨-⟩
<17>ut adinpleretur quod dictum est per esaiam pro⟨-⟩
gan cweþende henu cneht min þone ic geceas se leofa
fetam dicentem <18>ecce puer meus quem elegi dilectus
min
meus

5 scieritis] sciretis Y WW 7 etiam sabbati filius hominis] filius hominis etiam sabbati Y WW 8 et] + ecce Y WW | erat ibi] *om.* Y WW 9 liciet] licet Y WW 10 accussarint] accussarent Rᶜ Y accusarent WW 12 ciciderit] ceciderit Rᶜ Y WW | in foueam sabattis] sabbatis in foueam Y WW | tenebit eam et leuauit] tenebit et leuabit eam Y WW 15 manum suam] *om.* Y WW 16 ei] *om.* Y WW | Et euntes] exeuntes Y WW 18 secessit] recessit Xz Y WW=R 19 curabat] curauit Y WW 20 praecipit] praecepit Y WW

in þæm wel gelicade saule mine ic sette gast
in quo bene conplacuit anima mea ponam sp(iritu)m

minne ofer hine ⁊ he doemeð þeodum sægeþ
meum super eum et iudicium gentib(us) nuntiabit

ne fliteþ ne he ne cliopaþ ne geherað nænig
<19>**non contendet neq(ue) clamabit neq(ue) audiet aliquis**

stemn his on worðum hread þæt wagende
uocem eius in plateis <20>**arundinem quassatam**

ne tobreceþ ⁊ flæx .ł lin smikende ne adwæscet
non confringet et linum fumigans non extinguet

oþ þ ut asendeþ to sigor in dome ⁊ in noman
donec eiciat ad uictoriam in iudicium <21>**et in nomine**

his þeode hyhtaþ þa gebroht wæs him monn
eius gentes sperabunt:· <22>**Tunc oblatus est ei homo**

deofulseoke he wæs blind ⁊ dumb ⁊ deaf ⁊ þa gehæl⟨-⟩
demonium habens caecus et mutus surdus et cura⟨-⟩

de hine ⁊ swa þ he sprec ⁊ gesæh ⁊ geh\`o´erde
uit eum ita ut loqueretur et uideret et audiret:·

⁊ wundradun alle þa menigu ⁊ cwædon ah
<23>**Et stupebant omnes turbae et dicebant num⟨-⟩**

cweþest þu þis sie sunu dauiðes fariseas þa gehoerende
quid hic est filius dauid:· <24>**Farisei autem audien⟨-⟩**

cwedun þes ne awoerpeþ deoful nymþe in belzebub
tes dixerunt hic non eicit demones nisi in belzebul

þ is aldor deofla se helend þa witende þohtas
principe demoniorum:· <25>**ie(su)s autem sciens cogitati⟨-⟩**

heora cweþ to heom æghwilc rice gedęled wið
ones eorum dixit eis omne regnum diuissum contra

him seolfu(m) awóested biþ ⁊ æghwilc cæstre oþþa hus gedæled
sé desolabitur:· Et omnis ciuitas domus diuissa

wið him seolfum ne stondeþ ⁊ gif þonne wiðerweard se wiþerwearð
contra sé non stabit <26>**si enim satanas satanan**

ut weorpeþ wið him seolfum gedæled he is hu þonne ston⟨-⟩
eiecit aduersus sé diuissus est quomodo ergo sta⟨-⟩

deþ rice his ⁊ gif ic þonne in belzebub ut wyrpe deoful
bit regnum eius <27>**et si ego in belzebul eiecio demones**

bearn eowre in hwæm awyrpeþ forþon hię beoþ doeme
filii uestri in quo eiciunt ideo ipsi erunt iudices

eowre gif þonne in gaste godes ic ut wyrpe deoful þonne .ł cuþlice
uestri <28>**si autem in sp(irit)u d(e)i ego eicio demones igitur**

becymeþ in eow rice godes oþþa hu ænig
peruenit in uos regnum d(e)i:· <29>**Aut quomodo quis**

mæg gangan in huse stronges ⁊ fatu his
potest intrare in domum fortis et uassa eius

1 conplacuit] placuit Y WW | amima mea] animae meae Y WW 4 uocem eius in plateis] in plateis uocem eius Y WW 6 in[1]] *om.* Y WW 7 homo] *om.* Y WW 8 surdus] *om.* Y WW 9 et audiret] *om.* Y WW 12 belzebul] belzebub R[c] Y beelzebub WW 13 principe demoniorum] principem dæmonum Y principe daemonum WW Xz (dae-)=R 15 desolabitur] desolatur WW Y=R | ciuitas] + ł R[c] uel Y WW 16 si enim] et si Y WW 19 erunt iudices] iudices erunt Y WW 20 in sp(irit)u d(e)i ego] ego in spiritu dei Y WW 21 quis potest] potest quisquam Y WW

tobregdan nymþe ær gebindaþ se stronge ⁊ þon(ne)
Diripere nisi prius alligauerit fortem· et tunc

hus his tobręgdeþ se þe þonne nis mid mec
domum illius eripiet:· <30>Qui enim non est mecum

wið me is ⁊ se þe ne somnaþ mec se stenceþ
contra me est et qui non congregat mecum spargit

forþon ic sæcge eow æghwilc synne ⁊ efulsung .ł biþ
<31>ideo dico uobís omne peccatum et blasfemia re⟨-⟩

forleten monnum ⁊ swa hwælc swa cweþaþ word
mittetur hominib(us):· <32>et quicumque dixerit uerbum

wiþ sunu monnes f(or)leten bið þæm se þe þonne
aduersus filium hominis remittetur ei· qui autem

cweþaþ wið gaste þæm halgu(m) ne biþ forleten þæm ne in
dixerit contra sp(iritu)m s(an)c(tu)m non remittetur ei· neq(ue) in

ðisse weorlde ne in þære towarde oþþe wyrceþ treow
hoc saeculo neque in futuro:· <33>Aut facite arbore(m)

god ⁊ westem his godne oþþe wyrceþ treuw
bonam et fructum eius bonum aut facite arbore(m)

yfel ⁊ westem his yfelne forþon þe of westem
malam et fructum eius malum siquidem ex fructu

bið treow ongeten ge cynn nedrana hu
arbor agnoscetur <34>progenies uiperarum quomodo

magun ge god sprecan nu nu ge yfle sindun of nyhtnisse
potestis bona loquí cum sitis mali ex abundantia

f(or)þon heorta muð spreocaþ god monn of godu(m)
enim cordis ós loquitur <35>bonus enim homo de bono

horde heorta his bereþ god ⁊ yfel monn
thesauro cordis sui profert bona et malus ho⟨-⟩

of yfle horde heorta his bereþ yfel
mo de malo thesauro cordis sui profert mala:·

xƀ ic sæcge þon(ne) eow þæt ægwilc word unnytt
<36>Dico autem uobis quoniam omne uerbum otiosu(m)

þara þe gesprecan beoþan menn in dæg domes hie ageofaþ
quod locuti fuerint homines in die iudici reddent

bi þæm reht of wordum f(or)þon þinum þu bist gesoþfæsted
de eo rationem· <37>Ex uerbís enim tuis iustificaberis·

⁊ of wordum þinum þu bist niðrad þa ondswaradun
et ex uerbis tuís condempnaberis:· <38>Tunc respon⟨-⟩

him sumne bokere ⁊ fariseas cwæþende
derunt ei quidam de scribís et fariseis dicentes

lareu we willaþ from þe tacen geseon he ondswara⟨-⟩
magister uolumus á te signum uidere:· <39>Qui respon⟨-⟩

de heom cweþ cneorisse yfel ⁊ forlegene tacen
dens eis ait generatio mala et adulteria signum

soecet
querit

2 eripiet] diripiat Y WW | enim] *om.* Y WW 5 hominib(us)] + sp(iritu)s blasfemia non dimitetur R[Fa] (*the last word is corrected from* dimittetur; *with the gloss,* gastes efalsung ne bið forleten) spiritus autem blasphemia (-miæ Y) non remittetur Y WW 6 aduersus] contra Y WW 11 agnoscetur] agnoscitur Y WW 12 mali] + estis R[Fa] Y WW=R[*] 13 enim[2]] *om.* Y WW 14, 15 cordis sui] *om.* Y WW 17 in die iudici reddent de eo rationem] reddent rationem de eo in die iudicii Y WW 22 eis ait] ait illis Y WW

⁊ taken ne bið sald him nymþe tacen ionas se witga
Et signum non dabitur ei nisi signum ionae profetæ
swa swa f(or)þon wæs ione in wombe þæs hwales þreo dagas
<40>sicut enim fuit ionas in uentre caeti trib(us) diebus
⁊ þreo niht swa bið sunu monnes þreo daga
et trib(us) noctibus sic enim filius hominis trib(us) die(-)
⁊ þreo nęht in heorte eorðe weras mennisce
bus et trib(us) noctib(us) in corde terrae· <41>uiri ninuitae
arisaþ in domæ mið cneorisse þas ⁊ niðrigað
surgent in iudicio cum generatione ista et condempna(-)
hiæ f(or)þon þe hreunisse dydon in lare
bunt eam quia penitentiam egerunt in praedicatione
ionas ⁊ henu mara is her þon(ne) ionas dæles `ł cwæn´ suþ`an´ cuom ariseð
ionae et ecce plus hic quam iona· <42>regina austri surget
in domæ mið cneorisse þas ⁊ niðrað hiæ
in iudicio cum generatione ista et condempnabit ea(m)
f(or)þon þe hiu cuom fro(m) ende eorðe to geheranne snyttro salo(-)
quia uenit a finibus terrae audire sapientiam so(-)
mones ⁊ henu mara is her þon(ne) salomonn þonne
lomonis et ecce plus híc quam solomon:· <43>Cum autem
ut gáeþ gast unklene of menn he gæþ þurh stowe
exierit sp(iritu)s inmundus ab homine ambulat per loca
dryge soecende reste ⁊ ne gem`o´teþ þon(ne) cwęþ ic wille
arida querens requiam et non inuenit <44>tunc dicit
eft wendan in hus min þonan þe ic ut eode ⁊ cumende ge(-)
reuertar in domum meam unde exiui et ueniens in(-)
moeteþ hit emetig aswopen clæne ⁊ gefrętwad
uenit eam uacantem scopís mundatam et ornata(m)
þon(ne) gæþ ⁊ genimeþ mið him siofun oþre gastes
<45>tunc uadit et adsumit secum septem alios spiri(-)
wyrse þon(ne) he ⁊ ingangende eardigaþ ðęr ⁊ weorðaþ
tos nequiores sé et intrantes habitant ibi et fiant
þe ytmæste dæg þæs monnes wyrse þon(ne) þa erran swa bið éc
nouissima illius hominis peiora priorib(us) síc erit
⁊ cneorisse þas wyrresta þende he þa spręc
et generationi huic pessimæ· <46>Adhuc eo loquente
to þæ(m) mengum henu moder his ⁊ broþer utæ sto(-)
ad turbas ecce mater eius et fratres foris sta(-)
dan soecende ꝥ sprece wið him cwæþ þa to him sum monn
bant querentes loqui ei <47>dixit autem ei quidam
henu moder þin ⁊ broðer þin ute stondaþ soecende
ecce mater tua et fratres tui foris stant queren(-)
þe he sylfe ondwyrde to þæ(m) soecende ⁊ cwæþ hwelc is
tes té <48>at ipse respondens dicenti sibi aitq(ue) est
moder min
mater mea

3 enim] erit R^c (nim *is dotted and over-lined for cancellation*) Y WW **4** trib(us) diebus et trib(us) noctib(us) in corde terrae] in corde terrae tribus diebus et tribus noctibus Y WW **7** hic quam iona] quam iona hic Y WW **8** condempnabit] condemnabunt Y condemnabit WW **10** híc quam solomon] quam salomon hic Y WW **11** exierit sp(iritu)s inmundus] inmundus spiritus exierit Y WW **14** eam] *om.* Y WW **15** secum septem alios spiritos] septem alios spiritus secum Y WW **17** illius hominis] hominis illius Y WW **19** foris stabant] stabant foris Y WW **22** ipse] ille Y WW Xz=R | aitq(ue)] ait quae Y WW

⁊ broþer mine hwilce syndun ⁊ aþenende hond
Et fratres mei qui sunt <49>et extendens manum
in leornerum his cwæþ henu moder min ⁊ broþer
in discipulos suo dixit ecce mater mea et fratres
min swa hwa swa wyrceþ willan fæder mines
mei <50>quicumq(ue) fecerit uoluntatem patris mei
þe in heofunu(m) is se min ge broþer ⁊ swuster ⁊
qui in caelis est· ipse meus et frater et soror et
moder is on þæ(m) dæge gangende se hæl(end) of huse gesæt
mater est:· <XIII 1>In illo die exiens ie(su)s de domu sede⟨-⟩
bi sǽe ⁊ gesomnadun to him mengu
bat secus mare <2>et congregatae sunt et eum tur⟨-⟩
swa ꝥ he on scipe astigende gesett ⁊ all
bae ita ut in nauicula ascendens sederet· et om⟨-⟩
seo mengu stod on waraþe ⁊ he sprec to heo(m)
nis turbae stabat in litore <3>et locutus est eis
feola in gelicnissu(m) cweþende henu ut eode se sawend
multa in paruulís dicens· Ecce exit qui seminat
to sawenne ⁊ þa he seow sume gefeollun bi
seminare <4>et dum seminat quaedam ciciderunt secus
wæge ⁊ cuomun fuglas heofun ⁊ frætun þæt
uiam et uenerunt uolucres caeli et comederunt ea
oþere þonne gefeollon on stanig lond þær ne hęfde
<5>alii autem ciciderunt in petrosa ubi non habebant
eorðe miccle ⁊ hræþe cuomun upp f(or)þon þe hie
terram multam et continuo exorta sunt quia non ha⟨-⟩
næfdon heanisse eorðe sunne þa upp cuom ha⟨-⟩
bebant altitudinem terrae <6>sole autem ortu estu⟨-⟩
tedun ⁊ f(or)þon þe hie nęfdun wytryme forwisnadun
auerunt· et qui non habebant radicem aruerunt
sume þon(ne) gefetun in þornas ⁊ wexon þa þornas
<7>alia autem ciciderunt in spinas et creuerunt spinæ
⁊ smoradun hiæ Sume þonne gefetun on
et suffocauerunt ea:· <8>Alia uero ciciderunt in
eorðe gode ⁊ saldun wæstem sume hundteontig
terram bonam:· Et dabant fructum aliud ·c·
sume sextig sume þritig se þe hæbbe eara gehernesse
aliud ·lx· aliud ·xxx· <9>Qui habet aures audiendi
gehere ⁊ gangende to him þa leorneras his cwædun
audiat:· <10>Et accedentes discipuli eius dixerunt
forhwon in gelicnissum spreces þu heo(m) he þa onswarade
quare in parabulís loqueris eis <11>qui respondiens
cwęþ to heo(m) f(or)þon þe eow sald is gecunnan geryne rice
ait illís quia uobis datum est nosse misteria regni
heofuna heom þon(ne) ne is sald
caelorum illís (autem) non est datum:·

1 fratres mei qui sunt] qui sunt fratres mei Y WW 2 suo] *om.* Y WW suos Xz 3 quicumq(ue)] + enim Y WW 6 et^{2}] ad R^{Fa} Y WW | turbae] + multae Y WW 7 nauicula] nauiculam Y WW 8 turbae] turba Y WW 9 paruulís] parbolís R^{Fa} parabolis Y WW 11 uenerunt] uenenerunt Y WW=R | caeli] *om.* Y WW 12 alii] alia Y WW | habebant] habebat Y Xz WW=R 15 qui] quia Y WW 20 eius] *om.* Y WW | dixerunt] + ei Y WW 21 eis] *om.* Y WW=R | respondiens] respondens R^{c} Y WW

se þe þon(ne) hæfþ sald bið him ⁊ genyhtsumaþ se þe þon(ne)
<12>Qui enim habet dabitur ei et abundabit qui (autem)
ne hæfð ge þæt he æfð afirred bið him
non habet et quod habet auferatur ab eo:·
f(or)þon in gelicnissum ic sprece heom þe hie geseende ne ge(-)
<13>Ideo in parabulís loquor eis quia uidentes non
seoþ ⁊ geherende ne geh\`o´eraþ ne ongeotað
uident et audientes non audiunt neq(ue) intellegunt
ꝥ sie gefylled heo(m) witigdom esaias cweþende mid gehernisse
<14>ut adinpleretur eis profetia esaiae dicentis auditu
ge geherað ⁊ ne ongetaþ ⁊ geseende geseaþ ⁊ ne
audietis et non intellegitis et uidentes uidebitis et n(on)
geseoþ gefætted is f(or)þon heorte folkes þisses
uidebitis <15>incrasatum est enim cór populi huius
⁊ earu(m) heora hefiglice geherdun ⁊ egu heora
et aurib(us) suis grauiter aduierunt et oculos suos
fortyndon þy les hie hwanne geseo egum ⁊ earan
clusserunt ne quando uideant oculís et auribus
geheran ⁊ heorte ongeton ⁊ gecerrede ⁊ ic hælo
audiant et corde intellegant et conuertantur et sa(-)
hiae eower þon(ne) eadige ege þe hię geseoð ⁊ earan
ne illos:· <16>Uestri autem beati oculi qui uident et au(-)
eowre þe hiæ geherað soþ ic sæcge eow forþon
res uestræ quae audiunt <17>Amen dico uobis quia xƀ
monige witgu ⁊ soþfeste wilnadun ꝥ geseon þa þe ge seoþ
multi profetae et iusti cupierunt uidere quae uide(-)
⁊ ne gesegon ge forþon geherað gelicnisse
tis et non uiderunt:· <18>Uos ergo audite parabula(m)
þæs sawendes æghwilc þara þe geherað word rices
seminantis:· <19>Omnis enim qui audit uerbum regni
⁊ ne ongetaþ cymþ se wærgad ⁊ geriseð ꝥte
et non intellegit uenit malignus et rapuit quod
sawen wæs in heorte his ꝥ is se þe sawen
seminatum est in corde eius hic est qui seminat(u)s
wæs bi wæge se þe þon(ne) on þa stanige lond gesa\`u´wen
est secus uiam <20>qui autem supra petrosa semina(-)
wæs ꝥ is se þe gehereþ word ⁊ hraðe mid
tus est:· Hic est qui audit uerbum et continuo cum
gefea onfoehþ þæm ne hæfeþ þon(ne) in him wyrtryma ah is
gaudio accipit illud <21>non habet in sé radicem sed est
wilen geworden þonne swincnisse ⁊ oehtnisse
temporalis:· Facta autem tribulatione et perse
for þæ(m) wordum hraðe ⁊spurnisse þrowað
propter uerbum continuo scandalizatur:·

2 auferatur] auferetur Y WW 4 audiunt] audient Y WW=R 5 ut] et WW Y=R | adinpleretur] adimpleatur Y adimpletur WW | dicentis] dicens Y WW 6 intellegitis] intellegetis WW Y=R 8 suis] *om.* Y WW 10 sane illos] sanem eos Y WW 11 qui] quia Y WW 12 quae] qui Y WW | Amen] + quippe Y WW 14 uiderunt] + et audir[ ] que audi[ ] et n(on) audi[ ] R[Fa] (*supplied in margin, partly trimmed, with the gloss,* ⁊ gehera[ ] þa þe ge hoe[ ] ⁊ ne geh[ ], *for which the transcription in Harley 3449 reads* ⁊ geheran þa þe gehoerað ⁊ ne geherdon) et audire quae auditis et non audierunt in Y WW 15 enim] *om.* Y WW 16 malignus] malus Y WW | rapuit] rapit Y WW 17 seminat(u)s est secus uiam] secus uiam seminatus est Y WW 19 audit uerbum] uerbum audit Y WW 20 habet] + autem Y WW 21 perse] persecutione Y WW

xƀ se þe þonne in ðornum gesauwen wæs þæt is se þe word
<22>Qui autem in spinis seminatus est hic est qui uer⟨-⟩
gehereþ ⁊ behygdnis weorulde þisse ⁊ lygnisse
bum audit et solicitudo saeculi istius et fallacia
weolan asmoraþ þæt word ⁊ butan westemleas geweor⟨-⟩
diuitiarum suffocauit uerbum et sine fructu effi⟨-⟩
ðæd se þe þonne in eorðe godne gesauwen wæs ꝥ is
citur <23>qui uero in terram bonam seminatus est hic (est)
se þe gehereð word ⁊ ongeteð ⁊ westem forðbereþ
qui audit uerbum et intellegit et fructum adfert
⁊ wyrceþ sume þonne ł eowic hundteontig sume sextig
et facit aliud quidem centissimum aliud sexagis⟨-⟩
sume þritig oþer gelicnisse
simum porro aliud tricissimum:· <24>Aliam para⟨-⟩
gesette ˋł gesægdeˊ heom cwæþende gelic is rice
bulam possuit illís dicens:· Simile est regnum
heofunas menn ðæm þe seow god séd on
caelorum homini qui seminauit bonum semen in
lond his þa hie soþlice sleptun þa menn cuom
agro suo <25>cum autem dormierent homines uenit
feond his ⁊ oferseow wéod in midle
inimicus eius et superseminauit zizania in medio
þæs hwætes ⁊ hi(m) aweg eode þa soþlice weox se brord ⁊ wes⟨-⟩
tritici et abít <26>cum autem creuisset haerba et fruc⟨-⟩
tem dyde þa æteawde ek þa weod ⁊ cumende
tum fecisset tunc apparuit zizania <27>et accedentes
þa esnas to fæder þas heoredes cwedun to him drihten
autem serui ad patrem familias dixerunt ei d(omi)ne
no þu god sed geseowe on lond þin hwonan
nonne bonum semen seminasti in agro tuo:· Unde
þonne hæfð hit þæt weod ⁊ cweþ to heom unhold monn þæt
ergo habet zizania <28>et ait illis inimicus homo hoc
gedyde cwedun þa him esnas wiltu we gæn ⁊ gesomnige
facit dixerunt autem ei serui uís imus et colligim(u)s
hiæ ⁊ cweþ to heo(m) nic þy les gesomnende þa weod alucæ
ea <29>et ait eis non ne forte colligentes zizania era⟨-⟩
somed mið ðæm ⁊ ek þone hwete ah leteþ begen
dicetis simul cum eis et triticum <30>sed senite utraq(ue)
wexan oþþe to ripe ⁊ in tíd ripes
crescere usq(ue) ad missem et in tempore messis
ic cweðe to riftrum minum gesomnigæþ arest þa weod
dicam messorib(us) meis colligite primum zizania
⁊ gebindeþ hiæ sceafum to beornane hwete þonne
et alligate ea fasciculo ad comburendum triticu(m)
(autem)

1 in spinis seminatus est] est seminatus in spinis Y WW **3** suffocauit] suffocat Y WW **4** terram bonam] terra bona Y Xz WW=R **6** centissimum] centum Y WW | aliud[2]] + autem Y WW | sexagissimum] sexaginta Y WW **7** tricissimum] triginta Y WW **8** possuit] proposuit Y WW | Simile] + factum Y WW **10** dormierent] dormiervnt R^{c} Y WW=R* **13** apparuit] apparuerunt et Y WW | et] *om.* Y WW **14** ad patrem] patris Y WW **17** facit] fecit R^{c} Y WW | dixerunt autem ei serui] serui autem dixerunt ei Y WW **18** eis] *om.* Y WW **19** cum eis et triticum] et triticum cum eis Y WW=R | sed] *om.* Y WW | senete] senite R^{c} Y WW **21** meis] *om.* Y WW **22** fasciculo] fasciculos Y WW

gesomnigaþ in berern mine oþer gelicnisse
congregate in orreum meum:· <31>Aliam parabula(m)
sægde heom cweþende gelic is rice heofunas
propossuit eis dicens simile est regnum caelorum
corne sinapes þæt genimende mon seow
grano sinapis quod accipiens homo seminauit
on londe his þæt læsest þonne is alra seda
in agro suo <32>quod minimum quidem est omnib(us) semi(-)
⁊ hit þonne wexeþ mara is wyrtum
nibus cum autem creuerit maius est omnib(us) hole(-)
⁊ gewyrð treow swa þæt fluglas heofun cumaþ
ribus et fit arbor ita ut uolucres caeli ueniant
⁊ ea\r/digað in telgrum his oþer gelicnisse
et habitant in ramís eius:· <33>Aliam parabulam
sprec to heom cweþende gelic is rice heofunas
locutus est eis dicens· Simile est regnum caeloru(m)·
beorma þonne genimende wif gehydde
fermento quod acceptum mulier abscondit
in melwæs mittum ðrim oþ þæt gebeormad wæs
in farina satis tribus· donec fermentatum est
all þas all sprec hælend to mængum in gelicnissum
totum· <34>haec omnia locutus est ad turbas in para(-)
⁊ butan gelicnissum ne sprec he to heom þæt
bulís et sine parabulís non loquebatur eis· <35>ut
gefylled węre þætte gecweden wæs þurh esaias þone
adinpleretur quod dictum est per esaiam pro(-)
witgu cweþende ic ontyno in gelicnissum muð minne
fetam dicentem· aperiam in parabulís ós meu(m)
roketto forð \ł bilketto forð/ þa þe ahyded werun fro(m) setnisse middangeardes
eructabo absconsa á constitutione mundi:·
þa forletende þa mengu cuom in huse ⁊ eodun
<36>Tunc demissís turbís uenit in domum et acces(-)
to him leorneras his cwæþende arecce
serunt ad eum discipuli eius dicentes dissere
us þa gelicnisse hwæte ⁊ weode londes
nobis parabulam tritici et zezaniorum agri
he þa ondswarede ⁊ cwæþ se þe sauweþ god séd
<37>qui respondens ait qui seminat bonum semen
sunu monnes ꝥ is ꝥ lond þonne is middangeard ꝥ gode
filius hominis est <38>ager autem hic mundus bonu(m)
wiotudlice séęd sindun bearn rices þa weod þonne
uero semen hii sunt filii regni zezania autem
bearn syndon þa nænegu se fiond þonne se þe seow
filii sunt nequam <39>inimicus autem qui seminauit
hiæ is deoful
ea est diabulus·

6 et fit] effit Y WW=R 7 habitant] habitent WW Y=R 8 dicens] *om.* Y WW 10 farina] farinae Y WW 11 ad turbas in parabulís] iesus in parabolis ad turbas Y WW 13 adinpleretur] adimpleretur Y WW impleretur Xz | est] erat Y WW | esaiam] *om.* Y WW 15 eructabo] + qui R^{Fa} Y WW=R^{*} | absconsa] + erant R^{Fa} abscondita Y WW 18 tritici et] *om.* Y WW 19 semen] *om.* Y^{*} Y^{c} WW=R 20 filius hominis est] est filius hominis Y WW 20 hic] est Y WW

þa rip þonne endunge weorulde is þa riftra
messis uero consummatio saeculi est messores
þonne englas sydun swa beoþ gesomnad þa weod
autem angeli sunt· <40>si ergo colliguntur zezania
⁊ fyre forberned swa bið in endunge
et igni conburentur· Sic erit in consummatione
weorulde sendeþ sunu monnes englas his ⁊ hiæ asom⟨-⟩
saeculi· <41>mittet filius hominis angelos suos· et colli⟨-⟩
nigaþ of rice his all geswicu ⁊ þa fremmen⟨-⟩
gent de regno eius omnia scandala et eos qui fa⟨-⟩
de unreht ⁊ sendeþ þa in ofne fyres
ciunt iniquitatem· <42>et mittet eos in caminum ignis
beornende þær bið wop ⁊ gristbitung toþa þanne
ardentis illic erit fletus et stridor dentium· <43>tunc
þa soþfeste scinaþ swa swa sunne in rice fader heora
iusti fulgebant sicut sól in regno patris eorum
se þe hæbbe earan gehernisse geh`o´ęre gelic is
qui habet aures audiendi audiat:· <44>Simile est
rice heofunas goldhorde gehyded in eorðe
regnum caelorum thesauro abscondito in agro
þæm se þe findeþ þe monn ahydeþ ⁊ for gefea
quem qui inuenit homo abscondit et prae gaudio
his gæþ ⁊ bebygið .ł sellaþ all ꝥ he hæfeþ ⁊ bygiþ
illius· uadit et uendit omnia quae habuit et emit
lond þæt eft gelic is rice heofunas
agrum illum:· <45>Iterum simile est regnum caeloru(m)
menn ceape sohte gode ercnanstanas
homini· negotiatori querenti bonas margaretas
⁊ gemoetend þa ænne ercnastan diorwyrðe eode
<46>inuenta autem una margareta praetiosa abiit
⁊ salde eall þæt he hæfde ⁊ gebohte þanne
et uendidit uniuersa quae habuit et emit eam:·
eft gelic is rice heofunas nett asendun
<47>Iterum simile est regnum caelorum sanguine misae
in sáe ⁊ of æghwilce cynne fisca ꝥ somnendum þa hit
in mari· ex omni genere piscium congreganti <48>cumq(ue)
gefylled wæs upp teonde ⁊ bi waraðe gesittende
inplete essent ducentes et secus litus sedentes
gecuron þa gode in fatu þa yfle þonne sendun
elegerunt bonos in uassa· malos autem misse⟨-⟩
út swa bið in endunge weoruldes ⁊
runt foras· <49>Sic erit in consummatione saeculi· ex⟨-⟩
þon(ne) gæþ englas ⁊ asceadeþ yfle of midle soðfes⟨-⟩
ibunt angeli et separabunt malos de medio iusto⟨-⟩
tra
rum·

2 si] sicut Y WW 3 conburentur] comburuntur Y WW 6 mittet] mittunt Y mittent WW 7 ardentis] *om.* Y WW | illic] ibi Y WW 8 eorum] sui Y WW Xz=R 9 audiendi] *om.* Y WW 12 omnia] uniuersa Y WW | habuit] habet Y WW 15 margareta praetiosa] pretiosa margarita Y WW 16 uniuersa] omnia Y WW 17 sanguine] sagine R[c] saginae Y sagenae WW 18 piscium] *om.* WW Y=R | cumq(ue)] quam cum Y WW 19 inplete essent] impleta esset Y WW | ducentes] educentes Y WW 20 misserunt foras] foras miserunt Y WW

⁊ sendaþ hiæ in ofn fyres þęr bid wop ⁊ grist⟨-⟩
<50>et mittent eos in caminum ignis ibi erit fletus et stridor

bitung toþa ongetaþ ge þas eall cwedun hie la drihten cweþ
dentium <51>intellegitis haec omnia dicunt etiam d(omi)ne <52>ait

to heom forþon æghwilc bokere gelæred in rice heofunas
illis ideo omnis scriba doctus in regno caeloru(m)

is gelic menn fæder hina þæ(m) þe forðbereð of
similis homini patri familias qui profert de

goldhord his þa neowe ⁊ þa ealde ⁊ gelamp þa geen⟨-⟩
thesauro suo noua et uetera:· <53>Et factum est cum

dade se hælend gelicnisse þas foerde þonan ⁊ cuom
consummasset ie(su)s parabulas istas transit <54>et ue⟨-⟩

in oeþel his gelærde hiæ in gesomnungum
niens in patriam suam docebat eos in sinagogis

heora swa þæt hiæ wundradun ⁊ cweden hwonan þissum
eorum ita ut mirarentur et dicerent unde huic

þas sno`t´tre ⁊ mægen ah þis nis smiðes sunu
sapientia et uirtutes <55>nonne hic est fabri filius

iosep ah ne hatte maria moder his
ioseph· nonne dicitur maria ioseph· mater eius

⁊ broþer his iacob ⁊ iohannes ⁊ simon ⁊ iudas
et fratres eius iacob· et iohannis· et simon· et iu⟨-⟩

⁊ swæster his ah ne ealle mið us sindon
das· <56>Et sorores eius nonne omnes apud nos sunt

hwonan sindun þissum all þas ⁊ ⁊spurnissę þrowadun in him
unde ergo huic omnia ista <57>et scandalizabantur in eo·

se helend þa cwęþ nis witga butan are nymþe
ie(su)s autem dicit non est profæta sine honore nisi

in oeþel his ⁊ in hus his ⁊ forþon ne worhte þær
in patria sua et in domu sua· <58>Et ideo non fecit ibi

mægen monige for ungeleafa heora
uirtutes multas propter incredulitatem eorum:·

in þa tid gehoerde herodes tetrarcha hlisa
<XIV 1>In illo tempore audiuit herodis tetracha famam

se hælend ⁊ cweþ to ðægnum his ah þis is iohannes se xƀ
ie(s)u· <2>et ait puerís suís numquid hic est iohannis bab⟨-⟩

baezere þe ic heht heawan he aras fro(m) deaðe ⁊
tista quem decolaui· ipse surrexit a mortuis· et

forþon mægen sindun worht in him herodes forþon genom
ideo uirtutes operantur in eo· <3>herodis enim ten(u)it

iohannes ⁊ gebond hine ⁊ sette in carcern
iohannem et alligauit eum· Et possuit in carcere(m)

for herodiadi wif broþer his philippes
propter erodiadem uxorem fratris sui pilippi

1 mittent] emittent Y^{*} Y^{c} WW=R 2 intellegistis] intellexistis Y WW | dicunt] + ei R^{Fa} Y WW | d(omi)ne] *om.* Y WW 4 similis] + est Y WW 6 transit] transiit inde Y WW 9 sapientia] + haec Y WW | uirtutes] uirtus Y WW=R 10 ioseph^{1}] *om.* Y WW | dicitur maria ioseph mater eius] dicitur maria mater eius R^{c} mater eius dicitur maria Y WW 11 iohannis] ioseph Y WW | iudas] iuda Y WW=R 14 dicit] dixit eis Y WW 15 ideo] *om.* Y WW 16 eorum] illorum Y WW 17 tetracha] tetrarcha R^{Fa} Y WW 18 numquid] *om.* Y WW 19 quem decolaui] *om.* Y WW 20 operantur] inoperantur Y Xz WW=R 21 carcere(m)] carcere Xz Y WW=R 22 pilippi] *om.* Y WW

sægde him forþon ioh(anne)s nis alefed ðe to habban`n´e hire ⁊ wolde hine
<4>dicebat enim non licet tibi habere eam· <5>et uolens eu(m)
ofslean ⁊ dreord him ꝥ folc forþon swa swa witgu hine
occidere timuit populum quia sicut profetam ha⟨-⟩
hæfdun on dæg þa gebyrde herode pleagade dohter
bebant:· <6>Die autem natalis herodis saltauit filia
þara herodiade in midle ⁊ licade herodes þa
herodiadis in medio triclinio· et placuit herodi· <7>unde
mið aþe geheht þæt hire salde swa hwæt swa
cum iuramento pollicitus est ei dare quodcumq(ue)
hiu bede hine ⁊ hiu gemonade fro(m) moder hire
postulasset ab eo· <8>at illa præmonita a matre sua
cweð her sele me on disce heafod iohannes se bezere
inquid dá mihi in disco capud iohannis babtistae
⁊ wæs geunrotsed se cyning for þæ(m) aþe þonne ⁊
<9>et contristatus rex· propter iuramentum autem et
ðæm þe ætgędre hleonudun mið him heht sellan ⁊ sende
eos qui pariter recumbebant cum eo iusit dari· <10>misit⟨-⟩
⁊ ofslog iohannes in carcerne ⁊ broht wæs
q(ue) et decolauit iohannem in carcere <11>et allatum est ca⟨-⟩
heafud his on disce ⁊ sald wæs þæ(m) mægden ⁊ ꝥ mægden bęr ł salde
pud eius in disco et datum est puellae et puella dedit
moder hire ⁊ cumende leorneras his genomun
matri suae <12>et accedentes discipuli eius tollerunt
lichoma his ⁊ bebyrgedun hit ⁊ cumende cyddun
corpus eius et sepellerunt illud et uenientes nuntia⟨-⟩
ł sægdun se helend þa ꝥ þa geherde se helend gewat þonan
uerunt ie(s)u· <13>Quod cum audisset ie(su)s secessit inde
on scipe in stowe woesten sundor ⁊ ꝥ
in nauiculam in locum desertum seorsum· et cum
geherende mengu folgedun him on foeðe
audissent turbae secutae sunt eum pedestres
of cæstrum ⁊ he ut gangande gesæh mengu miccle ⁊
de ciuitatibus· <14>Et exiens uidit turbam multam et
⁊ milsade þære ⁊ gehelde untryme sundor .ł heora
misertus est eis et curauit languido sé orsum:·
on efen þonne geworden eodun to him leor⟨-⟩
<15>Uespere autem facto accesserunt ad eum disci⟨-⟩
neras his cweþende woestig is stowe þeos ⁊ tid ł hwil
puli eius dicentes desertus est locus híc et hora
forð gewat forlet þas mengu ꝥ hię gangende in cæstre
iam præteriit demitte turbas ut euntes in castella
gebycge heom mete se helend þa cwæþ to heom nabbaþ hię
emant sibi escas <16>ie(su)s autem dixit illis non habent

1 enim] + illi iohannes Y WW | eum] illum Y WW 2 profetam] + eum R[Fa] Y WW 4 triclinio] *om.* Y WW 7 inquid dá mihi] da mihi inquit hic Y WW 8 contristatus] + est Y WW 9 cum eo] *om.* Y WW 11 puella] *om.* Y WW | dedit] tulit Y WW 12 tollerunt] tullerunt R[c] tulerunt Y WW 13 eius] *om.* Y WW 14 ie(s)u] iesus Y WW=R 15 nauiculam] nauicula Y WW 18 eis] eius Y[*] WW + ł eis Y[Ald] | languido sé orsum] languidos eorum Y WW 20 desertus] desurtus Y[*] Y[c] WW=R | híc] *om.* Y WW 21 iam] eam Y WW=R 22 illis] eis Y WW

þearfe sella heom ge etan h'i'e andsware(-)
necessire date illis uos manducare <17>responde(-)
dun him nabbaþ we her nymþe fif hlafes ⁊ twegen fis(-)
runt ei non habemus hic nisi ·u· panes et duos pis(-)
cas he þa cweþ to heom gebringaþ þa me hider ⁊ heht
ces· <18>qui ait illis adferte illos mihi huc· <19>Et cum iussiset
þa mengu gesittan on hóeg ⁊ genom þa fif hlafas
turbam discumbere super fenum· acceptís ·u· panib(us)
⁊ twægen fiscas ⁊ locande in heofun bledsade ⁊ bręc
et duob(us) piscibus aspiciens in caelum· benedixit· et fregit
⁊ salde leorneras his þa hlafes leorneras þa mengu
et dedit discipulis suis panes· discipuli autem turbis·
⁊ etun alle ⁊ fulle wyrdun ⁊ genoman
<20>et manducauerunt omnes et saturati sunt et tullerunt
þa hlafe twælf monde þara gebroca fulle etendra
reliquias ·xii· cofinos fragmentorum plenos <21>mandu(-)
þara þonne wærun getala fif þusenð weora ek .ł butan·
cantium autem fuit numerus ·u· m(illa) uirorum exceptis
wifum ⁊ cnehtum ⁊ sona heht leorneras his
mulieribus et paruulis <22>et statim iusit discipulos suos
astigan on scipe ⁊ forðfere hine ofer
ascendere in nauiculam et praecedere eum trans
sae oþ ꝥ he forlet þa mengu ⁊ þa forlet þara mengu
fretum donec ipse demitteret turbas <23>et demisa turba
astag on dune ane him gebiddan efen þa
ascendit in montem solus orare· Uespere autem
'ł geworden' he ane wæs ðęr ꝥ scip þonne on middu(m) sáe
facto solus erat ibi· <24>nauicula autem in midio mari
wæs worpen yþum wæs forþon heom wind wiðer(-)
iactabatur fluctibus· erat autem illis uentus con(-)
wear feorðe þære wacone næhtes cuom to heom
trarius· <25>quarta autem uigilia noctis uenit ad eos
se helend gangende ofer þone sǽe ⁊ gesegun hine ofer þone
ie(su)s ambulans supra maræ <26>et uidentes eum supra
sáé gangandne gedryfed werun in mode cweþende þe þæt scinlac
mare ambulantem turbati sunt dicentes· quia fan(-)
wære ⁊ for ægsa cliopadun ⁊ sona
tasma est· Et prae timore clamauerunt· <27> continuo
se helend sprec to heom cwęþende habbaþ bęldu ic hit
quae ie(su)s locutus est eis dicens habete fiduciam ego
eam ne forhtaþ ge ondswarede þa petrus him
sum nolite timere <28>respondens autem petrus ei
⁊ cwæþ drihten gif þu ꝥ sių hat mec cume to þe ofer ꝥ wæt(er)
dixit d(omi)ne si tú és iube me uenire ad te super aquas·

1 necessire] + adeuntes (*in the upper margin with the gloss,* to gangenne) R[Fa] necesse ire Y WW 3 illis] eis Y WW 4 super] supra Y WW 6 suis] *om.* Y WW 10 suos] *om.* Y WW 11 nauiculam] nauicula Y Xz WW=R 12 ipse] *om.* Y WW 14 solus] salus Y* Y[c] WW=R | midio] medio R[c] Y WW 15 autem illis uentus contrarius] enim contrarius uentus Y WW 17 ie(su)s] *om.* Y WW 19 continuo quae] et continuo quae R[Fa] statimque Y WW 21 ei] *om.* Y WW 22 dixit] et dixit R[Fa] Y WW=R*

⁊ he cwæþ cum ⁊ astígende petrus of þæ(m) scipe
<29>Et ipse ait ueni· et discendiens petrus de nauicula· am(-)
eode ofer ꝥ he cuome to þæ(m) helende geseah þa þone wind swiðne
bulabat super ut ueniret ad ie(su)m <30>uidens uero uentum
frohtade ⁊ þa ingon sincan cegde cwęþende hæl
timuit et cum coepisset mergi clamauit dicens saluum
mec drihten ⁊ þa ræþe se helend aþenede hond his
me fac d(omi)ne <31>et continuo ie(su)s extendiens manum suam
⁊ gegrap hine cwęþ to hi(m) þu medmiccles gelefan f(or)hwon
adpraehendit eum· ait illi modicæ fidei quare du(-)
getwiodestu ⁊ þa hiæ astigan on scip þa blan
bitasti· <32>et cum ascendisset in nauiculam cessauit
se wind þa þe þonne on þæ(m) scipe werun ær cuomun ⁊ ge(-)
uentus· <33>Qui autem in nauicula erant uenerunt et ad(-)
bedun him cweþende soþlice sunu godes þu eart ⁊ þa hie
orauerunt eum dicentes uere filius d(e)i és tú <34>et cum
oferfæren hæfdon cuomon in lond genesara
transfretassent uenerunt in terram genessareth·
⁊ ondgetende hine weras þara stowe gebedun to hi(m)
<35>et cum cognouissent eum uiri loci illius adorauerunt eu(m)
⁊ sendun in eall lond þæt ⁊ brohtun
et miserunt in uniuersam regionem illam et obtulle(-)
him alle yfle hæbbende ⁊ bedun hine ꝥ hiæ oþþe
runt ei omnes male habentes· <36>et rogabant eum ut uel
fæss hrægles his mostun æthrinan ⁊ swa hwælc swa æt(-)
fimbriam uestimenti eius tangerent et quicumq(ue) titi(-)
hrinan hale wvrdon þa eodun to him
gerant salui facti sunt:· <XV 1>Tunc accesserunt ad eum
fro(m) hierosolimis bokere ⁊ fariseas cweþende forhwon
ab hierusolimís scribae et farissaei dicentes <2>quare
leorneras þine ofergæþ gesettnisse þara ældra
discipuli tui transgrediuntur traditionem seniorum
ne thuað honda heora þon(ne) hiæ hlaf etað
non enim lauant manus suas cum panem manducant
he þa ondswarade cwæþ to heo(m) f(or)hwon ⁊ ge ek ofer(-)
<3>ipse autem respondens ait illis quare et uos trans(-)
gæþ bebod godes for gesettnisse eowre
grediemini mandatum d(e)i· propter traditionem uestra(m)
forþon 'wiotudlice' god cwæþ are fæder þinum ⁊ moder þin
<4>nam d(eu)s dixit honora patrem tuum et matrem tuam·
⁊ se þe wærge fæder oþþe moder deaða swælteþ
et qui maledixerit patri uel matri morte morietur:·
ge þonne cweðaþ swa hwa swa cwið to fæder oþþe moder
<5>Uos autem dicitis quicumq(ue) dixerit patri uel matri

1 et[1]] at Y WW | de] *om.* Y WW=R 2 super] + aquam R[Fa] (*in the left-hand margin with the gloss,* ꝥ wæt(er)) Y WW | uentum] + ualidu(m) R[Fa] Y WW 3 mergi] mergeri Y WW=R | dicens] + domine Y WW 4 d(omi)ne] *om.* Y WW | suam] om. Y WW 5 eum] + et Y WW 6 ascendisset] ascendissent Y WW 8 tú] *om.* Y WW 10 adorauerunt eu(m) et] *om.* Y WW 13 titigerant] tetigerant R[c] tetigerunt Y WW 19 transgrediemini] transgredimini Y WW 20 tuum] *om.* Xz Y WW=R | tuam] *om.* Y WW 21 morietur] moriatur Y WW

lac swa hwilc swa is of me þe beðearfeþ ⁊ ne ariað
monus quodcumq(ue) est ex me tibi proderit <6>et non hono(-)
fæder his ⁊ moder his ⁊ ge ungænge
rificauit patrem suum et matrem suam· et inritum
gedydon bebod godes for settnisse eowrum
fecistis mandatum d(e)i· propter traditionem uestram·
ge licetheras wel witgade of eow essaias cweþende
<7>hyppochritae bene profetauit de uobis essaias dicens
folc þis weleru(m) mec weorðaþ heorte þonne eora feorr
<8>populus hic lapis me honorat cór autem eorum longe
is fro(m) me holunga þonne hiæ me begangeþ lærende lare
est á me <9>sine causa autem me colunt docentes doctri(-)
⁊ bebod monna ⁊ gecegende to him þæ(m) mængu(m)
nas et mandata hominum· <10>Et conuocatís ad se turbis
cwęþ to heo(m) geherað ⁊ ongeteþ nalles ꝥte ingæþ in muðe
dixit eís· audite et intellegite <11>non quod intrat in ós
smiteþ monnu ah ꝥte forðgæþ of muþe þæt
cóinquinant hominem sed quod procedit ex ore hoc
besmiteþ monnu þa hi(m) togangende leorneras
cóinquinant hominem:· <12>Tunc accedentes discipuli
his cwedun to him þu wast þætte fariseas geherde þis word
eius dixerunt ei· scis quia farisaei audito hoc uerbo
geincfullade werun ⁊ he ondswarade ⁊ cwæþ æghwilc
scandalizati sunt <13>at ille respondens ait omnis
wæstma seten þa þe ne sette fæder min se heofunlica
plantatio quam non plantauit pater meus cælestis
astęrfed bið forleteð hiæ blinde sindon lateuw blindra
eradicabitur· <14>sinete illos caeci sunt duces cæcoru(m)·
blind þonne gif blindne lædeþ begen
cæcus autem si caeco ducatum praestat ambo
in seaþ fallen andwyrde þa petrus
in foueam cadunt:· <15>Respondens autem petrus
cwæþ to him arecce us gelicnisse þas ⁊ he
dixit ei disere nobis parabulam istam· <16>at ille
cweþ nu geta ⁊ ge butan ondget sindun ⁊ ne ongetað
dixit adhuc et uos sine intellectu estis· <17>et non intel(-)
ge ꝥte gehwæt þæs þe in muðe ingæð in wombe gangeð
legis quia omne quod in ós intrat in uentrem uadit·
⁊ in leornisse bið út asended þa þe þonne gæð
et in secessum mittitur <18>quae autem procedunt
of muðe of heorta ut gaeþ geþohtas yfele morþur
de ore· <19>de corde exeunt cogitationes male homici(-)
unrihthæmed forlaegennisse stale lyge gewitnisse
dia· adulteria· fornicationes furta· falsa testi(-)
monia·

1 monus] munus R[c] WW manus Y 2 et[1]] *om.* Y WW | suam] *om.* Y WW 5 lapis] labis R[c] labiis Y WW 6 me colunt] colunt me Y WW | doctrinas] doctina Y[*] Y[c] WW=R 7 et[1]] *om.* Y WW 8 intellegite] intellegete Y WW=R 9 cónquinant] conquinat Y WW 10 cónquinant] conquinat R[c] Y WW 11 hoc] *om.* Y WW 15 praestat] praeset Y praestet WW 17 disere] edissere Y WW 18 et[2]] *om.* Y WW | intellegis] intellegitis Y WW 20 secessum] secessu Y WW=R | mittitur] emittitur Y WW 21 ore] + de corde exeunt et ea coinquinant (conci- Y) hominem Y WW 21 corde] + enim Y WW

hefalsunge þis sindon þa þe besmitaþ monnum
blasfemiae· <20>haec sunt quae quoinquinant homine(m)·
þæh unðwegenu(m) þonne hondum ete ne besmi⟨-⟩
non lotis autem manibus manducare non quoin⟨-⟩
taþ ꝥ monnum ⁊ gongende þonan se hælend gewat
quinat hominem:· <21>Et egresus inde ie(su)s secessit
in dæl tyre ⁊ sidone ⁊ henu wif cananisc
in partes tyri· et sidonis· <22>Et ecce mulier cannanea
of gemæru(m) þæm ut agongen cegde to him cweþende milt⟨-⟩
á finib(us) illis egressa clamauit ad eum dicens mise⟨-⟩
sa me drihten sunu dauiðes dogter min is yfle fro(m) deofle
rere mei d(omi)ne filii dauid· filia mea male á demonio
wæled he ne ondwyrde him worde ⁊ togangende
uexatur <23>qui respondit ei uerbum· Et accedentes
leorneras his bedun hine cwæþende forlet
discipuli eius rogabant eum dicentes dimitte
hiæ f(or)þon þe hiæ cægeþ æft(er) us he þa on`d´wyrde
eam quia clamat post nos <24>ipse autem respon
cweþ to heom ne ic wæs asended nymþe to scepu(m) þæ(m) þe forloren wyrdon
ait illis· non sum misus nisi ad oues quae perier(u)nt
husęs israheles ⁊ hiu cuom ⁊ gebed to him cwæþende
domus israhel· <25>at illa uenit et adorabat eum dicens
drihten fultume me he onwyrde cwæþ nis ꝥ god
d(omi)ne adiuua me <26>qui respondens ait non est bonum
þe monn genime hlaf bearna ⁊ weorpeþ hundum ⁊ hiu
sumere panem filiorum et mittere canibus· <27>at illa
cweþ la drihten forþon ⁊ welpas ek etaþ of cromum þe þe
dixit utiq(ue) d(omi)ne nam et catuli edunt de micis quae
falleþ of beode hlaferde heora þa andwyrde
cadunt de mensa demoniorum suorum· <28>Tunc res⟨-⟩
se hælend cweþ to hire la wif micel is geleafa þin geweorðe
pondens ie(su)s ait illi mulier magna est fides tua· fiat
þe swa ðu wille ⁊ gehæled wæs dohter hire of ðæm hwile
tibi sicut uís et sana facta est filia illius ex illa hora:·
⁊ þa þonan foerde se hælend cuo(m) æft bi sáe galilea
<29>Et cum transiset ie(su)s uenit iterum secus mare galileae
⁊ astigende on dune sett þær ⁊ eodun
et ascendens in montem sedebat ibi· <30>Et accesserunt
to him mengu monige hæbbende mid him dumbe ⁊ halte
ad eum turbae multae habentes secum mutos et clau⟨-⟩
⁊ blinde anhende ⁊ oþer monige ⁊ lægdun .ł feallan
dos et caecos debiles et alios multos· et proiecerunt
hiæ to fotum his ⁊ gehęlde hiæ swa ꝥ þa mengu wundradun
eos ad pedes eius et curauit eos <31>ita ut turbae mira⟨-⟩
rentur·

2 quoinquinat] coincinant Y coinquinat WW 5 illis] illius Y WW=R | ad eum dicens] dicens ei Y WW 7 qui] + non Y WW 9 respon] respondens Y WW 10 illis] *om.* Y WW 11 adorabat] adorauit Y WW 14 utiq(ue)] etiam Y WW 15 demoniorum] dominorum R^c Y WW 16 illi] + o Y WW 17 sana facta] sanata Y WW 18 transiset] transisset inde Y WW | iterum] *om.* Y WW 19 montem] monte Y WW=R 20 et] *om.* Y WW 21 et[1]] *om.* Y WW

gesægon þa dumbe sprecende ⁊ ða healte gangande ⁊ ða blinde
uidentes mutos loquentes claudos ambulantes· cæ⟨-⟩
segon ⁊ micladun god israhel hælend þa
cos uidentes· et magnificabant d(eu)m israhel· <32>ie(su)s autem
tosomne cliopade leorneras his cwæþ mec hreoweþ þas mengu
conuocatís discipulís suís dixit miserior huic turbae
ðe hie ˋł forðonˊ þreo dagas is nu þæt hie þurhwunadun mid mec ⁊
quia triduum est iam quod perseuerant mecum· et
nabbaþ þæt hie etaþ ⁊ ic forlete hie fæstende
non habent quod manducent· et demittere eos ieiunos
ne wille ðy les hię geteorige on wæge ⁊ cwædon hi(m) to þa leorneras hwonon þonne
nolo ne deficiant in uia:· <33>Et dicunt ei discipuli unde ergo
us on wæstenne hlafas to niomane ꝥ we gehreorde swa miccle
nobis in deserto panes ad tintos ut saturentur tantæ
mengu ⁊ cwæþ heo(m) to se hælend hwæt ˋł hu feolaˊ hlafas habbaþ ge hiæ cwedun
turbae <34>et ait illís ie(su)s quot panes habetis at illi dixer(u)nt
seofun ⁊ unmonige fiscas ⁊ þa bebead þæ(m) mengu ꝥ hie gesetun
uii· et paucos pisciculos <35>et praecipit turbae ut discu(m)⟨-⟩
on eorþan ⁊ genimende þa seofun hlafas ⁊ þa fiscas
berent super terram <36>et accipiens ·uii· panes et pisces
⁊ þongunge dˋoˊende ⁊ bræc ⁊ salde leorneras his ⁊ þa leor⟨-⟩
gratias egit et fregit et dedit discipulís suís· et dis⟨-⟩
neras saldun þæm folce ⁊ etun ealle ⁊
cipuli dederunt populo <37>et comederunt omnes et
fylde weron ł wurdun ⁊ ꝥte to lafe wæs þara gebroca ge⟨-⟩
saturati sunt et quod superfuit de fragmentís tul⟨-⟩
nomen siofun sperta fulle weron þonne þa þe etun
lerunt ·uii· sportas plenas <38>erant autem qui man⟨-⟩
siofun þusend weoras ˋł monnaˊ butan ˋł toekanˊ cnehtum ⁊
ducauerunt ·uii· milia uirorum extra paruulos et
wifum ⁊ þa forletende þara mengu astág on scipe
mulieres· <39>et demisa turba ascendit in nauiculam·
⁊ cuom in mæru magedan ⁊ eodun to him
et uenit in fines magedán:· <XVI 1>Et accesserunt ad eum
fariseas ⁊ sadduceas costende ⁊ bedon ꝥte he taken
farisaei et saducei temptantes et rogauerunt ut signu(m)
of heofune eaude heom ⁊ he andswarade ⁊ cwæþ geworden
de caelo ostenderet eis <2>at ille respondens ait facto
efenne ge cweoþað smylte þis biþ ⁊ an mergenne read is
uespere dicitis serenum erit cras rubicundum est
f(or)þon þe heofun ⁊ todæge biþ hreanis readaþ f(or)þon unrotlice
enim cælum· <3>et mane tempestas rutulat enim cum triste
þe heofun ge liceteras ondwliotu soþlice heofun doeme ˋł cunnaðˊ gedoemeˊ
caelum hyppochritae faciem ergo caeli uos iudicare
cunnað
nostis

1 mutos] multos Y WW=R 3 miserior] misserior R[c] misereor Y WW | huic] *om.* Y WW 4 triduum est] triduo Y WW | quod] *om.* Y WW 7 ad tintos] tantas Y WW | saturentur] saturemus Y WW | tantæ turbae] turbam tantam Y WW 9 praecipit] praecepit Y WW | discu(m)berent] discumberet Y WW 10 pisces] + et Y WW 11 egit et] agens Y WW 14 manducauerunt] manducauerant Y WW 15 uii] quatuor Y WW | uirorum] hominum Y WW 18 rogauerunt] + eum Y WW 19 respondens] + illis R[Fa] (illis *added in the margin with the gloss,* heom) + eis Y WW **(cont. on p. 138)**

tacen wiotudlice ⁊ tide ne magun gecnawan cneuris
signa autem et tempora non potestis cognocere <4>gene(-)
yfle tacen ⁊ sio forlegene soeceþ ⁊ tacen ne bið
ratio mala signum et adultera querit et signum non
sald hie nymþe tacen iona se witga ⁊ forletende hie
dabitur ei nisi signum ionae profetæ et relictís illís
aweg eode ⁊ þa cuomun leorneras his ofer sǽ
abiit:· <5>Et cum uenissent discipuli eius trans fretu(m)
forgetun ꝥ h'i'e hlafas genome cwæþ heom to behealdeþ
obliti sunt panes accipere <6>qui dixit illis adtendite
eow ⁊ warniaþ wið beorma farisseas ⁊ sadducea
uos et cauete a fermento farissaeorum et sadu(-)
⁊ hie þohtun betwion heom cweþende forþon 'ł ðy we'
cærum· <7>at illi cogitabant intra sé dicentes quia pa(-)
hlafas ne genoman ða wiste wiotudlice se hælend geþanc heora
nes non accipimus <8>sciens autem ie(su)s cogitationes eoru(m)
⁊ cwæþ hwæt þencaþ ge betwion eow medmiclæs geleafa menn f(or)þon ꝥ ge hlafas
dixit quid cogitatis intra uos modicæ fidei quia panes
ne habbaþ ne ge cuþlice ne ongetaþ ne ge ne myngað
non habetis <9>nondum enim intellegitis neq(ue) meministis
þara fif hlafa fif þusenda monna ⁊ hu monige monde
de quinq(ue) panibus ·u· milia hominum quot coffinos
genoman f(or)hwon ne ongetaþ ge ꝥ ic be hlafe
sumpsistis <11>quare non intellegistis quia non de pani(-)
cwæþ to eow bergaþ eow fro(m) bearma farisea
bus dixit uobis· cauete uos á fermento farisæoru(m)
⁊ saducea þa ongetun hie ꝥ he ne cwæþ
et saducæorum· <12>Tunc intellexerunt quod non dixerit
warnaþ eow fro(m) beorma hlafa ah wið lare farisea
cauete á fermento pauium· sed a doctrina farissæ(-)
⁊ sadducea to behealdene heom þa cwom
orum et saducæorum adtendere sibi:· <13>Uenit autem
se hælend in dæle cessariȩ filippes ⁊ frægn
ie(su)s in partes cessariae pilippi· Et interrogabat dis(-)
leorneras his cweþende huat cweoþaþ menn þæt
cipulos suos dicens quem me dicunt homines esse
monnes sunu siȩ hie cwædun sume iohannes se bædzere
filium hominis <14>at illi dixerunt alii iohannem babtis(-)
sume wiotudlice hieremias sume soþlice elias oþþe an
tam· alii autem heremiam· alii uero heliam· aut unum
þara witgana cwæþ heo(m) to se hælend ge þonne hwæt cweoþað hwæt
ex profetís· <15>Dicit illis ie(su)s uos autem quem me esse
ic seo ondswarade wiotudlice simon petrus cwæþ þu eart
dicitis· <16>respondens autem simon petrus dixit tú és

(f. 26r) 20 erit] + quia rebicundus (est) celum R^{Fa} (*in the lower margin with the gloss,* f(or)þon read is þe heofun) Y WW=R* | cras] *om.* Y WW **21** mane] + hodie Y WW | cum] *om.* Y WW **22** hyppochritae] *om.* Y WW | uos] *om.* Y WW | iudicare] diiudicare Y WW

(f. 26v) 1 et] *om.* Y WW | tempora] temporum Y WW | cognocere] cognoscere R^{c} *om.* Y WW **2** signum et adultera] et adultera signum Y WW **3** profetæ] *om.* Y WW **5** adtendite uos] intuemini Y WW **6** saducærum] saducæorum R^{c} sadducaeorum (sadu-Y) WW **7** intra] inter Y WW | accipimus] accepimus Y WW **8** cogtationes eoru(m)] *om.* Y WW **9** intra] inter Y WW **10** enim] *om.* Y WW | meministis de] recordamini Y WW **11** panibus] panum Y WW | milia] milium WW Y=R **(cont. on p. 139)**

crist godes sune þæs lifgenda þa ondsweorede se hælend cwæþ to hi(m) eadig
cr(istu)s filius d(e)i uiui· <17>respondens autem ie(su)s dixit illi bea⟨-⟩
þu eart simon sunu iona f(or)þon lic ⁊ blod ne onwreoþ
tus és simon bariona quia caro et sanguis non reue⟨-⟩
ðe ah fæder min se þe in heofunu(m) is ⁊ ic sæcge ðe
labit tibi sed pater meus qui in cælís est <18>et ego dico tibi
ꝥ þu eart petrus ⁊ on þæm petra ł stane ic getimbre mine
qui tú és petrus et super hanc petram ædificabo æcles⟨-⟩
circae ⁊ duru helle ne oferswiðiaþ wið
siam meam et portæ inferni non præualebunt aduer⟨-⟩
eo ⁊ ic þe selle selle kægen heofuna rices ⁊ swa hwæt swa þu
sus eam <19>et tibi dabo claues regni cælorum et quodcumq(ue)
bindes on eorðan gebunde biðon ⁊ in heofunum ⁊ swa hwæt swa þu
ligaueris super terram erunt ligata et in cælís et quaecu(m)q(ue)
unbindes on eorðan beoðan unbunde in heofunum þa
solueris super terram erunt soluta et in cælís· <20>Tunc
bebead leorneras his ꝥ hie nængum sægdun ꝥ he wære
præcipit discipulís suís ut nemini dicerent quia ipse
hælende crist æft(er) þon ingonn se hælend eawan his leorneras
esset cr(istu)s:· <21>Exinde coepit ie(su)s ostendere discipulís
þæt he scylde færan to hierusalem ⁊ feola geþrowigan
suís· quia oportet eum iræ in hirusolimam et multa pati
fro(m) þæ(m) ældru(m) ⁊ bokeru(m) ⁊ aldorsacerdum ⁊ ofslaegen beon
á seniorib(us) et scribís et principibus sacerdotum et occidi
⁊ ðridde dæg æftarisan ⁊ genimende hine petrus ongan
et tertia die resurgere <22>et adsumens eum petrus coepit
ðreiga hine cwæþende won siæ fro(m) þe dryht(en) ne biþ þe þæt se
increpare et dicere absit á te d(omi)ne· non erit tibi hoc <23>qui
ge\h/werfad cwæþ to petre gang æft(er) me þu wiþerwearde ⁊spyrnes
conuersus dixit petro uade post me satanas scanda⟨-⟩
eart me þi ðu ne const þa þe godes sindun ah þa þe
lum és mihi quia non sapis ea quae d(e)i sunt sed ea quæ
monna ða cwæþ se hæl(end) to his leorneras gif hwa
hominum:· <24>Tunc dixit ie(su)s discipulís suís si quis
wille æft(er) me cume ⁊sæcę him seolfum ⁊ bere his
uult post me uenire abnegat seipsum et tollat cru⟨-⟩
rode ⁊ folge me f(or)þon se þe þe wile his feorh
cem suam et sequar me <25>qui enim uoluerit animam
hal gedoa he f(or)leose þæt ⁊ se þe þon(ne) f(or)leoseþ
suam saluam facere perdat eam· et qui perdide
his feorh for me he gemoeteþ þæt forþon þe hwæt helpeð
animam suam propter me inueniet eam <26>quid enim
ł beþea\r/fað menn ðeah þe he middengeard ealne gestreone ⁊ feorh
prodest homini sí totum mundum lucretur animae

(f. 26v) 11 hominum] + et Y WW **12** sumpsistis] + et de uii panes iiii milia hominum ⁊ q(uo)t sporte accipistis R^{Fa} (*in the left-hand margin with the gloss,* ni þara siofun hlafas feower þusenda monna ⁊ hu monige sperta ge genoman) + neque septem panum quattuor milium hominum et quot sportas sumpsistis (sums- Y) Y WW | intellegistis] intellegitis Y WW | panibus] pane Y WW **13** dixit] dixi Y WW | uos] *om.* Y WW **14** quod] quia Y WW **15** cauete] cauendum Y WW | pauium] panum Y WW **16** adtendere sibi] *om.* Y WW **18** me] *om.* Y WW **20** heremiam] hieremiam R^{c} heliam Y WW | heliam] hieremiam Y WW **21** ie(su)s] *om.* Y WW **22** autem] *om.* Y WW

(f. 27r) 1 illi] *om.* Y WW ei Xz **2** reuelabit] reuelauit Y WW **4** qui] quia Y WW | et] *om.* Y WW=R **5** inferni] inferi Y WW | aduersus] aduersum Y WW **(cont. on p. 140)**

soþlice his ewyrdlu þrowiaþ oþþe hwælc seleþ
Uero suae detrimentum patiatur· aut quam dabit
monn geld for ferh his forðon sune
homo commercium pro anima sua· <27>Nam filius
monnes cymeþ ł cymende is in wuldor fæder his mið
hominis uenturus est in gloria patris sui cum an⟨-⟩
ænglum his ⁊ þon(ne) agæfeþ ł geldeþ anra gehwæm neh þon ‵ł æft(er)′ weorcæ his
gelís suís· Tunc reddet unicuiq(ue) iuxta opera sua·
soþ ic sæcge eow sindun sume of þæræ her stondendra þa þe
<28>amen dico uobis sunt quidam de híc stantibus qui
ne bergaþ deað ær þon he geseo sunu monnes
non gustabunt mortem donec uideant filium homi⟨-⟩
cymendę in rice his ⁊ geworden wæs æfter dagum
nis· uenientem in regno suo:· <XVII 1>Et factum est post dies
sex genom hælend ⁊ ⁊
sex· adsumpsit ie(su)s petrum· et iacobum· et iohanne(m)
broþer his ⁊ lædde hie on dune hea sund‵u′r ł niðer
fratrem eius· et dixit illos in montem excelsum seorsu(m)·
⁊ oferheowad wæs beforan heom ⁊ scán ondwliota
<2>et transfiguratus est ante eos et resplendeuit facies
his swa sunne hrægl þonne his wurdon
eius sicut sol uestimentua autem eius facta sunt
swa snau ⁊ henu æteawde heom ⁊ wiþ hælend
sicut nix· <3>et apparuit eis moyses· et helias· cum illo
sprecende ondswarade þa cwæþ to hælend
loquentes· <4>respondens autem petrus dixit ad ie(su)m
dryhten god his ꝥ we her sie gif þu wille gewyrce we her ðreo
d(omi)ne bonum est nobis híc esse si uis faciamus trea
selescotu ðe án ⁊ án ⁊ án
tabernacula tibi unum· et moysi unum· et heliae unu(m)
þende he þa gespræc henu wolken liht oferscuade hię
<5>adhuc eo loquente ecce nubs lucida obumbrauit eos·
⁊ henu stæfn of þæ(m) wolcne cweþende þis is sunu min se leofa
et uox de nube dicens· hic est filius meus dilectus in
in ðæm me wel gelicade him ge geherað ⁊ geherende
quo mihi bene conplacui ipsum audite <6>et audientes
þa leorneras feollan on ondwliotu hiora ⁊ heo(m) ondreordun swiðe
discipuli ciciderunt in faciam suam et timuerunt ualde
⁊ þa eode se hælend ⁊ æthran heom ⁊ cwæþ to heo(m) arísaþ ⁊ eow
<7>et accessit ie(su)s et tetigit eos dixitq(ue) eis surgite et nolite
ne ondredaþ hebben‵de′ .ł ahofan þa egan heora nænigne segun
timere <8>leuantes autem oculos suos neminem uiderunt
nymþe se hælend enne ⁊ niþerstigendum heom of dúne bebead
nisi solum ie(su)m <9>et discendentib(us) illís de monte præcipit
heo(m) se hælend
eis ie(su)s

(f. 27r) 7 erunt ligata et] erit ligatum Y WW | quaecu(m)q(ue)] quodcumque Y WW 8 erunt soluta et] erit solutum Y WW 10 esset] + iesus Y WW 11 oportet] oporteret Y WW | in] *om.* Y WW 14 et dicere] illum dicens Y WW 17 dixit ie(su)s] iesus dixt Y WW 18 abnegat] abneget Y WW | seipsum] semet ipsum Y WW 19 sequar] sequatur R[Fa] Y WW 20 perdat] perdet Y WW | et qui perdide] qui autem perdiderit Y WW 22 totum mundum] mundum uniuersum Y WW
(f. 27v) 2 commercium] commutationem Y WW 2 Nam filius] filius enim Y WW 4 Tunc] et tunc Y WW | iuxta opera sua] secundum opus eius Y WW **(cont. on p. 141)**

cweþende nænegum ge sæcgaþ gesihþe ðas ær ðon sunu
dicens nemini dixeritis uisionem hanc· donec filius
monnes fro(m) deadum arisę ⁊ frugnun .ɫ ascaden him
hominis a mortuis resurgat· <10>Et interrogauerunt eu(m)
leorneras his cweþende ah hwæt bokeras cweþað þæt
discipuli eius dicentes· quid ergo scribae dicunt quod
elias scyle ærest cuman he andswarade cwæþ to heom
heliam oportet primum uenire <11>at ille respondens ait eis
elias cymeþ ⁊ agefeþ eall sæcge þon(ne)
helias quidem uenturus est et restituet omnia <12>dico aute(m)
eowic þæt elias com ⁊ ne ongetun hine ah
uobis quia helias iam uenit et non cognuerunt eum sed
dydon in him swa hwælc swa h\`i´e waldun swa ⁊ monnes sune
fecerunt in eo quæcumq(ue) uoluerunt· sic et filius hominis
þrowende bið fro(m) heo(m) þa ongeton þa leorneras þæt he
passurus est ab eis· <13>tunc intellexerunt discipuli quia
bi iohanne þę(m) bædzere sægde heom ⁊ þa he cwom to mengu
de iohanne babtista dixisset eis:· <14>Et cum uenisset ad tur⟨-⟩
eode to him monn cneu begende beforan him
bas· accessit ad eum homo genibus prouolutus· ante eu(m)
cweþende miltse sune min forþon monsek he is ⁊
dicens <15>d(omi)ne miserere filio meo quia lunaticus est et
yfle þrowað forþon þe oft falleþ in fyre ⁊ gelome
male torquetur nam sepe cadit in ignem et crebro in
in wættre ⁊ ic brohte hine leornerum ðinum ⁊ ne mæhton
aquam <16>et obtulli eum discipulís tuís et non potuerunt
gehælen hine ondswarede þa se hælend cwæþ la \`ɫ eala´ cneoris un⟨-⟩
curare eum <17>respondens autem ie(su)s ait ó generatio in⟨-⟩
geleaf\`f´ullæ ⁊ miswerfde hu lánge beom ic eow mid hu lange
credula et peruersa usque quo ero uobiscum usque quo
ðrowa ic eow bringaþ hine hider to me ⁊ ðreatade hine
patiar uos· adferte illum huc ad me <18>et increpauit eum
se hæl(end) ⁊ eode fro(m) him ꝥ deoful ⁊ gehæled wæs se cneht þa
ie(su)s et exiit ab eo demonium et curatus est puer <19>Tunc
eodun þa leorneras to degullice ⁊ cwedun to him
accesserunt discipuli ad ie(su)m secrete dixerunt ei·
forwon we ne mæhton hit aweorpan út ⁊ he cwæþ to heom for
quare nos non potuimus iecere illum <20>et dicit illís prop⟨-⟩
ungeleafa eowrum soð ic sæcge eow
ter incredulitatem uestrum· Amen quippe dico uobis
gif ge habbað geleafa swa corn senepes ge cweoþað to dune
si habueritis fidem ut granum sinapis dicetis monti
þisse leor \`ɫ gewit´ heonan ⁊ gewitað ɫ liorað ⁊ nauwiht uneþe eow bið
huic transi hinc et transibit et nihil inpossibile erit
uobis

(**f. 27v**) **7** factum est] *om.* Y WW **9** dixit] duxit R[c] ducit Y WW **10** resplendeuit] resplenduit Y WW **11** sunt] + alba R[Fa] (*in the left-hand margin with the gloss,* hwit) Y WW **12** et[1]] + ecce R[Fa] ecce Y WW | eis] illis Y WW | illo] eo Y WW **14** nobis] nos Y WW | faciamus] + hic R[Fa] WW faciam hic Y | trea] tria R[c] Y WW **16** nubs] nubis Y WW nubes Xz **17** et] + ecce R[Fa] Y WW **18** conplacui] complacuit Y Xz WW=R **19** ciciderunt] ceciderunt R[Fa] Y WW **22** præcipit] praecepit Y WW **23** eis] *om.* Y WW (**f. 28r**) **1** hanc] *om.* Y WW **3** eius] *om.* Y WW **4** oportet] oporteat Y WW **9** eis] *om.* Y WW=R | turbas] turbam Y WW **10** prouolutus] prouolutis Y WW=R **11** filio meo] filii mei Y Xz WW=R **12** torquetur] patitur Y WW (**cont. on p. 142**)

þis þonne cynn ne bið ut aworpen nymðe þurh fæsten ⁊
<21>Hoc autem genus non iecitur nisi per ieiunium et o⟨-⟩
gebeodum ðende drohtadun þa hie in galilea cwæþ
rationem· <22>conuersantib(us) autem illis in galilea dixit
heo(m) to se hælend f(or)þon þe toward is wiotudlice þte sunu monnes bið sald
eis ie(su)s futurum est enim ut filius hominis tradetur
in honda monna ⁊ ofslægþ hine ⁊ he ðridde dæg æft⟨-⟩
in manus hominum <23>et occident eum et tertia die resur⟨-⟩
ariseþ ⁊ geunrotsad hie werun swiðe ⁊ þa hię cwoman
get et contristati sunt uehimenter:· <24>Et cum uenissent
to capharnaum eodun þa þe caseringe ondfengon
cafarnauum accesserunt qui dedragma accipie⟨-⟩
to petre ⁊ cwedun to him lareu eower ne gald
bant ad petrum· Et dixerunt ei magister uester non soluit
casering he cwæþ gæ ⁊ þa he eode in us forec\`u´om
dedragma <25>án utiq(ue) et cum intrasset in domum præuenit
hine se hælend cweþende hwæt ðynceþ þe petre \`simon´ cyningas eorðu fro(m) hwæm
eum ie(su)s dicens· quid tibi uidetur simon reges terrae á qui⟨-⟩
andfoað gæfle oþþe hernisse fro(m) bearnum heora þe fro(m)
bus accipiunt tributum· Uel censum á filís suís án ab
fremðum cwæþ he fro(m) fremðum cwęþ to hi(m) se hælend hwæt þon(ne) freo
alienís <26>dicente autem eo ab alienis dixit illi ergo liberi
sindun þa bearn we þon(ne) þy les geincfulligæ hiæ gang to sǽ
sunt filii <27>ut autem non scandalizemus eos uade ad ma⟨-⟩
⁊ send hoc ðin ⁊ þone fisc ðe þe ærest upp
re et mitte amum tuum et eum piscem qui primum· as⟨-⟩
astigað genim ⁊ ontyn muð his gem\`o´etest ðær scilling
cenderit tolle et aperto ore eius inuenies ibi staturam
genim þonne selle heo(m) for mec ⁊ ðec on þære hwile eodun
illam sumens dá eis pro me et té:· <XVIII 1>In illa hora accesse⟨-⟩
þa leorneras to hælend cwęþende hwa wenest nu mare sie
runt discipuli ad ie(su)m dicentes quis putas maior est
in heofuna rice ⁊ cwæþ soþ ic sæcge eow nymþe ge gewerfe
in regno cælorum <3>et dixit amen dico uobis nisi conuersi
beon ⁊ gefremmende swa cnehtas ne gæþ ge in rice
fueritis et efficiamini sicut paruuli non intrabis in reg⟨-⟩
heofunas forþon swa hwa eadmedaþ hine swa cneht
num caelorum· <4>Quicumq(ue) humiliauerit sé sicut paruu⟨-⟩
þios þe is mare in rice heofunas ⁊ se þe on\`d´foeþ
lus iste hic maior in regno cælorum <5>et qui susciperit
anum swælce in noma minum cnæhte me andfoeþ
unum talem in nomine meo paruolum me suscipit·
se þe þonne afælleþ enne lytlera þissa
<6>qui autem scandalizauerit unum de pussillís istís

(f. 28r) 14 autem] *om.* Y WW **15** usque quo[1]] quo usque Y WW **16** illum huc] huc illum Y WW | eum] ei Xz Y WW=R **17** puer] + de illa ma[ ] R[Fa] (*in the right-hand margin with the gloss,* of ðære yfle) ex illa hora Y WW **18** secrete] secreto Y secrete et WW | ei] *om.* Y WW **19** et] *om.* Y WW **20** uestrum] uestram Y WW **21** ut] sicut Y WW **(f. 28v) 1** ieiunium et orationem] orationem et ieiunium Y WW **2** illis] eis Y WW **3** eis] illis Y WW | futurum est enim ut] *om.* Y WW | tradetur] tradendus est Y WW **4** occident] occidunt Y WW=R | tertia] tertio Y WW **5** uenissent] uenisset Y WW=R **7** ei] *om.* Y WW **8** án utiq(ue)] ait etiam Y WW | in] *om.* Y WW **11** dicente autem eo] et ille dixit Y WW | illi] + ie(su)s R[Fa] YWW **13** amum tuum] chamum Y hamum WW | primum] primus Y WW **(cont. on p. 143)**

ðe in mec gelefaþ beðearfeþ him ꝥ ahongen się cwern esules
qui in me credunt expedit ut suspendatur mola assi⟨-⟩
on swira his ⁊ he se besenked on grunde seæs
naria in collo eius et demergatur in profundum maris·
wá soþlice midda\`n´g(earde) þios fro(m) fælnissum ned is forþon cumende
<7>**Uae enim mundo huic a scandalis necesse est enim ue⟨-⟩**
æswic hweþre þonne wá þæm menn þe þurh hine
nire scandala· Uerumtamen uae homini illi per que(m)
æswic cymeþ gif þon(ne) honde þine oþþe foet þine
scandalum uenit <8>**si autem manus tua uel pes tuus**
æswicęþ ł fælleþ ðec asceorf hine ⁊ weorp fro(m) ðe god
scandalizat té abscide eam et proiece abs te bonu(m)
is ðe anhende to life oþþe healt þon(ne)
est tibi ingredi debilem ad uitam uel clodum quam
twa honda oþþe twa foet hæbbende się sended in ecce
duas manus uel duos pedes habenti mitti in æter⟨-⟩
fyr ⁊ gif eagan ðin æswiceþ ðec ahloca .ł ateo\`h´ of
nam igne(m)· <9>**Et si oculus tuus scandalizat té erue**
þæt ⁊ aweorp fro(m) ðe god is ðe mid an ege
eum et proiece abs te bonum est tibi unum oculum
hæbbende in lif gæ þon(ne) twa eagan
habentem in uitam intrare quam duos occulos ha⟨-⟩
hæbbende ⁊ sie gesended in helle fyres beseoh ꝥ ðe ne reuwe
bentem mitti in gehennam ignis· <10>**Uidete né condempna⟨-⟩**
enne ðissum lytilra :· :· :· :· ic sæcge f(or)þon
mini unum ex hís pussillís qui credunt in me dico enim
eowic ꝥ englas heora on heofunu(m) á´ geseoð andwlitu fæder
uobis quia oculi eorum semper uident faciem patris
mines þæs þe in heofunu(m) is cuom forþon sune monnes to gehęlanne
uestri qui in caelís est· <11>**Uenit enim filius hominis sal⟨-⟩**
ꝥte ær forwearð hwæt ðincaþ eow gif hæbbe
uare quod perierat· <12>**quid uobis uidetur si fuerint**
hwa hundteontig scípa ⁊ gedwalige an of ðara ah ne forleteþ
alicui ·c· oues et errauerit una ex eís nonne relinq(u)et
hundnigontig ⁊ nigon on dunum ⁊ gað soece þætte
nonagenta nouem in montib(us) et uadet querere eam quæ
gedwalade ⁊ gif gelimpeþ þæt he hit finde soþ ic sæcge
errauerit <13>**et si contingerit ut inueniet eam· amen dico**
eowic þæt he mare gefeaþ be þæm þonne be þæm
uobís quia magis gaudebit super eam quam super
hundnigontig ⁊ nigon þe ne gedwaladun swæ þonne nis
nonagenta nouem quae non errauerunt <14>**síc non est**
willan beforan fæder minum þæm þe in heofunum is
uoluntas ante patrem uestrum qui in caelís est

(f. 28v) 14 ibi staturam illam] staterem illum Y WW **17** cælorum] + ad uocans [ ]s paruulos [ ]tatuit in medio eoru(m) R^{Fa} (*in the left-hand margin with the gloss,* ⁊ to cegende [ ]lend cnæhtas sette þon(e) in [ ]idlæ heora) + et aduocans iesus paruulum statuit eum in medio eorum Y WW **18** intrabis] intrabitis R^{Fa} Y WW | regnum] regno Y WW **19** Quicumq(ue)] + ergo Y WW **20** hic] + est R^{Fa} Y WW **21** talem in nomine meo parauulum] paruolum talem in nomine meo R^{c} (*indicated by* signes de renvoi) Y WW
(f. 29r) 1 expedit] + ei R^{Fa} Y WW **3** enim[1]] *om.* Y WW | huic] *om.* Y WW | uenire] ut ueniant Y WW **4** illi] *om.* Y WW **7** est tibi ingredi debilem ad uitam] tibi est ad uitam ingredi debilem Y WW **8** habenti] habentem Y WW | in] *om.* Y^{*} Y^{c} WW=R **(cont. on p. 144)**

ꝥ to lose weorðe an of þisse lytra þonne gif firnige ł syngige
ut pariat unus de pussillís istis:· <15>Quod si peccauerit
in ðec broðer ðin gang ⁊ þreata hine betwih ðe ⁊ him
in te frater tuus uade et corripe eum inter te et ipsu(m)
anum gif þe gehereþ þu gestreonest broþer ðin
solum si té audierit lucratus és fratrem tuum
gif he þanne þe ne gehereþ genim mið þec þonne geta ænne
<16>si autem te non audierit· Adhibe tecum adhuc unum
oþþe twegen ꝥ in muþe twegen oþþe þreo gewitnesse stonde gehwilc
uel duos ut in ore duorum uel trium testium stet omne
word ⁊ gif he ne geherað þæm sæcge circan
uerbum <17>quod si non audierit eos dic aeclessiæ
⁊ gif he circan ne geherað beo þe swa hæþenna
quod si æclissiam non audierit sit tibi sicut pupli⟨-⟩
⁊ eawisfirina soþ ic sæcge eow swa hwylce swa ge bindaþ
canus et gentilis <18>amen dico uobis quæcumq(ue) alligaue⟨-⟩
on eorðe beoþ gebunden swilce on heofunu(m) ⁊ swa hwælc swa
ritis super terram erunt ligata et in cælo· et quæcumq(ue)
ge unbindaþ on eordan beoþan unbunden swilce on heofunu(m) eft
solueritis super terram erunt soluta et in cælo· <19>iterum
soþ ic sæcge eow ꝥ gif twegen eower geþafigaþ
amen dico uobis quia si duo ex uobis consenserint
on eorþan be ængum þinge swa hwæs swa he gebiddan geweorþe heo(m)
super terram de omni re quacumq(ue) petierint fiet illis
fro(m) fæder minu(m) þæ(m) þe in hefonu(m) is f(or)þon þe þær twege oþþe þreo
á patre meo qui in caelís est· <20>Ubi sunt duo uel tres con⟨-⟩
gesomnade in minum noman þær ⁊ ic eam in midle heora
gregati in nomine meo ibi et ego sum in medio eorum:·
þa cumende petre to him cwæþ to hi(m) dryht(en) hú gif
<21>Tunc accedens petrus ad eum dixit ei d(omi)ne quod si
eorsaþ in mec broþer min hu oft ⁊ ic forlete to hi(m)
peccauerit in me frater meus quoties dimittam ei
oþþe seofun siþu(m) cwęþ to hi(m) hælend ne cwæþ ic to þe oþ seofun siðum
usq(ue) in septies· <22>dicit illi ie(su)s non dico tibi usq(ue) in septies
ah oþ hundseofuntigum siðum forþon ðe wiðermeten is
sed usq(ue) ad septies septuagies:· <23>Ideo adsimilatum (est)
rice heofunas menn cyninge þæ(m) þe walde gerihtes monige
regnum cælorum homini regi· qui uoluit rationem ponere
mid esnas his ⁊ þa he ingonn gerihtes monige
cum seruís suís· <24>Et cum coepisset rationem ponere
broht wæs him an se þe scalde ten þusende
oblatus est ei unus qui debebat ·x· milia tallenta
þa he þa næfde hwonan he agefe heht hine
<25>cum autem non haberet unde redderet iusit eum

(f. 29r) 8 æternam igne(m) (æter- *and* -ne(m) *in rasura*)] ignem æternam R[c] ignem aeternam Y WW 10 est tibi] tibi est Y WW tibi] + cum R[Fa] Y WW=R[*] | unum oculum habentem] uno oculo Y unoculum WW 12 condempnamini] contemnatis Y WW 13 qui credunt in me] *om.* R[c] (*cancellation marked by a series of three-dot signs above the Latin*) Y WW 14 oculi] angeli R[Fa] Y WW | eorum] + in celis R[Fa] in caelis Y(cæ-) WW 15 uestri] mei R[Fa] Y WW 18 uadet] uadit Y WW 19 errauerit] errauit Y WW=R | inueniet] inueniat Y WW 20 magis] *om.* Y WW | eam] ea magis Y eam magis WW 22 uestrum] meum R[Fa] Y WW=R[*]
(f. 29v) 1 pariat] pereat Y WW | Quod si] si autem Y WW 3 és] eris Y WW Xz=R 4 te non] non te Y WW 5 uel trium testium] testium uel trium Y WW (cont. on p. 145)

se hlaford his bebycgan ⁊ wif his ⁊ sunu
dominus eius uenundari et uxorem eius et filios

his ⁊ eall þætte he hæfde ⁊ agefnæ beon þa scylde
eius et omnia quae habebant et reddi debitum

swa micle forþfællende þa se esne bedd
tantum <26>procedens autem seruus ille rogabat

hine cwæðende geðyld hæfe in mec hlaford ⁊ eall
eum dicens patientiam habe in me d(omi)ne et omnia

agefe ic þe miltsende þa his hlaford þæ(m) esne his ⁊ for⟨-⟩
reddam tibi <27>misertus est autem d(omi)n(u)s serui illius di⟨-⟩

let hine ⁊ þa scyld forlet wið hine út gangende þa
misit eum· Et debitum remisit ei· <28>egressus autem

se esne gemoette ænne æfnþara his se þe sculde
seruus ille inuenit unum de conseruís suís qui de⟨-⟩

him hundred denera ⁊ genimende smorede hine
bebat ei ·c· denarios· Et tenens soffocabat eum

cwæþende agef þæt ðu scealt ⁊ forþfællende se his efnþeuw
dicens redde quod debes· <29>Et procedens conseruus

bed hine cweþende geþyld hæfe in mec ⁊
eius rogabat eum dicens patientiam habe in me et

eall ageofu ðe he þa ꝥ ne wolde ah eode ⁊ sende
omnia reddam tibi· <30>ille autem noluit sed habiit et mis⟨-⟩

hine in carcern oþ þæt he agæfe þa scyld geseonde
sit eum in carcerem donec redderet debitum <31>uidentes

þa ęfnðeuwe his þa þe þær gewurdun geunrotsade węron
autem conserui eius quae fiebant contristati sunt

swiðe cwoman ⁊ sægdon dryhtne heora eall ꝥ ðe ðær
ualde uenerunt et nuntiauerunt d(omi)no suo omnia quæ

gedoan weron þa gecægde him dryht(en) his ⁊ cwæþ to him
facta fuerant· <32>Tunc uocauit illum d(omi)n(u)s suus ait ille

þu esne nawiht ealle þa scylde ic forlet þe forþon
serue nequam omne debitum demisi tibi quoniam

ðe þu bede me ah þe ne gedæfnade ek ꝥte ðu miltsade ęfn⟨-⟩
rogasti me <33>nonne ergo oportuerat et té misereri con⟨-⟩

ðeuw þinum swa ic ðe miltsade ⁊ þa eorra his dryhten
seruo tuo· sicut et tui misertus sum· <34>et iratus est d(omi)n(u)s

wæs ⁊ salde hine tint(er)ga þægnu(m) oþ þætte he agefe
eius et tradidit eum tortoribus quoad usq(ue) redde⟨-⟩

ealle þa scylde swæ ⁊ swilce fæder min se heofunlica
ret uniuersum debitum· <35>síc et pater meus caelestis fa⟨-⟩

dóeþ eow gif ge ne forletaþ anra gehwylc broþer his
ciet uobis si non remiseritis unusquisq(ue) fratri suo

of eortum eowrum ⁊ gelamp þa geendade
de cordib(us) uestrís:· <XIX 1>Et factum est cum consummasset

se hælend
ie(su)s

(**f. 29v**) **7** quod si] si autem et Y WW | puplicanus et gentilis] ethnicus et publicanus Y WW **11** amen] *om.* Y WW **12** quacumq(ue)] quaecumque Y WW=R **13** ubi] + enim Y WW **14** et ego] *om.* Y WW **15** ei] *om.* Y WW | quod si] quotiens Y WW **16** peccauerit] peccabit Y WW | quoties] et Y WW **17** in[1, 2]] *om.* Y WW **18** ad septies septuagies] septuagies septies Y WW

(**f. 30r**) **1** eius[1]] *om.* Y WW **2** eius] *om.* Y WW | habebant] habebat Y WW | debitum tantum] debitum Y *om.* WW **3** rogabat] orabat Y WW **4** d(omi)ne] om. Y WW **5** est] *om.* Y WW **6** remisit] dimisit Y WW **(cont. on p. 146)**

word þas geleorde he fro(m) galilea ⁊
sermones istos transtullit sé a galilea et
cwom in mære iudeana be londe iordanen ⁊ fylgadun
uenit in fines iudae trans iodanen· <2>et secutae
him mængu monige ⁊ gehǽlde hie þær
sunt eum turbae multae· Et curauit eos ibi
⁊ cwomun to him fariseas costade
<3>et accesserunt ad eum farissæi· temptantes
his ⁊ cweþende mót monn forletan wif
eum dicebant· si licet homini dimittere uxore(m)
his for ænigum intinge he ondswarede cwæþ
suam quacumq(ue) ex causa <4>qui respondens ait
to heo(m) ah ge ne reordade þæt se þe worhte fro(m) fruman god wepned
eis non legistis quia qui fecit ab initio d(eu)s mas⟨-⟩
⁊ wif geworhte hiæ god ⁊ cwæþ for þon
culum et feminam fecit eos d(eu)s <5>et dixit propter
ðingu(m) forleteþ monn fæder ⁊ moder ⁊ ætclifað
hoc demittet homo patrem et matrem et adherebit
his wife ⁊ beoþ twægen in lice anum forþon ne
uxori suae et erunt duo in carne una <6>itaq(ue) non
sindun twægen ah án líc ꝥte þonne god gegadrade
sunt duo sed una caro· Quod ergo d(eu)s coniunxit
monn ne sceade cwædun hie ah hwæt moyses
homo non seperat· <7>Dicunt illi quid ergo moyses
bebead ꝥ monn salde boec aweorpnisse ⁊ forlete
mandauit dari libellum repudi et dimittere
cwęþ he to heo(m) forþon þe moyses to heardnisse heortan
<8>Ait illis quoniam moyses ad duritiam cordis
eowre let eowic forletan wif eowra
uestri permist uobis dimittere uxores uestras
fro(m) fruman þonne ne wæs swæ ic sæcge þanne eow
ab initio autem non sic fuit <9>dico autem uobis
ꝥ swa hwa swa forleteþ his wif nymðe fore
quia quicumq(ue) diserit uxorem suam sine causa
forlegernisse ⁊ him oþer lædeþ he forlegenisse fremmaþ
fornicationis et aliam duxerit iam mechatur
⁊ se þe forletnisse lædaþ forlægnisse fremmaþ
et qui demisam duxerit iam mechatur· <10>Di⟨-⟩
cwedon him to leorneras his gif swa is intinge menn
cunt ei discipuli eius si ita est causa homi⟨-⟩
wið wife ne beþærfeþ ꝥ monn hęme he cwæþ
nis cum uxore non expedit nubere <11>qui dixit
ne ealle nimaþ word þas ah ðæm
non omnes capiunt uerbum istum sed quib(us)
þe sald wæs
datum est

(f. 30r) 14 ualde] + et Y WW | nuntiauerunt] narrauerunt Y WW | fuerant] erant Y WW **15** suus] + et Y WW | ille] illi Y WW **17** nonne] non Y WW Y[Ald]=R | oportuerat] oportuit Y WW | consero tuo] conseri tui Y WW **18** et[1]] + ego Y WW | est] *om.* Y WW **19** et] *om.* Y WW
(f. 30v) 1 transtullit sé] migrauit Y WW **2** iodanen] iordanen R[Fa] Y WW **5** dicebant] et dicentes Y WW **7, 8** d(eu)s] *om.* Y WW **9** demittet] dimittit Y dimittet WW **10** itaque] + iam Y WW **12** seperat] separet Y WW **13** libellum] librum Y WW=R **17** diserit] dimiserit R[Fa] Y WW **(cont. on p. 147)**

f(or)þon sindun afyrde þa þe of moder hrife swa akende werun
<12>sunt iunuchi qui de matris utero sic nati sunt

⁊ sindun afyrde þa þe wurdon fro(m) monnu(m) ⁊ sindun
et sunt iunuchi qui facti sunt ab hominib(us) et sunt

afyrde þa þe hie sylfum afyrdun for
iunuchi qui sé ipsos iunuchauerunt propter

rice heofunas se þe mæg nioman nime
regnum caelorum qui potest capere capiat:·

þa brohte weron him cild ꝥ he honda hiæ on
<13>Tunc oblati sunt ei paruuli ut manus eis in⟨-⟩

sette ⁊ gebede þa leorneras þonne his
poneret· et curaret discipuli autem eius in⟨-⟩

geþreatadun ł steordon hie hælend þa cwæþ to heom leteþ
crepabant eos· <14>ie(su)s autem ait eis· sinite

þa cild ł lytlingan cuman to me ⁊ ne hię wernað ł forbeode
paruulos uenire ad me et nolite eos prohibere

swilce is forþon rice heofunas ⁊ þa
talium est enim regnum caelorum· <15>Et cum in⟨-⟩

sette on hiæ honda ⁊ eode ðonan ⁊ henu ł sihþe
possuisset eis manus abiit inde:· <16>Et ecce

an cumende cwæþ hi(m) to lareuw good hwæt godes
unus accedens ait illi magister bone quid boni

dóm ic ꝥ ic hæbbe lifes æce he cwæþ
faciam ut habeam uitam aeternam· <17>qui dixit

him to hwæt ðu mec geaxast ł frægnast be góde an is gód
ei quid me interrogas de bono unus (est) bonus

god gif ðu þonne wilt innga to life hald bebodu
d(eu)s· si autem uís uenire ad uitam serua mandata

cwæþ he hwælc hælend þa cwæþ to hi(m) ne þu
<18>dixit illi quae sunt· ie(su)s autem dixit ei non homi⟨-⟩

morður ne fremme ne do þu unrihthæmed ne fre(m)me stale
cidium facies non adulterabis· non facies fur⟨-⟩

ne lyge gewitnisse sæcge áre
tum· non falsum testimonium dices· <19>honora

fæder ðin ⁊ moder ðin ⁊ lufige þa nehstu(m)
patrem tuum et matrem tuam· Et dileges proxi⟨-⟩

ðinum swa þæc seolfne cwæþ hi(m) to se iungæ
mum tuum sicut te ipsum· <20>Dicit illi adoles⟨-⟩

eall ic þas geheold fro(m) iuguðe mine
cens omnia haec custodiui á iuuentute mea·

hwæt nu gęn is me woen cwæþ heo(m) to se hælend gif þu wilt wisfæstre
Quid adhuc mihi deest· <21>Dicit illi ie(su)s si uis per⟨-⟩

ł doefe beon ga ⁊ sylle ł bebycge eall þa gód
fectus esse uade et uende omnia bona

(f. 30v) 17 sine causa fornicationis] nisi ob fornicationem Y WW 18, 19 iam] *om.* Y WW 20 hominis] homini Y WW | uxore] muliere Y WW Xz=R 22 istum] istud Y WW

(f. 31r) 1 sunt[1]] + enim Y WW 2 qui] *om.* Y WW=R 3 iunuchauerunt] castrauerunt Y WW 6 curaret] oraret Y WW | eius] *om.* Y WW 7 eos] eis Xz Y WW=R | autem] uero Y WW 8 uenire ad me et nolite eos prohibere] et nolite eos prohibere uenire ad me Y WW 14 uenire ad uitam] ad uitam ingredi Y WW 15 dixit] dicit Y WW | sunt] *om.* Y WW | ei] *om.* Y WW 18 tuum] *om.* Y WW | tuam] *om.* Y WW 20 á iuuentute mea] *om.* Y WW 21 Dicit] ait Y WW 22 et] *om.* Y WW | ominia bona] *om.* Y WW

xƀ þæt þu hæfest ꝥ selle ðearfu(m) ꝥ þu hæfest hórd
Quae habes et da pauperib(us) et habebis thes⟨-⟩
in heofunu(m) ꝥ cym folga me þa gehýrde
aurum in caelo et ueni sequere· <22>Cum audisset
þæt se iunge word þæt eode awæg unbliðe
autem adolescens uerba haec habiit tristis
f(or)þon þe he monige hæfde æhte
Erat autem multas habens possessiones·
hælend þa cwæþ to leorneras his soð ic sæcge eow
<23>ie(su)s autem dixit discipulís suís· Amen dico uobis
þæt se weliga uneaþe gæþ in heofuna rice
quia diues dificile est intrare in regnum cælo⟨-⟩
ꝥ æft ic sæcge eow eþre is olbend
rum <24>et iterum dico uobis facilius est camellum
þurh ðyrel nedle to lioranne þon(ne) þæ(m) welgan
per foramen acus transire quam diuitem in⟨-⟩
to gangene in heofuna rice þa geyrdon þæt þa
trare in regnum cælorum· <25>Auditís autem his
leorneras wundradun ꝥ dreordun swiþe cweþende
Discipuli mirabantur et timebunt ualde dicen⟨-⟩
hwa þon(ne) mæg hal beon lokende
tes quis ergo potest saluus esse <26>aspiciens
þa se hæl(end) cwæþ to heo(m) mið monnu(m) þæt uneaðe
autem ie(su)s dixit illis apud homines hoc inpossi⟨-⟩
is mið god þonne eall eaðe sindun þa
bile est apud d(eu)m omnia possibilia sunt <27>tunc
andswarade ꝥ cwæþ to him sihþe we forleortun
respondit petrus et dixit ei· ecce nos relin⟨-⟩
eall ꝥ folgadun ðe hwæt þonne
quimus omnia et secuti sumus té quid ergo
biþ us hæl(end) þa cwæþ to heo(m) soþ ic secge
erit nobis <28>ie(su)s autem dixit illís Amen dico
eow þæt ge þe fylgende arun me in æftaken⟨-⟩
uobis quod uos qui secuti estis me in genera⟨-⟩
nisse ðisse þon(ne) sitteþ sunu monnes
tione ista· Cum sederit filius hominis in
in sedle ðrymmes his ge sittaþ ꝥ ek on
sede maiestatis suae sedebitis et uos super
sedlum twelfe doemende twelfe cynn israheles
sedes ·xii· iudicantes ·xii· tribus israhel·
ꝥ æghwilc þon(ne) ðe forleteþ hus oþþe broþer
<29>et omnis qui reliquerit domum aut fratres
oþþe swust(er) oþþe fæder oþþ moder oþþe
aut sorores aut patrem aut matrem aut
wif
uxorem

2 sequere] + me Y WW 3 uerba haec] uerbum Y WW 4 autem] enim Y WW | multas habens] habens multas Y WW 6 est intrare] intrabit Y WW | regnum] regno Y WW=R 10 mirabantur] mirantur Y* Y^c WW=R | et timebunt] *om.* Y WW 11 potest] poterit Y WW 13 d(eu)m] + autem R^Fa Y WW 14 respondit petrus et] respondens petrus Y WW | relinquimus] reliquimus WW Y=R 18 generatione ista] regeratione Y WW 21 reliquerit] relinquerit R^Fa reliquit Y WW | aut] uel Y WW

oþþe bearn oþþe lond for noman minu(m)
aut filios aut agros propter nomen meum·
hundteantigfalde onfooþ her ⁊ lif æce
centuplum accipiet hic· Et uitam aeternam
gesitteþ monige þon(ne) beoþan þa ærestu
possidebit· <30>Multi autem erunt nouissimi
nęhstu ⁊ þa næhstu ærestu gelice is rice
primi· et primi nouissimi:· <XX 1>Simile est regnum
heofunas monn fæder hina ðæ(m) ðe eode on ærne⟨-⟩
caelorum homini patri familias qui exít primo
morgen bycgæ wyrhta in wingeard his
mane conducere operarios in uineam suam·
⁊ þa geþingadun wið þæ(m) wyrhtu(m)
<2>Conuentione autem facta cum operarius
be dinere deglicu(m) sende hio in þone wingeard
ex denario deurno misit eos in uiniam suam·
⁊ ut eode æt þære ðridda tid ł hwile gesæh oþre
<3>et egresus circa horam tertiam uidit alios
standende on protbore unnytte ⁊ cwæþ to heom gæþ ge ek
stantes in foro otiosos <4>et dixit illís ite et uos
in wingeard mine ⁊ þætte reht biþ ic selle
in uineam meam et quod iustum fuerit dabo
eow hie þa eodun eft ut eode æt þæ(m)
uobis illi autem abierunt· <5>Iterum exiit circa
sextan ⁊ þæ(m) nigoþan tide ł hwile ⁊ dyde gelice
sextam et nonam horam et fecit similiter
æt þære ællefta soþlice tide þa eode ut ⁊ gemette oþre standende
<6>circa xi· uero horam exiit et uidit alios stan⟨-⟩
⁊ cwæð to þæm hwæt stondeþ ge her unnytte ealne
tes· et dixit illis quid hic statis otiosi tota
dæg cwædun hie f(or)þon nænig usic mið leane gebohte cwæþ to
die <7>dicunt ei quia nemo nos conduxit dicit
heom gáþ ge ek swilce in wingeard mine þa hit þa
illis ite et uos in uiniam meam· <8>Cum autem
efen geworden wæs cwæþ he se hlaford þæs wingeardes to his
serum factum esset dicit d(omi)n(u)s uiniae procu⟨-⟩
geroefa cege þæ(m) wyrhtum ⁊ gef heom
ratori suo uoca operarios et redde illis
heora lean ingingende fro(m) þæ(m) næhstum oþ þe
mercidem incipiens á nouissimís usq(ue) ad
ærestu þa cumende þa þe æt þære elleftan
primos· <9>Cum uenissent ergo qui circa ·ximam
hwile ł tide comen ⁊fengon æghwilc anum dinere
horam uenerant accipierunt singulos denarios

2 hic] *om.* Y WW 3 nouissimi primi et primi nouissimi] primi nouissimi et nouissimi primi Y WW 4 est] + enim Y WW 7 operarius] operariis Y WW 8 suam] *om.* Y WW=R 10 dixit illis] illis dixt Y WW 11 meam] *om.* Y WW 12 Iterum] + autem Y WW 14 xi uero horam] undecimam uero Y WW | uidit] inuenit R[Fa] Y WW 15 dixit] dicit Y WW | otiosi tota die] tota die otiose Y WW 17 meam] *om.* Y WW | autem serum] sero autem Y WW 22 accipierunt] acceperunt Y WW

cumende þa ek þa ærestu wendon þæt hie mare
<10>uenientes autem primi arbitrati sunt quod plus
sculdon onfoon onfengon ˥ hie þon(ne) swilce anum
essent accepturi acciperunt et ipsi singulos
xƀ dinere ˥ þa onfengon grornadun wið þæm
denarios· <11>Et accipientes murmurabant aduersus
fæder hina cweþende þas næhstu ane tide
patrem familias <12>dicentes hii nouissimi unam hora(m)
worhtun ˥ gelice þu hiæ us dydest we þe beron
fecerunt et pares illos nobis fecisti qui portaui⟨-⟩
mægen þisses dæges ˥ hǽtu ˥ he ondswarede anum
mus pundus diei et estum <13>at ille respondens uni
heora ˥ cwæþ freond ne do ic ðe teane ah ðu
eorum dixit amicae non facio tibi iniuriam nonne
be dinere dęglicu(m) geþingdest wið me genim þætte
ex dinario diurno conuenisti mecum <14>tolle quod
þin is ˥ ga ic wille ek ˥ ðissu(m) næhsta
tuum est et uade uolo autem et huic nouissimo
sellan swilce ˥ þe ah me is alæfed to sellan min þæt
dare sicut et tibi <15>aut non licet mihi dare mea quod⟨-⟩
ic wille doan þa egan þin nawiht is f(or)þon
q(ue) uolo facere án oculus tuus nequam est quia ego
þe god ic eam swa beoþ þa næhstu æreste ˥ þa eristu
bonus sum· <16>sic erunt nouissimi primi· et primi
næhstu monige forþon sindun gecęged ˥ feawe soðlice
nouissimi· multi enim sunt uocati pauci uero
gecoren ˥ astigende hæl(end) hierusolimis ge⟨-⟩
electi:· <17>Et ascendens ie(su)s hierusolimam ad⟨-⟩
nom þa twelf leorneras his degullice ˥ cwæþ to heo(m)
sumpsit xii discipulos suos secreto et ait illis
henu we astigað ˥ sunu
<18>ecce ascendimus hierusolimam et filius ho⟨-⟩
monnes bið sald aldorsacerd
minis tradetur principibus sacerdotum·
˥ bokerum ˥ gedoemeþ hine to deade ˥
et scribís et condempnabunt eum morte <19>et tra⟨-⟩
sellaþ hine ðeodum to bismerene ˥ to swinganne
dent eum gentibus ad deludendum et flagillan⟨-⟩
˥ to hóanne ˥ ðrydda dæg eftariseþ
dum et crucifigendum et tertia die resurget:·
þa eode to him moder sunu zebedes
<20>Tunc accessit ad eum mater filiorum zebedei
mid sunu hire to gebiddanne ˥ hine boensendu hwæthwugu fro(m) him
cum filís suís adorans et petiens aliquid ab eo

1 autem] + et Y WW 2 acciperunt] acceperunt autem Y WW 4 unam hora(m)] una hora Y WW 8 diurno] *om.* Y WW 10 dare mea quodq(ue)] quod Y WW 13 enim sunt] sunt enim Y WW | uero] autem Y WW 15 suos] *om.* Y WW 22 petiens] petens R^c Y WW

cwæþ he to hire hwæt wiltu cwæþ hio cwæþ þæt sittæ þas twægen
<21>Qui dixit ei quid uis· at illi ut sedeant hii duo
sunæ an on þa swiðran healfe þine ⁊ oþer on þa winstran healfe
filii unus ad dexteram tuam et unus et sinistra(m)
þin in rice þinum ondswarade þa heom se hælend
tuam in regno tuo· <22>respondens autem illis ie(su)s
⁊ cwæþ ge nytan hwæt ge bidaþ magon git ðene kælic
dixit nescitis quid petatis potestis calicem
drincan þe ic drincande beom cwædun hię wit
bibere quem ego bibiturus sum· Dicunt ei pos(-)
magun cwæþ he to heo(m) se hæl(end) kælic git minne drincan
simus <23>ait illis ie(su)s calicem quidem meum bibitis
sitte git þonne on þa swiðran halfe min ⁊ þa winstran
sedere autem ad dexteram aut ad senistra(m)
min nis me to sellanne inc ah ðęm ðe iarward
meam non est meum dare uobis sed quib(us) para(-)
is fro(m) fæder minum ⁊ geherende þa tene abolgenne
tum est á patre meo· <24>et audientes xii indigna(-)
werun be þæ(m) twæm broþru(m) hælend þa ceigde
ti sunt de dub(us) fratrib(us) <25>ie(su)s autem uocauit
þæm to him ⁊ cwæþ ge cunun þæt ðeoda aldormenn
eos ad sé ait scitis quia gentium principes
agun gewald þara .ł heora ⁊ þa þe mare sindun
Dominantur eorum· et qui maiores sunt potes(-)
mæhte begæþ ofer heo ne bið swa betwihc eow
tatem exercent in eos· <26>Non ita erit inter uos
ah swa hwa swa wille betwix eow mare geweorðan
sed quicumq(ue) uoluerit inter uos maior fieri
beo he eower ðægn ⁊ se þe wile betwix eow
sit uester minister· <27>et qui uoluerit inter uos
se forma beon beo he eower esne swa sunu
primus esse erit uester seruus· <28>sicut filius
monnes ne cwom ꝥ hi(m) wære ðægnad ah he ðægnade
hominis non uenit ministrari sed ministrare
⁊ salde ferh his for mongu(m) to alesnisse
et dare animam suam pro multis redemptione(m):·
⁊ þa ut eodun hiæ fro(m) hiericho folgadun him
<29>Egredientib(us) eis ab hiericho secutae sunt eu(m)
micel mengu ⁊ henu twægen blinde sittende bi ðæ(m)
turbae multae <30>et ecce duo ceci sedentes secus
wæge geherdun ꝥ se hælend foerde .ł liorde ⁊ cliopadun
uiam audierunt quia ie(su)s transiret et clama(-)
cwæþende dryht(en) miltsa unc sunu dauiðes
uerunt dicentes d(omi)ne miserere nostri fili dauid·

1 at] ait Y WW | illi] + dic R^{Fa} Y WW 2 filii] + mei R^{Fa} (*in the left-hand margin with the gloss,* mine) Y WW | et^{2}] ad R^{Fa} Y WW 3 tuam] *om.* Y WW | illis] *om.* Y WW 4 calicem bibere] bibere calicem Y WW 5 possimus] posumus Y possumus WW 6 ie(su)s] *om.* Y WW | bibitis] bibetis Y WW 7 dexteram] + mea(m) R^{Fa} Y WW | aut ad senistra(m) meam] et sinistram Y WW 9 xii] x R^{c} decem Y WW 10 dub(us)] duobus R^{Fa} Y WW 11 se] + et Y WW | gentium principes] principes gentium R^{c} (*indicated by* signes de renvoi) Y WW 18 pro multis redemptione(m)] redemptionem pro multis R^{c} (*indicated by* signes de renvoi) Y(redemt-) WW 19 Egredientib(us)] et egredientibus R^{c} Y WW | eis] illis Y WW Xz=R | secutae sunt eu(m) turbae multae] secuta est eum turba multa Y WW

sio mengu þa ðreattan hiæ ꝥ hí swigadun ⁊ hiæ
<31>turba autem increpabat eos ut tacerent at illi
swiðor cleopadun cweþende gemiltsa unc
magis clamabant dicentes misserere nostri
sunu dauiðes ⁊ gestód se hæl(end) ⁊ cliopade heom ⁊ cwæþ hwæt
filii dauid <32>et stetit ie(su)s et uocauit eos· Et ait quid
willaþ git ꝥ ic do eow cwædun heo dryht(en) ꝥ ontyned sie
uultis ut faciam uobis <33>dicunt ei d(omi)ne ut aperian⟨-⟩
egna ure miltsende þa heom se hælend ⁊ hrán
tur oculi ·n(ostr)i· <34>misertus est autem eorum ie(su)s et te⟨-⟩
egum heora ⁊ sona gesęgun ⁊ folgadun
tigit oculos eorum et confestim uiderunt secuti
him ⁊ þa hiæ nealehctun hierusalem ⁊ coman to beþfage
sunt eum:· <XXI 1>Et cum adpropinquassent beth⟨-⟩
to oelebearwes dune þa hæl(end) sende twægen leorneras
fage ad montem olieti· tunc ie(su)s misit discipulos
cwæþende to heo(m) gáð in þas cæstre þe beforan inc is ⁊ sonæ
<2>dicens ite in castellum quod contra uos est et sta⟨-⟩
git moeteþ ę\o/sul gesælde ⁊ folan mid
tim inuenietis assinam alligatam et pullum cu(m)
hire unsæleþ ⁊ ledað to me ⁊ gif hwa eow .ł inc
ea· soluite et adducite mihi· <3>et si quis uobis
awiht to cwæþe sæcgaþ þæt dryht(en) heora ðearf
aliquid dixerit dicite quia d(omi)n(u)s hís opus habet
⁊ sonæ forleteð heo þæt þonne eall
et confestim demittet uobis <4>hoc autem totum fac⟨-⟩
geworden wæs þæt gefylled wære þætte gecwæden wæs þurh essaia(m)
tum est ut adinplere quod dictum est per esseia(m)
se witga cwæðende sæcgaþ dohter sione henu cyningc
profetam dicentem <5>dicite filiae sión· Ecce rex
þin cymeþ ðe monnðwære ⁊ sittende on
tuus uenit tibi mansuetus et sedens super
eosule ⁊ on folan sunu þære teoma gangende þa
assinam et pullum subiugalem <6>euntes autem dis⟨-⟩
dydon swa bebead heom hæl(end) ⁊ to⟨-⟩
cipuli fecerunt sicut praecipit illís ie(su)s· <7>et ad⟨-⟩
brohtun eosula ⁊ fola ⁊ onbręddon
duxerunt assinam et pullum· et inpossuerunt
on heo hrægl heora ⁊ hine onufan sittende dydun
ei uestimenta sua· et eum desuper sedere fecerunt
sio mæste þa mængu strægdun hrægl
<8>plurimae autem turbae strauerunt uestimenta
heora on þæ(m) wege sume þon(ne) sneddun telgran of treowum
sua in uia· alii autem cedebant ramos de arboribus(us)

2 dicentes] + domine Y WW 4 ei] illi Y WW 5 est] *om.* Y WW | et] *om.* Y WW 7 adpropinquassent] + hierosolimis ⁊ uenissent R[Fa] hierosolymis et uenissent Y WW 8 misit] + duos R[Fa] Y WW 9 dicens] + illis R[Fa] + eis Y WW 13 uobis] eos Y WW | totum] *om.* Y WW 14 adinplere] adinpleretur R[Fa] impleretur Y WW | esseia(m)] *om.* Y WW 17 pullum] + filium R[Fa] Y WW | subiugalem] subiugalis Y WW 18 praecipit] praecepit Y WW 20 ei] super eis Y WW 21 plurimae autem turbae] plurima autem turba Y WW

xƀ ⁊ strægdun on þæ(m) wæge þa mengu þon(ne) þa þe beforaneodan
Et sternebant in uia· <9>Turba autem quae cedebat
⁊ þa þe æftereodun cleopadun cwæþende gehǽl
et quae secebatur clamabant dicentes ossi⟨-⟩
sunu dauiðes gebloetsad se þe cymeþ in noman
anna filii dauid benedictus qui uenit in nomine
dryht(nes) gehǽl in heanissum ⁊ þa he eode in hie⟨-⟩
d(omi)ni ossianna in excelsís· <10>Et cum introisset hie⟨-⟩
rusalem inhroered wæs eall sie ceastre cwæðende
rusolimam commota est uniuersa ciuitas· dicens
hwæt is þes ꝥ folc þa sægde þis is hælend se
quis est hic <11>populi autem dicebant· hic est ie(su)s pro⟨-⟩
witga fro(m) nazareþ galilea ⁊ eode se hæl(end) in tempel
feta a nazareth galileae· <12>Et intrauit ie(su)s in tem⟨-⟩
godes ⁊ wearp ut ealle þa sellende ⁊ gebycgende in
plum d(e)i et iecebat omnes uendentes et ementes in
þæm temple ⁊ béod þara mynetræ ⁊ settlas
templo· Et mensas nummulariorum· et cathedras
þa sellendum culfran afældę ⁊ cwæþ to heo(m) awriten is
uendentium columbas euertit· <13>Dicit eis scriptu(m) (est)
f(or)þon ꝥ hus min bið gebedes hus genemned
enim quia domus mea domus orationis uocabitur
eallum ðeodum ge þon(ne) gedydon hit to gescræfe
omnibus gentibus uos autem fecistis eam speloncа(m)
ðiofas ł scaþena ⁊ eodun to him blinde ⁊ healte
latronum· <14>Et accesserunt ad eum caeci et claudi
in þæ(m) temple ⁊ he gehælde þa gesegon þa aldur⟨-⟩
in templo et sanauit eos· <15>Uidentes autem princi⟨-⟩
sacerdos ⁊ bokeras ꝥ wundur ðe worhte
pes sacerdotum et scribae mirabilia quae fecit
se hæl(end) ⁊ cnæhtas clipigende in þæ(m) temple ⁊ cwæþende
ie(su)s et pueros clamantes in templo et dicentes
gehǽl sunu dauiðes hí þa abolgenne weron ⁊ cwædun
ossianna filii dauid indignati sunt· <16>et dixer(u)nt
to him geherest ðu hwæt þas sæcgaþ hæl(end) þa cwæþ to heo(m)
ei audis quid isti dicunt· ie(su)s autem dixit eis
hwæt ge næfre reordadun þæt of muðe cildra ⁊ sukendra ł diendra
utiq(ue) non legistis quia ex ore infantium et lactan⟨-⟩
þu gefylldęst lof ⁊ forletende hiæ eode ut
tium perfecisti laudem <17>et relictís illís abiit foras
of þara ceastræ in bethaniæ ⁊ þær wunade
extra ciuitatem in bethaniam et ibi mansit
on mærgne þa æft wę̨rfende in ceastre hungrig ł hingrade
<18>mane autem reuertens in ciuitatem esuriit·

1 Turba] turbae Y WW | cedebat] praecedebant Y WW 2 secebatur] sequebantur Y WW 3 filii] filio Y WW | uenit] uenturus est Y WW 4 excelsís] altissimis Y WW | introisset] intrasset Y WW 6 populi autem dicebant] populus autem dicebat Y WW=R 8 iecebat] eiciebat Y WW 10 euertit] et uertit Y WW=R 10 Dicit] et dicit Y WW 11 enim quia] *om.* Y WW 12 omnibus gentibus] *om.* Y WW | eam] illam Y WW Xz=R 16 ie(su)s] *om.* Y WW 17 filii] filio Y WW 18 dicunt] dicant Y WW | dixit] dicit Y WW 19 non] numquam Y WW 21 et ibi] ibique Y WW

⁊ sæh treow fices an bi wæge ⁊ cuom
<19>Et uidit arborem fici unam secus uiam· et uenit
to þæ(m) ⁊ nauwiht gemoette on hi(m) nymþe leaf efnæ
ad eam et nihil inuenit in ea nisi folia tantum·
⁊ cwæþ to him næfre of ðe siæ wæstim akenned in ek⟨-⟩
et ait illi numquam ex té fructus nascatur in se(m)⟨-⟩
nisse ⁊ forwisnade sonæ ł instyde se fic
piternum· et arida facta est continuo ficulnia·
⁊ gesegon ða leorneras wundradun cwæþende
<20>Et uidentes discipuli mirati sunt dicentes quo⟨-⟩
hu instyde adrugade se fic ondswarede þa
modo continuo aruit ficulnia· <21>respondens aute(m)
se hæl(end) soð ic sæcge eow gif ge hæfdon gele`a´fu ⁊ ne
ie(su)s amen dico uobis si habueritis fidem et non
twigaþ nælles be fice anum doaþ
hessitaueritis non solum de ficulnia facietis
ah swilce to dune þissere þæh þe ge cweðe hef ðæc ⁊ wearp in sǽ
et si monti huic dixeritis tolle té et mitte in mare
þ geweorþað ⁊ eallu(m) swa hwæt swa ge biddað in gebedę
fiet· <22>et omnia quaecumq(ue) petieritis in oratione
gelæfende ge ondfooð ⁊ þa he cwo(m) in tempel
credentes accipietis:· <23>Et cum uenisset in templum
eodun to him aldorsacerdas ⁊ eldre
accesserunt ad eum principes sacerdotum et seni⟨-⟩
þæs folcęs cwæþende in hwæs ł hwilcę mæhte þas ðu wircest .ł doest
ores populi dicentes in qua potestate haec facis
⁊ swa salde ðe þas mæht onswarade þa
et quis dedit tibi hanc potestatem <24>respondens aute(m)
se hæl(end) cwæþ to heo(m) ic ahsige eow ⁊ ek anes wordes
ie(su)s dixit illis interrogabo uos et ego unum sermone(m)
sæcgaþ me þ þon(ne) gif ge sæcgaþ me ⁊ ic ek eow sæcge
dicite mihi quem si dixeritis mihi et ego uobis dicam
in wilce mæhte ic þas do ł wyrce fullwiht iohan(nes)
in qua potestate haec facio· <25>baptismum iohannem
hwonan wæs of heofunu(m) ðe of monnu(m) hí þa þohtun
unde erat e caelo án ex hominib(us) at illi cogitabant
betwihs heo(m) cwæþende gif we cwęþaþ of heofunu(m) he cwæþ to us
intra sé dicentes sí dixerimus e caelo dicet nobis
forhwon ne gelefdan ge him gif we þon(ne) cweðaþ
quare non credidistis illi· <26>si autem dixerimus
of monnu(m) we us ondredaþ þas mængu ealle forþon
ex hominibus timemus turbam· omnes eni(m) habe⟨-⟩
habbaþ iohan(nem) swa witga ⁊ þa onswarade
bant iohannem sunt profetam·<27>et responden⟨-⟩
tes

1 uidit] uidens Y WW | arborem fici] fici arborem Y WW | et[2]] *om.* Y WW 4 arida facta] arefacta Y WW 6 ficulnia] *om.* Y WW 7 ie(su)s] + ait illis R^{Fa} (*in the left-hand margin with the gloss,* cwæþ to heo(m)) ait eis Y WW 8 facietis] + sed Y WW | té et mitte] et iacta te Y WW 12 eum] + docentem Y WW 14 dedit tibi] tibi dedit Y WW | aute(m)] *om.* Y WW 16 dicite mihi] *om.* Y WW | si] *om.* Y WW=R 18 e] *om.* R^{c} Y WW=R* 17 iohannem] iohannis Y WW 19 intra] inter Y WW | e] de R^{Fa} Y WW= R* 20 quare] + ergo Y WW 21 habebant] habent Y WW 22 sunt] sicut R^{Fa} Y WW

to þæ(m) hæl(ende) ⁊ cwedun niton we he cwæþ to heo(m) ⁊ ic no ek
ad ie(su)m dixerunt nescimus· ait illis et ipse non ego
sæcge eow in hwilce mæhte ic þas wyrce hwæt þon(ne)
dico uobis in qua potestate haec facio· <28>quid aute(m)
ðynce eow monn sum hæfde twægen sunes
uidetur uobis· homo quidam habebat duos filios·
⁊ gangande to þæ(m) ældra cwæþ sunu ga todæge wyrc
et accidens ad primum dixit filii uade operare
in wingeard minum he þa ondswarade cwæþ ic gánge dryht(en)
in uiam meam· <29>ille autem respondens dixit eo d(omi)ne
⁊ ne eode gangande þa to þæm oþru(m) cwæþ gelice
et non íít <30>accedens autem ad alterum dixit similiter
he ondswarade cwæþ nyll ic efter þa mid hreow⟨-⟩
at ille respondens ait nolo· postea autem pæneten⟨-⟩
nisse inhroered eode in wingeard hweþer þære twegra worhte willan
tia motus abiit in uiniam· <31>quis ex duob(us) fecit uolunta⟨-⟩
þæs fæderes cwædun hiæ se æftera ł nęrra cwæþ heo(m) to se hælend
tem patris· dicunt nouissimus dicit illis ie(su)s·
soð ic sæcge eow ꝥ æwisfirine ⁊ forlegnisse
Amen dico uobis quia puplicani et meritrices
beforangæþ eow in rice godes cwom f(or)þon to eow
praecedent uos in regno d(e)i:· <32>Uenit enim ad uos
iohan(nes) in wegæ soþfæstnisse ⁊ ge ne gelefdun him ewis⟨-⟩
iohannis in uia iustitiae et non credidistis ei· pup⟨-⟩
firinæ þon(ne) ⁊ forlægenisse gelefdun him ge
licani autem et meretrices crediderunt ei· uos
þon(ne) gesegon ne ge hreuwnisse hæfdun æft(er)
autem uidentes nec penitentiam habuistis post⟨-⟩
þon ꝥ ge gelefde him oþre bispell geherað
ea ut crederetis ei:· <33>Aliam parabulam audite
monn wæs fæder hina se þe sette wingeard
homo erat pater familias qui plantauit uinia(m)
⁊ he`a´ge .ł geard ymbtynde ðane ⁊ gedælf in ðæm torcul
et sepem circumdedit ei· et fodit in ea torcular
⁊ getimbrade torr .ł wall ⁊ gesette hine begengu(m)
et aedificauit turrem· et locauit eam agriculís
⁊ i(n) ellende .ł in elðiode gefoerde þa þæt tíd . to⟨-⟩
et peregre profectus est <34>cum autem tempus ad⟨-⟩
nealehte wæstma þæs wintreowes sende esnas his
propinquasset fructum uiniae missit seruos tuos
to þæ(m) begængu(m) ꝥ hi onfengon þæ(m) wæstmu(m) ⁊ þa begengu
ad agriculas ut acciperent fructum eius· <35>et agri⟨-⟩
gegripan ł fengon esnas his sume cnidun
culae adpraehensís seruís eius· alium cederunt

1 ad ie(su)m] iesu Y WW | non ego] nec ergo Y nec ego WW 2 qua potestate] quam potestatem Y WW=R | facio] faciam Y WW Xz=R 3 uidetur uobis] uobis uidetur Y WW | quidam] *om.* Y WW 4 uade] + hodie R^{Fa} Y WW 5 uiam meam] uineam meam R^{Fa} uinea mea Y WW | dixit eo d(omi)ne et non íít] ait nolo postea autem paenitentia motus abiit Y WW 8 nolo postea autem pænetentia motus abiit in uiniam (uineam R^{Fa})] eo domine et non iuit Y WW 9 dicunt] +ei R^{Fa} Y WW=R | nouissimus] primus WW Y Xz=R 11 praecedent] praecedunt WW Y=R 13 regno] regnum Xz Y WW=R 17 sepem] saepae Y saepe WW Xz=R 19 adpropinquasset fructum] fructuum adpropinquasset (app- Y) Y WW 20 uiniae] *om.* Y WW | tuos] suos Y WW 21 ad] et Y WW=R **(cont. on p. 156)**

sume soþlice stændun ⁊ sume ofslogan ⁊
alium uero lapidauerunt et alium occiderunt <36>et ite(-)
æft sende oþre esnas mænigu þæ(m) ærrum ⁊ dydun
rum missit alios seruos plures prioribus et fece(-)
ðæm gelice æt nehsta þa sende to heo(m)
runt illís similiter· <37>Nouissime autem missit ad eos
sunu his cweþende hio ofwitun sunu min þa begengu
filium suum· dicens reuerebuntur filium meum· <38>agri(-)
þa geségun þone sunu cwedun in innan heom
culae autem uidentes filium dixerunt intra sé
þis is se erfeweard cymeþ wutu ofslan þane ⁊ uru ˋł ⁊ habbe we usˊ bið
hic est heres uenite occidamus eum· Et nostra erit
erfe his ⁊ þa gegripon hine ⁊ wurpon hine butan
hereditas eius <39>et adpraeso eo iecerunt eum extra
þone wingeard ⁊ ofslogan þæne nu cymeþ dryhten þæs wingeardes
uiniam et occiderunt <40>cum ergo uenerit d(omi)n(u)s uiniae
hwæt doeþ he begengum þæm cwædun hiæ yflu yfle abreoþeð
quid faciet agriculís illís <41>aiunt illi malos male per(-)
⁊ þone wingeard geseteþ oþru(m) begengum þæm þe ageofað him
det et uiniam locabit alís agriculís qui reddent ei
wæstim tidum his cwæþ to heo(m) se hælend hwæt ˋł ahˊ ge næfre reordun
fructum temporib(us) suís <42>dicit illís ie(su)s quid non legistis
in gewritum stan þæm thi wiðcurun timbrade
in scripturís· lapidem quem reprobauerunt ædifi(-)
sé gewarð in heafod hwommes fro(m) dryhtne gewarð
cantes hic factus est in capud anguli· a d(omin)o factus
þis ⁊ is wundurlic in egum urum forþon
est istud hoc est mirabile in occulis nostrís· <43>ideo
ic sæcge eow þæt afirred bið fro(m) eow rice godes ⁊ salde
dico uobis quia auferetur á uobis regnum d(e)i et da(-)
þara ðiode þe wyrceþ wæstim his ⁊ se þe afalleþ
bitur genti facienti fructum eius <44>et qui ciciderit
on stáne þæm ne biþ gebroken on þone þanne
super lapidem istum non confringetur super que(m)
þe he falleþ gehnyscet hine ⁊ þa geherdun
uero ciciderit conteret eum· <45>Et cum uenissent
þa aldorsacerdas ⁊ fariseos bispell
principes sacerdotum et farissæi parabulas
his ongetun þæt he be heo(m) sægde ⁊ soecende
eius cognouerunt quod de ipsis diceret <46>et uolen(-)
hiæ ꝥ hine genoman ⁊ dreordun him mængu f(or)þon þe hiæ
tes eum tenere Timuerunt turbas quoniam
swa wihtga hinę hæfdun
sicut profetam eum habebant:·

(**f. 35r**) **21** acciperent] acciperunt Y WW=R | fructum] fructus Y WW **22** cederunt] ceciderunt R[Fa] WW Y=R[*]

(**f. 35v**) **1** alium uero lapidauerunt et alium occiderunt] alium occiderunt alium uero lapidauerunt Y WW | et[2]] *om.* Y W **4** reuerebuntur] uerebuntur Y WW **6** nostra erit hereditas eius] habebimus hereditatem eius Y WW **7** adpraeso eo] adpraehenso eo R[Fa] adprehensum eum Y(app-) WW | iecerunt] eiecerunt Y WW | eum *om.* Y WW **10** reddent] reddant Y WW **11** quid non] numquam Y WW **13** factus[2]] factum Y WW **14** hoc] et Y WW **16** fructum] fructus Y WW **17** non] *om.* Y WW **18** uenissent] audissent R[Fa] Y WW **20** uolentes] querentes R[Fa] Y WW (quae-)

⁊ ondswarade se hælend cwæþ ęfter bispellum heora
<XXII 1>Et respondens ie(su)s dixit iterum in parabulis eis·
gelice wearð rice heofunas monn cyninge þæ(m) þe worhte
<2>simile est regnum cælorum homini regi qui fecit
gemunge sunu his ⁊ sende esnas his cegan þæm
nuptias filio suo <3>et misit seruos suos uocare in⟨-⟩
gelaðadum to þæ(m) gemunge ⁊ noldan cuman ⁊ æft
uitatos ad nuptias· Et noluerunt uenire <4>et iterum
sende oþre ęsnas cwæþende sæcgað þæ(m) gelaðadum henu
missit alios seruos dicens dicite inuitatís· ecce
undernmete min geiarwad fearras mine ⁊ fóedelfuglas mine
prandium meum· paraui tauri mei· et altilia mea
ofslægene ⁊ all iara cumaþ to þæ(m) gemungæ hiæ þa
occissa et omnia parata uenite ad nuptias· <5>illi (autem)
ne rohtun ⁊ eodun awæg sum in his tunę sum þon(ne)
neglexerunt· et abierunt alii in uillam alii aute(m)
to ceapunge his elle genoman ęsnas
ad negotiationem suam <6>reliqui uero tenuerunt ser⟨-⟩
his ⁊ geonrettæ ofslogun se cyning ða
uos eius et contumilia adflictos occiderunt· <7>rex (autem)
he ꝧ geherde eorre wæs ⁊ sende hergas his
cum audisset iratus est· Et missit exercitum suum
⁊ abriodde myrðra heora ⁊ burg heora for⟨-⟩
et perdidit homicidias illos· et ciuitatem eorum suc⟨-⟩
bernde þa cwæþ to æsnum his gemunge wæs iare
cendit:· <8>Tunc ait seruís suis nuptiae quidem para⟨-⟩
ah þa þe gelaþade weron ne werun wyrðe gáþ
tae sunt· sed qui inuitati erant non sunt digni· <9>ite
nu to utgengum weogas ⁊ swa hwilce swa ge moete cliopað
ergo et exitus uiarum et quoscumq(ue) inueneritis· uo⟨-⟩
to þæ(m) gemungæ ⁊ þa ut gangende þa esnas on weogas somnadun xƀ
cate ad nuptias· <10>Et egressi serui eius in uia congre⟨-⟩
alle þa þe hi gemettun gode
gauerunt omnes quotquot inuenerunt· bonos
⁊ yfle ⁊ gefylled wæs ꝧ gemung sittendra
et malos et inpletæ sunt nuptiae discumbentibus:·
eode inn þa cyning ꝧ he gesæge þa sittendu ⁊
<11>Intrauit autem rex ut uideret discumbentes· et
gesæh ðær monnu ungegeradne hrægle gemunglice ⁊ cwæþ
uidit ibi hominem non uestitum ueste nuptiali· <12>et ait
hi(m) to freond hu eodest þu hider inn ⁊ þu \`ne' hæfest
illi amicae quomodo huc intrasti non habens
wéde ł hrægl gemunglic ⁊ he adumbede þa cwæþ se cyning to þægnu(m)
uestem nuptialem· at ille obmotuit· <13>tunc dixit minis⟨-⟩
gebindað him
trís ligatís

1 eis] + dicens Y WW 2 simile] + factum Y WW 4 noluerunt] nolebant Y WW | et²] *om.* Y WW 6 mea] *om.* Y WW 8 alii¹] alius Y WW | uillam] + suam Y WW | alii aute(m)] alius uero Y WW 10 adflictos] adfectos R^Fa Y WW 11 missit exercitum suum et] missis exercibus suis Y WW 12 homicidias] homicidas Y WW | eorum] illorum Y WW 14 sunt] fuerunt Y WW 15 et¹] ad R^Fa Y WW 16 uia] uias Y WW 17 quotquot] quos Y WW | bonos et malos] malos et bonos Y WW 18 discumbentibus] discumbentium Y WW 22 dixit] + rex R^Fa Y WW

foet ⁊ honda ⁊ sendeþ hine in ðiostre ꝥ ytmæst
pedibus et manibus mittite eum in tenebras exte⟨-⟩
ł yterræ þær bið wop ⁊ gristbitung toþa monige
riores illic erit fletus et stridor dentium· <14>multi
f(or)þon sendun gecægde ⁊ feawe gecorænę þa awæg gangænde þa fariseas
enim uoci pauci uero electi·<15>Tunc abeuntes faris⟨-⟩
geþæhtungę dydun ꝥ gefenge hinæ in worde
sæi consilium fecerunt ut caperent eum in sermo⟨-⟩
⁊ sendon him leorneras heora mið herodes þægnu(m)
ne <16>et mittunt ei discipulos suos cum herodianís
cwæþende lareu we wutan þæt þu soþfest eart in wæg
dicentes magister scimus quia uerax és in uiam
godes ⁊ in soþfestnisse lærest ⁊ nis ðe gemnis be ængum
d(e)i in ueritate doces· Et non est tibi cura de aliquo·
forþon þe þu ne locast to hadum monna sæg þon(ne)
non enim respicis ad personas hominum· <17>Dic ergo
us þæt þe ðyncę is alæfed to sellane gæfel kasere
nobis quid tibi uidetur licet dare censum cessari
oþþe nis ongetende þa se hælend hete heora cwæþ for⟨-⟩
án non <18>cognita autem ie(su)s nequitia eorum ait quid
won ge min costigaþ licetteras eawaþ me mynet
me temptatis hippochritae <19>ostendite mihi nu(m)⟨-⟩
þæs gæfles hiæ þa brohtun him dinere
misma census· At illi obtullerunt ei denarium·
⁊ cwæþ to heo(m) se hælend hwæs gelicnis his þæt ⁊ gewrit
<20>et ait illís ie(su)s cuius est imago haec et superscri⟨-⟩
cwædun hiæ kaseres þa cwæþ to heo(m) se hælend ageofaþ
ptio· <21>Dicunt ei cessaris· tunc ait illis ie(su)s reddite
þon(ne) kasere þa þe kasere sindun ⁊ þa þe godes sindun gode
ergo cessari quae cessaris sunt et quæ sunt d(e)i d(e)o:·
⁊ hiæ geherende wundradun ⁊ forleten hine eodun awęg
<22>Et audientes mirati sunt et relicto eo abierunt:·
on þæ(m) dæge him eodun to saduceas þa þe cwædun þæt
<23>In illa die accesserunt saducei qui dicunt non
seo æriste ł uparisnisse ⁊ frugnon .ł axsadun hine cwæþende
esse resurrectionem· interrogauerunt eum <24>dicen⟨-⟩
lareu moyses cwæþ gif wa swylte
tes magister moyses dixit· si quis mortuus fuerit
⁊ ne hæfde sunu þæt is broþer foe to his wife
non hens filium· Ut ducat frater uxorem illius
⁊ wæcce sed his broðer weron þonne mid
et suscitet sen fratri suo· <25>erant autem apud
us siofun broþre ⁊ se æreste ꝥ wif hæfde ⁊ 'a'swalt
nos ·uii· fratres· et primus uxorem duxit defunc
est

1 pedibus] + eius Y WW 2 illic] ibi Y WW 3 enim] + sunt R^{Fa} autem Y WW | uoci] uocati R^{Fa} Y WW 4 fecerunt] inierunt Y WW 6 in] et Y WW 8 ad personas] personam 9 uidetur] uideatur Y WW | dare censum] censum dari Y WW censum dare Xz 14 ie(su)s] *om.* Y WW 15 cessari quae cessaris sunt] quae sunt caesaris caesari Y WW 17 illa] illo Y WW | accesserunt] + ad eum Y WW 18 resurrectionem] + et Y WW 20 hens] habens R^{Fa} Y WW | frater] + eius Y WW 21 sen] semen R^{Fa} Y WW 22 uxorem duxit defunc est] uxorem duxit defuncta (ta *supplied in the running-on*) est R^{c} uxore ducta defunctus est Y WW

ꝥ næfde nan sed læfde his wif his broþer
non habens semen reliquit uxorem suam fratri
swa ꝥ gelice ꝥ se oþer ꝥ se þridde oþ to þæm siofund
suo· <26>similiter et secundus et tertius· usq(ue) ad uii⟨-⟩
þe lætest þon(ne) ealra ꝥ ꝥ wif ek aswalt
mum· <27>Nouissime autem omnium et mulier defunc⟨-⟩
in æriste hwylces þara siofuna bið ꝥ wif
tus est <28>in resurrectione ergo cuius erit de uii· uxor
forþon þe alle hæfdun hire þa ondswarade se hælend
omnes enim habuerunt eam· <29>Respondens (autem) ie(su)s
ꝥ cwæþ to heo(m) ge dwaligað ne cunnan gewritu ne mægen
ait erratis nescientes scripturas neq(ue) uirtu⟨-⟩
godes þe in æriste forþon ne hæmeþ ne hæmde bioþ
tem d(e)i· <30>in resurrectione ergo neq(ue) nubent neq(ue) nu⟨-⟩
ah sendon swa godes englas on heofonu(m) bi æriste
bentur sed erunt sicut angeli d(e)i in caelo· <31>de resur⟨-⟩
þon(ne) deadra ah ge ne hreordun ꝥ acwæden wæs
rectione ergo mortuorum non legistis quod dictu(m) (est)
fro(m) dryhtne cwæþendu(m) to eow ic eam god abrahames ꝥ god
a d(omi)no dicente uobis· <32>Ego sum d(eu)s abracham· et d(eu)s
isaces ꝥ god iacobes nis god deadra ah lifgendra
isaac· Et d(eu)s iacob· non est d(eu)s mortuorum sed uiuen⟨-⟩
god ꝥ þa geherende þa mengu wundradun in
tium d(eu)s:· <33>Et audientes turbae mirabantur in
lare his fariseos þa geherdun þæt
doctrina eius· <34>farissaei autem audientes quod
he stillnisse gesettun saduceas gesomnadun
sillentium inpossuisset saduceis congregaue⟨-⟩
in an ꝥ axsade hine an heora æ⟨-⟩
runt in unum <35>et interrogauit eum unus ex eis legis
laruw costænde his cwæþ lareu hwilc bebod
doctor temptans dixit <36>magister· quid est manda⟨-⟩
is micel in ae ꝥ cwæþ him to se hæl(end) lufa dryhten god
tum magnum in lege <37>et ait illi ie(su)s dileges d(omi)n(u)m d(eu)m
þinne of alre heortan þines ꝥ of alra saule þinre ꝥ of
tuum in toto corde tuo et in tota anima tua et in
alra mode þinu(m) f(or)þon þe þis is bebod ꝥ mæste ꝥ ꝥ æreste
tota mente tua <38>hoc est mandatum magnum et pri⟨-⟩
ꝥ æftere þon(ne) is gelic þæm lufa þon(e) næh⟨-⟩
mum· <39>secundum autem simile huic dileges proxi⟨-⟩
stu þinne swa þec seolfne in þissu(m) twæm bebodum
mum tuum sicut té ipsum <40>in his duobus mandatís
ealle ae hongað ꝥ witga þa gesomnade weron þa
tota lex pendet· et profetae <41>congregatís autem

1 non] et non Y WW 2 et[1]] *om.* Y WW 3 defunctus] defuncta Y WW 6 ait] + illis Y WW 7 ergo] enim Y WW 8 erunt] sunt Y WW 9 ergo] autem Y WW 10 d(omi)no] deo Y WW 12 d(eu)s] *om.* Y WW 14 sillentium] silentium R[c] Y WW | congregauerunt] conuenerunt Y WW 16 temptans] + eum R[Fa] Y W | dixit] *om.* Y WW | Quid] quod Y WW 17 et] *om.* Y WW 18 in[1]] ex Y Xz WW=R | in[2]] ex Y WW=R 19 est] + enim Y WW=R | mandatum magnum et primum] maximum et primum mandatum Y WW 20 simile] + est Y WW 22 tota] uniuersa Y WW

fariseas gefrægn hiæ hælend cwæþende hwæt
farissæis interrogauit eos ie(su)s <42>dicens quid
ðynceþ eow be criste hwæs sunu he się cwædun hiæ
uobis uidetur de cr(ist)o cuius filius est dicunt ei
dauiðes cwæþ heo(m) to se hælend hu þonne dauid in gaste nemneþ
dauid· <43>ait illis ie(su)s quomodo ergo dauid in sp(irit)u uoca⟨-⟩
hine dryht(en) cwæþende cwæþ dryhten hlaferd minne site on þa
uit eum d(omi)n(u)m dicens· <44>Dixit d(omi)n(u)s d(omi)no meo sede á dex⟨-⟩
swiþran halfe mine oþ ꝥ ic sette feondas þine tæppilbred
trís meis donec ponam inimicos tuos scabellum
fota þinra nu nu dauid nemneþ hine dryhten
peduum tuorum· <45>si ergo dauid uocauit eum d(omi)n(u)m
hu is he his sunu ⁊ nænig mæhte geandwyrdan
quomodo filius eius est <46>Et nemo poterat respon⟨-⟩
him worde ne heora nænig dyste of ðæm
dere ei uerbum neq(ue) ausus quis fuerat ex illa
dæge hine mæ geascigan þa se hæl(end) spræc
die eum amplius interrogare <XXIII 1>Tunc ie(su)s locutus (est)
to mongum ⁊ to leorneras his cwæþende on
ad turbas et ad discipulos suos <2>dicens super
setule moyses setun bokeras ⁊ fariseas
cadhedram moysi sedent scribae et farissæi
all soþlice swa hwæt swa ic sægce eow doð ⁊
<3>omnia ergo quaecumq(ue) dixerint uobis facite et
haldeþ æft(er) þonne wærcu(m) heora ne doð
seruate secundum uero opera eorum· nolite
ge sægcaþ þanne ⁊ hi sylfe ne doð bindaþ
facere dicunt enim et ipse non faciunt· <4>alligant
þon(ne) byrþenne hæfige ⁊ un⁊hoife ⁊ setteþ
enim honera grauia et inportabilia· Et inpo⟨-⟩
on exlan monna fringre þon(ne) heora nylleþ
nunt in humeros hominum digito autem suo nolunt
þa styrgan all heora wærc þon(ne) wyrcaþ ꝥ h'i'ę siæ
ea mouere <5>omnia uero opera faciunt ut uidi⟨-⟩
gesænę fro(m) monnu(m) ðe hiæ brædaþ f(or)þon þwæng'a'e
antur ab hominibus· Dilatant enim filactiria
heora ⁊ micclaþ fasu hiora lufigaþ þon(ne)
sua· et magnificauit fimbrias suas· <6>amant enim
ꝥ æreste sætil æt efengereordu(m) ⁊ forþmestu setulas
primos recubitos in cænís et primas cathedras
on heora somnungu(m) ⁊ hælettungæ on gemote ⁊ beon nemde
in snagogís <7>et salutationes in foro et uocari
fro(m) monnu(m) lareu ge þon(ne) nyllaþ beon nemde larewas
ab hominib(us) rabbi· <8>uos enim nolite uocari rabbi·

1 quid] quod Y WW=R 2 filius est] est filius Y WW=R 3 ie(su)s] *om.* Y WW | uocauit] uocat Y WW 6 peduum] pedum Y* WW Y^{c}=R | uocauit] uocat Y WW 8 quis fuerat] quisquam fuerat R^{Fa} fuit quisquam Y WW 11 sedent] sederunt R^{Fa} Y WW 11 farissæi] + dicentes (*in the left-hand margin, glossed* cwæþende) R^{Fa} Y WW=R* | facite et seruate] seruate et facite Y WW 13 uero opera] opera uero Y WW 14 ipse] *om.* Y WW 15 enim] autem Y WW 17 opera] + sua Y WW 19 magnificauit] magnificant Y WW | suas] *om.* Y WW | enim] autem WW Y=R 20 recubitos] recubitus WW Y=R 22 enim] autem Y WW

an is forþon eower lareuw alle þon(ne) ge broþre
unus enim magister uester omnes enim uos fra⟨-⟩
sindun ⁊ fæder ne nemnaþ eow on eorðan an is
tres· <9>et patrem nolite uobis super terram· unus (est)
forþon fæder eower se þe in heofunu(m) is ne sculon ge nemnan
autem pater uester qui in caelís est <10>neq(ue) uocemini
lareu f(or)þon lareu eower an is crist se þe
magistri· quia magister uester unus est cr(istu)s· <11>qui
mare is eower he beo eower þægn se þe hine þon(ne)
maior est uestrum erit uester minister <12>qui sé aute(m)
áhæfæþ he bið genægeþ ⁊ se þe hine genægeþ
exaltauerit humiliabitur et qui sé humiliauerit
he bið ahæfen wá eow þon(ne) bokeras ⁊ fariseas licet⟨-⟩
exaltabitur:· <13>Uae uobis scribae et farissæi hip⟨-⟩
teras þe ge lucaþ rice heofona beforan
pochritae quia cluditis regnum caelorum ante
monnum ge þonne ne gæþ ínn ne þa ingangende
homines uos autem non intratis nec introeuntes
letaþ ingangen wæ eow boceras ⁊
sinitis intrare:· <15>uae uobis scribae et farissæi
licetteras þe ge ymbgangaþ sæ ⁊ eordu
hippochritae quia circumitis mare et aridam
ƿ ge dóþ ænne hæþne iudiscne ⁊ þon(ne) he biþ gedóan
ut faciatis unum prosilitum· Et cum fuerit factus
ge dóþ hine sunu helles twæ(m) fældu(m) mare þon(ne) eow
faciatis eum filium gehenae duplo quam uos:·
wa eow bokeras ⁊ fariseas licetteras f(or)þon
<14>Uae uobis scribae et farissæi hippochritae q(uonia)m
ge etaþ hus widuwana set feorranne
commeditis domus uiduarum occassione longe
biddende for þon ge onfoeþ forþor domes
orantes propter hoc accipietis amplius iudiciu(m):·
wa eow latewas blinde se þe cwæþad swa hwa swa sweræþ
<16>Uae uobis duces cæci qui dicitis quicumq(ue) iuraue⟨-⟩
þurh tempel nis ƿ næht se þe þon(ne) sweraþ in gólde
rit in templum nihil est· qui autem iurauerit in au⟨-⟩
þæs temples scyldyg is dysig ⁊ blinde forþon the hweþ'r'e is mare
rum templi debitor est <17>stulti caeci· Quid enim maius (est)
góld oþþæ tempel ƿte halgaþ ƿ gold ⁊ swa
aurum án templum quod s(an)c(t)ificat aurum· <18>Et qui⟨-⟩
hwa swa swæraþ on wifode ƿ is nauwiht se þe þon(ne)
cumq(ue) iurauerit in altare nihil est· Qui autem
að sellaþ in þære geofu þe is on him se his scyldig
iurauerit in dono quod est super illud debitor est·

1 enim[1]] + est Y WW | enim[2]] autem WW Y=R | fratres] + estis R[Fa] Y WW 2 nolite] + uocare R[Fa] Y WW | (est) autem] est enim R[Fa] enim est Y WW 3 neq(ue)] nec Y WW 5 uester minister] minister uester Y WW | sé autem] autem se Y WW 6 humiliauerit] humiliabitur Y WW 7 Uae] + autem Y WW 9 autem] enim Y WW 13 faciatis] facitis Y WW 14 *The whole verse (23.15=14) is omitted in* Y WW 18 in[1]] per Y WW | aurum] auro WW Y Xz=R 19 debitor est] debet Y WW | stulti] + et Y WW 21 altare] altari Y WW | Qui] quicumque Y WW 22 debitor est] debet Y WW

blinde hwæþer soþlice mare is geofu oþþe wibed
<19>caeci quid enim maius est donum· án altare
þte halgaþ ðа geofu ah se þe aþ selð on wibede
quod s(an)c(t)ificat donum· <20>qui ergo iurauerit in altare
he sweraþ on þæm ⁊ in allum þæm ðe on him sindun ⁊ se þe
iurat in eo et in omnib(us) quae super illud sunt <21>et qui
sweraþ on tempel he sweraþ ⁊ in him ⁊ in ðæm ðe eardaþ
iurauerit in templo iurat et in illo et in eo qui habitat
in him ⁊ se þe sweraþ be heofune swerat be sedle godes
in ipso <22>et qui iurauerit in caelo iurat in throno d(e)i
⁊ in ðæm se þe siteþ on him wa eow bokeras
et in eo qui sedit super eum:· <23>Uae uobis scribae
⁊ fariseas liceteras f(or)þon ge þe tægþigaþ mintæ
et farissæi hippochritæ· Qui decimatis menta(m)
⁊ dile ⁊ cymen ⁊ forletun þa þe hæfi⟨-⟩
et annetum· et cimminum· Et reliquistis quae gra⟨-⟩
gra sindun þara ǽ ⁊ dóm ⁊ mildheortnisse
uiora sunt legis· et iudicium· Et misericordiam·
⁊ geleafu þas gedęfnade þe monn dyde ⁊ þa ne forletan
et fidem· haec oportuit facere et illa non omittere
latuwas blinde flega asiendę ⁊ olbendu wiotudlice
<24>duces caeci culicem exspuentes camellum autem
glendrende wa eow bokeres ⁊ farisseas liceteras
deglutientes:· <25>Uae uobis scribae et farissæi hip⟨-⟩
f(or)þon ðe ge clænsigaþ þte utan is cælces
pochritae qui mundatis quod de foris est calicis
⁊ binne þon(ne) fulle sindun nednimende
et parabsidis· intus autem pleni estis rapina
⁊ unclennisse þu farissea blindę geclænsa ær þte
et inmunditia:· <26>Farissae cæce munda prius quod
binnan is cælcæs ⁊ ⁊ ek geweorþæ þte butan
intus est calicis et parabsidis· et fiat quod de
bið clæne wa eow bokeras ⁊
foris est mundum:· <27>Uae uobis scribae et faris⟨-⟩
þe ge sindun gelice byrgennum behwitum
sæi hippochritae quia similes sepulchrís dealba⟨-⟩
þa þe utan eaweþ monnu(m) wlitige
tís quae á foris apparent hominib(us) speciosa·
binnan þanne fulle sindun bana deadra ⁊ æghwilcre
intus uero plena sunt ossibus mortuorum· et omni
unsyfernissę swa ⁊ eow utan ek æteaweþ
spurcitia· <28>sic et uos á foris quidem apparietis
monnu(m) soþfestę innan þon(ne) fulle sindun liceteras
hominibus iusti· intus autem pleni estis hippochrissi·
⁊ unryhtæs
et iniquitate:·

2 iurauerit] iurat Y WW | altare] altari WW Y Xz=R 4 et[1]] *om.* Y WW | habitat] inhabitat Y WW 5 iurauerit] iurat Y WW 6 sedit] sedet Y WW 7 qui] quia Y WW 9 et[1]] *om.* Y WW 11 culicem exspuentes] + et R[Fa] excolantes culicem Y WW 12 deglutientes] glutientes Y WW 13 qui] quia Y WW 14 estis] sunt Y WW 16 et[2]] ut Y WW | fiat] + et id Y WW 18 similes] + estis Y WW 19 apparent] parent Y WW 21 apparietis] apparetis R[c] paretis Y WW

ge þe
<29>Uae uobis scribæ et farissæi hippochritae qui
timbraþ byrgenne witgana ⁊ frętwæþ
ædificatis sepulchra profetarum et ornatis
gemynde soðfestra ⁊ cwæþað þær wę wærun
munumenta iustorum· <30>Et dicitis quia si fuessemus
on dagum fædra ure ne wæron we foéran
in diebus patrum nostrorum· Non essemus socii
eora in blódgyte uitgana hwæt ge in cyþnisse
eorum in sanguine profetarum· <31>itaq(ue) testimoniu(m)
sindun eow seolfum ꝥ ge bearn sindun heora se ðe witgan
estis· uobismet· ipsis· quia filii estis eorum qui pro⟨-⟩
slógun ⁊ ge ek gefyllaþ gemet fæd`e´ra
fetas occiderunt· <32>et uos inpletis mensuram patruu(m)
eowra ge nedra cynn uiperana hu
uestrorum· <33>serpentes genimina uiperarum· quomodo
fleaþ ge fro(m) dome helle forþon ic sende to eow witgan
fugietis á iudicio gehennae <34>ideo ego misi ad uos pro⟨-⟩
⁊ snottre ⁊ bokeras ⁊ of þæm ge ofslæþ
fetas et sapientes et scribas et ex illís occidistis
⁊ hóaþ ⁊ of þæm ge swingaþ in somnunge
et crucifigistis· Et ex eis flagillastis in sinagogís
eowrum ⁊ oehtaþ of ceastre in ceastre
uestrís et persequemini de ciuitate in ciuitatem·
ꝥ cymaþ on eow æghwilc blód soþfæst ꝥ þe ago⟨-⟩
<35>ut ueniat super uos omnis sanguis iustus qui ef⟨-⟩
ten wæs on eorðan fro(m) blóde soþfest abeles
fussus est super terram á sanguine iusti abel
oþ to blod zacharias sunu barachias
usq(ue) ad sanguinem zachariae filii barachiae
þæs þe ge ofslogun betwion tempel ⁊ wibæd soþ
quem occidistis inter templum et altare <36>amen
ic sæcge eow cymeþ þas eall ofer cneorissę
dico uobis uenient haec omnia super generatione(m)
þas þu þe slægst
istam:· <37>Hierusalem hierusalem· quae occidis
witga ⁊ stænęst þa þe to þe sende werun hu
profetas et lapidas eos qui ad te misi sunt quo⟨-⟩
oft ic wolde gesomnian bearn þin swa
tiens uolui· congregare filios tuos quemadmodu(m)
henne somnaþ ciken hiræ under feþran hire ⁊ ge naldun
gallina congregat pullos suos sub alís suís et nolu⟨-⟩
sihþe forleten e`o´w biþ hus eowra woestig
isti· <38>ecce relinquetur uobis domus uestra deserta

1 qui] quia Xz Y WW=R 3 quia] *om.* Y WW 5 testimoniu(m)] testimonio Y WW 7 inpletis] implete Y WW | mensuram] mensura Y WW=R | patruu(m)] patrum Y WW 9 ideo] + ecce Y WW | misi] mitto Y WW 10 et[3]] *om.* Y Xz WW=R | occidistis] occidetis Y WW 11 crucifigistis] crucifigetis Y WW | flagillastis] flagillabitis Y WW 12 persequemini] persequimini Y WW=R 14 iusti abel] abel iusti Y WW 20 tuos] suos Y WW=R 21 alís suís] alas Y WW 22 relinquetur] relinquitur Y WW

ic sæcge forþon eow ne geseoþ ge mec sie þæt ær þon
<39>dico autem uobis non me uidebitis ámodo donec

ge cweoþan gebloetsad se þe cwome in noman dryhtnes ⁊ ut gangande
dicatis benedictus qui uenit in nomine d(omi)ni· <XXIV 1>Et egres⟨-⟩

hælend of temple eode ⁊ him eodun to leorneras his
sus de templo· ibat et accesserunt discipuli eius·

ꝥ eawden him getimbru þæs temples he þa
ut ostenderent ei aedificationem templi· <2>ipse (autem)

⁊swarade ⁊ cwæþ heo(m) to ge geseoþ þas eall soþ
respondens dixit illís uidetis haec omnia· amen

ic eow sæcge ne bið læfed her stán ofer stanę
dico uobis non relinquetur hic lapis super lapidem

þæt he sy toworpen sæt þa he on oelebear⟨-⟩
qui non distruatur:· <3>Sedente autem eo super mon⟨-⟩

wes dúne eodun to him leorneras his degullice
tem olieti· accesserunt ad eum discipuli eius secre⟨-⟩

cweþende sæge us hwanne þas beoþ ⁊ hwylc
to dicentes dic nobis quando haec erunt et quod

tacun þines cymes ⁊ geendunge weorulde
signum aduentus tui et consummatione saeci:·

⁊ þa ⁊swarade se hælend cwæþ heo(m) to geseáeþ ꝥ nænig eow forlære
<4>Et respondens ie(su)s ait eis uidete ne quis uos sedu⟨-⟩

forþon þe monig cumaþ in minu(m) noma cwæþende
cat· <5>Multi enim uenient in nomine meo dicentes

ic eam crist ⁊ monige forlæræþ forþon þe ge bioþ geherende gefæht
ego sum cr(istu)s et multos seducent· <6>Audietis proelia

⁊ hlisu gefæhta geseáeþ ꝥ ge sy gedræfde
et opinniones proeliorum· Uidete né turbemini

sculon forþon þas weorþan ah nis þonne get ende ariseþ
oportet enim haec fieri sed nondum est finis· <7>con⟨-⟩

forþon þeod on ðeode ⁊ rice on rice ⁊
surget enim gens in gentem et regnum in regnum et

beoþ adle ⁊ hunger ⁊ eorþhroernisse geond
erunt pestilentiae et fames et terrae motus per

stowa þas þon(ne) eall onfruma sindun sares þon(ne) sellaþ
loca· <8>haec omnia initia sunt dolorum· <9>Tunc tradent

eow in ðrycnisse ⁊ slæhþ eow ⁊ ge bioþ in fiunge
uos in tribulationem et occident uos et eritis odio

eallu(m) þeodum for minum noma ⁊ þon(ne)
omnibus gentibus propter nomen meum· <10>et tunc

⁊spurnaþ .ł. æswicende monige ⁊ betwig hię sellaþ
scandalizabuntur multi· Et inuicem sé tradent

⁊ f'i'egaþ hæbbende heo(m) betwig ⁊ monige lyge ł lease witga
et odio habebunt inuicem· <11>et multi seodoprofetæ

1 autem] enim Y WW **2** egressus] + iesus R[Fa] Y WW **4** ostenderent] ostenderunt Y WW=R aedificationem] aedificationes Y WW **5** illis] eis Y WW **8** eius] *om.* Y WW **10** consummatione] consummationis Y WW | saeci] saeculi R[Fa] Y WW **11** ait] dixit Y WW **13** Audietis] audituri enim (autem Xz) estis Y WW **18** haec] + autem Y WW **19** tribulationem] tribulatione Y WW=R **21** se] *om.* Y WW

arisaþ ⁊ forlæreþ monige forþon genyhtsumaþ
insurgent et seducent multos <12>quoniam habundabit
unreht ⁊ acolaþ lufu monegra se þe
iniquitas· Et refrigerescit caritas multorum· <13>qui
þon(ne) þurhwunaþ on godes willan oþ ende se
autem perseuerauit in ámore d(e)i usq(ue) in finem hic
biþ hal ⁊ bodad bið þis godspell rices
saluus erit· <14>Et praedicabitur hoc euangelium regni
geond alnę ymbhwyrft in cyþnisse allu(m)
in uniuerso orbe terrarum· in testimonium omnibus
þeodum ⁊ þon(ne) cymeþ endunge weoruldes þon(ne) þis
gentibus· Et tunc ueniet consummatio sæculi:· <15>Cu(m) ergo
geseoþ ⁊ustrungæ þara awoestednisse þe acweden
uideretis abhominationem desolationis quæ dicta
wæs fro(m) daniele þæ(m) wihtga stondende in stowe halig se þe rędę
sunt á danielo profeta stantem in loco s(an)c(t)o· qui legit
⁊gete þon(ne) þa þe in iudea sint fleoþ to dunum
intellegat· <16>Tunc qui in iudea sunt fugiant in montes
⁊ se þe on þæce siæ ne stigað he niðer to genimanne owiht of his
<17>et qui in tecto non discendat tollere aliquid de do⟨-⟩
huse ⁊ se þe on londæ sy ne cerraþ he eft to nimene his
mu sua <18>et qui in agro non reuertatur tollere to⟨-⟩
tunican wa þon(ne) eknum ⁊ cildfóedendum
nicam suam· <19>Uae autem prignantib(us) et nutrian⟨-⟩
in ðæ(m) dagu(m) gebiddaþ ge þon(ne) eow ꝥ ne werþe fleam eower
tib(us) in illís diebus· <20>orate ergo né fiat fuga uestra
on wintre oþþe on restedæge biþ forþon þon(ne) ðrycnisse micelu
cheme uel sabbato· <21>erit enim tunc tribulatio magna
swilce ne wæs fro(m) fruman middangeardes oþ þis nu ne æft(er) ne weorþaþ
qualis non fuit ab initio sæculi usq(ue) modo neq(ue) fiet
⁊ þær ne wære scýnde þa dagas ne wyrðe hal
<22>et nisi breuiati fuissent dies illi non fuerit salua
ænig lic ah for þæ(m) gecorenum beoþ scynde .ł scorte
omnis caro· sed propter electos breuiabuntur
þa dagas þon(ne) þeah þe hwa eow sæcge sihðe her crist
dies illi· <23>Tunc si quis uobis dixerit ecce híc cr(istu)s
oþþe geond ne gelefaþ ge forþon þe arisaþ lyge crist
aut illic nolite credere <24>surgent enim seodocr(ist)i
⁊ lyge witgu ⁊ sellaþ tacen micel
et seudoprofetae et dabunt signa magna
⁊ forebecun swa ꝥ in gedwolan sien gelædde monigra
et prodigia ita ut in errorem inducant multos
þær ꝥ beon mæge ge þa gecorenan geta sihþe ic sæcge eow
si fieri pot(est) etiam elecos <25>ecce praedixi uobis

1 insurgent] surgent Y WW | quoniam] et quoniam Y WW 2 Et] *om.* Y WW | refrigerescit] refrigescet Y WW 3 perseuerauit] perseuerauerit Y WW permanserit Xz | in amore dei] *om.* Y WW 5 terrarum] *om.* Y WW 6 sæculi] *om.* Y WW 7 uideretis] uideritis Y WW 8 sunt] est Y WW 9 in[2]] ad Y WW 11 domu] domo Y WW 13 ergo] autem Y WW | ne] ut non Y WW 15 sæculi] mundi Y WW 16 fuerit] fieret Y WW 21 errorem] errore Y WW=R | inducant multos] inducantur Y WW 22 elecos] electos R[c] electi Y WW

forþon þæh þe sæcge eow sihþe 'ł henu' in węstene he is ne gæþ ge
<26>si enim dixerint uobis ecce in deserto est nolite
ut henu in cofu(m) innæ ne ge ꝥ ne lefað forþon
exire ecce in penetrabilib(us) Nolite credere <27>sicut
ðe swa læget ut gæþ fro(m) eastdæle ⁊ eaweþ oð
enim fulgor exiit ab oriente et apparet usq(ue)
westdæle swa bið æc se cyme sunu monnes
ad occidentem ita erit aduentus filii hominis
swa hwær swa bið lic þider somnigað
<28>ubicumq(ue) fuerit corpus illuc congregabuntur
earnes ræþe þon(ne) æft(er) ðrycnissum dagana
aquilæ:· <29>Statim autem post tribulationem dieru(m)
þara sunne áþiostraþ ⁊ mona ne seleþ his
illorum sól obscurabitur et luna non dabit lumen
leoht ⁊ steorran falleþ of heofune ⁊ mægen heofunas
suum et stelle cadent de caelo· et uirtutes cæloru(m)
bioþ gehróered ⁊ þon(ne) eaweþ tacen sune
commouebuntur <30>et tunc apparebit signum filii
monnes in heofune ⁊ þon(ne) wépaþ ofer hie all
hominis in caelo et tunc plangent super sé omnes
getalu ł cynn eorðu ⁊ geseaþ sunu monnes cumende
trib(us) terrae et uidebunt filium hominis uenientem
in heofunas wolcnum mid mægen miccle ⁊ ðrymme hea⟨-⟩
in nubibus caeli· Cum uirtute multa et maiestate ex⟨-⟩
nisse ⁊ sendeþ englas his mid beman ⁊ stæfne
celsa· <31>Et mittet angelos suos cum tuba et uoce
micle ⁊ gesomnaþ ða gecorenu(m) his fro(m) feowre
magna et congregabunt electos suos a quatuor
windu(m) heofunas fro(m) heanissu(m) heofunas oþ to gemęru eora
uentís cælís a summis cæloru(m) usq(ue) ad terminos eoru(m):·
from treo þon(ne) fices leornaþ bispell þon(ne)
<32>Ab arbore autem uici discite parabulam· cum
telgra his merwe biþ ⁊ leaf akenned ge witan
iam ramos eius tener fuerit et folia nata· scitis
þæt neh is sumer swa ge ek þanne geseoþ þas
quia prope est estas <33>ita et uos cum uideretis hæc
eall wite ge þæt he is in durum soþ ic sæcge
omnia· scitote quia prope est ianuis· <34>Amen dico
eow ꝥ ne geleoraþ cneorisse þeos ær þon
uobis quia non praeteribit generatio haec donec
eall ðus geweorþað heofun ⁊ eorþe geleoraþ word
omnia fiant· <35>Caelum et terra transibunt uerba
þon(ne) min næfre ne leoraþ be ðæ(m) dæge þonne
autem mea non praeteribunt <36>de die autem illa

1 enim] ergo Y WW | penetrabilibus] penetralibus Y WW Xz=R 3 apparet] paret Y WW 4 ad occidentem] in occidentem Y WW in occidente Xz | erit] + et Y WW 8 stelle] stellae Y WW 9 apparebit] parebit Y WW 10 super se] *om.* Y WW 12 excelsa] *om.* Y WW 14 suos] eius Y WW 15 cælís] *om.* Y WW 16 uici] fici Y WW 17 ramos] ramus Y WW 18 uideretis] uideritis Y WW 19 est] + in Y WW 20 generatio haec] haec generatio Y WW 21 omnia] + haec Y WW 22 autem[1]] uero Y WW

⁊ þara hwile nænig wat ne englas in heofunu(m) nymþe fæder
et hora nemo scit neq(ue) angeli cælorum nisi pater
ane swa þon(ne) wæs in noes dagu(m) swa bið ek se tocyme
solus· <37>sicut enim fuit in diebus noe ita erit aduen(-)
monnes sune forþon swa si hi weron in ˋðæmˊ dagu(m) ær þa
tus filii hominis· <38>sicut enim erant in diebus ante
flodes etende ⁊ drincende ⁊ to hęmde sellende
diluium comedentes· Et bibentes et nuptum tradentes
oþ þone dæg ðe eade noe in ða arkę
usq(ue) ad illum diem quo intrauit noe in arcam·
⁊ ne ongeotun ær þon ðe flod com ⁊ genom
<39>et non cognuerunt donec uenit diluium et tullit
ealle swa bið ek se cyme monnes sunę þon(ne) beoð
omnes· ita erit aduentus filii hominis <40>tunc er(u)nt
twegen on londe oþer bið genumen ⁊ oþer bið forleten
duo in agro unus adsumetur et unus relinquetur
twa grindende æt cweorne oþere bið genumen ⁊ oþere
<41>duæ molentes ad molam una adsumetur et una
forleten twegen on bedde oþeru biþ genumen ⁊ oþer
relinquetur· Duo in lecto unus adsumetur et unus
bið forleten wæccaþ ge forþon þe ge ne cunnan hwilc dæg
relinquetur· <42>Uigilate ergo quia nescitis qua die
oþþe hwilc hwile ˋɫ tidˊ dryht(en) ure cymˊiˋd þæt ge þon(ne)
uel qua hora d(omi)n(u)s uester uenturus est:· <43>Illud autem
witaþ ꝥte ꝥ þær se hinefæder wiste on hwilce hwile
scitote quoniam si sciret pater familias qua hora
se þeof cuman walde he wæcende beon walde ⁊ ne letan
fúr uenturus esset uigilaret utiq(ue) et non sineret
þurhdelfan his hus forþon ge ek beoþ gearwe
perfodiri domum suam· <44>ideo et uos estote parati
þe ge ne witan hwilce tid monnes sunu cymeþ
quia nescitis qua hora filius hominis uentura est
hwælc wenest þu sie getrewe esne ⁊ snotter þęne gesette
<45>Quis nam est fidelis seruus et prudens quem con(-)
dryht(en) his of heorod his ꝥ selle heom
stituet d(omi)n(u)s suus super familiam suam ut det illis
mete in tide eadig is se esne þon(e) cymeþ
cibum in tempore <46>beatus ille seruus quem cum uene(-)
dryht(en) is ⁊ gemoeteþ swa dónde soþ ic eow
rit d(omi)n(u)s eius inuenerit síc facientem· <47>Amen dico
sęcge þæt ofer all his god gesetteþ
uobis quoniam super omnia bona sua constituet
hine gif þanne cwæþ se yfle esne in heorte his
eum· <48>Si autem dixerit ille seruus in corde suo

2 enim] autem Y WW | fuit] *om.* Y WW | erit] + et Y WW 4 bibentes] + et nubentes R^{Fa} (*in the right-hand margin with the gloss*, ⁊ hemende) + nubentes Y WW 5 illum] eum Y WW | intrauit] introivit Xz Y WW=R | noe in arcam] in arcam noe Y WW 7 erit] + et Y WW | erunt duo] duo erunt Y WW 9 ad molam] in mola Y WW 10 Duo in lecto unus adsumetur et unus relinquetur] *om.* Y WW 11 qua die uel] *om.* Y WW 12 est] sit Y WW 15 ideo] ideoque Xz Y WW=R 16 nescitis qua] qua nescitis Y WW | uentura] uenturus Y WW 17 nam] putas Y WW | constituet] constituit Y WW 18 super] supra Y WW 22 ille seruus] + male R^{Fa} malus seruus ille Y WW

aeldingę doeþ dryht(en) min to cumene ⁊ onginnaþ slán
moram fecit d(omi)n(u)s meus uenire <49>et coepit percuterit
efnþeu his manducat hi(m) þon(ne) ⁊ drinceþ mid druncennu(m)
conseruos suos· manducat autem et bibit cu(m) ebrís
cymþ þon(ne) dryht(en) þæs esnes on þæ(m) dæge þe he ne wenaþ
<50>ueniet autem d(omi)n(u)s serui illius in die qua non sperat
⁊ þære tide þe he ne wat ⁊ hine gedælaþ ⁊ dæl his seteþ
Et hora qua ignorat <51>et diuidiuit partem eiusq(ue) ponet
mið liceteru(m) þær biþ heaf ⁊ gristbitung toða
Cum hippochritís illic erit fletus et stridor dentiu(m):·
ða gelic biþ rice heofunas tén femnan þa
<XXV 1>Tunc simile erit regnum cælorum ·x· uirginib(us) quæ
genimende leohtfatu ł ðecele heora eoden ut ongǽgn brydguma
accipientes lampades suas exierunt obiam sponso
⁊ brýde fife þon(ne) þaræ werun dysige ⁊ fife snottre
et sponsae <2>·u· autem ex eis erant fatuae et u· pruden⟨-⟩
ah ða fife dysige genimænde þa leohtfatu heora ne ge⟨-⟩
tes· <3>sed ·u· fatuae acceptís lampadib(us) suís non su(m)⟨-⟩
noman oele mid hiæ þa snottre þon(ne) genoman
pserunt oleum secum <4>prudentes autem acciper(u)nt
oele in fatu heora mið þæ(m) lehtfatum ǽlde þa
oleum in uassís suís cum lampadib(us)· <5>Moram (autem)
se brydguma slepade ealle ⁊ slep ofer⟨-⟩
faciente sponso dormitauerunt omnes et dormi⟨-⟩
eode æt middere niht þa cirm .ł cleopung geworden wæs ⁊
erunt· <6>media autem nocte clamor factus est et
henu brydguma cymeþ gæþ ut ongǽgn him þa arisan
ecce sponsus uenit exite obiam ei <7>tunc surrexer(u)nt
ealle þa femnan ⁊ ingunnon fretwan le`o´htfatu heora
omnes uirginis illæ et ornauerunt lampades suas
þa dysege to þæ(m) snottru(m) cwedun sellaþ us
<8>fatuae autem sapientib(us) dixerunt date nobis
of oeles eowres forþon þe lehtfætu ure adwæsced sindun
de olo uestro quia lampades nostre extinguntur
andswaredun þa snottre cwæþende nese `ł nic´ ðy les
<9>responderunt prudentes dicentes non né forte
ne nyhtsum´i`gæ us ⁊ eow gæþ mæ to bebycgendu(m)
non sufficiat nobis et uobis· ite putius ad uen⟨-⟩
⁊ gebycgæþ eow ðenden hiæ þa eodun bycgan
dentes et emite uobis· <10>dum autem irent emere
com se brydguma ⁊ þa þe gearwe weron ineodun
uenit sponsus et quae parate erant intrauer(u)nt
mid hine to gemungæ ⁊ belocen wæs se dure æt nihste
cum eo ad nuptias et clausa est ianua· <11>nouissime
þa
autem

1 fecit] facit Y WW | coepit percuterit] coeperit percutere Y WW 2 manducat] manducet Y WW | bibit] bibat Y WW 3 autem] *om.* Y WW 4 diuidiuit partem eiusque] diuidet eum partemque eius Y WW 9 suis] *om.* Y WW 10 autem] uero Y WW 13 et] *om.* Y WW 15 uirginis] uirgines Y WW 17 olo] oleo R[Fa] Y WW 18 non] *om.* Y WW 21 parate] *om.* Y paratae WW 23 autem] *om.* Y WW

comun ⁊ ec þa oþre femnan cwæþende dryht(en) dryht(en)
uenerunt et relique uirgines dicentes d(omi)ne d(omi)ne
ontyn us ⁊ he ⁊swarade ⁊ cwæþ soþ ic sæcge
aperet nobis· <12>at ille respondens ait· amen dico
eow forþon ne con ic eow wæceþ nu forþon þe ge
uobís quia nescio uos· <13>Uigilate itaq(ue) quia nesci(-)
cunnan dæg ne þa hwile forþon þe swa se monn on ellende færende
tis diem neq(ue) horam:· <14>Sicut homo perigre profi(-)
cęgde esnas his ⁊ salde þæm his
ciscens uocauit seruos suos et tradidit illis bona
god ⁊ anum salde fif oþrum þon(ne) twegen sumu(m)
sua· <15>et uni dedit ·u· talenta· alii autem duo· alii
soþlice an æghwilce æfter his mægene
uero· unum· unicuiq(ue) secundum propriam uirtu(-)
⁊ foerdon sona þa eode se þe fif
tem· et profectus est statim <16>autem abiit qui ·u·
ondfeng ⁊ worhtæ in þæm ⁊ gestrionde
talenta acciperat et operatus est in eis· et lucra(-)
oþre fife swilce þe ⁊ se þe twægen onfeng
tus est alia ·u· <17>similiter autem et qui duo accipe(-)
gestrionde oþre twægen se þe þonne onfeng
rat lucratus est alia duo <18>qui uero acciperat
anum eode bedælf in eorþe ⁊ ahydde feoh
unum abiens fodit in terra et abscondit pecunia(m)
dryhten his æfter micclum fæce þa cwom dryhten es(-)
d(omi)ni sui· <19>post multum uero temporis uenit d(omi)n(u)s ser(-)
na þara ⁊ monade rehtæs heo ⁊
uorum illorum· Et possuit rationem cum eis <20>et
þa cumende se þe fif onfeng brohte oþre
accedens qui ·u· talenta acciperat obtullit alia
fif cweþende dryht(en) fif saldest þu me henu oþre fife
u· dicens d(omi)ne ·u· talenta tradidisti mihi alia ·u·
ic toeke gestrionde ⁊ cwæþ him to dryht(en) his wel þec goda
superlucratus sum· <21>Et ait illi d(omi)n(u)s meus· euge serue
esne ⁊ getreowa forþon ofer fæawum węre getreuwe
bone et fidelis quia super pauca fuisti fidelis
ofer monegu ic þe gesette gang in gefea dryhtnes
super multa té constituam intra in gaudium d(omi)ni
þines þa cwom ec oþer se þe twægen onfeng
d(e)i tui· <22>accessit Et alter qui duo talenta acciperat
⁊ cwæþ dryht(en) twægen me þu saldest sihþe twegen
dicens d(omi)ne duo tallenta mihi tradidisti et ecce duo
oþre ic gestrionde cwæþ hi(m) to his dryhten wel þec godu esne
alia superlucratus sum· <23>ait illi d(omi)n(u)s eius serue bone

1 uenerunt] ueniunt Y WW 2 aperet] aperi R^c Y WW 3 quia] *om.* Y WW 4 sicut] + enim Y WW | perigre] peregre Y WW *om.* Xz 8 autem abiit] abiit autem Y WW 10 autem et] *om.* Y WW 11 uero] autem Y WW | acciperat unum] unum acceperat Y WW 16 u[1]] + talenta Y WW | tradidisti mihi] + ecce R^Fa mihi tradidisti et (*om.* Xz) ecce Y WW 17 Et] *om.* Y WW | meus] eius R^c Y WW | serue bone] bone serue Y Xz WW=R 19 super] supra WW Y Xz=R 20 d(e)i] R^c (*expunct*) Y WW | accessit] + autem Y WW | alter] *om.* Y WW 21 dicens] et ait Y WW | mihi tradidisti] tradidisti mihi Y WW | et] *om.* R^c (*expunct*) Y WW | duo alia] alia duo Y WW 22 superlucratus] lucratus Y WW | eius] + euge R^c (*below the line*) Y WW | serue bone] bone serue Y WW

⁊ getreowa forþon þu ofer feawum wȩre getreowe ofer monegu
et fidelis quia super pauca fuisti fidelis super multa
ic þe gesete ga in gefea ðines dryht(nes) þa cumende ek
té constituam· intra in gaudium d(omi)ni d(e)i tui· <24>accedens
se þe an onfeng cwæþ dryhten ic wat ꝥte
autem qui unum tallentum acciperat ait d(omi)ne scio quia
þu eart eard monn ⁊ ripes þær þu ne sewe ⁊ somnast
homo durus és metis ubi non seminasti· et congregas
þær þu ne stenctȩs ⁊ frohtende ic eode ⁊ ahydde
ubi non sparsisti· <25>et timens ego abii et abscondi· tal⟨-⟩
þine in eorþe henu hæfȩþ ꝥte þin is
lentum tuum in terra· Ecce habes quod tuum est
⁊swarade þa his dryhten cwæþ him to þu yfle esne
<26>respondens autem d(omi)n(u)s eius dixit ei serue male
⁊ swǽr wistȩs ꝥ ic ripe þær ic ne seow ⁊ somnige
et piger sciebas quia meto ubi non semino et congrego
þær ic ne strægde hwæt þe þa geras ꝥ þu sendest min
ubi non sparsi· <27>oportuit ergo te committere pec⟨-⟩
feoh myneterum ⁊ ic cumende onfenge
cuniam meam nummularís· Et ego ueniens requi⟨-⟩
cuþlice þæt þe min is mid ofersceatta genimað
pissem utiq(ue) quod meum est cum ussura· <28>tollite
him æt þæne ⁊ sellað þæ(m) þe hæfð ten æghwilc
ab eo tallentum et date qui habet x tallenta <29>omni
forþon hæbbende selleþ ⁊ genyhtsumað þæ(m) þon(ne)
enim habenti dabitur et habundauit ei autem
þe næfeþ ⁊ ꝥ hi(m) þynce ꝥ he hæbbe bið afyrred fro(m) him ⁊ þene
qui non habet et quod habet auferetur ab eo· <30>et in⟨-⟩
unnytte esne weorpað in þeostra ꝥ ytterre þær
utilem seruum iecite in tenebras exteriores illic
bið heaf ⁊ toþa gristbatung ⁊ mið þy cymeþ þon(ne)
erit fletus et stridor dentium:· <31>Et cum uenerit
sune monnes in ðrymme his ⁊ ealle englas
filius hominis in maiestate sua et omnes angeli
mið hine þon(ne) gesitæþ on sedle his þrymmes
cum eo· tunc sedet super sedem maiestatis suae
⁊ gesomnede beoð beforan him ealle þeode ⁊ gesceadiþ
<32>et congregabuntur ante eum omnes gentes· et sepa⟨-⟩
hiæ in tu swa hiorde ascadeþ scép
rabit eos ab inuicem· sicut pastor segregat oues
fro(m) ticnum ⁊ seteþ þa scæp on þa swiðran healfe his ticcen
ab hedís <33>Et statuit quidem oues a dextrís hedos
þon(ne) on þa winstran healfe þon(ne) cwæþ se cyning þæm þe on þa swiþran halfe
autem a sinistrís· <34>Tunc dicet rex hiis qui a dextrís
his beon
eius erunt·

1 super[2]] supra Y WW 2 d(e)i] *om.* Y WW 3 autem] + et Y WW 4 es] + et Y WW Xz=R 5 ego] *om.* Y WW 9 committere] mittere Y WW 10 ego ueniens] ueniens ego Y WW | requipissem] recipissem R[c] recepissem Y WW 11 tollite] + itaque Y WW 12 date] + ei Y WW 13 habundauit] abuntabit Y WW 14 habet] uidetur habere Y WW 16 Et cum] cum autem Y WW 18 sedet] sedebit R[Fa] Y WW 21 statuit] statuet Y WW | quidem oues] oues quidem Y WW | dextris] + suis Y WW

cymeþ gebletsade mines fæder gesi\t/tað rice
Uenite benedicti patris mei possedite regn(u)m
þte eow geiarwad wæs fro(m) setnisse middang(eardes) forþon ðe mec
quod uobis paratum est ab oregine mun <35>esuriui
yngrade ⁊ ge saldun me etan mec þyrste ⁊ ge salden
enim et dedistis mihi manducare sitiui et didistis
me drincan cuma ic wæs ⁊ ge feormadun mec nacud
mihi bibere hospis eram et colligistis me <36>nudus
ic wæs ⁊ ge wriogan mec untrum ⁊ ge neosadun mín
eram et cooperuistis me infirmus et uisitastis me
in carkærn ic wæs ⁊ ge coman to me þon(ne) ⁊swærigaþ
in carcere fui et uenistis ad me· <37>Tunc responde⟨-⟩
him þæ(m) soþfæste cwæþende dryht(en) hwonne gesagun we ðe hyngrende
bunt ei iusti dicentes d(omi)ne quando té uidimus essu⟨-⟩
⁊ we foeddan þe oþþe þyrstigne ⁊ we þe drincan
rientem et pauimus té aut sitientem· et dedimus
saldun hwanne þon(ne) gesagun we þe cuman
tibi potum· <38>quando autem té uidimus hospite(m)
⁊ gefeormadun ðe oþþe nacudne ⁊ we þec wreogan oþðe
et collegimus te aut nudum et cooperuimus <39>aut
hwonne we þe segun untrymne oþðe in quartern ⁊
quando té uidimus infirmum aut in carcere et
we coman to þe ⁊ andswarade se cyningc cwæþ to heo(m) soþ ic
uenimus ad te <40>et respondens rex dicet illís amen
sæcge eow swa longe swa ge dydun anu(m) þe læsesta þara
dico uobis quandiu fecistis uni ex minimís hís
broþre mine me ge dydon þon(ne) cwæþ se cyning ec to þæ(m) þa þe
fratrib(us) meis mihi fecistis· <41>Tunc dicet rex hiís qui
on þæ(m) winstran halfe beoþan gewitaþ fro(m) me awærgede
á sinistris eius erunt discedite á me maledicti
in ece fyr þte wæs geiarward fæder min
in ignem æternum· quem praeparauit pater meus
deofle ⁊ his englas forþon þe mec hyngrede ⁊ ge ne saldun
diabulo et angelís eius· <42>esuriui enim et non dedistis
me etan mec ðyrste ⁊ ge ne saldun me drincan
mihi manducare sitiui et non dedistis mihi bibere
cuman ic wæs ⁊ ge ne feormadun mec nacud ⁊ ge ne wreogan
<43>hospis eram et non colligistis me nudus et non co⟨-⟩
mec untrum ⁊ in carkern ⁊ ge ne neosadun
operuistis me infirmus· et in carcere et non uisi⟨-⟩
min þon(ne) ⁊swarigað hiæ swilce cwæþende
tastis me <44>tunc respondebunt et ipsi dicentes
dryht(en) hwanne gesagun we ðe hyngrende oþþe þyrstigne
d(omi)ne quando te uidimus esurientem aut sitientem·

1 regnum quod uobis paratum est] paratum uobis regnum Y WW 2 ab oregine] a constitutione Y WW | mun] mundi R[c] (di *added in red ink*) Y WW 3 dedistis] dedisti Y WW=R 4 hospis] hospes Y WW | colligistis] collexistis Y Xz collegistis WW 5 eram] *om.* Y WW | cooperuistis] operuistis Y WW 6 fui] *om.* Y erat WW 8 te] *om.* WW Y=R | aut] *om.* Y WW 10 collegimus] colleximus Y WW Xz=R 11 aut] et Y WW=R 13 ex minimis his fratribus meis] de his fratribus meis minimis Y WW 14 rex] et Y WW 15 a[1]] ad Y WW=R | eius] *om.* Y WW | discedite] discendite Y WW=R 16 quem praeparauit pater meus] qui praeparatus (paratus Xz) est Y WW 18 bibere] potum Y WW 19 hospis] hospes Y WW | colligistis] collexistis Y Xz collegistis WW | cooperuistis] operuistis Y WW

oþþe cuman oþðe untrum oþþe in carcrænnæ ⁊ we ne
Aut hospitem aut infirmum uel in carcere et non

þegnnedun þe þon(ne) ⁊swareþ heom cweþende
ministrauimus tibi <45>tunc respondebit illis dicens

soþ ic sæcge eow swa longe swa ge ne dydun anum meoduma
Amen dico uobis quandiu non fecististis uni de mino⟨-⟩

þissa ne me ge ne dydun ⁊ gaþ hiæ in æce tintergu
ribus hís nec mihi fecistis <46>et ibunt hii in supplicium

þa soþfeste þon(ne) in æce lif ⁊ geworden wæs
æternum iusti autem in uitam æternam:· <XXVI 1>Factum (est)

þa geendade se hælend word þas eall
autem cum consummasset ie(su)s sermones hos omnes

cwæþ se hælend to his leorneras ge wutan þæt æft(er) twæ(m) dagu(m) beoþ eastran ⁊ monnes
dixit· <2>Scitis quia post biduum pascha fiet et filius

sunu bið sald ꝥ he się áhongen /—/ þa werun gesomnade
hominis tradetur ut crucifigatur·ꝛ <3>Tunc congregati

alduras sacerdas ⁊ þa aeldra þæs folkes in
sunt principes sacerdotum et seniores populi in

cæfertun þæs aldorsacerdæs se þe wæs haten caifas
atrium principis sacerdotum qui dicebatur cai⟨-⟩

⁊ geþæhtungę dydon ꝥ hy se hælend inwit noman ⁊ of⟨-⟩
fas· <4>et consilium fecerunt ut ie(su)m dolo tenerent· et oc⟨-⟩

slogen hy cwædun þon(ne) nællæs in symbeldæge þy les
ciderent·, <5>dicebant enim non in die festo ne forte

ungerec ł ungeþwære in þæ(m) folce gewyrde mid þy þon(ne) þende se hæl(end) wæs
tumultus in populo fieret:·, <6>Cum autem esset in be⟨-⟩

in bethania þæ(m) tune in huse simonis þæs hreofan þa cwom to him
thania in domu simonis leprosi <7>accessit ad eum

an wif hæbbende stæna fullę smirenisse deorwyrþe
mulier habens alabastrum unguenti praetiosi

⁊ ageat ofer his heafud hlengendes æt gereordu(m)
et infudit super capud eius recumbente ipso·

ꝥ gesægon þa leorneras abælgede werun cwæþende
<8>uidentes autem dicipuli indignati sunt dicentes·

to hwon is ðeos forwyrd forþon þe þis mæhte beon beboht in micel
ut quid per haecꝛ <9>potuit enim istud uenundari prætio

⁊ sald þearfum witende þa se hæl(end) cwæþ heo(m) to
magno et dari pauperibus·, <10>sciens autem ie(su)s ait illis·

†for`h´won sindun ge swæncende þæm wife werc þon(ne) god hio worhte in mec
quid molesti estis mulieri bonum operata est in me,

forþon þe ge á´ þearfan habbad mid eow mec þon(ne)
<11>nam semper pauperes habebitis uobiscum· me (autem)

á ne habbaþ þas þon(ne) sendendu smerenisse
non semper habebitis·, <12>haec autem mittens unguen⟨-⟩
tum

1 hospitem] + aut nundum Y WW 3 fecististis] fecistis Y WW 5 factum] et factum Y WW 6 autem] *om.* Y WW 7 dixit] + iesus disciplis suis R^{c} + disciplis suis Y WW 12 enim] + ł autem R^{c} autem Y WW 13 in populo fieret] fieret in populo Y WW 13 esset] + iesus R^{Fa} Y WW 14 domu] domum R^{c} (*suspension stroke added above* u) domo Y WW 15 alabastrum] alabavstrum R^{c} alabastrum Y WW 16 infudit] effudit R^{c} effudit Y WW | eius] ipsius Y WW | recumbente ipso] recumbentis R^{c} Y WW 17 dicipuli] discipuli R^{c} Y WW 18 per] perdictio R^{c} perditio Y WW | prætio mango] multo Y (+ pretio Y^{Ald}) WW 20 estis] + huic R^{c} Y WW=R^{*} | mulieri] + opus enim R^{c} + opus Y WW 21, 22 habebitis] habetis Y WW 22 haec autem mittens] mittens enim haec Y WW

þis on min lic to bebyrgenne mec iarwede soþ ic
hoc in corpus meum ad sepeliendum me fecit, <13>amen

eow sæcge swa hwær swa bodad bið þis god(-)
dico uobis ubicumq(ue) praedicatum fuerit hoc euan(-)

spel in allu(m) middang(earde) ek bið sægd ⁊ ꝥte þios dyde
gelium in toto orbe narrabitur· et quod haec fecit

in gemynd hiræ /—/ þa eode awæg an þara twælfe se þe is nemned
in memoriam ipsius·, <14>Tunc abiit unus de ·xii· qui dici(-)

iudas scarioth to aldursacerdæs
tur iudas scarioth· ad principes sacerdotum

⁊ cwæþ to heo(m) hwæt willað ge me sellan ⁊ ic hine eow sellan
<15>et ait illis, quid uultis mihi dare et ego uobis trada(m)?

⁊ hiæ gesettun hine ðritig scillinga ⁊ seoþþan
eum at illi constituerunt ei ·xxx· argenteos· <16>et exinde

he gesohte sel þæt he hinæ salde heo(m)
querebat oportunitatem ut eum traderet illis·,

formæ dæge þa þara ðefra metta eodun ða leorneras
<17>prima die autem azemorum accesserunt discipuli

to hælend cweþende hwær uuiltu we iarwan þe eastra to etanne
ad ie(su)m dicentes, ubi uís paremus tibi pascha come(-)

ða cwæþ hæl(end) to h`i´ę †gæþ in cæstre to sumu(m) men ⁊ cwæþað
dere? <18>at ie(su)s dixit ei·, ite in ciuitatem ad quendam et dicite

hi(m) to lareu cwæþ tid min neh is mið þe
ei·, magister dicit·, tempus meum prope est apud te

ic wyrce eastra mid minu(m) leorneru(m) ⁊ /—/ ða dydon þa leorneras
facio pascha cum discipulis meis·, <19>et fecerunt disci(-)

swa hi(m) bebead ł gesette heo(m) se hæl(end) ⁊ gearwadun eastran
puli sicut praecipit illis ie(su)s et parauerunt pascha:·

þa efen þa cwom he hleonede mið ðæ(m) twælf leorneras
<20>Uespere autem facto discubuit cum xii· discipulis

⁊ etendum heo(m) to cwæþ †soþ ic eow sæcge ꝥ an eower
<21>Et ædentib(us) illis dixit·, Amen dico uobis quia unus ues(-)

me sellende bið ⁊ /—/ geunrotsade wærun swiðe ⁊
trum me traditurus est, <22>et contristati sunt ualde et

ingunnun anlepum cweþan ah ic hit eam dryht(en) ⁊
coeperunt singuli dicere, numquid ego sum d(omi)ne? <23>at

he ⁊swarade cwæþ †se ðe depið mid me honde in
ipse respondens ait, qui intingit mecum manum in

þas parabside se mec sellaþ sunu monnes gæð
parabside hic me tradet, <24>filius quidem hominis uadit:·

swa awriten wæs be hi(m) hweþre þonne wa þæ(m) menn
sicut scriptum est de eo· uerumtamen uæ homini

þe þurh hine sunu monnes bið sald god hi(m) wære
illi per quem filius hominis tradetur, bonu(m) erat

3 orbe] mundo Y WW | narrabitur] dicetur Y WW 4 ipsius] eius Y WW | qui dicitur] dicebatur Y qui dicebatur WW Xz=R 6 tradam eum] tradam R^c (eum *cancelled by dots*) eum tradam Y WW 8 illis] *om.* Y WW 9 die autem] autem die Y autem WW 10 pascha comedere] comedere pascha R^c (*marked by* signes de renvoi) Y WW 11 ei] *om.* Y WW 14 praecipit] + ł constituit R^c constituit Y WW 15 discubuit] discumbebat Y WW 17 sunt] *om.* Y WW | et²] *om.* Y WW 21 eo] + illo R^c illo Y WW | uerumtamen uæ] uae autem Y WW 22 tradetur] traditur Y WW

þær he akenned ne wære se monn ⁊swarade þa iudas se þe
non nasci ille homo <25>respondit autem iudas qui
sellende wæs hine cwæþ ah ic hit eam lareu
traditurus erat eum· numquid ego sum rabbi?
cwæþ hi(m) to hæl(end) þu†þæt cwæde /—/ þende hiæ þa æt þæ(m) efenmete werun genom
ait illi ie(su)s, tu dixisti·, <26>cannantib(us) autem eis· acci⟨-⟩
se hælend hlaf ⁊ bletsade ⁊ bræc ⁊ salde his disci⟨-⟩
pit ie(su)s panem et benedixit ac fregit deditq(ue) disci⟨-⟩
lum ⁊ cwæþ † ondfóþ ⁊ etæþ þis is
pulis suis diciens, accipite et manducate hoc est
forþon min lichoman ⁊ /—/ þa genom cælic þongade
enim corpus meum·, <27>Et accipiens calicem· gratias
⁊ salde heo(m) cwæþende † drincaþ of þas ealle ꝥ is
egit et dedit illis· diciens, bibite ex hoc omnes, <28>hic est
forþon blod min þara neowe gewitnisse þæt for mongum
enim sanguis meus noui testamenti qui pro multis
bið agoten in forletnisse synne ic sæcge þonne
effundetur in remisionem peccatorum·, <29>dico autem
eow forþon ne drince ic siðet of þissu(m) cynne wintreos
uobis quia non bibam amodo de hoc genimine uitis
oð þæne dæg þon(ne) ic hit drince eow mid neowe
usq(ue) in diem illum·, quod illud bibam uobiscum nouum
in rice fæder mines ⁊ /—/ ymne acwædene eodun ut on oelebearwes
in regno patris mei·, <30>et imno dicto exierunt in montem
dune þa cwæþ to his disc(i)p(ulum) † ealle ge æswic ł ⁊spyrnnisse
olieti·, <31>Tunc ait discipulís suís·, omnes uos scanda⟨-⟩
þrowigaþ on me to þisse næhte awriten is forþon
lum patiemini in me in ista nocte·, scriptum est enim·,
ic slæ heorde ⁊ tostænced beoþ scep þæs edæs
percutiam pastorem et dispergentur oues gregis·,
æfter þon þanne ðe ic æftarise ic forega eow
<32>postquam autem resurrexero praecidam uos
in galilea /—/ ⁊swarade þa petre cwæþ hi(m) to
in galileam·, <33>respondens autem petrus dixit ei·,
⁊ þæh þe ealle æswice þrowige on þe ic næfræ
Et si omnes scandalizati fuerint in te ego numqua(m)
þrowe cwæþ hæl(end) to him þæt to ðisse niht ær þon
scandalizabor·, <34>ait illi ie(su)s·, quia in hac nocte ante⟨-⟩
hona cræd þriowa me onsæcest cwæþ hi(m) petrus to
quam gallus cantet ter me negabis·, <35>ait illi petrus·,
þæh þe ic scyle sweltan mið ðe ne ⁊sace ic ðe swa ge⟨-⟩
etiamsi oportuerit mori tecum non te negabo·, simili⟨-⟩
lice ⁊ ealle þa leorneras cwædun þa cwo(m) se hælend
ter et omnes discipuli dixerunt·, <36>tunc uenit ie(su)s

1 non nasci ille] ei si natus non fuisset R^{c} (*added above the line with the original dotted*) Y WW | homo] + ille R^{c} Y WW | respondit] respondens Y WW 2 traditurus erat] tradidit Y WW | eum] + dixit R^{c} Y WW 3 iesus] *om.* Y WW | cannantibus] cænnantibus R^{c} cenantibus Y WW | accipit] accepit Y WW 5 diciens] dicens R^{c} et ait Y WW | manducate] comedite Y WW 6 enim] *om.* Y WW 7 diciens] dicens R^{c} Y WW 9 effundetur] effunditur Y WW 10 quia] *om.* Y WW 11 illum] *om.* Y WW=R | quod illud] cum illum Y cum illud WW 13 olieti] oliueti R^{c} Y WW | ait discipulís suís] dicit illis iesus Y WW | omnes] omnis R^{c} Y WW=R^{*} 16 praecidam] praecedam R^{c} Y WW 17 dixit ei] ait illi Y WW 19 iesus] + amen dico tibi R^{Fa} *(in the left-hand margin with the gloss,* soþ ic sæcge þe) Y WW 21 oportuerit] + me R^{Fa} Y WW

mid heo(m) in tún þone þe hatte gezemani ⁊ cwæþ to his
Cum illis in uillam qui dicitur gethsamani· ait disci⟨-⟩
† sittaþ her oþ ꝥ ic gange geond ⁊ gebidde me
pulís suís·, sedite hiic donec uadam illuc adorare·,
⁊ /—/ genom petrus ⁊ twægen sunas zebedeo ongan
<37>et adsumpto petro et duob(us) filiis zebedei coepit
beon unrot ⁊ in unbliðu(m) mode cwæþ ða to heo(m) † unrot is
contristari et mestus esse·, <38>tunc ait illís·, tristis est
min saul oð to deaðe abidęþ her ⁊ wæccaþ
anima mea usq(ue) ad mortem·, sustinete híc et uigilate
m'i'd me ⁊ /—/ forþor hwæne gangende on his ondwliotu
mecum·, <39>et progressus pussillum procidit in facia(m)
gebiddende ⁊ cwæþende † fæder min gif þæt beon mæge leore
suam orans et dicens·, Pater si possibile est tran⟨-⟩
fro(m) me þes calic hweþre þon(ne) nalles swa ic wille
seat a me calix iste·, sed tamen non sicut ego uolo
ah swa þu wilt ⁊ /—/ cwom to þæ(m) ⁊ ge⟨-⟩
sed sicut tú uís·, <40>et uenit ad discipulos suos et in⟨-⟩
mette hiæ slepende ⁊ cwæþ to petre swæ ne mæhtest
uenit eos dormientes·, et dicit petro·, sic non posuisti
ane hwile ł tid awæccan mid me † wæcceþ ⁊ gebiddaþ eow ꝥ ge
unam horam uigilare mecum,ɼ <41>uigilate et orate né
ne gangan in costunge min gast gearo is
intretis in temptationem·, sp(iritu)s quidem prumptus (est)
ꝥ lic þon(ne) is untrum /—/ eft oþre siðe eode ⁊ gebęd
caro autem infirma·, <42>iterum secundo abiit· et ora⟨-⟩
cweþende † fæder min gif ne mæge þeos cælic leoran
uit dicens·, pater meus si non potest hic calix transire
fro(m) me nymþe ꝥ ic of him drince beo hit þin willæ ⁊ /—/ cwom
á me nisi ut illum bibam fiat uoluntas tua·, <43>et uenit
æft ⁊ gemette heo slepende forþon þe heora eagun
iterum et inuenit eos dormientes·, erant enim ocli
wærun swiþe áhæfgad ⁊ hiæ forletende æft eode ⁊ gebed
eorum grauati·, <44>Et relictís iterum abiit et orauit
ðridde siðe þæt ilce word cwæþende þa cwom to his
tertio· eundem sermonem dicens·, <45>tunc uenit ad dis⟨-⟩
⁊ cwæþ heo(m) to † slepað nu ⁊ eow restęþ
cipulos suos et ait illis·, dormite iam et requiescite·,
henu tonealiceþ hwil ⁊ monnes sune bið sald
ecce adpropinquabit hora et filius hominis trade⟨-⟩
in honda synfulra arisaþ wutu gángan
tur in manus hominum peccatorum·, <46>surgite eamus
henu toneoliceþ se þe mec sellað /—/ þenden hiæ þa swa sprecun x(ƀ)
ecce adpropinquauit qui me tradet·, <47>adhuc eo loquen⟨-⟩
te

1 qui] quae Y WW | ait] et dixit R^c Y WW 2 adorare] et orem Y WW 7 pater] + mi R^{Fa} Y WW=R^* mi pater Xz 8 a me] *om.* Y WW=R | sed tamen] ueruntamen R^c Y WW 9 uis] *om.* Y^* WW Y^c=R 9 suos] *om.* Y WW 10 posuisti] potuisti R^c potuistis Y WW 11 unam horam] una hora Y WW | ne] ut non Y WW 12 prumptus] promitus Y promtus WW 14 meus] mi R^c Y WW 15 a me] *om.* Y WW | nisi ut illum bibam] nisi bibam ut illum R^c (*marked by* signes de renvoi) nisi bibam illum Y WW 16 ocli] oculi R^c Y WW 17 relictis] + illis Y WW 19 ait] dicit Y WW 20 adpropinquabit] adpropinquauit Y (app-) WW | tradetur] traditur Y Xz WW=R 21 hominum] *om.* R^c Y WW 22 tradet] tradit Y WW | eo] illo Y WW

xƀ henu iudas an of þære twelfe cwom ⁊ mid him mengu micel
Ecce iudas unus de xii· uenit et cum eo turba multa
mid sweordum ⁊ stængum asended fro(m) aldorsacerdum
cum gladís et fustibus misi á principibus sacerdotu(m)
⁊ þæ(m) ældran þæs folces se þe þon(ne) salde ł sellend hine salde
et seniorib(us) populi·, <48>qui autem tradidit eum dedit
heo(m) tacun cwæþende swa hwilc swa ic cysse
illis signum diciens·, quemcumq(ue) osculatus fuero
se hit is gen'i'meþ hine ⁊ sonæ gangende to hæl(ende) cwæþ
ipse est tenete eum <49>et confestim accidens ad ie(su)m dixit,
hal lareu ⁊ he cyste hine cwæþ hi(m) to se hælend †freond
haue rabbi⁓ et osculatus est eum·, <50>dixitq(ue) ie(su)s·, amice⁓
to hwon cwome ðu /—/ þa eoden ⁊ honda
ad quod uenisti⁓ fac Tunc accesserunt et manus ini(-)
fengon on þone hæl(end) ⁊ genomun hine ⁊ henu an of þara
ecerunt in ie(su)m et tenuerunt eum·, <51>et ecce unus ex hiis
þe werun mið þæ(m) hæl(ende) aþenende honda gebrægd his sweord
qui erant cum ie(s)u extendens manum eximit gladiu(m)·
⁊ slog esne þæs aldorsacerdos ⁊ heow
et percussit seruum principis sacerdotum et absci(-)
eara his þe swiðræ þa cwæþ hæl(end) heo(m) to †gecer
dit auriculam eius dexteram·, <52>tunc ait illi ie(su)s·, conuer(-)
þin sweord in his stowe ealle forþon þa þe niomaþ
te gladium tuum in locum suum·, omnes enim qui acci(-)
sweord in sweorde forweorþað þu wenest þæt
piunt gladium in gaudio peribunt·, <53>án putas quia
ic næ mæge biddan fæder min ⁊ he selle me nu
non possim rogare patrem meum et exibit mihi
mæ þon(ne) twælf þusend herigæs ængla ah hu þon(ne) bioþ
plus quam xii· legiones angelorum·,⁓ <54>quomodo ergo
gefylled gewritu þe þus sceal beon
inplebuntur scripturae quia sic oportet fieri·,⁓
/—/ on þære hwile cwæþ se hælend to þæ(m) mængu(m) †swa to
<55>in illa autem hora dixit ie(su)s turbis·, quassi ad la(-)
scaþe ge eoden ut mid sweordum ⁊ stængum to fóne
tronem uenisti cum gladís et fustib(us) conpræhen(-)
me dæghwæmlice mid eow ic sætt in templæ
dere me·, cotidie apud uos sedebam in templo
lærende ⁊ mec ne noman /—/ þis þon(ne) eall gewarð
docens et non me tenuistis·, <56>hoc autem totum fac(-)
þæt wære gefylled gewriotu witgana
tum est ut adinplerentur scripturæ profetaru(m)·,
þa þa leorneras ealle forletende hine flugen ⁊ hiæ genoman
tunc discipuli eius relicto eo fugerunt·, <57>at illi tenentes
hine
eum

2 misi] missi Y WW *om.* Xz 4 diciens] dicens R^c Y WW 6 dixitque] + illi Y WW 7 fac] *om.* R^c Y WW 9 eximit] exemit R^c Y WW | gladium] + suum R^Fa Y WW 10 percussit] percutiens Y WW | et abscidit] amputauit Y WW 11 dexteram] *om.* Y WW 12 omnes] omnis R^c Y WW=R^* | accipiunt] acciperint Y WW 13 in gaudio] gladio R^c Y WW 14 possim] possum Y WW | exibit] exibebit R^Fa exhibebit Y WW | mihi] + modo R^Fa Y WW 15 xii] + milia R^c Y WW=R^* 17 autem *om.* R^c Y WW | quassi] quasi R^c tamquam Y WW 18 uenisti] existis Y WW 19 in templo docens] docens in templo R^c (*marked by* signes de renvoi) Y WW 21 adinplerentur] implerentur Y WW 22 discipuli eius] discipuli omnes R^Fa Y WW 23 eum] iesum Y WW

⁊ læddon to caifan þæm aldorsacerdos
adduxerunt ad caifam principem sacerdotum·
þær þe bokeras ⁊ þa ældru werun ær gesomnade petrus þon(ne)
ubi scribæ et seniores conuenerunt·, <58>petrus aute(m)
folgade hine feorran oþ cæfertun þæs aldur⟨-⟩
sequebatur eum a longe usq(ue) in atrium· princi⟨-⟩
sacerdæs ⁊ ingangende gesæt betwih
pis sacerdotum et ingressus intro sedebat
mið þæ(m) þægnum þ he gesæge endunge þa aldor
cum ministrís ut uideret finem eius rei·,· <59>Principes
þa sacerdæs ⁊ ealle þ gemot sohtun
autem sacerdotum et omne concilium querebant
lyge gewitnisse wið þone hælend þ hine deaðe salde
falsum testimonium contra ie(su)m ut eum morti tra⟨-⟩
⁊ ne funden ⁊ þon(ne) monige lyge gewitu
derent <60>et non inuenerunt·, et cum multi falsi testes
cwomun æt næhste þa cwoman twægen lyge
accessisent nouissime autem uenerunt duo falsi
gewitu ⁊ cwædun þes cwæþ ic mæg toweorpan þas
testes <61>et dixerunt·, hic dixit·, possum distruere hoc
tempel godes ⁊ æft(er) ðrim dagum getimbre þæt ⁊
templum d(e)i· et post triduum ædificabo illud·, <62>ex⟨-⟩
arisende aldursacerd cwæþ to hi(m) nawiht ⁊wyr⟨-⟩
surgens princeps sacerdotum ait illi·, nihil res⟨-⟩
dest to þæm þe þas cyþan wið þe
pondes ad ea quae isti testificantur aduersum
hælend þa swigade ⁊ aldur sacerdæs
te·, <63>ie(su)s autem tacebat· et princeps sacerdotum·
cwæþ to hi(m) ic halsio þe þurh god þone lifgende þ þu sæcge us gif
ait illi·, adiuro té per d(eu)m uiuum ut dicas nobis si
þu sy crist godes sunu þæs lifgende cwæþ heo(m) to hæl(end) þu† þ cwæde hwæþre
tú és cr(istu)s filius d(e)i uiui·, <64>Dicit ei ie(su)s·, tú dixisti· ueru(m)
þon(ne) ic sæcge eow æft(er) þisse geseoþ sunu monnes sittende
tamen dico uobis a modo uidebitis filium hominis
on þa swiðran halfe godes mægænes ⁊ cumende in wolcnum heofunas
ad dexteram uirtutis et uenientem in nubib(us) caeli·,
þa / — / se aldur sacerdæs slat hrægl
<65>tunc princeps sacerdotum scidit uestimenta
his cwæþende he efalsade hwæt ðurfe wæ leng gewitnisse
sua dicens·, blasfemauit·, quid adhuc egimus testib(us)·ꝛ
henu ge nu geherdun efalsunge hwæt ðynceþ
ecce nunc audistis blasfemiam·, eius, <66>quid uobis
eow hiæ ⁊swaredun ⁊ cwædun he his scyldig dead
uidetur·ꝛ at illi responderunt et dixerunt· reus (est) mor⟨-⟩
tis·,

1 adduxerunt] duxerunt Y WW 2 conuenerunt] conuenerant Y WW 5 eius rei] *om.* R[c] (*by encircling*) Y WW 8 et[2]] *om.* Y WW 10 hoc] *om.* Y WW 11 ædificabo] aedificare Y WW | exsurgens] et exsurgens R[c] et surgens Y WW 12 respondes] respondens Y WW=R 13 testificantur aduersum te] aduersum te testificantur Y WW 16 uiui] *om.* Y WW | ei] illi Y WW 17 hominis] + sedentem R[Fa] Y WW 18 ad dexteram] a dextris Y WW | uirtutis] + dei R[c] Y WW= R[*] 20 egimus] egemus Y WW 21 blasfemiam] blasphemia Y blasphemiam WW | eius] *om.* R[c] (*crossed out*) Y WW 22 responderunt et] respondentes Y WW

þa spittadun on his ondwliotu ⁊ mid hondu(m) hine
<67>Tunc expuerunt in faciem eius et colophís eum
slogun sume þon(ne) mid brade honde on his ondwliotu hine
cederunt·, Alii autem palmas in faciem eius dede(-)
slogun cwæþende witga us crist hwa is ꝥ þe
runt <68>dicentes·, profetiza nobis cr(ist)e quis est qui
slog petrus þon(ne) sætt þærúte in cæfertune
té percussit·⁏ <69>petrus uero sedebat foris in atrio·
⁊ eode to him an menen ł þeowæ cwęþende ⁊ þu ek mid
et accessit ad eum una ancella dicens·, tú cum
hælend þone galiliscu were ⁊ he onsóc beforan eallum
ie(s)u galileo eras·, <70>at ille negauit coram omnibus
cwæþende ne wat ic hwæt þu sægest þa he þa ut eode beforan dure
dicens·, nescio quid dicis·, <71>Exeunte autem illo ianua
gesæh hine oþer ⁊ cwæþ to þæ(m) þe þær weron ⁊ þes wæs ek
uidit eum alia et ait hiis qui erant ibi·, Et hic erat
mid þæ(m) hælend þone nazarenisco ⁊ æft ⁊soc mid haþe
cum ie(s)u nazareno·, <72>et iterum negauit cum iura(-)
ꝥ ic ne conn þone monn ⁊ ymb lytle hwile
mento dicens non noui hominem·, <73>Et post pussillu(m)
þa þe stodun eodun forð ⁊ cwædun to petre soþlice
qui stabant accesserunt· et dixerunt petro·, ue(-)
⁊ þu eart \`ec´ heora ⁊ reord þin ek þæc gecyþæþ
re et tú ex illis és·, nam et loquella tua manifes(-)
þa ongon he ⁊ustriga ⁊ swerige
tum té facit·, <74>Tunc coepit detestare et iurare
ꝥ he ne cuðe þone monn ⁊ hræðe hona
quia non nouisset hominem·, et continuo gallus
creow ⁊ þa gemunde petrus word þæs hæl(endes) þe
cantauit·, <75>et recordatus est petrus uerbi ie(s)u quod
he cwæþ ær þon hona crǽd þriuwa me ondsacast
dixerat priusquam gallus cantet ter me negabis·,
⁊ gangende út weop bitterlice þa hit þa morgen
et egressus foras fleuit amarissime·, <XXVII 1>mane
wæs in þæhtunge eodun ealle aldur(-)
iam facto consilium fecerunt omnes principes
sacerdæs ⁊ ældre þæs folces wið þæ(m) hælend
sacerdotum et seniores populi aduersus ie(su)m
ꝥ hine to deaþe salden ⁊ gebundene læddun
ut eum morti traderent· <2>et uinctum adduxe(-)
hine ⁊ saldun pontiscan pylato þæm ge(-)
runt eum et tradiderunt pontio pylato præs(-)
roefæ þa geseah iudas se þe hine salde
sidi <3>tunc uidens iudas qui eum tradidit

1 colophis] colaphis R^c Y WW 2 cederunt] ceciderun Y WW | eius] ei Y WW 5 dicens] + et R^c Y WW 7 ianua] ianuam Y WW 8 alia] ancilla Y WW=R 10 dicens] quia R^Fa (*original expuncted, addition above the line*) Y WW 11 qui stabant accesserunt] accesserunt qui stabant Y WW 12 et[1]] *om.* Y WW=R 14 detestare] detestari Y WW 17 fleuit] plorauit Y WW | amarissime] amare R^c Y WW 18 iam] autem Y WW | fecerunt] inierunt Y WW

ꝥ he niðrad wæs mid hreownisse lædde ⁊ brohte
quia dampnatus est penetentia ductus re⟨-⟩
eft ðritig scyllinga aldursacerdum
tullit xxx· argenteos principibus sacerdotu(m)
⁊ þa eldran þæs folces ⁊ cwæþ ic gefirinade sellende
et seniorib(us) populi <4>dicens·, peccaui tradens
blod ꝥ soþfæste cwædun hye hwæt is us
sanguinem iustum·, At illi dixerunt·, quid ad nos
ꝥ locæ þu ⁊ þa wearp he þa scillingas in templ gewat
tú uideris·⸵ <5>et proiectís argenteis templo reces⟨-⟩
⁊ þonan gangende awyrgde hine þa aldur⟨-⟩
sit· et abiens laqueo sé suspendit <6>Tunc prin⟨-⟩
sacerdas þa genoman þa scillingas ⁊ cwedun
cipes sacerdotum aceptis argenteís dixerunt·,
ne mot heo mon sende in temples feh forþon þe ꝥ is weorð blodes
non licet eos mitti in corban· quia prætium est san⟨-⟩
⁊ þa ˋtoˊ geþæhtunge eodun gebohtun mið þæ(m) tigle ˋꝉ lamˊ wyrhte lond
guinis· <7>Consilio autem initio emerunt ex illis agru(m)
to bebyrgenne elðeodigra forþon wæs næmned
in sepulturam perigrinorum·, <8>propter hoc uoca⟨-⟩
ꝥ lond acheldemach ꝥ is blodes lond
tus est ager ille acheldemach·, quod est ager san⟨-⟩
oð þeosne dæg ⁊ þa gefyllad wæs
guinis usq(ue) in hodiernum diem·, <9>Tunc inpletum est
ꝥte cwæden wæs þurh hieremiam þone witgan cwæþen⟨-⟩
quod dictum est per heremiam profetam dicen⟨-⟩
de ⁊ genoman ðrittig scillinga weorþ þæs ge⟨-⟩
tem·, et accipierunt xxx argenteos prætium ad⟨-⟩
bohtæ þæs þe gebohtum æt israheles bearnum
prætiati quem adpraetiauerunt filii israhel·,
⁊ saldun þa in londe lamwyrhtæ swa me gesette
<10>et dederunt eos in agrum figuli sicut constituit
dryhten hælend þa stód beforan þæ(m) gehróefa ⁊ hine
mihi d(omi)n(u)s·;· <11>Ie(su)s autem stetit ante præsidem· et in⟨-⟩
frægn se geroefa cwæþende þu eart cyning iudeana
terrogauit eum praesis·, tú és rex iudæorum·,
⁊ cwæþ to heo(m) se hæl(end) þu † ꝥ cwiðst ⁊ / — / þa þe he wæs gewroeged fro(m) aldur⟨-⟩
et dicit ei ie(su)s·, tu dicis·, <12>et cum accussaretur· a prin⟨-⟩
sacerdum ⁊ eldran nauwiht ⁊swarede
cipib(us) sacerdotum et seniorib(us) nihil respondebat·,
þa cwæþ hi(m) to pilatos ah þu ne gehoerest hu miccle wið þe
<13>tunc dicit ei pilatus·, non audis quanta aduersu(m)
sægcaþ cyðnisse ⁊ ne andwyrde him to anu(m)
te dicunt testimonia·, <14>et non respondit ei ad ullu(m)
worde
uerbum·,

1 quia] quod Y WW | est] esset Y WW 3 populi] *om.* Y WW 5 argenteis] + in R^{Fa} Y WW 6 Tunc principes] principes autem Y WW 7 aceptis] acceptis R^{c} Y WW 8 eos mitti] mittere eos R^{c} (mitti *corrected to* mittere; *the word order marked by* signes de renvoi) Y WW | corban] corbanan R^{c} Y WW | est sanguinis] sanguinis est R^{c} (*marked by* signes de renvoi) Y WW 9 agrum] + figuli R^{Fa} Y WW 11 quod est] *om.* Y WW 12 tunc] et tunc Y WW Xz=R 14 accipierunt] acceperunt Y WW 15 adpraetiauerunt] + a R^{c} Y WW | filii] filiis Y WW 18 praesis] + dicens R^{c} Y WW 19 et^{1}] *om.* Y WW 20 respodebat] respondit Y WW 21 ei] illi Y WW 22 dicunt] dicant Y WW

swa þæt he wundrade se geroefa swiðe on dæge
ita ut miraretur praesis uehimenter·, <15>per diem
þa heora symbel gewunede sé geroefæ þe he
autem sollempnem constituerat praesis dimit⟨-⟩
forlete þæ(m) folce enne gebundenne þene þe he walden
tere populo unum uinctum quem uoluissent·,
hæfdun þanne þa enne gebundenne mernæ monn
<16>habebant autem tunc unum uinctum insignem
se wæs haten barrabas heo heo(m) þa gesomnadun
qui dicebatur barrabbas·, <17>Congregatis autem
cwæþ pilatus hwæþer willaþ ge ic forlete eow
illis dixit pylatus·, quem uultis dimittam uobis
barrabas oþþe se hælend þone þe cweden crist forþon he wiste
barrabban· An ie(su)m qui dicitur cr(istu)s·,r <18>sciebat eni(m)
ꝥ hiæ þurh æfeste saldun hine þa he þa sett
quod per inuidiam tradidissent eum·, <19>sedente (autem)
on hehsettle sende to him his wif cwæþende
eo pro tribunali missit ad eum uxor eius dicens·,
nawiht þe siæ on þæ(m) soþfæste gemænes feola ic forþan þrowade
nihil tibi sit et iusto illi· multa enim passas sum
todæge in gesihþe for him þa aldur⟨-⟩
hodie per uisum propter illum·, <20>principes aute(m)
sacerdum ⁊ þa ældran lærdun þæ(m) folce
sacerdotum· et seniores persuasserunt populo
þæt hiæ abeden barrabban ⁊ hælend soþlic fordydun ł slogan þa
ut peterent barabban· ie(su)m uero perderent·, <21>res⟨-⟩
⁊wyrde se geroefa cwæþ heo(m) to hwæþer willaþ ge eow
pondens autem præssis ait illis·, quem uultis uobis
þara twegra forleten beon hiæ þa cwædun cwæþ
de duob(us) dimitti·r at illi dixerunt barabban·, <22>dixit
heo(m) to pilatus hwæt dom ic þanne be hæl(ende) þæ(m) þe cwæden
illis pylatus·, quid igitur faciam de ie(s)u qui dicitur
is crist cwedun ealle sy ón rode genæglad cwæþ heo(m) se roefa to
cr(istu)s·r dicunt omnes crucifigetur·, <23>ait illis pylatus·,
hwæt dyde untale ⁊ heo swiðor cleopadun
quid enim mali fecit·, At illi magis clamabant
⁊ cwædun siæ nægled on róde þa gesæh þa pilatus
dicentes·, crucifigatur·, <24>uidens autem pylatus
þæt hi(m) nauwiht speou ah swiðor ungereo gewarð in þæ(m) folce
quia nihil proficeret sed magis túmultus in po⟨-⟩
genom wæt(er) ⁊ ðwog his honda beforan
pulo fieret· accepta aqua lauauit manus cora(m)
þæ(m) folcę cwæþende unsceþþende ic eam fro(m) blóde þisses soþfæste
populo· dicens·, innocens ego sum á sanguine iusti

2 constituerat] consueuerant Y WW 4 habebant] habebat Y WW | unum] *om.* WW 5 27.16 + qui propter homicidium misus fuerat in carcerem Y^Ald Y* WW=R | autem] ergo Y WW 9 eo] illo R^c (eo *is altered to* eum, *then marked for interchange with* illo *in line 11, which is altered from* illum) Y WW | eum] illum Y WW 10 sit] *om.* Y WW | passas] passa Y WW 11 illum] eum R^c Y WW 12 principes] princips Y Xz WW=R 13 populo] populis Y WW 15 dixit] dicit Y WW 17 crucifigetur] crucifigatur Y WW | pylatus] praeses Y WW 18 mali] male R^c Y WW=R* 20 in populo fieret] fieret in populo R^c (in *and* fieret *are marked with* signes de renvoi) fieret (*om.* in populo) Y WW 21 lauauit] lauit Y WW

ge lokigæþ eow ⁊ þa ⁊wyrdan eall ꝥ folc cwæþende
huius uos uidetis·, <25>Et respondens omnis populus
blod his ofer us ⁊ ofer bearn ure þa
sanguis eius super nos et super filios nostros·, <26>tunc
forlet he heo(m) hælend þon(ne) geswunganne salde
dimisit illis barabban· ie(su)m autem flagillatum tra⟨-⟩
heo(m) ꝥ he were on rode nægled þa þæs geroefe kęmpe ge⟨-⟩
didit eis ut crucifigetur, <27>Tunc milites præsidis sus⟨-⟩
noman hælend in gemote gesomnadun to him
cipierunt ie(su)m in prætorio congregauerunt ad eum
ealne þone þreat ⁊ gærwende hine gegærelum
uniuersam cohortem· <28>et exeuntes eum calamidem
reade ryfte ymbsaldun him ⁊ widende bæg
cocineam circumdederunt ei·, <29>Et plectentes corona(m)
of þornum gesettun on his heafud ⁊ hreod
de spinís inpossuerunt super capud eius· et arun⟨-⟩
in þa swiðran hond ⁊ kneu begende beforan hi(m) bismeradun
dinem in dexteram et genu flexu ante eum inludebant
cweþende hal cyning iudeana ⁊ þa spittende on him heor spaðl
dicentes·, aue rex iudæorum·, <30>tunc expuentes in eum
⁊ genoman ꝥ hreod ⁊ slogun his heafud
et accipierunt arundinem et percutierunt capud
⁊ æft(er) þon þe hiæ hine bismeradun ungeredun hine ðy ryhte
eius· <31>et postquam inlusserunt eum exuerunt cala⟨-⟩
⁊ gegearwadun hine his agene wede ⁊ læddun
midem· Et induerunt eum uestimentís eius· et addux⟨-⟩
hine ꝥ he þrowigan salde ⁊ þa hiæ þa ut eoden gemoettun
erunt eum ut crucifigeretur·, <32>Exeuntes autem inue⟨-⟩
monn cyreniscnę cymende ongæn heom
nerunt hominem cyrineum uenientem obiam sibi·
þæ(m) węs noma symon þone hiæ næddun ꝥ he bere
nomine simonem·, hunc angarizauerunt ut tollerent
his rode ⁊ þa cwoman in stowę se þe hatte golgoþa
crucem eius·, <33>et uenerunt in locum qui dicitur golgotha·
þæt is heafodpanne stouw stede genæmned ⁊ saldun
quod est caluariae locus nominatus·, <34>Et dederunt
him win drincan wið gallan gemænged ⁊ þa he inbergde
ei uinum bibere cum felle mixtum·, et cum gustasset
nolde he drincan æft(er) þon þa þe hiæ áhengon
noluit bibere·, <35>postquam autem crucifixerunt
hine gedældun his hrægl tán sendende
eum diuiserunt uestimenta eius sortem mittentes·,
⁊ sittende heoldun hine ⁊ settun
<36>et sedentes seruabant eum· <37>et inpossuerunt

1 uidetis] uideritis Y WW | omnis] uniuersus Y WW | populus] + dicens R[c] dixit Y WW 4 crucifigetur] crucifigeretur Y WW | suscipierunt] suscipientes Y WW 6 calamidem] clamidem Y (+ et induerunt eum tunicam purpuream clamydem) WW 8 inpossuerunt] posuerunt Y WW 9 dexteram] + eius R[c] dextra eius Y WW | flexu] flexo WW Y=R 10 tunc] et Y WW 11 et[1]] *om.* Y WW | accipierunt] acciperunt R[c] acceperunt Y WW | percutierunt] percutiebant Y WW 12 eum] ei Y WW | exuerunt] + eum R[Fa] Y WW | calamidem] clamidem R[c] clamyde Y WW clamydem Xz 13 adduxerunt] duxerunt Y WW 14 crucifigeretur] crucifigerent Y WW 15 uenientem obiam sibi] *om.* WW Y=R 18 nominatus] *om.* Y WW **(cont. on p. 182)**

ofer his heafud intinge his awritene þas
super capud eius causam ipsius scriptam·, hæc (est)
þis is hæl(end) crist cyningc iudeana þa wærun ahongenne
hic est ie(su)s cr(istu)s rex iudeorum·,· <38>Tunc crucifixerunt
mid hinę twægen scaþe oþre on þa swiðran ⁊ oþer on þa winstran
cum eo duos latrones unus á dextrís et unus á sinis⟨-⟩
hiæ þon(ne) foreliorende hefa\`l´sadun
trís <39>praetereuntes autem blasfemabant eum·
hroerende ł styredun heora heafud ⁊ cwædun se þe breceþ
Mouentes capita sua <40>et dicentes ·uá· qui distru⟨-⟩
templ ⁊ on þrim dagum æft getimbrað
ebas templum· et in triduo illud reaedificabas·,
hǽl þec seolfne gif godes sune siæ astig nu of
salua té ipsum si filius d(e)i és· discende nunc de
rode swa ek ⁊ ealle þa aldursacerdun
cruce <41>similiter et omnes principes sacerdotu(m)
bismerende mið bokeru(m) ⁊ þæ(m) eldrum cwæþende
inludentes· cum scribís et seniorib(us) dicentes·,
oþre he hælde ⁊ hine selfne ne mæg gehælun
<42>alios saluos fecit se ipsum non potest saluu(m)
gif he cyning syæ israhela astigæ nú of rode
facere·, si rex israhel est discendat nunc de cru⟨-⟩
⁊ we gelefæþ him getriowe in god ⁊ nu gefreoge
ce et credimus ei· <43>confidet in d(eu)m et nunc liberet
hine gif he wile forþon þe he cwæþ ꝥ ic godes sune eam ꝥ ilce
eum si uult·, dixit enim·, quia filius d(e)i sum·, <44>id ipsu(m)
þon(ne) ⁊ ek þa þeofes þe ahongenne werun mid hinę
autem et latrones qui crucifixerunt cum eo
ætwitun him æft(er) þon þe he þrowad wæs
inproperant ei· postquam crucifixus est:·
fro(m) þære syxta tid ł hwile þon(ne) geþriostra wyrdun
<45>A sexta autem hora tenebræ factae sunt
ofer ealle middang(eard) oþþe nigoþan tíd ł hwile
super uniuersam terram usq(ue) in horam no⟨-⟩
⁊ æt þære nigoþan tíd þa cliopade hælend
nam·, <46>et circa horam nonam· exclamauit ie(su)s
miclæ stæfnę cwæþende ·in g(recis)c † god min god min forhwon forletes þu mec
uoce magna dicens·, heli· heli· lama sabactha⟨-⟩
ꝥ is in lat(in) god min god min forhwon forletes þu me
ni·, hoc est d(eu)s meus· d(eu)s meus· quare me dereli⟨-⟩
/—/ sume þa þær stondende ⁊ þa geherende
quisti·, <47>quidam autem illic stantes et audientes
cwedun elia(m) cleopaþ ðeos ⁊ instyde arn
dicebant heliam uocat iste·, <48>et continuo occurrens

(f. 48r) 21 mittentes] + ut impleretur quod dictum est per prophetam diuiserunt sibi uestimenta mea et super uestem meam miserunt sortem Y WW=R
(f. 48v) 1 hæc] hic R^c *om.* Y WW | est] *om.* Y WW **2** cr(istu)s] *om.* Y WW | crucifixerunt] crucifixi sunt Y WW | duos] duo Y WW **5** ua] *om.* Y WW | distruebas] destruebat Y destruit WW **6** templum] + dei Y WW=R | reaedificabas] reaedificabat Y reaedificat WW **7** té ipsum] temet ipsum Y WW | nunc] *om.* Y WW **8** omnes] *om.* Y WW | principes] princips Y WW=R **9** dicentes] dicebant WW Y Xz=R **12** credimus] credemus Xz Y WW=R | confidet] confidit WW Y Xz=R | deum] deo Y WW | et²] *om* Y WW | nunc liberet] liberet nunc Y WW **13** uult] + eum Y WW Xz=R | filius dei] dei filius Y WW **(cont. on p. 183)**

an of heora genom spynge ⁊ gefylde
unus ex eis acceptam spongiam et inpleuit
ecedes ⁊ sette on hreod ⁊ salde hi(m) drincan
accæto· et inpossuit arundini et dabat ei bibe⟨-⟩
þa oþre þon(ne) cwædun abid hwute geseon hwæþer
re·, <49>cæteri uero dicebant·, sine uideamus án
cume elias ⁊ gefreoge hine
ueniat helias et liberat eum·, alius autem ac⟨-⟩

cepta lancia popungit latus eius· et exiit aqua
hælend þa æft cegde miccle stæfne
et sanguis·, <50>ie(su)s autem iterum exclans uoce
asende his gast ⁊ henu wágryft þæs temples to⟨-⟩
magna emissit sp(iritu)m·, <51>et ecce uelum templi sci⟨-⟩
berst in twægen dæles fro ufawarde to neoþewearde
sum est in duas partes a summo usque de⟨-⟩
⁊ eorþe styred wæs ⁊ stanes brustæn
orsum:· Et terra mota est et petræ scise sunt
⁊ byrgenne ontynde werun ⁊ monig lic
<52>et monumenta aperta sunt et multa corpora
haligra þære ðe ær sleptun arisen ⁊ gangende
s(an)c(t)orum· dormientium surrexerunt·, <53>et exeuntes
of byrgennum æfter his ærist̨ę cwoman
de monumentís post resurrectionem eius uene⟨-⟩
in þa halgan cæstræ ⁊ æteawdun monigvm
runt in s(an)c(t)am ciuitatem· et multís apparuerunt:·
se centurio þon(ne) ⁊ þa þe mid hinæ werun haldende
<54>Centorio autem et qui cum eo erant custodien⟨-⟩
hælend ⁊ gesegun þa eorðhroernisse ⁊ þa þe þęr gewurdun
tes ie(su)m· et uiso terrae motu et ea quae fiebant
frohtadun swiþe cwæþende soþlice godes sune `bearn' þes wæs
timuerunt ualde dicentes·, uere filius d(e)i erat
werun þon(ne) þær wif monige gesægun
iste·, <55>erant autem ibi mulieres multae uidentes
feorran þa þe ær fylgende werun hælend fro(m) galilea
á longe quae secutae fuerant ie(su)m a galilea
þægnende him betwix þæm wæs maria siu magda⟨-⟩
ministrantes illi·, <56>inter quas erat maria mag⟨-⟩
lenisca ⁊ maria iacobes ⁊ iosepep moder ⁊ moder sunena
dalena et maria iacobi et ioseph· et mater filio⟨-⟩
zebedeæs æt æfenne geworden wæs
rum zebedei·, <57>cum autem sero factum esset
cwom sum monn wælig fro(m) arimaðia se wæs haten
uenit quidam homo diues ab arimathia nomine
ioseph
ioseph·

(f. 48v) **14** crucifixerunt] fixi erant Y Xz crucifixi erant WW **15** inproperant] inproperabant R^{Fa} Y WW | postquam crucifixus est] *om.* Y WW **17** in] ad Y WW **18** et] *om.* Y WW=R | horam] + uero Y WW=R | exclamauit] clamauit Y WW **20** quare] ut quid Y WW | me dereliquisti] dereliquisti me Y WW **22** occurrens] currens Y WW (**f. 49r**) **1** et] *om.* Y WW **4** et liberat] liberans Y WW | alius … et sanguis (l.6)] *om.* Y WW **6** exclans] exclamans R^{Fa} clamans Y WW **11** dormientium] qui dormierunt R^{c} qui dormierant Y WW **13** multis apparuerunt] apparuerunt multis R^{c} (*marked by* signes de renvoi) Y WW **14** centorio] centori Y centurio WW **(cont. on p. 184)**

se ec wæs leornere þæs hælend se eode
Qui et ipse discipulus erat ie(s)u·, <58>hic accessit
to pilatus ⁊ bæd þæs hælendes lic þa pilatæ
ad pylatum et petit corpus ie(s)u·, tunc pylatus ius⟨-⟩
heht ageofan þæt lic ⁊ þa genoman þæs hælendes lic iosep bewand
sit dari corpus ie(s)u·, <59>et accepto corpore ie(s)u inuo⟨-⟩
in clæne scetan ⁊ alægde in
luit illud in sindone munda· <60>et possuit illud in
his byrgenne neowe ꝥte he ær geheu on stane ⁊
monumento suo nouo quod exciderat in petra·, et
towælede stan micelne to dure þære byrgenne
aduoluit saxum magnum et hostium monumenti
⁊ awæg eode wæs þa þær maria se magdalenisca ⁊ oþer
et abiit·, <61>erat autem ibi maria magdalena et al⟨-⟩
maria sittende togægnes þara byrgenne
tera maria sedentes contra sepulchrum:·
† þa oþer dæg se þe is æft(er) þæ(m) gearwunga dæge
<62>Altera autem die quae est post parasceuen
cwomun þa alduras sacerdæs ⁊ fariseas
conuenerunt principes sacerdotum et faris⟨-⟩
to pilatu(m) cwæþende dryhten gemynest þu
sæi ad pylatum <63>dicentes·, d(omi)ne rememorati sumus
þæt se forlænd cwæþ ꝥ he get lifde æft(er) þrim
quod seductor ille dixit adhuc uiuiens post tertiu(m)
dagu(m) ic æftarise hat forþon gehaldan þa byrgenne oþ
diem resurgam·, <64>iube ergo custodiri sepulchrum usq(ue)
ðridde dæg þy les cuman leorneras his ⁊ for⟨-⟩
in diem tertium· Ne forte ueniant discipuli eius et furen⟨-⟩
stælan hine ⁊ sæcgað folce he rás fro(m) deaþe ⁊ bið se æftera
tur eum· et dicent plebi surrexit á mortuis·, Et erit nouis⟨-⟩
gedwola wyrse þone þæ(m) ærran cwæþ heo(m) to pilatus ge habbaþ gehæld
simus error peior priori·, <65>ait illís pylatus·, Habetis mili⟨-⟩
gæþ ⁊ haldeþ swa ge cunnun hiæ þa awæg gangende mid
tes ite custodite sicut scitis·, <66>illi autem abeuntes cum
heordu(m) geoldun þa byrgenne gemerkade
custodibus munierunt sepulchrum·, signantes
þon stan mid heordum
lapidem et discesserint:·
on efenne þa þæs restedagas þæ(m) þe inlihte in forma dæg
<XXVIII 1>Uespere autem sabbati quae luciescit in prima
æft(er) restedæg cwom maria magdalenisca ⁊ oþer
sabbati· uenit maria magdalena et altera
maria to sceawenne þa byrgenne ⁊ henu eorþstyrennis
maria uidere sepulchrum· <2>Et ecce terræ motus

(f. 49r) 15 et[1]] *om.* Y WW | ea] his Y WW **16** filius dei] dei filius Y WW **17** uidentes] *om.* Y WW **18** fuerant] erant Y WW **19** illi] ei R[c] Y WW **20** ioseph] + mater Y WW **21** autem sero] sero autem Y WW
(f. 49v) 3 dari] reddi Y WW | ie(s)u[1]] *om.* R[c] Y WW | ie(s)u[2]] ioseph Y WW | inuoluit illud] *om.* Y WW=R **4** in[1]] *om.* Xz Y WW=R | munda] mundo Y WW=R **6** et] ab R[c] ad Y WW **9** post] *om.* Y WW=R **11** rememorati] recordati Y WW **12** quod] quia Y WW | tertium diem] tres dies Y WW **15** dicent] dicant R[c] Y WW **16** milites] custodia R[c] custodiam Y WW **17** cum custodibus] *om.* Y WW **19** et discesserunt] cum custodibus R[c] Y WW **20** prima] primam Xz Y WW=R

gewarð micelu ængel forþon dryhtnes astag of heo⟨-⟩
factus est magnus angelus enim d(omi)ni discendit de cæ⟨-⟩
funu(m) ⁊ togangende awælede þone stan ⁊ gesett on
lo et accedens reuoluit lapidem et sedebat super
þæm wæs þa his onseone swa leget ⁊ wæda ł rægl
eum· <3>erat autem aspectus eius sicut fulgor· et ues⟨-⟩
his hwit swa snau for h'i's ægsa þon(ne)
timenta eius candita sicut nix· <4>Præ timore aute(m)
afirde werun þa weardas ⁊ geworden swa
eius exterriti sunt custodes· et facti sunt uelud
deade andswarade þa se engel cwæþ to þæ(m) wifu(m)
mortui· <5>respondens autem angelus dixit mulie⟨-⟩
ne forhtige eow ic wat forþon ꝥ git hælend þone
rib(us) nolite timere uos· scio enim quod ie(su)m qui
þe hongen wæs gesoecaþ nis he her forþon þe he aras swa
crucifixus est quaeritis <6>non est hic surrexit enim si⟨-⟩
he cwæþ cumaþ ⁊ geseoþ þa stowe þær aseted wæs
cut dixit uenite et uidete locum· ubi possitus erat
dryhten ⁊ hræþe gangaþ sæcgaþ discipulas his ꝥ he aras
d(omi)n(u)s· <7>et cito euntes dicite discipulis eius quia surrexit
fro(m) deade ⁊ henu beforangæþ eow in galilea ðær
á mortuís· et ecce praecidit uos in galileam ibi
ge hine geseoþ henu swa ic foresægde ⁊ hiæ eodun hraþe
eum uidebitis et ecce dixi uobís· <8>et exierunt cito
of byrgenne mið egsa ⁊ mið gefea micel eornende
de monumento cum timore et gaudio magno cur⟨-⟩
secgan disc(ipu)l(as) his ⁊ henu hælend quom
rentes nuntiare discipulís eius· <9>et ecce ie(su)s occur⟨-⟩
heo(m) ongægn cwæþende beoþ hale hiæ þa stopen forþ
rit illis dicens auete ille autem accesserunt
⁊ genomen his foet ⁊ gebedun to him
et tenuerunt pedes eius et adorauerunt eum·
þa cwæþ heo(m) to se hæl(end) ne ondredeþ inc ah gæþ sæcgaþ
<10>tunc ait illís ie(su)s nolite timere sed ite nuntiate
broþru(m) minum ꝥ hiæ gangan in galilea þær hi me geseoþ
fratribus meis ut eant in galileam ibi me uide⟨-⟩
þa hí þa awæg eodun henu sume þara
bunt· <11>quae cum abissent ecce quidam de cus⟨-⟩
wearda cwomun in cæstre ⁊ sægdun
todibus uenerunt in ciuitatem et adnuntiaue⟨-⟩
þa aldursacerdum eall ꝥ þe þær
runt principibus sacerdotum omnia quae
gedóen werun ⁊ hiæ gesomnade mið ðæm ældrum
facta fuerant· <12>et congregati cum senioribus

3 eum] eam Y[Ald] Y* WW=R | autem] enim Y WW=R | uestimenta] uestimentum Y WW 4 candita] *om.* Y WW 9 et] *om.* Y WW 10 euntes] eunte Y WW=R 11 a mortuis] *om.* Y WW 12 et[1]] *om.* R[c] Y WW | dixi] predixi R[c] praedixi Y WW 13 gaudio mango] mango gaudio Y WW 15 ille] illae Y WW 17 sed] *om.* Y WW 20 adnuntiauerunt] nuntiauerunt Y WW

geþæhtunge ineoden onfengon feoh geny`h´tsum saldun
consilio accepto pecunia(m) copiosam dede⟨-⟩
þæ(m) kempum cwæþende sæcgaþ þæt his discip(u)l(as)
runt militibus <13>dicentes dicite quia discipuli
on næht cwomun ⁊ forstælen hinæ us
eius nocte uenerunt et furati sunt eum nobis
slepende ⁊ gęf þ gehoered bið fro(m) geroefe
dormientibus· <14>Et si hoc auditum fuerit á prae⟨-⟩
we getæceþ ł scyaþ him ⁊ orsorge eow gedoaþ
side nos suadebimus ei et securos uos faciamus
⁊ hię onfengon þæ(m) feo dydun swa hiæ werun
<15>at illi accepta pecunia fecerunt sicut erant
gelærde ⁊ gemæred wæs word þis mið iudeum
docti· et deuulgatum est uerbum istud apud iu⟨-⟩
oþ þisne ondwardan dæg þa enlefan
deos usq(ue) in hodiernum diem:· <16>Undecim (autem)
his þa eodun on dune
discipuli eius abierunt in galileam in montem
þær gesætte ær heo(m) se hæl(end) ⁊ geseonde hine to him
ubi constituerat illís ie(su)s· <17>et uidentes eum ad⟨-⟩
bedun sume þon(ne) tweodun ⁊ heo(m) to⟨-⟩
orauerunt· Quidam autem dubitauerunt <18>et ac⟨-⟩
gangende se hæl(end) spræc to heo(m) cwæþende gesald is me
cedens ie(su)s locutus est eis dicens data est mihi
æghwilc mæht on heofune ⁊ on eorþe gæþ forþon
omnes potestas in cælo et in terra· <19>euntes ergo
nu læreþ alle ðeode dyppende hiæ in
nunc docete omnes gentes babtizantes eas· in
noman fæder ⁊ sunu ⁊ þæs halgan gastes lærende hiæ
nomine patris et filii et sp(iritu)s s(an)c(t)i· <20>Docentes eos
to healdene eall swa hwæt swa ic bebead
obseruare omnia quaecumq(ue) mandaui
eow ⁊ henu ic mid eow eam ealle
uobis Et ecce ego uobiscum sum omnibus
dagas oð to ende weorulde
diebus usque ad consummationem saeculi:·
endeþ soþlice endeþ soþ endeþ
finit amen finit amen finit:·:·

Farᛗ p(res)b(yte)r þas boc þus gleosede dimittet ei d(omi)n(u)s omnia peccata sua si fieri po(test) ap(ud) d(eu)m:·

1 consilio] consilium Y WW=R 5 faciamus] faciemus Y WW 9 eius] *om.* Y WW 13 omnes] omnis WW Y=R 14 nunc] *om.* Y WW | eas] eos Y WW 15 spiritus] spiritu Y WW=R 16 obseruare] seruare Y WW 19 finit amen finit amen finit] amen Y *om.* WW

incipit
euange⟨-⟩
lium
secun⟨-⟩
dum·
mar⟨-⟩
cum

onfruma
<I 1>**Initium**
godspelles hælendes
euangelii ie(s)u
cristes sunu godes swa awriten is
cr(ist)i filii d(e)i <2>**sicut scriptum est**

in esaia þone witgu henu ic sende engel
in esaia propheta· Ecce mitto angelu(m)
min beforan onseone þine se þe f(or)egearwað
meum ante faciem tuam qui praepara⟨-⟩
weg þinre stemn cliopande in westenne
bit uiam tuam:· <3>Uox clamantis in deserto
gearwigað weig drihtnes rehte wyrcaþ ł doað stige ł gongas his
parate uiam d(omi)ni rectas facite semitas eius:·
wæs ioh(anne)s in westenne gefulwade ⁊ bodade
<4>Fuit iohannis in deserto babtizans et prae⟨-⟩
fullwiht hreownisse in forgefnisse
dicans babtismum paenitentiae in remisi⟨-⟩
synna ⁊ færende wæs ł foérde to him
onem peccatorum· <5>Et egrediebatur ad illu(m)
alle iudeas londe ⁊ ða hierosolimisca alle
omnis iudeae regio· et hierusolimitæ uniuersi:·
⁊ gefullwade fro(m) him in iordanes streame
Et babtizabantur ab illo in iordanis flu⟨-⟩
ondetende synna heora ⁊ wæs iohannes
mine confitentes pecca sua:· <6>Et erat iohannis
gegerelad ł gewedad mið herum cameles ⁊ gyrdels fellenne ymb
uestitus pylis camelli et zona pillicia circa
lendenu his ⁊ waldstapan ł lo\p/pestra ⁊ wuduhuniges ꝥ wæxeþ on wudebendum
lumbos eius et lucustas et mel siluestræ
⁊ ꝥ brucende wæs ⁊ bodade cweþende cymeþ dom
ædebat <7>Et praedicabat dicens uenit
strongre mec æft(er) me ðæs ł his nam ic wyrðe
fortior me post me cuius non sum dignus
forehlutende undon ł loesan þwongas gescoas
procumbens soluere corrigiam calcia⟨-⟩
his ic fulwade eowic in wætre
mentorum eius <8>ego babtizaui uos aqua
he wiotudlice gefulwað ⁊ aworden wæs in
ille uero babtizabit <9>et factum est in
dagum ðæm cwom þe hælend fro(m) nazareð þære byrig to galilea
diebus illís uenit ie(su)s a nazareth galileae
⁊ gefulwad wæs in iordanen fro(m) iohanne
et babtizatus est iordane ab iohanne
⁊ onstyde astag of wætre geseh
<10>et statim ascendens de aqua uidit

5 iohannis] iohannes Y WW 9 iordanis] iordane Y WW 10 pecca] peccata R^{Fa} Y WW | iohannis] iohannes Y WW 11 pillicia] pellicia R^{c} Y WW 12 lucustas] locustas R^{c} Y WW=R 17 babtizabit] + uos in sp(irit)u s(an)c(t)o R^{Fa} (*in the left-hand margin with the gloss*, eowic mið gaste halgu(m)) uos spiritu sancto Y WW 19 est] + in R^{c} Y WW | ab] a R^{c} Y WW=R^{*}

ontynde heofunas ⁊ gastes halga swilce culfra
apertos caelos et sp(iritu)m tamquam colu(m)⟨-⟩

ofdunestigende ⁊ wuniende in him ł in ðæm ⁊
bam discendentem et manentem in ipso <11>et

stæfn geworden wæs of heofune þu eart sunu min
uox facta est de caelis tú és filius meus

leof on ðe ic wel licade ⁊ sona ðe gast
dilectus in te conplacui:· <12>Et statim sp(iritu)s

draf hine on westen ⁊ wæs on westen
expulit eum in desertum <13>et erat in deser⟨-⟩

feowertig daga ⁊ feowertig næhta ⁊ wæs acunnad
to ·xl diebus· et xl noctib(us) et temptabatur

fro(m) þæm wiðerwearda wæs mið wildedeorum ⁊ englas
a satana:· Eratq(ue) cum bestis et angeli

geþegnedon ł herdon him æfter þon wutudlice gesald wæs
ministrabant ei:· <14>Postquam traditus (est)

iohannes com se hæl(end) in galilea bodade
iohannis uenit ie(su)s in galileam:· Praedicans

godspelles rice godes ⁊ cweþende forþon gefylled
euangelium regni d(e)i <15>et dicens quoniam inple⟨-⟩

is tide ⁊ togenealacede rice
tum est tempus et adpropinquauit regnu(m)

godes hreowsiaþ ⁊ gelefaþ in godspell ⁊ færende
d(e)i paenitemini et credite euangelio <16>et prae⟨-⟩

bi sæ galilea gesæh simone(m) ꝥ is petrus
teriens secus mare galileae uidit simone(m)

⁊ andreas broðer his hia sendende nett
et andream fratrem eius mittens retia

on sæ werun forþon fisceres ⁊ cwæþ heom to
in mare erant enim piscatores:· <17>Et dixit

se hæl(end) cumaþ æfter me ⁊ gedoa eowic ꝥ ge beoþan ł ge seon
ie(su)s uenite post me et faciam uos fieri

fisceres monnu(m) ⁊ ricenlice mið þy forleten
piscatores hominum <18>et protinus relictís

nett fylgende werun him ⁊ foerde
retibus secute sunt eum:· <19>Et progressus

þonan lytel hwon gesæh iacobus zebedes sunu ⁊ iohan⟨-⟩
in pussillum uidit iacobum zebedei et io⟨-⟩

nes broðer his ⁊ þa ilca ł hia in scip
hannem fratrem eius et ipsos in naui

1 sp(iritu)m] + s(an)c(tu)m R^{Fa} Y WW=R 2 discendentem] descendentem R^{Fa} Y WW 3 caelis] celis Y^{*} Y^{Ald} WW=R 5 expulit] expellit Y WW 8 ei] illi Y WW | Postquam] + aut(em) R^{Fa} Y WW 9 iohannis] iohannes Y WW 10 inpletum] impletum R^{c} Y WW 14 mittens] mittentens R^{Fa} mittentes Y WW 15 dixit] + eis R^{Fa} Y WW 18 secute] secuti Y WW 19 in] inde R^{Fa} Y WW

gesetton þ nett ⁊ sona ł ðariht geceigde hia
conponentes retia sua <20>et statim uocauit eos
⁊ mið þy f(or)let fæder his zebedeus in scipe mið þæ(m) hyre(-)
et relicto patre suo zebedeo in naui cum mer(-)
monnum fylgende wærun him ⁊ infoerdun caphar(-)
cinarís secuti sunt eum:· <21>Et ingredietur cap(-)
naum þære byrg ⁊ sona restedagas infoerde ł ineode to somnu(-)
harnauum et statim sabbatis ingressus in sina(-)
gum gelærde hia ⁊ swigadun ł stylton ofer lære
gogam docebat eos:· <22>Et stupebant super doc(-)
his wæs forþon lærende hia swilce ł swa hæ mæhte
trinam eius· Erat enim docens eos quasi potes(-)
hæfde ⁊ no swa uðwutu ⁊ wæs in
tatem habens et non sicut scribae:· <23>Et erat in
somnungum heora monn in gaste unclænum ⁊ oft cleopade
sinagoga eorum homo in sp(irit)u inmundo et exclama(-)
cwæþende hwæt us ⁊ ðe þv hælend ðæ nazarenisca come þu
uit <24>dicens quid nobis et tibi ie(s)u nazarene uenisti
to losane ł lorene usic ic wat hwæt þu þu eart halig god ⁊ bebeod ł beboden
perdere nos· scio quis sis s(an)c(tu)s d(e)i· <25>Et comminatus
is him se hæl(end) cwæðende swiga þu ⁊ gaa of ðæm menn gast
est ei ie(su)s dicens obmutuesce et exii de homine sp(iritu)s
unclæne ⁊ bitende ł bat hine gast ðe unclæne ⁊ of(-)
inmunde <26>Et discerpiens eum sp(iritu)s inmundus· et ex(-)
cliopande stæfne micelre ł miccle ⁊ ofeode fro(m) him ⁊ wundrende wærun
clamans uoce magna exiuit ab eo <27>et mirati sunt
alle þus þte hie frugno ł ascadun betwihc heom cweþende
omnes ita ut conquirerent inter sé dicentes
hwæt þ is þis hwilc lar þios ł ðas niowa is
Quidnam est hoc quae doctrina haec noua est
forþon in mæhte ⁊ gastum unclænum hataþ
quia in potestate et spiritib(us) inmundis imperat
⁊ edmodað him ⁊ sprang ł foerde mersung ł merðo his sona ł ˋinˊstyde ł ræþe
et oboediunt ei· <28>et processit rumor eius statim
in eallum þę(m) londe galilæę ⁊ recene
in uniuersam regionem galileae:· <29>Et protinus
foerde of somnunga comon in hus þ is pe(-)
egredientes de sinagoga uenerunt in domum sy(-)
trus ⁊ andreas mið iacob ⁊ iohannes gelegen wæs
monis et andreae cum iacob et iohanne <30>decumbe(-)
wutudlice swægre þ is petrus feferdrifende ⁊ ræþe
bat autem socrus symonis febricitans et statim
cwedun to him of þæ(m) ł of þære ⁊ com geneolacede ahof ða ilca ⁊ mið þy gegripen
dicunt ei de illa· <31>et accedens leuauit eam adpræ(-)
wæs
chensa

1 sua] *om.* Y WW | eos] illos Y WW 3 ingredietur] ingrediuntur Y WW 4 in] *om.* Y WW 5 doctrinam] doctrina Y WW 10 quis] qui WW Y=R | sis] es R[Fa] Y WW=R* 11 obmutuesce] ommutesce Y* obmutesce Y[c] WW | exii] exi Y WW | sp(iritu)s inmunde] *om.* Y WW 12 discerpiens] discerpens Y WW 15 est[2]] *om.* Y WW 18 uniuersam] omnem Y WW 22 lauauit] elauauit Y WW | eam] + et Y WW=R | adpræchensa] et praehensa Y adprehensa WW

hond his ⁊ ricenlice forlet hio hal fro(m) ridesohte ˋł gedrifˊ ⁊ geþæignade
manu eius et continuo dimisit eam febris et minis⟨-⟩
heom æfen wutudlice þa gewarð mið þy to sete eode sunne
bat eis· <32>Uespere autem facto cum occidisset sol
gefoerdun ł brohtun to him alle þa yfle hæbbende ⁊ deoful
adferebant ad eum· omnes male habentes et dæ⟨-⟩
hæbende ⁊ wæs alle cæstre ł burg gesomnad
monia habentes <33>et erat omnis ciuitas congregata
to dore ł geat ⁊ lecnade monige þa þe werun geswæncte
ad ianuam <34>et curauit multos qui uexabantur
missenlicum adlum ⁊ deofles monige he f(or)draf ł afirde
uaris langoribus et dæmonia multa eiciebat:·
⁊ ne let him sprecan forþon he wisten hine
Et non sinebat ea loqui quoniam sciebant eum:·
⁊ on æringe swiðe aras ⁊ foerde ł færende eode in
<35>Et diluculo ualde surgens et egressus abiit in
westige stowe ł stede ⁊ ðer gebęd ⁊ fylgende wæs him
desertum locum ibiq(ue) orabat <36>et persecutus est eum
simon ⁊ þa ðe mið him wærun ⁊ mið þy onfundun hine
symon et qui cum eo erant· <37>Et cum inuenissent eum
cwædun to him f(or)þon alle soecaþ ðe ⁊ cwæþ to heom se hæl(end) gá we ł wutu
dixerunt ei quia omnes quærunt té <38>et ait illis ie(su)s ea⟨-⟩
gangan in þa nehsto lond ⁊ ða cæstre þte ⁊ ec ðær ic bodige
mus in proximos uicos et ciuitatesunt et ibi praedi⟨-⟩
⁊ to ðisse forþon ic com ⁊ węs bodande in somnungum
cem ad hoc enim ueni <39>et erat prædicans in sinagogis
heora ⁊ alle galile ⁊ deoflas fordraf ł f(or)warp ⁊ com
eorum et omni galilea et dæmonia eiciens:· <40>Et uenit
to him licþrowere bed ł bidende him ⁊ mid cneu begende ł beginge
ad eum leprosus depraecans eum et genu flexu
cwæþ gif ðu wilt þu mæh me geclensige se hælend witudlice þa wæs miltsende
Dixit si uís potes me mundare <41>ie(su)s autem miser⟨-⟩
him gerahte honda his ⁊ hran him
tus eius extendit manum suam et tangens eum
cwæþ to him ic wille geclænsie ⁊ mið þy cwæþ hræþe foer⟨-⟩
ait illi uolo mundare <42>et cum dixisset statim dis⟨-⟩
de from him þe hriofal ⁊ geclensad wæs ⁊ beboden
cessit ab eo lepra et mundatus est <43>et commina⟨-⟩
wæs him hræþe ⁊ draf hine ⁊ cwæþ to him gesih ðu nænegum menn
tus est statim et eicit illum· <44>Et dicit ei uide nemini
sæcge ł cweþe ah gaa æteaw þe ðæm aldorsacerd
dixeris sed uade ostende te principi sacerdotu(m)
⁊ agef for clænsunga þine þa þe heht
et offer pro emundatione tua quae praecipit

1 minisbat] ministrabat Y WW 3 eum] + et erat R^{c} (erased later) Y WW=R* 7 ea loqui] loqui ea Y WW 8 et[2]] *om.* Y WW 9 persecutus] secutus R^{c} Y WW=R* 10 eo] illo Y WW 11 ie(su)s] *om.* Y WW 12 ciuitatesunt] ciuitates ut R^{c} Y WW ciuitates ut ut R^{Fa} 13 ad] et Y WW=R 15 flexu] flexo Y WW 20 est] + ei R^{Fa} ei (*om.* est) Y WW | et[1]] *om.* Y WW

moyses in cyþnisse ðæm soð he foerde ongan
moyses in testimonium illis:· <45>At ille egressus cæpit
bodige ⁊ mærsige word þus ꝥ wutudlice
praedicare et defamare sermonem ita ut iam
ne mæhte eawunga in ða ceastre ingangan ł ineode ah
non posset manifeste in ciuitatem introire sed
butan in westigum stowum wære ⁊ gesomnadun ł efnecomon to
forís in desertís locís esse et conueniebant ad
him æghwonan fro(m) æghwilcu(m) halfe ⁊ æft(er)sona ł hraeðe infoérde ł ineode capharnau(m) þe byrig
eum undique:· <II 1>Et iterum intrauit capharnauu(m)
æft(er) dagum ⁊ gehered wæs ꝥte in huse wære ⁊ efne⟨-⟩
post dies et auditum est quod in domu esset <2>et con⟨-⟩
comon monige þus ꝥte ne mæhte foan ł nioman ne to dore ł to gete
uenerunt multi ita ut non caperet neq(ue) ad ianua(m)
⁊ sprecende wæs heom ˋł him´ word ⁊ comon toferende ł brengende
et loquebatur eis uerbum <3>et uenerunt ferentes
to him þone eorðcrypel se ðe fro(m) feowrum wæs geboren
ad eum paraliticum qui a quatuor portabatur
⁊ mið þy hí ne mæhtun gebringan hine him for mengo genacadun
<4>et cum non possent offere eum illi prae turba nuda⟨-⟩
ł unwreogon ꝥ hus ł þa bére þær he wæs ⁊ openedon ł ˋopnende´ dydon adune sendun
uerunt tectum ubi erat et patefacientes submisi⟨-⟩
ł settun þa bere in ðære þe eorðcrypel læg ł licgende wæs
erunt grabattum in quo paraliticus iacebat
mið þy gesæh þoˋn´ne se hælend geleafa heora cwæþ to þæ(m) eorð⟨-⟩
<5>cum uidisset autem ie(su)s fidem illorum ait parali⟨-⟩
crypele sunu forgefen beoþan ðe synne þine weron wutudlice
tico filii dimittuntur tibi peccata <6>erant autem
ðær sume of uþwutum sittende ⁊ ðencende ł smeande
illíc quidam de scribís sedentes et cogitantes
in heortum heortu(m) hwæt þes ðus ł swa sprecaþ heofolsaþ
in cordibus suis <7>quid hic sic loquitur blasfemat
hwa mæg f(or)geofan ł f(or)letan synne nymþe ane god of þon
quis potest dimittere peccata nisi solus d(eu)s <8>quo
sona onget se hælend gast his ꝥte swa þohton ł smeadon
statim cognito ie(su)s sp(irit)u suo quia sic cogitarent
betwih heom cwæþ to heom hwæt þas ge þencaþ in heortum
intra sé dicit illís quid ista cogitatis in cordib(us)
eowrum hwæt is eþre ł eaður to cweþanne þæm eorðcryple forgefen
uestris· <9>Quid est facilius dicere paralitico dimit⟨-⟩
beoþun þe synne þine oþðe cweþan aris ⁊ nim ł ber
tuntur tibi peccata tua aut dicere surge et tolle
bere þine ⁊ gaa þæt witud witaþ ge
grabbatum tuum et ambula:· <10>Ut autem sciatis

1 ille] illae Y[*] Y[c] WW=R | cæpit] coepit Y WW 2 defamare] difamare R[c] diffamare Y WW 5 domu] domo Y WW 10 cum] eum Y WW=R 11 submisierunt] summiserunt Y WW 12 grabattum] grauatum Y WW=R 14 peccata] + tua R[Fa] Y WW=R* 19 intra] inter Y WW=R 21 tua] *om.* Y WW | aut] an R[c] Y WW 22 grabattum] grauatum Y grabattum WW

ꝥte he mæhte hæfeð sunu monnes on eorþa f(or)gefnisse
quia potestatem habet filius hominis in terra dimit(-)
synne cwæþ to þæ(m) eorðcryple þe ic sægce aris ⁊ nim
tendi peccata ait paralitico <11>tibi dico surge et tolle
bere þine ⁊ gaa to huse þinum ⁊ instyde
grabattum tuum et uade in domum tuam <12>et statim
he aras ⁊ underleat bere eode beforan
ille surrexit et sublato grabatto abiit coram
allum swa ꝥte ofwundradun alle ⁊ þa worþadun
omnib(us) ita ut mirarentur omnes et honorifica(-)
god cweþende ꝥte hia næfre þus ł swilc ne gesegun
rent d(eu)m dicentes quia numquam síc uidimus:·
⁊ færende wæs æftersona ec to sæ eall þa þreat
<13>Et egressus est rursus ad mare omnis quæ turba
cymende to him ⁊ lærde hia ⁊ mið þy þonan
ueniebat ad eum et docebat eos· <14>et cum praete(-)
foerde gesæh sittende to geafolmonunge
riret uidit leuin alphei sedentem ad telonum
⁊ cweþ to him folgam ł fylge me ⁊ aras fylgende wæs him
et ait illi sequere me et surgens secutus est eum:·
⁊ geworden wæs mið þy gehlionade in huse ðæs monige
<15>Et factum est cum accumberet in domo illius multi
openlice synnige ł hehsun\`n´e ⁊ synnfulle ætgædre gereston ł hleonadun
puplicani et peccatores simul discumbebant
mið ðon(e) hæl(end) ⁊ ðegnum his weron forðon monigu ða ðe
cum ie(s)u et discipulis eius· erant enim multi qui
⁊ fyligdun ł fylgende werun him ⁊ uðwutu ⁊ ða aldu
et sequebantur eum· <16>Et scribae et pharisæi
gisegun forðon ðæt he ett ł etende wæs mið ðæm synfullum
uidentes quia manducaret cum peccatorib(us)
⁊ bærsynnigum hię cwedun ðegnum his for hwon
et publicanis dicebant discipulis eius quare
mið bærsunnigum ⁊ synfullum etest ⁊
cum publicanis et peccatoribus manducat et
drinces larow iower mið ðy giherde ðis ðe hæl(end) cwæð to him
bibit magister uester:· <17>Hoc audito ie(su)s ait illis
ne nedðærfe habbas hælo to lece ah ða ðe yfel
non necesse habent sani medico sed qui male
habbas ne forðon com ic to ceganne soðfæste ah synn(-)
habent· non enim ueni uocare iustos sed pecca(-)
fylle ⁊ werun ðegnas iohannes ⁊ ða aldu
tores· <18>et erant discipuli iohannis et pharisæi
fæstende ⁊ comun ⁊ cwedun him f(or)hwon ðegnas
ieiunantes et ueniunt et dicunt illi cúr discipuli
iohannes
iohannis

2 et] *om.* Y WW 3 grabattum] grauatum Y WW=R 4 et] *om.* Y WW=R | grabatto] grauato Y WW=R 5 mirarentur] admirarentur Y(amm-) WW 7 rursus] rursum R[Fa] Y WW=R* | ad] et Y WW=R | omnis quæ] omnisque Y WW 9 telonum] theloneum R[Fa] teloneum Y WW 11 accumberet] acumberet Y* Y[c] WW=R 19 medico] medicum Y WW 21 iohannis] iohannes Y WW=R 22 cur] quare Y WW Xz=R

⁊ cuð ic dyde him noma ðinne ⁊ cyð ic doe ðæm ꝥ
<26>et notum feci eis nomen tuum et notum faciam ut
ic lufo ꝥte ðu lufades mec in ðæm sie ⁊ ic in ðæ(m)
dilectio quia dilexisti me in ipsis sit et ego in ipsis:·
þa mið ðy cwæþ se hæl(end) eode þa mid his þægnu(m)
<XVIII 1>Haec cum dixisset ie(su)s egressus est cum discipulís
his ofer þah hlynne þe mon cedron nemneþ þær wæs fæger gewyrtun in þæ(m)
suis trans torrentem cedron ubi erat hortus in que(m)
he eode sylf ⁊ his þægnas **his** þa wiste soþlice ⁊ iudas
introiit ipse et discipuli eius· <2>sciebat autem et iudas
þe hine to deaþe sellan walde **hine** þa stowe f(or)þon þider gelome se hæl(end) cwom
qui tradebat eum locum quia frequenter ie(su)s conue⟨-⟩
ðer mið his ðægnum **his** iudas wiotudlice gefeng
nerat illuc cum discipulís suís:· <3>Iudas ergo cum acci⟨-⟩
mið þreate ⁊ fro(m) þa biscopas ⁊ fariseos ealdormen
pisset cohortem et á pontificibus et farisaeis minis⟨-⟩
cwomun þidera mid lehtfatu ⁊ **brondum** ⁊ wepenu
tros uenit illuc cum lanternís et faucibus et armís:·
hæl(end) wutudl(ice) wiste alle ða ðe toworde werun ofer
<4>Ie(su)s itaq(ue) sciens omnia quae euentura erant super
hine gifeoll ⁊ cwæð him hwæt soecas ge ondsworadun
eum processit et dicit eis quid quaeritis <5>respon⟨-⟩
him ðe hæl(end) nazarenisca cwæð to him ðe hælend ic am gistod
dierunt ei ie(su)m nazarenum· dicit eis ie(su)s· ego sum sta⟨-⟩
wutudlice ⁊ iudas se ðe salde hine mið ðæm ꝥte
bat autem et iudas qui tradebat eum cum ipsis· <6>ut
forðon cwæð him ic am eodun onbæc ⁊ feollun
ergo dixit eis ego sum abierunt retrorsum et cecide⟨-⟩
on eorðo eftersona forðon hię gifrægn hwelcne
runt in terram <7>iterum ergo eos interrogauit quem
soecas ge hia wutudl(ice) cwedun ðon(e) hælend nazarenisca ondswora⟨-⟩
queritis· illi autem dixerunt ie(su)m nazarenum· <8>res⟨-⟩
de him ic cweð iow ꝥte ic am gif forðon mec soecas
pondit eis dixi uobis quia ego sum si ergo me quae⟨-⟩
forletas ðas gaa ꝥte sie gifylled word ðe ic cwæð
ritis sinite hos abire <9>ut impleretur sermo que(m) dixit
forðon ðu me saldes me ne spil ł ne ˋloˊsa of ðæm æniht
quia quos dedisti mihi non perdidi ex ipsis quemqua(m):·
simon forðon petr(us) hæfde sword gibrægd hine ⁊ slog
<10>simon ergo petrus habens gladium eduxit eum· et per⟨-⟩
aldormonnes esne ⁊ ofceorf his earliprica
cussit pontificis seruum et abscidit eius auricula(m)
ðæt swiðra wæs wutudl(ice) nemned ðe esne malchus cwæð forðon
dexteram· erat (autem) nomen seruo malchus· <11>dixit ergo
ðe hæl(end) to petre
ie(su)s petro·

5 introit] introiuit Y WW **7** accipisset] accepisset WW Y=R **10** euentura] uentura Y WW **11** quid] quem Y WW | respondierunt] responderunt Y WW **17** eis] iesus Y WW **20** habens] haben Y habens Y[Ald] WW

COMMENTARY

Each of the entries below comments on Farman's gloss from both palaeographical and linguistic perspectives, in addition to miscellaneous features that may help deepen our understanding of the gloss. Reference is made by line numbers on each folio followed by chapter-verse numbers in brackets. Corrections and alterations made to the Old English gloss, mostly by Farman himself, are reported, and discussed where possible, when the original reading is retrievable with some certainty. Illegible erasures will not be reported, unless the existence of such trace itself would encourage useful speculation and contribute to the understanding of the gloss.

The nature of the Latin text of the Rushworth manuscript (R) will be discussed only in relation to the analysis of the gloss. In the process, the R text will often be compared with 'the standard Vulgate', a term that lacks precision, especially in the context of biblical textual studies. However, given the nature and focus of the present edition, comparison with printed standard editions, such as the Oxford Vulgate edited by Wordsworth and White (WW) and the Stuttgart Vulgate (Xz), would still serve its purpose, if the risk of oversimplification is understood. The textual apparatus of WW and Fischer's extensive collations (1988–91) of selected excerpts are made full use of when appropriate. Because the Matthew portion of the Vetus Latina edition is yet to be published, the *Itala* edition by Jülicher et al. (referred to as *Itala*) is used. For the Vulgate manuscripts, Houghton (2016) serves as the most up-to-date manual; for the Vetus Latina manuscripts, see Gryson (1999) and (2004).

As discussed in the Introduction (III.1.3), Farman's gloss often reflects Latin readings other than R. Care is taken to signal such instances, but by no means all the instances are discussed, partly because such an approach would result in too many repetitive notes, and also because readers will have naturally become accustomed to identifying such instances by the use of the textual apparatus.

As regards linguistic notes, it must be remembered that modern readers of Old English glosses tend to attribute the instances that cannot easily be accounted for too readily to glossators' *errors*. This is partly because the existence of the Latin text on the same page makes us expect *correct* forms in Old English; for example, one could call a gloss in a different grammatical case from its Latin lemma an error, but it may simply reflect a syntactic requirement in Old English. It should also be understood that there may have been glossing practices that are unfamiliar to modern readers. Therefore, the linguistic comments try not to be too theoretical, but to give more emphasis to interpreting the intention of Farman's gloss in each given context.

All the previous editions of the Rushworth Gospels are compared in producing the text and various points will be discussed below, especially on such issues as word division and emendations. The Surtees Society edition by Stevenson and Waring (1854–65) is hardly mentioned, as it had been long superseded by Skeat, except for those cases where their readings at odds with Skeat were adopted by Bosworth in his *Dictionary* (BT). Since Tamoto (2013) mostly accepts Skeat's readings uncritically, apart from pointing out some typographical errors, his edition is also sometimes omitted from comparison. McAllister's unpublished edition (1952) has by far more important insights into the text and is duly noted. It is often tantalizing that he did not provide fuller commentary than short footnotes to his text to explain his editorial judgement, one shortcoming that the present edition avoids repeating by providing this commentary.

Citations from the present edition will be presented in simplified forms in the commentary, i.e., without accent marks and in expanded forms, unless such marks and abbreviations are the main concern of the discussion. For comparison, the corresponding Gospel passage is often cited from the West Saxon Gospels (from WSCp, Cambridge, Corpus Christi College 140, with DOE's punctuation and capitalization, unless otherwise noted) and Aldred's gloss in the Lindisfarne Gospels (Li). References to other verses in Matthew will be made simply by chapter and verse (e.g., 6:9), while those in other Gospels will be preceded by Mk, Lk and Jn. Old English texts other than the Gospels are cited by DOE's short titles and reference numbering, supplemented, when necessary, by relevant editions. To identify comparable passages in Old English texts, Cook (1898) and (1903) still remain indispensable.

f. 1r

The manuscript opens with Matthew's incipit page, possibly once preceded by an evangelist portrait as in the other three Gospels. Liuzza and Doane (1995: 22) postulate that a 'quire [is] missing before **I** [i.e., the first quire consisting of ff. 1–10] containing prefaces, canon tables and Matthew portrait'. However, we do not know whether the manuscript once contained a Matthew portrait alone in an irregular quire, a set of prefatory materials in a complete quire, or even nothing at all. There are no prefaces, chapter lists, etc., between the Gospels in this manuscript; neither is the Latin text supplied with Eusebian numbers or any set of chapter numbers. Such lack of prefatory materials is the tendency found in some Irish gospel manuscripts, as shown by McGurk (1961) and (1987).

See Farr (2007) for a detailed art-historical analysis of the incipit pages of the manuscript. The erroneous use of the Greek *pi* for *rho* in *XΠI* is found not only here, but also on f. 2v (1:18) and f. 52r (Mark incipit); see Tilghman (2011: 98).

The Matthew incipit page is neatly glossed by Farman, including the three-line Latin incipit written in red ink at the upper right corner of the framed space.

1 (INCIPIT) Skeat prints Ru1's incipit as if a variant reading to Li's incipit for the genealogy in particular (*onginneð godspelles cynnreccenis* for *incipit euangelii geneologia mathei*). The incipit for the Gospel itself appears on f. 29r, the 'Chi-rho page', in the Lindisfarne Gospels.

her onginneþ godspell to cyþenne for *incipit euangelium* is a rather free translation, echoing a conventional opening found frequently in Old English texts, which can be contrasted with the more literal glossing of the same incipit in Li (*onginneð godspell*).

3 (INCIPIT) *æfter matheus tosagan* for *secundum matheum*. The grammatical case of *matheus* is uncertain, as noted by Schulte (s.v. *matheus*); in Ru1, *matheus* occurs three times, always in this spelling, and the instances in 9:9 (where the final *s* may have been corrected from *m*) and 10:3 are in the nominative. Furthermore, *tosagan*, treated as one word by Skeat (followed by DOE Corpus) and Schulte (with a question mark), is apparently a hapax legomenon, whereas McAllister and Tamoto read *to sagan* without comment. The latter reading requires *matheus* to be taken as dative, or less likely accusative (see Page 1958: 147–48), governed by *æfter*. The noun *saga*, related to the verb *secgan* along with the more common feminine *sagu* (cf. Holthausen, s.v. *saga* 2 and *sagu* 1), is attested only once in Old English: ÆLS (Agnes) [0072 (192)], *þin saga bið geswutelod* … 'Thy saying will be manifested …' in Skeat's translation (1881–1900: i, 181), and BT regards *saga* as weak masculine. Thus, the sense of the entire phrase *æfter matheus to sagan* may be 'according to Matthew, as a story'. In contrast, when *tosagan* is taken as one word (presumably a noun), *matheus* is to be read as genitive, and the entire phrase may be compared to the opening of WSCp, i.e., *æfter matheus gerecednysse* ('according to Matthew's narrative'). Also comparable is *æfter Mathees gesetnysse* translating Latin *secundum Matheum* in Ælfric's *Grammar* (ÆGram [1911 (270.2)]). The sense of *tosagan* may be assumed to be comparable to that of *gerecednes* or *gesetnes*, given the sense of the root *sag-*, though the force of the prefix *to-* is not entirely clear. The formation of the compound may be compared with *foresaga*, an element-by-element translation used in Li for Latin *praefatio*, *prooemium* and *prologus* 'prologue, preface' (see DOE s.v. *fore-saga*).

f. 1v

ff. 1v–3r have a border surrounding the text, in red for the verso pages and green on recto pages. The text has accordingly 20 lines on these pages (19 on f. 2r), as against normal 22. The genealogy passage is only sporadically glossed.

2 (1:2) *blo\`e'þrę*. Between *þ* and *rę*, *æs* is erased. No other instances with *bl-* for *broþer* 'brother' are recorded in Old English according to DOE. Brown (1892: §10) notes this substitution of *l* for *r* is 'by dissimulation'. In the manuscript, there are comparable cases where *bl-* is likely to have been corrected to *br-*, though their phonological significance is not clear (see further Introduction III.2.1.3). The superscript *e*, missed by Skeat, is recorded by McAllister. The umlaut is not necessary historically for the accusative plural form. The ending *rę* is of unknown origin, as Ross (1976: 497–98) points out; cf. 1:11 *broeþre* (accusative plural).

4 (1:3) *ðamar*. The initial *ð* is transformed from *t*.

12 (1:6) *of þære þe urias ahte* translates *ex ea quae fuit uriae* rather freely, using *agan* 'to possess', which has no Latin equivalent. *urias* is to be taken here as nominative, the literal translation of the Old English relative clause being 'from the one whom Uriah possessed [as wife]'. Li supplies *wif* here (*of ðære ðe ðy wæs u(u)ries wif*), followed by an appropriate historical account of Uriah in the margin; see Boyd (1975: 6).

f. 2r

2 (1:11) Several letters have been erased before *in babilonia*, which appear to have read *⁊ æft*, possibly with a stroke over *t* to indicate the contraction for *æfter*, as used elsewhere (e.g., 3:11). The erased reading agrees with the gloss in the next line, and this kind of misplaced glosses, implying an eye-skip, appears to reinforce the likelihood that Farman used an Old English exemplar, as discussed in Introduction III.1.3.

fære for *transmigratione* (also in line 3). As DOE s.v. *fær* 1.b.i. shows, the use of *fær* for this specific meaning is found only in Ru1. See also the note on line 16 below.

14 (1:17) Farman's script becomes smaller with narrower pen strokes from this line, where the Latin text starts to be glossed more consistently.

The Latin nominative *omnes … generationes* is translated into different cases, *ealra … kneorissum* 'for the generations of all'. The intention is not clear and there is no recorded Latin variant reading that might lie behind the syntax of the gloss.

16 (1:17) *and* for *et* is the sole spelled-out instance in Ru1; the Tironian note ⁊ is used consistently elsewhere.

Ru1's *from* for the first *ad* in this line apparently translates the standard Vulgate reading *a*. See also line 18, where R has a contaminated reading, *ad*, instead of *a*, followed by an ablative.

færennisse, recorded twice in this verse, is unique to Ru1 (see DOE s.v. *farennes*). Li has a triple gloss (*forworpnise ł ymbcerr ł oferfaer*) and a double (*from ymbcerr ł from oferfaer*) in the same verse.

17 (1:17) *kneo*. DOE s.v. *cneoris* regards this instance as an abbreviated form of *cneoris*, though not marked for abbreviation in the manuscript. It is possible instead to regard it as a form of DOE s.v. *cneow*, as it includes the sense '2. generation'; see also its reflexes in MED s.v. *kne* n. 3. Generation, degree of relationship' and OED2 s.v. *knee* '11. *figurative*. A degree of descent in a genealogy'.

Bottom margin There are marginal writings (*cr(istu)m*, *ad*), perhaps *probationes pennae*, above the bottom line of the border. The letter forms appear to imitate those found in the last line of the text.

f. 2v

1 (1:18) *kennisse* is to be taken as nominative. The ending *-nisse* (or *-nesse*) for the nominative singular of abstract nouns ending with *-niss*, *-ness* is frequent in Ru1. See Campbell (OEG §592 (f)).

þus wæs was erased above *-atio* of *generatio*, and the same phrase is written above *sic*. This correction appears to have been intended to adjust the position of the gloss, suggesting the involvement of copying procedure rather than translating word-for-word. A similar correction is also found in line 9, where *þohte* for *cogitante* is preceded by an erasure of the same word in the identical spelling.

2 (1:18) *þa þe* for *cum*, as against more common *þa* or *þa þa*, as a conjunction 'when' is attested only occasionally in Old English prose and is absent in poetry, as discussed by Mitchell (OES §2580). *þa þe* occurs also for *cum* in 27:12.

esset disponsata receives a triple gloss (*wæs bewedded ł befest ł in sceat alegd*) in Ru1, whereas Li actually has a quadruple gloss (*wæs biwoedded ł beboden ł befeastnad ł betaht*). Between Ru1 and Li, lexical agreement is found only for the first item *beweddian*, the word most commonly used for the sense 'engage, betroth' in Old English (see Fischer 1986: 25–26). Ru1's second item *befest*, from *befæstan* (etymologically related to Li's third item *befæstnian*), is also a common word, but, according to DOE s.v. *be-fæstan* 2.d., the use specifically designating 'engage, betroth' appears to be confined to Ru1 and Li (and Ru2). The third item *in sceat alegd* has received much attention in previous scholarship. One controversial point is whether *sceat* means 'lap, bosom' (i.e., *scēat*) or 'money'. DOE adopts the latter (s.v. *alecgan* 1.b.1 'to betroth [i.e., to put down the bride price]'). For a summary of the two interpretations (esp. Roeder 1907a and 1907b for the 'lap' theory), see Fischer (1986: 34–35).

7 (1:19) *traducere* receives no gloss; cf. Li *gebreng ł geləda* and WSCp *gewidmærsian*. This omission could be a mistake, but *hie* may as well be read as an accusative object of *ne walde* 'and he did not desire her'.

8 (1:20) Skeat prints *ł þis* as a gloss to *haec*, supplied with the marginal note 'ðendi he þa ꝥ þohte (*above*)'. In the manuscript, however, *ł þis* appears to have been squeezed below the original gloss *ðendi he þa ꝥ þohte*, which is a free translation ('while he then was thinking about that') of the Latin ablative absolute construction *haec autem eo cogitante*. In contrast, the alternative reading produces a word-by-word gloss (*þis soþlice he þohte*) to the Latin phrase. What Farman intended is seemingly a combination of free and literal translations, i.e., *ðendi he þa ꝥ þohte ł þis soþlice he þohte.*

The spelling *ðendi* for *þenden* is not recorded elsewhere in Old English. In Ru1, more common is *þende*, with loss of final *-n* (see Hogg 1992: § 7.100 and Brown 1892: §12). Lexically, *þenden* is preferred in verse and examples in prose are relatively rare; see Mitchell (OES §§2634–35) and references cited there for details.

11 (1:20) *ne ondred þu þe* for *noli timere*. The avoidance of literal rendering of Latin '*noli(te)* + infinitive' into '*nellan* (or *ne willan*) + infinitive' is characteristic of Ru1, as discussed by Ogura (1988: esp. the table presented in §13).

There are morphological and syntactic difficulties as regards *onfoh ł onfoiæ*. While the corresponding Latin is the infinitive (*accipere*), as literally translated in both Li (*nelle ðu ðe ondrede ł forht bian to onfoanne*) and WSCp (*nelle þu ondrædan Marian þine gemæccean to onfonne*), the first item in the double gloss is unambiguously imperative (see Campbell OEG §745). It seems necessary therefore to construe as *ne ondred þu þe; onfoh maria...* 'do not fear; take Maria ...', when read with the first alternative in the double gloss. The second item *onfoiæ* is classed as the subjunctive present singular by Brown (1892: §27) and Schulte (s.v. *onfoan*). The reason why the subjunctive was chosen here is not clear, but it may be related to the fact that *ondrædan* can be used with a *þæt*-clause in which the subjunctive mood tends to be chosen (though not compulsory). See BTS s.v. *ondrædan* II (c) for the use with a *þæt*-clause.

17 (1:22) *þe witgu*, part of the second word written on erasure. Being in apposition with *esaiam*, governed by *þurh*, the expected case of the phrase is the accusative. The form *witgu* prevails as an accusative singular in Ru1. As to inflexions of *-an* nouns in Ru1, see Ross (1976: 497), Campbell (OEG §617), and Hogg and Fulk (2011: §3.109). On the other hand, the use of *þe*, where the masculine accusative form of *se* might be expected, may appear striking, found only once elsewhere in Ru1: 8:17 *þurh esaiam þe witgu* glossing the identical Latin. One caveat about taking these forms as accusative in strict terms is found, for example, in 21:4 *þurh essaiam se witga cwæðende* for *per esseiam profetam dicentem*, where *se witga* is unambiguously in the nominative. Farman sometimes gives a nominative form of a generic noun after a proper noun. See also discussion about case-endingless forms used by Farman in Introduction III.2.2.3.

18 (1:23) *ecce* receives a triple gloss. The first item *henu* is the word used most frequently in Ru1 for *ecce*. The Anglian colouring of the word (also spelled *heonu* [in Li] and *ono* [in Bede]) has been pointed out; see Wenisch (1979: 170–72) for distribution. The phrase *her is* as a translation of *ecce* is found only in this example in Ru1, but occurs frequently in WSCp (e.g., 12:18 *Her is min cnapa þone ic geceas* for *ecce puer meus quem elegi*; see also BTS s.v. *her* II.). *sihþe*, written above the two items, is used ten times in Ru1, but its distribution in Old English is limited. There is no relevant instance in Li; in contrast, PsGlA uses only *sihþe* for *ecce*, mostly spelled as *sehðe*.

f. 3r

2 (1:24) *feng* for *accipit*. R often confuses the perfect form *accepit* with the present *accipit* and Ru1 tends to translate the standard Vulgate reading as in this example.

3 (1:24) Farman's use of *u* in *wiue* is noted by Brown (1892: §16) as the sole instance of Farman's use of *u* for the voiced sound /v/ in native Old English words. This may be compared with the fact that he usually keeps the *-u-* of Latin spellings in his Old English gloss, as in *dauid* or *dauið*. Clark (1970: lxiv) notes in discussing the language of the final continuation of the Peterborough Chronicle that even 'in Old English, Latin influence sometimes led scribes to replace medial *f* by *u*'. In fact, DOE Corpus yields 14 instances of *wiue(s)* spellings, including those in charters, which may suggest the need of scrutiny about how much Latin influence would indeed account for the *u* spelling in Old English.

3 (1:25) *ne groette hire* for *non cognosebat eam*. DOE s.v. *gretan* lists the present instance under '1.c. to have carnal relations or sexual intercourse with (someone *acc.*)'. Though there is no explicit comment on the case of *hire*, the definition suggests that DOE takes it as the accusative. Although the use of feminine dative forms for the accusative in later Old English is well known (cf. OED3 s.v. *her*, pron.2 and n.2, A.1.c, of which the present instance is the first citation, and Mustanoja 1960: 129), there is no unambiguous accusative instance of *hire* (or its variant spellings) in Ru1. One possible instance is *hire* used with *habban* in 14:4; Mitchell (OES §1092) notes that the verb can take genitive objects and Ru1 has an apparently mixed structure *ic hæbbe lifes æce* for *habeam uitam aeternam* in 19:16. See Introduction III.2.2.3 for further discussion.

7 (2:1) The distribution of *tungolcræftiga* (in BT's spelling) as a translation of *magi* is restricted to texts with Anglian colouring. Apart from Li and Ru1, where the word is used exclusively for *magi*, it is found in Mart 5 (Kotzor) [0019 (Ja 6, A.6)] *þreo tungolcræftegan coman fram eastdæles mægðum to Criste*. More common is *tungolwitega*, as used in WSCp.

quomon for *uenerunt*. For the *qu*- spelling for more usual *cu*- or *cw*-, see Introduction III.2.1.2.

11 (2:3) *wæs gedroefed in mode* for *turbatus est*. Note the use of *in mode*, which has no corresponding word in the Latin (cf. Li *gedroefed węs*; WSCp *wearð he gedrefed*). This insertion presents no semantic difficulty (see also 14:26 *gedryfed werun in mode* for *turbati sunt*), but, when seen as a work of interlinear glossing, the insertion stands out, indicating that Farman at times translates the Latin text very freely. See also note on 2:9.

15 (2:5) *cwædon* appears to have been altered from *cwæddon* by erasing the first *d*.

19 (2:6) *ræc\c/et* is regarded as a form of *ræcan* 'to reach' by both Schulte and McAllister. However, while the stem vowel *æ* may support this interpretation, the sense of the verb is not appropriate to translate *regere* 'to govern' in this context (the prefixed *geræcan* 'obtain, seize' would fit better). The superscript *c* may suggest that the verb is a form of *reccan* 'to rule' as used in the corresponding passage in WSCp (*se heretoga se þe recð min folc israhel*). The distinction between *e* and *æ* in Ru1 is notoriously confused, as discussed in Introduction III.2.1.4. The *-et* ending for the third person singular is found in Ru1, exclusively for weak verbs (Campbell OEG §734 (b)).

20 (2:7) *acægde*. According to DOE s.v. *a-cigan*, the verb occurs nine times in Old English and it is used 'mainly in Angl. and poetic texts'. Ru1 has two instances, both of which translate Latin *uocare* (cf. 2:15).

f. 3v

1 (2:7) *dedicit*. *de*- protrudes into the left-hand margin, apparently in the main scribe's hand.

2 (2:8) *gæþ ⁊ ahsiað* for *ite interrogate*. Although the use of ⁊ may reflect the standard Vulgate reading *ite et interrogate*, such an addition could have easily been made in the process of translation, reducing its significance as evidence for Farman's knowledge of the purer Vulgate.

4 (2:8) *swilce* is written entirely on erasure. The erased letters are illegible. Though written above *ego*, *swilce* translates Latin *et*, used here as an adverb 'also, likewise'.

5 (2:9) Old English translators and glossators seem to have been reluctant to translate Latin *audissent regem* literally, with Aldred's *geherdon ðone cyning* being an exception. Farman inserts *word* and renders the Latin by *ðæs kyninges word*, with *ðæs* written above the line. This can be compared to the prose translations: WSCp, as Liuzza notes (1994–2000: ii, 52), paraphrases the Latin as *þæt gebod* 'the command', whereas Ælfric, translating the same passage, renders the temporal clause into a prepositional phrase *æfter þæs cinges spræce* (ÆCHom I, 5 [0013 (217.24)]).

8 (2:10) R originally reads *uidens*, which Farman corrects to *uidentes*, supplying *te* above *-ns*. The gloss *geseænde*, present participle form, appears to have been altered from the finite form *gesegon*, judging from the trace of erased *g* after *gese-* and the curious letter form of *æ*, apparently transformed from *o*.

10 (2:11) The *a* in *forþfallende* is altered from *æ*. The verb is used by Farman in two other instances, both in the present participle, spelled with *æ* instead of *a* (18:26, 29). DOE s.v. *forþ-feallan* notes that the verb is used only in Ru1.

20 (2:14) R wants *eius* after *matrem* and Ru1 *his moder* reflects the Vulgate reading *matrem eius*, though such an addition could have easily been made from the context.

f. 4r

5 (2:16) *ł finibus* is added above *regionibus* by Farman. The original reading is unique to R amongst the Vulgate manuscripts examined by WW, but is witnessed by some Old Latin manuscripts as recorded in *Itala*. Ru1 *gemoerum*, apparently from *gemære*, is likely to translate *finibus*, as *regio* is usually glossed with *lond* in Ru1. The spelling with *-oe-* for *(ge)mære* is striking and not found elsewhere in Ru1.

8 (2:18) *heanisse* for *rama*. The gloss reflects an interpretation of the Hebrew word which, originating from exegetical writings, appears to have been well established, as paralleled by other Old English writings; see Liuzza (1994–2000: ii, 52) and Godden (2000: 41) for parallels and possible sources of this interpretation in WSCp and ÆCHom I, 5, respectively. In contrast, Li has *tuigga ł* (no alternative gloss supplied) in the corresponding passage, which apparently takes *rama* as a form of *ramus* 'twig'.

14 (2:20) *þe þe*. Mitchell (OES §2149) notes 'Doubled *þe* [as a relative pronoun] occasionally occurs in the prose', but all the examples listed there are construed with a singular verb. Here, *þe þe* for *qui* (plural) may simply be for *þa þe*. See also 15:27.

17 (2:22) *⁊ geherdun*. The plural verb form disagrees with Latin singular *audiens*, which may have been prompted by taking both Joseph and Mary as the subject. Note also that ⁊ has no corresponding word in Latin.

18 (2:22) *ne durste … gangan ƚ færan* for *timuit … ire* is semantically an appropriate translation ('did not dare to go' for 'was afraid to go'), but it is exceptional amongst the Old English translations of the passage; Li *ondreard … fara ƚ to færenne* and WSCp *ondred … to farende*. Ælfric uses an expression similar to Ru1 in a homily dealing with the same Gospel passage: ÆCHom I, 5 [0082 (222.172)] *⁊ ne dorste his neawiste genealæcan*.

19 (2:22) *gemynga* for *admonitus*. Skeat reads *gemyngad*. The final *d* is, however, hardly legible and McAllister reads *gemynga*. Some residue of ink is still visible after *a* and the loss may have been accidental due to the condition of the parchment surface rather than erasure. Tamoto also reads *gemyngad* in his text, noting that Junius transcribed it as *gemynegade* (the *e* after *n* is inserted by Junius). Tamoto does not specify the source, but the reading is found on f. 47v of Junius MS 76. The transcripts by Thwaites and Todhunter in Harley MS 3449 read *gemynegade* on f. 8r (the entire transcript has been crossed out for cancellation) and *gemynga* on f. 19r.

20 (2:23) Farman supplies *et* at the beginning of the verse as well as the gloss ⁊.

f. 4v

1 (3:1) *bezera* 'baptist' is used only in Ru1, Li and Rit, in 14 occurrences in total (DOE s.v. *bæzere*; see Campbell OEG §53 for spelling variations). Its etymology is variously interpreted: see Falluomini (2010: 400) for a summary of the previous scholarship. Whereas this word is the usual choice for Farman in glossing Latin *baptista*, Aldred's use is limited (2 occ.): it is used in this verse as one of double glosses (*bæstere ƚ fuluihtere*), and the other instance is found in the *Capitula lectionum* to Matthew (*bæðcere* for *baptistae*, Skeat p.16, line 6). See also the note on line 22 below for the vocabulary related to the baptism.

3 (3:2) The present tense *neoliceþ* for Latin perfect *adpropinquauit* may be due to a variant reading *adpropinquabit* (for the full list of manuscripts with this reading, see Fischer 1988–91: i, 24), but the use of the present tense here is contextually and semantically not surprising even without support of Latin variant readings: cf. WSCp *Soðlice genealæceð heofona rice* and the Authorized Version *for the kingdome of heauen is at hand*.

4 (3:3) The insertion of the inorganic or unhistoric *h* in *his* (instead of *is*) for *est* is one of characteristic features of Farman's orthography; see Introduction III.2.1.3.

8 (3:4) Ru1 uses *olbend* (BT s.v. *olfend*) for 'camel' throughout Matthew, as is general in most Old English texts; in contrast, Li consistently uses *camel*, a word not used in Old English texts other than Li, Ru1 and Ru2. The single occurrence of the latter word in Ru1 is in Mk 1:6 (*cameles* for *cameli*). For the etymology of *olbend*, see OED3 s.v. *olfend*, n. The word is normally spelled with *f* in Old English, but in Ru1 it is consistently spelled with *b*, a spelling found only twice elsewhere in DOE Corpus: CorpGl 2 (Hessels) [2542 (4.361)] *Dromidus afyred olbenda* and Mart 5 (Kotzor) [1128 (Se 27, A.26)] *Þa com ðær yrnan sum olbenda*.

9 (3:4) *lendu* is taken as an accusative plural form of *lendenu* by Schulte and McAllister, a noun always used as plural. OED2 (s.v. *lend*, n.[1]) also lists the form *lendu* alongside *lendenu* and *lændenu* as Old English plural forms. It is difficult, however, to account for the absence of *-en-*. Even the syncopation of *-e-* before *-n-* is not attested in this word, except for PsGlB 44:4 *lendna* (acc.pl.), glossing *femur*; cf. Hogg and Fulk (2011: §3.57, n. 7), where the Vespasian Psalter (PsGlA) has *lendan* and Kuhn (1965: 236) regards it as an accusative singular form of weak feminine *lende*, which is a hapax legomenon, unless Ru1's *lendu* is taken as another instance. This may, in fact, be an alternative interpretation, because Ru1 shows confusion in unstressed vowels and loss of final *-n*, which lead to oblique cases of weak nouns ending with *-u*. See Introduction III.2.1.6.

10 (3:4) *wudehuniges*. The genitive ending is hard to account for in the present instance, whether the word is taken as a compound or two separate words. It is unlikely to be a variant of the plural ending *-as*, both because of the singular form in the Latin and because *hunig* is otherwise neuter (see DOE s.v. *hunig*). The same ending occurs in Mk 1:6 *wuduhuniges* where the genitive is required by the verb *brucan*.

12 (3:6) The omitted Latin at the beginning of the verse is noticed by Farman and marked with a *signe de renvoi*, formed with three dots lined vertically. Old English alone is supplied for the missing part in the left-hand margin, which is trimmed partially and usually restored as *[wer]un depte in ior[da]ne*, as in Skeat, translating the missing Latin *et baptizabantur in iordane ab eo*. The transcription by Francis Junius in MS Junius 76, f. 48r, reads ⁊ *werun depte in iordane* without noting any loss, though it is not certain whether Junius transcribed the manuscript before it suffered the loss by trimming.

On the use of *depte*, see note on line 22 below.

16 (3:8) *wyrþe westem* for *dignum fructum*. Judging from the form of the adjective, *westem* is here treated as neuter, while the same noun in line 21 below, *godne woestim*, is apparently masculine. See Introduction III.2.2.2 for discussion on the weakening gender distinctions in Ru1.

17 (3:9) *wellað*. For the vowel *-e-* in the root and comparable instances in Anglian texts, see Hogg and Fulk (2011: §6.162).

The second gloss *ł in innan eow* to *inter uos* is written above *betweon eow*. The phrase *in innan* is found in four instances in Ru1, three times as a prepositional phrase and the fourth as an adverb. Elsewhere this phrase is recorded only in poetic texts, most frequently in the formulaic half line, *burgum in innan* (4 occ.), while *on innan* is more frequently used both in prose and verse.

19 (3:10) *þe nu*, written above *iam* at the beginning of the verse is treated as one word by Skeat. His reading is adopted by Schulte, who lists *þenu* as a headword in his glossary with this unique occurrence. Spacing in the manuscript may have led to this word division, but, as *þenuis* in fact is written without any clear division, it is unwise to rely upon the manuscript spacing. McAllister's text has *þe nu* as separate words, which seems more appropriate; *iam* is glossed by *nu* twice in Ru1 (15:32, 26:45), though it is often left unglossed as the meaning can be understood contextually (5:28, 14:15, 17:12, 19:9 *bis*, 24:32, 27:1). Farman uses *þe* as an adverb glossing *quia* and *quoniam*. It is possible, therefore, that this *þe* is in effect a gloss to *enim*, to which *soþlice* is given as a word-for-word gloss, though somewhat redundantly.

is. There is no word corresponding to *is* in the Latin original, as the Latin verb *possita est* is glossed word-for-word with *aseted his* (for *h*-, see the note on line 4 above). Interestingly, there are two Old English translations of this verse (or its corresponding passage in Lk) that start with *Nu is*: CP [1665 (45.339.14)] *Nu is ðonne sio æxs aset on ðane wyrttruman ðæs treowes*; WSCp Lk 3:8 *Nu is seo æx asett to ðæs treowes wyrtruman*. Ru1's reading apparently echoes such conventional translation.

22 (3:11) *depu ł dyppe* for *babtiszo*. Farman's use of *dypan* and *dyppan* (the distinction made in DOE is followed here) for *baptizare* has evoked much discussion. See Gneuss (1993: 120–22) for a summary of the earlier tendency to regard these forms as an example of loan-formations from Greek spread through Gothic, and for his argument against such explanations. More recently, Falluomini (2010) considers that the use of *fullwiht*, the usual noun for baptism in Old English, is originally related to the episcopal *confirmatio* in Roman baptismal practices, and suggests that Farman's use of *dypan* and *dyppan*, instead of verbs related to *fullwiht* (e.g., *fullian*, *fullwian*), may point to the background related to non-Roman missionaries, where the process of *confirmatio*, she believes, was lacking. It is unfortunate that she regards Farman's gloss as Northumbrian, stating that these verbs 'occur only in Northumbrian glosses' (p. 399), especially because she discusses the distance from the area in which Roman missionary activity was more intense. Aldred's gloss, for example, has no instance of *dypan* or *dyppan* to translate *baptizare*, but he uses the verbs related to *fullwiht*. In this regard, her theory needs reconsideration, but there remains the possibility that Farman's gloss places more emphasis on the process of immersion in water than other ritual processes of baptism. Alternatively, as Gneuss (1993: 122) mentioned, Farman's gloss may have been affected either directly or indirectly by a source that explains the etymology of the Latin, and ultimately Greek, term (Gneuss cites Isidore's *Etymologiae*, VI.xix.43, *Baptismus Graece, Latine tinctio interpretatur* as an example). In an attempt to link Farman's choice of words to liturgical contexts, it should not be underestimated that *fullwiht*-type vocabulary is also used in his gloss: e.g., 3:14, where *dypan* is paired with *fullwihtian*.

f. 5r

1 (3:11) *æfter me* agrees with *post me* in the standard Vulgate, which is wanting in R. Because the reading with *post me* is universally found (only two other Old Latin manuscripts are reported to omit the phrase by Fischer 1988–91: i, 57), it is likely that Farman was familiar with the correct reading and may have supplied its gloss from memory.

2 (3:11) *þ* is not a literal translation of the Latin relative pronoun in the genitive case *cuius*. It is probably to be taken as a consecutive conjunction rather than a form of the relative *se*. The literal translation of the gloss in this part would be 'he who is to come after me is stronger than I in that I am not worthy to carry [his] shoes'.

4 (3:12) *winduiscoful* for *uentilabrum*. Skeat, followed by DOE Corpus and Tamoto, transcribes this as *windiuscoful*, but the three minims after *wind-* are better taken as *-ui-*, as transcribed by McAllister. Much earlier than McAllister, BT, using Kemble's text, which was to be re-edited by Skeat, suggests that Farman's form may in fact be *windui-* rather than *windiu-*, and lists the word under *windwig-scofl*, a hapax legomenon. A similar compound for the same Latin word, *windsobl* (cf. BT s.v. *wind-scofl*), is found in ClGl 3(Quinn) 108 (p.75), a mid-tenth-century Latin-Old English glossary in BL, Cotton MS Cleopatra A iii. (Ker no. 143).

5 (3:12) *bęreflor*. According to DOE (s.v. *bere-flor*), there are only two other instances of the word in Old English: Ru2 *bereflor* and Li *berern ł bereflor* (Lk 3:17). Li reads *beretun* in this verse.

6 (3:12) An erasure is visible between *þa* and *ceaf*, which is mostly illegible apart from trace of a descender. McAllister suggests *s* with a question mark.

ceaf has no grammatical ending for the accusative plural of a light-stemmed neuter (normally *-u* or *-o* in Ru1; see Hogg and Fulk 2011: §3.11, and Brown 1892: §55). See Introduction III.2.2.3 for discussion on case-endingless forms.

8 (3:14) The word order of *iohannes þonne werede him* agrees more closely with that of the standard Vulgate reading *iohannes autem prohibebat eum* than with that of R (R's word order is unique amongst the manuscripts examined by Fischer 1988–91: i, 66).

10 (3:15) *let þus nu* for *sine modo*, with the addition of *þus*, which has no exact equivalent in the Latin, gives a smooth reading.

11 (3:15) Farman renders the Latin impersonal structure *decet nos … inplere* into the Old English personal structure *we sculon gefyllan*; both WSCp and Li keep the impersonal structure by using *gedafnian*. The word order *gefyllan æghwilce* agrees with the standard Vulgate reading rather than R.

12 (3:16) *he þa gedeped* for *baptizatus est autem*. Skeat and DOE Corpus place *he* at the end of the preceding verse, where there is no expressed subject (*þa forlet hine* for *Tunc dimissit eum*). The word order and the layout of the gloss, however, strongly suggest that Farman intends to write *he* as part of verse 16, as transcribed by McAllister and Tamoto; the pronoun subject can be used in apposition to the noun subject *se hælend*. It should also be noted that *est* is not glossed, perhaps reflecting the standard Vulgate reading. Skeat's emendation *gedeped [wæs]*, followed by Tamoto, is not necessary even without support of Latin textual variants, because the gloss can still be read without difficulty as it stands, with *gedeped* being a past participle in apposition to the subject.

21 (4:3) *beon ł gewærþe* for *fiant*. The form of the second gloss is difficult to explain. The ending may be considered as plural, with loss of final *-n*, but the vowel *æ* appears to be inexplicable.

22 (4:4) *lifgaþ menn* for *uiuit homo*. The use of plural *menn* is likely to be independent from the Latin; no Latin variant readings are recorded for the plural reading. Although the use of plural is somewhat unexpected when seen as a word-for-word translation, the sense itself is clear, reflecting the indefinite sense 'one, people'. Cf. note on 5:15.

f. 5v

1 (4:4) *æghwelceum* for *omni*. There is illegible space for about two letters after *c*. The present edition adopts the reading proposed by McAllister. Skeat reads *æghwelcicum* in the manuscript, which he emends to *æghwelcum*. McAllister notes that Skeat's *i* is 'one leg of the *m* in *me*, 5R1, shining through' and that 'the following letter is certainly *e*, not *c*'. He regards the illegible portion as 'a greasy spot, which Farman avoided, in the parchment'.

3 (4:5) *hehstowe* for *pinnaculum* is printed as two words *heh stowe* by Skeat, reflecting word division in the manuscript, followed by Schulte, Tamoto and DOE Corpus. Although the compound **heahstow* is not recorded elsewhere in Old English (hence there is no entry for the word in DOE), compounding may be supported by the fact that no clear ending of *heh* is observable. The present edition, following McAllister, reads this as a compound. Farman also employs two more *heh*-compounds, *hehsetl* (27:19) and *hehsynn* (12:5), which are attested in other Old English texts. For Aldred's term used here, see DOE s.v. *horn-sceaþ*.

5 (4:6) *englum* is altered from *englas*, of which *as* is dotted below and *um* is written above. Interestingly, Li shows a similar correction in the corresponding verse, where Aldred's original gloss reads *engla*, but *a* is subpuncted and *u(m)* is written beside it (f. 32vb, 24). The dative gives a smoother syntax with *bebeodan* than the accusative.

The present tense *bebeodeþ* may reflect the Latin reading that has the future tense, *mandabit*, as adopted by WW (cf. *mandauit* in Y, glossed with *bebead*).

6 (4:6) *ut custodiant te in omnibus uis tuis* is a reading found in a limited number of manuscripts; see Fischer (1988–91: i, 99). Cf. Ps 90:11. In Farman's gloss to this portion, the subject *he* appears to disagree with the plural verb ending (*gehalden*), but there are several instances of *he* used as the nominative plural in Ru1; see glossary s.v. *he* and Hogg and Fulk (2011: §5.17, n. 6). There is also a mixture of different grammatical markers in the prepositional phrase, *in allum weogas þine*. Curiously, the same pattern is found in the twelfth-century Eadwine Psalter gloss: PsGlE 90:11 *Forþan englum his bebead be ðe ðette gehealdon þe on eallum wegas þine* (*Quoniam angelis suis mandavit de te ut custodiant te in omnibus viis tuis*).

weogas. In the nominative/accusative plural forms of this word, forms with the back umlaut are the norm in Ru1: see 22:9 and 22:10.

8 (4:7) Note the sole instance of *ie(su)s* being used in the gloss by Farman, as against normal *hælend*.

10 (4:8) *þune* for *montem* is probably to be taken as a form of *dune*, as suggested by Schulte (s.v. *dun*). Farman's use of *ð* and *þ* for *d* is noted by Brown (1892: §18), although the instances of *þ* for *d* are mostly confined to *-eþ* ending for expected past participles; see Introduction III.2.1.2. The present instance may be compared in particular with *geþo* to Latin *eice* (the imperative of *eicere*) in 7:5, which is likely to be a form of *gedon*.

11 (4:8) *rice* for *regna* is preceded by two letters that are smudged and difficult to read. Skeat and Tamoto report nothing, while DOE Corpus reads *us*. McAllister reads *re* with a question mark. The first letter is likely to be *r*, though the descender is hardly visible. The second letter may be an unfinished *e* without a horizontal stroke added.

14 (4:10) *onbæclinc*, written without any word division, is treated as one word here, following DOE's practice that 'instances of the adverbs / adverbial phrases *on bæcling* and *under bæcling* are treated under *onbæcling* and *underbæcling*' (DOE s.v. *bæclinge*). Note, however, that DOE Corpus records this as two words, following Skeat's text.

Latin *retro* does not appear in this passage in the standard Vulgate. Some Old English writers seem to have been familiar with the reading with *retro*: e.g., WSCp *gang þu sceocca onbæc* and HomS10 (BlHom3) [0008 (17)] *Ga þu onbæcling, wiþerwearda*. See also Liuzza (1994–2000: ii, 34), who cites another relevant instance from Ælfric's *Catholic Homilies*.

15 (4:10) *ðu ł to gebidde* for *adorabis*. The linked glosses present difficulties, because *ðu* and *to* do not appear to form an interchangeable pair. *ðu* is taken as the subject of the verb *gebidde*, which can be either the imperative or the subjunctive (with jussive sense), translating the Latin future tense. (The subjunctive may be ruled out on the basis of Mitchell [OES §883], who notes that the jussive subjunctive of the second person singular can be used only either without a pronominal subject or with a pronominal subject following the verb.) The use of *to*, on the other hand, may be compared with a similar instance in 8:2, where *to-* is used as a prefix: *to<->gebedd him* for *ado<->rabat eum*, divided by a line break (Schulte lists therefore *togebiddan* as a headword in his glossary). Alternatively, it may be compared with *tu*, the second person nominative singular, contracted with the preceding verb (e.g., *wiltu*, *cweþestu*; see the glossary s.v. *þu* for further examples). As the imperative gives a smooth translation as seen above, it is not inconceivable that some form like **gebiddestu* may underlie this confusing double gloss. Cf. MED s.v. *thou* pron., for some variants starting with *t-* instead of *th-* in contractions.

20 (4:13) *sæcaestrae* for *maritimam* is probably to be taken as an otherwise unattested compound. Skeat, DOE Corpus and Tamoto read as two words, while BT appears to suggest compounding, as noted in the entry of *sæ-burh*, which is used by Aldred in the corresponding verse. CH (s.v. *sæceaster* 'seaport town'), Schulte, and McAllister list as a compound.

f. 6r

3 (4:16) *þeode londe*, a seemingly two-word gloss to *regione*, puzzles Schulte (s.v. *þeod*), who takes *þeode* as genitive plural with an exclamation mark, and McAllister, whose glossary lists it as dative singular with a question mark. The possibility of taking the two words as a compound has not been considered by them, presumably because the ending *-e* of *þeode* is unexpected in the formation of the compound *þeodland* (see Campbell OEG §341, Hogg and Fulk 2011 §3.144). Ru1's spelling *þeodelond* may be an otherwise unrecorded variant spelling of the compound, with the *-e-* being an example of what Carr (1939: 281–82) terms 'sporadic glide-vowel', which, occurring 'frequently in the combination of a *l* or *r* and another consonant', is one of the causes of abnormal forms of compounds in Old English. In fact, *þeodland* often translates Latin *regio*, as exemplified in BT (s.v. *þeod-land*). See also Waite (1984: ii, 603) for the use of the word in Bede. In the Psalter glosses, it occurs once in PsGlB 114:9 *Ic licige dryhtne on ðeodlonde uiuorum* (*sic*) for *placebo domino in regione vivorum* (cf. PsGlA *londe*, D-type glosses and PsGlC *rice*, PsGlI *eþele ł earde*).

deade scade ł scua for *umbre* (*umbra* Y WW) *mortis*. The form *deade* is probably to be taken as the adjective *dead* in the instrumental case, although, given the Latin phrase, it is tempting to take Ru1's *deade* as a form of the noun, because Farman sometimes uses *d* for *ð* (cf. Brown 1898: §18 and Introduction III.2.1.2). However, it would become difficult to explain why the dative rather than the genitive was used. It may be taken as the first element of a compound with a glide vowel as seen above. McAllister indeed suggests this possibility: *deaþscua* is found in Beo 160, referring to Grendel; see DOE s.v. *deaþ-scua* and *dæd-scua*.

A dialectal contrast is discernible between the two paired, alliterating words *scade ł scua*, as *scua* has been considered as an Anglian word. See Wenisch (1979: 215–16) and Fulk (2008: 88, under §29). In Psalter glosses, while PsGlA consistently uses *scua* for Latin *umbra*, PsGlB, despite its close textual relationship with PsGlA, uses *sceadu* in Ps 43:20, 79:11, 87:7, 106:14.

6 (4:18) *He* is written with an enlarged *h*. The verse opens a new chapter in some medieval chapter divisions (see De Bruyne 1914: 500). For its potential significance, see Introduction III.1.3.3.

11 (4:19) *ic gedom þ git beoþan monna fisceres* for *faciam uos fieri piscatores hominum*. The Latin infinitival construction is translated into a clausal expression. The causative use of *(ge)don* with *þ*-clause occurs in two other instances in Ru1 (5:32, Mk 1:17). The latter is in a corresponding context to the present instance. *beoþan* is a form idiosyncratic to Farman. Whereas the significance of the form *beoþon* is discussed at length by Hogg (2003: 74–78), it is not certain how closely Farman's *beoþan* can be compared with the examples of *beoþon*.

12 (4:20) *foletend*. For the possible significance of the omission of *r* in this example, see Introduction III.2.1.3.

14 (4:21) *zebedeaes sunu* for *zebedei*. *sunu* has no corresponding word in the Latin original, but the addition clarifies the sense, and Li reads similarly (*zebeðes sunu*). For similar instances, see note on 4:25.

17 (4:22) The clearly legible erasure *þ nett* precedes *heora nett*. This needs to be considered with *þ nett heora* for *retibus suis* in 4:20 (line 12), because the standard Vulgate reading wants *suis* in these two instances. Farman's *heora* corresponds with *suis* in the Latin text he was glossing, while *þ nett* would naturally be expected as a gloss to the Vulgate reading without *suis*. *þ nett heora* in line 12 appears to be the mixture of the two readings, while the erasure in line 17 is likely to be a correction that brings the gloss closer to its own Latin text.

19 (4:23) *in heora synagogum ł somnungum* for *sinagogis eorum*. The first gloss *synagogum* is inflected as an Old English word. The word is not listed in standard dictionaries of Old English such as BT (and its supplements) and CH. The earliest instance in OED2 (s.v. *synagogue*, n.) is cited from the Lambeth Homilies, which OED2 dates to '*c.* 1175', but OED3 to '*c.* 1225' in updated entries. For the dating of London, Lambeth Palace Library, MS 487, see Ker (1957: xix) 'may have been written before 1200' and Ganz and Roberts (2007: 62) '*c.* 1200'. The Ru1 instance, if indeed taken as an Old English word, would bring the earliest attestation of the word backwards by more than two centuries. The second item of the double gloss may be explanatory, which can be compared with ÆHom15 [0023 (89)] *Þæt Iudeisce folc wæs gehaten Sinagoga, þæt is gegaderung on Engliscere spræce*, where *Sinagoga* is 'introduced by Ælfric as the technical name of the Jewish congregation' (Pope 1967–68: ii, 911). Elsewhere in Ru1, *(ge-)somnung* is used to translate the Latin word.

bodende godspelles rice for *praedicans euangelium regni*. As DOE notes (s.v. *bodian*, 2.b.i.), there appears to be some confusion in translating this Latin phrase. Farman's gloss reads 'preaching the kingdom of the Gospel' rather than 'the Gospel of the kingdom', and this appears again in Mk 1:14, which reads *bodade godspelles rice godes*, with some erasure visible after *rice*, for *praedicans euangelium regni dei*. Furthermore, the same Latin phrase is translated into *bodede godspelles rices* in 9:35, where the *-es* ending may be a variant of *-as* for the accusative plural, as the noun is used as masculine occasionally (see DOE s.v. *god-spell*).

f. 6v

1 (4:24) *ter* is written above *-tre-* of *tintregum*. As McAllister observes, no cancellation is indicated for the original reading. The added spelling would produce the form with metathesis, which Campbell regards is promoted by low stress (OEG §459 (4)). According to DOE Corpus, forms with metathesis, including corresponding verb forms, are found mostly in the texts with Anglian colouring, such as Li, Ru1, Ru2, Mart and GD. The use of *tintreg*/*tinterg* is confined mostly to prose works apart from four instances in poetry, of which two in GuthA show metathesis.

3 (4:24) *monsekae* for *lunaticos* occurs only in Ru1, but cf. BT s.v. *monaþseoc*. Li reads *bræcsec*, a word found mostly in Anglian texts; see DOE s.v. *bræc-seoc*. In OED3 s.v. *moonsick*, this instance from Ru1 is the sole medieval attestation, followed by presumably historically unrelated instances from the sixteenth and seventeenth centuries. Farman uses the word also in 17:15.

loman for *paraliticos*. *lome* is used by Farman, while Aldred consistently uses forms of *eorðcrypel* for the Latin word. Farman uses the latter only in Mk. See Roberts (2006) for further details.

4 (4:25) *fylgendun* for *secuti* (*secutae* WW) *sunt*. The unexpected medial *-n-* may be caused by confusion with present participle forms. Farman sometimes translates periphrastic perfect forms of a Latin deponent verb into the Old English periphrasis of a present participle with BE-verb: e.g., 19:28 *fylgende arun* for *secuti estis* and 27:55 *ær fylgende werun* for *secutae fuerant*.

5 (4:25) *⁊ of iudea ⁊ of londe begeonda iordane* for *et de iudea trans iordanen*. The repetition of *⁊ of* is closer to the standard Vulgate reading *et de iudaea et de trans iordanen* than R itself. The use of *londe*, which cannot be accounted for by Latin variant readings, can be considered as a semantic addition to clarify the meaning: 'from the land beyond the river Jordan' instead of 'from beyond the river Jordan'.

6 (5:1) Farman's use of an enlarged *h* coincides not only with the modern chapter division, but with the beginning of the pericope assigned to the feast of All Saints (1 November); see Introduction III.1.3.3 for further details.

7 (5:1) The periphrastic form *wæs gesett* is apparently to be taken as passive of *(ge)settan*, as suggested by Schulte (s.v. *gesettan*). However, an intransitive verb is usually expected to translate *sedere*, and accordingly *(ge)settan* is not used to gloss the Latin verb elsewhere in Ru1. McAllister lists this instance under *sittan* as a past participle without further comment. While a weak past participle for the strong verb requires further explanation, the periphrastic construction may denote the pluperfect. Farman tends to focus on tense relationships such as this, and a similar structure with an intransitive verb is used immediately after the Sermon of the Mount: 8:1 *þa he þa wæs astigen of dune folgedun him menga monige* for *cum autem discendisset de monte secuti sunt eum turbae multae*.

his discipuli ł his þægnas. The pairing of a loan word with its native alternative may be compared with the double gloss to *sinagogis* in 4:23. Unlike the case of *synagogum*, *discipulus* is more frequently attested in Old English texts, with either Old English or Latin (as in this instance) inflections; see DOE s.v. *discipul*.

8 (5:2) The present participle *ontynde* reflects the standard Vulgate reading *aperiens* rather than R itself.

10 (5:4) *þa milde* for *mites.* The ink has been lost for a large portion of these two words, seemingly due to the 'greasy' surface of the parchment, as McAllister observes. Both Junius (Junius MS 76, f. 49r) and Thwaites and Todhunter (Harley MS 3449, f. 21r) read *þa milde,* and so does Skeat. The remnant strokes now visible in the manuscript support, though in a very limited way, this reading.

11 (5:5) *þa wepende* for *qui lugent.* Skeat reads *...de* and McAllister *nen--de,* noting *nen* is 'doubtful'. The two early modern transcripts cited in the preceding note agree with one another in having *þa wepende.* In fact, Farman uses *wepan* in glossing *lugere* in 9:15. Although the present condition of the parchment does not allow confirmation of this reading, the traces of letters and remaining strokes do not appear to contradict it.

12 (5:6) *þa þe hie hyngriþ ⁊ ðyrsteþ soðfæstnisse* for *qui esuriunt et sitiunt iustitiam.* Unlike the Latin, in which the two verbs, *esuriunt* and *sitiunt,* are personal with the plural subject, the corresponding Old English verbs have singular endings, and they are apparently used as impersonal verbs (hence *hie* is accusative and a retained pronoun in the relative clause). Mitchell (OES §1038) suggests the possibility that the personal construction of these verbs 'was Latin rather than native idiom', which may account for Farman's use of impersonal verb forms, possibly reflecting a more native construction. WSCp uses the personal construction (*Eadige synt þa ðe rihtwisnesse hingriað ⁊ þyrstað*), while Ælfric uses adjectival forms derived from the related Old English verbs (ÆCHom I, 36 [0072 (491.158)] *Eadige beoð ða þe sind ofhingrode ⁊ ofþyrste. æfter rihtwisnysse*).

13 (5:7) *þa mildheortnisse* for *missericordes.* Ru1's use of the abstract noun here, which can be contrasted with the substantive use of adjectives, as in WSCp *þa mildheortan* and Li *miltheorte,* may have been affected by the following *mildheortnisse* glossing *misericordiam.*

15 (5:9) *þa sibsume ł friðsume* for *pacifici.* The second gloss is a hapax legomenon. See DOE s.v. *friþsum.*

16 (5:10) *hoehtnisse* for *persecutionem.* There is a trace of another stroke before the word, which may be the first stroke of *o.* Farman may possibly have started with *o,* but then restarted with inorganic *h,* given his uncertainties about the use of initial *h.* See Introduction III.2.1.3.

18 (5:11) *homines* is not adopted in the standard Vulgate, while it is found in some Irish texts. Ru1's *mennisc* is apparently treated as plural. Both Li and WSCp insert third person plural pronominal subjects, whereas Ælfric uses the impersonal pronoun *man* as the subject: ÆCHom I, 36 [0077 (491.164)] *Ge beoð eadige. þonne eow man wyrigð ⁊ eower eht.*

20 (5:11) *ligende*. Between *li-* and *-gende*, there is a trace of erasure of two letters, of which the second was an *l*. The spelling *-i-* instead of *-eo-*, or *-e-* with smoothing, see Campbell (OEG §227).

21 (5:12) *lean ł meard*. The second gloss is often regarded as Anglian: see Wenisch (1979: 183–84). *meord* is always paired with *lean* in Ru1; see 6:1 and 10:41. In the other occurrences of Latin *merces*, *lean* is used (7 occ.).

is genihtsumað. As classified by Schulte, *genihtsumað* may be taken as a past participle (instead of *-ad* ending), though the sense expressed by the periphrastic form is not entirely clear. The gloss, in fact, reads well with *genihtsumað* alone, with *is* possibly added by the influence of *est*.

f. 7r

1 (5:13) *gif ꝥ salt þonne awerdað* for *quod si sal euanuerit*. There is a trace of erasure after *gif*. The use of *þonne*, which apparently has no equivalent in the Latin, may be compared to Farman use of the combination of *gif* and *þonne* to translate *quod si* in 5:29 (*gif þanne*) and 18:15 (*þonne gif*).

Schulte and DOE regard *awerdað* as the present third person singular of *aweorþan* 'become worthless' (*-að/þ* ending for the third person singular of strong verbs is found in Ru1). McAllister instead regards it as a form of *awierdan*, presumably because of the medial *-d-* instead of the expected *-ð-* for *aweorþan*. This is unlikely, however, because all the instances of the verb recorded in DOE (s.v. *a-wyrdan*) are used transitively. *aweorþan* is frequently used as a gloss to *fieri* in Li, which DOE calls the 'Northumbrian' use (s.v. *a-weorþan*, I.). In Ru1, the 'Northumbrian' use is found only once in Mk 1:9, where Farman's gloss shows similarities to Li. The use of *aweorþan* in the present context (translating *euanescere*) is paralleled in WSCp *Gyf þæt sealt awyrð*.

2 (5:13) *in þæm þe hit bið salten* for *in quo sallietur*. Farman appears to take *in quo* as a relative rather than an interrogative. Similar renderings are found also in WSCp and Li, and Liuzza (1994–2000: ii, 83) discusses the former as an example of 'Errors and bad translation'.

nymþe þæt for *nisi ut*. For the Anglian, perhaps more specifically Mercian, nature of *nymþe*, see Mather (1894), Jordan (1906: 46–48) and Fulk (2008: 88, item 29 [k]). As to the functions of the two words, Mitchell (OES §3656, and also §§3628, 3641–46) considers *þæt* is a conjunction introducing a noun clause, while he is unwilling to decide whether *nymþe* is a preposition or a conjunction.

5 (5:15) Latin *homines* and its gloss *menn* are added by Farman after *ne*. The gloss *ne menn blæcern inbeornað* gives a smooth reading, which is comparable to King Alfred's translation of the Gospel verse in Gregory's *Pastoral Care*: *ne scyle nan mon blæcern ælan under mittan* (CP [0116 (5.43.1)]). Latin *homines*, however, is not found among the variant readings recorded by WW and *Itala*, suggesting the possibility that *homines* might have resulted from a back-translation from *menn*. See Introduction III.1.3.2. (esp. citation 18) for further discussion.

inbeornað is transcribed as two words by Skeat and Tamoto. The text here follows DOE, which cites this instance under *in-byrnan*, a verb otherwise recorded only once in DurRitGl as an intransitive verb. DOE suggests that the transitive use of the verb in Ru1 'may be due to confusion with *inbærnan*'. The transitive verb occurs only once in Old English (GD).

6 (5:15) *hine* for *eam*. Glossing the feminine pronoun *eam* referring to *lucerna*, *hine* refers to *blæcern*, which is generally neuter, with DOE noting two unambiguously masculine instances (*-as* plural in one of the Vercelli Homilies [HomS 36]).

candeltreow for *candillabrum*. A unique compound in Old English; see DOE s.v. *candel-treow*.

7 (5:15) *he gelihte* for *luceant*. *he* may be written on erasure. R reads *luceant* instead of the standard Vulgate *luceat*, which may account for Farman's use of the singular *he gelihte*.

9 (5:16) *fæder eowrum* for *patrem uestrum*, glossing the Latin accusative, is in the dative case; BT's citation includes no instances of *(ge)wuldrian* being used with a dative object. Nor does Mitchell (OES §1092) include the verb in his list of verbal rections.

10 (5:17) *the*, instead of *þe* or *ðe*. There are seven instances of *th* in native words in Farman's gloss; see further Introduction III.2.1.2.

c\u/ome for *ueni*, with *u* written as suprascript. In Anglian texts, the past forms of *cuman* tend to have *-w-* (or *-u-*), except for Ru2; see Campbell (OEG §742) and Hogg and Fulk (2011: §6.59). This insertion highlights Farman's use of *-u-/-w-* spellings, whereas it can be contrasted with sporadic instances without *-u-/-w-* in Ru1 (*com* 17:12, 24:39, 25:20; *coman* 21:1, 25:36, 25:39; *comun* 25:11; *comen* [ind./subj.pret.pl.] 20:9).

11 (5:17) *eþþa*. See also the same spelling in line 13 and *eþa* in 6:24 (f. 9v, in the lower margin). The spelling with *e-* may be compared with *aeththa* in *Bede's Death Song* (BDSN, line 4). Smith (1933: 27) regards *eðða* as 'Nb'. *eðþa* is found in Rid 43 (line 16), whose editors, e.g., Tupper (1910: 176, his Riddle no. 44), Williamson (1977: 280, his Riddle no. 41) and Muir (2000: ii, 646), agree in regarding the spelling as Northumbrian (or at least northern). These comments appear to depend on Sievers (cf. Sievers-Cook 1903: §317), who lists *eðða* and *oðða* as Northumbrian, but without any proper attestation, and, in fact, no *e*-spellings are found in Li. BDSN's *aeththa* may be sound evidence for early Northumbrian, given that *ae-* is an orthographical variation for *e-* as Smith argues, but the absence of the *e-* spelling from Li (where *oðe*, *oðða* and *oððæ* are found) points to the difficulty in attributing *eþþa* to Northumbrian without fuller consideration.

13 (5:18) *hol stæfes.* Skeat, Schulte, McAllister and Tamoto all take *holstæfes* as one word, though McAllister expresses uncertainty in his glossary. As DOE now lists under *hol,* 3.b., it is better read as two words. While BT has an entry for 'hol, es; n. *A covering* [?]', citing the Rushworth instance as the sole instance, Campbell notes in the *Addenda* that the instance should be under 'hol, *hole,* III', 'an aperture passing through anything; a pore' (as defined by BTS), comparing it with another instance from the Corpus Glossary glossing Latin *spiramentum* (which is cited under DOE *hol,* 3.a. and OED2 *hole,* II. 7.a. 'An aperture passing through anything; a perforation, opening'). Ross (1979b: 497–98) lists the present instance as one of Farman's glosses that are 'obscure and without solution', but a footnote added by E[ric] G. S[tanley] (p. 479, n. 5) accepts Meritt's solution (1954: 138), who suggests *hol* as 'aperture' as noted above.

14 (5:18) *þus.* No Latin word, either in R or other manuscripts examined by WW, corresponds with this gloss. The adverb gives a smooth reading. WSCp instead adds a noun, *ærþam ealle þing gewurðan.*

15 (5:19) *an of þisse beboda læsest* for *unum de mantatis istis minimis* shows the mixture of two different grammatical constructions. Whereas *of* corresponds with *de* in the Latin, *þisse beboda* is likely to be the genitive plural, suggesting the use of the partitive genitive instead of an *of*-phrase, though *læsest* is seemingly undeclined. Mitchell (OES §1201) notes that the partitive use of *of* in Old English is found mostly in the 'texts in which Latin influence is at least a strong possibility'.

17 (5:19) *micel.* The use of the positive for the Latin superlative *maximus* suggests that Ru1 reflects *magnus* as in the standard Vulgate.

19 (5:20) *mæ.* For the comparative of the adverb *micel, mæ* and *mae* are used in Ru1; see Campbell (OEG §676, n.5).

21 (5:21) *iumonnum* for *antiquis.* See DOE s.v. *geo-mann,* which gives six instances of the word in poetry and prose, along with one possible emended instance in the prose life of Guthlac; see Roberts (2009: 182–83).

22 (5:21) *reus erit iudicio* is doubly glossed by *scyldig he biþ dome* and *he bið doma scyldig,* the latter being written above the former. Although the difference in ending between *dome* and *doma* may be simply due to confusion in unstressed syllables, it is possible that the former is the dative singular ending and the latter the genitive plural, as *scyldig* can be used with both genitive and dative (see BT s.v. *scyldig*). In terms of word order, the second gloss deviates from the Latin, resulting in the word order which occurs also in the gloss to *reus erit* in the following verse (5:22).

f. 7v

1 (5:22) *æghwilc þara eorsaþ his broþer* for *omnis qui irascitur fratri suo.* Farman's use of the genitive plural relative pronoun *þara* can be contrasted with more literal translations in WSCp *ælc þe yrsað hys breþer* or Li *eghuelc seðe uraeðes broðere his.* The verb *eorsaþ* is construed with a singular subject, either because of the Latin influence, or – probably more importantly – because the relative clause refers to one of what Mitchell calls 'indefinites', the condition where the verb in the relative clause introduced by *þara þe* 'is more often singular than plural' (OES §2346).

DOE A-I does not record the form *eorsaþ,* presumably choosing *yrsian* for the headword. CH has *iersian,* whereas BTS has several headwords in BT integrated into *irsian.* The verb can be used with a dative object as in the citation from WSCp cited above; the grammatical case of Ru1's *broþer* is ambiguous, without mutation in the root syllable.

3 (5:22) *patri suo* is not recorded elsewhere, and accordingly corrected to *fratri suo* by Farman.

4 (5:22) *dysig ł dole* for *fatuae.* According to DOE, the second gloss *dol* is less frequently found in Old English (22 occurrences) than *dysig* (*c.* 250). Farman uses *dol* twice; in both instances, the word is paired with *dysig* (the other instance is in 7:26, glossing *stultus*).

hellefyres for *gehenne ignis.* The present edition follows DOE in taking *hellefyres* as a compound (s.v. *helle-fyr*), although it notes that it 'may alternatively be taken as two words', as treated so by Skeat, McAllister and Tamoto.

5 (5:23) *weofud ł wibede*; see also *weofud ł wibed* in line 7 below. These double glosses combine variant forms reflecting two distinct dialectal developments of an etymologically identical word, with the first item being West Saxon and the second Anglian. The word in its etymology can be analyzed as *wīg* 'idol, sacrifice' compounded with either *beod* 'table' or *bed* 'bed'. See Holthausen (s.v. *wioh, wih*) and BT (s.v. *wig-bed*). Whereas the former cites only *beod* as the second element, the latter, followed by Campbell (OEG §461, n. 3), leaves the two possibilities. The first element had the back consonant *χ* at the end, and this caused the sound change from the original vowel *ī* to *īo.* This *īo*, however, was affected by smoothing and became *ī* in Anglian, whereas it was retained or further became *ēo* in the other dialects. Furthermore, as to the consonants, *f* and *b*, when the compound was formed, the back consonant *χ* came to stand before the voiced consonant *b*, causing the loss of the back consonant. While Anglian kept *b* between vowels, West Saxon replaced the intervocalic *b* with *v*, which was spelled out with *f.*

gemyne for *recordatus.* The adjective form is often cited as an instance of *i*-adjectives (Campbell OEG §654; Hogg and Fulk 2011: §4.7); this example in Ru1 is apparently the sole instance in Old English, alongside *gemun*, found only once in Or.

6 (5:23) *boþer* lacks *r* for *broþer*. See note on 1:2 for Farman's treatment of *r* in this word.

9 (5:24) *agefes* for *offeris*. *f* is overwritten on *o*, presumably cancelling the *o*, though McAllister adopts *ageofes*. Farman uses both *-e-* and *-eo-* spellings in the present tense forms of *gyfan* (including prefixed ones), as note by Campbell (OEG §210.2). The *-eo-* spelling, showing back mutation, is characteristic to Anglian dialects.

9 (5:25) Skeat, followed by Tamoto, supplies the second *ł* in *wæs ł beo ðu gemod [ł] þencende* for *esto consentiens*. However, the emendation is not necessary, because the manuscript layout suggests that the gloss should be read as *wæs gemod ł beo ðu þencende*, as adopted by DOE Corpus. *wæs* is an imperative form, as Ru1 often has *æ* instead of *e*, and *gemod* is an adjective meaning 'in agreement with', found mostly in Alfredian texts; see BT and BTS, s.v. *gemod* (cf. *ungemod* 'disagreeing'). The use of *þencan* in this context is hardly explicable, unless it is a translation of the Latin stem *sentio*; cf. Li *ðæm ðencende* for *consentibus* (for *consentientibus*), to which *ł ðafendu(m)* is added in the margin (MtHeadGl (Li) 63, f.22rb, 20).

9 (5:25) *þinum þæm wiðerwearde* for *aduersario tuo*. Mitchell (OES §106) notes that the word order of 'possessive + demonstrative + noun' is rare in Old English (attested in Bo), unless the last element is an adjective used as a noun. Ru1's *wiðerwearde* is regarded as adjective by Schulte, but the dative singular form is apparently declined as noun (not weak adjective *wiðerweardan* or strong *wiðerweardum*, although it cannot be ruled out fully that *wiðerwearde* is a variant of the former, with confusion of unstressed vowels and loss of final *-n*). Hence, the glossary, following CH, adopts the masculine noun *wiþerwearda* as a headword.

12 (5:25) *his dægne* for *ministro*. The use of *his* is not supported by Latin variant readings recorded in WW, but is semantically appropriate and can be compared with ÆLet 6 (Wulfgeat) [0025 (85)] *se dema þe betæce his underþeoddum* (Assmann 1889: 4, line 98). For *dægne* instead of *ðægne*, see Introduction III.2.1.2.

carcern for *carcerem*. Ru1 almost exclusively uses this word for 'prison' as against *cweartern*, a word used mainly in late West Saxon. The only exception is *quartern* in 25:39. Fulk (2008: 88, item 30 (b)) regards *carcern* as one of 'Anglian words not normally found in Late West Saxon'.

16 (5:28) *þæs* written above *hire* is probably intended as an alternative gloss, the former referring to *wif* in the grammatical gender and the latter in the natural gender. The case of *hire* is ambiguous, but it is reasonable to take it as genitive, as required *gitsian*, but, being an alternative gloss, its syntactic relationship with the entire sentence may not be rigid, as suggested by the lack of the inflected infinitive ending; cf. Introduction III.2.2.3.

17 (5:28) *gewemmed is* apparently reproduces the Latin periphrasis *mechatus est*, the perfect form of the deponent verb *moechari*. Unlike the Latin counterpart, however, *gewemmed is* cannot be read as active, because *wiþ* precedes its object. Farman may have intended the verb to be read as passive, meaning 'he is corrupted against her in his heart'.

18 (5:29) *æswicað þe ł fælle þec* for *scandalizat te*. Farman uses the combination of *æswician* and *fyllan* (DOE s.v. *fyllan*[2], 7; see also *a-fyllan*) in two other instances, 5:30 and 18:8. In the two successive examples in Chapter 5, *æswician* is in the indicative mood, while *fyllan* in subjunctive, though there appears to be no clear reasons for this differentiation. See De Smet (1987, especially 125) for a detailed survey on Old English equivalents to *scandalizare/scandalum*.

ahloca for *erue*. DOE s.v. *a-hlocian* counts four instances in Old English, of which two are in Ru1. The other two are found in the Erfurt and Corpus glossaries as a gloss to *effodere*.

19 (5:29) *forþon þe þe beþerfeð þ to lore weorðe an þine lioma* deviates syntactically from Latin *expedit enim tibi unum membrorum tuorum ut pereat*. The Old English word order in the *þæt*-clause should be considered in the light of Latin variant readings, because the gloss appears to reflect more closely the standard Vulgate reading *ut pereat unum membrorum tuorum*.

The spelling of the possessive *þine* apparently contradicts the expected genitive plural, making both Schulte (s.v. *þin*) and Brown (1892: §79 (c)) express uncertainties in classifying this and another example in the following verse.

21 (5:30) McAllister's text reads *æswicæð* instead of *æswicað*, but the second *æ* is likely to be *a* touched accidentally by the cross stroke of *ð*.

f. 8r

1 (5:30) *to lose wearþe*, with *ł lore beon* written above, for *pereat*. Both *lore* and *lose* occur only in the phrases *to lore/lose weorþan* in Ru1: *to lore weorþan* 5:29, 9:17, 10:6; *to lose weorþan* 18:14. Jordan (1906: 15–16) regards *lose* as Anglian and *lore* West Saxon. Waite (1984: 499) reports instances of replacement of *lose* with *lore* in some manuscripts of the Old English Bede. See also Grant (1989: 64) for the changes in MS B (CCCC 41). The phrase *to lose/lore weorþan* is confined mostly to earlier texts, such as CP, GD, and Bede. The exact meaning and grammatical form of *beon* in the alternative gloss are not clear.

2 (5:31) *Gecwæden*. The initial letter is enlarged, whereas no comparable emphasis is given to the Latin text. See Introduction III.1.3.3 for further details.

3 (5:31) *swa hwa swa*. The first *swa* is followed by erasure of a letter, which may have been a wynn.

4 (5:31) *þare aweorpnisse*. The phrase is preceded by erasure of *a*, and there is also erasure of another letter between *a* and *w* in *aweorpnisse*.

4 (5:32) *eow*, with *ł iu* written above, for *uobis*. The spelling *iu* for the dative of the second person plural pronoun is not recorded elsewhere in Ru1. Major grammars, such as Campbell (OEG §702), Hogg and Fulk (2011: §§5.30–32) and Brunner (1965: §332), do not list *iu* in discussing variant forms of the pronoun. Whereas the dative plural *iu* is found in some of the West Germanic languages, comparison may perhaps be made with Aldred's forms (notably *iuh ł iw* in Lk 22:10).

5 (5:32) *forletep*. *r* is written over erasure. The erased letter had a descender. In 6:14, the same word is spelled without *r* with the omission signalled by a caret. See Introduction III.2.1.3 for further details.

7 (5:32) *he fæþ unrehthæmeþ* for *adulterium committit*. All the previous editions, as well as DOE Corpus, read *hefæþ* as one word. However, it presents difficulties, especially because *unrehthæmeþ* (the third person present form of *unrihthæman* 'commit adultery') by itself would have translated the Latin phrase. Schulte regards *hefæþ* as a form of *habban* and *unrehthæmeþ* as a variant spelling of the noun *unrehthæmed* 'adultery' (for the examples of interchange between *d* and *ð*/*þ* in Ru1, see Introduction III.2.1.2). McAllister, instead, suggests *hebban* in his glossary. The use of these two verbs in this collocation is not paralleled in Ru1; cf. 19:12 *ne do þu unrihthæmed* for *non adulterabis*. An alternative explanation, which the present edition follows, is suggested in DOE (s.v. *don* I.A.1.k.; for the headword E. G. Stanley is named as being responsible). It regards *he* and *fæþ* as separate words and suggests that the latter may result from miscopying a form of *don* or possibly *fremman*, a verb used by Farman in the sense of 'commit (a crime, murder)' (see the glossary). Whereas it is difficult to judge whether such a miscopying is palaeographically feasible, the use of the pronominal subject, referring back to *se þe*-clause, is paralleled in Li *seðe forleteno lædæs he synnieð*.

9 (5:33) For the inorganic initial *h* in *haþas*, see Introduction III.2.1.3. See also note on line 14 below, where another instance of *aþ* was written with *h*, which is now erased.

10 (5:34) *ne sellaþ hað ł swerge* for *non iurare*. Farman uses the collocation *aþ sellan* to translate *iurare* in four instances, where *aþ* is always used as singular (see the glossary s.v. *aþ*). For the function of the second gloss, see the following note.

As to *ł eower nan*, written above *allunga*, McAllister suggests in his glossary that *nan* might be an error for *man*, as found in line 8 above, but this is unlikely because *swerian man* translates *periurare* not *iurare*. Instead, *eower nan* should probably be read with the second item of the preceding double gloss (*ł swerge*), i.e., *ic cweþe to eow þ swerge eower nan* 'I say to you that none of you should swear…'

11 (5:34) *seþel.* The spellings with *þ/ð*, instead of *t*, have been regarded as Anglian (e.g., Campbell OEG §420) and they are predominant in the Old English Bede (Waite 1984: ii, 562). However, this is the only instance with *þ* in Ru1 and Farman's spelling of the word shows a surprising degree of inconsistency, as listed in the glossary, s.v. *setl.*

11 (5:35) R omits *est* in the *quia*-clause, which Ru1 translates along with the pronoun subject, *hio is.*

fotscamel for *scabillum* is paired with *ł tæppelbred* written in the next line. The former word is commoner, used in Ru1, Li and WSCp in this verse (DOE s.v. *fot-sceamol*), whereas the second gloss (BT s.v. *tæppel-bred*) is idiosyncratic to Farman (another instance in 22:44). The first element *tæppel* can be associated with the Latin loan word *tæpped* (from Latin *tapete* or *tapetum* 'carpet, tapestry'); see Holthausen s.v. *tæppel-bred.* Durkin (2014: 121–22) accordingly lists *tæppelbred* among the examples of 'derivatives and compounds of loanwords' in Old English.

14 (5:36) *aþ selle ł swerigę.* An erased inorganic *h* is legible before *aþ*. See note on line 9 above.

15 (5:37) *ł is ł hit is.* Although all previous editions have ignored or overlooked it, another *ł* sign precedes *is ł hit is*, with the second gloss protruding into the right-hand margin. The first *ł* sign is somewhat lifted above the line and is short, suggesting that Farman first intended to squeeze the entire second gloss into the space above the first.

The use of the formal subject *hit* in the alternative glosses in the verse can be compared with WSCp *hyt ys hyt ys, hyt nys hyt nys.* The following citation from Ælfric's *Grammar* (with Zupitza's punctuation, adopted by DOE) is also comparable: ÆGram [1496 (227.7–9)] *Ac Crist sylf us forbead ælcne að and het us ure spræce þus afæstnian:* est? *is hit swa?* est *hit is;* non? *nis hit swa?* non *hit nis.*

16 (5:37) *þæm wordum* for *his.* The addition of *wordum* to translate the Latin pronoun is paralleled in Li *from daem* (sic) *wordum* in this verse.

The positive *genyhtsume* for the Latin comparative *amplius* (*abundantius* WW) obscures the syntactic relationship with the preceding phrase in the dative.

21 (5:40) The grammatical case of *dom* for *iudicio* appears to be the accusative singular, disagreeing with the Latin. DOE accordingly cites the current instance under *dom* '1.a. in collocation with verbs forming legal expressions (not necessarily established legal idioms)', and suggests *dom geflitan* 'to contend, sue' (s.v. *dom* 1.a.xiii), though, even without *dom*, the verb phrase *wið þe geflitan* conveys the needed meaning (cf. DOE s.v. *geflitan*, *flitan*). Both WSCp (*on dome*) and Li (*to dome*) use prepositional phrases.

22 (5:40) *ł swilce* is written above *him*, but they can hardly form a pair of alternative glosses to *ei*. *swilce* is probably intended as an alternative to the following ⁊ for *et*, specifying the sense of 'too, as well'. For other instances of *swilce* glossing *et*, see 2:8 (and note to the verse) and 6:14.

hryft for *pallium* is spelled with an inorganic *h*. According to Owen-Crocker (2004: 336), *rift* is 'popular' in Anglian. In this verse, all the three Old English versions use different words to translate *pallium*. Li has a triple gloss (*hrægl ł hæcla ł bratt*); WSCp *wæfels*. For details of these terms, see Owen-Crocker's useful list (2004: 332–41). In glossing *pallium* in Ps 103:6 (only in the Roman version; Gallican *uestimentum*), *rift* is used in all A-Type Psalter glosses, whereas PsGlD has *pæll*.

22 (5:41) The double gloss *to lædenne ł to ferganne* is a semantic addition that has no exact equivalent in the Latin text. It may be compared with MS A of the West Saxon Gospels (f. 9r, line 4), where *to ganne* is added by a different hand than the main hand (*swa hwa swa ðe genyt þusende stapa* `*to ganne*´).

f. 8v

1 (5:41) *þusend steppan* with *þæt his an mil* written above. *stæpe* is given as a gloss to *passus* also in the Antwerp-London glossary (see OED2 s.v. *step*, n.[1], 7.a.).

1 (5:42) *all ł se þe* for *omni*. The second gloss apparently reflects the relative clause in the standard Vulgate reading *qui petit a te da ei*. The first gloss *all* lacks a case ending, suggesting that Farman may have given only a lexical equivalent to *omni*. The gloss, when read with *se þe*, agrees closely with the Vulgate reading, especially in the use of the finite form *bidde* instead of a participle that would have translated R's *petenti*. However, see also note on the next line, where Farman translates a Latin participle into an Old English relative clause without support from Latin variant readings.

2 (5:42) The Latin participle *uolenti* is glossed with the relative clause *þæm ðe wille*. Unlike the instance in the previous line, the use of a relative clause is not supported by Latin variant readings, a caveat against attributing the syntactic discrepancy between the gloss and R in the previous instance too readily to the possibility that Farman translated the Vulgate instead of R.

DOE (s.v. *borg*, 2.b.) defines *on borg niman* for *mutari* as 'to take / receive (something) on loan', citing only the present instance in Ru1. More examples of the same collocation are cited for the legal sense 'to take (someone *acc.*) in surety, stand surety for (someone)' (s.v. *borg*, 1.a.ii.).

3 (5:43) *Ge geherdun*. As in 5:31, the beginning of another pericope is marked with a tall *g*. See Introduction III.1.3.3 for further details.

There appears to be no clear reason why the plural form *þine þa nexstan* is used to translate *proximum tuum*. Likewise, *þine fiond* in the next line may also be plural, judging from *þine* and given the original declension of the masculine nouns in *-nd-* (Campbell OEG §632). However, note that the nominative/accusative plural forms of *fiond* have the *-as* ending elsewhere in Ru1 as in line 5 below (cf. Campbell OEG §633).

6 (5:44) *hateþ*, with *ł fieg꞉* written above, for *oderunt*. It is not clear whether *hateþ* should be regarded as singular (for *-aþ*) or plural (for *-iaþ*), because the relative pronoun *þæm þe*, though glossing Latin plural *his qui*, can be either singular or plural in Old English. Similarly, *fieg꞉*, which is probably a subjunctive form, can be either singular or plural with loss of *-n*. Lexically, *feogan* is listed as one of 'Anglian words not normally found in West Saxon' by Fulk (2008: 88, item 29(e)); see also DOE s.v. *feogan*, which also notes that the word is used in 'mainly Angl[ian]' texts. See also 6:24, where *feogan* is again paired with *hatian* (*fiað ł hateþ*).

for hearmcuidele .ł oihtende eowic ⁊ for ehtendum ł hoelende eowic for *pro calumpnientibus uobis et persequentibus uos*. The standard Vulgate reads *pro persequentibus et calumniantibus uos*. Above *hearmcuidele*, there is a trace of an erased gloss, presumably starting with a *ł* sign. On this portion, Menner (1934: 25) presents an interesting, though complicating, argument, which may be quoted in full:

> Farman seems to gloss Rushworth's reading first in *for hearmcuidele ł oihtende eowic*, and then adds *⁊ for ehtendum ł hoelende eowic*, changing both the word for *calumniantibus* and the form of *oihtende*. At first sight, it is easy to conceive of the first rendering as a direct translation of Rushworth in Farman's own language, and the second (with the reversed order) as a copy of another gloss with WS. *ehtendum* instead of his own Angl. *oihtende*. But actually we find that Farman's usual form is *oehtan*, and that *(h)ehtan* occurs in two other passages (5.11, 10.23).

This interpretation involves some questionable assumptions: that *ł* is used to gloss *et* and that *⁊* introduces a set of alternative glosses. It is at least equally possibly, if not more likely, that the first items of the two double glosses, i.e., *hearmwidele* and *ehtendum*, are the glosses given to R, and the alternative glosses, *oihtende* and *hoelende*, were given to reflect the Vulgate word order. Therefore, Menner's speculations about copying procedure and dialectal forms should be treated with caution.

Lexically, *hearmcuidele* is an adjective, recorded twice in Old English, and here it is used as a substantive (DOE s.v. *hearm-cwedol*). For *hoelende*, see DOE s.v. *hēlan*, a hapax legomenon, but it is related to the noun *hol* 'vain speech', and the verb *holian* is once recorded in the Lambeth Psalter (PsGlI) in the triple gloss (*holiendum ł hyspendum ł teoniendum*) to *calumpniantibus* (corresponding to *persequentibus* in the Roman version) in Ps 118:121.

8 (5:45) *upp gangan*. The word division reflects the fact that DOE does not include *up(p)-* in the prefixed forms of *gan* and *gangan*, suggesting that it takes *up(p)* as an adverb; DOE Corpus has Skeat's *uppgangan*. For the collocation with *upp* in the specific meaning of 'the sun rises', see DOE s.v. *gangan* III.B.1.d.i. and *gan* III.B.1.a.i. Fulk (2008: item 30 (e)) regards the use of the infinitive *gangan* as one of the 'Anglian words not normally found in Late West Saxon, though they occur in Early West Saxon'.

10 (5:46) There is erasure of at least a few letters between *þa* and *þe*, which may have read *þe eow*. The erasure stands in the space above Latin *eos*; the extant gloss *þe eow* corresponds with Latin *qui uos* in terms of their position. The correction may have been intended to have aligned the position of glosses to that of the corresponding Latin words.

lufigaþ (second instance in line) for *diligunt* shows a trace of erasure between *i* and *g*, and the original reading appears to have been *lufiaþ*, suggesting that a non-Anglian form may have been corrected to the Anglian form as it stands now; see Campbell (OEG §757).

11 (5:46) *gæfelgeroefe* (DOE s.v. *gafol-gerefa*) for *puplicani* is a word that occurs only Ru1. There are four instances, along with one without *-ge-* (DOE s.v. *gafol-refa*), all of which translate *publicanus*.

14 (5:48) An erased wynn precedes *beoþ*, which suggests the possibility that Farman may have started to write a *w-* form of the imperative such as *wesaþ*. The two possible forms of imperative sometimes form a double gloss elsewhere: *wæs ł beo* for *esto* in 5:25 and *bioþ ł wesaþ* for *estote* in 10:16.

swa swilce. In the manuscript, *swa* is written above *perfecti* and *swilce* above *sicut*. However, *swa* translates the sense of *sicut* and *swilce* appears to reflect *et* in the Vulgate reading (*sicut et pater…*) 'too, as well'.

17 (6:1) *from heom from him*. The second phrase *from him* is written above *alio-* of *alioquin* in the manuscript. Because the meaning of the adverb *alioquin* is properly translated by *elles ł elcur* (see the next note), the second phrase is probably caused by misunderstanding of the Latin word.

elles ł elcur. The second gloss (DOE s.v. *elcor*, *ellicor*) is regarded as an Anglian word; see Waite (1984: ii, 407) and Wenisch (1979: 124–28).

The same pair is used again to gloss *alioquin* in 9:17 in the reverse order. That these two words are used as a double gloss may be compared with the fact that *elcor* is often substituted with *elles* in later West Saxon copies of those texts with Anglian colouring, such as GD and Bede, as noted by Wenisch (1979: 125).

20 (6:2) *heora* has no corresponding word in R or variant readings recorded by WW. Although the insertion is not paralleled in WSCp or Li, Ru1's insertion of *heora* is semantically appropriate.

f. 9r

1 (6:3) *se winstrae hond þin* for *sinistra.* For the form *se* used with historically feminine nouns, see Introduction III.2.2.2.4. The use and position of *þin* suggests that the gloss may reflect the standard Vulgate reading *sinistra tua.* The use of *hond,* though contextually appropriate, is not supported by any Latin variant readings and can be contrasted with more literal translations in WSCp *þin wynstre* and Li *winstra ðin*; cf. CP [1580 (44.323.12)] *ðæt is ðæt sio winestre hand ne scyle witan hwæt sio suiðre do.*

2 (6:4) *in abscondito* with the gloss *in degulnisse* is added after *tua* between the lines. Because R consistently uses *in absconso* instead of *in abscondito* in this passage, Farman's insertion suggests his knowledge of another Latin text with the reading *in abscondito.*

4 (6:5) *stalle. ł stonde* for *stare.* R is contaminated with an Old Latin reading (see *Itala*), having *stare* after *amant,* a rare reading amongst the Vulgate manuscripts examined by WW. The double gloss appears to have resulted from the effort to translate this variant reading, with *stonde* being an infinitive with loss of final *-n.* The first gloss is more problematic. Schulte lists the instance under the masculine noun *stall,* while pointing out the uncertainty about the form. Although Schulte does not explain the sense of the head word, it probably refers to *steall* 'standing point', whose exact intention in this context remains unclear. It may in fact be a form of the otherwise unattested verb *stællan*; its prefixed form (see BT s.v. *gestællan* 'to stall, stable') occurs only once in Mart 5 (Kotzor) [0060 (Ja 16, A.4)] *Ða he þæt ne geðafode, þa het he on ðæs papan ciericean gestællan his blancan ond monig oðer neat.*

worþana for *platearum* is taken as a genitive plural form of *worþ* 'court, street' by Schulte and McAllister. However, there is no unambiguous example of the word being declined as a weak noun elsewhere. The form in Ru1 may have been affected by *worþign* (cf. OED3 s.v. *worthine,* n.); its genitive plural form *worðigna* occurs in the Vespasian Psalter (Ps 17:40), also glossing *platea.* If Ru1's form is in fact affected by *worþign,* that the two texts are Mercian may be of some relevance to the fact that *worþign* (and its reflex) is 'most prolific' in West Midland as a place-name element (Smith 1956: ii, 277).

7 (6:6) The Latin ablative absolute *cluso* (corrected to *clausso*) *hostio tuo* is rendered into the imperative (*betun þine dure*), which gives a smooth reading (cf. the New International Version: *when you pray, go into your room, close the door and pray to your Father, who is unseen*), unlike the other Old English versions that attempt to imitate the Latin structure.

8 (6:6) After *tuum* in the Latin text, the omission is marked by a *signe de renvoi*, and Farman added both Latin and Old English gloss in the right-hand margin.

degulnisse for *absconso*. *l* is altered from *g* by overwriting.

10 (6:7) *þæt him sie ...gehered*. Whereas *him* can be read as a possessive dative duplicating *heora* in the prepositional phrase, it may be tempting, given that Farman often places a pronominal subject at the beginning of a subordinate clause (see Kotake 2022), to assume that *him* may have resulted from miscopying a nominative plural subject; cf. WSCp *þæt hi sin gehyrede on hyra menigfealdan spæce*.

feolasprece has been treated as two words in the previous editions, but all major dictionaries have listed it as a compound (BT, CH and DOE s.v. *fela-spræc*). This is the only recorded instance of the noun, whereas the adjective form (DOE s.v. *fela-spræce*) is recorded seven times, mostly in CP. See also Schreiber (2003: 522) for the distribution of the adjective and its related forms in comparison with *felasp(r)ecol*.

11 (6:8) *forþon þe eower fæder* for *scit enim pater uester*. The gloss fails to translate *scit*, which may have been caused by placing *forþon þe* at the beginning of the clause, thus occupying the space above *scit*. See 6:32, where the same Latin is translated into *forþon þe eower fæder wat*.

13 (6:9) The word order *þu þe in heofunum earð* agrees with the standard Vulgate reading *qui in caelis es* rather than R *qui es in caelis*. As being part of the Lord's Prayer, with which Farman by all means must have been familiar, it is not wise to place too much emphasis on this word order as evidence of his knowledge of another Latin text.

14 (6:10) *cume to þin rice* for *adueniat regnum tuum*. Because *þin rice* is nominative, *to* is an adverb, presumably an element-by-element gloss of *ad-*. It is not clear why *to* is postposed, but two points may be noted: that Farman does not use *tocuman* elsewhere and that a good number of Vulgate manuscripts have *ueniat* instead of *adueniat*, as adopted by the Stuttgart Vulgate.

16 (6:11) *dæghwæmlicu ł instondenlice* for *substantialem* (*super-* WW). The first gloss is corrected from *dæghwæmlice*, with the final *e* dotted below and *u* written above. The corrected form is probably the weak masculine accusative singular with loss of *-n*. Semantically, the first gloss corresponds more closely with *cotidianum*, a variant reading reflected in some other Old English versions; see Liuzza (1994–2000: ii, 34). Whereas this may be interpreted as his knowledge of another Latin text with *cotidianum*, the corresponding passage in Lk 11:3 *panem nostrum cotidianum da nobis hodie* (cited from R) could also have influence on the choice of words.

The second gloss *instondenlice* is a hapax legomenon, and DOE's definition (s.v. *in-standenlic*) as 'present / essential' is based on the Latin equivalent. Middle English *instonding* 'need, urgency' (only one instance is cited by MED s.v. *instonding*) may support this interpretation.

17 (6:12) *swa swa we ec forleten þæm þe scyldigat wið us* for *sicut et nos remittimus debitoribus nostris*. The Latin noun phrase *debitoribus nostris* is expanded into an Old English relative clause. This practice is rare in Old English interlinear glosses (cf. Li *suæ uoe forgefon scyldgum usum*), and in this verse, even WSCp uses a noun phrase (*swa swa we forgyfað urum gyltendum*). Ru1's solution can be compared more closely with ÆCHom I, 19 [0072 (329.128)] *swa swa we forgyfað þam mannum þe wið us agyltað*; BenR [0285 (13.38.14)] *swa swa we forgifað þam, þe wið us gyltað*; or a verse version (LPr III [0006 (19)]) *swa swa we forlætað leahtras on eorþan þam þe wið us oft agyltað*.

18 (6:13) *constungae* for *temptationem*. The spelling *con-* is not attested elsewhere according to DOE s.v. *costung*.

20 (6:14) *heow swilce foletep* for *dimittet (+ et* WW*) uobis*. *heow* is likely to be an instance of inorganic *h*, added to *eow*, rather than an error for *he eow*, with *he* anticipating the subject *eower fæder*. Ru1 *swilce* agrees with *et* in the standard Vulgate; see note on 5:40. *foletep* lacks *r*, as found in 5:32, but here the omission is noted by a caret. It is not entirely certain whether it was added by Farman himself.

f. 9v

2 (6:16) *weorfaþ* lacks the initial *h*. Farman always spells *hweorfan* without *h-* when not prefixed. See Introduction III.2.1.3 for further details.

5 (6:18) *þy les þu sie gesene monnum* for *ne hominibus uidearis* corresponds more closely with the word order of the standard Vulgate *ne uidearis hominibus*, though it cannot be ruled out that the word order of the gloss is a result of the syntactic adjustment to place a pronominal subject at the beginning of the clause.

9 (6:19) The order of *om* ⁊ *mohþa* suggests that Farman follows the Vulgate reading *erugo et tinea* rather than R *tinea et erugo* both here and in the following verse.

16 (6:23) *ne bið nan* for *nequam* may have resulted from Farman's failure to grasp the sense of *nequam* 'worthless', and Skeat's rare note that 'ne bið nan *is the gloss to* nequam' appears to suggest such an interpretation. The gloss, though not a precise translation, still makes sense as it stands: 'but if there is no eye of yours'. Farman duly glosses *nequam* with *nawiht* in 18:32 and 20:15, whereas a sign of confusion is detected in 13:38.

18 (6:23) *þæt þeostre* for *tenebrae* is probably an instance of the use of the neuter *þeostre*, as against the feminine *þeostru* (for the distinction, see BT s.v. *þeostru*), unless it is taken as another instance of *þæt* used with a feminine noun as discussed in Introduction III.2.2.2.5. Despite the Latin plural form, the use of *þæt* appears to suggest that *þeostre* is singular, agreeing with the verb *biþ* in the next line. The seemingly neuter instances of the noun are also found in 22:13 and 25:30.

20 (6:24) *forþon þe he þa oþerne fiað. ł hateþ* for *aut enim unum odio habebit. þa* is unlikely to be a form of *se*, because it does not agree with *oþerne* in gender and number. McAllister takes it as an adverb corresponding with *enim*, adding 'or aut?'; Schulte considers that *þa* translates *aut*. The gloss apparently fails to translate *aut*, which correlates with another *aut* in the portion added in the bottom margin, glossed with *eþa*, a variant form of *oþþe*. Because the correlation 'either … or …' is not likely to be expressed by *þa* … *eþa*…, it may be tempting to suppose that *þa* is a miscopying of a form similar to *eþa*. On the spellings *eþa* and *eþþa*, see note on 5:17.

22 (6:24) *dwale* for *mammone*. DOE (s.v. *dwola*, 2.) lists this occurrence under *dwola* 'error, doubt', suggesting that the word 'perhaps refer[s] to the exaltation of wealth as a form of spiritual delusion or as a false god'. It also suggests the possibility that the word is in fact a corrupted form of *deofol* or *woruldwela*, the latter of which occurs in WSCp *Ne magon ge gode þeowian ⁊ woruldwelan*. The former possibility can be compared with Aldred's marginal note to the verse: MtMarg (Li) [0013 (6.24)] *Mamon, þæt is gidsunges hlaferd ðe diowl; He is sua genemned Mammonis*, on which see Boyd (1975: 15–19).

22 (6:25) *þ ge sorgige* for *ne soliciti sitis* lacks the negative particle in the gloss. When the Latin conjunction *ne* is glossed with *þæt*, negation is expected to be expressed in the *þæt*-clause.

f. 10r

4 (6:26) All the previous editions read *heofunfuglas* as two words, but the present edition treats it as a compound, following DOE (s.v. *heofon-fugel*), especially because of the absence of a case ending in the first element. All other instances of the compound occur in poetry.

7 (6:27) *hwilc eower mæg þonne þencende ætece* for *quis autem uestrum cogitans potest adicere*. In the gloss, *eower* is written partly on erasure, which appears to have read *mæg*, suggesting that Farman adjusted his gloss to have the partitive *eower* placed next to *hwilc*. The position of *mæg* is dislocated from the position of its Latin equivalent *potest*.

ætece. The verb occurs only in Anglian texts. Li has *æt ł toece* in this verse. DOE (s.v. *æt-ican*) counts nine occurrences of the verb, noting 'mainly in Bede', along with one instance (with 'unaccented prefix' *ot-*) in the Vespasian Psalter.

12 (6:30) *nu nu* for Latin *si* is also found in 7:11 and 22:45, along with a further instance in 12:34, glossing *cum*. There is another instance in Bede 1 [0362 (16.80.19)] *Ono nu nu þæm mete ne bið clæne, þam þet mod ne bið clæne, forhwon þonne þæt wiif þæt heo clæne mode of gecynde þrowað, sceal hire in unclænnesse geteled beon?* corresponding to Latin *Si ergo ei cibus inmundus non est, cui mens inmunda non fuerit, cur, quod munda mente mulier ex natura patitur, ei in inmunditiam reputetur?* (Colgrave and Mynors 1969: 94).

13 (6:30) *to mærgen ł marne* for *cras*. The first gloss lacks the dative ending, while *marne* is the dative singular form found frequently in Bede, PsGlA. It occurs only here in Ru1.

21 (6:34) *sorgaþ beoþ* for *sollicitus erit. beoþ*, written on illegible erasure, is redundant, because *sollicitus esse* is fully translated by *sorgaþ*.

f. 10v

1 (7:2) All the previous editions read *in ðæm* for *in quo* without comment, but in the manuscript, the gloss was written twice, with the second gloss written above the first. Given the poor parchment condition in this area, the second gloss may simply have been rewriting of the first, but the first gloss appears to be *on ðæm*, as adopted in the present edition.

Similarly, they read *weotudlice* for *enim*, but it should read *wiotudlice*, with the first *i* having been confused with *e* due to show-through from the back of the folio.

3 (7:3) *broþer þine* for *fratris tui. þine* lacks the *-s* ending for the expected masculine genitive.

5 (7:4) After *tuo*, the omission is marked by a cross, and both the Latin text and the gloss are added by Farman in the left-hand margin (see the apparatus, p. 107). The addition begins with *frat(er)*, glossed with *broþer*, functioning as a vocative that does not occur in the standard Vulgate. WSCp also has the vocative *broþur*, which Liuzza (1994–2000: ii, 74–75) discusses as an example of harmonization, reflecting the use of *frater* in Lk 6:42.

6 (7:5) Schulte regards *geþo* for *eice* as a form of *gedon*, which McAllister adopts with a question mark. The spelling is not listed in the attested spellings recorded by DOE s.v. *gedon*. The confusion between *þ* and *d* is found in Ru1 elsewhere (*þune* instead of *dune* in 4:8), and the use of *gedon* can be compared with *ofdon*, which is used in the previous verse (in the marginal addition) as a gloss to the same Latin verb, and *adon* used in WSCp *ado ærest ut þone beam of þinum agenum eagan*.

8 (7:6) Ru1 consistently uses *ercnanstanas* for *margarita*, which can be contrasted with Li and WSCp, which use the loan word *meregrot*. See DOE s.v. *eorcnan-stan*.

10 (7:6) *gehwerfeþ* is transcribed as *-æþ* by Skeat, Tamoto, and DOE (s.v. *gehwyrfan*); with McAllister, the present edition reads *-eþ*, as the supposed *æ* is apparently caused by the prolonged tongue of the preceding *f* touching the *e*.

Skeat, followed by Tamoto and DOE Corpus, reads *to slite* as two words, but Skeat uses prefixed forms in WSCp (*toslyton*) and Li (*toslitas*) in the same verse. Given the relatively large number of occurrences of the prefixed form, and to remove the inconsistency in Skeat's treatment, the present edition reads *toslite* as one word.

14 (7:9) *monn þe hine bidde sunu his* for *homo quem si petierit filius suus*. *hine* is to be understood as what Mitchell discusses as the instances of 'indeclinable particle [*þe*] followed by pronoun showing the case relation' (OES §§2198–200).

17 (7:11) *cunneþ* for *nostis* is an example of a preterite-present verb that shows 'by-forms with the endings of strong presents' (see Hogg and Fulk 2011: §6.135; see also Campbell OEG §767).

19 (7:11) Ru1 glosses the Latin participle structure *petentibus se* into the relative clause *þæm þe biddaþ hine*. There is erasure of *hine* between *þæm þe* and *biddaþ*.

f. 11r

2 (7:13) For the possible significance of the occurrence of both feminine and masculine forms in the double gloss *þære ł þæne*, referring to *weg* glossing *uia*, see Introduction III.2.2.2.6, esp. n. 124.

3 (7:14) Between *hu* and *naru*, there is erasure of *nearu*, still largely legible.

The use of the word *wiðerdune* as part of the double gloss for *angusta* is discussed in Kotake (2017: 92–93), who points out that the rare adjective occurs twice in this specific biblical context of the 'narrow gate', both of which are paired with forms of *nearu* (in GD and one of the Vercelli Homilies [HomU 11]).

arta is altered to *arcta*, possibly by the main scribe of the Latin text. While the standard Vulgate adopts *arta*, several manuscripts examined by WW, including some Irish ones, have *arcta*.

4 (7:14) The second gloss *cymeð in þara*, written above *gemoetaþ þane* for *inueniunt eam* (*þane* being corrected from *þanne*, by erasing the first *n*), appears to be an element-by-element translation of *inuenire*, with *þara* reflecting the gender of the Latin pronoun.

7 (7:15) *risænde ł woedende* for *rapaces*. Both words are found in collocation with *wulf* elsewhere, for example Bede 1 [0429 (18.92.10)] *Beniamin is risende wulf* and HomU 36 (Nap 45) [0039 (101)] *ic sende ofer eow wedende wulfas and wedende hundas, þe etað eowerne lichaman to deaðes tocyme*. See Klaeber (1902–4: 1902, 314) for the Bede citation and the verb *(ge)risan*. The second gloss gives alliteration with *wulf*, which may be compared with the series of double glosses given to *facere* and *fructus* in verses 17 and 18, see below.

8 (7:16) *winbegęr* for *uuas*. *winbeger*, instead of *winberge*, occurs only here in Ru1 and twice in Li (in the marginal addition to 21:33 and Lk 6:44). For the second element, see DOE s.v. *beger*, which lists four instances in Latin-Old English glossaries, glossing *vaccinum* 'whortleberry', and also Pheifer (1974: 69). OED2 (s.v. *bay*, n.[1]) suggests that *beger* and similar forms in the glossaries 'might be an archaic plural of an original *-is*, *-os* stem'.

gorstum for *tribulis* is altered from *grorstum* by erasing the first *r*.

9 (7:16) *ficos ł nyte* for *ficos*. The first gloss is the only example of the Old English noun *fic* inflected as Latin according to DOE s.v. *fic*. It may indeed be taken as a Latin word copied in as a gloss, because there are a few instances in Ru1 where a Latin word appears as if an Old English gloss; e.g., *manducat* in 24:49 and *parabside* in 26:23. See also note to 8:3 on the use of *centurio*. The second gloss is apparently a form of *hnute* with loss of *h*; this glossing instance is the sole attestation for DOE s.v. *hnute*, 1.d. 'fig'.

9 (7:17) *godne węstmas* for *bonos fructus* shows lack of concord in number. In verses 17 and 18, if we read with the second glosses for the four double glosses, there will be alliteration between the verbs and their objects, as discussed in Kotake (2017: 92). Note also that *blæd*, which alliterates with forms of *beran*, is noted as 'disproportionately frequent in poetry' by DOE s.v. *blæd*.

13 (7:19) *þara* written above *ergo* does not translate the Latin word, which does not occur in the standard Vulgate. *þara* is likely to be a misplaced gloss, which was to be used with *þe* as a translation of the relative *quae*. The gloss may be reconstructed as *æghwilc treow þara þe* …

f. 11v

11 (7:28) *þa* is erased immediately after *gewarð*. Another *þa* is written above *est*, presumably to make the gloss stand closer to *cum*.

15 (8:1) On the periphrastic verb phrase *wæs astigen*, see note to 5:1.

16 (8:2) The Latin nominative *quidam*, which is a reading peculiar to the mixed Irish family according to WW, is glossed with the masculine accusative *sumne*. This confusion in grammatical case may have arisen due to the textual difference between R and Farman's source presumably reflecting a purer Vulgate reading without *quidam*.

18 (8:3) *et* is supplied at the beginning of the verse by Farman along with its gloss, bringing the R reading closer to the Vulgate.

21 (8:4) *æteaw þe* apparently translates the Vulgate reading *ostende te* rather than R, which lacks *te*.

f. 12r

1 (8:5) Farman left *centorio* unglossed here, which may be compared with the fact that he uses the Latin loanword *centurio* twice elsewhere in his gloss, in both instances preceded by Old English demonstratives (8:8 *þæm centurione*; 27:54 *se centurio*). Aldred similarly uses the Latin word, but he supplies an explanatory note (e.g., 8:5 *ðe centur þæt is hundraðes monna hlaferd*), presumably indicating that he is not entirely satisfied with the use of the word as English. See further DOE s.v. *centur, centurio, centurius.*

3 (8:6) *is yfle wælid* for *male torquetur. (ge)wælan*, used by Farman in three instances, is rare elsewhere and considered to be an Anglian word. See Jordan (1906: 57). The only other occurrence is found in GuthA 424–25 ... *þæt hy his lichoman leng ne mostan witum wælan*; cf. DOE s.v. *a-wælan* and *be-wælan.*

5 (8:8) *þacu minne* for *tectum meum. þacu*, accusative plural of the neuter noun *þæc*, is followed by *minne*, apparently masculine accusative singular. An alternative interpretation may be to take *þacu* as a form of the weak noun *þaca* 'covering, roof' with loss of *-n*.

9 (8:9) *ł ðeow*, written above *to esne* for *seruo*, is the only occurrence of *þeow* in Ru1 (the feminine form *þeowe* and the compound *efenþeow* are used; see the glossary). Farman constantly uses *esne* in glossing *seruus*, which is often associated with early West Saxon and Anglian (cf. Jordan 1906: 91). In considering dialect vocabulary (see Introduction III.2.3), it is important to note that the first occurrence of *esne* in Ru1 here is in fact supplied with another word of wider distribution, *þeow*. The form *ðeow* apparently lacks the case ending.

10 (8:10) *wundriende wæs* for *miratus est.* The present participle form is corrected from *wundrade* with *a* erased incompletely and *ien* written above. The correction appears to intend to make the gloss closer to the Latin periphrastic form. Farman usually uses simple preterite forms even when glossing the deponent verb *(ad)mirari* in periphrastic forms (see 8:27, 21:20, 22:22); the only other instance of the periphrastic preterite of *wundrian* is found in Mk 1:27.

fylgendun him to þæm cwæþ for *sequentibus se dixit*. In the manuscript, *to þæm* appears to have been squeezed in, perhaps as an afterthought. This sequence should be read as *cwæþ to þæ(m) fylgendun him*, which would account for the apparently unexpected *-n* ending in *fylgendun*. Instead of taking *-un* as an error for the strong dative plural *-um*, it is to be taken as a variant spelling of the weak dative plural ending *-an*, for which Ru1 has one comparable instance (the weak noun *eagun* in 26:43).

11 (8:10) *swa micel geleafa* for *tantum fidem*. While the loss of final *-n* would allow the reading of *geleafa* as accusative, *micel* clearly lacks the case ending for the masculine accusative. Cf. Introduction II.2.2.

14 (8:12) *rice þeos* for *regni huius*. The gloss does not reflect the genitive case of the Latin phrase and there is apparently lack of gender concord between the neuter *rice* and the feminine *þeos*. While this may be an example of weakening gender and case distinctions in Ru1, it should also be noted that *huius* is a non-Vulgate reading found in some manuscripts aligned to the mixed Irish family, which appears to be reflected also in WSCp *þises rices bearn beoð aworpene*.

16 (8:13) *ða* has no corresponding word in either R or variant readings recorded in WW, but the insertion can be compared with ÆCHom I, 8 [0059 (244.101)] *Ða cwæð eft se hælend to þam hundredes ealdre*.

19 (8:15) *sio drif* for *febris*. DOE s.v. *drif* 'fever' lists only two instances, with the other instance taken from in Chron E 1086, whereas the prefixed *gedrif* occurs more frequently; cf. note on Mk 1:30–31.

20 (8:16) Above *autem*, there is a trace of erasure of two words; the legible portions suggest that it is likely to have read *þa wæs*. While *þonne* translates *autem* in the current state, the use of *þa wæs* is probably to be taken as part of Farman's attempt to translate the Latin ablative absolute construction by using a *þa*-clause (cf. WSCp *Soþlice þa hyt æfen wæs hig brohton him manege defolseoce*). The two *þa* forms in the next line, both of which lack equivalents in the Latin text, appear to be related to this attempt. See Introduction III.2.4.

21 (8:16) *brohtun*. *r* appears to have written over *o*. For the potential significance of the correction, see Introduction III.2.1.3.

deofulseoke habbende. *deofolseoc* is usually used as an adjective or a substantive denoting 'one possessed by devils', but Farman uses the word as an abstract noun, for which *deofolseocnes* 'insanity' is more frequently employed in Old English.

22 (8:16) *þurh his worde* for *uerbo*. The manuscript layout gives the impression that *þurh his* was probably added later than *worde*, especially because of the *i* of *his* written under the baseline, a space-saving practice derived from the Insular tradition (see Introduction III.3). *þurh* is used here to denote the instrumental sense of the Latin ablative (cf. Mitchell OES §825), but this is the only occurrence of inserted *þurh* in Ru1, while *mid/mið* is more frequently used for the sense. Note also that *worde* appears to be in the dative. This is the only unambiguous instance in Ru1 where *þurh* is used with a dative. If *þurh his* was indeed written after *worde*, then the dative may simply have been Farman's attempt to give a literal translation of *uerbo*. Elsewhere, the dative after *þurh* is preferred in Ælfric's *Catholic Homilies* (cf. Mitchell OES §1207).

f. 12v

2 (8:17) *wiotudlice* corresponds with no Latin in R or other variant readings; see Introduction III.1.3.1 for the discussion on the possible influence of the Old Testament source (Is 53:4 *Vere languores nostros ipse tulit, et dolores nostros ipse portavit*).

5 (8:18) *sae ł brymstream* for *fretum*. The first *r* of the second gloss is apparently overwritten on *y*. The word, supplied as an alternative gloss to the more usual *sae*, occurs elsewhere only in poetry. See DOE, under two separate headings, *brymm-stream* and *brim-stream*.

6 (8:19) *ic wille folgian* for *sequar*. The use of *wille* to translate the Latin future can be contrasted with WSCp *ic fylige þe* and Li *ic fylgo ðe ł ic ðeh sohte* (the intention of Aldred's second gloss is not sure). For similar uses of *willan* in Ru1, see 10:14 and 24:43; for the use of *sculan*, see note to 11:3.

hwider swa is a rare instance of the absence of the first *swa* in *swa … swa …* phrases. See DOE s.v. *hwider, hwæder* 4.b.iii. and Mitchell (OES §2486).

7 (8:20) *selescota* for *tabernacula*; see also 17:4. Both *selesceot* and *selegesceot*, considered to be Anglian, are found in PPs, PsGlA, B, C (14:1), and Christ. See Lendinara (1993: 313–14).

9 (8:21) *of* is written *in rasura*; the erased word appears to have read *his*, translating *eius* in the next line. *leornere* has no dative plural ending to form the partitive phrase after *of*, unlike in WSCp *oþer of hys leorningcnihtum*; for the partitive use of *of*, see Mitchell (OES §§1201–2). Neither does it appear to be the genitive plural. Farman's initial attempt may have been to use the nominative phrase *oþer his leornere* (for syntactic ambiguities of such phrases, see Mitchell OES §517), but his finished gloss was affected by the corresponding Latin, which made him add *of* for *de* and change the position *his*, while leaving *leornere* unchanged.

11 (8:21) *fæder minum.* It is not clear why the dative is chosen after *bebyrgen*, which usually governs an accusative object; see DOE s.v. *be-byrgan*.

14 (8:24) *geworden* for *facta* involves correction with *o* and *d* written *in rasura*. The former is apparently written over *a*, making it difficult to confirm the corrected reading (hence McAllister reads *gewerden*); the original reading for the *d* may have been *ð* with a trace of the cross-stroke somehow still visible. The correction, therefore, may have been intended to alter the simple preterite form *gewarð* into the periphrastic phrase agreeing with Latin *facta est*.

16 (8:25) *uero* is given effectively a triple gloss composed of *wiotudlice*, *soþ* and *þonne* (cf. WSCp *Witodlice he slep*; Li *he soðlice geslepde ł slepende wæs*). Statistically, Farman prefers *þonne* as an equivalent to *uero*. The adverb may have had somewhat dramatic effect in this specific context, contrasting the violent tempest with the calmness of Christ, making Farman seek for an appropriate adverb. A small number of Latin manuscripts have *autem* instead of *uero*; see Fischer (1988–91: i, 203).

19 (8:26) All the previous editors read *gefrohte* as one word, which the present edition follows; DOE (s.v. *geforht*), while adopting the one-word reading, suggests the possibility of taking it as *ge frohte*. There is no decisive evidence with which to choose from the two alternative interpretations. The pronoun reading may appear to be more likely, given the rarity of the prefixed *geforht* (DOE gives only one other instance, against *c.* 120 instances for *forht*); however, in terms of word order of questions, an inserted pronominal subject tends to follow the verb to form the VS order.

22 (8:27) *gehęraþ* is corrected from *-eþ*, with the *e* dotted below and *a* written above.

f. 13r

1 (8:28) *gerasinga* for *gerasenorum*. The suffix *-ing* is productive with non-Germanic names to form patronymics and placenames in Ru1 (see DOE s.v. *-ing*[2] and OED3 s.v. *-ing*, suffix[3]; cf. Sprockel 1965–73: ii, 43): see also *gomorringa* (10:15), *samaringa* (10:5), *sodominga* (10:15, 11:24), *sodomingum* (11:23). There are a small number of similar instances in Old English: *adaming* (Li, Luke 3:38, spelled with contraction as *a'ing*), *Moabitingas* (PPs 107:8; cf. O'Neill 2016: 686), *Idumingum* (Widsith 87; cf. Hill 2009: 114).

3 (8:28) *þyrh* is corrected from *þurh* by writing *y* over *u*. DOE Corpus records only two other instances of *þyrh*: in a homily recorded in a twelfth-century manuscript (Oxford, Bod.L, Bodley 343), where *y* is sometimes used for Old English *u* (see Irvine 1993: lix) and in a twelfth-century copy of a charter (Sawyer no. 817). The colour of ink suggests that it was Farman's correction, but the intention of choosing deliberately *y* is not clear.

6 (8:30) *suner* for *grex* is found only in Ru1/2 and Li (cf. *heord* in WSCp). See Jordan (1906: 24–25). See also OED3 s.v. *sounder*, n.[1], which derives from a later Old French loan of the related Germanic origin. See also note on *wræð* in line 10 below.

8 (8:31) *þas sunrae swina*. *þas* is partially written *in rasura* which is not legible. The final *-a* of *swina* is blurred, perhaps as erasure (so treated by McAllister), but the text adopts the original reading as required by the sense.

9 (8:32) *⁊ hię* for *at illi* is written entirely *in rasura*, which apparently had been a dittography of the gloss to *ait illis* in the previous line. Although the legible strokes are not sufficient to reconstruct the erased reading completely, it is likely that the erased gloss was something similar to *cweþ to heom*.

in swinum ł in þassum for *in porcos*. The second gloss does not present a lexical variant to the first. The combined reading of the two alternative glosses, i.e., *in þassum swinum*, would produce a possible solution, though no Latin variant recorded in Fischer (1988–91: i, 225) supports it. The dative plural form *þassum* is recorded only in this instance in Ru1, while it is found in Ru2 and Li. See Ross (1967: 286–87) and (1977: 304).

10 (8:32) *suner ł wræð* for *grex*. The second gloss *wræð*, related to the verb *wriþan* 'twist, bind', usually means 'bandage, band, fillet' (cf. Mod.E. *wreath*). For its use for the specific meaning 'flock, company', see BT (s.v. *wræd, wræð*, III); for an instance of the word specifically referring to a flock of pigs, see Alex [0201 (28.8)] *Þa het ic sona þa hors gerwan ⁊ eoredmen hleapan up, ⁊ het geniman swina micelne wræd ⁊ drifan on horsum ongean þæm elpendum*. For the dialectal nature of the text (especially its Anglian nature), see Vleeskruyer (1953: 55–56) and Bately (1988: 99).

deade wurdon is preceded by erasure of *wurdon*. The correction alters the word order of the gloss to match that of the Latin text.

13 (8:33) *deofulseoke werun ł æfdon ær* for *abebant*. As noted in 8:16, the second gloss (for the lack of *h-*, see Introduction III.2.1.3, and note the Latin *abebant*) indicates that *deofulseoc* can be used as an abstract noun in Ru1, while the first gloss reflects its more usual use as an adjective.

15 (9:1) *oferlaþ þone sæe* for *transfretauit*. *oferliþan* occurs always in sea-faring contexts, in Prose Guthlac (LS 10.1 (Guth) [0011 (0.31)] *swa swa <ic> strange sæ and mycele oferliðe*), and in the entry for St Erasmus in Martyrology (Mart 5 (Kotzor) [0547 (Ju 2, A.20)] *ond þa gemette he scip ond he astag on þæt scip ond mid ðy oferlað þa mægðe*). The Martyrology instance is replaced with *oferfor* in the revised C (CCCC 196). In poetry, it occurs in the Noah episode in Ex 362 *Niwe flodas Noe oferlað*.

16 (9:2) The *r* of *brohtun* is apparently written on an *l*.

18 (9:2) *for-* of *forletne* is written at the end of the line; the *r* is written with an unusually long vertical stroke, which may have originally an *l*.

19 (9:2) *þe* is erased and still legible above *tibi*, which is translated in the previous line before the verb phrase. The cancelled gloss follows the Latin word order more closely.

19 (9:3) *of* is erased above *de*. Farman's gloss often betrays uncertainties about how to translate Latin partitive phrases using *de*. Here, literal translation of *de* into *of* is cancelled and *þara bocera* is clearly inflected as the genitive plural.

20 (9:3) Skeat reads *he-falsaþ* with no explanation about the use of the hyphen, which Tamoto uncritically follows. Schulte, McAllister and DOE read it as one word and a form of *eofulsian*; the inorganic *h-* is frequently inserted in this word.

21 (9:4) *ðohtas*. OED3, s.v. *thought*, n. (but not OED2) notes in the etymology section that 'In Old English the unprefixed form *þōht* is chiefly (although not exclusively) attested in Northumbrian'. Ru1 has both forms; see the glossary.

22 (9:5) *ł eaþe*, an alternative gloss to *eþre* glossing *facilius*, is erased.

In the righthand margin, Farman added *xb* (with an abbreviation stroke through the ascender of *b*) mark, for which see Introduction III.3.

f. 13v

6 (9:8) *ן dreordun heom* for *timerunt*. Skeat, followed by McAllister and Tamoto, reads *ןdreordun*, presumably as a form of *ondrædan*, though the reading does not account for the repetition of *d* in the resulting *onddreordun*. Skeat, again followed uncritically by Tamoto but not by McAllister, mistakenly reads *ןdreordun* for *et timebunt* instead of *ן dreordun* in 19:25 (for details, see note to the passage). In the present instance, because Ru1 translates the preceding participle *uidentes* into the finite form *gesegon*, the insertion of the conjunction ן gives the smoother reading. See Introduction III.2.4. For the other possible occurrences of *ןdrædan*, see notes on 14:5 and 21:46. DOE s.v. *drædan* notes that the instances of *ןdrædan* in Ru1 may 'perhaps' be taken as examples of *drædan*.

8 (9:9) *monnu*, the object of the verb *gesæh*, is probably to be taken as an accusative singular of the weak noun *manna*, with the loss of final *-n*. As Terasawa (2010: 30–32) discusses, the weak noun tends to be restricted to the accusative singular, which is also true in Ru1. See the glossary s.v. *manna*.

matheus is apparently altered from *matheum*. Cf. note to INCIPIT.

9 (9:9) *fylgæ* is corrected from *folgæ*, by dotting *o* below and writing *y* above. Similarly, *fylgænde* appears to have been corrected from *fo-* by simply writing *y* over *o*.

10 (9:10) *þær* has no corresponding word in the Latin text. Given the finite verb form *hlionede* glossing the Latin ablative absolute construction, *þær* appears to function as a conjunction introducing an adverbial clause. A more frequent practice is to use *þa* for similar purposes; see Introduction III.2.4 for details.

11 (9:10) *gæfelhroefe* for *puplicani*. For the inorganic *h-* at the beginning of the second element of the compound, see Introduction II.2.1.3. The compound without the medial *-ge-* occurs only here (see DOE s.v. *gafol-refa*); cf. line 13 *gæfelgehrefum*.

15 (9:12) *ł vntrymum* is written above *yfle*, but the double gloss should be understood as *yfle hæbbende ł vntrymum*, as the latter word alone translates the entire phrase *male habentibus*.

f. 14r

1 (9:15) The use of *þæt* for the conjunction *cum* is found only in this instance in Ru1 and it can be contrasted with more frequent *þonne* or *mid/miþ þy* (latter especially in Mk); cf. Li *cymes uutedlice dagas miððy genummen bið*. The use of *þæt* in similar constructions, however, is well attested as discussed by Mitchell (OES §§2784–88); cf. WSCp *Soðlice þa dagas cumað þæt se brydguma …*

2 (9:15) *þonne* is altered from *þanne* with *o* written above *a* with no sign of cancellation.

3 (9:16) *enim* is glossed with *þonne*, which is more frequently used for *autem*. WW has *autem*. See Introduction III.1.3.1.

claþ flyhti neowenne for *commisuram panni rudis*. DOE, listing this instance under *flyhte*, suggests that it may in fact be intended as the compound *flyhte-claþ*, for which DOE lists three instances from Latin-Old English glossaries. All that can be said of the gender of *flyhti* is that it is not feminine. The masculine accusative form of *neowenne* is in agreement with *claþ*, reinforcing the possibility of taking *claþ flyhti* as being based on the Old English compound, yet rearranged according to the Latin word order.

5 (9:17) For the use of the plural *menn* for an indefinite subject, see note on 5:15.

6 (9:17) The compound *winbeligas* is not recorded elsewhere in Old English; Ross (1979b: 496) compares the Old Icelandic *uinbelgr*.

Note that the passage contains both *(win)beligas* and *belgas*, forms with and without the epenthesis (*-i-*). Hogg (1992: §6.44, n.1) notes that the form with epenthesis might be due to West Saxon influence. For a similar contrast involving correction, see note to 9:35.

8 (9:17) *geotaþ ł gedoaþ* for *ponunt*, with the second gloss written on illegible erasure. For the possibility that the first gloss reflects *mittunt* in the standard Vulgate (as in line 5) as against the second gloss being an attempt to translate R's *ponunt*, see Kotake (2017: 88–89).

11 (9:18) *is nu aswolten is* for *modo defuncta est*. The second *is*, which is written above *est*, is redundant, as it is already written before *nu*; the repetition indicates a mixture of phrasal and literal approaches of glossing.

15 (9:20) *fæss hrægl his* for *fimbriam uestimenti eius*. *hrægl* lacks the expected genitive singular ending. It is tempting to suggest that this may be seen as indicating the otherwise unattested compound **hrægl-fæss*, but unlikely. The noun *fæss* itself occurs infrequently (see DOE s.v. *fæs*, *fæsn*, which counts 15 occurrences); for its possible Anglian nature, see Wenisch (1979: 133–34) and the references cited there.

18 (9:22) *halne* is clearly declined as masculine, but it does not fit the context.

19 (9:22) *ða*, written neatly above *est*, does not have a corresponding word in the Latin text (even in variant readings). The use of the adverb is not out of place semantically and would be effective in emphasizing the immediate recovery.

21 (9:23) *ruxlende*, glossing *tumultuantem*, is a hapax legomenon, probably cognate with the noun *gehruxl* 'tumult, noise'. DOE lists *ruxlende* under the heading *hruxlende* as the present participle 'of otherwise unattested **hrūxlian*'. OED3 has a detailed etymological note for *rustle*, v., which, citing Förster (1908: 344–47), refers to the unattested Old English verb as a possible etymon of *rustle*.

f. 14v

2 (9:26) *se hlisa þis* for *fama haec*. See Introduction III.2.2.2.6 for the neuter form *þis* used with the historically masculine *hlisa* (cf. DOE s.v. *hlisa*).

3 (9:26) *in uniuersam terram illam* is in its current state glossed with *in all ꝥ lond*, but this involves several corrections: between *all* and *ꝥ*, the erasure of *þæ(m)* is visible; *lond* is corrected from *londe*; and *þæt* is erased above *illam*. The original reading is likely to have been a dative phrase following *in*, with a literal rendering of *illam* written above it. The corrected reading follows the Latin in choosing the accusative, while the resulting word order is the one expected in Old English.

3 (9:27) *forþfoerde ł liorde* for *transeuntes*. It is impossible to decide whether to read the second gloss as the simplex *leoran* or the compound *forþleoran*, for the latter of which DOE records four instances in Bede. The glossary lists this instance under *leoran*. The Latin *transeuntes … ie(su)s* is a defective reading for *transeunte … iesu*. Farman understands the passage correctly, glossing the verb with the finite form with the singular ending, followed by the nominative *se hælend*.

4 (9:27) *twa*, usually neuter or feminine, is used where a masculine form is expected. See further note on line 6 below.

5 (9:27) *unc* is corrected from *hunc*.

5 (9:28) ⁊ is erased above *-et* of *ueniset*.

6 (9:28) *tu* is written above *twa*, glossing *duo*, which is omitted in the standard Vulgate. *twa* can be either neuter or feminine, whereas *tu* is a rare neuter form, found only once elsewhere in Ru1 in the phrase *in tu* glossing *ab inuicem* in 25:32 (involving correction). It is not clear why masculine forms are not used in this passage. See Hogg and Fulk (2011: §§4.83–84) for the declension and variant forms of *twegen*.

9 (9:30) *statim* is not reflected in the gloss. The Latin adverb is not in the standard Vulgate and it occurs only in R amongst the versions examined by WW.

10 (9:30) *ł biatadae* is written above *forbead* for *comminatus est*. The verb *beotian* 'threaten' is found only here in Ru1. Waite (1984: ii, 358) reports that Jackson J. Campbell 'claims that *beotian* may be Anglian' in his dissertation ('The Differences in Vocabulary in the Manuscripts of the Old English Version of Bede's "Ecclesiastical History"', Yale University, 1950, p. 61 [not seen]).

11 (9:30) The use of *þis* is not supported by R or variant Latin readings, but the addition of an object for *witan* gives a smooth reading. Cf. WSCp *ge hyt nanum men ne secgeon*.

13 (9:32) *dumb ⁊ deaf* for *mutum et surdum* (*mutum* WW). *et surdum* derives from Old Latin readings and is frequently found in the manuscripts aligned to the mixed-Irish family. Both *dumb* and *deaf* have their endings erased; in both cases, the erased space is too small to contain the expected *-ne* ending for the masculine accusative singular. See Introduction III.3.2.2.3 (esp. citation 52) for further discussion.

17 (9:34) There is an *i* erased between *d* and *e* of *deoful*.

18 (9:35) There is an *i* erased between *r* and *g* of *burgas*. Farman betrays his uncertainties about whether to include the epenthesis elsewhere. See note on 9:17.

19 (9:35) *bodede godspelles rices*. See note to 4:23 for possible interpretations of the phrase.

22 (9:36) *þæm þe hie.* While the relative phrase *þæm þe* is in the case required in the main clause, *hie* appears to be used to indicate the nominative case required in the relative clause. See also note to 7:9.

f. 15r

1 (9:36) *swa scep heordeleas* for *sicut oues non habentes pastorem.* The use of *heordeleas* can be contrasted with more literal translations of the Latin phrase in WSCp (*swa swa sceap þe hyrde nabbað*) and Li (*suæ scip næfdon hiorde*). For the use of the adjective in similar contexts, see DOE s.v. *hyrde-leas* which counts five occurrences in Old English. See also note on *westemleas* in 13:22.

1 (9:37) *cwæþ to leorneras* for *dicit discipulis* contains a rare example of the accusative after *to*, which cannot be attributed to Latin influence. However, its value as evidence for the construction must be dealt with reservation, as this apparently nominative/accusative plural form *leorneras* occurs repeatedly where the dative is expected. See the glossary for further instances and Mitchell (OES §1215) for the accusative after *to*.

2 (9:37) Farman glosses the adverb *quidem* with the phrase *þis is* instead of using an Old English adverb (cf. Li *soðlice*). Ælfric's translation of the passage is comparable to some extent: ÆCHom II, 41 [0002 (304.5)] *Þæt gerip is micel. and ða ryfteras feawa.*

8 (10:2) The position of *þonne*, dislocated from its corresponding Latin *autem* in the previous line, appears to suggest Farman's reluctance to interrupt the noun phrase by following the Latin word order.

14 (10:5) *n* is written above Latin *ne* with no indication of abbreviation or trace of erasure. The required reading is *ne*, as emended by Skeat and others.

15 (10:5) *samaringa.* See note to 8:28.

DOE lists *iongaþ* as a variant spelling of *in-gan.* The *ion* spelling occurs for the preposition *in* in PsGlC (Ps 75:2) and PsGlF (Ps 88:36), both glossing Latin *in*; in both cases, no sign of correction or erasure is found in the manuscripts, though the editor of PsGlF (Kimmens 1979: 172) suggests that the 'scribe began to write *in*, then changed his mind and wrote *on*, erasing nothing'. In the present instance, however, Farman appears to have no obvious reason to correct it to *on-*, as there is no instance of *ongan* or *ongangan* in Ru1.

20 (10:8) For *arwunga* and *arwunge*, glossing *gratis*, see DOE s.v. *earwunga*: all occurrences other than these Ru1 examples are in PPs, also corresponding to *gratis* in the sense 'without (just) cause'.

22 (10:10) *bisæc* for *peram* is a hapax legomenon, which DOE (s.v. *bisacc, bisæcc*) compares with Latin *bisaccium.* See also Ross (1979b: 497).

f. 15v

3 (10:11) *burh* for *ciuitatem* is preceded by *cæstre ł*, which is erased. The erasure is apparently prompted by *cæstre* for *castellum* in the same line.

4 (10:12) *ɣ ge gangan* for *intrantes. ge* is treated in this edition as a pronominal subject rather than the *ge-* prefix, although the latter reading is adopted by Skeat, McAllister and Tamoto. In addition to the fact that *gangan* is never used with the *ge-* prefix in Ru1, the subjunctive present form of the verb would give a smoother reading with a subject. The function of the subjunctive mood in glossing a Latin participle may not be entirely clear, but a temporal clause structure as in WSCp (*Þonne ge ingan soþlice on þæt hus*) might underlie it. The subjunctive tends to be employed in the temporal clause which accompanies a main clause containing the imperative; see Mitchell (OES §2616).

5 (10:13) The double gloss *sibb ł frið* for *pax* (see also *frið ł sibb* in 10:34) may be compared with the 'repetitive word pair' *sibb ɣ frið* (also in the reverse order) found in Or; see Koskenniemi (1968: especially 148, for the list of instances).

6 (10:13) *sibb* is preceded by erasure. Given the double gloss noted above, it is tempting to assume that it was a form of *friþ*, but it is impossible to confirm it from remaining strokes. The visible portion appears to contain three letters, which may have been *fið*, though the last letter might lack the cross stroke.

7 (10:13) The feminine form *hiæ* appears to reflect the gender in the Latin (*eam* referring to *domus*) rather than the neuter of Old English *hus*. Similarly, in *frið eowra* for *pax uestra*, *eowra* is apparently feminine, while *frið* is masculine or neuter.

11 (10:14) The end of verse 14 is marked with a *signe de renvoi* formed by three dots lined vertically. Farman added in the left-hand margin (now partially trimmed) *[ ]n testimoniu(m) [ ]llorum* with the gloss *in cyþnisse heora*. While the standard Vulgate does not have the corresponding phrase, several manuscripts, including the Lindisfarne Gospels and the Codex Amiatinus, have *in testimonium eorum*. The reading with *illorum* is not recorded in the apparatus of WW, an indication that Farman may have back-translated his gloss into Latin. See further the discussion in Introduction III.1.3.2.

11 (10:15) As DOE s.v. *a-ræfnendlic* suggests, Ru1's *arefrendlicre* is 'apparently for *arefnendlicre* with *n* / *r* confusion'. This may be interpreted as evidence for Farman's copying from an Old English exemplar in which *r* could have had a short descender. Amongst Old English glosses, what Ker (1957: xxx) describes as a form of *r* 'with a very short descender so that the letter looks like **n**' occurs in the Vespasian Psalter gloss, as well as very occasionally in Farman's own gloss (see Introduction III.3). See also Roberts (2005: 25, with plate 2a).

13 (10:16) *in midde* is used with a dative as if a phrasal preposition. Mitchell (OES §1178) lists *onmiddan* and *tomiddes* in his list of prepositions, but not *inmidde* or similar forms. A comparable instance with accusative is found in Bede 5 [0266 (13.428.3)] *Tugon heo ða wergan gastas ⁊ niðer mid geweotan in midde ða niolnesse ðæs byrnendan leges*, translating *Trahentes autem eos maligni spiritus descenderunt in medium baratri illius ardentis* (Colgrave and Mynors 1969: 492). For *in midle* with a genitive, see DOE s.v. *in*, I.A.5.d. *in midle / midlene*.

20 (10:19) *biþ sald forþon eow* for *dabitur enim uobis*. The phrase is preceded by erased *eow*, while the *eow* written above *uobis* is apparently altered from *eowic*.

21 (10:20) *ne forþon ge sindun ꝥte ge sprecaþ* for *non enim uos estis qui loquemini* presents two difficulties that are interrelated. Skeat, Tamoto and McAllister read *gesprecaþ* as one word, which the present study prints as two words. The other uncertainty is the function of *ꝥte*, written above the Latin relative pronoun *qui*. It would not be convincing to argue that *ꝥte* functions not as a relative on the basis of the lack of concord, as Mitchell (OES §§2135–44) lists and discusses some examples of the relative pronoun *þæt(te)* that may show lack of concord. Furthermore, in this specific passage, there is no reasonable alternative interpretation. The previous editors, therefore, appear to take *ge* as a prefix on the grounds that no subject is required in the relative clause. However, Farman sometimes uses a redundant pronoun in the relative clause, as discussed in notes to 7:9 and 9:36. Given the two preceding instances in verse 19 that are treated as simplexes (*ge sprece*, *ge sprecan*), it is unwise to rule out the possibility of reading *ge* as a pronominal subject retained in the relative clause.

f. 16r

1 (10:21) Ru1's *oþerne* for *fratrem* gives a smooth reading, though it is exceptional among Old English translations in avoiding direct translation; WSCp *Soþlice broþur sylþ hys broður to deaðe* and Li *geseleð uutedlice broðer ðone broðer in deað*. The following citation from a text in the Blickling Homilies, based on the same gospel passage, is comparable: LS 32 (Peter & Paul) [0007 (17)] *Þonne læweþ broþer oþerne hæþnum on deaþ*.

2 (10:21) *freondum* for *parentes*. See DOE s.v. *freond* 3. for the use of the word denoting 'kinsman, relative', which lists Li examples of *freond* glossing *cognatus*; Aldred uses *aldrum* for *parentes* in the present instance. The etymology section in OED3 (s.v. *friend*, n. and adj.) notes that 'the meaning "relative" [is shown] by Old Frisian, Old Dutch, Old Saxon, and Old High German and "relative" is the only sense of the word in the Scandinavian languages'.

4 (10:22) The use of *his* in *oþ his ende* is not supported by Latin; compare it with LS 32 (Peter & Paul) [0008 (20)] *Swa hwylc þonne soþlice swa on elne ⁊ on mines noman andetnesse oþ his ende wunað.*

7 (10:23) *monnæs.* While Farman's spelling betrays uncertainties about unstressed vowels, this is the only example of the genitive singular of *monn* with the *-æs* ending. In fact, *æs*, written as a ligature with the *e* part of *æ* being tall and upright, may have been a result of alteration from *a*, whose back is elongated to the right, as if no letter is expected to follow.

10 (10:25) Note that *nu* is used to translate Latin *si*, a rare instance of the conjunction *nu* apparently meaning 'if'. See also note to 6:30 about the use of *nu nu* for *si*.

fæder heora for *patrem familias.* DOE s.v. *hiwan* notes *fæder heora* is probably a corrupt form of *fæder hina* 'with confusion of *n* and *r*'. On the possible confusion of *n* and *r*, see note to 10:15 above. Elsewhere, Farman uses *hina* (genitive plural) for *familia* and once the unique compound *hinefæder* (24:43; cf. DOE s.v. *hina-fæder*).

11 (10:25) *hiwæ ł hine.* Ru1 has both of the alternative spellings *hiwan* and *higan* (e.g., *higu*, *hine*, *hina*) that arose through Verner's Law; see Hogg (1992: §4.9 (3)). For a triple gloss that contains three variant forms, see 10:36.

12 (10:26) *vnwrigan* originally read *onwrigan*, with *v* being written above *o*. Farman uses both *on-* and *un-* forms elsewhere; see the glossary. Farman's use of *v* for *u* is rare; see Introduction III.2.1.2.

16 (10:28) *þa se þe slæhþ se lichoma* for *eos qui occidunt corpus.* There appears to be some confusion in the gloss. First, *þa*, glossing *eos*, is written *in rasura*, which appears to have read *eow*, a reflexive pronoun appearing in the preceding line. The corrected reading *þa se þe* shows lack of concord, and *þa þe* would produce a reading closer to Latin *eos qui.* Besides, the relative clause also contains uncertainty: the accusative *corpus* is glossed with the apparently nominative *se lichoma* and the verb form is also singular as against *occidunt.*

saule, glossing *animam*, is followed by erasure of an alternative gloss introduced by *ł*, which is likely to have been a form of *feorh.* Lockett (2011: 51) notes that *sawol* and *feorh* are used to distinguish contextual meanings of *anima* in Ru1. For the two words used as a double gloss, see 10:39.

19 (10:29) *cumende* for *a se ueniunt*, with *ne beoþ þunde bohte* written above the gloss. R's reading is defective, for which WW reads *asse ueneunt.* Farman's first gloss *cumende* is probably an attempt to translate R itself, while the alternative gloss added without a *ł* sign translates the expected reading. Li, where the Latin text also reads *ueniunt* instead of *ueneunt*, contains a similar error (*of anum cymas*) as noted by Ross (1932: 391).

The use of *pund* to translate Latin *as* can be contrasted with WSCp's *pennig* (*Hu ne becypað hig twegen spearwan to peninge*); cf. WSCp Lk 12.6 *Ne becypað hig fif spearwan to helflinge* (*nonne quinque passeres ueneunt dipundio*).

of is erased above *ex*. Another instance of the uncertainty between the partitive genitive and close translation of Latin *ex* or *de* into *of*.

20 (10:30) The gloss for *uestri* is mostly missing in the current state, with the first few letters completely lost, followed by two partially legible descenders and then by the final *e*. The loss is apparently accidental due to the condition of the parchment. The transcripts by both Junius in Junius MS 76 (f. 34r) and Thwaites and Todhunter in Harley MS 3449 (f. 34r) read *eowre*, without noting difficulty. Skeat's *[eo]wre* suggests that the loss had already been caused when he examined the manuscript.

22 (10:31) *forhtigaþ* is corrected from *frohtigaþ*, by adding *o* as suprascript above *fr* and then adding a dot below the original *o*. Ru1 has forms both with and without metathesis for *forhtian*. The metathesis found in this word is a case of 'post-vocalic /r/ [being] metathesized to stand before a short vowel metathesis', which is 'mainly restricted' to late Northumbrian, according to Hogg (1992: §7.95).

f. 16v

9 (10:36) For the effectively triple gloss *higu ł hine* with *hiwen* added above, see note on 10:25.

20 (10:42) *cælc fulne wættres galdes* for *calicem aquae frigide*. Farman's use of *fulne*, not supported by the Latin, gives a smooth reading. See DOE s.v. *full*, 1.a.i for the use of the adjective with a genitive. Neither WSCp nor Li use the adjective in this verse, but the former translates *calicem aquae* into *calic fulne wæteres* in Mk 10:41 in a comparable context.

21 (10:42) *galdes* instead of *caldes*. The use of *g* for initial *c* is unlikely to be accounted for by palaeographical confusion. OED2 s.v. *cold*, adj. records the spelling *gold* from ME; MED s.v. *cold*, adj. 3 (a) has one quotation with the spelling *golde* [a1450 St.Editha (Fst B.3) 3354]).

f. 17r

4 (11:2) *twægen leorneras his* for *duos de discipulis suis*. Ru1's translation of the Latin partitive structure with *de* into 'numeral + noun' can be contrasted with the partitive genitive in WSCp *twegen hys leorningcnihta* and with the *of*-phrase in Li *tuoege of ðegnum his*.

5 (11:3) Note the use of *scalt* to translate the Latin periphrastic future. See also 11:14. In general, Li inserts *sculan* to express futurity more frequently than Ru1 and WSCp. See note to 8:19 on Farman's use of *willan* to translate the Latin future tense. See Yamamoto (2013: 133–34) and Sundaram (2003: 43–44) for detailed statistics. Despite the use with a modal auxiliary, *cwome* is apparently a finite form rather than an infinitive. Although the glossary lists it under infinitives for the sake of its syntactic environment, the form may have resulted from a mixture of two different approaches to translate the Latin periphrastic future.

8 (11:5) *clænsade* is corrected from *clænsande* by erasing the second *n*.

10 (11:6) *geincfullad* for *scandalizatus*. The verb *geincfullian* is recorded in three instances in Ru1; see DOE s.v. *geincfullian* and separately under *geincfullod* for past participle forms. Elsewhere, it is recorded only once in the occasional gloss to the so-called Augsburg Gospels (Ker no. 287*; see Ó Cróinín 1988 for the manuscript), spelled with abbreviation *incful* for *scandalizat* in 5:39; see DOE s.v. *incfullian* and Hofmann (1963: 39–40).

11 (11:7) The correlative construction *þa* … *þa* … is used to translate the ablative absolute construction (see Introduction III.2.4). *þonan*, written above *autem* with a trace of erasure between *þon-* and *-an*, appears to reflect the prefix of *abeuntibus* rather than *autem*.

14 (11:8) *oþþe*, here and at the beginning of the next verse, corresponds with *sed*, the only instances of Farman's use of *oþþe* for the Latin conjunction. The use of *oþþe* is fitting in this context, connecting the questions introduced by *forhwon*. WSCp also employs *oþþe* at the beginning of 11:8 (*ac* in 11:9), which is the sole instance of *oþþe* used to translate *sed* in WSCp according to Liuzza's glossary (1994–2000: ii, 306).

næscum is corrected from *næsce*, with *ce* erased and followed by *cum*. The entire phrase *monnu næscum hræglum gearwæd* for *hominem mollibus uestitum* may be compared with WSCp *mann hnescum gyrlum gescrydne* in that both supply, perhaps influenced by *uestiuntur* in the following part, past participles of the verbs meaning 'to clothe'; Li takes a similar solution, but omits the noun, *ðone monno mið hnescnisum geweded ł gegearuad*. For Ru1's *monnu*, see note to 9:9.

f. 17v

1 (11:12) *iohannes se bęzeres* for *ihannis* (corrected to *iohannis*) *baptistae* is another instance of lack of concord between the phrases put in apposition. See also a similar instance in 11:7. While *bęzeres* has the expected genitive ending, it is preceded by the nominative *se*.

oþ þis nu is written above *usque nunc*. Farman's usual choice for *usque* is *oþ* alone (see the glossary). The use of *þis* is probably an attempt to translate *nunc*, if somehow redundantly with *nu*. Cf. WSCp *Soþlice fram Iohannes dagum fulwihteres oð þis*.

2 (11:12) *nedniomu*, though written as if a gloss to *rapiunt*, corresponds with *uiuolenti*, being the nominative plural of the weak masculine noun *nydnima* 'one who takes by force' (CH s.v. *nydnima*; BT s.v. *nid-nima*) with the loss of *-n*.

3 (11:13) *þe alle* for *omnes* is written above the cancelled (by crossing out) gloss *æghwilc*.

4 (11:14) *andfoa*. There are several instances of *ondfon* and *andfon*, besides *⁊fon*, for *onfon* in Ru1 (see the glossary s.v. *onfon*). DOE does not have **andfon* as a headword, presumably taking all *and-/ond-* forms as variants of *onfon*, an entry yet to be published.

5 (11:14) *cume* is corrected from *cuome* by erasing *o*.

8 (11:16) *prodbore* for *foro*. Ross (1979b: 497) calls *prodbore* the 'oddest' of the rare compounds used by Farman. He agrees with BT (s.v. *prodbor*) in taking the second element as related to Old English *bor* 'gimlet', caused by associating *foro* with the Latin verb *forare* 'to bore, plough'. This interpretation leads to associating the first element to Modern English *prod*, but OED3 (s.v. *prod*, v.) considers it 'very unconvincing'. OED3 also rejects, probably rightly, Merrit's suggestion that the first element may have derived, with some copying errors involved, from *wroht* 'accusation'. See Merrit (1954: 31–32) for details. This leaves us a crux; the same word (spelled *protbore*) occurs in 20:3, glossing the same Latin word.

clipende is corrected from *clippende* by erasing the first *p*, after which a dot, or possibly a start of another stroke, is also erased.

9 (11:17) R omits *et non saltastis lamentauimus* after *uobis*, for which only Old English (*ge ne plagadun cwiddun*) is supplied in the left-hand margin without any sign noting the insertion. There is erasure above *plancxisti*, which is likely to have read *plagadun*, though the ending is not legible due to the corrected gloss *weopun* written over it. This clearly suggests that Farman at first did not recognize the defective Latin text and continued writing the gloss corresponding to the expected Latin reading. After writing *plagadun* above *plancxisti*, he noticed the disagreement, and then corrected the gloss and supplied Old English glosses for the missing portion in the margin.

12 (11:19) *glendrende ł swelgande* for *deuorator*. Both words in the double gloss appear to have received corrections. The *r* in *glendrende* appears to be written over another letter, while the *e* of the second word is clearly altered from *i*. The verb *glendrian* is used twice in Ru1 (cf. 23:34), while it is recorded elsewhere only once in LibSc; see DOE s.v. *glendrian*. DOE s.v. *for-glendrian* shows that the prefixed verb is slightly more frequent (nine occurrences).

13 (11:19) *firenfullra* is altered from *firyn-* by writing *e* over *y*.

18 (11:21) *þær* is one of several instances of the word used to gloss *si/nisi* in Ru1 (see the glossary for details). For detailed analysis of the use of *þær* to introduce conditional clauses, see Mitchell (OES §§ 3615–25) and works quoted there. While the use is widely attested, the distribution appears to be uneven with Alfredian texts having a preponderance of examples; cf. Schreiber (2003: 489) for CP and Godden and Irvine (2009: i, 201) for Bo.

19 (11:21) For *wite* for *cylicio*, DOE s.v. *hwit*, noun, 4.a. 'white (? undyed) cloth / clothing', cites this instance in Ru1 as the sole attestation with the note on the loss of initial *h-* (cf. OED3 *white*, adj. (and adv.) and n., B.6). The DOE entry also refers to the adjective *hwit* used with *hrægl*, translating the same Latin word (cf. DOE s.v. *hwit*, adj. 2.c.). While the loss of *h-* in the *hw* cluster is frequent in Ru1 (see introduction III.2.1.3), whether to follow the DOE's suggestion is a subtle question. Both Schulte and McAllister list the present instance under the neuter noun *wite*, and the resulting reading ('repented in punishment'), though not an accurate translation of Latin, seems acceptable in the context. Note further that the compound *witehrægl* 'sackcloth' occurs in PPs [0225 (68.11)] as *Gif ic mine gewæda on witehrægl cyme cyrde* (cf. Ps 68:12 *et posui uestimentum meum cilicium*). On the possible occurrences of the same compound in the Prose Paris Psalter (Pss 29:12, 34:13) that involve some emendation, see O'Neill (2001: 221, 230).

21 (11:22) *forletendre bið* for *remisius erit* is preceded by an erased *b*, suggesting that Farman may have started to write the gloss in the reverse order, but then he chose to follow the Latin word order.

f. 18r

2 (11:23) *wen þe*. The exact function *þe* is not entirely clear, but phrasal expressions such as *wen is þæt* … apparently underlie this gloss rendering *forte*. See BT s.v. *wen*, IIIa.

4 (11:24) *forletendæ* is altered from *forletennæ*. The comparative ending is missing; cf. 11:22 *forletendre*. The *r* is written over a partially written ascender.

4 (11:25) *in þa tid* for *in illo tempore*. The use of *in* (as against *on*) with the accusative, judging from the form *þa* (as against the dative *þære*, or even *þæm*; see Introduction III.2.2.2.1, for the use of the latter), appears to be restricted to Anglian texts. The form *tid* is probably to be taken as an example of case-endingless forms. Apart from Ru1 instances, *in þa/ða* *tid* is found almost exclusively in GD, Bede, and texts in the Vercelli and Blickling Homilies according to DOE Corpus.

5 (11:25) *ondetu* is followed immediately by erased *þe*, which would have looked as if part of the word. *þe* is again written on *tibi*.

7 (11:25) *forðonclum* for *prudentibus* is a relatively rare adjective (see *foreþancol* in the glossary), here used as a substantive; see DOE s.v. *fore-þancol*, which lists instances from CP, Sol, ChristC.

11 (11:28) *gebyrde* for *honorati* is listed as past participle of the otherwise unattested verb *gebyrþan* 'burden, oppress' in the glossary; see DOE s.v. *gebyrd*.

12 (11:29) *habbaþ .ł nimaþ* for *tollite*. The first gloss is the only instance of *habban* translating *tollere* in Ru1, for which *(a)hebban* is Farman's usual choice (see the glossary s.v. *ahebban* and *hebban*); cf. Li *ahebbas geoc minne*.

16 (12:1) *akcras* for *sata*. The *c* is written as suprascript, which may have been intended as correction, especially because, while the use of *k* is frequent in Ru1, the sequence *kc* is not found for either the velar or the palatal.

The syntactic structure concerning *hyngrede* is ambiguous. Although it corresponds with the Latin participle *essurientes*, the glossary takes it as preterite third person singular of the impersonal use of the verb. Accordingly, *leorneras* is classified as accusative plural. Alternatively, *hyngrede* could be the nominative plural of the past participle in apposition with the nominative plural *leorneras*. See also note to 5:6.

17 (12:1) *æchir* for *spicas* is a form of *ear* 'ear of grain'; see DOE s.v. *ear*[1]. As to the *-ch-* spelling which indicates that it retained the original velar fricative, OED3 s.v. *ear*, n.[2] gives a detailed account and points out that it is an Anglian feature.

eton is altered from *etan*, by dotting below *a* and writing *o* above.

18 (12:2) *gesęgon* is altered from *gesęgen* by writing *o* above the *e* of *-en* without noting the cancellation.

20 (12:3) *hreordeþ* for *legistis*. The initial *h-* is presumably inorganic; cf. *reordaþ* for *legistis* in 12:5. Given the preterite instances, *reordade* (19:4) and *reordadun* (21:16), both glossing forms of *legere*, Ru1 appears to have the weak verb *reordian* (or *reordan*?) 'to read', which is not recorded elsewhere apart from two doubtful manuscript variants in Bede. Miller's text (1890–99: 316, line 8), based on MS T (Oxford, Bodleian Library, MS Tanner 10), reads *reordan* (reduplicated preterite of *rædan*), for which MSS O (Oxford, Corpus Christi College 279) and Ca (Cambridge, University Library, MS Kk.3.18) read *reordedon*. BT (s.v. *hreodian* II), using Smith's edition (based on Ca), includes the latter reading alongside Ru1 instances. Ru1 and Bede are the only prose texts listed by Campbell

(OEG §746) as having reduplicated preterites of the verb *rædan* (i.e., *reord-*). While the two Bede instances may be dismissed as scribal confusion caused by the unfamiliar preterite form rather than a preterite form of the weak verb, Ru1 instances suggest that the weak verb is productive for Farman. It is impossible to determine whether the unique verb arose as a result of back-formation from reduplicated preterite forms of *rædan* or it was somehow related to *reordian* 'to speak, utter' (cf. OED3 s.v. *reird* v. and n., but no trace of the meaning 'to read').

22 (12:4) *hlaf* for *panes* lacks a plural ending, though it is referred to by the plural relative *þa þe*.

f. 18v

3 (12:5) *templ* apparently lacks a dative ending.

9 (12:10) *cweþende mot monn* for *dicentes si liciet* (*licet* WW). The frequent use of indefinite pronoun *mon(n)* in translating Latin impersonal structures is a feature of Farman's gloss; see Introduction III.2.4. That *si* is not clearly reflected in the gloss, unlike Li *cuoede gif is gelefed*, is probably because Farman intends to render the clause into direct speech as in WSCp *cweðende; Ys hyt alyfed* (in Skeat's punctuation); see also 19:3.

10 (12:10) *cwæmdon ł acuste* for *accussarint* (altered to *-rent*). The second gloss is taken as a form of the otherwise unattested verb *acusan*; see DOE s.v. *acusan* and OED3 s.v. *accuse*, v. (cf. OED2 does not include this unique Old English instance). See also Durkin (2014: 133–34) for the list of Latin loanwords in Old English classified according to their frequency. The first gloss *cwæmdon* is even more problematic, as Ross (1979b: 497–98) regards it as one of 'those glosses which are obscure and without solution'. DOE s.v. *cweman* 2. suggests that it was 'perhaps by confusion with *accurare* "to take care of"', while Campbell in the *Addenda* to BT includes the headword *cwæman* without any detailed account. It remains a crux, as no solution proposed so far is entirely convincing.

16 (12:13) *ei* is a rare reading not recorded in the apparatus of WW and is probably a remnant of an Old Latin reading (cf. *Itala*). Farman may have simply provided a word-for-word gloss to the unfamiliar reading so that the function of *þęm* in his gloss is not clear.

20 (12:16) *ł ewisade*, written above the line, is effectively an alternative gloss to the phrasal expression *gecuðne … dydon*, corresponding to *manifestum … facerent*. The verb *eawisian* is not recorded elsewhere. Whereas the related adverb *eawunga* 'openly, manifestly' is relatively frequent (DOE counts *c.* 55 occ.), such derivatives as *eawislic* and *eawslice* are rare and restricted to Anglian texts. Farman also uses *eawisfiren* 'one who commits manifest sin' in glossing *publicanus*, a word that is not found outside Ru1; see note to 18:17.

f. 19r

2 (12:18) *doemeð* for *iudicium* is perhaps a slip in translation, possibly caused by the preceding nominative *he*, which is the subject of *sægeþ*.

5 (12:20) It is not certain whether *smikende* is from the weak verb *smican* (as treated in the glossary), or the class II strong verb *smeocan*, with *i* for the expected *e* as a result of smoothing; Campbell (OEG §227; cf. *ligende* from *leogan* in 5:11).

6 (12:20) *sigor* for *uictoriam* is a word found disproportionally, though not exclusively, in poetry (cf. *sige* in both WSCp and Li). See Jordan (1906: 107).

8 (12:22) *wæs* is written *in rasura*. The use of *wæs* to gloss *habens* suggests that *deofulseoke* is used as an adjective here. See note to 8:33.

⁊ þa gehæled for *et curauit*. Although there is no corresponding word in Latin, *þa* is probably taken as an adverb, which emphasizes the sequence of events told in the narrative. See Lenker (2018: 499–500) for similar instances and their analysis from the perspective of discourse markers.

10 (12:23) *ah cweþest þu* for *numquid*. While the use of *cweþan* to translate *numquid* is the norm in many Old English texts, this is the only instance in Ru1, where *cweþest þu* is preceded by *ah*, which Farman usually uses by itself for *numquid*. See Ogura (1984) for a detailed account of various Old English counterparts to *numquid* and *nonne*.

16 (12:26) *⁊ gif þonne* for *si enim* (*et si* WW). *þonne* is written on erasure, which had a descender at the beginning. If Farman's exemplar followed the standard Vulgate, it is likely to have wanted an adverb corresponding to *enim*, and the erasure of a descender may have been part of a wynn of *wiðerweard*.

18 (12:27) *⁊ gif ic þonne* for *et si ego*. *þonne*, for which there is no equivalent word in R, may have been either Farman's spontaneous addition or reflecting a variant reading with *ergo* recorded in a few manuscripts examined by WW.

19 (12:27) *doeme* for *iudices* apparently lacks a plural ending.

f. 19v

1 (12:29) *se stronge* for *fortem* appears to be the nominative singular rather than the expected accusative.

3 (12:30) *somnaþ* for *congregat*. There is a large gap between *som-* and *-naþ* and there is erasure in between, which is likely to have ended with *-gaþ*. In Ru1, spellings both with and without *-g-* are found for Class II weak verbs.

se stenceþ for *spargit*. *se* refers anaphorically to *se þe*, which is comparable to the use of *he* in WSCp *se þe ne gaderaþ mid me he towyrpð*.

4 (12:31) *efulsung* for *blasfemia* is followed by *ł* with the second gloss being erased and illegible. Farman consistently uses *eofulsung* in glossing the Latin word, and there no other instance of double gloss involving *eofulsung*.

5 (12:31) Farman supplies the missing Latin with Old English gloss in the left-hand margin, indicated by a *signe de renvoi* at the end of the verse (see the apparatus for detail). *dimitetur* (apparently corrected from *dimittetur*) instead of *remittetur* is not recorded elsewhere according to WW.

7 (12:32) *gaste þæm halgum*, if arranged in Old English word order, may be seen as an example of 'demonstrative + strong form of adjective + noun', the existence of which Mitchell (OES §118) thinks is 'a matter of considerable doubt' in Old English. As Mitchell observes, this pattern tends to involve 'the possibility of *-um/-an* confusion in dative singular masculine [...] or neuter' and it is frequent in Ælfric's *Catholic Homilies*, where the majority of *þam/ðam halgum gaste* instances are found according to DOE Corpus.

12 (12:34) *nyhtnisse* for *abundantia*. The Old English word is not recorded elsewhere; cf. BT *(ge)nyhtsumnes*.

13 (12:35) *enim* receives no gloss with the space above it left empty. The standard Vulgate wants the adverb here.

15 (12:35) *of yfle horde* for *de malo thesauro*. The form of the adjective *yfle* is apparently the feminine dative singular, disagreeing with the expected masculine or neuter of the noun as seen in *of godum horde* in the same verse.

17 (12:36) *gesprecan beoþan* for *locuti fuerint*. While *gesprecan* is presumably a past participle with *-an* for *-en*, the intention of using the periphrastic verb form of 'past participle + *beon*' is not entirely clear; it might be an attempt to reflect the future sense. Cf. Li *sprecende biðon* and WSCp *specað*. On the form *beoþan*, see note to 4:19.

20 (12:38) *sumne bokere ⁊ fariseas* for *quidam de scribis et fariseis*. The absence of a gloss to translate *de* suggests that Farman is likely to employ '*sum* + noun' rather than the partitive structure, but the use of *sumne*, apparently the masculine accusative singular followed by the singular *bokere*, instead of nominative plural, is hardly explicable.

f. 20r

2 (12:40) *þreo dagas ⁊ þreo niht*, and in the following line *þreo daga ⁊ þreo nęht*, both for *tribus diebus*. The two phrases appear to show different grammatical details. The contrast between the accusative *dagas* and the genitive *daga* is likely to be due to the two different uses of the numeral. For the former, *þreo* is in the dependent use, whereas the latter reflects the use of cardinal numbers with the partitive genitive (cf. Mitchell OES §548). The spelling difference in *niht* and *nęht* may indicate the variation between the unmutated and mutated vowels (cf. Campbell OEG §628). The absence of the *-a* ending appears to suggest that both are to be taken as accusative plural with the numerals dependent on them.

4 (12:41) *weras mennisce* for *uiri ninuitae* has been considered by Menner (1934: 25) as an example of 'errors and peculiarities that make one suspect the possibility of the earlier gloss' that Farman might have relied on. In fact, a spelling similar to WSCp's *niniuetisce*, for instance, would have contained so many minims that it may be confusing enough to lead to such a copying error. If caused by palaeographical confusion, the choice of the word *mennisce* is not surprising, as its use for the meaning 'a race of people' is attested in Old English (see OED3 s.v. *mannish*, n.).

7 (12:42) *dæles ł cwæn suþan* for *regina austri*. The second gloss *cwæn*, squeezed above *dæles*, provides the expected sense. *dæles* should probably be read with *suþan*, as in WSCp *suþdæles cwen* and Li *cuen suð-dæles*; note, especially, that *-an* of *suþan* is written as suprascript in Ru1. The misplacement of *dæles* may have been caused by erroneously associating *regina* with *regio*.

cuom is out of context and may have been added in relation to the confusion discussed in the previous note.

13 (12:44) *hus* is corrected from *huse* by erasing *e*.

14 (12:44) *aswopen clæne* for *scopis mundatam*. *clæne* can be either an adjective in the neuter accusative singular referring to *hus*, or an adverb 'swept cleanly' (the glossary adopts the latter interpretation). In either case, *scopa* 'broom' is not reflected in the gloss; cf. WSCp *geclænsod mid besmum* and Li *mið besmum geclænsad*.

17 (12:45) *þe ytmæste dæg*. The use of *dæg* in glossing *nouissima* appears to reflect how Farman interpreted the passage. Aldred here uses a triple gloss (*ða endo ł lætmæsta ł ða lattera*); cf. WSCp *ytemestan*.

18 (12:45) *cneorisse þas wyrresta* for *generationi huic pessimæ*. Erasure precedes *cneorisse*, which appears to have read *þas*, apparently to correct the word order. In glossing the dative phrase in the Latin, the use of *þas* suggests that the phrase is the accusative singular (or, less likely, nominative/accusative plural). The exact intention is not clear.

18 (12:46) *þende he þa spręc* for *adhuc eo loquente*. The same construction with '*þende* + S + *þa* + V' renders the same Latin ablative absolute in 17:5 and 26:47. The sense conveyed by *adhuc* is not clearly reflected in Ru1 (cf. WSCp *gyt* and Li *geonæ*) unless the use of *þa* is intended for that purpose. See the glossary s.v. *gen*, *gyt* and *gyta* for the words used to gloss *adhuc* elsewhere in Ru1.

22 (12:48) *soecende* for *dicenti* is written entirely on erasure. The use of *secan* instead of a verb of saying to render *dicere* is not found elsewhere in Ru1. It is semantically fitting here, especially given the context in which Christ's mother and brothers were 'seeking to speak to him'.

f. 20v

5 (13:1) *gangende* for *exiens* is corrected from *ingangende* by erasing *in*.

11 (13:4) *fuglas heofun* for *uolucres caeli*. *heofun* apparently had an ending which is now erased. The cancellation of the case ending of *heofun* may imply that the compound *heofunfugel* underlies Farman's gloss. See note to 6:26, where he uses the compound.

16 (13:7) *gefetun* for *ciciderunt*. DOE s.v. *gefetan* records that the verb, etymologically related to *fot* 'foot', is a rare word recorded only in Ru1; there is one other instance in the following verse. Ross (1979b: 496) compares it with OHG *gifëzzan*.

17 (13:7) *smoradun* for *suffocauerunt*. While the prefixed *asmorian* is found outside Ru1 (cf. DOE counts 7 occ. including one in Ru1 [13:22]), the simplex *smorian* is found only in Ru1; see also 18:28. As Ross (1979b: 496) observes, the verb appears in later English; see MED s.v. *smoren* and OED2 s.v. *smore*, v.

20 (13:10) *gangende to him* for *accedentes*. There are no Latin words in R or variant readings that would account for *to him*, but the addition gives a smooth reading. Besides, the standard Vulgate has *dixerunt ei* instead of R *dixerunt*, which may have prompted the insertion of the *to*- phrase in the gloss.

22 (13:11) *gecunnan* is altered from *gecunnen* by transforming the *e* of *-en* to an *a*.

f. 21r

7 (13:15) *þisses*. *i* is written on erasure. The original reading is likely to have been *þas*.

9 (13:15) *fortyndon* is altered from *fortyndun* with the *u* dotted below and *o* written above.

11 (13:16) *þe hię geseoð* for *qui* (*quia* WW) *uident*. It is difficult to determine the function of *þe*, especially because of R's variant reading. While *þe* is often used to translate *quia* in Ru1 (hence *þe* as a conjunction), it is impossible to rule out the possibility that *þe* is a relative pronoun, translating R's *qui*, with the retained pronoun *hię*. The same ambiguity applies to *þe hiæ geherað* in the following line.

13 (13:17) *wilnadun ꝥ geseon þa þe ge seoþ* for *cupierunt uidere quae uidetis*. Although both Schulte and McAllister classify *geseon* as infinitive agreeing with the Latin equivalent, it is possible that *þ* is a conjunction introducing a noun clause in which *geseon* is the subjunctive present plural with the subject unexpressed. In fact, reading *geseon* as infinitive would make *þ* redundant, the *þa þe*-clause being the object of *geseon*. Skeat, followed by Tamoto, reads *ge-seoþ* for *uidetis* with a hyphen, apparently to show that *geseoþ* is a single word, which is written with space between *ge* and *seoþ*, caused by the tall upright stroke of *d* of *uidetis* as a space saving measure. Here, *ge* is more likely to be the subject of the verb because it would emphasize the second person plural subject in contrast to the other third person plural forms.

14 (13:17) The marginal addition of both Latin and Old English by Farman is substantially trimmed and can be supplied from the transcript in Harley MS 3449, f. 41r, as cited in the apparatus.

15 (13:19) *enim*, which is wanting in the standard Vulgate, is not reflected in the gloss.

word for *uerbum* has its ending erased and appears to have read *wordum*.

20 (13:21) *þonne*, without equivalent word in R, may reflect *autem* in the standard Vulgate.

21 (13:21) *wilen* (for *hwilen*) for *temporalis* is a rare word, for which DOE s.v. *hwilen* counts three occurrences. See Squires (1988: 96) for its use in Whale with a list of examples of the more common antonym *unhwilen* 'eternal'.

f. 21v

2 (13:22) *behygdnis*, with the *g* apparently written on *d*, is another instance of a rare *-ness* word in Ru1; see Ross (1979b: 497). DOE s.v. *be-hygdignes*, *be-hygdnes* counts seven instances, most of which are found in glossing contexts.

lygnisse is also a rare *-ness* word in Ru1, found elsewhere in the Harley glossary: HlGl (Oliphant) F377 *Figmenta .i. plasmatio mendacia hiwunga lignes uaria figura compositio.*

3 (13:22) *butan westemleas* for *sine fructu* is tautological. There appears to have been confusion between word-by-word and phrasal translations. The use of *westemleas* can be compared with *heordeleas* glossing *non habentes pastorem* in 9:36.

4 (13:23) *eorðe godne* for *terram bonam*. For the use of the masculine accusative singular form *godne* with the historically feminine *eorðe*, see Introduction III.2.2.2.2.

6 (13:23) *wyrceþ* for *facit* is preceded by erased *d*, which may have been an aborted attempt to use a form of *don*; cf. WSCp *deð* and Li *doas ł wyrcas*.

þonne ł eowic for *quidem*. The second gloss is puzzling. Li has *soðlice ł ec* here; *quidem* is once translated by *eac* (*ek* in 23:28) in Ru1, but it is hardly possible to regard *eowic* as resulting from a copying error of *eac*.

8 (13:24) *gesette ł gesægde* for *possuit* (*proposuit* WW) may be an attempt to reflect Latin variant readings in the double gloss. While the first gloss *gesette* is likely to reflect R's *possuit*, which is a defective reading not recorded elsewhere, the sense of *gesecgan* is closer to *proponere* 'relate, tell' (cf. *sægde* for *propossuit* in 13:31).

12 (13:25) *hwætes* is preceded by an erased letter, which appears to have been a wynn. The correction may have been intended to supply the initial *h-*, which Farman tends to omit in the *hw-*cluster (see Introduction III.2.1.3).

se brord for *haerba* is preceded by erased *þa*.

13 (13:26) *ӕteawde ek þa weod* for *apparuit zizania* (*apparuerunt et zizania* WW). The apparent lack of concord in grammatical number between the plural subject and the singular verb is probably affected by R's *apparuit* instead of *apparuerunt* in WW. In contrast, the use of *ek* reflects the standard Vulgate reading *et* 'too'.

15 (13:27) The use of *no* (see the glossary s.v. *na*) to translate *nonne* is recorded only here in Ru1. Ogura (1984: 20, Table 2) finds several examples of *na* translating *nonne* in psalter glosses.

on lond þin for *in agro tuo*. *lond* is preceded by erased *þ*, suggesting that Farman may have started to write *þin* (or *þæt*) *lond*. There is also erasure before *þin*, which may have been *t*.

16 (13:28) *unhold monn* for *inimicus homo*. Farman makes a clear distinction between *inimicus* used as a substantive and as an adjective. For the former, he uses the noun *feond*, but he does not use it in this instance, unlike Aldred (*ðe fiond monn*). Cf. WSCp *unhold mann*.

18 (13:29) See Hogg (1992: §5.152, n.1) for the use of the rare form *nic* for *non*. Despite its etymological interpretation (from *ne ic*), it appears to mean simply 'no' rather than 'not I' in this instance, as Hogg points out. Farman uses *nic* in one other instance as an alternative gloss; see 25:9.

f. 22r

3 (13:31) *sinapes* is corrected from *senepes*, by subpuncting the first two instances of *e* and adding corrections above them. The corrections alter the usual Old English spelling *senep*, which Farman employs in 17:20, to the Latin one, while retaining the Old English case ending.

5 (13:32) There is an erased *þ* between ⁊ and *hit* above *cum*. The cancelled *þ* may have been an abandoned attempt to write *þonne*, which would have introduced a temporal clause, corresponding to *cum*, as in

WSCp *soplice þonne hit wyxþ hit is ealra wyrta mæst.* The attempt may have been abandoned to avoid the repetition of *þonne* glossing *autem.*

6 (13:32) *fluglas* (*sic*) *heofun* for *uolcres caeli.* The spelling with the initial *fl-* in this word is also recorded in the Erfurt Glossary, corresponding to *fu-* in the Épinal (1068 and 1085); cf. DOE s.v. *fugel.* Whether the *fl-* spelling is a simple error or due to the influence of etymologically related 'fly' words (cf. Li *flegendo heofnes* in this verse or related adjective *flugol*) is not clear. For the etymology, see OED2 s.v. *fowl.* For the lack of the genitive ending for *heofun* and its implication, see note to 13:4.

9 (13:33) *þonne* for *quod* is to be read as a variant form of *þone*, the masculine accusative singular relative pronoun.

10 (13:33) *gebeormad* is a hapax legomenon, a past participle of the otherwise unattested *gebeormian* (DOE s.v. *gebeormod*), which DOE compares with *gebyrman*, found mostly in poetry. OED2 s.v. *barm*, v., a word attested otherwise only after the fifteenth century, lists this example in Ru1 in square brackets.

11 (13:34) *hælend* appears to reflect *iesus* in the standard Vulgate, which is wanting in R.

15 (13:35) R *eructabo absconsa* (*eructabo abscondita* WW) is corrected by Farman to *eructabo qui absconsa erant*, a unique reading not recorded elsewhere (including variant readings of its source Ps 77:2). Farman's gloss *þa þe ahyded werun* 'what were hidden' is appropriate for the neuter plural of the past participle (*absconsa*), and, given the discussion presented in Introduction III.1.3.2, the Latin correction may have been an instance of Farman's back-translation from his Old English gloss. The use of the relative clause to render *absconsa* may be compared to the translation of the psalm alluded here: PPs 77:2 *Ic on anlicnessum ærest ontyne mines sylfes muð, secggean onginne, þa on worldricum wæron æt frymðe*, translating (cited from *Romanum*) *aperiam in parabolis os meum loquar propositiones ab initio saeculi.*

roketto forð ł bilketto forð for *eructabo* is a rare example of the paired words in a double gloss apparently rhyming. The same pairing is found in the Harley Glossary: HlGl E342: *eructuat.i. a corde emittit bylcetteþ rocceteþ.* The second verb in Farman's double gloss, *bealcettan* in DOE's spelling, occurs somewhat more frequently (DOE counts *c.* 35 occ.; cf. OED2 s.v. *belch*) than *roccetan*, which is etymologically related to the Latin verb *eructare* (see Holthausen s.v. *roccetan*) and tends to occur in texts with Anglian colouring (cf. the compound *forþrocettan* is also included in DOE with a single instance recorded in PsGlG). The dialectal contrast can be observed in psalter gloss examples, where A-type glosses have *(ut)roccetan*, while D-type ones *bealcettan*; see citations in DOE s.v. *bealcettan.* Aldred does not use either of the verbs in the present instance, having *ic loccete ł ic geyppe ł* with the third gloss not supplied, unless *loccete* should be associated with *rocettan* as Jordan (1906: 77) suggests. The glossary in *Cod. Lind.* lists it under *hloccetan*, apparently associating it with *hloccetung* 'sigh' recorded only once in the Aldhelm glosses; see DOE s.v. *hloccetung*, which refers to the yet-to-be-published *loccetan*. Aldred uses *roccetan* in the gloss to the colophon which *Cod. Lind.* calls 'the five sentences': *rocgetede ł gisprunt* (in DOE Corpus's transcription; the latter may be *gisprant* with an open **a**, as Roberts [2005: 34] transcribes) for *eructauit*. WSCp's approach is distinct, using *bodian* to render *eructare*.

18 (13:36) *hwæte* appears to lack the genitive singular ending; cf. 13:25.

22 (13:38) *nænegu* for *nequam* is likely to be a mistranslation resulting from Farman's failure to understand the indeclinable adjective *nequam* 'worthless, wretched'. Cf. WSCp *þa manfullan bearn*; Li *suno [...] yfelwyrcende <ł> wohful*. See also note to 6:23.

f. 22v

2 (13:39) *sydun* for *sunt* shows no sign of abbreviation or correction. Skeat emends it to *sy[n]dun*.

2 (13:40) *swa beoþ* for *si ergo* (*sic ergo* WW). *bið* is erased between *swa* and *beoþ*. Given *swa bið* in the next line, the erased reading may have resulted from eye-skip. The lack of an equivalent to *ergo* in Ru1 may also have been caused by the same reason.

5 (13:41) *þa* for *eos* is written on erased *hie* or *hiæ*.

8 (13:43) *scinaþ* is altered from *scineþ* with a dot under *e* and *a* written above.

14 (13:45) *menn ceape* for *homini negotiatori*. The glossary follows DOE s.v. *cypa, ceapa,* weak masculine noun 'merchant', whose list of attested spellings includes the spelling *ceape* from Ru1. The form should probably be understood as the dative singular with loss of final *-n*. Schulte adopts *ceap monn* as headword, and it is not inconceivable that the compound underlies Farman's gloss. See DOE s.v. *ceap-mann*, *cype-mann*, which includes the exact spelling *ceapemenn* among attested spellings.

The finite form *sohte* for the present participle *querenti* may appear to be out of place (cf. Li *soecende*), but the use of a relative clause, though not reflected in the gloss, may underlie Farman's choice; cf. WSCp *þam mangere þe sohte þæt gode meregrot.*

16 (13:46) *þanne* above *eam* is to be taken as a variant spelling of the masculine accusative singular *þone*, referring to *ercnanstan*. This marked spelling may reflect the emphasized stress that the independent use of *se* could have received (cf. Mitchell OES §315).

17 (13:47) *nett asendun … ꝥ somnendum* for *sanguine* (corrected to *sagine*) *misae … congreganti*. It is probably more effective to read these glosses as a word-for-word rendering than to try to construe them syntactically. *nett* appears to have no dative case ending required by *gelic*; the position of *þ* is also hard to account for, and if it refers to *nett*, it is clearly not dative; and, in contrast, the two past participles *asendun* and *somnendum* may be weak dative singular forms (variants of *-an*).

18 (13:48) *hit gefylled wæs* does not reflect R's plural verb *inplete essent*, but instead the standard Vulgate *impleta esset*.

21 (13:49) *weoruldes* is one of a small number of analogical *-es* genitives in Ru1; see Introduction III.2.2.3.

22 (13:49) *þonne*, written as *þon* with a suspension stroke, has no Latin equivalent in R or other variant readings.

asceadeþ. Between the initial *a-* and *-sc-*, there is erasure of two or three letters, of which the first two may have read *se*.

f. 23r

2 (13:51) Farman added *ei* after *dicunt*. The corrected reading agrees with the standard Vulgate reading. His gloss *hie* written above the added *ei*, however, is more likely to be the subject of the verb than a translation of *ei*. For a similar instance, see note to 21:31.

9 (13:54) *þas snottre* for *sapientia* (+ *haec* WW). The glossary takes *snottre* as a variant spelling of the feminine noun *snyttru*, as in Schulte and McAllister. The use of *þas* may reflect *haec* in the standard Vulgate, and the form suggests that it is the nominative plural despite the Latin singular.

10 (13:55) The first *ioseph* in the line of the Latin text is a variant reading found in several mixed-Irish family texts and accordingly received the Old English gloss. The second one is probably defective, duly crossed out and not glossed.

11 (13:55) *iohannis*, instead of WW *ioseph*, is recorded also in the Book of Kells and in the marginalia to the Echternach Gospels, both aligned to the mixed-Irish family texts. WW notes that the *iohannes* reading is also found in multiple Greek manuscripts; see also Metzger (1994: 28). Ru1 follows its own Latin text and shows no sign of correction.

18 (14:1) *se hælend* for *iesu* is an example of the nominative used where an oblique case is expected. Similarly, *se hælend* is used where the dative is expected in 14:12.

19 (14:2) *þe ic heht heawan* for *quem decolaui*. The Latin phrase is not in the standard Vulgate, though recorded in a number of manuscripts, presumably as a result of harmonization with Mk 6:14. Hence, WSCp *se fulluhtere þe ic beheafdode* (see Liuzza 1994–2000: ii, 75–76). The use of *heht*, without an equivalent word in the Latin, is semantically fitting, reflecting the interpretation that Herod himself is unlikely to be the actual executioner. According to DOE s.v. *heawan*, 5.b., the present instance is the only example of the verb specifically referring to beheading, for which *be-heafdian* is more frequently employed as in the citation from WSCp.

f. 23v

1 (14:4) *sægde him forþon iohannes* clearly reflects the standard Vulgate reading *dicebat enim illi iohannes* rather than R, which omits *illi iohannes*.

to habbanne hire is an example of the genitive used with the verb *habban*, unless *hire* is taken as the feminine accusative singular; see note to 1:25. For a comparable instance in which *habban* is used with a genitive object, see 19:16.

2 (14:5) *ꝛ dreord.* The Tironian note is likely to be intended as a conjunction rather than the prefix. Although there is no corresponding Latin, ꝛ can connect the two finite verbs, *wolde* and *dreord*, the former being a translation of the Latin participle *uolens*. Skeat, followed by Tamoto, adopts two-word reading, while McAllister reads as one word. For further discussion, see note to 9:8.

4 (14:6) *triclinio* 'dining-room', a reading not adopted by WW but found in multiple manuscripts, is not translated by Farman.

7 (14:8) *cweð her sele me* for *inquid da mihi* (*da mihi inquit hic* WW). Ru1's *her* appears to reflect *hic* in the standard Vulgate reading.

12 (14:11) *moder. d* is written on another letter having a descender.

13 (14:12) *cumende* is altered from *cumenne*, by writing *d* over *n*.

15 (14:13) *sundor* is altered from *sundur*, by dotting under the second *u* and writing *o* above.

18 (14:14) ꝛ at the beginning of the line is likely to be due to dittography, repeating the ꝛ at the end of the previous line. Skeat's text has only one ꝛ, while DOE Corpus reads <*ondmilsade*>, but there is no instance of **andmil(t)sian* or **onmil(t)sian* in the corpus.

languido sé orum (*languidos eorum* WW). Ru1's *sundor ł heora* is probably an attempt both to reflect *seorsum*, a reading arising from erroneous word division, with the first gloss (cf. *sundor* in 14:13), and to translate the correct reading with the second gloss *heora*. The accent stroke above *se*, which is often applied to a monosyllabic word in R, may have prompted the erroneous word division.

f. 24r

1 (14:16) The significance of *necessire* (*necesse ire* WW) and Farman's correction *adeuntes* with his gloss *to gangenne* is discussed in Introduction III.1.3.2. as a possible instance of Farman's back translation from Latin.

It is ambiguous whether *sella* is an imperative form or (jussive) subjunctive. Although the verb is not immediately followed by the subject pronoun, it is still possible that the conventional word order *sella ge* underlies Farman's gloss, which could have been rearranged according to the Latin word order. Cf. Mitchell's rigorous distinction about the ambiguity (OES §§879–919)

3 (14:18) *he þa cweþ* for *qui ait.* The use of *þa*, which has no exact equivalent in the Latin, can be compared with WSCp *Þa cwæð se Hælend.* The function of the Latin relative as a 'connecting link', noted by Plater and White (1926: 128) as a constant Vulgate feature, may have invited the two independent translators to use the adverb *þa* here.

3 (14:19) *heht* for *cum iussiset.* The apparent lack of an equivalent to *cum* in the gloss is resolved by the use of ⁊ in the next lines, turning the hypotactic structure into paratactic: *heht* … ⁊ *genom* (corresponding to Latin absolute ablative) … ⁊ *(locande)* … *blesade…*

6 (14:19) *leorneras* for *discipulis*; see note to 9:37 on the use of *leorneras* where the dative plural is expected.

8 (14:20) *hlafe* for *lafe* is a rare example of inorganic *h* before *l* in Ru1. See Introduction III.2.1.3.

monde for *cofinos. mand* 'basket' is also found in Li, though in the present instance it has *ceawlas ł foðer* (see DOE s.v. *cawl* and s.v. *fodder, fodor, foþer*, respectively). OED3 s.v. *maund*, n.[1] points out that Modern English *maund*, found chiefly in regional English, is likely to have derived from a later loan from Middle French, because of the large gap in attestation between the Old English period and the fifteenth century.

The use of *gebroc* specifically referring to the fragment of bread is also found in GD. See DOE s.v. *gebroc.*

13 (14:23) *astag* for *ascendit.* The final *g* appears to be written on *h*.

After *efen*, there is erasure of *wæs*, which is again written above *facto*, then crossed-out and supplied with *ł geworden* above it. Farman appears to have been trying to follow the Latin text closely. The reading with *wæs* would have stood without difficulty; cf. WSCp *Soþlice þa hyt æfen wæs.*

14 (14:24) *middum* for *midio* (corrected to *medio*). There is erasure of *le* between *midd-* and *-um.*

15 (14:24) *forþon* above *autem* appears to reflect *enim* in the standard Vulgate. See further Introduction III.1.3.1.

16 (14:25) *feorðe þære wacone* for *quarta autem uigilia.* Note *autem* is not reflected in the gloss. It may have been accidentally missed in translation, especially due to its position within a noun phrase, or it might reflect some other Latin text wanting *autem* (e.g., the Lichfield Gospels omits it according to WW).

18 (14:26) As to the use of *in mode*, see note to 2:3.

22 (14:28) *wæter* is written as *wæt* with a suspension mark above. There is erasure of a few letters after *wæt*, suggesting that it might have had a different ending originally.

f. 24v

1 (14:29) *ambulabat* was originally glossed with *gangende*, with *gan-* written above *am-* and *-gende* above *-abat* in the next line. Farman erased it, though still legible, and added *eode* in the remaining space above *-bu-*.

6 (14:32) *blan* for *cessauit*. The distribution of *blinnan* is summarized by Wenisch (1979: 112–14), who classified the verb to 'gemainanglisches Wortgut', though with some examples found also in CP. See Schreiber (2003: 593) for further details and the distribution of related words.

11 (14:35) While *eall lond þæt* in its current state follows the Latin word order *uniuersam regionem illam*, there is an erased *þ* before *lond*, suggesting that the word order more natural in Old English *eall þæt lond* may have been intended at first.

14 (14:36) *hale wvrdon* for *salui facti* is altered from *hæle wyrdon*, by erasing involving strokes in the respective letters, *æ* and *y*.

15 (15:1) *bokere* for *scribae*. The apparently singular form translates the Latin plural.

16 (15:2) *gesettnisse* is altered from *gesettenisse* by erasing the *e* in *-ten-*.

17 (15:2) *enim* is not translated in Ru1; there is no variant reading omitting *enim* recorded in WW. The omission is more likely to be related to semantic factors than textual variants, because readings without an equivalent to *enim* would present a smooth reading, as in WSCp *Hwi forgymað þine leorningcnihtas ure yldrena lage; Ne þweað hi hyra handa þonne hig mete þicgeað.*

thuað for *lauant* is preceded by an erased *þ*, suggesting a correction from *þ* to *th*. See Introduction III.2.1.2 for Farman's use of *th* instead of *þ/ð* and that of *u* instead of *w*.

21 (15:4) *deaða swælteþ* for *morte morietur*. *deaða* is likely to be taken as the genitive plural in the light of BTS s.v. *sweltan* IV 'to die from something (gen.)', which cites one instance from GD [0034 (3.264.10)] … *ne magon sweltan þæs ecan wites deaðes* (Hecht's text adopts the reading from MS O [BL, Cotton MS Otho C. i.] f. 102r; DOE Corpus has the C text [CCCC 322, f. 112v], *ne magon sweltan þæs ecan lifes*). Mitchell's list of verbal rections (OES §1092) gives '*sweltan* (i) die to s[ome]t[hing] (gen.)'.

f. 25r

2 (15:6) *ungænge* for *inritum* is a hapax legomenon. BT s.v. *ungenge* compares it with Old Icelandic *úgengr* 'not fit to walk on'; Ross (1979b: 496) notes that the sense does not agree. The sense of the adjective *genge*, especially in such phrases as *genge beon* 'to prevail' or *genge weorþan* 'to come to prevail' as noted by DOE (s.v. *genge*, adj.), appears to suggest that the prefix *un-* is negative, resulting in 'not prevailing, not valid', an element-for-element translation Latin *irritus* 'not valid'.

6 (15:9) *holunga* for *sine causa*. Jordan (1906: 59, n.1) suggests that the adverb may be Anglian. Citations in DOE s.v. *holinga*, *holunga* indicate that it occurs disproportionately in texts with Anglian colouring such as Bede and GD. Note, however, the Junius Psalter (PsGlB) has *holinga* for *in vano* (Ps 126:1), as against *in idelnisse* in the Vespasian Psalter (PsGlA), suggesting the risk of overgeneralization as to its Anglian nature.

9 (15:11) *smiteþ monnu* and *besimteþ monnu* (line 10) for *coninquinant hominem*. As noted in 9:9, the spelling *monnu* occurs in Ru1 where the accusative singular of the weak noun *manna*. See, however, also note to 15:20 below.

13 (15:13) *wæstma seten* for *plantatio*. Skeat, Schulte, Tamoto and McAllister treat *wæstmaseten* as an otherwise unrecorded compound. BT s.v. *seten* II, however, lists *wæstma seten*, presumably based on the Surtees Society edition. In fact, given a few instances of *seten* as a gloss to *plantaria* in Latin-Old English glossaries cited in BT, in conjunction with the inflected *wæstma*, it is reasonable to treat *wæstma seten* as two words. TOE ('04.02.04.02.04 (n.) Planting') also adopts the two-word reading.

20 (15:17) *in leornisse* for *in secessum*. Given the small size of attestation of *leornes* (cf. Ross 1979b: 496–97), it is not clear whether the noun could mean specifically the late Latin sense of *recessum* 'privy, latrine', or it was chosen for a more general meaning 'going away, departure'. The use of derivatives of verbs of motion for the specific meaning can be observed in *gang* (see DOE s.v. *gang* 14.) and its compounds; cf. WSCp *forþgang*. TOE ('04.05.03.05.02 (n.) A privy') does not list *leornes*. Li has *feltun*, for which see DOE s.v. *fel-tun*.

21 (15:18) R omits *de corde exeunt et ea coninquinant hominem* at the end of the verse, presumably due to homeoteleuton (cf. 15:19 *de corde exeunt*...). Farman's gloss shows no sign of confusion or correction related to this omission.

f. 25v

1 (15:20) *besmitaþ monnum* and *besmitaþ ꝥ monnum* (line 2) for *quoinquinant hominem*. In 15:9, *(be)smitan* is used with *monnu*, which may be understood as the accusative singular of the weak *manna* as noted in 9:9 (found also in 9:32, 10:35, 11:8, 22:11). Given that neither DOE nor Mitchell (OES §1092) records the use of *bemitan* with dative object, *monnum* in the present verse may also be understood as a variant of the accusative singular of the weak noun, perhaps with some confusion with the dative plural form of *mann*. For *þ*, see below.

2 (15:20) *þæh unðwegenum* is partially written on illegible erasure. While *þæh* has no equivalent in the Latin, it appears to function as a conjunction ('even though'), turning the infinitival construction (*non lotis … manibus manducare*) into a clause, as in WSCp *Ne besmit þone mann þeah he unþwogenum handum ete*.

ete is corrected from *eteþ* with the final letter erased. This alteration reinforces the interpretation of *þæh* presented in the previous note, as the use of the subjunctive is more expected in a clause of concession.

3 (15:20) *þ monnum*. The use of *þ*, when read as a demonstrative, lacks concord in gender, a possible sign for the expansion of *þæt* to non-neuter, for which see Introduction III.2.2.2.5. Alternatively, *þ* may possibly be taken as the subject of the main clause, referring to 'eating with unwashed hands'. For a comparable use of *þ*, see note to line 13 below.

7 (15:23) *ne* reflects *non*, which is omitted in R; there is no sign of correction to the Latin text.

13 (15:26) The Latin infinitival construction (*sumere … mittere*) is rendered into a clause introduced by *þe* and the subject *þ* is supplied in the main clause (*nis þ god*). The indefinite pronoun *monn* is used to supply a subject in the subordinate clause, in which there is discrepancy in mood between *genime* and *weorpeþ*, with the latter partially written on illegible erasure.

14 (15:27) For *þe þe*, see note to 2:20.

17 (15:28) *ðæm hwile* is one of several instances in Ru1 where feminine nouns in the dative singular are used with *ðæm/þæm*, the historically masculine or neuter forms; cf. 20:5, 25:41. See Introduction III.2.2.2.1 for further details.

21 (15:30) *hiæ* is erased before the double gloss *lægdun ł feallan*. The third person plural subject would give a smooth reading. While *lægdun* is used as a transitive verb (hence *hiæ* glossing *eos* as a reflexive pronoun), *feallan* is used elsewhere intransitively, requiring a different syntactic structure. The form *feallan* appears to be infinitive, unless it is taken as a variant spelling of the past plural (e.g., *feollun*, *fellun*). Farman sometimes gives a bare form in the second gloss, to give only a lexical alternative.

f. 26r

4 (15:32) *ðe hie* is written above *quia* with *ł forðon* (Skeat's *forþon* is an error, as noted by Tamoto) squeezed above *ðe hie*. The double gloss should probably be interpreted as *hie ł forðon ðe*. The use of *hie* here is difficult to account for because another *hie*, the subject of *þurhwunadun*, stands within the *þ*-clause. However, there may have been confusion between literal rendering of the Latin and a freer translation as in WSCp *ðisse menegu ic gemiltsige forþam hig þry dagas mid me wunodon*.

5 (15:32) *etaþ* is altered from *eteþ* by dotting under *e* and writing *a* above.

6 (15:33) *him to* for *ei*. Although postposed prepositions are a well-known syntactic feature in Old English (see, for example, Mitchell [1978: 248–55] and Lapidge [2006]), one thing that should be noted as regards Ru1 is that the phrase *him to*, especially used with forms of *cweþan*, is frequent in the latter half of Matthew, and the present instance is the first of such instances.

7 (15:33) *hlafas* is altered from *hlafes* with *a* written above *e*. No cancellation is signalled.

to niomane for *ad tintos*. The Latin reading is defective (*tantos* WW). The gloss, entirely written on an illegible erasure, is apparently a result of confusion caused by the defective reading. The gloss still makes sense somehow, and may be translated 'Whence then should we have loaves *to take* in the desert…'

we gehreorde, written above *saturentur*, is closer to the standard Vulgate reading *saturemus*. R's *saturentur* is shared by some manuscripts aligned to the mixed-Irish family.

14 (15:37) *sperta* for *sportas* is a Latin loan word (see BT s.v. *spyrte*), as listed by Durkin (2014: 112). Ælfric uses it in his homily for the Eighth Sunday after Pentecost (ÆCHom II, 29), which deals with the same story as the present verse, but based on Mk 8:1–9.

15 (15:38) R has the erroneous numeral *uii* for *quattuor*, but Farman's gloss *siofun* follows R.

16 (15:39) *forletende* for *demisa*. *r* is apparently written over an *l*.

20 (16:2) The addition made in the bottom margin by Farman, *quia rebicundus est celum*, is apparently caused by R's *cras*, which does not occur in the standard Vulgate, but does occur in some other manuscripts aligned to the mixed-Irish family. In fact, R's text was complete in its original state and Farman's addition is clearly redundant. The use of *quia* in the marginal addition, which is not attested elsewhere, suggests that his Latin addition may have been a back-translation from the Old English gloss *forþon*, which originally corresponds with *enim*. See Introduction III.1.3.2 for other possible instances of back-translation.

21 (16:3) *todæge* is written as if a gloss to *mane*, but it reflects *hodie*, which is missing in R. Accordingly, *mane* is not reflected in the gloss.

hreanis. *r* is written on erasure where an ascender is visible.

22 (16:3) *heofun* for *caeli* lacks the expected genitive ending.

f. 26v

2 (16:4) The first *tacen* in the line is corrected from *tacun* by dotting under *u* and writing *e* above it.

3 (16:4) *hie* for *ei*. The apparently nominative/accusative plural *hie* is used where the dative is expected.

12 (16:10) The entire verse is missing in R and it is supplied in the margin by Farman with Old English gloss as presented in the apparatus. Farman's Latin addition betrays the possibility of back-translation, as discussed in Introduction III.1.3.2.

12 (16:11) *þ ic be hlafe cwæþ* for *quia non de panibus dixit* (*dixi* WW). Whereas *ic* clearly reflects the standard Vulgate reading, Farman fails to reflect Latin *non* in his gloss.

14 (16:12) *þa ongetun hie* for *Tunc intellexerunt*. From the perspective of glossing practice, to supply a pronominal subject after the verb (leading to the VS order) in the statement (i.e., not questions or imperatives) is exceptional; on the other hand, the resulting word order in this instance reflects the norm after *þa* or *þonne* as an adverb (see Mitchell OES §§3922–23).

21 (16:15) *hwæt cweoþað hwæt ic seo* for *quem me esse dicitis*. The gloss here appears to show the mixture of a freer translation and a word-for-word approach. The gloss would give a smooth reading without the first *hwæt*, which was apparently added redundantly in an attempt to give an equivalent to *quem* in its position.

f. 27r

2 (16:17) *sunu iona* for *bariona*. Farman gives an etymological translation for *bariona*, which can be compared with *culfran bearn* in both WSCp and ÆCHom I, 26, based on another etymological interpretation; see Liuzza (1994–2000: ii, 55) and Godden (2000: 211). Aldred does not gloss the word in Li.

4 (16:18) *petra ł stane* for *petram*. The first gloss is apparently a Latin word, paired with a more direct translation of the Latin. The pairing appears to highlight the reference to *petra* as the etymology of Peter.

5 (16:18) *oferswiðiaþ* for *prævalebunt*. The present plural ending *-iaþ* suggests that the verb may in fact be from *oferswiþrian* rather than *oferswiþan*, the latter of which conjugates as either Class I weak verb or occasionally Class I strong verb. Semantically and syntactically, too, *oferswiþrian* gives a better reading because of its meaning 'prevail' and its tendency to be used intransitively. The glossary, following Schulte, therefore lists this example under *oferswiþrian*. It is not clear whether the possible omission of *r* in this example is related to occasional loss of *r* found in other instances in Ru1 as discussed in Introduction III.2.1.3.

6 (16:19) *ic þe selle selle* for *tibi dabo. ic þe selle* is written about *tibi* and *dabo* is again glossed with the redundant *selle.*

13 (16:21) *æftarisan* for *resurgere.* There is uncertainty about whether to regard this as a compound or two words in Skeat's edition; even DOE has both the compound (s.v. *eft-arisan*; note the use of a swung dash which DOE uses to indicate 'quasi-compounds') and the collocation *eft arisan* (s.v. *arisan* A.4.a.i and *eft* 2.b.ii). As it is not reasonable to distinguish them on the basis of word division in the manuscript, the present edition treats all relevant instances as compound (see the glossary).

18 (16:24) *⁊sæcę* for *abnegat.* DOE s.v. *and-sacian* does not include this instance in the four instances it identifies, while the other two occurrences in Ru1 (*⁊sace* 26:35 and *ondsacast* 26:75) are included. As DOE suggests, it is possible that these forms may be forms of *onsacan*, but there is no reason for this instance in 16:24 to be distinguished from the others apart from the uncertain root vowel *æ*.

19 (16:25) *forþon se þe þe wille* for *qui enim uoluerit.* The repetition of *þe* is puzzling at first glance, but one of the particles may have been a misplaced gloss which was to form the phrase *forþon þe.*

22 (16:26) *feorh* for *animae* apparently wants a genitive ending.

f. 27v

4 (16:27) *neh þon ł æfter* for *iuxta* (*secundum* WW). Although the *ł* sign clearly precedes *æfter*, the actual order of the double gloss is likely to be the reverse. The layout in the manuscript indicates that Farman first wrote *æfter*, which is just above *iuxta*, and then he squeezed *neh* below *æfter*, with the *ł* added to indicate that these two words form a double gloss, which reflects both *secundum* (*æfter*) in the standard Vulgate and R's *iuxta* (*neh*).

9 (17:1) *sundur ł niðer* for *seorsum.* The second gloss may be due to the confusion between *seorsum* and *deorsum*, the latter constantly being glossed with *niþer* elsewhere in Ru1.

10 (17:2) *oferheowad wæs* for *transfiguratus est.* Both Farman and Aldred use *oferhiwian* for *transfigurare* in this verse. Aldred has a double gloss *oferhiuad wæs ł megwlitgad wæs*; for the second gloss, cf. related noun *mægwlite*, frequent especially in poetry. While WSCp reads *wæs gehiwod* in this verse, *oferhiwian* occurs in Mk 9:1 *⁊ wearð beforan him oferhiwud.*

12 (17:3) *hælend* for *illo* (*eo* WW) is a rare instance of a Latin pronoun being glossed with its referent.

20 (17:7) *⁊ þa eode* for *et accessit.* The use of *þa*, which has no equivalent in the Latin text, emphasizes the narrative sequence, as in WSCp *He genealæhte þa.*

22 (17:8) *se hælend enne* for *solum iesum*. Note the mixed cases between *se* and *enne*.

f. 28r

3 (17:10) *ah hwæt* for *quid ergo*. From the perspective of word-for-word agreement, *ah* may be interpreted as corresponding to *ergo*, which is glossed with such adverbs as *soþlice*, *þonne*, *witodlice*, etc., elsewhere. DOE (s.v. *ac*) lists comparable instances of *ac* under H.1. 'used to introduce questions either with or without an interrogative pronoun', a usage which appears to underlie Farman's choice (similarly in 19:7)

5 (17:11) The adverbs *quidem* and *iam* (in the next line, verse 12) are not translated. Latin textual variants are unlikely to cause such omissions in these cases. Old English translations would read smoothly without equivalent adverbs; in particular, *iam* is not reflected in either WSCp (*Helias com*) or Li (*helias cuom*).

6 (17:12) *eowic* is used as the dative plural; this occurs elsewhere in Ru1, always glossing *dico [...] uobis* with *(ic) sæcge [...] eowic* (18:10 and 18:13). Otherwise, Farman restricts *eowic* to accusative instances, unlike Owun and Aldred, for which see Ross (1933).

8 (17:13) *ongeton* is altered from *ongetan* by dotting under *a* and adding *o* above it.

11 (17:15) *sune min* for *filio meo*. *min* is not inflected for the dative.

17 (17:18) Farman supplied the missing Latin in the right-hand margin with *de illa ma[ ]* for *ex illa hora* in WW. Judging from his gloss *of ðære yfle*, the trimmed part is likely to have been *mala* (neither Junius MS 76 nor Harley MS 3449 serves to supply the missing portion in the Latin). Whatever the exact reconstruction, the Latin phrase is not recorded in variant readings, though the sense 'recovered from the evil' might stand. Note, also, that *ðære* is apparently feminine, whereas *yfel*, if indeed a noun, is neuter, a possible instance of unhistorical gender congruence (see Introduction III.2.2.2.7).

21 (17:20) The present edition reads *ge cweoþað* instead of *ge-* as prefix as in Skeat and Tamoto, though there is no absolute reasoning to rule out the latter possibility. *gecweþan* is recorded in Ru1, but it is infrequent and limited to imperative singular and inflected infinitive forms (three instances in total, excluding past participles). McAllister reads as two words.

22 (17:20) *þisse* is corrected from *þissere* by erasing the ending. The feminine dative singular *þissere* is found in 21:21, again collocated as *dune þissere*. The use of the adjectival ending *-re* is compared with either the late West Saxon form (*þissere*) or Aldred's forms (e.g., *þissre*, with the omission of medial *-e-*); see Hogg and Fulk (2011: §5.12) and, for Aldred's forms of *þes*, Ross (1967).

f. 28v

2 (17:22) *drohtadun* for *conuersantibus* is the sole occurrence of the verb *drohtian* in Ru1. DOE s.v. *drohtnian, drohtian* notes that forms without medial *n*, as in this instance, 'predominate in Alfredian translations'.

10 (17:25) *hernisse* for *censum*. DOE s.v. *hyrnes* 6. compares this use of the noun, apparently meaning 'tax, duty', for which the current instance in Ru1 is the only attestation, with the verb *hyran* (7.d.), which in legal contexts could mean '(of a fee / duty) belong to, be due to', as recorded in LawICn [0049 (13.1)] *gyf man ænig lic of rihtscriftscire elles hwær lecge, gelæste man þone sawlsceat swa þeah into þam mynstre, þe hit to hyrde.*

11 (17:26) *hwæt* is apparently an interjection having no obvious Latin equivalent, which can be compared with Ælfric's translation of the passage in the homily for the dedication of the Church of St Michael: ÆCHom I, 34 [0083 (470.163)] *Hwæt la: sind heora siblingas frige?*

15 (18:1) There is erasure of *þa* before *eodun*.

16 (18:1) *wenest nu* for *putas*. WW's apparatus records no Latin variant that would account for the use of *nu* here. It is not inconceivable that *nu* is an error for *þu* (or part of contracted forms such as *wenstu*) given the usual word order in questions, as found in both WSCp and Li.

17 (18:2) The entire verse is missing and added by Farman in the margin with the gloss, indicated in the main text by a *signe de renvoi* made of three dots aligned vertically. In the marginal addition, *ad uocans* is written with space (for *aduocans* WW); its gloss *to cegende* appears to follow the spacing. The plural reading *paruulos* (*paruulum* WW) is not recorded elsewhere.

20 (18:4) *þios*, apparently the feminine nominative, refers to the masculine *cneht*; see Introduction III.2.2.2.6 for further discussion.

20 (18:5) *onfoeþ* is altered to *ondfoeþ* by adding suprascript *d*, possibly suggesting Farman's preference of *ond-* forms over *on-* as regards *on(d)fon.*

f. 29r

1 (18:6) *cwern esules* for *mola assinaria. eosol* 'ass, donkey' is a loanword associated with Latin *asellus* by Durkin (2014: 109), which is less frequent (*c.* 20 occ. including CP and GD) than another loanword *assa* related to Latin *asinus*, or possibly via Celtic loans (see Durkin 2014: 78); see DOE s.v. *eosol* and *assa*. Aldred employs his characteristic *asal, asald* (in DOE's spelling) not recorded outside his works. Farman's gloss can be compared with the compound *eosol-cweorn*, for which see DOE and Schreiber (2003: 483).

3 (18:7) *middangearde þios* for *mundo huic*. Skeat and Tamoto expand *middang* (*n* as a suprascript) with a suspension mark to *middangeard*, but given the phrase 'woe to…', the present edition reads it as a dative form (cf. WSCp *Wa þysum middangearde*). For the unexpected use of the feminine nominative *þios*, see Introduction III.2.2.2.6.

fælnissum for *scandalis*; cf. *æswic* for *scandalum/-a* in the following lines. It is not certain whether there is any semantic distinction between the two Old English words. For the former, see DOE s.v. *fylnes*[2], which is a hapax legomenon, related to the verb *fyllan*[2] 'cause to fall' (cf. *fælleþ* in 19:8). See note to 5:29 and De Smet (1987) for related vocabulary.

6 (18:8) *asceorf* for *abscide* contains an inorganic *s*, perhaps to indicate the palatalized sound, unless it is affected by the *sc-* spelling in the Latin; see Brown (1892: §20).

7 (18:8) Note that *ingredi* is not reflected in the gloss. While this may be an accidental omission, it may be remembered that the infinitive of a verb of motion is often omitted after an auxiliary verb (Mitchell OES §§1006–8). Although the syntactic environment is different here, it cannot be ruled out that a similar kind of ellipsis underlies this instance, especially because the direction of movement is clearly expressed by the prepositional phrase *to life*.

9 (18:9) *eagan* for *oculus* is to be taken as the nominative singular; for similar instances, including *willan* in 18:14 (in line 22 on this folio) and *egan* in 20:15, see Ross (1976: 497).

10 (18:9) *unum oculum* (*unoculum* WW) is corrected by Farman *cum unum oculum*. Although the resulting reading is rare due to the unusual case after *cum*, the use of *cum* itself is found in multiple manuscripts (*cum uno oculo*). WSCp has *mid* (*Betere þe ys mid anum eage on life to ganne*), though the preposition could be used even without support of Latin variants.

12 (18:9) *⁊ sie gesended* for *mitti*. It is not entirely clear why *⁊* is used here, but the intention may have been to connect two participles (*hæbbende* and *gesended*). The Old English verbs *gæ* and *sie gesended* are likely to be the present subjunctive forms rather than infinitive as in the Latin. The use of the subjunctive forms may be seen as a sign of expanding the Latin infinitives into Old English clauses, as in the *þonne*-clause in WSCp here: *Betere þe ys mid anum eage on life to ganne þonne þu si mid twam asend on hellefyr*.

12 (18:10) *beseoh ꝥ ðe ne reuwe* for *uidete ne condempnamini*. Farman translates the Latin second person plural with the singular *beseoh* and *ðe*.

13 (18:10) *qui credunt in me* is a reading recorded in some mixed-Irish family texts. Farman added the words *þa þe* above *qui*, but then erased them. The cancellation of the Latin phrase is signalled by three dots arranged in the triangle form, each written above *cre-*, *-dunt*, *in* and *me*. It is not possible to determine with any certainty whether the cancellation was marked by Farman.

16 (18:12) *gif hæbbe hwa* for *si fuerint alicui*. The Latin structure of *esse* + dative expressing possession is rendered by using *habban*. As a translation method, it is not surprising, as is found also in WSCp (*gyf hwylc mann hæfð…*), but the contrast is clear when it is compared with a more literal approach by Aldred in Li (*gif he biðon ł weron ængum*).

f. 29v

1 (18:15) *firnige ł syngige* for *peccauerit*. DOE s.v. *firenian* notes that the verb is 'disproportionately freq[uent] in poetry', while the prefixed form *gefirenian* is found in prose and glosses. Li also uses *firenian* paired with *syngian* in 27:4 *ic synngade ł ic firinade*, where Ru1 has the prefixed *gefirinade*.

7 (18:17) *hæþenna ⁊ eawisfirina* for *puplicanus et gentilis (ethnicus et publicanus* WW). The order of the gloss appears to reflect the standard Vulgate reading. According to DOE s.v. *eawis-firen*, the adjective, used as a substantive, occurs only in Ru1 (see also 21:31, 32), whose literal meaning is 'openly sinful'; cf. note on the verb *eawisian* 'to manifest' in 12:16.

13 (18:20) *forþon þe þær twege oþþe þreo gesomnade* for *ubi* (+ *enim* WW) *sunt duo uel tres congregati*. *forþon þe* appears to reflect *enim* in the standard Vulgate. Although the passive structure is expected, there is no equivalent to *sunt* in the gloss.

15 (18:21) *hu gif* for *quod si* (*quotiens* WW). The use of *hu* above *quod* betrays Farman's attempt to translate *quotiens* there, as suggested by *hu oft* glossing *quoties* in the next line. The ⁊ that follows *hu oft* reflects the standard Vulgate reading *et dimittam*.

18 (18:23) *wiðermeten* for *adsimilatum*. *wiþermetan* 'compare' is less frequent than *wiþmetan*, occurring only in ClGl 3 (Quinn) and HlGl (Oliphant) other than Ru1.

19 (18:23) *rationem ponere* is always glossed with *(ge)rihtes manian* in Ru1 (18:24, 25:19). For the use of *manian* with a genitive object in the sense 'claim (what is due)', see BT and BTS s.v. *manian*, IV.

f. 30r

7 (18:28) *ænne æfnþara* for *unum de conseruis*. DOE s.v. *efen-þeow* lists *æfnþara* as a spelling variant with no comment. The partitive genitive structure in Old English requires a genitive plural form, but the actual spelling is hardly explicable unless the noun is confused with the genitive plural demonstrative *þara*.

8 (18:28) *denera* for *denarios*. Farman uses the Latin-derived word (see DOE s.v. *diner*) as a gloss. The use of the loanword in Old English is mostly confined to Ru1, apart from one instance in Ælfric's *Grammar* which may suggest that *diner* was recognized as an Old English word: ÆGram 285.1 [2107 (285.1)] denarius *tynfeald* denarius *is eac se dinor, þe awehð* DECEM NVMMOS, *þæt sind tyn penegas.* See also Durkin (2014: 112).

9 (18:28) An erased *þ* is still visible above *-de* of *redde*, cancelled probably to adjust the following gloss *þæt* to the position matching to the Latin.

13 (18:31) *þa þe þær gewurdun* for *quae fiebant.* Note that *þær* has no equivalent Latin, which Schulte (s.v. *þær*) calls 'Füllwort'. It is not sure whether the adverb is completely 'expletive', as the reading as a full adverb 'what happened there' would give a smooth reading. Similarly, *quæ facta fuerant* in line 14 is glossed with *þ ðe ðær gedoan weron.* For similar instances, see 27:54 and 28:11.

18 (18:34) There is erasure of *w* between *eorra* and *his*, presumably a cancellation of *wæs*, which was to be written in the next line. The fact that *est* is omitted in the standard Vulgate may have contributed to the rewriting.

19 (18:34) *tinterga þægnum* for *tortoribus.* The first word is written as *tintga* with a suspension stroke above the second *t.* For the forms with and without metathesis in this word, see note to 4:24. BT s.v. *tintregþegn* treats the present instance as a compound for which there is only one other instance recorded in ClGl 1 (Stryker) [0120 (129)] Ac lictoribus *tinterðegnum* (*sic*). The present edition, following Skeat, adopts the two-word reading, especially because of the genitive plural case ending for the first word.

f. 30v

2 (19:1) *be londe iordanen* for *trans iodanen* (corrected to *iordanen* by Farman). The use of *londe* in glossing *trans iordanen* is also found in 4:25, where Farman's gloss reads *of londe begeonda iordane* 'from the land beyond the river Jordan'.

5 (19:3) For the want of an equivalent to *si*, see note on 12:10.

8 (19:5) *for þon þingum* for *propter hoc.* The use of the noun *þing* in translating prepositional phrases introduced by *propter* is also found in WSCp; e.g., Jn 11:15 *⁊ ic eom bliþe for eowrum þingon* for *et gaudeo propter uos.* In the present instance, *for þon* alone would be an equivalent to *propter hoc* (note the singular form *þon* against plural *þingum*), suggesting a possible mixture of two different approaches to translate the phrase.

9 (19:5) *ætclifað* for *adherebit*. The Old English verb is rare and elsewhere found only in psalter glosses; see DOE s.v. *ætclifian*.

21 (19:10) The use of *hæman* to mean specifically 'to marry' is found only in Ru1. DOE s.v. *hæman* 1.b. For a detail account of the words related to the stem *hæm-*, see Fischer (1986: 63–75).

f. 31r

5 (19:13) *he honda hiæ on sette* for *manus eis inponeret*. Although Skeat and Tamoto read *onsette* as a verb with prefix, the present edition takes *on sette* as two words; McAllister's position is equivocal because his transcription does not employ hyphens at the end of lines. Farman elsewhere uses *(ge)settan* with prepositional phrases with either *on* or *ofer* to translate *inponere* (cf. 9:28, 19:15, 23:4, 27:29 27:48), and the use of postposed prepositions is not infrequent in Old English in general (cf. note to 15:33).

6 (19:13) *gebede* for *curaret* (*oraret* WW). Farman's gloss reflects the standard Vulgate reading.

8 (19:14) *þa cild ł lytlingan* for *paruulos*. The alternative gloss is elsewhere declined as a strong noun and this apparently weak plural is noted as a 'perhaps transmission error' by OED3 (s.v. *littling*, n.[1]), which has removed this Ru1 instance from the citations quoted in OED2. The inclusion of this word in OED is based on the word's use in regional dialects; it was 'apparently re-formed in the 18th cent[ury]'.

ne for *nolite* is followed by erasure, which appears to have read *wernað*. The erased reading would have resulted in a more usual Old English word order, with the imperative immediately following the negative particle. The correction is likely to have been intended to match the gloss with the Latin word order.

wernað ł forbeode for *prohibere*. The form of the second gloss is not entirely clear, but it is probably an infinitive with loss of *-n*, as one of the examples of bare forms that are used in the second gloss.

12 (19:16) *dom ic* for *faciam*. For the first person present form *dom*, with the analogical *-m* ending, see Campbell (OEG §735 (a)) and Ross (1976: 505).

lifes æce for *uitam aeternam*. For the use of *habban* with the genitive object of *habban*, see note on 14:4. *æce* lacks the genitive ending.

15 (19:18) *iesus autem dixit* is treated as the beginning of verse 18 by Skeat, followed by DOE Corpus and Tamoto. There is no reason to deviate from the traditional verse division at *dixit illi quae sunt* in modern editorial contexts; McAllister and Liuzza (1994–2000) adopt the traditional verse division.

There is erasure of *fr-* between *ne* and *þu*. It may have been part of *fremme*, which was to be written above its Latin equivalent in the next line.

18 (19:19) *lufige þa nehstum ðinum* for *deleges proximum tuum*. The object of *lufige* shows the mixture of the accusative (*þa*) and the dative. *lufian* is not listed in Mitchell's list of verbal rections (OES §1092), and the dative may have been influenced by the preceding *arian*, which is constantly used with the dative.

21 (19:21) *wisfæstre ł doefe* for *perfectus*. There is no clear reason why the first gloss has the comparative ending. The form without prefix *ge-* is rare for *defe*; DOE s.v. *defe* counts only two occurrences (the other is in ÆHomM 8).

f. 31v

2 (19:21) *folga* is altered from *fylga* by writing *o* over *y*.

3 (19:22) *þæt* is written above *autem*, but *þæt* is not used for the Latin adverb elsewhere in Ru1 (for a similar instance, see Introduction III.2.2.2.5, esp. citation 31). Thus, the function of the *þæt* in this verse is not entirely clear. It is not certain whether it is of relevance that there are some Vulgate and Old Latin manuscripts that omits *autem* here. It may possibly be a redundant demonstrative *þæt* referring to *word*, which is followed by another *þæt* glossing *haec*.

6 (19:23) *se weliga uneaþe gæþ* for *diues dificile est intrare*. Ru1 reflects the standard Vulgate reading *diues difficile intrabit*. For the gloss that would translate the infinitival construction, see the gloss for *facilius est … transire* the next verse.

17 (19:28) *æftakennisse* for *generatione* (*regeneratione* WW). The gloss is an element-for-element gloss to the standard Vulgate reading. The Old English compound (DOE s.v. *eft-acennes*) is recorded elsewhere only once in DurRitGl, also glossing *regeneratio*.

19 (19:28) *ge sittaþ* for *sedebitis*. Both Skeat and Tamoto read *gesittaþ*, but *et uos* in the Latin strongly suggests the use of the subject pronoun, emphasizing the contrast between 'the son of man' and 'you too'; McAllister reads *ge sittaþ*.

f. 32r

3 (19:30) R's *nouissimi primi et primi nouissimi* is in the reverse order of the standard Vulgate reading. Farman's gloss follows the latter.

5 (20:1) *monn* for *homini* appears to be the nominative, where the dative is expected. It may be construed, though very awkwardly, as the subject, 'the man is like the kingdom of heaven', if the following relative pronoun *ðæm ðe* were ignored, which, however, is clearly dative and referring to *monn*. For another instance of *monn* used in the same syntactic environment, see 22:2.

8 (20:2) *þone wingeard* for *uiniam suam* (*uineam* WW). The use of the demonstrative rather than a possessive in the gloss may reflect the standard Vulgate reading, which omits *suam*.

12 (20:5) *æt þæm sextan ⁊ þæm nigoþan tide ł hwile* for *circa sextam et nonam horam*. For the use of *þæm* with the historically feminine *tid* and *hwil*, see Introduction III.2.2.2.1, esp. citation (24).

14 (20:6) *ællefta* for *xi* (*undecimam*) shows the assimilation of *n* with *l*; see Hogg (1992: §7.91 (2)).

16 (20:7) *mið leane gebohte* for *conduxit* (WW reports that R originally reads *conducit*, corrected to *conduxit* by R[sax], i.e., Farman. However, there is no sign of correction in the manuscript). While *conducere* 'to hire' is glossed with *bicgan* alone in 20:1, the sense is clarified with *mið leane* 'with remuneration' in the present instance. DOE s.v. *gebicgan* A.4 cites only this example for the collocation.

22 (20:9) *æghwilc* has no exact equivalent in the Latin and is presumably the nominative singular used 'to indicate distribution of a plurality of things among the members of a set' as defined by OED3 (s.v. *each*, adj. and pron., B. *pron.* 2). The citations in OED3 (under B.2.a) include the present verse from WSCp *þa onfengon hig ælc his pening*.

f. 32v

3 (20:11) *grornadun* for *murmurabant*. Ru1 has only *grornian* of the double forms *grornian* and *gnornian* (both in DOE's spelling). On the development of these forms, see Stanley (1952–53: 111–14).

5 (20:12) *we þe* for *qui*. Both Skeat and Tamoto mistakenly read *se þe*.

8 (20:13) *dęglicum* for *diurno* is written with two erased letters between *g* and *l*, which read probably *ul*. The spelling with *-ul-* can be compared with *degullice* in line 15; see the glossary s.v. *digollice*.

11 (20:15) *þa eagan þin* for *an oculus tuus*. *þa* is not a precise translation of Latin *an*, but the adverb *þa* could fit the context, connecting two questions. For the nominative singular use of *eagan*, see note to is 18:9.

12 (20:16) *beoþ* is altered from *beoþan* by erasing *an*. On the form *beoþan*, see note to 4:19.

14 (20:17) *hierusolimis* is altered from *hierosolimis*, by writing *u* (with the *v* form) above the first *o*. There is no sign of cancellation of the original reading.

22 (20:20) *boensendu* for *petiens* (corrected to *petens*). The verb occurs in texts with Anglian colouring according to DOE s.v. *bensian*. See also Rauh (1936: 17), who identifies the verb as Anglian. Aldred uses it in DurRitGl, but not in Li, which has *giwude* in this verse; *giwian* is a verb used exclusively in Aldred's gloss and Ru2.

f. 33r

3 (20:22) There is erasure of *þa* before *andwarade*, which was apparently repositioned to match the position of *autem*.

5 (20:22) *drincan* for *bibere* is probably corrected from *drincað* by erasing *ð* and writing *n* on it.

6 (20:23) *drincan* for *bibitis* (*bibetis* WW) is corrected from *drincað* in the same manner as the above. While the original form would have been read without difficulty (cf. WSCp *witodlice gyt minne calic drincaþ*; Li *ðe calic ec soð min gie drinces*), the corrected form *drincan* is likely to be a subjunctive present plural form, reflecting futurity.

8 (20:23) *iarward* for *paratum* is preceded by erasure of *ge*, which may have been intended as either the prefix *ge-* or the alternative spelling *gear-*. For the latter interpretation, see Introduction III.2.1.3. Note also that the *r* in *-ward* is inorganic (cf. 25:41).

12 (20:25) *agun gewald* for *dominantur*. For the collocation, see DOE s.v. *agan*, I.A.5.f.i. and I.A.11.h.i.

17 (20:28) *ꝥ him wære ðægnad ah he ðægnade* for *ministrari sed ministrare*. The contrast of the active and passive voices of the Latin infinitives is expressed by using the different finite verb forms in the *þæt*-clause; WSCp also uses a *þæt*-clause, but the indefinite pronoun *man* enables the parallel syntactic structure for both Latin infinitives. See Introduction III.2.4, esp. citation 58.

18 (20:28) At the end of verse 28, WSCp has a long section that reflects an Old Latin reading; see Liuzza (1994–2000: ii, 36) for details. Farman's gloss here shows no trace of such non-Vulgate readings.

f. 33v

1 (20:31) *ðreattan* for *increpabat*. The grammatical form of *ðreattan* is uncertain. Ross (1976: 509) assumes 'a loss of the medial vowel between the two dentals', suggesting forms like *ðreatadon*. While the subject *sio mengu* is grammatically singular, the use of the plural verb is not unexpected because of the sense, as found in line 21 *sio mæste … mængu strægdun*.

4 (20:32) *do* for *faciam* is followed by erasure of one letter, which may have been *m*. Farman elsewhere uses the form *dom* for the first person present singular; see note to 19:16.

8 (21:1) *oelebearwes dune* for *montem olieti*. For the first word, see DOE s.v. *ele-bearu*, a compound which occurs only in Ru1/2 and Li. The latter does not use the compound in this verse (*mor oliuetes*), but it has *on mor ł on duni olebearuas* in 26:30.

12 (21:3) *to cwæþe* for *dixerit*. Skeat, followed by Tamoto, transcribes *to-cwæþe* with hyphen. This is probably unnecessary because *to* is the preposition separated from its object (*eow ł inc*), a normal syntactic pattern required for *cweþan*.

13 (21:3) *forleteð heo* for *dimittet uobis* (*eos* WW). Farman's *heo* follows the standard Vulgate reading *eos*; there is no sign of correction in R's Latin.

19 (21:7) *onbręddon* for *inpossuerunt* (Skeat and Tamoto print as *on-bręddon*). The prefixed verb *onbrædan* does not occur elsewhere and is not recorded in CH, BT and BTS; Campbell's *Addenda* lists the word, referring to this specific instance; cf. DOE s.v. *brædan*[2] and Ross (1979b: 496).

f. 34r

1 (21:9) *beforaneodan* for *cedebant* reflects the standard Vulgate reading *praecedebant*. Skeat prints both *beforan eodan* and *æfter eodun* (line 2) as two words, while DOE has the headword *beforan-gan*, under which the present instance is listed. DOE, however, does not have **æftergan* as a headword, while there are several compound verbs with *æfter-* in DOE (e.g., *æfter-cweþan*, *æfter-fylgan*, *æfter-spyrian*). The present edition regards both as compounds, partly because of DOE's *beforan-gan* and also because of the clear contrast between the two verbs in the context, thus creating a verb not recorded in DOE. The validity of the decision should be considered by lexicographers along with several instances of *æfter* + *gan* that can be found in DOE Corpus.

9 (21:12) *mynetræ* for *nummulariorum*. *y* is written on another letter, which may have been *u*.

settlas þa sellendum culfran for *cathedras uendentium columbas*. *þa sellendum* shows the disagreement in case, but they clearly stand together written above *uendentium*. There is one more unambiguous instance of *þa* used with a dative plural form (*sægdun þa aldursacerdum* for *adnuntiauerunt principibus* in 28:11), a possible sign of weaking case distinctions (cf. Introduction III.2.2.3).

11 (21:13) *bið gebedes hus genemned* for *domus orationis uocabitur*. *hus* is erased above *domus*, and written again as it now stands, apparently to have the phrase *gebedes hus* uninterrupted by other words. Where Farman translates the Latin phrase by the two words *gebedes hus* as indicated by the genitive ending of *gebedes*, WSCp has the compound *gebedhus*. In Li, Aldred cancels the genitive ending of *hus gebedes*, by expuncting *-es* (f. 69ra, 5–6), which may suggest that he had the compound in mind.

17 (21:15) *hi þa abolgenne weron* for *indignati sunt*. The layout suggests that Farman is likely to have squeezed *hi þa* in after having written the rest of the gloss. There is no equivalent to *þa* in the Latin text, including variant readings. The adverb certainly emphasizes the narrative sequence, as also found in WSCp *ða wæron hig yrre*.

19 (21:16) *næfre* for *non* appears to reflect the standard Vulgate reading *numquam*, for which Ru1 uses *næfre* elsewhere.

sukendra ł diendra for *lactantium*. The second gloss is from **deon* (cf. Holthausen s.v. *dion*, and Ross [1979b: 496], who compares it with modern Swedish *dia* 'to lactate'), for which finite forms are not recorded, apart from the prefixed *gediides* in Li (Lk 11:27, glossing *suxisti*; see DOE s.v. *gedeon*). Li has *diendra* in the present verse.

f. 34v

1 (21:19) *sæh* for *uidit* is altered from *sæg*, by writing *h* on *g*.

4 (21:19) *sonæ ł instyde* for *continuo*. The adverb *instyde* in the alternative gloss is found only in Ru1. See note to Mk 1:28.

9 (21:21) *þæh þe*, translating *si*, is dislocated from its Latin equivalent and placed before the 'S + V' sequence. For similar instances in other interlinear glosses and their significance, see Kotake (2022).

ge cweðe for *dixeritis*. Skeat and Tamoto print *gecweðe* as one word, but *ge* as the subject gives a smoother reading, especially because of its position (see the previous note).

13 (21:21) *in hwæs ł hwilcę mæhte* for *in qua potestate*. The first gloss *hwæs* may not be regarded as an accurate translation of the Latin, but it gives a smooth reading 'in whose authority'; cf. ÆHomM 6 (Irv 1) (from the twelfth-century Oxford, Bodleian Library, Bodley 343) *Sæge us, we biddæþ, on hwæs mihte ðu wurcæst þas syllice wundræ*, translating Lk 20:2 *dic nobis in qua potestate haec facis*. As to the second gloss, the apparently masculine or neuter form is used with *miht*, which is historically feminine; see also *in (h)wilce mæhte* in 21:24 and 21:27. Note that Li shows some signs of unhistoric gender congruence of the word, including the dative singular used with *ðæm* as in this verse *(in ðæm mæht*) or the *-es* genitive singular (*ðæs mæhtes* for *uirtutis* in Mk 14:62); cf. Jones (1967: 105–106) and (1988: 92–93). See also Introduction III.2.2.2.1 for comparable instances in Ru1.

14 (21:23) It is not clear why *swa* is used for *quis* instead of *hwa*, a striking reinterpretation of the verse. Palaeographical confusion is unlikely between *s* and *h*.

16 (21:24) *þ þonne* for *quem*, with *þonne* written as *þon* with a suspension stroke. Because the Latin relative pronoun *quem* refers to *unum sermonem*, the direct translation would need only *þ*, referring to *anes wordes*. The *þon* may be expanded to *þone* and is interpreted as an alternative relative pronoun agreeing with the masculine in the Latin. Skeat, McAllister and Tamoto all expand it to *þonne*, which may simply be taken as a variant of *þone*.

17 (21:24) *þas* for *haec* is altered from *þis*, by writing *a* above *i* with no sign of cancellation.

f. 35r

5 (21:29) R's version of the verses 29–31, containing the parable of the two sons, shows significant textual variants. The actions of the brothers are presented in the revised order (i.e., the first said 'yes' and did not go; the second said 'no', but did go moved with repentance) and therefore the answer of the chief priests and the elders of the people is *nouissimus* 'the last' as against *primus* 'the first' in the standard Vulgate reading (though there are texts with the Vulgate order and yet having *nouissimus* as in Y, which Jerome in his commentary on Matthew condemns by saying 'the authentic copies do not have "the last" but "the first" [cited in Scheck's translation 2008: 243–44]). Farman's gloss follows R while adding minor corrections and shows no sign of confusion caused by the textual issue. For the nature of the textual transmission in the Greek tradition, see Metzger (1994: 44–46). See also Berger (1893: 42) for other Irish manuscripts that contain the same textual variant.

7 (21:30) *efter* for *postea*. As McAllister observes, *e* may have been altered from *æ*, by erasing the loop.

9 (21:31) Farman inserted *ei* after *dicunt*, a reading that is found in multiple manuscripts, but not adopted by WW (see Appendix I). His gloss *hiæ*, written just above the inserted *ei*, does not translate *ei*, but functions as the subject of the verb; cf. note to 13:51.

10 (21:31) *forlegnisse* for *meretrices*. While the usual sense of the noun is abstract 'fornication, adultery', DOE, s.v. *for-legennes* 2. records two instances of the noun used for the sense 'prostitute'. The other instance is taken from a manuscript variant in CP, which may have been an error for *forlegis*, used more frequently for the sense 'prostitute, harlot, adulteress' in CP (see DOE s.v. *for-legis, for-leges*, and Schreiber 2003: 588).

14 (21:32) *ne ge hreuwnisse hæfdun* for *nec penitentiam habuistis*. Skeat, McAllister and Tamoto all print *gehreuwnisse* as one word. DOE s.v.

gehreownes counts only two instances (the other instance in DurRitGl). The present edition reads *ge* as the pronominal subject of the verb *hæfdun*. I have argued elsewhere (Kotake 2022) that a pronominal subject is often dislocated from the verb and placed in the clause opening, grouped with the conjunction, even in interlinear glosses. Although the manuscript layout has limited value as evidence for word division, it may also be pointed out that *ge* is written closer to *ne* than *hreuwnisse*.

17 (21:33) *heage .ł geard* for *sepem* (*saepe* WW). The second gloss is without any case ending, giving only a lexical alternative, as against the dative *heage* required by the Old English syntax (note the accusative *ðane* for *ei*). The use of *geard* for the sense 'hedge' is recorded elsewhere only in GD; see DOE s.v. *geard* 3.

torcul for *torcular*. The Latin loan *torcul* is not recorded elsewhere in Old English. OED2 s.v. *torcular*, n. is a seventeenth-century loan and does not refer to the present instance. Although Ross (1979b: 497) lists it under rare loan words found in Ru1, it is impossible to determine from this single occurrence whether *torcul* was established as an Old English word. Durkin (2014) does not deal with it.

19 (21:33) *in ellende ł in elðiode* for *peregre*. *ellende*, as both a noun and an adjective, is relatively rare with the noun found in four occurrences, two of which are in Ru1 (the other two in Bo); see DOE *ellende*, n. In contrast, *elðeod* is somewhat more frequent (14 occ. according to DOE s.v. *elþeod*, n.), found in both prose and poetry. OED3 newly includes *althede*, n., on the basis of its occurrence in Laȝamon's *Brut*.

19 (21:34) *þæt*, though written above *autem*, is not a word to be used by Farman to gloss the Latin adverb. If *þæt* is to be taken as a demonstrative, there would be unhistorical gender congruence with the feminine *tid*, a possible sign of *þæt* being used with non-neuter. See Introduction III.2.2.5.

tid for *tempus* is followed by erasure of *ł h-*, which may be conjectured as an abandoned form of *hwil*. While the pair of *tid* and *hwil* (in both orders) occurs frequently as a double gloss in Ru1, all the instances of the double gloss are given to *hora*. For further details, see Kotake (2017: 89–90 and n. 19).

22 (21:35) *sume* for *alium* (also in line 1 on f. 35v) appears to disagree with the Latin in number, but a plural form gives a smooth reading as a free translation.

cnidun for *cederunt* (corrected to *ceciderunt* by Farman). DOE s.v. *gnidan* takes *cnidun* as a form of *gnidan*, listing it under the specific subheading '3. glossing *caedere* "to beat, flog", ? here interpreted "to crush, dash down"'. Spellings with *cn-* instead of *gn-* are also listed by DOE for the prefixed verb *forgnidan* from PsGlF. In contrast, Schulte, CH, BT and

Holthausen, all include *cnidan* 'to beat' as a headword and Ross (1979b: 497) lists this instance as one of Ru1's rare words, noting that the etymology is 'obscure'. The glossary adopts the headword *cnidan*, but does not intend to rule out DOE's suggestion, not least because Farman's gloss betrays the alteration of *c* and *g*, though not always under similar conditions; cf. note on *caldes* in 10:42.

f. 35v

2 (21:36) *mænigu* for *plures*. The use of the positive degree for the comparative in the Latin is paralleled in the first gloss of Li's double gloss *monigo ł micla maa*.

4 (21:37) *ofwitun* for *reuerebuntur* (*uerebuntur* WW). R's text has the prefixed *reuereor* 'respect, honour', which may have been confused with a form of *reuerberare* 'to repel' by Farman; BTS compares Ru1's *ofwitun*, a verb not recorded elsewhere, with such verbs as *ætwitan* and *oþwitan* that have meanings closer to *reuerberare*.

6 (21:38) On the double gloss given to *et nostra erit*, see Introduction III.1.3.1, esp. citation 16.

8 (21:40) *nu* for *cum* is the only instance of *nu* glossing the conjunction *cum* in Ru1. It is probably intended as a conjunction 'now that, when'.

12 (21:42) *þæm thi*. The use of *th* instead of *þ*/*ð* is probably a remnant of early orthographical practice as noted in Introduction III.2.1.2. While there is no other instance of the spelling *thi* in Ru1, *þi* is found elsewhere (*þi* glossing *quia* in 16:23 and as part of *forþon þi* in 5:33). DOE Corpus yields only one other instance of *thi* in the so-called *A Proverb from Winfrid's Time*, recorded in a continental manuscript (Vienna, Nationalbibliothek, Lat 751); see Dobbie (1942: lxvii–lxix, 57).

timbrade for *ædificantes* may be a corrupted form of a present participle form of the same verb, which both Li and WSCp use in this verse (Li *stan ðone eftedwidon timbrende*; WSCp *Se stan þe ða timbriendan awurpon*). Some of the Old English glosses to the psalm alluded to here (Ps 117:22) also use the same participle (e.g., PsGlA *Stan ðone widcurun timbrende* for *Lapidem quem reprobauerunt aedificantes*).

17 (21:44) R's *non confringetur* is a defective reading for *confringetur* (WW); Farman gives a word-for-word gloss to R.

18 (21:44) *gehnyscet* for *conteret* is a hapax legomenon according to DOE s.v. *gehnyscan*, unless the adjective form *gehnysta* (*se gehnysta gast*) in KtPs (line 127) is taken as a past participle of the verb (cf. DOE s.v. *gehnyst*). Ross (1979b: 497) regards the etymology of the verb as 'obscure'. As to the *-et* ending, see Introduction III.2.1.2.

20 (21:46) *soecende hiæ þ hine genoman* for *uolentes* (corrected to *querentes* by Farman) *eum tenere*. *þ* is erased between *hine* and *genoman*. Another *þ* now stands before *hine*, for which see note below.

21 (21:46) *ꝛ dreordun* for *timerunt* is treated here as two words; see also note to 9:8. Unlike the other instances discussed there, there is no clear syntactic reason why *ꝛ* is used here. Although the preceding Latin infinitive *tenere* is glossed with the finite form *genoman*, this is due to the expansion of the infinitive into a *þæt*-clause ('seeking that they would capture him, they feared…'). However, as there is no explanation for the doubled *d* resulting from reading *ꝛ* as a prefix, the present edition treats this example as two words as in the other cases discussed at 9:8 and 14:5.

hine is erased at the end of the line, presumably because it is written above its Latin equivalent *eum* in the next line.

f. 36r

1 (22:1) *heora* for *eis* is not an accurate translation. Note that *dicens*, which follows *eis* in the standard Vulgate, is missing in R, possibly obscuring the function of *eis*.

2 (22:2) *wearð* for *est* appears to reflect more closely the standard Vulgate reading *factum est*.

3 (22:2) *gemunge* for *nuptias*. The use of the word in the meaning 'marriage, wedding' is identified as Anglian by Klaeber (1902–4: 1904, 399); see also DOE s.v. *gyming, gymung*, 5. Li does not share this Anglian use of the word (*færmum* in this verse; see DOE s.v. *feorm* 2.a. 'marriage feast, wedding'; all the citations are from Li for this specific sense of the word), though DurRitGl has instances of *gyming*. In Ru1, in lines 4 and 7, the word is used with *þæm* and in line 18 with *þ*, suggesting unhistorical gender congruence for the word in Ru1, which is feminine elsewhere. See also Fischer (1986: 44–49) for detailed analysis of related nouns.

6 (22:4) *foedelfuglas* for *altilia* is a hapax legomenon (DOE s.v. *fedel-fugel* 'fattened fowl'), whose first element can be compared with DOE s.v. *fedels* 'fattened animal', a word found mostly in Latin-Old English glossaries. OED3 s.v. *feddle*, n. replaces two Old English examples cited from glossaries in OED2 with the present instance in Ru1, noting that it is 'recorded earliest in the Old English compound *fēdelfugel* fattened fowl'.

9 (22:6) *elle* for *reliqui*. DOE s.v. *ell* records only two instances of *el-* as a word, with the other occurring in Beo (752) in the comparative form *elran* 'other', which is sometimes emended to *eldran*, but the emendation is rejected by Klaeber (1905–6: 1905, 252). See also Dobbie (1953: 153).

10 (22:6) *geonrettæ* written above *contumilia* is a past participle form of *georrettan* 'put to shame, disgrace', with *-nr-* caused apparently by dissimilation (if not due to palaeographical confusion between *n* and *r*; see note to 10:15), translating the phrase *contumilia adfectos* (corrected by Farman from *adflictos*).

12 (22:7) *abriodde* for *perdidit*. The verb *abreoþan* is a class II strong verb, and, according to DOE s.v. *a-breoþan*, this is the only instance of it being treated as a weak verb.

15 (22:9) *utgengum* for *exitus*. BT has a separate heading *utgeng* for this example, therefore creating a hapax legomenon (no correction is suggested in BTS); similarly, CH has *utgenga*, referring to this specific instance. While the glossary adopts CH's headword, it cannot be ruled out that it is a variant spelling of *utgang/utgeong*. OED3 s.v. *outgang*, n. cites both Li *utgeong* and the present instance in Ru1 from this verse with the latter put in square brackets as a variant to the former.

weogas for *uiarum* is apparently the nominative/accusative plural form, where the genitive plural is expected.

16 (22:9) *gemungæ* for *nuptias*. Both Skeat and Tamoto print the word as *gemunge*, but the manuscript has *gemungæ*, as McAllister reads.

20 (22:11) *ungegeradne* for *non uestitum*. The adjective is not recorded elsewhere in the same spelling in Old English. BT s.v. *ungegearwod* lists the present instance along with an instance from the Durham Ritual (DurRitGl 1 [0783 (107.21)] *vngigearvad woede* for *non uestitum ueste* [cited from the DOE Corpus rather than the actual BT entry]).

f. 36v

5 (22:16) *mið herodes þægnum* for *cum herodianis*. While both Ru1 and Li (*mið heroðes ðegnum*) use *þegn* to translate the Latin, WSCp has a more literal rendering by using the Latin word with an Old English case ending, *mid þam herodianiscum*.

15 (22:21) The second *kasere* for *cessaris* appears to want the genitive case ending, unless it is taken as the possessive dative.

17 (22:23) *cwædun þæt seo ærist ł uparisnisse* for *dicunt non esse resurrectionem*. Note that the negative sense is lost in expanding the Latin infinitival structure into the Old English clause.

18 (22:23) *æriste ł uparisnisse* for *resurrectionem*. The second gloss *uparisnisse* is found elsewhere only in the twelfth century PsCaE (Liles) [0234 (18(14).6)] *uparisnesse* for *resurrectionem*, while other earlier versions have forms of *ærist* in the corresponding verse. MED does not contain the exact reflex of *uparisnes*; cf. MED s.v. *uparising(e*.

19 (22:24) *swylte* is altered from *swælte* by adding a dot under *æ* and writing *y* above it.

f. 37r

2 (22:26) *swa ⁊ gelice* for *similiter*. While *swa gelice* is a phrase frequently found in Old English (also in Ru1, 26:35 glossing *similiter*), there is no instance of *swa and/ond gelice* in DOE Corpus.

siofund for *uiimum* (*septimum*). Note the use of the ordinal *siofund* instead of *seofoþa* forms, a feature shared by Northumbrian and Ru1; see Campbell (OEG §692) and Hogg and Fulk (2011: §4.90, n. 2).

7 (22:30) *ne hæmde bioþ* for *neque nubentur*. *hæmde* is written on erasure which is likely to have read *mægen*, suggesting that Farman at first mistakenly repeated the gloss *ne mægen* for *neque uirtutem* in the previous line due to the repetition of *neque* followed by letters formed with minims.

14 (22:34) *gesettun* for *inpossuisset*. There is no reason to expect the plural form of the verb here.

18 (22:37) *alre heortan þines* for *toto corde tuo* shows the mixture of the feminine *alre* and the masculine/neuter *þines*. While DOE s.v. *heorte* notes that neuter or masculine examples of *heorte* are found occasionally in Northumbrian, this kind of mixture seems to indicate that gender distinctions were weakening in Farman's language to some degree. See also *alra mode þinum* for *tota mente tua* in line 19, which shows the unexpected *alra* for the expected neuter dative singular. See Introduction III.2.2.2 for further discussion.

19 (22:38) Both *forþon þe*, agreeing with *enim* in the standard Vulgate, and *mæste* for *magnum* (*maximum* WW) clearly indicate that Ru1 follows the standard Vulgate reading here.

f. 37v

4 (22:44) *hlaferd minne* for *domino meo*. It is not clear why the accusative form is used instead of the dative or a prepositional phrase with *to*.

7 (22:46) *mæhte* for *poterat* is written in the current state with a large space between *mæh-* and *-te*, where *dyrs* appears to have been erased, suggesting that it was corrected from *dyrste*. Given *nænig dyste* (*sic*, see note below) in the next line, it is likely that eye-skip was involved.

8 (22:46) *ne heora nænig dyste* for *ausus quis* (corrected to *quisquam* by Farman) *fuerat*. *dyste* for *dyrste* is presumably an error, as, in the erasure noted above, there are two descenders for *r* and *s* clearly visible. Although there is no exact equivalent in the Latin, the partitive genitive *heora* gives a smooth reading.

10 (23:1) *mongum* for *turbas*. The spelling of the gloss could suggest that it is a form of *manig*, but, given that all the instances of *turba* are glossed with *menigu* in Matthew (cf. *þreat* in Mk 2:13), *mongum* should probably be treated as unexpected spelling variant of the noun *menigu*, as treated by Schulte s.v. *mengu*.

12 (23:3) *swa hwæt swa ic sægce* for *quaecumque dixerint*. Ru1's *ic sægce* for *dixerint* in this context is hardly explicable other than as an error.

15 (23:4) *un⁊hoife* for *inportabilia* is a hapax legomenon; cf. BT *unandhefe*. Ross (1979b: 497) compares the formation with Gothic *unandsoks* 'irrefutable'. The element *-hoife* is apparently related to *hebban*, but the exact interpretation of the etymology is not clear.

16 (23:4) *fringre* for *digito* is emended by Skeat to *fingre*. It is impossible to determine whether the inorganic *r* is an error or is caused by some phonological feature. The *fr-* spelling for *finger* is found at least in two instances. The one in the thirteenth century manuscript (London, BL, Harley MS 6258, f. 58v) of *Peri didaxeon* is emended by its editor (Löweneck 1896: 27). The fragment of the Old English prose Exodus in New York, Pierpont Morgan Library, G. 63 has *fringre* (s. xi[2]; see Ker's additional transcription in Crawford 1969: 460; for the manuscript, see no. 418 in Ker's 'Supplement' and Marsden 2008: lxi–lxiii, though his edition does not report the variant *fringre* on p. 121). These instances suggest the need of taking into consideration manuscript variants that are emended or are not adopted in edited texts in order to give a fuller consideration to the irregular spelling. (It is regretted that *The MANCASS C11 Database: An Inventory of Script and Spellings in Eleventh-Century English* has been unavailable for a long time now.) OED3 s.v. *finger*, n. also records some *fr-* spellings from the early Middle English period, noting that they are 'transmission error[s]'.

18 (23:5) *þwængae* for *filactiria*. The word is written as *þwænge* with *a* written as a suprascript between *g* and *e*, which appears to alter the original to either *þwængae* or *þwænga* (there is no sign of cancellation of the original *e*). The use of *þwang* specifically for the sense 'phylactery' is shared by Li in this verse (*ðuuencgu*); WSCp has *healsbæc*, a hapax legomenon (DOE s.v. *healsboc*). The occasional gloss to the Gospels in Cambridge, Fitzwilliam Museum MS 45–1980 (Ker no. 7*) has *wrædas* (see Napier 1900: 235).

19 (23:6) *þonne* for *enim* (*autem* WW; *enim* Y). As discussed in Introduction III.1.3.1, Farman's *þonne* appears to reflect *autem* in the standard Vulgate. Here, Y also has *enim* (Li *forðon*), indicating that the standard Vulgate readings reflected in Farman's gloss cannot always be found in the text of the Lindisfarne Gospels.

20 (23:6) *setulas* for *cathedras* is altered from *settlas*, by dotting the second *t* below and writing *u* above. On the *-u-* spelling, see Hogg (1992: §5.105 (2)). It should be noted that Farman uses the spellings with *-u-* only when the word translates Latin *cathedra* (see 23:2).

22 (23:8) *nyllaþ* is altered from *nellaþ* by adding *y* above *e* with no sign of cancellation.

f. 38r

8 (23:13) *þe ge lucaþ* for *quia cluditis.* Skeat and Tamoto print *þe gelucaþ* with *ge-* as a prefix, but *þe* functions here as a conjunction 'because' and the use of a pronominal subject in the clause gives a smooth reading; cf. line 15 *þe ge ymbgangaþ* for *quia circumitis.* McAllister reads *ge lucaþ* as two words.

9 (23:13) *gæþ* is altered from *gangæþ* by dotting below *gan-*.

10 (23:15) The verse numbering follows that of WW. Verse 14 is an interpolation from Mark 12:40 or Luke 20:47 and omitted in authoritative manuscript witnesses in the Greek tradition and accordingly in the standard Vulgate; see Metzger (1994: 50). R, as well as the Book of Kells, places verse 14 after verse 15, whereas both WSCp and Li (i.e., Y itself) omit the verse.

12 (23:15) *hæþne iudiscne* for *prosilitum.* Farman's use of the two adjectives is likely to be an attempt to give a precise gloss to *proselytus* 'one that has come over from heathenism to the Jewish religion' (in Lewis and Short's definition). Aldred leaves the Latin word unglossed here and in his gloss to *capitula lectionum* (Skeat, p. 21, line 16). WSCp has *elþeodine*; for the use of the adjective for this specific sense, see DOE s.v. *elþeodig* 2.a.ii.

13 (23:15) *helles* for *gehenae* is an instance of the analogical *-es* genitive; see Introduction III.2.2.2.3.

twæm fældum for *duplo.* The inflected form *twæm* suggests that the phrase is treated as two words. DOE s.v. *-feald* is an entry specifically as a suffix, and it does not contain *feald* as an independent word (cf. related *fyld* does not refer to the current instance).

15 (23:14) *set feorranne* for *occassione longe*, which is a corrupted reading for *occasione longa* 'for a long time' (see WW's apparatus and *Itala*). Farman's *feorranne* clearly suggests that he takes *longe* as the adverb 'at a distance'. His use of *set* also betrays his uncertainty, which appears to render the etymological meaning of *occasio*, i.e., *occidere*, given his *to sete eode* glossing *occidisset* in Mk1:32. As noted above in the note to line 10, it is possible that his exemplar does not contain the verse, which may have caused some confusion.

16 (23:14) *for þon* for *propter hoc.* There is erasure immediately after *for*, which appears to have read *þæm*.

f. 38v

1 (23:19) There is erasure of *is* between *hwæþer* and *soþlice*.

4 (23:21) *in him* for *in illo*. *him* is apparently corrected from *ðæm* by erasing the original reading. The first two letters *ðæ-* are still legible.

7 (23:23) *forþon ge þe tægþigaþ* for *qui* (*quia* WW) *decimatis*. The gloss appears to reflect both R and WW with *forþon* for *quia* and *ge þe* for *qui*.

10 (23:23) *þas* for *haec* is altered from *þis*, by dotting *i* below and writing *a* above. The plural is a more accurate translation of the Latin.

forletan for *omittere* is probably an infinitive, which agrees with the Latin. However, because the gloss turns the Latin infinitival structure with *oportuit* into a *þe*-clause with *gedęfnade*, the expected verb is a finite form, coordinate with *dyde* for *facere*. WSCp also use a clausal structure, though the subject in the clause is *ge* against *monn* in Ru1: *þas þing hyt gebyrede þæt ge dydon ⁊ þa oðre ne forletun*.

11 (23:24) *asiendę* for *exspuentes* (*excolantes* WW) is from *aseon* 'strain' (DOE s.v. *a-seon*[2]), which is recorded mostly in medical recipes, and reflects the standard Vulgate reading. Farman uses *spittan* for *exspuere* elsewhere.

14 (23:25) *parabsidis* is not glossed here or in line 16. Both Li and WSCp use forms of *disc*. In 26:23, Farman simply repeats the Latin word as a gloss. Farman may have used the Latin term even in English contexts, thus finding no need for giving an equivalent here. See note to 26:36 for a similar situation about *discipulus*.

nednimende for *rapina*. See note to 11:12 on the related noun *nydnima*.

18 (23:27) *behwitum* for *dealbatis*. DOE (s.v. *be-hwitt*) regards *behwitum* is a past participle form of the otherwise unattested verb **behwitan* 'whiten'. While the present edition adopts DOE's interpretation, it cannot be ruled out that Farman's *be* was an element-for-element glossing of *de-* added to the simple adjective *hwitum*; the same adjective is used in WSCp *(hwitum byrgenum)* in this verse.

22 (23:28) *innan* is altered from *binnan*, by erasing *b* and elongating *i*. It is not clear why this particular instance is corrected, while *intus* is constantly glossed with *binne* and *binnan* in the present passage (lines 14, 16 and 20).

f. 39r

8 (23:33) *uiperana* for *uiperarum*. Both BTS and CH list *vipere* with specific reference to the present instance. The weak genitive plural ending indeed suggests that Farman may have treated it as an Old English word. OED2 s.v. *viper* is yet to be fully updated for OED3 and, currently, it does not include any medieval instance of the word, with the first attested instance from the sixteenth century.

11 (23:34) *somnunge eowrum* for *sinagogis uestris* shows the mixture of a singular noun and a plural possessive form, unless *somnung*, elsewhere feminine, is thought to show gender shift to masculine or neuter.

17 (23:36) There is erasure of *þas* between *eow* and *cymeþ*, which is apparently rewritten to match the Latin word order.

22 (23:38) *hus eowra* for *domus uestra*. The apparently genitive plural form *eowra*, instead of *eower*, is not explicable.

f. 39v

1 (23:39) *sie þæt* for *amodo* should be considered in conjunction with *siðet* for the same Latin in 26:29; see note to the verse.

3 (24:1) *him eodun to* for *accesserunt*. Although *to* is written closer to the subject *leorneras*, it should be read as a postposed preposition with *him*. As seen in 22:23, *him … to* is likely to reflect a Latin variant with *ad eum*, a variant reading recorded in this verse in some manuscripts examined by WW. WSCp also betrays a similar reading: *him togenealæhton hys leorningcnihtas* (instead of *togenehlæhton*, Liuzza reads *to genealæhton*).

7 (24:2) *þæt he sy toworpen* for *qui non distruatur*. Farman apparently renders the Latin relative clause into a *þæt*-clause, in which a negative particle is not included. A comparable approach, though a negative particle is included in the *þæt*-clause, is found in HomS 21 (BlHom 6) [0079 (218)] *⁊ her ne bið forlæten stan ofor stan, þæt ælc ne sy fram oþrum adon.*

8 (24:3) *eodun* is altered from *heodun*; see Introduction III.2.1.3.

13 (24:6) *forþon þe ge bioþ geherende* for *audietis* (*audituri enim estis* WW) is a clear case of Ru1 following the standard Vulgate, as suggested by the use of *forþon þe* (for *enim*) and the periphrastic verb.

14 (24:6) *ꝥ ge sy gedræfde* for *ne turbemini*. While the Latin conjunction *ne* is glossed with *ꝥ*, there is no negative particle in the clause, resulting in the opposite meaning to the Latin. Cf. note to line 7 above.

18 (24:8) *onfruma* for *initia*. DOE s.v. *fruma* suggests that Ru1's *onfruma* (also in Mk 1:1) is an anomalous form of *fruma* resulting from 'a mechanical gloss' of the first element of the Latin.

19 (24:9) *ðrycnisse* for *tribulationem*. The noun is found only in Ru1; Ross (1979b: 496) compares it with Old High German *druknissí*.

22 (24:10) *fiegaþ hæbbende* for *odio habebunt*. Farman elsewhere uses *feogan* or *hatian* to render the Latin phrasal expression *odio habere*. In this verse, *fiegaþ* alone would fully translate the Latin.

f. 40r

3 (24:13) *in amore dei* is a reading not recorded elsewhere, even in Old Latin manuscripts. The use of *willa* for *amor* may be unexpected, but Farman may have felt the need of another word than *lufu* because it is used for *caritas* in the previous verse.

6 (24:15) *þis* for *ergo* is hardly explicable, unless it refers to *⁊ustrungæ* with the clearly feminine ending *-ung* in the next line; the use of *þes* showing historically wrong gender congruence is not entirely absent in Ru1 (e.g., *þeos* with masculine nouns; see Introduction III.2.2.2.6).

7 (24:15) *⁊ustrungæ* for *abhominationem* is a hapax legomenon, whose etymology is uncertain (cf. DOE s.v. *and-ustrung*). See note to 26:74, where the related verb *andustrian* is used.

awoestednisse for *desolationis*. DOE s.v. *a-westednes* records only one other instance, *awestednysse*, in PsGlI (72:19), which also translates *desolatio*. The choice of the Lambeth Psalter glossator is unique amongst the psalter glosses as noted in DOE (ABJ forms of *tolysnes*, C *tolysydnysse*, DEFGHK forms of *forlætnes*).

9 (24:15) *⁊gete* for *intellegat* originally read *⁊ on gete* with *on* now erased. The erasure appears to be intended to alter the superfluous conjunction ⁊ into the prefix. The verb is listed under *ongietan* in the glossary.

10 (24:17) *se þe on þæce siæ* for *qui in tecto*. Farman may have supplied *siæ* spontaneously where there is an ellipsis of a Latin copulative verb, or it could have been due to the influence of Latin variant readings with *est* as recorded in WW's apparatus. WW also reports that *est* is added by an Anglo-Saxon corrector in O; for its possible significance, see Introduction III.1.3.

11 (24:18) *se þe on londæ sy* for *qui in agro*. See the note above; in this instance, variants with a copulative verb are not recorded by WW, whereas some variants with *est*, *erit* or *sunt* are recorded in Old Latin manuscripts according to *Itala*.

12 (24:19) *cildfoedendum* for *nutriantibus*. While the sense and the formation are self-evident, the compound is not recorded elsewhere. See DOE s.v. *cild-fedende*.

15 (24:21) There is no exact equivalent to *æfter* in the Latin, which appears to function as an adverb 'afterwards' to help express the future tense of the Latin verb *fiet*. See DOE s.v. *æfter* I.B.

21 (24:24) *sien gelædde monigra* for *inducant multos* (*inducantur* WW). R's reading is unique. The use of the passive in Ru1 indicates that it reflects the standard Vulgate reading, while Farman at the same time tries to give a corresponding word to *multos*, providing the seemingly genitive plural *monigra*.

f. 40v

5 (24:28) *þider* for *illuc*. There is an erased *ð* before *d*. OED2 s.v. *thither* notes that the *-th-* for the medial consonant is found 'first in manuscripts of *Cursor Mundi*, but rare before 1525'. It is impossible to tell whether the erased spelling was a harbinger of the later change or due to the possible influence of Old Norse *paðra*, or indeed a slip in copying.

14 (24:31) *gesomnaþ ða gecorenum his* for *congregabunt electos suos*. *gecorenum* is expanded from *-u* with the usual suspension mark, but the dative form does not agree with *ða*, if it is taken as a form of *se*, not an adverb. Furthermore, the dative is not expected for an object of *(ge)somnian*, which Mitchell's list of verbal rections (OES §1092) does not include. The *-um* form may be a rare instance of *-um* / *-an* levelling in Ru1, here used instead of the weak accusative form *gerorenan* (cf. Campbell §378 n.1 notes that Ru1 'preserve[s] *-um* prevailingly').

15 (24:31) *to* for *ad* is written on erasure. The erasure is likely to have read *eora*, which was to be written again above *eorum*.

f. 41r

1 (24:36) *englas in heofunum* for *angeli cælorum*. Although the gloss gives a smooth reading, the use of the *in*-phrase instead of the genitive is not a slavish translation of the Latin text. No Latin variant reading having an equivalent *in*-phrase is reported by WW, apart from a correction of *caelorum* to *in caelo* by an Anglo-Saxon corrector in O.

3 (24:38) *forþon swa si hi weron* for *sicut enim erant*. The function of *si* in the gloss is uncertain.

10 (24:41) *twegen on bedde oþeru biþ genumen ⁊ oþer bið forleten* for *duo in lecto unus adsumetur et unus relinquetur*. The Latin text is an interpolation from Luke 17:34 and accordingly omitted in the standard Vulgate reading (the portion is treated as verse 42 in WW and its verse numbering henceforth in this chapter accordingly differs from the modern version). While Y does not have the Latin, WSCp's reading clearly reflects this interpolation: *Twegen beoþ on bedde, an byð genumen ⁊ oþer byð læfed*. Farman's use of the apparently feminine form *oþeru* for the first *unus* may be affected by the preceding feminine forms (*oþere* for *una*; his use of *oþeru* for the feminine nominative singular, see 12:13).

12 (24:42) *cymid* for *uenturus est* is preceded by an erased *is*, which may have been a trace of Farman's attempt to reflect the Latin periphrastic future. *cymid* is to be treated as the present third person singular (for *d* for *ð*, see Introduction III.2.1.2).

13 (24:43) *hinefæder* for *pater familias*. DOE s.v. *hina-fæder* takes this instance as a unique instance of the compound, which the present edition adopts. In fact, this compound may underlie some of the other instances of Farman's gloss of *pater familias*, which are taken as two words *fæder hina*, because the gloss agrees with the Latin word order element-for-element. See the glossary s.v. *hiwan*.

14 (24:43) *he wæccende beon walde ⁊ ne letan* for *uigilaret utique et non sineret*. All three Old English versions agree in using *wolde* (or *nolde*) in translating the Latin subjunctive imperfect: WSCp *he wolde wacigean ⁊ nolde geþafigen*; Li *waecca he walde uutedlice ⁊ ne walde gelefa*. That all versions use *wolde* without the corresponding lexical item in the Latin appears to indicate the shared need for expressing the sense conveyed by the Latin subjunctive here. See Yamamoto (2013: especially 132–33) for comparison of use of modal verbs in the three versions.

15 (24:44) ⁊ is erased above *et*, whose sense is translated by *ek*.

17 (24:45) *hwælc wenest þu sie* for *quis nam* (*putas* WW) *est*. Farman's gloss clearly reflects the standard Vulgate reading, while there is no sign of correction to the Latin text.

18 (24:45) *of* for *super*. *of* is not used for *super* elsewhere in Ru1; given the accusative *heorod* instead of the dative, *of* may have been intended as *ofer*, the usual choice for *super* in Ru1.

19 (24:46) *þone* for *quem*. *þon* with a suspension mark here is expanded to *þonne* by Skeat, McAllister and Tamoto, who apparently consider it as a gloss to *cum*. However, it should probably be read as a relative pronoun *þone* because the insertion of ⁊ in the next line makes it unnecessary to use a temporal clause. Farman's intension was clearly 'Blessed is the servant whom his master comes and finds so doing'.

f. 41v

2 (24:49) *manducat him* for *manducat*. The Latin word is repeated as a gloss for no obvious reason, followed by *hi* with the usual suspension mark, expanded as *him*. The use of *him* may be compared with CP [0541 (17.121.13)] *itt him ðonne ⁊ drincð mid ðam <druncenwillum> monnum*, where, referring to the same Gospel passage, *etan* is used with the reflexive pronoun; cf. DOE s.v. *etan* I.B.1.a.

drinceþ for *bibit* is corrected from *drigð*, by erasing *-gð*. The correction alters the syncopated form to one without syncopation.

8 (25:2) *fife þonne þaræ* for *u autem ex eis*. There is erasure of *þara* between *fife* and *þonne*. The correction appears to attempt to match the word order of the gloss to that of the Latin.

9 (25:3) *genimænde* for *acceptis*. The *i* in the gloss is altered from *o*, suggesting that Farman may have started to write a finite form (e.g., *genoman*).

12 (25:5) *slepade* for *dormitauerunt* and *slep ofereode* for *dormierunt*. Farman appears to attempt to differentiate the frequentative-derived *dormitare* and *dormire*. Whereas Li uses *geslepan* for both, WSCp has *þa hnappudon hig ealle ⁊ slepun* (cf. ÆCHom II, 44 [0004 (327.9)] *ða mædenu begunnon to hnappienne. oð þæt hi ealle slepon*). The collocation *slæp ofergan* is found mostly in poetry and their context suggests both suddenness of the sleep (three instances are used with *semnninga* [And 464, 820, Rid40 10]) and its completeness (four instances are used in an *oþ þæt*-clause [And 464, 820, 826; Mart 5 (Kotzor) [0565 (Ju 9, A.7)]]).

15 (25:7) *ingunnon* has no clear equivalent in the Latin, apparently governing both *arisan* and *fretwan*. This is the only instance of *inginnan* or *onginnan* used without a Latin equivalent in Ru1 and it apparently intensifies the inchoative aspect, which would fit the current context, though not paralleled in other Old English versions.

17 (25:8) *of oeles eowres* for *de olo* (corrected to *oleo* by Farman) *uestro*. Ogura (2008: 520–21), while pointing out that this instance may be a 'contamination of the "*of* + dative" and the genitive object [of the verb *sellan*]', regards it as the sole example of '*of* + genitive' in Old English. Farman's gloss tends to mix Old English and Latin syntactic features in general, and in particular as regards the partitive genitive. While it remains unclear whether *sellan* can be used with a genitive object (Mitchell's list of verbal rections does not include *sellan*; see OES §1092), the 'contamination' interpretation appears to be closer to the actual situation.

19 (25:9) *nyhtsumigæ* for *sufficiat* is corrected from *nyhtsumaþ*. The original *-aþ* is erased and *i* is added below *m* tucked into its last minim and *gæ* added after the erasure.

22 (25:10) *se dure* for *ianua*. DOE s.v. *duru* notes that it is used as masculine once in Ru1, apparently referring to this instance. See Introduction III.2.2.2.2 for further instances of the *se* form used with feminine nouns.

f. 42r

7 (25:15) *æfter his mægene* for *secundum propria uirtutem*. The gloss does not reflect the Latin fully, having no exact equivalent to *propria*; cf. WSCp *be hys agenum mægene* and Li *æfter agenlic ł syndrig mægn*.

8 (25:15) *foerdon* for *profectus est*. Note the unexpected use of the plural verb form for the Latin singular.

10 (25:17) *þe* for *autem* (omitted in WW). The use of *þe* for *autem*, which is not recorded elsewhere in Ru1, may be related to the fact that *autem* does not occur in the standard Vulgate.

14 (25:19) *monade rehtæs heo* for *possuit rationem cum eis*. See note to 18:23 for the collocation *manian (ge)rihtes*, where a Latin *cum*-phrase is glossed with a *mid*-phrase. In the present instance, the accusative *heo* is used.

15 (25:20) *brohte* for *obtullit. r* is written *in rasura.*

f. 42v

6 (25:25) *hæfęþ* for *habes* appears to be the present third person singular, where the second person singular is expected.

9 (25:27) *hwæt* is apparently an interjection. It is difficult to discern a word-for-word agreement, but the combination of the interjection and the adverb *þa* appears to translate *ergo* in this instance.

11 (25:27) *ofersceatta* for *ussura.* The noun (cf. BT s.v. *ofersceatt*) is a hapax legomenon. While WSCp has *þam gafole*, whose use as 'interest, usury' is shared by Ælfric (cf. DOE *gafol*, 4.a.), Li has another hapax legomenon *frico* (cf. DOE s.v. *frico*).

12 (25:28) *hæfð* for *habet.* McAllister reads *hæð* and Tamoto notes 'a space between "æ" and "ð"', where there is 'no trace' of *f*; however, there are parts of strokes visible that do suggest an *f.* The Surtees Society edition and Skeat do not indicate any uncertainty about the letter, simply reading *hæfð*. The current condition of the manuscript suggests that the loss occurred in modern times by the time McAllister used it.

12 (25:29) *æghwilc forþon hæbbende selleþ* for *omni enim habenti dabitur* fails to translate the passive voice of *dabitur* and accordingly *æghwilc* appears to be the nominative.

14 (25:29) *ꝥ him þynce ꝥ he hæbbe* for *quod habet* clearly reflects the standard Vulgate *quod uidetur habere*, with the expansion of the infinitive into a *þæt*-clause.

20 (25:32) *in tu* for *ab inuicem.* While both WSCp and Li use forms of *betweonan* (WSCp *he asyndrað hi hym betwynan*; Li *tosceades hia betuih*), Farman's gloss can be compared to Ælfric's *he toscæt hi on twa* in ÆCHom II, 7 [0075 (64.131)], based on the same Gospel passage.

f. 43r

13 (25:40) *anum þe læsesta þara broþre* for *uni ex minimis his fratribus.* Part of the gloss is written on erasure; the original reading cannot be retrieved. The Latin prepositional phrase is rendered into the partitive genitive; the function of *þe* may be compared with the possible instances of the indeclinable demonstrative *þe* discussed in Introduction III.2.2.3.

15 (25:41) *on þæm winstran halfe* for *a sinistris eius.* Here, as well as in Mk 1:45 (*æghwilcum halfe*), the noun *healf* is treated as masculine or neuter as against feminine elsewhere. See Introduction III.2.2.2.1.

16 (25:41) *þte wæs geiarward* for *quem praeparauit* (*qui praeparatus est* WW). The passive reflects the standard Vulgate reading. Note the inorganic *r* in *-ward.*

21 (25:44) *hiæ swilce* for *et ipsi.* There is erasure of ⁊ above *et*, apparently avoiding redundancy, as the sense of *et* is translated by *swilce* 'they, too'.

f. 43v

1 (25:44) *carcrænnæ* for *carcere* shows the metathesis of a post-vocalic /r/. See note to 10:31.

7 (26:2) This verse is the beginning of the passion narrative in Matthew. For the significance of the textual unit, see Introduction III.1.2.2. In the left-hand margin, there is a cross made by vertical and horizontal strokes, two for each arranged in parallel, written with dry-point, signalling the beginning of the passion. The Matthew, as well as Luke, passion narrative in the Rushworth manuscript is marked also with the so-called liturgical signs and additional punctuation, which had been added before the Old English gloss was written. The present edition reproduces the signs and punctuation in approximate positions. The signs used in the Rushworth manuscript are (1) a cross indicating the words of Christ and (2) a horizontal line (transcribed as /–/ in the edition) indicating the beginning of narrative passages. For the history and purposes of the signs, see Introduction II.2 and references cited there. For the corrections occurring in this section by an Anglo-Saxon hand that may be different from Farman, see Introduction III.1.3.2 (b) and Appendix II. It should also be kept in mind that Aldred's gloss bears similarity to Ru1 in this section, as discussed by Ross (1979a) and reviewed by Kotake (2012b). There are two independent Old English homilies that are effectively a translation of Matthew chapters 26–27 with some extra-biblical elements in them. The texts adopted by DOE (HomS18 and HomS19) are used for comparison in the following notes and references to these texts will be presented in a simplified manner, i.e., based on chapter and verse, though the DOE texts are numbered according to their own system. For these texts, see Introduction III.1.2.2. and also Kotake (2021).

eastran for *pascha*. Farman uses the weak form of *eastre*. DOE s.v. *eastre* notes that the nous is 'mainly f. wk. in West-Saxon' and 'mainly n. st. in Northumbrian'.

9 (26:3) *alduras sacerdas* for *principes sacerdotum*. Farman usually translates *princips sacerdotum* into the compound *ealdor-sacerd* with the first element having no case ending. The glossary treats this instance under the compound, because, if it is to be taken as two words, *sacerdas* is expected to be the genitive plural. Alternatively, it might be possible to read the two words as two independent nominative plural subjects, which, though not an accurate translation of the Latin, presents a smooth reading 'leaders, priests and the elders'. For a similar instance, see 26:59 and 27:62.

11 (26:4) *hy se hælend inwit noman* for *iesum dolo tenerent*. The gloss appears to lack grammatical precision, e.g., the use of the nominative *se hælend* for the accusative *iesum* and *inwit* without a case ending or preposition (cf. Li *hia ðone hælend mið inwite genome ł hia gehealdon*).

13 (26:5) *ungerec ł ungeþwære* for *tumultus*. The second gloss *ungeþwære* is elsewhere used as an adjective and its noun use is recorded only here (cf. BT s.v. *ungeþwære*).

13 (26:6) *miþ þy þonne þende* for *cum autem*. The conjunction *cum* appears to be translated redundantly by both *miþ þy* and *þende*. Li has simply *ðende ðonne*.

14 (26:7) *þa cwom to him an wif* for *accessit ad eum mulier*. The adverb *þa* has no equivalent word in the Latin; WSCp, HomS18 and HomS19 all begin the verse with *þa*.

15 (26:7) *stæna fullę* (cf. Li *stænna fulle*) for *alabastrum* (corrected apparently to *alabavstrum* in R with *v* written above the line between *a* and *s*, which WW reads *alabastrum*). Ru1's *stæna* and Li's *stænna* have been taken as forms of the adjective *stænen* 'made of stone, stony' (cf. BT *stænen*, III.). It is possible, however, that it is actually a weak feminine noun recorded only once elsewhere; see OED2 s.v. *stean*, n., which records the sole Old English instance from the Cleopatra glossary, *stænan* glossing *gallione* (for its medieval Latin meaning 'vessel', see OED2 s.v. *galleon*, n.). OED2's definition of *stean* 'A vessel for liquids' fits the context here and the form in both Ru1 and Li can be taken as the accusative singular with the usual loss of final *-n*. For the use of *fullę*, see note to 10:42.

18 (26:9) *beon beboht* for *uenundari*. There is erasure of *in* between *beon* and *beboht*.

in micel for *prætio magno* (*multo* WW). The standard Vulgate reading omits *prætio*, and Farman's gloss appears to reflect such a reading, having no equivalent to *prætio*. In contrast, Aldred supplies *pretio*, which is not in Y in the original state, and glosses it with *feh*. Liuzza (1994–2000: ii, 38) considers WSCp's *to myclum wurþe* as reflecting a reading with *praetio*.

22 (26:11) *ne* is erased above *non*, apparently to get the negative particle positioned next to the verb.

22 (26:12) *þas þonne sendendu smerenisse þis* for *haec autem mittens* (*mittens enim haec* WW) *ungentum hoc*. The Latin *haec* is the feminine nominative singular, as Li has *ðas ł ðios*, of which the second is truer to the Latin. Farman's gloss appears to show some confusion; rather clumsily, *þas smirenisse* may be read as the accusative object and *þis* as the neuter nominative singular referring to *wif.*

f. 44r

1 (26:12) *to bebyrgenne mec iarwede* for *ad sepeliendum me fecit.* The use of *gearwian* for *facere* is a contextual translation, which may be compared to WSCp *þæt ic wære gesmyryd to bebyrgynne* and contrasted with a more literal approach in Li *to bibyrgenne mec dyde.*

6 (26:15) *ic hine eow sellan* for *ego uobis tradam eum* (*eum* is cancelled by dots; *eum tradam* WW). While *eum* is cancelled in the Latin text, the gloss has *hine.* The apparently infinitive form *sellan* is used where a finite form is expected.

9 (26:17) *þara ðefra metta* for *azemorum. ðefra* is apparently the genitive plural form of the adjective *þeorf* 'unleavened' (cf. Li *ðorofra*), but the spelling lacks *r* in the root.

11 (26:18) *to hię* for *ei* (omitted in WW). There is erasure between the two Old English words, which is not legible. The gloss in its current state presents an unambiguous instance of '*to* + accusative'. See also note to 9:36 and Mitchell (OES §1215).

14 (26:19) *swa him bebead ł gesette heom se hælend* for *sicut praecipit illis iesus.* The Latin verb *praecipit* is provided with an alternative reading *ł constituit,* which is the standard Vulgate reading, and Farman's double gloss appears to reflect the two readings in the same order. Both *him* and *heom* are to be taken to translate *illis.*

15 (26:20) *þa efen þa cwom* for *uespere autem facto.* The Latin ablative absolute is rendered into a temporal clause introduced by the conjunction *þa.* Whereas the use of *cuman* fits the context and is probably idiomatic (cf. *æfen c(w)om* in poetry; see also OED3 s.v. *cuman,* v. III. 26.a.), the use of the verb to translate *fieri* is rare, as the present instance is listed by DOE s.v. *cuman* under 'K. glossing Latin words other than *venire* "to come" (rarely)'. DOE mistakenly reports in the citation that WSCp (and MS H) uses 'forms of *settan'* instead of Ru1's *cwom,* but the verb is *sittan* translating *discumbebat* (for R's *discubuit*); instead, it uses a prepositional phrase *On þam æfene sæt se Hælynd mid hys twelf leorningcnihtum æt gereorde.* WSCp uses *cuman* in Mk 14:17 in the same context: *Soðlice þa æfen com him twelfum mid him* (*uespere autem facto uenit cum duodecim* WW).

20 (26:23) The use of *parabside* 'dish' as a gloss can be compared with the fact that Farman left the Latin unglossed earlier. See note to 23:25. The use of the Old English demonstrative *þas* may imply that the word could be used as an Old English word.

f. 44v

4 (26:26) *his discilum* for *discipulis suis*. Note the unusual spelling *discilum* for a form of *discipul* in the gloss, which may in face have been simple error. There is no sign of abbreviation in this example; see note to line 13 below. See also note on the forms of this Latin-derived noun as an Old English word in 5:1.

7 (26:27) *drincaþ of þas* for *bibite ex hoc*. The gloss appears to show an example of '*of* + accusative', but the referent *cælic* is usually masculine (though once with a feminine demonstrative, *þeos cælic* in 26:42). It seems more likely that it shows the mixture of word-for-word translation of the Latin and the genitive object of *drincaþ* with *þas* being a variant of *þæs*. See also note to 25:8.

10 (26:29) *siðet* for *amodo*. As Campbell suggests in the *Addenda* to BT (s.v. *siþ*, adv.), this form may be understood as *sið ðæt* in a formation comparable to *siþþan*. While this interpretation is likely to be valid, it is possible that Farman did not understand the Old English phrase, given the spelling he uses here, and the impression is further reinforced by his use of *sie þæt* for the same Latin in 23:39. His gloss *æfter þisse* for *amodo* in 26:64, in contrast, is a straightforward gloss to the Latin. See also Roberts (1979: 132) for a similar discussion about *siþþam* (or *siþ þam*) in GuthA 136.

13 (26:31) *discp* with a suspension stroke above *cp* for *discipulis* is expanded in the edition to *discipulum*, with the Old English dative plural ending; cf. *discpl* with a suspension stroke above *cp* and a cross stroke over *l* in 28:8, where the dative plural is also expected. Lindsay (1915: 61) notes a variety of abbreviation of the word in the Latin manuscript tradition, and it is hardly possible to associate the form of abbreviation with a specific scribal background.

f. 45r

1 (26:36) *discipulis* and also *discipulos* in line 9, are left unglossed, apparently suggesting that Farman finds no need to supply a gloss as the Latin word itself can be used as a gloss. See note to 23:25 for a similar situation.

4 (26:37) *(beon…) in unbliðum mode* for *mestus esse*. The use of *mod* without any Latin equivalent to refer to a state of mind is probably a characteristic feature of Farman's language, as discussed in the note to 2:3. Li appears to take a similar approach, presumably affected by a shared source, though using an instrumental phrase (*unbliðe moede wosa*) rather than an *in*-phrase.

12 (26:41) *min gast* for *spiritus* is corrected from *se gast*, by dotting *se* below and adding *min* above. Although there is no reading with *meus* in

WW's apparatus, HomS19 has a comparable reading: *Min gast is swiðe fuus.*

14 (26:42) *þeos cælic* for *hic calix*. As noted in 26:27, *cælic* is used with the apparently feminine *þeos*, which may have been a variant of *þes*. See Introduction III.2.2.2.6.

17 (26:43) *wærun swiþe ahæfgad* for *erant … grauati*. There is no exact equivalent of *swiþe* in the Latin; both HomS18 (*wæron swiðe gehefegode*) and HomS19 (*hi wæron swiþe gehefgude*) use the adverb here, while WSCp and Li follow the Latin closely.

f. 45v

15 (26:53) *mæ þonne twælf þusend herigæs ængla* for *plus quam xii* (+ *milia* R[c]) *legiones angelorum*. The addition of *milia* by an Anglo-Saxon hand is not paralleled in the standard Vulgate text, while it is found in some of the manuscripts aligned to the mixed-Italian family; see Appendix II. HomS18 also reflects the non-Vulgate reading: *ma þonne twelf þusenda weroda engla on fultum to gefeohte.*

18 (26:55) *eoden ut* for *uenisti* appears to reflect the standard Vulgate reading *existis*.

19 (26:55) There is a dry-point addition of *nne* with a suspension stroke above the first *n* for *nonne* before *cotidie*. Farman apparently did not care to avoid it, writing *d-* of *dæghwæmlice* on the final *-e*. According to Fischer's collation (1988–91: i, 428), the reading with *nonne* is found in a few Breton manuscripts. This is one of the two dry-point corrections (excluding other kinds of marking as discussed in the note to 26:2) to the Latin text that the present editor has noticed in the Rushworth manuscript: the other is in Lk 2:25, the end of line 10, f. 90r, altering *timoratus* to *timens*, the latter reading found in, for instance, Codex Usserianus Primus.

f. 46r

2 (26:57) *þær þe* for *ubi*. Mitchell (OES §2456) notes that the combination is not common and occurs mostly in the early prose, including Bede and GD.

4 (26:58) *ingangande gesæt betwih mið þæm þægnum* for *ingressus intro sedebat cum ministris*. The space above *intro* is blank, but the sense is reflected by the *in*-prefix. In contrast, *betwih* has no clear Latin equivalent, and it may be read as an adverb intensifying the sense of 'among' of the prepositional phrase introduced by *mið*, though DOE s.v. *betweoh* does not record such collocation.

5 (26:59) *þa aldor þa sacerdæs* for *principes autem sacerdotum*. Although the two elements of the compound are separated by *þa* above *autem* as a result of following the Latin word order, the first element still lacks the case-ending, suggesting that the compound may underlie this example. As noted in 26:3, *þa aldor* and *þa sacerdæs* may be taken as two coordinate noun phrases.

6 (26:59) *gemot* for *concilium* is preceded by erasure, which is not legible, and is altered from *gemote*, by erasing the final *-e*.

10 (26:61) *þas tempel* for *hoc templum* (*hoc* omitted in WW). Because Old English *tempel* is historically neuter, *þas* may be plural as against the Latin singular form, but there is no clear reason for the use of plural here. It is probably another instance of historically wrong gender congruence, as discussed in Introduction III.2.2.2.7.

13 (26:63) *aldur sacerdæs* for *princeps sacerdotum*. See also *se aldur sacerdæs* for the same Latin in line 19. These two instances are probably better to be read as two words, because the compound would have the unaccountable *-æs* ending for the nominative singular. Instead, the ending is the genitive singular ending of the second word. The glossary nevertheless lists these instances under *ealdorsacerd*, as they are clearly comparable to the compound instances.

16 (26:64) *heom* for *ei* (*illi* WW). The apparently plural form is used for the Latin singular for no obvious reason.

18 (26:64) *on þa swiðran halfe* for *ad dexteram* (*a dexteris* WW). *on* is altered from *to*, by erasing *t* and adding *n*.

dei added after *uirtutis* by an Anglo-Saxon corrector. Although *dei* is a non-Vulgate reading, WSCp (*Godes mægenþrymmes*) and HomS18 (*Godes mægenes*), and probably HomS19 (*his fæder mægenþrimmes*), reflect the reading. See Appendix II and Liuzza (1994–2000: ii, 38) for Latin manuscripts with *dei*.

f. 46v

2 (26:67) *mid brade honde on his ondwliotu hine slogun* for *palmas in faciem eius* (*ei* WW) *dederunt*. Farman gives a free translation rather than restrained by the Latin as in Li *hondbreodo in onsione hine saldon*. Note especially the use of the *mid*-phrase for the Latin accusative and the choice of the verb *slogun*. WSCp has a very similar translation: *Sume hyne slogon on his ansyne mid hyra bradum handum*. For *brad hand* 'the palm of hand', see DOE s.v. *brad*, 8.

8 (26:71) *weron* is altered from *weran* by dotting *a* below and writing *o* above.

9 (26:71) *mid þæm hælend þone nazarenisco* for *cum iesu nazareno* presents a mixture of different cases for no obvious reasons.

13 (26:74) *ȝustriga* for *detestare*. As noted about the related noun in 24:15, the etymology of *andustrian* is unclear. See Ross (1979b: 498) and

Holthausen s.v. *and-ustrian*. Jordan (1906: 24) points out that both Li and Ru1 use the verb in this verse, but Li's *ad-* spelling instead of *and-* (*adustriga*) may point to Aldred's unfamiliarity with the word, if the spelling in Ru1, which also uses the noun form *ȷustrungæ*, is taken to be authentic.

15 (26:75) *ȷ þa gemunde petrus* for *et recordatus est petrus*. There is no exact equivalent to *þa* in the Latin, and accordingly Li reads simply *ȷ gemyste ł eftgemyndig wæs*. In contrast, all the prose versions, WSCp, HomS18 and HomS19 employ *þa* instead of *and* for *et*, presumably to emphasize the dramatic narrative sequence.

17 (26:75) There is erasure of *ut* before *gangende*. The cancellation was presumably prompted by the use of another *ut* for *foras*.

18 (27:1) *eodun* for *fecerunt* reflects the standard Vulgate reading *inierunt*.

21 (27:2) *pontiscan pylato þæm geroefæ* for *pontio pylato præsidi*. There is erasure of *þæ(m)* before *pontiscan*. The cancelled demonstrative is found in WSCp (*þam Pontiscean Pilate þam deman*), HomS18 (*ðam Pontiscan Pilate, þam gerefan*) and HomS19 (*þam Pontiscan Pilate þam gerefan*).

f. 47r

6 (27:5) *awyrgde hine* for *laqueo se suspendit*. Farman's gloss fails to reflect *laqueo* (cf. Li *mið sade hine awurigde*; WSCp *mid gryne hyne sylfne aheng*). Ru1 and Li share the use of *awyrgan* here as against *ahon* in WSCp, HomS18 and HomS19.

8 (27:6) *ne mot heo mon sende* for *non licet eos mitti* (corrected to *mittere eos* in R). The Latin passive infinitive is corrected to the active, and the gloss reflects the active voice of the infinitive by using the indefinite pronoun *mon* as a subject.

9 (27:7) *tigle ł lam wyrhte lond* for *agrum* (+ *figuli* by Farman). The double gloss produced by squeezing *ł lam* above the first gloss should be read as *tiglewyrhte ł lamwyrhte*. The first alternative is used in WSCp and HomS18, while Li has *lamwrihta ł smiðes*.

12 (27:8) The masculine accusative singular *þeosne*, which is the form used in the Vespasian Psalter, is used only in this example in Ru1. Vleeskruyer (1953: 140) notes that the form is 'primarily non-West-Saxon'.

12 (27:9) *gefyllad* for *inpletum* is preceded by erasure of *wa* or *wæ*, which was to be written above *est*, following the Latin word order.

f. 47v

1 (27:14) There is erasure of *swiþe* after *wundrade*, apparently to match the position of the adverb with its Latin equivalent.

1 (27:15) *on dæge þa heora symbel* for *per diem autem sollempnem*. Despite their positions being arranged according to the Latin equivalents, the compound *symbeldæg* is likely to underlie the gloss. Note especially the uninflected form *symbel* and the use of *heora*, which has no Latin equivalent, before the first element. Cf. WSCp *Hig hæfdon heom to gewunan to heora symbeldæge.*

10 (27:19) *nawiht þe siæ on þæm soþfæste gemænes* for *nihil tibi sit* (*sit* omitted in WW) *et iusto illi*. There is no equivalent for *gemænes* in the Latin, but it can be compared with WSCp *ne beo þe nan þing gemæne ongen þisne rihtwisan.*

16 (27:22) *be hælende þæm þe cwæden is crist* for *de iesu qui dicitur cristus.* There is erasure of *of* before *be*. The abbreviation *hæl* with a cross stroke on *l* is expanded to *hælend* in Skeat, McAllister and Tamoto, but the dative is more likely, as expanded in the edition, given the form of the relative pronoun. There is a caveat against too grammatical an approach, however, because Farman occasionally uses case-endingless forms for the dative, as noted in Introduction III.2.2.3.

20 (27:24) *ungereo* for *tumultus* is apparently a copying error for *ungerec*. While the transcription by Thwaites and Todhunter in Harley MS 3449, f. 76r and the Surtees Society edition reproduce the manuscript reading *ungereo*, all the modern editions after Skeat have *ungerec*, effectively incorporating a silent emendation. DOE Corpus adopts *ungereo*.

f. 48r

1 (27:25) *⁊ þa ⁊wyrdan eall ꝥ folc cwæþende* for *et respondens omnis populus* (+ *dicens* R[c]; cf. *dixit* WW). The form *⁊wyrdan* is probably the preterite plural; the subject is grammatically singular, but the referent may be taken as plural semantically. Thus, after a finite verb, the use of the participle *cwæþende* is fitting in the Old English syntax. In contrast, the addition of *dicens*, a reading not recorded elsewhere, leaves the Latin sentence without a finite verb. It is not inconceivable that *dicens* may be a back-translation from the gloss, because it cannot be ruled out that the Anglo-Saxon corrector active in the passion section, to whom the present edition attributes the addition, may in fact have been Farman.

4 (27:27) *þæs geroefe kęmpe* for *milites præsidis. geroefe* is written on erasure which appears to have started with *k[ ]m-*, suggesting a form of *kempa* (listed as *cempa* in the glossary). The word order in the current state reverses that of Latin, resulting in 'genitive + headword', though both words lack the final *-n* of weak noun declensions.

6 (27:28) *gærwende* for *exeuntes*. DOE s.v. *gyrwan* defines '3. glossing *exuere* in sense "to strip (a person of garments)"', citing only the present example (Li *gearwende* is treated as a form of *gearwian* classified to the same category without no other attestation). However, while the semantic development of the verb from 'to prepare' to 'to clothe' (DOE's category 2) is clear, the use of the same verb for the opposite action 'to strip' is hardly explicable. DOE fails to note that in 27:31 *exuerunt* is glossed by *ungeredun*, a form of *ungierwan* (in CH's spelling; BT s.v. *ungyrwan*); cf. Li *ongeredon*. This strongly suggests that *gærwende* here is likely to be an error for *ungærwende*, shared by Li presumably through a common source.

⁊ gærwende hine gegærelum reade ryfte ymbsaldun him. If the interpretation presented in the previous note is valid, *gegærelum*, though written above *calamidem*, should probably be read with the preceding portion as 'and stripping off [his] garments', because *calamidem* is properly translated into *ryfte* in the next line, which is also used, though in the unusual spelling *ryhte*, to translate the same Latin in 27:31.

7 (27:29) *widende* for *plectentes* is probably for *windende* from *windan* 'to plait'. There is erasure of *bęg* after *widende*, which appears to have been repositioned to match the Latin equivalent.

9 (27:29) *kneu* for *genu* is preceded by erasure of *g*.

10 (27:30) *spittende on him heor spaðl* for *expuentes in eum*. There is no clear equivalent for *heor* (for *heora*) *spaðl* in the Latin. The *sp-* alliteration may indicate some underlying collocation; there are several instances where *spatl* is used with *spiwan* instead of *spittan* in similar contexts, e.g., HomS 12 (A homily for the Second Sunday in Lent uniquely preserved in Oxford, Bod.L., Hatton MSS 113 and 114; Ker no. 331, art. 44) [0002 (5)] *hi hine slogon mid bradum handum on his neb and hi mid heora spatlum spiwon on his andwlitan*. For the first half of the citation, see also note to 26:67.

12 (27:31) *ðy ryhte* for *calamidem*. Skeat and Tamoto print *ðy-ryhte* with a hyphen and McAllister as one word. As discussed in the note to 27:28, if *ryhte* is taken as a variant spelling of *ryft(e)*, *ðy* is the neuter instrumental singular of the demonstrative *se*. Confusion between *f* and *h* is unlikely both phonologically and palaeographically, but the existence of another word *riht* may have contributed to the error.

13 (27:31) *his agene wede* for *uestimentis eius*. The use of *agen* without any Latin equivalent can be compared with WSCp *mid hys agenum reafe*, HomS18 *his ægenum hrægle* and HomS19 *his agenum hrægle*. The morphological form of *agene* is not clear; with *wede* being historically feminine, it may be another example of unhistorical gender congruence, if it is not an error for *agenre* or a rare instance of the weak form of the adjective with loss of *-n*.

18 (27:33) *heafodpanne stouw stede* for *caluariae locus. stouwe* and *stede* appear to form a double gloss without a *ł* sign, which Skeat supplies in square brackets; cf. Li *heafudponnes styd ł stowa*. Skeat also supplies a hyphen in *heafodpanne-stouw*, apparently based on the lack of the *-es* ending that occurs in Li. However, the noun is usually weak feminine (DOE s.v. *heafodpanne*) and Ru1's spelling can be taken as the genitive singular with the loss of *-n*.

f. 48v

1 (27:37) The original reading *hæc (est)*, which is corrected to *hic (est)*, is redundant, as *hic est* follows in the next line. The gloss *þas* appears to be confused with this corrupted Latin reading.

5 (27:40) The gloss in the verse clearly reflects the standard Vulgate reading. Note the unglossed *ua* (omitted in WW) and the use of the third person singular verb forms, *brecep* and *æft getimbrað*, for *distruebas* (*destruit* WW) and *reaedificabas* (*reaedificat* WW).

8 (27:41) *þa aldursacerdun* for *principes sacerdotum* has the unexpected ending *-un* for the nominative plural.

16 (27:45) *geþriostra wyrdun* for *tenebræ factae sunt*. The first *r* of *geþriostra* is inorganic. The Old English noun *þeostru* is not used with *ge-* elsewhere, and Campbell includes the headword *geþeostru* in BT in his *Addenda*, referring to the present instance. Given the rarity of the prefixed noun, one may be tempted to assume that it may have been a copying error for a past participle form; cf. Li (Mk 13:24) *sunna bið geðiostrod* for *sol contenebrabitur*.

17 (27:45) *ealle middangeard* for *uniuersam terram. middangeard* is written as *middang* with a suspension stroke above *g* (also in 25:34 for the genitive and dative in 18:7 and 26:14). Here, the case of the masculine noun can be either accusative or dative governed by *ofer*, but *ealle* would lack concord in either case. Note that *terra* is usually glossed with the feminine *eorþe* in Ru1 while *middangeard* is most frequently used for *mundus*.

19 (27:46) The two abbreviations, *in gc* and *in lat* in the following line, both with a suspension stroke written above, are expanded to *in grecisc* and *in latin*, respectively, although it is not entirely clear whether they are intended as abbreviations of Old English or Latin. Cf. Robinson (1994) for the use of Latin for Old English. The *gc* abbreviation is not recorded by Lindsay (1915: 427) from the Latin tradition (cf. *g*, *gr*, *gre*, *grc*); when it is taken as an Old English word, it should be expanded to *in grecisc* (see DOE s.v. *grecisc*, 2.b). The *lat* abbreviation is ubiquitous in the Latin tradition; the use of *t* in *lat* may point to the Latin reading, as against *d* as in *læden* in Old English (cf. OED2 s.v. *leden*); however, Aldred uses the *latin* spelling in his gloss (Mk 5:41 *ꝥ is getrahtad in latin*).

f. 49r

3 (27:49) *hwute geseon* for *uideamus*. *hwute* is the only instance of inorganic *h* inserted before *w* in Ru1, while *h* is often dropped in the initial *hw-* cluster.

4 (27:49) R has an interpolation based on Jn 19:34 in this verse, which is not glossed. No other translations or homilies based on the Matthew passion include the account. See Metzger (1994: 59) for textual notes and WW's apparatus for the Latin manuscripts that include the interpolation.

7 (27:50) *asende his gast* for *emissit spiritum*. Because no Latin variant that would account for *his* is recorded in WW or *Itala*, *his* is likely to have been a result of contextual translation. It is shared by WSCp and HomS18, but not Li.

9 (27:51) *stanes brustæn* for *petræ scise sunt*. The use of an intransitive verb instead of the passive structure is paralleled in WSCp *stanas toburston*. DOE s.v. *berstan* notes that *brustæn* is the only example of the verb without metathesis. It is uncertain whether it is due to a simple error or is affected by other languages that do not show metathesis for the word. See OED2 s.v. *burst*, v. for the etymology.

13 (27:53) *monigvm* for *multis* is altered from *monige*, by dotting *e* below and adding *vm* above.

15 (27:54) For the use of *þę̨r*, see note to 18:31.

20 (27:56) *sunena* for *filiorum* shows the genitive plural form of the weak declension. DOE Corpus finds only five instances of the spelling *sunena*, of which two are from Ru1 and WSCp in this verse. Two of the other three occur in the Old English Heptateuch (Gen and Lev) and the other in Sol. See also Hogg and Fulk (2011: §3.121).

21 (27:57) *æfenne* for *sero* is preceded by an erased *h*.

f. 49v

5 (27:60) *ꝥte* for *quod*, referring to the feminine *byrgenne*, may be an instance of *þæt* used with non-neuter nouns, for which see Introduction III.2.2.2.5, unless it is due to the influence of the gender of the Latin lemma.

6 (27:60) *towælede* for *aduoluit*. *towyltan*, which Ross (1979b) regards as an element-for-element calque of the Latin verb, is not recorded elsewhere. Cf. DOE s.v. *a-wyltan*, which Farman uses in 28:2, glossing *reuoluit*.

et is corrected to *ab* rather than *ad* as in WW. Its gloss *to* appears to reflect the standard Vulgate reading.

7 (27:61) *þa* for *autem* is preceded by another *þa* erased above *-at* of *erat*, presumably to match the position of the gloss to the corresponding Latin.

9 (27:62) *þa oþer dæg* for *altera autem die*. Another *þa* is erased above *-m* of *autem*, probably because *autem* is already translated with the initial *þa*. *oþer dæg* appears to lack a case ending, obscuring its intended function.

11 (27:62) *to pilatum* for *ad pylatum* is written with a suspension mark above *u*, which is expanded to *pilatum* as in Skeat. Note, however, in line 2, the same Latin is glossed as *to pilatus*.

11 (27:63) *gemynest þu* for *rememorati sumus*. While there are no Latin variant readings recorded that would account for the use of the second person singular in the gloss, the word order and the context seem to suggest that Farman's gloss is intended as a question 'Do you remember…?' A similar translation is adopted in HomS19 *Wæs þu gemindig, lareow…*

12 (27:63) *forlænd* for *seductor* is corrected from *forlærd*, by erasing the descender of *r*. Skeat, Tamoto and DOE s.v. *forlæran*, 1.a. all read *forlærd*, while McAllister has *forlænd*. The erasure of the descender is clearly visible and unlikely to be accidental. The transcription by Thwaites and Todhunter in Harley MS 3449, f. 78r also reads *forlænd*. DOE points out the uncertainty about the use of the seemingly past participle form *forlærd* for the sense 'seducer' instead of 'seduced'. The corrected form is probably still to be taken as a form of *forlæran*, but as DOE suggests, it was probably 'miswritten for otherwise unattested **forlærend*'.

15 (27:64) *dicent* is corrected to *dicant* by writing *a* above *e* with no cancellation marked. WW's apparatus and Tamoto report *dicunt* as the corrected reading, but the added letter is more likely to be an open *a*, as reported by Skeat and McAllister.

18 (27:66) There is erasure of *ge healdadun* between *heordum* and *geoldun*. The glossary lists the latter under *gehealdan*, following DOE (s.v. *gehealdan*, A.2.a.).

20 (28:1) *restedagas* for *sabbati* is altered from *restedægas* by erasing the raised (for ligaturing) top loop of the *æ*.

f. 50r

12 (28:7) *et ecce dixi uobis*. *et* is crossed out by three diagonal strokes in ink and *dixi* is altered to *p(re)dixi* by Farman by inserting the usual abbreviation for *pre* (*p* with a suspension mark above). Presumably prior to these alterations, the entire phrase had been crossed out by dry-point. Farman's gloss *henu swa ic foresægde* reflects the corrected reading, having no equivalent to the cancelled *et* and using *fore-* for the added *pre-*. The use of *swa* in the gloss may reflect a Latin variant reading with *sicut* found in some manuscripts aligned to the mixed-Irish family. For the dry-point cancellation, it may be compared with the Echternach Gospels where the entire phrase is reported to be missing by WW.

14 (28:8) There is uncertainty about how to expand *discpl.* The syntax would require a dative plural form, but it cannot be straightforwardly expanded to *discipulum*, because *discipulas* (line 10 above) and the apparently imperfect *discilum* (in 26:26) are used where the dative plural is expected. The edition follows Skeat in expanding it to *discipulas*, but other possibilities should not be ruled out.

21 (28:11) *þa aldursacerdum* for *principibus sacerdotum.* For the use of *þa* with the dative plural, see note to 21:12.

eall ꝥ þe þær gedoen werun for *omnia quae facta fuerant.* For the use of *þær*, see note 18:31.

f. 50v

f. 50v has a border surrounding the text in red as on ff. 1v–3r.

1 (28:12) *geþæhtunge ineoden onfengon* for *consilio accepto.* The two Old English verbs appear to form a double gloss without a *ł* sign. While *onfengon* clearly agrees with *accepto*, the use of *ingan* can be compared to 27:7, where *consilio … initio* is glossed with to *geþæhtunge … eodun.*

5 (28:14) *getæceþ ł scyaþ* for *suadebimus.* For the second gloss, see BT s.v. *scyan*, which Waite (1984: ii, 556) suggests may be Anglian, reporting that Jackson J. Campbell regards the verb as 'obsolete in late WS' in his dissertation (see note to 9:30 for the dissertation).

gedoaþ for *faciamus* is altered from *gedoeþ*, by dotting *e* below and writing *a* above.

14 (28:19) *ðeode* for *gentes* has a space between *o* and *d*, where a trace of a vertical stroke with ascender is visible.

16 (28:20) *ic bebead* for *mandaui* is followed by erasure of *eow*, which is written again above *uobis* in the next line.

19 (Mt Explicit) The use of *finit*, instead of *explicit*, is generally a feature of Irish manuscripts. The Rushworth Gospels uses also *explicit* in Luke. For details, see Lindsay (1923: 5–10).

Bottom of the bordered space (Farman's colophon) As noted in Introduction III.3, the name is spelled with the *man* rune as *Farᛗ*, which is the only use of runes in the manuscript.

presbyter is abbreviated as *pbr* with a cross stroke through the ascender of *b*. This type of abbreviation is recorded in the Latin tradition (see Lindsay 1915: 436–37); its use in Old English contexts may deserve scrutiny. See also Robinson (1994: 163).

potest is written with *po-* rather than *pot-* followed by the usual abbreviation of *est*.

f. 51r

There is an added drawing of a portrait of St Mark, for which two descriptions available differ significantly in their implications. Alexander (1978: no. 54) attributes it to 'a later, (?) 12th-century hand' and notes that it 'differ[s] slightly from' the Mark portrait on f. 51v, with a reference to his no. 36, the Barberini Gospels, whose Mark portrait is included as fig. 177 in his *Survey*. In contrast, Doane in the description of the Rushworth Gospels in the Anglo-Saxon Manuscripts in Microfiche Facsimile series (Liuzza and Doane 1995: 22) states that the 'added portrait of Mark (f. 51r) has writing in the book that is the same hand and ink as the gloss of Mark and is simply a tracing with "Italian" stylistic traits of the earlier "Irish" portrait on the other side of the leaf'. Doane lacks precision in saying 'the gloss of Mark', as both Farman and Owun wrote the gloss there, but the writing is similar to that of Farman. The most crucial difference in the two interpretations is the chronology; if the writing is indeed Farman's, the portrait must have been added by the time he was working on his gloss. This portrait clearly awaits further scrutiny of art-historians.

f. 51v

There is the original portrait of St Mark. The fullest description of the Evangelist portraits in the Rushworth Gospels remains that of Alexander (1978: no. 54) with a list of references. A short description in the catalogue from the British Library's recent exhibition (Breay and Story 2018: no. 75) does not add to such seminal studies as Pächt and Alexander (1973: no. 1269), Alexander (1978: no. 54) and Watson (1984: no. 43). No trace of the glossators' activity can be found on the page.

f. 52r

This folio is the Mark Incipit page, containing the incipit as well as the first verse and part of the second verse of the Gospel according to Mark. Unlike the Matthew Incipit page, the short incipit written in red at the top of the page is not glossed. See note to the Matthew incipit for related references, especially Farr (2007).

8 (Mk 1:1) For *onfruma* for *initium*, see note to 24:8.

f. 52v

ff. 52v and 53r have a border surrounding the text in red and green respectively.

3 (Mk 1:2) *weg þinre* for *uiam tuam*. See Introduction III.2.2.2.6 for discussion of unhistorical gender congruence.

6 (Mk 1:6) *forgefnisse* for *remisionem* is one of the examples in which Farman's lexical preference changes from Matthew, where *forlætness* and its verb *forlætan* are used consistently. Instead of making comments on all such changes, the glossary notes the words that occur only in Mark. See the introductory comments in the glossary.

11 (Mk 1:6) *gegerelad ł gewedad* for *uestitus*. As DOE s.v. *gegyrelod* suggests, the first gloss is probably a past participle form of 'otherwise unattested wk. 2 vb. **(ge)gyrelian*'. Apart from Ru1 and Li, the verb is found only once in PsGlI, where the Lambeth Psalter glossator uniquely uses *gegerlad* for *indutus* (for the choices of the other versions, see DOE's citation).

12 (Mk 1:6) *lendenu* for *lumbos* is a lexical choice disagreeing with Li *sido*. See note to 3:4 on the word used by Farman.

waldstapan ł loppestra for *locustas*. While the second gloss agrees with Li *lopestro*, the first gloss is a hapax legomenon. Farman uses *gærshoppa* in Matthew (3:4). Although both words in the double gloss are taken as accusative plural by Schulte, they may possibly be genitive (*waldstapan* being possibly singular), as the verb *brucan* is often used with a genitive object.

wuduhuniges þ wæxeþ on wudubendum for *mel siluestræ* is a rare case of an explanatory gloss being shared with Aldred, whose gloss reads *wudu hunig þ wæxes on wudu binde*. The genitive *wuduhuniges* is apparently required by the verb *brucan*, despite some uncertainties noted below. See also note to 3:4. Boyd (1975: 37–38) suggests attributing Aldred's explanatory gloss to Pseudo-Jerome's remark in his *Commentarius in Evangelium secundum Marcum*.

13 (Mk 1:6) *⁊ þ brucende wæs* for *ædebat*. The function of *⁊ þ*, written protruding to the left, is unclear, because the objects of *brucan* are already expressed in the previous line, presumably in the genitive forms.

dom after *cymeþ* does not make any sense, unless it is thought to be copied erroneously from something similar to the second gloss in Li *cymes ł cwom*.

15 (Mk 1:7) *forehlutende* for *procumbens*. See DOE s.v. *fore-lutan*, which is recorded only in this verse in Ru1 and Li, both sharing the inorganic *h*.

gescoas his for *calciamentorum eius*. *gescoas* is preceded by erasure *his*, suggesting that Farman first intended to employ the 'possessive +

headword' order. The spelling of *gescoas* where the genitive plural is expected is not explicable; cf. Li *scoe his*.

17 (Mk 1:8) The marginal addition to supply the defective Latin differs from the standard Vulgate, including Y, which wants *in* for Farman's *uos in spiritu sancto*. See Appendix I for the readings with *in*.

20 (Mk 1:10) *onstyde* for *statim* disagrees with Li *sona* and is not recorded elsewhere; cf. *instyde*, which occurs five times exclusively in Ru1 (see DOE s.v. *in-styde*).

f. 53r

1 (Mk 1:10) Farman's addition of *sanctum* after *spiritum* is not paralleled in WW or Y. Its gloss *gastes halga* has an inexplicable grammatical form, where the accusative singular is expected. WSCp *haligne gast* also appears to reflect the reading with *sanctum*. See Liuzza (1994–2000: ii, 76–77).

2 (Mk 1:10) *ofdunestigende* for *discendentem* is here treated as a single word. Searches through DOE Corpus show that the same combination is treated variously in different texts; e.g., Skeat transcribes the present instance as three separate words *of dune stigende*, while there are a number of instances of *ofdune (ge)stigan* and several of *ofdunestigan*.

4 (Mk 1:11) *ðe* for *te*. Tamoto reports that the manuscript has *ða* and Skeat's *ðe* is an emendation. DOE Corpus also reads *ða*. However, the manuscript has *ðe* with the *e* somewhat ill-formed with the top stroke, or hook, being small, and the tongue not touching the back of the letter, leaving some space in the inner part of the letter. Yet, it is clearly intended as an *e*, as Skeat and McAllister read.

5 (Mk 1:12) *expulit* is likely to have been corrected from *expellit*. The trace of the first *l* is still legible, but the original vowel that precedes the trace is not legible due to the overwriting.

7 (Mk 1:13) There is erasure of another *mið* before *mið* for *cum*, apparently to match the position of the gloss to its Latin equivalent.

wildedeorum for *bestis* is treated as a compound as against *wilde deorum* in Skeat, McAllister and Tamoto. Although forms without the vowel after the first element (cf. BT *wilddeor*, *wildeor*) are more frequent, BT also has *wildedeor* as a separate headword and DOE Corpus finds several instances with medial *-e-* treated as a compound.

10 (Mk 1:14) For *godspelles*, see note to 4:23.

rice for *regni* is written partially on erasure, whose original reading is illegible apart from *g* at the end of the erasure.

12 (Mk 1:15) *godspell* for *euangelio* is altered from *godspelles* by erasing the *-es* ending.

13 (Mk 1:16) *simonem ꝥ is petrus* for *simonem*. The brief explanatory note is not found in Li. Farman appears to have wanted to emphasize the identification; see similar instances in Mk1:29 and 30.

16 (Mk 1:17) *me* for *me* is altered from *mec* by erasing *c*.

f. 53v

1 (Mk 1:20) *sona ł ðariht* for *statim*. The second gloss is not in Li. Following BT s.v. *þærrihte*, under which the present instance is listed, the glossary regards *ðariht* as a variant form of *þærrihte*.

2 (Mk 1:20) *mið ðy forlet fæder his* for *relicto patre suo*. The use of the singular forms, *forlet* and *his*, is not an accurate translation of the Latin in the context, but it is shared by Li.

hyremonnum for *mercinaris* disagrees with Li *celmertmonnum*. While the latter is found in Li and Ru2 (see DOE s.v. *celmert-mann*), the word employed by Farman (DOE s.v. *hyr-mann*[2]) is also found in Ælfric's texts.

5 (Mk 1:22) *swigadun ł stylton* for *stupebant* is discussed by Ross (1979a: 195) as an important piece of evidence that 'shows that Aldred must be influencing Farman and not vice versa', because of the only occurrence of the second verb in Ru1, which is frequently used in Li. Kotake (2012b) reviews Ross's argument for direct copying between the two glosses; see also Introduction III.1.2.

6 (Mk 1:22) *hæ mæhte* for *potestatem*. While McAllister prints it as two words, Skeat and Tamoto read *hæmæhte*, a reading adopted also by DOE, which lists it under *heah-miht*. Kuhn (1945: 661) compares the *hæ-* spelling of the first element with Farman's *þæh* for *þeah*. While some confusion must have been involved to introduce the *æ* spelling and to cause the lack of word division in the manuscript, the intended reading appears to have been *he mæhte* as in Li (*he mæht*), given the clause initial position where a pronominal subject is often supplied. Farman consistently translates *potestas* by *miht* and there appears to be no reason to differentiate the present instance.

8 (Mk 1:23) *oft cleopade* for *exclamauit*. The use of *oft* for the prefix *ex-* may simply be an error for *of*; see Mk 1:26.

10 (Mk 1:24) *to losane ł lorene* for *perdere*. While the first gloss appears to be the inflected infinitive of *losian*, the second gloss presents a crux. It is likely to be related to the neuter noun *lor*, which Farman uses in Matthew as *to lore weorþan* in glossing *perire*, but the intended form of the spelling *lorene* is not clear. Li has *losige ł losane*.

hwæt þu þu eart for *quis sis* (corrected to *es* by Farman; *qui sis* WW). The Latin correction to *quis es* by Farman brings the R text identical with Y, but it cannot be used as evidence for direct copying from the Lindisfarne Gospels, because the reading with *es* is recorded in multiple manuscripts.

The repetition of *þu* in the gloss appears to have been dittography caused by writing, respectively, *hwæt þu* above *quis* and *þu eart* above *es.*

17 (Mk 1:28) *sona ł instyde ł ræþe* for *statim.* Of the triple glosses, the last agrees with Li *hraðe.* As noted in Mk 1:10, *instyde* is found only in Ru1.

21 (Mk 1:30) *feferdrifende* for *febricitans* disagrees with Li *febrende wæs.* Skeat and Tamoto read *fefer drifende* as two words, while McAllister treats it as an otherwise unrecorded compound; DOE has no entry for the compound. Basing his analysis on McAllister's text, Ross (1979b: 497) compares the second element with one of the senses recorded for Middle English *driven* 'to afflict, torment' (MED s.v. *driven* b, 8b(b)). In addition, it must be remembered that both *drif* (8:15) and *gedrif* (Mk 1:31) are used by Farman in the sense 'fever'.

f. 54r

1 (Mk 1:31) *forlet hio hal from ridesohte ł gedrif* for *dimisit eam febris.* While both Ru1 and Li translate *dimittere* by supplying *hal from* (Li *forleort hia hal from februm*), their choice of the words for 'fever' differs. For Farman's second gloss, see DOE s.v. *gedrif.* The first element of the first gloss *ridesohte* is apparently *hriþ* 'fever', for which DOE s.v. *hriþ* notes three instances in Old English (see also *hriþ-adl*). The second element can probably be compared with *suht* 'disease', occurring only in GenB 472, in the phrase *ne suht sware,* which Doane (1991: 279) considers to be Old Saxon. As Doane reports, BT considers that Farman's compound may be borrowed from Old Norse *riðusott,* but Ross (1979b: 497, fn.4) disagrees with the argument.

3 (Mk 1:32) After *eum,* there is the Latin addition *et erat* with its gloss *⁊ wæs,* both of which are now erased. The Latin addition was probably by Farman, though it cannot be confirmed due to the erasure. The correction was first made apparently because *omnes* was mistaken for *omnis* in the next verse, which is preceded by *et erat.*

8 (Mk 1:35) *on æringe* for *diluculo.* Li has *on æring* and also uses the word in Mk 13:35 (*on æring* for *mane*), where Ru2 has *on merne.* The only other occurrence is in Jul 160. See DOE s.v. *æring.*

9 (Mk 1:35) *stede* is altered from *styde* by writing *e* above *y* with no sign of cancellation.

12 (Mk 1:38) The Latin text had originally the defective *ciuitatesunt,* written as if one word. It had been corrected to the expected *ciuitates ut,* by crossing out the *-n-* of *-unt,* but it was further corrected by adding *ut* between the lines. The latter correction appears to have been by Farman who also wrote the gloss *ꝥte* with the Latin.

13 (Mk 1:38) *⁊ to* for *ad.* The use of *⁊* here could be seen as a rare indication that there may have been direct relationship between the

Rushworth and Lindisfarne Gospels, the latter of which has *et* instead of *ad* here, a reading not otherwise recorded in WW (glossed by Aldred as ⁊ *to*). One may argue that ⁊, for which there is no equivalent word in R, could have been derived from *et* in Y. However, its significance will probably be dwarfed by the great number of instances of Farman's use of ⁊ even without support of Latin as recorded in the glossary.

15 (Mk 1:40) *mid cneu begende ł beginge* for *genu flexu*. The second gloss can be compared with Li *cnewbeging*, which is taken as a compound by DOE s.v. *cneow-biging*, recorded three times in Old English (not including the instance in Ru1; the other two instances are in RegCGl).

22 (Mk 1:44) *clænsunge* for *emundatione* is altered to *clænsunga*, by writing *a* above *e* with no sign of cancellation.

f. 54v

3 (Mk 1:45) *ingangan ł ineode* for *introire*. While the form of the second gloss is not expected as a gloss to the Latin infinitive (cf. Li *ingeonga ł incuma*), the following infinitive *esse* is also glossed with an apparently finite form *wære*. Li's gloss to *esse* reads *wæs ꝥ wære*, showing comparable uncertainty.

5 (Mk 1:45) *æghwonan from æghwilcum halfe* for *undique* is probably to be treated as a double gloss with a *ł* sign missing, as in Li *eghuona ł from halfe gehuelc*. Note that the masculine/neuter singular form *æghwilcum* is used with the historically feminine *halfe*.

7 (Mk 2:2) *to dore ł to gete* for *ad ianuam*. *gete* is altered from *gæte* by writing *e* above *æ* with no sign of cancellation. Li has simply *to duru*.

8 (Mk 2:3) *toferende ł brengende* for *ferentes*. *brengende* is altered from *bringende* by writing *e* above *i* with no sign of cancellation. Li also uses *brengan* in the second gloss: *feredon ł brengende*.

11 (Mk 2:4) *ꝥ hus ł þa bere* for *tectum*. The second gloss, from *bær* 'bed', does not translate the sense of *tectum* (cf. Li *ꝥ hus*; Farman uses *þæc* for *tectum* in Matthew). It may have been a misplaced gloss for *grabattum*, as found in the next line, though it is not clear how such confusion could arise.

14 (Mk 2:5) After *peccata*, Farman supplies *tua* with its gloss *þine*, a reading not found in the standard Vulgate. See Appendix I for the manuscripts with the reading.

16 (Mk 2:6) *heortum heortum* for *cordibus suis*. The second *heortum* was probably written in error for *heora*; cf. Li *heartum hiora*.

22 (Mk 2:10) *witud* for *autem* lacks any sign of abbreviation.

f. 55r

6 (Mk 2:12) *þte hia næfre þus ł swilc ne gesegun* for *quia numquam sic uidimus*. The use of *hia* as the subject is probably a translation error. Aldred appears not to share the same error in his gloss *þte næfra ðus ł sua we gesegon*, but there is erasure, which is illegible, between *þte* and *næfra* in the manuscript (f. 98rb, 7).

7 (Mk 2:13) *rursus* is corrected to *rursum* by Farman who wrote *m* above *s* with no sign of cancellation. The corrected reading is attested by only one of the manuscripts examined by WW. See Appendix I.

omnis quæ is for *omnisque*; similarly, Y has *omnis quae*. While Aldred, rendering it by *⁊ all*, appears to understand the Latin correctly despite the defective Latin, Farman's *eall þa* is a mechanical translation of the same Latin, apparently taking *quæ* as a form of the relative pronoun.

9 (Mk 2:14) *to geafolmonunge* for *ad telonum*, which is corrected to *theloneum* by Farman (for the manuscripts having the *th-* spelling, see Appendix I). Farman's compound is a hapax legomenon (see DOE s.v. *gafol-manung*); it can be compared to *gæflaes monunge* for the same Latin in 9:9. Aldred leaves the Latin word unglossed here as well as in the Matthew example.

10 (Mk 2:14) *folgam ł fylge me* for *sequere me*. The form of the first gloss is not explicable unless it is taken as an error for *folga me*. Li here reads *soec mec ł fylg me*.

12 (Mk 2:15) *openlice synnige ł hehsunne* for *puplicani*. Neither of the double glosses agree with Li *bærsynnigum*, which is used only in Li and Ru2; see DOE s.v. *bærsynnig*. The first gloss in fact can be seen as representing the etymology of *bærsynnig*. The second gloss is a hapax legomenon, though its literal sense '[one who is] highly sinful' is obvious; see DOE s.v. *heahsunn*. This double gloss is discussed in Kotake (2017: 86), where I mistakenly reported *synninge* instead of the correct *synnige*; the same error occurs in DOE Corpus.

f. 162r

Farman glossed the first three verses of Chapter 18 of John's Gospel, where, as noted by Ker, Owun added the six words which are given in bold face in the present edition. Owun supplied glosses for the space left blank above Latin words, even for those that were glossed properly in a position deviating from the Latin equivalent; in fact, five out of the six words (i.e., apart from *brondum*) are therefore redundant; see Introduction III.2.4.

It has not been discussed why Farman's hand reappears in this section, and it is impossible to find an absolute answer to the question. However, it should be pointed out that Jn 18:1 is the beginning of the Good Friday pericope, dealing with the Passion narrative. For an Old English example, see Scragg (1992: 1–47). Given the special nature of Farman's gloss and also the Latin text in the Matthew passion, the connection may have led him to the related passage. The Gospel Harmony of Tatian combines Jn 18:1–2 with Mt 26:36; see Ranke (1868: 146) for an edition of the Latin version in Fulda, Hochschule- und Landesbibliothek, Bonifatianus 1 and Sievers (1892: 250) for the Latin and Old High German versions in St Gall, Stiftsbibliothek 56.

4 (Jn 18:1) *ofer þah hlynne* for *trans torrentem*. *þah* is probably to be taken as the feminine accusative of the demonstrative *se*, with an inorganic *h* inserted, presumably affected by the following word. Both DOE s.v. *hlynn*[2] and OED2 s.v. *linn*, n.[1] suggest the possible connection of the hapax legomenon *hlynn* with the masculine noun *hlynn* 'sound, noise', though the semantic connection is not entirely clear. Ru1's instance is an isolated attestation in OED2, where all other citations are from the sixteenth century and later. It also suggests the influence of Celtic words such as Gaelic *linne* and Irish *linn*, but it is not clear how far they are relevant to the present instance. Li has a double gloss *þæt burna ł .i. uinterburna*; the second gloss appears to be an explanatory gloss whose intention is not clear. The word is not recorded elsewhere other than as place names recorded in charters.

fæger gewyrtun for *hortus*. The adjective *fæger* is clearly an extra-biblical element.

7 (Jn 18:2) Owun's *ðer* for *illuc* is redundant, because Farman had already translated the Latin with *þider* in the previous line.

9 (Jn 18:3) *brondum* for *faucibus* is the only substantial addition by Owun in this section and therefore should be taken as part of Ru2 rather than Ru1, agreeing with Li *brondum*. DOE s.v. *brand*, 2a, cites only these Li and Ru2 examples as referring specifically to 'torch'. Latin *fax* does not occur elsewhere in the section which Farman glossed.

GLOSSARY

The inconsistent spellings of Ru1 as discussed in the Introduction force a compromised approach to the choice of headwords. For the sake of consistency and ease of consultation of major dictionaries, the present glossary adopts headwords of DOE (for A–I) and CH. For this reason, *o* before nasal, for example, appears as *a* in the glossary, despite the predominance of *o* in the text. This approach must result in the undesirable situation where forms adopted as a headword never occur in Ru1, but cross-references are supplied to facilitate the use of the glossary. Forms with the *ge-* prefix are grouped under separate headings, which follow the unprefixed ones.

The words that occur only in Mark are marked with [MK] before the headword. Hapax legomena are marked with † and the words that occur in multiple instances in Ru1 but do not occur elsewhere with (†). The corresponding headword in OED, when available, is given in square brackets at the end of each entry (when the relevant entry is not updated for OED3 as of the time of finalizing the glossary in several months up to August 2022, the headword is preceded by 'OED2').

Only chapter and verse numbers are quoted for Matthew examples; Mark instances are marked by Mk, followed by chapter and verse numbers. In each entry, citations are arranged according to Latin equivalents, which are presented by the order of frequency (and, when occurring at similar frequency, that of alphabet). When Old English words are used without exact Latin equivalents, they are listed under NL. Conventional abbreviations are used in providing grammatical information; note the use of the Roman numerals for strong verb classes and Arabic for weak.

a *adv.* 'always' SEMPER ~ 18:10, 26:11 (*bis*) [o, *adv.*]

abel *prop.n.* *gs.* **abeles** 23:35

abelgan *v.III* 'offend, anger' INDIGNARE *pp.p.* **abolgenne** 20:24, 21:15 [abelghe, *v*]

abidan *v.I* 'await' SINERE *imp.s.* **abid** 7:4 (margin), 27:49 || SUSTINERE *imp.p.* **abidęþ** 26:38 [abide, *v.*]

abiddan *v.V* 'ask for, request' PETERE *subj.pt.3p.* **abeden** 27:20

abraham *prop.n.* ~ *as.* 3:9, 8:11; *gs.* **abrahames** 1:1, 22:32; *ds.* **abrahame** 1:17, 3:9

abreoþan *v.II* (or *v.1*?) 'destroy' PERDERE *ps.3s.* **abreoþeð** 21:41; *pt.3s.* **abriodde** 22:7 [n.]

abylgan *v.1* 'anger, offend' INDIGNARE *pp.p.* **abælgede** 26:8

ac *conj.* 'but' SED **ah** 4:4, etc. || NONNE **ah** 5:46, 5:47, 6:25, 6:26, 7:22, 10:29, 12:11, 13:55 (*bis*), 13:56, 18:12, 18:33, 20:13 || NUMQUID **ah** 7:9, 7:10, 7:16, 9:15, 11:23, 12:23, 14:2, 26:22, 26:25 || NON (in question) **ah** 12:3, 19:4, 20:15, 21:42, 22:31, 27:13 || ERGO **ah** 17:10, 19:7, 23:20 || QUOMODO **ah** (*hu*) 26:54 || NL **ah** 21:21 (SED in WW) [ac, *conj.*]

acennan *v.1* 'bear, bring forth' NASCI *pp.s.* **akenned** 1:16, 1:20, 2:1, 2:2, 2:4, 21:19 26:24; *pp.p.* **akende** 19:12; **akenned** 24:32 [akenned, *adj.*]

aceorfan *v.III* 'cut out' ABSCIDERE

imp.s. **aceorf** 5:30; **asceorf** 18:8 [n.] || EXCIDERE *pp.s.* **acorfen** 3:10, 7:19

acheldemach *prop.n.* ~ *ns.* 27:8

acigan *v.1* 'call' VOCARE *pt.1s.* **acægde** 2:15; *pt.3s.* **acægde** 2:7

acolian *v.2* 'become cold' REFRIGESCERE *ps.3s.* **acolaþ** 24:12

[MK]**acunnian** *v.2* 'test, tempt' TEMPTARE *pp.s.* **acunnad** Mk1:13

†**acusan** *v.1* 'accuse' ACCUSARE *pt.3p.* (*subj.*?) **acuste** 12:10 [n.] [accuse, *v.*]

acweþan *v.V* 'say, tell' DICERE *pp.s.* **acweden** 1:22, 2:15, 2:23, 24:15; **acwedan** 12:17; **acwæden** 4:14, 22:31; *pp. mds.* **acwædene** 26:30 [OED2 aqueath, *v.*]

adelfan *v.III* 'dig' EFFODERE *ps.3p.* **adelfaþ** 6:19, 6:20

adl *f.* 'ailment, disease' LANGUOR *as.* **adle** 4:23, 9:35, 10:1; *dp.* **adlum** 4:24, Mk1:34 || PESTILENTIA *np.* **adle** 24:7 [adle, *n.*]

adrugian *v.2* 'become dry' ARERE *pt.3s.* **adrugade** 21:20; *pp. fas.* **adrugade** 12:10 [adrowe, *v.*]

adumbian *v.2* 'become dumb, speechless' OBMUTESCERE *pt.3s.* **adumbede** 22:12

[MK]**adune** *adv.* 'down, downward' SUB- ~ Mk2:4 [adown, *adv.* and *prep.*]

adwæscan *v.1* 'extinguish' EXSTINGUERE *ps.3s.* **adwæscet** 12:20; *pp.p.* **adwæsced** 25:8 [adwesch, *v.*]

aeldingę, see **ielding**

afeallan *v.VII* 'fall' CADERE *ps.3s.* **afalleþ** 21:44 [afall, *v.*]

afon *v.VII* 'seize, receive' TRADERE *pp.s.* **afongen** 4:12 [afang, *v.*]

afrefran *v.1* 'console, comfort' CONSOLARE *pp.s.* **afreofred** 2:18; *pp.p.* **afreofrede** 5:5

afyllan *v.1* 'cause to fall, stumble, overturn' EVERTERE *pt.3s.* **afældę** 21:12 || SCANDALIZARE *ps.3s.* **afælleþ** 18:6 [afell, *v.*]

afyran *v.1* 'castrate, (*pp.* used as subst.) eunuch' EUNUCHUS *pp. mnp.* **afyrde** 19:12 (x3) || EUNUCHARE *pt.3p.* **afyrdun** 19:12

afyrran *v.1* 'remove, put far away' AUFERRE *pp.s.* **afirred** 9:15, 13:12, 21:43; **afyrred** 25:29 || EICERE *pt.3s.* **afirde** Mk1:34 || EXTERRERE *pp.p.* **afirde** 28:4 [afferre, *v.*]

agan *pret.pres.v.* 'possess, own' POSSIDERE *inf.* ~ 10:9 || part of DOMINARI *ps.3p.* **agun** (*gewald*) 20:25 || NL *pt.3s.* **ahte** 1:6 [n.] [own, *v.*]

agen *adj.* 'own' NL *fds.* **agene** 27:31 [n.] [own, *adj.* and *pron.*]

ageotan *v.II* 'pour' EFFUNDERE *pt.3s.* **ageat** 26:7; *pp.s.* **agoten** 9:17, 23:35, 26:28 [ayet, *v.*]

agyfan *v.V* 'give' REDDERE *ps.1s.* **agefe** 18:26; **ageofu** 18:29; *ps.3s.* **agæfeþ** 16:27; *ps.3p.* **ageofaþ** 12:36; **ageofað** 21:41; *subj.ps.3s.* **agefe** 5:26; *subj.pt.3s.* **agefe** 18:25, 18:34; **agæfe** 18:30; *imp.s.* **agef** 5:33, 18:28; *imp.p.* **ageofaþ** 22:21; *pp.s.* **agefnæ** 18:25 || OFFERRE *ps.2s.* **agefes** 5:24 [n.]; *imp.s.* **agef** Mk1:44 || RESTITUERE *ps.3s.* **agefeþ** 17:11; *pp.s.* **agefen** 12:13 || DARE *inf.* **ageofan** 27:58 (REDDERE in WW) [agive, *v.*]

ah, see **ac**

ahebban *v.VI* 'lift, raise' EXALTARE *ps.3s.* **ahæfæþ** 23:12; *pp.s.* **ahæfen** 11:23, 23:12 || LEVARE *ps.3s.* **ahefeþ** 12:11; *pt.3s.* **ahof** Mk1:31; *pt.3p.* **ahofan** 17:8 || TOLLERE *ps.3s.* **ahefeþ** 9:16; *ps.3p.* **ahebbaþ** 4:6 [aheave, *v.*]

ahefigian *v.2* 'make heavy, wight down' GRAVARE *pp.p.* **ahæfgad** 26:43

ahlocian *v.2* 'pluck out' ERUERE *imp.s.* **ahloca** 5:29, 18:9

ahon *v.VII* 'hang' CRUCIFIGERE *pt.3p.* **ahengon** 27:35; *pp.s.* **ahongen** 26:2; *pp.p.* **ahongenne** 27:38, 27:44 || SUSPENDERE *pp.s.* **ahongen** 18:6 [ahang, *v.*]

ahydan *v.1* 'hide, conceal' ABSCONDERE *ps.3s.* **ahydeþ** 13:44; *pt.1s.* **ahydde** 25:25; *pt.2s.*

ahyddest 11:25; *pt.3s.* **ahydde** 25:18; *pp.s.* **ahyded** 5:14; *pp.p.* **ahyded** 13:35

ahyldan *v.1* 'bend down, rest' RECLINARE *subj.ps.3s.* **ahelde** 8:20

akcras, see **æcer**

al-, see also **eal-**

alecgan *v.1* 'lay, put down' PONERE *pt.3s.* **alægde** 27:60 || part of DESPONSARE 'to betroth' *pp.s.* (*in sceat*) **alegd** 1:18 [n.] [allay, v.1]

alfees *prop.n.* - *gs.* 10:3

alucan *v.II* 'pluck out, uproot' ERADICARE *subj.ps.2p.* **alucæ** 13:29

alyfan *v.1* 'allow' LICERE *pp.s.* **alefed** 12:2, 12:12, 14:4; **alæfed** 20:15, 22:17

alysnes *f.* 'redemption, release' REDEMPTIO *ds.* **alesnisse** 20:28 [aleseness, *n.*]

an *adj.* 'one, sole' UNUS *mns.* - 5:18, 8:19, 9:18, 10:29, 16:14, 18:14, 18:24, 19:16, 19:17, 20:21, 22:35, 23:8, 23:9, 23:10, 26:14, 26:21, 26:47, 26:51, 27:48; *mas.* **ænne** 5:36, 13:46, 18:16, 18:28, 23:15; **enne** 18:6, 18:10, 27:15, 27:16; *mds.* **anum** 10:42, 18:5, 20:13, 25:15, 25:40, 25:45; *fns.* - 5:41, 26:69 (*nns.*?); *fas.* **ane** 6:27, 20:12, 26:40; *nns.* - 5:18, 5:29, 5:30, 6:29, 18:12, 19:6; *nas.* - 5:19, 12:11, 17:4 (x3), 18:9, 21:19, 22:34, 25:15 (gender uncertain), 25:24 (gender uncertain); *ngs.* **anes** 21:24 *nds.* **anum** 19:5, 25:18 (gender uncertain), 27:14 || SOLUS *mns.* **ane** 14:23 (*bis*), 24:36, Mk2:7; *mas.* **enne** 17:8; *mds.* **anum** 4:4, 4:10, 18:15; *dp.* **anum** 12:4 || SINGULI *mds.* **anum** 20:9 [n.], 20:10 || part of UNUSQUISQUE *gp.* **anra** 16:27, 18:35 || NL *nns.* - 26:7; *mds.* **anum** 21:21 [n.] [one, *adj.*, *n.*, and *pron.*]

and *conj.* 'and' ET **and** (spelled-out) 1:17; ⁊ (Tironian note) elsewhere || AT ⁊ 4:20, 8:32, 9:12, 9:22, 14:8, 15:13, 15:16, 15:25, 15:27, 16:2, 25:12, 26:23, 26:57, 26:70, 27:23, 28:15 || -QUE ⁊ 14:10, 17:7 (f. 27v, 20^{2}), 26:26, Mk1:35 (f. 54r, 9) || QUOD (SI) ⁊ 18:17 (*bis*, f. 29v, 6, 7) || ⁊ AC 26:26 || NL ⁊ 2:7, 2:8 (ET in WW), 2:22, 2:23, 4:22; 4:24 (f. 6v, 1^{1}), 6:7, 8:26 (f. 12v, 19), 9:8 (f. 13v, 6^{1}) [n.], 9:10 [n.], 9:22 (f. 14r, 18^{1}), 9:37, 10:4 (f. 15r, 12^{2}), 10:7, 10:12, 11:25 (f. 18r, 5), 12:22 (f.19r, 9^{1}), 12:26 (ET in WW), 13:37, 13:47, 14:5, 14:14 (f. 23v, 18^{1}) [n.], 14:19 (f. 24r, 4), 14:19 (f. 24r, 5), 14:27 (ET R^{Fa}; -QUE in WW), 14:28, 14:31, 15:13 (f. 25r, 12^{2}), 15:31 (*bis*, f. 26r, $1^{1,2}$), 15:36 (f. 26r, 11^{1}, ET in WW), 16:2 (f. 26r, 19^{2}), 16:8, 16:9 (ET in WW), 16:27 (ET in WW), 17:19 (ET in WW), 18:12 (f. 29r, 18^{1}), 18:13 (f. 29r, 21), 18:32 (ET in WW), 19:3 (f. 30v, 5), 20:2, 20:13 (f. 32v, 7), 20:22, 20:25 (ET in WW, f. 33r, 11), 21:13 (ET in WW), 21:27 (f. 35r, 1^{1}), 21:42 (ET in WW), 21:46 (f. 35v, 21) [n.], 22:13 (f. 36v, 1^{2}), 22:23, 22:24 (f. 36v, 20), 22:25, 22:26 (f. 27r, 2^{1}) [n.], 22:29, 23:17, 24:2, 24:46 [n.], 24:51 (f. 41v, 4), 25:12 (f. 42r, 2^{2}), 25:22, 25:24 (f. 42v, 4^{1}), 26:1 (ET in WW), 26:26 (f. 44v, 5, ET in WW), 26:36 (f. 45r, 2, ET in WW), 26:57 (f. 46r, 1), 27:3 (f. 47r, 1), 27:4, 27:6, 27:7, 27:9 (f. 47r, 12, ET in WW), 27:20 (f. 47v, 13), 27:23 (f. 47v, 19), 27:24, 27:30 (f. 48r, 10, ET in WW), 27:32, 27:42 (f. 48v, 10), 27:65, Mk1:6 (f. 52v, 13), Mk1:38 (f. 54r, 13) [n.] [and, *conj.*1, *adv.*, and *n.*1]

andettan *v.1* 'confess' CONFITERI *ps.1s.* **ondetu** 7:23, 11:25; **ondeto** 10:32; *ps.3s.* **ondeteþ** 10:32; *pp. mnp.* **ondentende** 3:6; **ondetende** Mk1:5

andgyt *n.* 'understanding' INTELLECTUS *as.* (or *d.*?) **ondget** 15:16 [anyit, *n.*]

andreas *prop.n. ns.* - 10:2; *as.* - 4:18, Mk1:16; *gs.* - Mk1:29

andsacian *v.2* 'deny' NEGARE *ps.1s.* **⁊sace** 26:35; *ps.2s.* **ondsacast** 26:75

|| ABNEGARE *subj.ps.3s.* ⁊sæcę 16:24 [n.] [see also **onsacan**]

andspurnan *v.III* (or *v.I?*) 'stumble' OFFENDERE *subj.pres.2s.* **⁊spurne** 4:6 || SCANDALIZARE *ps.3p.* **⁊spurnaþ** 24:10

andspurnnes *f.* 'scandal, offence' SCANDALUM *ns.* **⁊spyrnes** 16:23; *as.* **⁊spyrnnisse** 26:31 || part of SCANDALIZARE *as.* **⁊spurnisse** (*þrowian*) 13:21, 13:57

andswarian *v.2* 'answer' RESPONDERE *ps.3s.* **⁊swareþ** 25:45; *ps.3p.* **⁊swærigaþ** 25:37; **⁊swarigað** 25:44; *pt.3s.* **ondswarade** 11:4, 12:39, 15:3, 15:13, 16:16, 17:4, 20:22, 21:29, 21:30, 22:29; **ondswarede** 13:37, 14:28, 17:17, 19:4, 20:13, 21:21, 22:1; **ondsweorde** 16:17; **onswarade** 13:11, 21:24, 21:27; **andswarade** 16:2, 17:11, 19:27, 25:40, 28:5; **⁊swarade** 24:2, 24:4, 25:12, 25:26, 26:23, 26:25, 26:33; **⁊swarede** 27:12; *pt.3p.* **ondswaradun** 12:38; **andswaredun** 14:17, 25:9; **⁊swaredun** 26:66; *ps.p. mns.* **ondswarende** 3:15; **ondswarande** 8:8; **⁊swarande** 4:4 [answer, *v.*]

andswaru *f.* 'answer' RESPONSUM *a/ds.* **andsuari** 2:12 [answer, *n.*]

andustrian *v.2* 'curse, repudiate' DETESTARE *inf.* **⁊ustriga** 26:74 [n.]

†**andustrung** *f.* 'abomination' ABOMINATIO *as.* **⁊ustrungæ** 24:15 [n.]

andweard *adj.* 'present, actual' part of HODIERNUS *mas.* **ondwardan** 28:15

andwlita *m. wk* 'face' FACIES *ns.* **ondwliota** 17:2; *as.* **andwlitu** 6:17, 18:10; **ondwliotu** 16:3, 17:6, 26:39, 26:67 (*bis*); *ap.* **andwliotu** 6:17; *ds.* **ondwliota** 11:10 [OED2 anleth, *n.*]

andwyrdan *v.1* 'answer' RESPONDERE *ps.2s.* **⁊wyrdest** 26:62; *pt.3s.* **ondwyrde** 11:25, 12:48, 15:23, 15:24; **andwyrde** 15:15, 15:28, 27:14; **⁊wyrde** 27:21; **onwyrde** 15:26; *pt.3p.* **⁊wyrdan** 27:25 [n.] [OED2 andwurde, *v.*]

geandwyrdan *v.1* 'answer' RESPONDERE *inf.* ~ 22:46

andwyrde *n.* 'answer' RESPONSUM *a/ds.* ~ 2:12

anfeald *adj.* 'simple, single' SIMPLEX *ns.* **anfald** 6:22 [aefauld, *adj.*]

anhende *adj.* 'one-handed, lame' DEBILIS ~ 18:8 (grammatical form uncertain; see note); *ap.* **anhende** 15:30

anlipig *adj.* 'single, (used advervially) each in turn' SINGULI *dp.* **anlepum** 26:22 [onlepy, *adj.*, *n.*, and *adv.*]

ansyn *f.* 'face, countenance' ASPECTUS *ns.* **onseone** 28:3 || FACIES *a/ds.* **onseone** Mk1:2 [onsene, *n.*]

apostol *m.* 'apostle' APOSTOLUS *gp.* **apostola** 10:2 [OED2 apostle, *n.*]

ar *f.* 'honour' HONOR *ds.* **are** 13:57 [ore, *n.1*]

ar-, see also **ear-**

aræfnendlic *adj.* 'tolerable' TOLERABILIS *comp. nns.* **arefrendlicre** 10:15 [n.]

arc *f.* 'ark' ARCA *as.* **arkę** 24:38 [OED2 ark, *n.*]

archelaus *prop.n. ns.* ~ 2:22

areccan *v.1* 'narrate, explain' DISSERERE *imp.s.* **arecce** 13:36, 15:15

arian *v.2* 'show honour, respect' HONORARE *imp.s.* **are** 15:4, 19:19 || HONORIFICARE *ps.3s.* **ariað** 15:6

arimaðia *prop.n.* ~ *ds.* 27:57

arisan *v.I* 'rise' SURGERE *ps.3s.* **arisеð** 12:42; *ps.3p.* **arisaþ** 12:41, 24:24; *pt.3s.* **aras** 8:15, 9:7, 9:19, 9:25, 11:11, 14:2, 28:6, 28:7, Mk1:35, Mk2:12, Mk2:14; *pt.3p.* **arisen** 27:52; *imp.s.* **aris** 2:13, 2:20, 9:5, 9:6, Mk2:9, Mk2:11; *imp.p.* **arisaþ** 17:7, 26:46; *inf.* ~ 25:7 [n.]; *ps.p. mns.* **arisende** 8:26 || CONSURGERE *ps.3s.* **ariseþ** 24:7; *ps.p. mns.* **arisende** 2:14 || EXSURGERE *ps.p. mns.* **arisende** 1:24, 2:21, 26:62 || INSURGERE *ps.3p.* **ariseþ** 10:21; **arisaþ** 24:11 || RESURGERE *ps.3p.*

arisaþ 11:5; *subj.ps.3s.* **arisę** 17:9 [OED2 arise, *v.*]

†**asamnian** *v.2* 'gather together' COLLIGERE *ps.3p.* **asomnigaþ** 13:41

asægdnes *f.* 'sacrifice' SACRIFICIUM *as.* **asægdnisse** 9:13, 12:7

ascan, see **axe**

asceacan *v.VI* 'remove by shaking' EXCUTERE *imp.p.* **ascakeþ** 10:14 [OED2 ashake, *v.*]

asceadan *v.VII* 'separate, exclude' SEGREGARE *ps.3s.* **ascadeþ** 25:32 || SEPARARE *ps.3p.* **asceadeþ** 13:49

ascian, geascian, see **axian, geaxian**

asecan *v.1* 'seek, try to find' EXQUIRERE 'learn, discover by inquiring' *pt.3s.* **asohte** 2:16 [OED2 aseek, *v.*]

asendan *v.1* 'send out, send forth' MITTERE *pp.s.* **asended** 15:17, 15:24 26:47; *pp. nds.* **asendun** 13:47 || EICERE *ps.3s.* **asendeþ** 12:20 || EMITTERE *pt.3s.* **sende** 27:50 [OED2 asend, *v.*]

aseon *v.I* 'strain, strain out, remove' EXSPUERE *ps.p. mnp.* **asiendę** 23:24 (EXCOLARE in WW) [n.]

asettan *v.1* 'set' PONERE *pp.s.* **aseted** 3:10, 5:14 28:6 [OED2 aset, *v.*]

asmorian *v.2* 'choke, suffocate' SUFFOCARE *ps.3s.* **asmoraþ** 13:22

astigan *v.I* 'go up or down, ascend or descend' ASCENDERE *ps.3s.* **astigað** 17:27 [n.]; *ps.1p.* **astigað** 20:18, *pt.3s.* **astag** 3:16, 14:23, 15:39, Mk1:10; **astahg** 5:1; *subj.pt.3p.* **astigan** 14:32; *inf.* ~ 14:22; *ps.p. mns.* **astigende** 9:1, 13:2, 15:29, 20:17 || DESCENDERE *ps.2s.* **astigest** 11:23; *pt.3s.* **astag** 7:25, 7:27, 28:2; *subj.ps.3s.* **astigæ** 27:42; *imp.s.* **astig** 27:40; *ps.p. mns.* **astigende** 14:29; *pp.s.* **astigen** 8:1 [OED2 asty, *v.*]

astyrfan *v.1* 'kill, destroy' ERADICARE *pp.s.* **astęrfed** 15:13 [OED2 asterve, *v.2*]

aswapan *v.VII* 'sweep, clean by sweeping' SCOPIS MUNDERE *pp. nas.* **aswopen** 12:44 [n.]

asweltan *v.III* 'die' DEFUNGI *pt.3s.* **awalt** 22:25, 22:27; *pp.s.* **aswolten** 9:18 [OED2 aswelt, *v.*]

ateon *v.II* 'pull out' ERUERE *imp.s.* **ateoh** 18:9 [OED2 atee, *v.*]

aþ *m.* 'oath' IURAMENTUM *ds.* **aþe** 14:7, 14:9, 26:72; *ap.* **haþas** 5:33 [n.] || part of IURARE *as.* **aþ** 5:36 [n.], 23:20; **hað** 5:34; **að** 23:18 [oath, *n.*]

aþenian *v.2* 'stretch out' EXTENDERE *pt.3s.* **aþenede** 12:13, 14:31; *imp.s.* **aþene** 12:13; *ps.p. mns.* **aþenende** 8:3, 12:49, 26:51

aþeostrian *v.2* 'grow dark' OBSCURARE *ps.3s.* **aþiostraþ** 24:29 [OED2 a-thester, *v.*]

awæccan *v.1* 'awake, watch' VIGILARE *inf.* ~ 26:40 [OED2 awake, *v.*]

awægan *v.1* 'deceive' ILLUDERE *pp.s.* **awæged** 2:16

aweccan *v.1* 'awaken, rouse' SUSCITARE 'raise up' (cf. DOE aweccan 4.h., 'to engender, produce (an heir)' *inf.* **awęccan** 3:9 [awecche, *v.*]

aweg *adv.* 'away' AB- prefix ~ 13:25, 16:4, 27:60, 27:66; **awæg** 19:22, 22:5, 22:15, 26:14, 28:11; **awęg** 22:22 [away, *adv.*, *adj.*, and *n.*]

aweorpan *v.III* 'throw, cast forth' EICERE *ps.3s.* **aweorpeþ** 12:24; *ps.3p.* **awyrpeþ** 12:27; *pt.3s.* **awearp** 8:16; *subj.ps.2s.* **awearpe** 7:5 (or *inf.*?); **awearpa** 8:31; *subj.pt.3p.* **awurpe** 10:1; *pp.s.* **aworpen** 9:25, 17:21; *pp.p.* **aworpenne** 8:12; *inf.* ~ 17:19 || PROICERE *imp.s.* **awerp** 5:29; **aweorp** 5:30, 18:9 [OED2 awarp, *v.*]

aweorpness *f.* 'casting out' REPUDIUM *gs.* **aweorpnisse** 5:31, 19:7

aweorþan *v.III* 'come to pass, happen' FIERI *pp.s.* **aworden** Mk1:9 || EVANESCERE 'become worthless' *ps.3s.* **awerdað** 5:13 [n.] [OED2 aworth, *v.*]

awestan *v.1* 'lay waste, destory' DESOLARE *pp.s.* **awoested** 12:25

awestednes *f.* 'desolation, destruction' DESOLATIO *gs.* **awoestednisse** 24:15

awiht *pron.* 'anything, aught' ALIQUIS *nas.* **awiht** 21:3; **owiht** 24:17 || part of NIHIL *nns.* **owiht** 10:26 [aught, *pron.*, *adj.*, and *adv.*]

awritan *v.1* 'write' SCRIBERE *pp.s.* **awriten** 2:5, 4:4, 4:7, 4:10, 11:10, 21:13, 26:24, 26:31, Mk1:2; *pp. mas.* **awritene** 27:37 [awrite, *v.*]

awylwan *v.1* 'roll aside' REVOLVERE *pt.3s.* **awælede** 28:2

awyrgan *v.1* 'curse' MALEDICERE *pp. np.* **awærgede** 25:41 [OED2 awarie, *v.*]

awyrgan *v.1* 'strangle, suffocate' SUSPENDERE *pt.3s.* **awyrgde** 27:5 [n.] [OED2 aworry, v.]

axe *f. wk* 'ash' CINIS *ds.* **ascan** 11:21 [OED2 ash, *n.2*]

axe, see **æxe**

axian *v.2* 'ask' INTERROGARE *ps.1s.* **ahsige** 21:24; *pt.3s.* **axsade** 22:35; *pt.3p.* **ahsadun** 12:10; **ascaden** 17:10; **axsadun** 22:23; *imp.p.* **ahsiað** 2:8; **ahsigaþ** 10:11 || CONQUIRERE *pt.3p.* **ascadun** Mk1:27 || SCISCITARI *pt.3s.* **ahsade** 2:4 [ask, *v.*]

geaxian *v.2* 'ask' INTERROGARE *ps.2s.* **geaxast** 19:17; *inf.* **geascigan** 22:46

æ *f.* 'law' LEX *ns.* **ae** 7:12, 11:13, 22:40; *as.* **ae** 5:17; *gs.* ~ 23:23; *ds.* **ae** 5:18, 12:5, 22:36 [e, *n.2*]

æcer *m.* 'field' SATA *ap.* **akcras** 12:1 [n.] [acre, *n.*]

æchir, see **ear**

æfen *m.* or *n.* VESPER *ns.* ~ Mk1:32; **efen** 8:16, 14:23, 26:20; *ds.* **efenne** 16:2, 28:1; **efen** 14:15 (endingless?) || SERUM *ns.* **efen** 20:8; *ds.* **æfenne** 27:57 [n.] [even, *n.1*]

æfengereord *n.* 'evening meal, supper' CENA *dp.* **efengereordum** 23:6

æfenmete *m.* 'evening meal' CENA *ds.* **efenmete** 26:26 [evenmeat, listed under even, *n.1*]

æfest *m.* 'envy, jealousy' INUIDIA *ds.* **æfeste** 27:18 [evest, *n.*]

æft-, see also **eft-**

æfter *prep.* 'after' POST ~ 1:12, 4:2, 4:19, 8:5, 15:23, 16:23, 16:24, 17:1, 24:29, 26:2, 26:61, 27:53, 27:62, 27:63, Mk1:7, Mk1:17, Mk2:1 || SECUNDUM 'according to' MtINCIPIT, 2:16, 9:29, 23:3, 25:15, 25:19 || IUXTA ~ 16:27 (SECUNDUM in WW) || NL ~ 3:11 [n.], 28:1

æfter þon *adv.* 'after that' EXINDE ~ 16:21 || POSTEA ~ 21:32 || POSTQUAM ~ Mk1:14 (conj.)

æfter þisse 'after this' A MODO ~ 26:64

æfter þon þe 'after' POSTQUAM ~ 27:31, 27:44; **æfter þon ... þe** 27:35; **æfter þon ... ðe** 26:32 [n.] [after, *adv.*, *prep.*, and *conj.*]

æfter *adv.* 'after, afterwards' POSTEA **efter** 21:30 || ITERUM **ęfter** 22:1 || NL ~ 24:21 [n.] [see previous]

†**æftergan** *anom.v.* 'go after' SEQUI *pt.3p.* **æftereodun** 21:9 [n.]

æfterra *adj.* 'latter, second' NOUISSIMUS *mns.* **æftera** 21:31 [n.], 27:64 || SECUNDUS *nns.* **æftere** 22:39 [after, *adj.* and *n.1*]

[MK]**æftersona** *adv.* 'again, once more' ITERUM ~ Mk2:1 || RURSUM ~ Mk2:13 [OED2 eftersoons, *adv.*]

[MK]**æghwanon** *adv.* 'from all sides' UNDIQUE **æghwonan** Mk1:45

æghwilc *adj.* 'each, all' OMNIS *mns.* ~ 5:22, 5:28, 5:32, 7:8, 7:21, 7:24, 7:26, 10:32, 13:52, 19:29, 25:29; *nns.* ~ 3:10, 7:19, 12:25, 13:19, 23:35; **ægwilc** 7:17; *nas.* ~ 5:11; **ægwilc** 12:36; *nds.* **æghwelceum** 4:4 [n.]; **æghwilce** 13:47 (or *i.*?); *fns.* ~ 12:25, 12:31, 15:13, 28:18; *fas.* **æghwilce** 3:15, 4:23 (*bis*), 9:35 (*bis*), 10:1 (*bis*); *fgs.* **æghwilcre** 23:27 || UNUSQUISQUE *mds.* **æghwilce** 25:15 || NL *mns.* ~ 20:9 [n.]; *f?ds.* **æghwilcum** Mk1:45 [n.] [each, *adj.* and *pron.*]

ægypt *prop.n. a/ds.* **ægypti** 2:13, 2:14; *ds.* **ægypto** 2:15, 2:19

æht *f.* 'possession' POSSESSIO *ap.* **æhte** 19:22 [aucht, *n.*]

ælareow *m.* 'teacher of the law' LEGIS DOCTOR *ns.* **ælaruw** 22:35

ælde, ældingę see **ieldan, ielding**

ællefta, see **endlyfta**

ælmes *f.* 'alms' ELEMOSINA *ns.* ~ 6:4; *as.* **ælmisse** 6:2, 6:3 [alms, *n.*]

æmtig *adj.* 'empty' VACANS *nas.* **emtig** 12:44 [empty, *adj.* and *n.*]

ænig *pron.* 'any, anyone' (ALI)QUIS *ns.* ~ 12:29; *ds.* **ængum** 22:16 || NEMO 'no one' *mns.* **ænig** (w. *ne*) 6:24

ænig *adj.* 'any' OMNES *nns.* **ænig** 24:22; *nds.* **ængum** 18:19 || QUICUMQUE *ds.* **ænigum** 19:3 [any, *adj.*, *pron.*, and *n.*, and *adv.*]

ær *adv.* 'before, earlier' PRIUS ~ 12:29, 23:26 || NL ~ (w. past verbs for pluperfect) 2:9, 2:16, 8:33, 14:33, 18:11, 26:57, 27:52, 27:55, 27:60, 28:16

ær *prep.* 'before' ANTE ~ 5:12, 8:29, 24:38

ær þon 'before' DONEC ~ 5:18, 5:26, 10:23, 16:28, 23:39, 24:34, 24:39; **ær ðon** 17:9 || ANTEQUAM ~ 1:18, 6:8, 26:34 || PRIUSQUAM ~ 26:75 [OED2 ere, *adv.1*, *prep.*, *conj.*, and *adj.*]

ærest *adj.* 'first' PRIMUS *mns.* **æreste** 22:25; *nns.* **æreste** 22:38; *nas.* **æreste** 23:6; *mnp.* **æreste** 20:16; **eristu** 20:16; **ærestu** 19:30 (*bis*), 20:10; *a/dp.* **ærestu** 20:8 [OED2 erst, *adj.* and *adv.*]

ærest *adv.* 'first' PRIUS ~ 5:24 || PRIMUM ~ 6:33, 8:21, 10:2, 17:10, 17:27; **aræst** 7:5; **arest** 13:30 [see previous]

[MK]**æring** *f.* 'daybreak, dawn' DILUCULUM *ds.* **æringe** Mk 1:35 [n.]

ærist *f.* 'resurrection' RESURRECTIO *ns.* **æreste** 22:23; *ds.* **æriste** 22:28, 22:30, 22:31; **æristę** 27:53 [arist, *n.*]

ærnemorgen *m.* 'early morning' PRIMO MANE *ds.* **ærnemorgen** 20:1 (endingless?) [OED2 arne-morwe, *n.*]

ærra *adj.* 'earlier' PRIOR *mds.* **ærran** 27:64; *mnp.* **erran** 12:45; *mdp.* **ærrum** 21:36 [erer, *adj.* and *adv.*]

æswic *m.* 'offence, scandal' SCANDALUM *ns.* ~ 18:7 (*bis*); *as.* **æswic** 26:31 || part of SCANDALIZARE *as.* **æswice** 26:33

æswician *v.2* 'offend, cause to stumble' SCANDALIZARE *ps.3s.* **æswicað** 5:29 [n.], 5:30; **æswiceþ** 18:9; *ps.3p.* **æswicęþ** 18:8 [n.]; *ps.p. mnp.* **æswicende** 24:10

æt *prep.* 'at, from, around' CIRCA ~ 20:3, 20:5, 20:6, 20:9, 27:46 || AB/A ~ 2:7, 5:42, 11:29, 25:28 (postposed), 27:9 || IN ~ 9:9, 10:15, 23:6 || AD ~ 4:6, 24:41 || NL ~ 21:37, 25:6, 25:11, 26:7, 26:26, 26:60, 27:57 [OED2 at, *prep.*]

ætclifian *v.2* 'cleave to' ADHAERERE *ps.3s.* **ætclifað** 19:5 [n.]

æteowan *v.1* 'appear, show' APPARERE *ps.2p.* **æteaweþ** 23:28; *pt.3s.* **æteaude** 2:19; **æteawde** 1:20, 2:7, 2:13, 9:33, 17:3; *pt.3p.* **æteawde** 13:26 [n.]; **æteawdun** 27:53 || OSTENDERE *pt.3s.* **æteawde** 4:8; *imp.s.* **æteaw** 8:4, Mk1:44 || ORIRI *pt.3s.* **æteawde** (*upp*) 4:16 [OED2 atew, *v.*]

ætgædere *adv.* 'together' PARITER **ætgędre** 14:9 || SIMUL **ætgædre** Mk2:15

æthrinan *v.1* 'touch' TANGERE *pt.3s.* **æthran** 8:3, 8:15, 9:20, 9:29, 17:7; *subj.ps.3p.* ~ 14:36; *inf.* ~ 14:36 [OED2 atrine, *v.*]

ætican *v.1* 'add' ADICERE *inf.* **ætece** 6:27 [n.]

ætwitan *v.1* 'blame, reproach' EXPROBARE *inf.* ~ 11:20 || IMPROPERARE *pt.3p.* **ætwitun** 27:44 [atwite, *v.1*]

æwyrdla *m. wk* 'damage, loss' DETRIMENTUM *as.* **ewyrdlu** 16:26

æxe *f.* 'axe' SECURIS *ns.* **axe** 3:10; [OED2 axe, *n.1*]

babilonia *prop.n. gs.* ~ 1:11, 1:12; **babilonie** 1:17; **babylonie** 1:17

ban *m.* 'bone' OS *gp.* **bana** 23:27

[bone, *n.1*]

barachias *prop.n. gs.* ~ 23:35

barrabas *prop.n. ns.* ~ 27:16; *as.* ~ 27:17; **barrabban** 27:20

bartholomeus *prop.n. ns.* ~ 10:3

[MK]**bær** *f.* 'bed' GRABATUS *as.* **bere** Mk2:4, Mk2:9, Mk2:11, Mk2:12 || TECTUM *as.* **bere** Mk2:4 [n.] [OED2 bier, *n.*]

bæzere *m.* 'baptist (referring to John)' BAPTISTA *ns.* **bezera** 3:1 [n.]; **baezere** 14:2; **bezere** 14:8; **bædzere** 16:14; *gs.* **bęzeres** 11:12; *ds.* **bæzere** 11:11; **bædzere** 17:13

be *prep.* 'by, about' DE ~ 4:6, 6:28, 8:33, 11:10, 16:11, 18:19, 19:17, 20:24, 21:21, 22:16, 22:42, 24:36, 26:24, 27:22; **bi** 2:8, 11:7, 12:36, 17:13, 22:31 || SECUS **bi** 13:1, 13:4, 13:19, 13:48, 20:30, 21:19, Mk1:16 || EX ~ 20:2, 20:13 || IN ~ 23:22 (*bis*) || SUPER ~ 7:28, 18:13 (*bis*) || IUXTA **bi** 4:18 || TRANS ~ 19:1 [OED2 by, *prep.* and *adv.*]

beag *m.* 'crown' CORONA *as.* **bæg** 27:29 [OED2 bee, *n.2*]

bealcettan *v.1* 'belch, utter' ERUCTARE *ps.1s.* **bilketto** 13:35 [n.]

beam *m.* 'beam' TRABS *ns.* ~ 7:4; *as.* ~ 7:3, 7:5 [OED2 beam, *n.1*]

bearn *n.* 'child, son' FILIUS *ns.* ~ 8:20, 27:54; *np.* ~ 5:9, 5:45, 8:12, 9:15, 12:27, 13:38 (*bis*), 17:26, 23:31; *ap.* ~ 2:18, 3:9, 19:29, 23:37, 27:25; *gp.* **bearna** 15:26; *dp.* **bearnum** 11:19, 17:25, 27:9; **beaearnum** 7:11 || NATUS *dp.* **bearnum** 11:11 [OED2 bairn, *n.*]

bebeodan *v.II* 'command' PRAECIPERE *pt.3s.* **bebead** 1:24, 8:4, 12:16, 15:35, 16:20, 17:9, 21:6, 26:19; *ps.p. mns.* **bebeodende** 10:5, 11:1 || MANDARE *ps.3s.* **bebeodeþ** 4:6 [n.]; *pt.1s.* **bebead** 28:20; *pt.3s.* **bebead** 19:7 || IMPERARE *ps.3s.* **bebead** 8:26 || COMMINARI *pt.3s.* **bebeod** Mk1:25; *pp.s.* **beboden** Mk1:25, Mk1:43 [OED2 bibede, *v.*]

bebicgan *v.1* 'sell, give in exchange' VENDERE *ps.3s.* **bebygið** 13:44; *imp.s.* **bebycge** 19:21; *ps.p. dp.* **bebycgendum** 25:9 || VENUNDARE *inf.* **bebycgan** 18:25; *pp.s.* **beboht** 26:9

bebod *n.* 'command' MANDATUM *ns.* 22:36, 22:38; *as.* ~ 15:3, 15:6, 15:9 (or *p.*?); *ap.* **bebodu** 19:17; *gp.* **beboda** 5:19; **bebodum** 22:40 [OED2 bibod, *n.*]

bebyrgan *v.1* 'bury' SEPELIRE *pt.3p.* **bebyrgedun** 14:12; *inf.* **bebyrgen** 8:21, 8:22; *infl.inf.* **bebyrgenne** 26:12, 27:7 [OED2 bebury, *v.*]

becuman *v.IV* 'come' PERVENIRE *ps.3s.* **becymeþ** 12:28 [OED2 become, *v.*]

gebed *n.* 'prayer, praying' ORATIO *gs.* **gebedes** 21:13; *ds.* **gebęde** 21:22; *dp.* **gebeodum** 17:21

bedd *n.* 'bed, couch' LECTUS *as.* ~ 9:6; *ds.* **bedde** 9:2, 24:41 [OED2 bed, *n.*]

bedelfan *v.III* 'dig, bury' FODERE *pt.3s.* **bedælf** 25:18 [OED2 bedelve, *v.*]

befæstan *v.1* 'entrust' DESPONSARE 'betroth' *pp.s.* **befest** 1:18 [n.]; [cf. OED2 befast, *s.v.* be-, *pref.* sense 5.a.]

beforan *prep.* 'before, in front of' ANTE ~ 5:24, 7:6, 11:10, 11:26, 17:2, 17:14, 18:14, 23:13, 25:32, 27:11, 27:29, Mk1:2 || CORAM ~ 10:32, 10:33 (*bis*), 26:70, 27:24, Mk2:12 || CONTRA ~ 21:2 || NL ~ 26:71 [before, *adv.*, *prep.*, *conj.*, and *n.*]

beforangan *anom.v.* 'go before' CEDERE *pt.3p.* **beforaneodan** 21:9 (PRAE- in WW) || PRAECEDERE *ps.3s.* **beforangæþ** 28:7; *ps.3p.* **beforangæþ** 21:31 [cf. before]

began *anom.v.* 'worship, revere, exercise' COLERE *ps.3p.* **begangeþ** 15:9 || EXERCERE *ps.3p.* **begæþ** 20:25 [OED2 bego, *v.*]

begen *adj.* 'both' AMBO *np.* **begen** 15:14; *np.* **bu** 9:17 || UTERQUE *ap.* ~ 13:30 [OED2 bo, *adj.* (and *pron.*)]

begende, see **bigan**
begeondan *prep.* 'beyond' TRANS **begeonda** 4:25 [OED2 beyond, *adv.*, *prep.*, and *n.*]
begytan *v.V* 'obtain' CONSEQUI *ps.3p.* **begetaþ** 5:7 [beget, *v.*]
behealdan *v.VII* 'behold, beware' ATTENDERE *imp.p.* **behaldeþ** 6:1, 7:15; **behealdeþ** 16:6; *infl.inf.* **behealdene** 16:12 || CAVERE *imp.p.* **behaldeþ** 10:17 || RESPICERE *imp.p.* **behaldeþ** 6:26 [OED2 behold, *v.*]
behindan *adv.* 'behind' RETRO **behyndan** 9:20 [OED2 behind, *adv.*, *prep.*, and *n.*]
behwitt *adj.* 'whitened' DEALBATUS *fdp.* **behwitum** 23:27 [n.]
behydnes *f.* 'care, concern' SOLLICITUDO *ns.* **behygdnis** 13:22
belg *m.* 'bag, leather bottle' UTER *np.* **belgas** 9:17; **beligas** 9:17; *ap.* **belgas** 9:17 [OED2 belly, *n.* and bellows, *n.*]
belucan *v.II* 'shut, close' CLAUDERE *pp.s.* **belocen** 25:10 [belouk, *v.*]
belzebub *prop.n. as.* ~ 10:25; *ds.* ~ 12:24, 12:27
beman, see **byme**
bend *m.* 'bond, fetters, confinement' VINCULUM *dp.* **bendum** 11:2 [OED2 bend, *n.1*]
beneoþan *adv.* 'below' INFRA **beniuþa** 2:16 [OED2 beneath, *adv.*, *prep.*, and *adj.*]
bensian **v.**2 'supplicate, petition' PETERE *ps.p. fns.* **boensendu** 20:20 [n.] [? OED2 bensy, *v.*]
beod *m.* 'table' MENSA *as.* ~ 21:12; *ds.* **beode** 15:27 [OED2 beod, *n.*]
beon, see **wesan**
beorma *m. wk* 'yeast, leaven' FERMENTUM *ds.* **beorma** 13:33, 16:6, 16:12; **bearma** 16:11 [OED2 barm, *n.2*]
†**gebeormod** *adj.* 'leavened' FERMENTATUS *mns.* **gebeormad** 13:33 [n.] [cf. OED2 barm, *v.*]
beorgan *v.III* 'protect, guard against' CAVERE *imp.p.* **bergaþ** 16:11 [OED2 bergh | berȝe | berwe, *v.*]
beornende, beornane, see **byrnan**
beotian *v.2* 'threaten' COMMINARI *pt.3s.* **biatadae** 9:30 [n.] [OED2 beote, *v.*]
beran *v.IV* 'bear, carry, bring forth' FACERE *ps.3s.* **bereþ** 3:10, 7:17 (*bis*), 7:19; *inf.* **beoran** 7:18 (*bis*) || PORTARE *pt.3s.* **bær** 8:17; *pt.1p.* **beron** 20:12; *infl.inf.* **beranne** 3:11 || TOLLERE *subj.ps.3s.* **bere** 16:24; *subj.pt.3s.* 27:32; *imp.s.* **ber** Mk2:9 || PARERE *ps.3s.* **bereþ** 1:21, 1:23 || PROFERRE *ps.3s.* **bereþ** 12:35 (*bis*) || DARE *pt.3s.* **bęr** 14:11 [bear, *v.1*]
geberan *v.IV* 'bear (a child), carry' PARERE *pt.3s.* **gebær** 1:25 || PORTARE *pp.s.* **geboren** Mk2:3 [i-bere, *v.1*]
bereern *n.* 'barn, granary' HORREUM *as.* **berern** 3:12, 6:26 (*p.*?), 13:30 [OED2 bar, *n.*]
bereflor *m.* 'threshing-floor' AREA *as.* **bęreflor** 3:12
berstan *v.III* 'break apart' SCINDERE *pt.3p.* **brustæn** 27:51 [n.] [OED2 burst, *v.*]
besencan *v.1* 'cause to sink' DEMERGERE *pp.s.* **besenked** 18:6 [OED2 besench, *v.*]
beseon *v.V* 'see, behold' VIDERE *imp.s.* **beseoh** 18:10 [n.] [OED2 besee, *v.*]
besmitan *v.I* 'defile, polute' COINQUINARE *ps.3s.* **besmiteþ** 15:11; *ps.3p.* **besmitaþ** 15:20 (*bis*) [n.] [besmite, *v.*]
betan *v.1* 'make good, repair' REFICERE *ps.p. mnp.* **boetende** 4:21 [OED2 beet | bete, *v.*]
bethania *prop.n. ds.* ~ 26:6; **bethaniæ** 21:17
bethlem *prop.n. ds.* ~ 2:5, 2:8, 2:16
bethsaidæ, *prop.n. ns.* ~ 11:21
betweonan *prep.* 'between, among' INTER/INTRA **betweon** 3:9, 11:11; **betwion** 16:7, 16:8, 23:35; **betwih** 18:15, Mk2:8; **betwihc** 20:26, Mk1:27; **betwix** 20:26, 20:27, 27:56; **betwihs** 21:25 || INVICEM **betwig** 24:10 (*bis*) || NL **betwih** 26:58 [n.] [OED2 between, *prep.*, *adv.*, and *n.*]

betynan *v.1* 'close, shut' CLAUDERE *imp.s.* **betun** 6:6 [OED2 bitun, *v.*]

beþeccan *v.1* 'cover' COOPERIRE *pp.s.* **beþæht** 6:29 [OED2 bithecche, *v.*]

beþfage *prop.n. ds.* ~ 21:1

beþurfan *pret.pres.v.* 'need' EXPEDIRE 'be profitable, benefit' *ps.3s.* **beþerfeð** 5:29; **beðęrfeþ** 5:30; **beðearfeþ** 18:6; **beþærfeþ** 19:10 || PRODESSE *ps.3s.* **beðearfeþ** 15:5, **beþearfað** 16:26

beweddian *v.2* 'betroth' DESPONSARE *pp.s.* **bewedded** 1:18 [OED2 bewed, *v.*]

bewindan *v.III* 'wrap, enfold' INVOLVERE *pt.3s.* **bewand** 27:59 [OED2 bewind, *v.*]

bewreon *v.I* or *v.II* 'cover, conceal' OPERIRE *pp. ngs.* **bewrigenes** 10:26 (subst. 'what is concealed') [OED2 bewry, *v.2*]

biatadae, see **beotian**

bicgan *v.1* 'buy' EMERE *ps.3s.* **bygiþ** 13:44; *inf.* **bycgan** 25:10 || CONDUCERE 'hire' *inf.* **bycgæ** 20:1 || VENIRE (VEN-EO) *pp.p.* **boht** 10:29 [OED2 buy, *v.*]

gebicgan *v.1* 'buy' EMERE *pt.3s.* **gebohte** 13:46; *pt.3p.* **gebohtun** 27:7; *subj.pt.3p.* **gebycge** 14:15; *imp.p.* **gebycgæþ** 25:9; *ps.p. map.* **gebycgende** 21:12 || APPRETIARE *pt.3p.* **gebohtum** 27:9; *pp. ngs.* **gebohtæ** 27:9 || CONDUCERE *pt.3s.* **gebohte** 20:7 [n.] [see previous]

bidan *v.I* 'wait, expect' EXPECTARE *ps.1p.* **bideþ** 11:3 [OED2 bide, *v.*]

biddan *v.V* 'ask, pray' ROGARE *pt.2s.* **bede** 18:32; *pt.3s.* **bedd** 18:26; **bed** 18:29; *pt.3p.* **bedun** 8:31, 8:34, 14:36, 15:23; **bedon** 16:1; *imp.p.* **biddaþ** 9:38; *ps.p. mns.* **biddende** 8:5; *mnp.* **biddende** 9:28; *inf.* **biddan** 26:53 || PETERE *ps.3s.* **bit** 7:8; **biddeth** 7:10; *ps.2p.* **biddað** 21:22; **bidaþ** 20:22; *ps.3p.* **biddaþ** 7:11; *pt.3s.* **bæd** 27:58; *subj.ps.3s.* **bidde** 5:42, 7:9; *imp.p.* **biddaþ** 7:7 || (AD)ORARE *pt.3p.* **bedun** 28:17; *subj.ps.2p.* **bidde** 6:5 (w. refl.); **biddan** 6:8; *imp.s.* **bidde** 6:6; *ps.p. mnp.* **biddende** 23:14 || DEPRECARE *pt.3s.* **bed** Mk1:40; *ps.p. mns.* **bidende** Mk1:40 || POSTULARE *subj.pt.3s.* **bede** 14:7 [OED2 bid, *v.1*]

gebiddan *v.V* 'pray' ADORARE 'worship, pray to' (usu. w. *to* + dat.) *ps.1s.* **gebidde** 2:8 (or *subj.*?), 26:36; *ps.2s.* **gebiddes** 4:9; *ps.2p.* **gebiddað** 6:9; *subj.ps.1s.* **gebidde** 4:10 [n.]; *pt.3s.* **gebęd** 9:18; **gebed** 15:25; *pt.3p.* **gebedun** 2:11, 14:33, 14:35, 28:9; *subj.ps.3p.* **gebiddan** 18:19; *infl.inf.* **gebiddenne** 2:2; **gebiddane** 20:20 || ORARE *pt.3s.* **gebęd** 26:42, Mk1:35; **gebed** 26:44; *subj.ps.2s.* **gebidde** 6:6; *imp.p.* **gebiddaþ** 5:44, 24:20, 26:41; *inf.* **gebiddan** 14:23; **gebidde** 6:5; *ps.p. mns.* **gebiddende** 26:39; *mnp.* **gebiddendae** 6:7 || CURARE (ORARE in WW) *subj.pt.3s.* **gebede** 19:13 [OED2 i-bid, *v.*]

bifian *v.2* 'shake, tremble' FEBRICITARE 'shake with a fever' *ps.p. fas.* **bifigende** 8:14 [n.] [OED2 bive, *v.*]

bigan *v.1* 'bend' PROVOLVERE *ps.p. mns.* **begende** 17:14 || FLECERE *ps.p. mnp.* **begende** 27:29; *nds.* **begende** Mk1:40 [OED2 bey, *v.*]

biggenga *m. wk* 'inhabitant' AGRICOLA *np.* **begengu** 21:35, 21:38; *dp.* **begengum** 21:33, 21:40, 21:41; **begængum** 21:34

bigspell *n.* 'parable' PARABOLA *as.* **bispell** 21:33, 21:45 (or *p.*?), 24:32; *dp.* **bispellum** 22:1 [OED2 byspel | bispel, *n.*]

bilewite *adj.* 'pure, innocent' SIMPLEX *np.* **bilwite** 10:16 [OED2 bilewhit, *adj.*]

bilketto, see **bealcettan**

bindan *v.III* 'bind together' (AL)LIGARE *ps.2s.* **bindes** 16:19; *ps.2p.* **bindaþ** 18:18; *ps.3p.* **bindaþ** 23:4 [OED2 bind, *v.*]

gebindan *v.III* 'bind together' (AL)LIGARE *ps.3s.* **gebindaþ** 12:29; *pt.3s.* **gebond** 14:3; *imp.p.*

gebindađ 22:13; **gebindeþ** 13:30; *pp.p.* **gebunde** 16:19; **gebunden** 18:18 || VINCIRE *pp. mas.* **gebundene** 27:2; **gebundenne** 27:15, 27:16 [see previous]

binnan *adv.* 'within, inside' INTUS ~ 23:26, 23:27; **binne** 23:25 [OED 2 bin | binne, *adv.* and *prep.*]

†**bisæcc** *m.* 'wallet, bag' PERA *as.* **bisæc** 10:10 [n.]

bisceop *m.* 'bishop' PONTIFEX *ap.* **biscopas** Jn18:3 [OED2 bishop, *n.*]

bismeradun etc., see **bysmorian**

[MK]**bitan** *v.I* 'bite' DISCERPERE *pt.3s.* **bat** Mk1:26; *ps.p. mns.* **bitende** Mk1:26 [OED2 bite, *v.*]

biterlice *adv.* 'bitterly, sorely' AMARE **bitterlice** 26:75 [OED2 bitterly, *adv.*]

blawan *v.VII* 'blow' FLARE *pt.3p.* **blewan** 7:25; **bleowan** 7:27 || CANARE *imp.s.* **blau** 6:2 [OED2 blow, *v.1*]

blæc *adj.* 'black' NIGER *mas.* **blæcne** 5:36 [black, *adj.* and *n.*]

blæcern *n.* or *m.* 'lamp, lantern' LUCERNA *ns.* ~ 6:22; *as.* ~ 5:15 (referred to by *hine*)

bled *f.* 'fruit' FRUCTUS *ap.* **blęd** 7:17, 7:18 [OED2 blede, *n.*]

bletsian *v.2* 'bless' BENEDICERE *pt.3s.* **bledsade** 14:19; **bletsade** 26:26 [OED2 bless, *v.1*]

gebletsian *v.2* 'bless' BENEDICERE *pp. mns.* **gebloetsad** 21:9, 23:39; *np.* **gebletsade** 25:34 [see previous]

blind *adj.* 'blind, a blind person (used as substantive)' CAECUS *mns.* ~ 12:22, 15:14; *mns.* **blindę** 23:26; *mas.* **blindne** 15:14; *np.* **blinde** 9:27, 9:28, 11:5, 15:14, 20:30, 21:14, 23:16, 23:17, 23:19, 23:24; *ap.* **blinde** 15:30, 15:31; *gp.* **blindra** 15:14 [OED2 blind, *adj.* (and *adv.*)]

blinnan *v.III* 'cease' CESSARE *pt.3s.* **blan** 14:32 [n.] [OED2 blin | blinn, *v.*]

geblissian *v.2* 'rejoice, exult' EXULTARE *imp.p.* **geblissiađ** 5:12 [cf. OED2 bliss, *v.*]

blod *n.* 'blood' SANGUIS *ns.* ~ 16:17, 23:35, 26:28, 27:25; *as.* **blod** 23:35, 27:4; *gs.* **blodes** 9:20, 27:6, 27:8; *ds.* **blode** 23:35, 27:24 [blood, *n.* (and *int.*)]

blodgyte *m.* 'bloodshed, blood' SANGUIS *ds.* **blodgyte** 23:30

boc *f.* 'book' LIBER *np.* **boec** 1:1 || LIBELLUM *ap.* (or *s.*?) **boec** 5:31, 19:7 || NL *as.* ~ MtCOLOPHON [book, *n.*]

bocere *m.* 'scribe, scholar' SCRIBA '(Jewish) scribe' *ns.* **bokere** 13:52; *as.* **bokere** 12:38 [n.]; *np.* **bokeras** 17:10, 21:15, 23:2, 23:13, 23:14, 23:23, 23:27, 26:57; **bokeres** 23:25; **boceras** 23:15; **bocera** 7:29; **bokere** 15:1; *ap.* **bokeras** 2:4, 23:34; *gp.* **bokera** 8:19; **bokere** 5:20; **bocera** 9:3; *dp.* **bokerum** 16:21, 20:18, 27:41 [booker, *n.*]

bodian *v.2* 'proclaim, announce' PRAEDICERE *ps.1s.* **bodige** Mk1:38; *pt.3s.* **bodede** 9:35; **bodade** 11:1, Mk1:4, Mk1:7, Mk1:14; *inf.* **bodige** Mk1:45; *imp.p.* **bodigađ** 10:7; **bodigaþ** 10:27; *pp.s.* **bodad** 24:14, 26:13; *ps.p. mns.* **bodende** 3:1, 4:23; **bodande** Mk1:39 [OED2 bode, *v.1*]

borg *m.* 'loan, debt' MUTUARI *as.* (*on*) ~ (*niman*) 5:42 'take (something) on loan' [n.] [OED2 borrow, *n.*]

brad *adj.* 'broad' PALMA *fap.* **brade** (*honde*) 26:67 [OED2 broad, *adj.*, *n.1*, and *adv.*]

brædan *v.1* 'spread, enlarge' DILATARE *ps.3p.* **brædaþ** 23:5 [brede, *v.2*]

brecan *v.IV* 'break' FRANGERE *pt.3s.* **bręc** 14:19; **bræc** 15:36, 26:26 || SOLVERE *infl.inf.* **brecanne** 5:17, **breccane** 5:17 || DESTRUERE *ps.3s.* **breceþ** 27:40 [OED break, *v.*]

gebrecan *v.IV* 'break apart' CONFRINGERE *pp.s.* **gebroken** 21:44 [see previous]

gebregdan *v.III* 'draw, unsheathe' EXIMERE *pt.3s.* **gebrægd** 26:51

brengan *v.1* 'bring' OFFERRE *pt.1s.*

brohte 17:16; *pt.3s.* **brohte** 25:20 [n.]; *pt.3p.* **brohtun** 2:11, 4:24, 8:16 [n.], 9:2 [n.], 9:32, 14:35, 22:19; *ptp.s.* **broht** 18:24; *pp.p.* **brohte** 19:13; *imp.s.* **breng** 8:4 || AFFERRE *pt.3p.* **brohtun** Mk1:32; *pp.s.* **broht** 14:11 || REFERRE *pt.3s.* **brohte** (*eft*) 27:3 || FERRE *ps.p. mnp.* **brengende** Mk2:3 [n.] [OED2 bring, *v.*]

gebrengan *v.1* 'bring' OFFERRE *pp.s.* **gebroht** 12:22 [see previous]

bringan *v.III* OFFERE *subj.ps.2s.* **bringa** 5:23 || AFFERRE *imp.p.* **bringaþ** 17:17 [OED2 bring, *v.*]

gebringan *v.III* 'bring' AFFERRE *imp.p.* **gebringaþ** 14:18 || OFFERE *inf.* **gebringan** Mk2:4 [see previous]

gebroc *n.* 'fragment, piece of bread' FRAGMENTUM *gp.* **gebroca** 14:20 [n.], 15:37 [cf. OED2 breach, *n.*]

brord *m.* 'blade of grain' HERBA *ns.* ~ 13:26 [OED2 brerd, *n.*]

broþor *m.* 'brother' FRATER *ns.* **boþer** 5:23 [n.]; **broþer** 7:4 (margin) [n.], 10:2 (*bis*), 10:21, 12:50, 18:21, 22:24; **broðer** 18:15; *as.* **broþer** 4:18, 4:21, 5:22 (or *d.*? see note), 17:1, 18:15; **broðer** Mk1:16, Mk1:19; *gs.* **broþer** 7:3, 7:5, 14:3; *ds.* **broþer** 5:22, 5:24, 7:4, 18:35, 22:25; **broðer** 22:24; *np.* **broþer** 12:46, 12:48, 12:49, 13:55; **broðer** 12:47; **broþre** 22:25, 23:8; *ap.* **broþer** 5:47, 19:29; **bloeþrę** 1:2 [n.]; **broeþre** 1:11; *gp.* **broþre** 25:40; *dp.* **broþrum** 20:24, 28:10 [brother, *n.* and *int.*]

gebroþor *m.* 'brothers' FRATER *ap.* **gebroþer** 4:18, 4:21 [i-brotheren, *n.*]

[MK]**brucan** *v.II* 'use, partake of food' EDERE *ps.p. mns.* **brucende** Mk1:6 [OED2 brook, v.*1*]

bryd *f.* 'bride' SPONSA *ds.* **bryde** 25:1 [bride, *n.1*]

brydguma *m. wk* 'bridegroom' SPONSUS *ns.* ~ 9:15 (*bis*), 25:5, 25:6, 25:10; *gs.* **brydguma** 9:15; *ds.* **brydguma** 25:1 [bridegroom, *n.*]

brymmsteam *m.* 'sea, sea-current, estuary' FRETUM *as.* **brymstream** 8:18 [n.]

bufan *prep.* 'over' SUPRA ~ 2:9 [bove, *adv.* and *prep.*]

burh *f.* 'town, city' CIVITAS *ns.* **burg** Mk1:33; *as.* **burg** 22:7; *ds.* ~ 10:11; *ap.* **burgas** 9:35 || NL *as.?* **byrig** Mk2:1; *ds.* **byrig** Mk1:9, Mk1:21 [OED2 burg, *n.*; burgh, *n.*; borough, *n.*]

butan *prep.* 'without, except' SINE ~ 10:29, 12:5, 13:22 [n.], 13:34, 13:57, 15:16 || EXCEPTUS ~ 5:32, 14:21 || EXTRA ~ 15:38, 21:39 [OED2 bout, *prep.* and *adv.*; but, *prep.*, *adv.*, *conj.*, and *n.2*]

butan *adv.* 'outside' DE FORIS ~ 23:26, Mk1:45 [see previous]

byldu *f.* 'boldness, courage, faith' FIDUCIA *as.* **bęldu** 14:27 [OED2 bield, *n.*]

byme *f. wk* 'trumpet' TUBA *as.* **beman** 6:2; *a/ds.* **beman** 24:31 [OED2 beme, *n.*]

gebyrd *f.* 'birth' NATALIS *gs.* **gebyrde** 14:6

byrgan *v.1* 'taste' GUSTARE *ps.3p.* **bergaþ** 16:28

byrgen *f.* 'burial place, grave' MONUMENTUM *gs.* **byrgenne** 27:60; *ds.* **byrgenne** 27:60, 28:8; *np.* **byrgenne** 27:52; *dp.* **byrgennum** 8:28, 27:53 || SEPULCHRUM *as.* **byrgenne** 27:64, 27:66, 28:1; *a/ds.* **byrgenne** 27:61; *ap.* **byrgenne** 23:29; *dp.* **byrgennum** 23:27 [OED2 burian, *n.*]

byrian *v.2* 'be lawful, be permitted' LICERE *pt.3s.* **byrede** 12:4 [OED2 bir, *v.*]

byrnan *v.1* 'burn up' ARDERE *ps.p. ngs.* **beornende** 13:42 || COMBURERE *infl.inf.* **beornane** 13:30 [OED2 burn, *v.1*]

†**gebyrþan** *v.1* 'burden, oppress' ONERARE *pp.p.* **gebyrde** 11:28 [n.]

byrþen *f.* 'burden' ONUS *ns.* **byrðen** 11:30; *ap.* **byrþenne** 23:4 [OED2 burden | burthen, *n.*]

bysmorian *v.2* 'mock, deride'

ILLUDERE *pt.3p.* **bismeradun** 27:29, 27:31; *ps.p. mnp.* **bismerende** 27:41 || DELUDERE *infl.inf.* **bismerene** 20:19 || DERIDERE *pt.3p.* **bismeradun** 9:24 [OED2 bismer, *v.*]

cafarnaum *prop.n. ns.* ~ 11:23; *as.* ~ 8:5; *ds.* ~ 4:13; **capharnaum** 17:24, Mk1:21, Mk2:1 (or *a.*?)

cafertun *m.* 'forecourt, enclosure' ATRIUM *as.* **cæfertun** 26:3, 26:58; *ds.* **cæfertune** 26:69

caifas *prop.n. ns.* ~ 26:3; *ds.* **caifan** 26:57

calic *m.* 'drinling vessel, cup' CALIX *ns.* ~ 26:39, 26:42; *as.* **cælc** 10:42; **cælic** 26:27; **kælic** 20:22, 20:23; *gs.* **cælces** 23:25; **cælcæs** 23:26 [OED2 chalice, *n.*]

[MK]**camel** *m.* 'camel' CAMELUS *gs.* **cameles** Mk1:6 [OED2 camel, *n.*]

cananeisc *adj.* 'of Canaan, Canaanit' CANANAEUS *mns.* **cananisca** 10:4; *nns.* **cananisc** 15:22 [Canaanitish, *adj.*]

candeltreow *n.* 'candlestick' CANDELABRUM *as.* ~ 5:15

carcern *n.* 'prison' CARCER *as.* ~ 5:25, 14:3, 18:30; *ds.* **carcerne** 14:10; **carcrænne** 25:44 [n.]; **carkærn** 25:36; **calkern** 25:43

casere *m.* 'emperor' CAESER *gs.* **kaseres** 22:21; *ds.* **kasere** 22:17, 22:21 (*bis*) [OED2 kaser, *n.*]

casering *m.* '(Roman) coin' DIDRAGMA *as.* ~ 17:24; *ds.* caseringe 17:24

cæg *f. wk* 'key' CLAVIS *ap.* **kægen** 16:19 [key, *n.1* and *adj.*]

ceace *f.* 'jaw, jawbone' MAXILLA *as.* **ceke** 5:39 [cheek, *n.*]

ceaf *n.* 'chaff' PALEA *ap.* ~ 3:12 [OED2 chaff, *n.1*]

ceald *adj.* 'cold' FRIGIDUS *ngs.* **galdes** 10:42 [n.] [OED2 cold, *adj.*]

ceapa *m. wk* 'merchant' NEGOTIATOR *ds.* **ceape** 13:45 [n.] [cf. OED2 cheap, *n.1*]

ceapung *f.* 'trade' NEGOTIATIO *ds.* **ceapunge** 22:5 [OED cheaping, *n.*]

ceaster *f.* (note *-as* plural in 9:35) 'city' CIVITAS *ns.* **cæstra** 5:14, 5:35, 8:34; **cæstre** 12:25, Mk1:33; **ceastre** 21:10; *as.* **cæstre** 4:5, 10:23, 28:11, Mk1:38; **caestrae** 4:13; **cæstræ** 8:33, 27:53; **ceastre** 23:34, Mk1:45; *ds.* **cæstre** 2:23, 10:14, 10:15, 26:18; **ceastræ** 21:17; **ceastre** 21:18, 23:34; *ap.* **cæstra** 10:5; **cæstre** 10:23 (or *s.*?); *dp.* **cæstrum** 11:1, 11:20, 14:13 || CASTELLUM *as.* 10:11 [n.], 21:2; *ap.* **cæstre** 14:15; **cæstras** 9:35 [OED2 chester, *n.1*]

cedron *prop.n. as.* ~ Jn18:1

cempa *m. wk* 'warrior' MILES *np.* **kęmpe** 27:27; *ap.* **cempa** 8:9; *dp.* **kempum** 28:12 [OED2 kemp, *n.1*]

cennan *v.1* 'beget, bring forth' GIGNERE *pt.3s.* **kende** 1:2, 1:16 || PARERE *ps.3s.* **kenneþ** 1:21, 1:23 [OED2 ken, *v.2*]

cennes *f.* 'generation' GENERATIO *ns.* **kennisse** 1:18 [n.]; *gs.* **kennisse** 1:1

centurio *m.* 'centurion' CENTURIO *ns.* ~ 8:8, 27:54; *ds.* **centurione** 8:13 [centurion, *n.*]

geceosan *v.II* 'choose' ELIGERE *pt.1s.* **geceas** 12:18; *pt.3p.* **gecuron** 13:48; *pp.p.* **gecoren** 20:16; **gecorænе** 22:14; *pp. np.* **gecorenan** 24:24; *dp.* **gecorenum** 24:22, 24:31 [n.] [cf. OED2 choose, *v.*]

cessarię *prop.n. gs.* ~ 16:13

chorazam *prop.n. ns.* ~ 11:21

cicen *n.* 'young chicken, chick' PULLUS *ap.* **ciken** 23:37 [chicken, *n.*]

cigan *v.1* 'cry, call out' (EX)CLAMARE *ps.3s.* **cægeþ** 15:23; *pt.3s.* **cegde** 14:30, 15:22, 27:50; **cęgde** 25:14; *infl.inf.* **ceganne** 9:13; *ps.p. mnp.* **cegende** 8:29 [n.], 9:27; *fns.?* **cegende** 3:3 || VOCARE *pt.3s.* **ceigde** 20:25; *imp.s.* **cege** 20:8; *inf.* **cegan** 22:3; *ps.p. mns.* **cegende** 18:2 (margin) || CONVOCARE *ps.p. mns.* (*tosomne*) **cegende** 10:1

gecigan *v.1* 'cry, call out' VOCARE

pt.3s. **gecægde** 4:21, 18:32; **geceigde** Mk1:20; *pp.p.* **gecęged** 20:16; **gecægde** 22:14 || CONVOCARE *ps.p. mns.* **gecegende** 15:10

cild *n.* 'child' PARVULUS *np.* ~ 19:13; *ap.* ~ 19:14 || INFANS *gp.* **cildra** 21:16 [child, *n.*]

†**cildfedende** adj. 'suckling a child' NUTRIENS *dp.* **cildfoedendum** 24:19 [n.]

cirm *m.* 'cry, shout' CLAMOR *ns.* ~ 25:6 [OED2 chirm, *n.*]

claþ *m.* 'cloth' COMMISSURA *as.* ~ 9:16 [n.] [OED2 cloth, *n.*]

clæne *adj.* 'clean, pure' MUNDUS *nns.* ~ 23:26; *fds.* ~ 27:59; *mnp.* ~ 5:8 [OED2 clean, *adj.*]

clæne *adv.* 'cleanly' MUNDARE ~ 12:44 [n.] [OED2 clean, *adv.*]

clænsian *v.2* 'cleanse, purge' MUNDARE *ps.2p.* **clænsigaþ** 23:25; *imp.p.* **clænsigæþ** 10:8; *pp.p.* **clænsade** 11:5 [OED2 cleanse, *v.*]

geclænsian *v.2* 'cleanse, purge' MUNDARE *imp.s.* **geclænsa** 23:26; *inf.* **geclęnsie** 8:2; **geclænsige** 8:3; **geclensige** Mk1:40; **geclænsie** Mk1:41; *pp.s.* **geclensad** 8:3, Mk1:42 [see previous]

[MK]**clænsung** *f.* 'cleansing' EMUNDATIO *as.* **clænsunga** Mk1:44 [n.] [OED2 cleansing, *n.*]

clipian *v.2* 'cry, call out' (EX)CLAMARE *ps.3s.* **cliopaþ** 12:19; *pt.3s.* **cliopade** 27:46; **cleopade** Mk1:23; *pt.3p.* **cliopadun** 14:26, 20:30; **cleopadun** 20:31, 21:9, 27:23; *ps.p. mgs.* **cliopande** Mk1:3; *mnp.* **clipigende** 21:15 || VOCARE *ps.3s.* **cleopaþ** 27:47; *pt.3s.* **cliopade** 4:21, 20:32; *imp.p.* **cliopað** 22:9; *ps.p. mnp.* **clipende** 11:16 [n.] || CONVOCARE *pt.3s.* (*tosomne*) **cliopade** 15:32 [OED2 clepe, *v.*]

clipung *f.* 'cry, shout' CLAMOR *ns.* **cleopung** 25:6 [OED2 cleping, *n.*]

gecnawan *v.VII* 'recognize' COGNOSCERE *inf.* ~ 16:3 [yknow, *v.*]

cneoris *f.* 'generation' GENERATIO *ns.* ~ 17:17; **cneorisse** 12:39, 24:34; **cneuris** 16:4; *as.* **cneorisse** 11:16, 12:41, 12:42, 12:45 (? see note); **cneorissę** 23:36; *np.* **kneorisse** 1:17 (*bis*); **kneo** 1:17 [n.]; *dp.* **kneorissum** 1:17

cneow *n.* 'knee' GENU *as.* **kneu** 27:29; *ap.* **cneu** 17:14 [knee, *n.*]

[MK]**cneowbiging** *f.* 'bending of the knee, kneeling' GENU FLEXO *ds.* (*mid*) **cneu ... beginge** Mk1:40 [n.]

†**cnidan** *v.I* 'beat' CAEDERE *pt.3p.* **cnidun** 21:35 [n.]

cniht *m.* 'boy' PUER *ns.* **cneht** 2:9, 8:6, 8:8, 8:13, 12:18, 17:18; *as.* **cneht** 2:11, 2:13 (*bis*), 2:14, 2:20, 2:21; *gs.* **cnehtes** 2:20; **cnęhte** 2:8; *ap.* **cnehtas** 2:16; **cnæhtas** 21:15; *dp.* **cnehtum** 11:16 || PARVULUS *ns.* **cneht** 18:4; *ds.* **cnæhte** 18:5; *np.* **cnehtas** 18:3; *ap.* **cnæhtas** 18:2 (margin); *dp.* **cnehtum** 14:21, 15:38 [OED2 knight, *n.*]

cnyssan *v.1* 'knock (on the door)' PULSARE *imp.p.* **cnyssaþ** 7:7; *ps.p. mds.* **cyssande** 7:8 [OED2 knush, *v.*]

cofa *m. wk* 'room, chamber' CUBICULUM *as.* **cofan** 6:6 || PENETRABILIS *dp.* **cofum** 24:26 [OED2 cove, *n.1*]

corn *n.* 'seed, grain' GRANUM *ns.* ~ 17:20; *ds.* **corne** 13:31 [OED2 corn, *n.1*]

costere *m.* 'tempter, the devil' TEMPTATOR *ns.* ~ 4:3

costian *v.2* 'try, tempt' TEMPTARE *ps.2p.* **costigaþ** 22:18; *pt.3s.* **costade** 19:3; *imp.2g.* **costa** 4:7; *ps.p. mns.* **costænde** 22:35; *mnp.* **costende** 16:1; *pp.s.* **costad** 4:1 [costen, *v.1*]

costung *f.* 'temptation' TEMPTATIO *as.* **constungae** 6:13 [n.]; **costunge** 26:41 [costning, *n.1*]

crawan *v.VII* 'crow' CANTARE *ps.3s.* **cræd** 26:34, 26:75; *pt.3s.* **creow** 26:74 [crow, *v.1*]

crist *m.* 'Christ, title applied to Jesus

of Nazareth' CRISTUS *ns.* ~ 16:16, 16:20, 23:10, 24:5, 24:23, 26:63, 26:68, 27:17, 27:22, 27:37; **krist** 1:16, 2:4; *gs.* **cristes** Mk1:1; **kristes** Mt INCIPT, 1:18, 11:2; *ds.* **criste** 22:42; **kriste** 1:17 || part of PSEUDOCRISTUS *np.* (*lyge*) **crist** 24:24 [Christ, *n.* and *int.*]

crum *m.* 'crumb, morsel of food' MICA *dp.* **cromum** 15:27 [OED2 crumb, *n.*]

culfre *f. wk* 'dove, pigeon' COLUMBA *as.* ~ 3:16; *as.* **culfra** Mk1:10; *np.* **culfra** 10:16; *ap.* **culfran** 21:12 [OED2 culver, *n.1*]

cuma *m. wk* 'visitor, guest' HOSPES *ns.* ~ 25:35; **cuman** 25:43; *as.* **cuman** 25:38, 25:44 [comer, *n.*]

cuman *v.IV* 'come' VENIRE *ps.1s.* **cume** 8:7; *ps.2s* **cumest** 5:24; **cymest** 3:14; *ps.3s.* **cymeþ** 8:9, 16:27, 17:11, 18:7, 21:5, 21:9, 21:40, 24:14, 24:44, 24:46, 25:6, 25:31, Mk1:7; **cymeð** 3:11; **cymþ** 13:19, 24:50; **cymaþ** 23:35; **cymid** 24:42 [n.]; *ps.3p.* **cumaþ** 7:15, 8:11, 9:15, 13:32, 24:5; *ps.3p.* **cymeþ** 23:36; *pt.1s.* **cwom** 9:13, 10:34, 10:35; **com** Mk1:38; **cuom** 5:17; *pt.2s.* **cwome** 8:29, 26:50; **come** Mk1:24; *pt.3s.* **cuom** 2:21, 3:1, 3:13, 8:14, 8:28, 11:18, 11:19, 12:9, 12:42, 13:25, 13:36, 13:54, 14:25, 15:25, 15:29, 15:39, 18:11, 21:19; **cwom** 4:13, 9:1, 9:23, 9:28, 16:13, 17:14, 19:1, 20:28, 21:23, 21:32, 25:19, 26:36, 26:40, 26:43, 26:45, 26:47, 27:57, 28:1, Mk1:9; **com** 17:12, 24:39, 25:10, Mk1:14, Mk1:40; *pt.1p.* **cuomon** 2:2; **coman** 25:39; *pt.2p.* **coman** 25:36; *pt.3p.* **cuomun** 7:25, 13:4, 14:33, 16:5; **cuomon** 7:27, 14:34; **cwomon** 9:10; **cwoman** 17:24, 18:31, 26:60, 27:33, 27:53; **cwomun** 28:11, 28:13, Jn18:3; **quomon** 2:1 [n.]; **comun** 25:11; **comen** 20:9; **coman** 21:1; **comon** Mk1:29, Mk2:3; *subj.ps.3s.* **cyme** 10:13; **cume** 10:23, 27:49; *subj.ps.3p.* ~ 27:64; *subj.pt.1s.* **cuome** 5:17 [n.]; **cwome** 10:34; *subj.pt.3s.* **cuome** 14:29; **cwome** 23:39; *imp.s.* **cym** 9:18, 19:21; **cyme** 8:9; **cum** 14:29; *imp.p.* **cumaþ** 4:19, 22:4, 28:6, Mk1:17; **cumeþ** 11:28; **cymeþ** 21:38, 25:34; *inf.* ~ 17:10, 19:14, 22:3, 24:43; **cume** 14:28, 16:24; **cwome** 11:3 (? see note); *infl.inf.* **cumene** 24:48; *ps.p. mns.* **cumende** 2:9, 2:23, 3:16, 8:2, 12:44, 18:7, 25:27; **cymende** 2:8, 16:27, Mk2:13; *mas.* **cymendę** 16:28; **cumende** 24:30, 26:64; **cymende** 27:32; *np.* **cumende** 8:33, 10:29 (? see note), 14:12, 20:9, 20:10; *ap.* **cumende** 3:7 || ACCEDERE *pt.3s.* **cuom** 8:5; **cwom** 9:18, 25:22, 26:7; **com** Mk1:31; *pt.3p.* **cwoman** 4:11; **cwomun** 19:3, 26:60; *ps.p. mns.* **cumende** 8:19, 18:21, 19:16, 25:20, 25:24; *mnp.* **cumende** 13:27, 14:12 || CONVENIRE (*tosomne*) 'come together' *pt.3s.* **cwom** Jn18:2; *pt.3p.* **cwomun** 27:62; *pt.3p.* **cwoman** 1:18 || (EX)ORIRI *pt.3s.* **cuom** 13:6; *pt.3p.* **cuomun** 13:5 || ADVENIRE *subj.ps.3s.* **cume** 6:10 || INVENIRE *ps.3p.* **cymeð** 7:14 [n.] || OCCURRERE *pt.3s.* **quom** 28:9 || FIERI *pt.3s.* **cwom** 26:20 || NL *pt.3s.* **cuom** 12:42 [n.] [come, *v.*]

cunnan *pret.pres.v.* (but note *-eþ*, *-aþ* present forms) 'know' NOSCERE *ps.1s.* **conn** 26:72; *ps.3s.* **con** 11:27 (*bis*); *ps.2p.* **cunneþ** 7:11 [n.]; **cunnað** 16:3 (*bis*); **cunun** 20:25; *pt.1s.* **cuþe** 7:23; *pt.3s.* **cuðe** 26:74 || NESCIRE (w. negative) *ps.1s.* **con** 25:12; *ps.2p.* ~ 22:29, 24:42, 25:13 || SCIRE *ps.2p.* **cunnun** 27:65 || SAPERE *ps.2s.* **const** 16:23 [can, *v.*]

gecunnan *pret.pres.v.* 'know' NOSCERE *inf.* ~ 13:11 [see previous]

gecuþ *adj.* 'known' MANIFESTUS *mas.* **gecuðne** 12:16

cuþlice *adv.* 'indeed, truly' IGITUR ~ 1:17, 7:20, 12:28 || ENIM 16:9 (*om.* in WW) || UTIQUE ~ 25:27

[OED2 couthly, *adv.*]

cweartern *n.* 'prison' CARCER *as.* **quartern** 25:39 [quartern, *n.1*]

cweman *v.1* 'please' ACCUSARE 'accuse (?)' *pt.3p.* **cwæmdon** 12:10 [n.] [?queem, *v.*]

cwen *f.* 'woman, queen' REGINA *ns.* **cwæn** 12:42 [queen, *n.*]

cweorn *f.* 'mill' MOLA *ns.* **cwern** 18:6; *ds.* **cweorne** 24:41 [quern, *n.1*]

cweþan *v.V* 'say, tell' DICERE *ps.1s.* **cwæþe** 5:39, 5:44; **cweþe** 5:34, 6:25, 8:9; **cweðe** 8:9, 13:30; **cwæþ** 18:22; *ps.2s.* **cwiðst** 27:11; (w. contracted subject) **cweþestu** 7:4; *ps.3s.* **cweþ** 7:21, 8:25; **cwęþ** 12:44, 13:57; **cwið** 15:5; **cwæþ** 21:25, 26:18; *ps.1p.* **cwęþaþ** 21:25; **cweðaþ** 21:26; *ps.2p.* **cweðaþ** 15:5; **cweoþað** 16:2, 16:15, 17:20; **cwæþað** 23:30; **cwæþad** 23:16; *ps.3p.* **cweþað** 7:22, 11:17, 17:10; **cweðaþ** 12:32 (*bis*); **cwæþað** 11:18, 11:19; **cweoþaþ** 16:13; *pt.1s.* **cwæþ** 16:11; *pt.2s.* **cwæde** 26:25, 26:64; *pt.3s.* **cwæþ** (the distinction between *pr.* and *pt* is not entirely clear) 2:8, etc.; **cwæð** 20:6; **cweþ** 9:22, 11:25, 12:25, 15:16, 15:27; **cweð** 12:3; **cwęþ** 4:4, 17:26, 18:22; **cwaeþ** 5:22; *pt.3p.* **cwædon** 2:5, 9:28, 12:23, 15:33, 21:31; **cwædun** 13:10, 16:14, 19:7, 20:7, 20:22, 20:33, 21:16, 21:27, 22:21, 22:23, 22:42, 26:5, 26:35, 26:61, 26:66, 26:73, 27:4, 27:21, 27:23, 27:40, 27:49, Mk1:37; **cwedun** 9:3, 9:11, 9:34, 12:2, 12:24, 13:27, 13:28, 13:51, 15:12, 15:34, 17:19, 17:24, 21:38, 25:8, 27:6, 27:22, 27:47, Mk1:30; **cwedon** 19:10; **cweden** 13:54 (or *subj.*?); *subj.ps.2s.* **cweþe** Mk1:44; *subj.ps.3s.* **cwæþe** 5:22, 21:3; *subj.ps.2p.* **cweoþan** 23:39; **cweðe** 21:21; *subj.ps.3p.* **cwæþan** 5:11; *imp.s.* **cwæþ** 20:21, 26:18; *imp.p.* **cweþaþ** 10:27; **cwæþað** 26:18; *inf.* ~ 3:9, 4:17, 11:7, 26:22, Mk2:9; *infl.inf.* **cweþane** 9:5; **cweþanne** Mk2:9; *ps.p. mns.* **cweþende** 1:20 [n.], etc.; **cwæþende** 8:27, etc.; **cwæðende** Mk1:25; **cwęþende** 14:27, 14:30; *mas.* **cweþende** 1:22, 2:5, 2:15, 2:17, 3:3, 4:14, 8:17, 12:17, 13:35; **cwæþende** 27:9; **cwæðende** 21:4; *mgs.* **cweþende** 13:14; *mds.* **cwæþendum** 22:31; *nns.* **cweþende** 15:22; **cwæþende** 27:19; *fns.* **cwæþende** 15:25; **cwæðende** 21:10; **cweþende** 17:5; **cwęþende** 26:69 (or *n.*?); *nns.* **cwæþende** 27:25; *np.* **cweþende** 2:2, etc.; **cwæþende** 8:29, etc.; **cwęþende** 10:7, 18:1; *pp.s.* **cwæden** 5:21, 5:27, 5:38, 27:9, 27:22; **cweden** 2:17, 3:3, 27:17; **cwęden** 5:33, 5:43 || AIT *pt.3s.* **cwæþ** 4:10, etc.; **cwęþ** 4:7, 11:4, 13:11, 14:31, 19:8, 21:21 (margin); **cweþ** 8:4, 8:7, 8:8, 8:19, 8:22, 8:32, 12:39, 13:28, 13:29, 13:52, 14:2, 14:18, 15:24, 15:28, Mk2:14; *pt.3p.* **cwædun** 21:41 || INQUIT *ps.3s.* **cweð** 14:8 || PART of NUMQUID *ps.2s.* **cweþest** 12:23 [n.] [queath, *v.*, quoth, *v.*]

gecweþan *v.V* 'say, tell' DICERE *imp.s.* **gecwæþ** 4:3; **gecweþ** 8:8; *infl.inf.* **gecweþanne** 9:5; *pp.s.* **gecwæden** 5:31, 8:17, 21:4; **gecweden** 13:35 [OED2 i-quethe, *v.*]

cwiþan *v.2* 'lament' LAMENTARE *pt.1p.* **cwiddun** 11:17 (margin)

cwylman *v.1* 'torture, kill' AFFICERE *pt.3p.* **cwelmaþ** 10:21 [quelm, *v.*]

cyme *m.* 'coming, advent' ADVENTUS *ns.* ~ 24:27, 24:39; *gs.* **cymes** 24:3 [come, *n.1*]

cymen *m.* 'cumin' CUMINUM *as.* **cymen** 23:23 [OED2 cumin, *n.*]

cyning *m.* 'king' REX *ns.* ~ 14:9, 22:7, 22:11, 22:13, 25:34, 25:41, 27:11, 27:29, 27:42; **king** 2:3; **kining** 2:2; **cyningc** 21:5, 25:40, 27:37; *as.* ~ 1:6; *gs.* **kyninges** 2:1, 2:9, 5:35; *ds.* **cyninge** 18:23, 22:2; *np.* **cyningas** 17:25; *gp.* **kyninga** 11:8; *dp.* **kyningum** 10:18 [king, *n.*]

cynn *n.* 'lineage, race' GENIMEN *ns.* ~ 23:33; *ds.* **cynne** 26:29 || GENUS *ns.* ~ 17:21; *ds.* **cynne** 13:47 ||

PROGENIES *ns.* - 3:7, 12:34 || TRIBUS *np.* - 24:30; *ap.* - 19:28 [OED2 kin, *n.1*]

cyrce *f.* 'church, congregation' ECCLESIA *as.* **circae** 16:18; *ds.* **circan** 18:17 (*bis*) [church, *n.1* and *adj.*]

cyreneisc *adj.* 'of Cyrene' CYRENAEUS *mas.* **cyreniscnę** 27:32

cyrran *v.1* 'turn, go/come back, return' REDIRE *pt.3p.* **cerdun** 2:12 || REVERTI *ps.3s.* **cerraþ** 24:18 [OED2 chare | char, *n.1*]

gecyrran *v.1* 'turn' CONVERTERE *pt.3s.* **gecerde** 9:22; *pt.3p.?* **gecerrede** 13:15 (or *pp.p. mnp.*?); *imp.s.* **gecer** 26:52 || REVERTERE *subj.ps.3s.* **gecerre** 10:13 || SECEDERE 'turn aside to, withdraw' *pt.3s.* **gecerde** 2:22 [OED2 i-cherre, *v.*]

cyssan *v.1* 'kiss' OSCUARI *ps.1s.* **cysse** 26:48; *pt.3s.* **cyste** 26:49 [OED2 kiss, *v.*]

cyþan *v.1* 'tell' NUNTIARE *pt.3p.* **cyðdon** 8:33; **cyddun** 14:12 || RENUNTIARE *imp.p.* **cyþaþ** 11:4 || TESTIFICARI *subj.ps.3p.* - 26:62 || NL 'proclaim, preach' *infl.inf.* **cyþenne** Mt INCIPIT; [OED2 kithe | kythe, *v.*]

gecyþan *v.1* 'tell, make known' MANIFESTUM FACERE *ps.3s.* **gecyþæþ** 26:73 [see previous]

cyþnes *f.* 'witness, testimony' TESTIMONIUM *a/ds.* **cyþnisse** 8:4, 10:14 (margin), 10:18, 23:31, 24:14, Mk1:44; *ap.* **cyðnisse** 27:13

gedafenian *v.2* 'be appropriate, fitting' OPPORTERE *pt.3s.* **gedæfnade** 18:33; **gedęfnade** 23:23

daniele *prop.n. ds.* - 24:15

dauid *prop.n. ns.* - 22:43, 22:45; **dauið** 12:3; *gs.* **dauiðes** 1:1, 9:27, 12:23, 15:22, 20:30, 20:31, 21:9, 21:15, 22:42; **dauiþes** 1:20; *ds.* **dauide** 1:17; **dauiðe** 1:17

dæg *m.* 'day' DIES *ns.* - 6:34, 27:62 [n.]; *as.* - 11:23, 20:6, 24:38, 25:13, 26:29, 27:8, 28:15; *gs.* **dæges** 20:12; *ds.* **dæge** 6:34, 7:22, 13:1, 22:23, 22:46, 24:36, 24:50, 26:17, 27:15; - 12:36, 14:6, 16:21, 17:23, 20:19, 24:42, 27:64; *np.* **dagas** 9:15, 24:22 (*bis*); *ap.* **dagas** 12:40, 28:20; *gp.* **daga** 4:2, 12:40, Mk1:13; **dagana** 24:29; *dp.* **dagum** 2:1, 3:1, 11:12, 17:1, 23:30, 24:19, 24:37, 24:38, 27:63, Mk1:9, Mk2:1 || part of BIDUUM *dp.* **dagum** 26:2 || part of TRIDUUM *np.* **dagas** 15:32; *dp.* **dagum** 26:61, 27:40 || NL *ns.* - 12:45 [n.]; *as.* - 28:1; *ds.* **dæge** 27:62 [day, *n.*]

dæghwamlic *adj.* 'daily' SUBSTANTIALIS *mas.* **dæghwæmlicu** 6:11 [n.] [daiwhomly, *adj.*]

dæghwamlice *adv.* 'daily, every day' COTIDIE - 26:55

dæglic *adj.* 'daily' DIURNUS *mds.* **deglicum** 20:2; **dęglicum** 20:13 [daily, *adj.* and *n.*]

dæl *m.* 'part' PARS *as.* - 15:21, 24:51; *ds.* **dęle** 2:22; **dæle** 16:13; *ap.* **dæles** 27:51 || part of QUADRANS *as.* (*feorþan*) - 5:26 || REGINA *gs.*? **dæles** 12:42 (mistranslation or misplaced gloss? see note) [OED2 deal, *n.1*]

dælan *v.1* 'divide' SEPARARE *infl.inf.* **delanne** 10:35 [OED2 deal, *v.*]

gedælan *v.1* 'divide' DIVIDERE *ps.3s.* **gedælaþ** 24:51; *pt.3p.* **gedældun** 27:35; *pp.s.* **gedæled** 12:26; *pp. nns.* **gedęled** 12:25; **gedæled** 12:25 [see previous]

dead *adj.* 'dead' MORTUUS *nns.* **dead** 9:24; *m/nis.* **deade** 4:16 (or noun? see note); *np.* **deade** 8:32, 11:5, 28:4; *ap.* **deaða** 8:22; **deaðe** 10:8; **deada** 8:22; *gp.* **deadra** 22:31, 22:32, 23:27 || DEFUNGI *mns.* - 2:19; *np.* **deaðe** 2:20 [OED2 dead, *adj.*, *n.*, and *adv.*]

deaf *adj.* 'deaf' SURDUS *mns.* - 12:22; *mas.* - 9:32 [n.]; *np.* **deafe** 11:5 [OED2 deaf, *adj.*]

dearnunga *adv.* 'secretly' CLAM **dernunga** 2:7; part of MOECHARI 'fornicate, commit adultery' (*licgan*) **dernunge** 5:27, 5:32

deaþ *m.* 'death' MORS *as.* **deað** 16:28; **dead** 10:21; *ds.* **deaþe** 10:21, 27:1; **deaðe** 26:38, 26:59; **deade** 20:18; **dead** 26:66; *gp.* **deaða** 15:4 [n.]; *dp.* **deadum** 17:9 || MORTUUS *ds.* **deaþe** 14:2, 27:64; **deade** 28:7 || OBITUS *as.* **dead** 2:15 || part of TRADERE *ds.* **deaþe** Jn18:2 [death, *n.*]

decapoli *prop.n. ds.* ~ 4:25

defe *adj.* 'fitting, proper' PERFECTUS *mns.* **doefe** 19:21 [n.]

gedefe *adj.* 'fittting, righteous, perfect' PERFECTUS *mns.* **gedoefe** 5:48; *mnp.* **gedoefe** 5:48

gedelfan *v.III* 'dig' FODERE *pt.3s.* **gedælf** 21:33 [cf. OED2 delve, *v.*]

dema *m. wk* 'judge' IUDEX *ns.* **doeme** 5:25; *ds.* **doeme** 5:25; *np.* **doeme** 12:27 [OED2 deme, *n.1*]

deman *v.1* 'judge' IUDICARE *ps.2p.* **doemeþ** 7:2; *imp.p.* **doemeþ** 7:1; *inf.* **doeme** 16:3; *ps.p. mnp.* **doemende** 19:28; *pp.p.* **doemed** 7:1; **doemde** 7:2 || IUDICIUM *ps.3s.* **doemeð** 12:18 [n.] [OED2 deem, *v.*]

gedeman *v.1* 'judge' CONDEMNARE *ps.3p.* **gedoemeþ** 20:18 || IUDICARE *inf.* **gedoeme** 16:3 [i-deme, *v.*]

deofol *n.* or *m.* 'devil, Satan' DAEMONIUM *ns.* **deoful** 17:18; *as.* **deoful** 11:18, Mk1:32; *ds.* **deofle** 15:22; *ap.* **dioful** 4:24; **deoful** 7:22; **deoflas** Mk1:39; **deofles** Mk1:34; *gp.* **deofla** 9:34, 12:24 || DAEMON *as.* **deoful** 9:33; *np.* **deoful** 8:31; *ap.* **deoful** 9:34, 12:24, 12:27, 12:28 || DIABOLUS, ZABULUS *ns.* **deoful** 4:5, 4:11, 13:39; **deaful** 4:8; *ds.* **deofle** 4:1, 25:41 [devil, *n.*]

deofolseoc *adj.* 'possessed by devils, insane, (subst.) one possessed by devils, insanity(?)' DAEMONIUM *ns.* **deofulseoke** 12:22; *as.* **deofulseocne** 9:32; *adj. np.* or *n.ap.*? **deofulseoke** 8:33 [n.]; *ap.?* **deofulseoke** 8:16 [n.]; **deofulseoka** 8:28; **deofulsoece** 10:8

deon *v.1* 'suck' LACTARE *ps.p. gp.* **diendra** 21:16 [n.]

digol *n.* 'secret' OCCULTUM *gs.* **degles** 10:26

digollice *adv.* 'secretly, privately' OCCULTE **degullice** 1:19 || SECRETE **degullice** 17:19, 20:17, 24:3 [cf. OED2 dighel, *adj.*]

digolnes *f.* 'secret, (*in degulnisse*) in secret, secretly' ABSCONSUM, ABSCONDITUM *ds.* **degulnisse** 6:4 (*bis*), 6:6, 6:18 (*bis*)

dile *m.* 'dill, anise' ANETHUM *as.* **dile** 23:23 [OED2 dill, *n.1*]

diner *m.* 'coin, denarius' DENARIUS *as.* **dinere** 22:19; *ds.* **dinere** 20:2, 20:9, 20:10, 20:13; *gp.* **denera** 18:28 [n.] [OED2 denar | denare, *n.*, denarius, *n.*]

disc *m.* 'dish' DISCUS *ds.* **disce** 14:8, 14:11 [OED2 dish, *n.*]

discipul *m.* 'disciple' DISCIPULUS *np.* **discipuli** 5:1; **discipulas** 8:25, 12:2; **discpl** 28:13; *dp.* **discilum** 26:26 [n.]; **discp** 26:31 [n.]; **discipulas** 28:7; **discpl** 28:8 [disciple, *n.*]

dohtor *f.* 'daughter' FILIA *ns.* **dohter** 9:18, 9:22, 14:6, 15:28; **dogter** 15:22; *as.* **dohter** 10:35, 10:37; *ds.* **dohter** 21:5 [daughter, *n.*]

dol *adj.* 'foolish, stupid' FATUUS *mns.* **dole** 5:22 || STULTUS *mds.* **dolum** 7:26 [OED2 dull *adj.*]

dom *m.* 'judgement' IUDICIUM ~ 5:40 [n.], 23:23; *gs.* **domes** 12:36 (cf. *domesdæg*), 23:14; *ds.* **dome** 5:21, 7:2, 12:20, 23:33; **domæ** 12:41, 12:42; *gp.* **doma** 5:21, 5:22 [OED2 doom, *n.*]

dom ? Mk1:6 (see note)

domdæg *m.* 'Doomsday, the day of judgement' DIES IUDICII *ds.* **domdæge** 11:22, 11:24 [cf. OED2 doomsday, *n.*]

domesdæg *m.* 'Doomsday, the day of judgement' DIES IUDICII *ds.* **domesdæge** 10:15 [OED2 doomsday, *n.*]

don *anom.v.* 'do' FACERE *ps.1s.* **do** 20:13, 20:32 [n.], 21:24; **dom** 19:16 [n.], 27:22; *ps.2s.* **doest** 21:23; *ps.3s.* **doeþ** 5:32 (causative with *þæt*-clause), 5:45 (causative with inf.), 8:9, 18:35, 21:40, 24:48; *ps.2p.* **doaþ** 5:47, 21:21; **doþ** 23:15 (*bis*); *ps.3p.* **doeþ** 5:46; **doaþ** 5:47 (*bis*), 12:2; **doð** 23:3; *pt.2s.* **dydest** 20:12; *pt.3s.* **dyde** 1:24, 9:22, 12:3, 13:26, 20:5, 23:23, 26:13, 27:23; *pt.2p.* **dydun** 25:40, 25:45 (*bis*); **dydon** 25:40; *pt.3p.* **dydun** 12:14, 12:16, 21:7, 21:36, 22:15, 28:15; **dydon** 17:12, 21:6, 26:4, 26:19; *subj.ps.3s.* **doa** 6:3; *subj.ps.2p.* **doan** 6:1; *subj.ps.3p.* **doan** 6:2, 6:7; **doa** 7:12; *imp.s.* **do** 8:9; *imp.p.* **doaþ** 7:12; **doað** Mk1:3; **doð** 23:3 (*bis*); *inf.* **doan** 20:15; *infl.inf.* **doanne** 12:2, 12:12; *ps.p. mas.* **donde** 24:46 || AGERE *pt.3p.* **dydon** 11:20, 11:21, 12:41; *imp.p.* **doeþ** 3:2; **doaþ** 4:17; *ps.p. mns.* **doende** 15:36 || BENEFACERE *imp.p.* **doeþ** (*wel*) 5:44 'do well' || COMMITTERE(?) *ps.3s.* **fæþ** 5:32 (miscopy? see note) || part of ADULTARE *imp.s.* **do** 19:18 || NL *pt.3p.* **dydon** Mk2:4 [do, *v.*]

gedon *anom.v.* 'make, bring it about that…' FACERE *ps.1s.* **gedom** 4:19 (causative, with a *þæt*-clause); **gedoa** Mk1:17 (causative, with a *þæt*-clause); *ps.1p.* **gedoaþ** 28:14; *pt.3s.* **gedyde** 13:28; *pt.3p.* **gedydon** 15:6, 21:13; *inf.* **gedoa** 9:28, 16:25; *pp.s.* **gedoan** 23:15; *pp.p.* **gedoan** 18:31; **gedoen** 28:11 || EICERE *imp.s.* **geþo** 7:5 [n.] || PONERE *ps.3p.* **gedoaþ** 9:17 (MITTERE in WW) [n.]

drædan *v.VII* 'dread, fear' TIMERE *pt.3s.* **dreord** 14:5 [n.]; *pt.3p.* **dreordun** 9:8 [n.], 19:25, 21:46 [OED2 dread, *v.*]

gedrefan *v.1* 'disturb, vex' TURBARE *pp.s.* **gedroefed** 2:3; *pp.p.* **gedryfed** 14:26; **gedræfde** 24:6

drif *f.?* 'fever' FEBRIS *ns.* ~ 8:15 [n.]

[MK]**gedrif** *n.* 'fever' FEBRIS *ds.* **gedrif** Mk1:31 [n.]

[MK]**drifan** *v.I* 'drive out, expel' EICERE *pt.3s.* **draf** Mk1:43 || EXPELLERE *pt.3s.* **draf** Mk1:12 [drive, *v.*]

drincan *v.III* 'drink' BIBERE *ps.1s.* **drince** 26:29 (*bis*); *ps.3s.* **drinceþ** 24:49; *ps.1p.* **drincaþ** 6:31; *subj.ps.1s.* **drince** 26:42; *subj.ps.2p.* ~ 20:23; *imp.p.* **drincaþ** 26:27; *inf.* ~ 20:22, 25:35, 25:37, 25:42, 27:34 (*bis*), 27:48; *ps.p. mns.* **drincende** 11:18, 11:19; **drincande** 20:22; *np.* **drincende** 24:38 || POTARE *ps.p. mns.* **drincande** 11:19 || EBRIUS *pp. dp.* **druncennum** 24:49 [OED2 drink, *v.1*]

drohtian *v.2* 'dwell, live' CONVERSARI *pt.3p.* **drohtadun** 17:22 [n.]

dryge *adj.* 'dry' ARIDUS *fap.* ~ 12:43 [OED2 dry, *adj.* and *adv.*]

dryhten *m.* 'lord' DOMINUS *ns.* ~ 7:21, 7:22 (*bis*), 8:25, 11:25, 16:22, 17:4, 18:21, 18:32, 18:34, 20:30, 20:33, 21:3, 21:29, 21:40, 22:44, 24:42, 24:45, 24:46, 24:48, 24:50, 25:11 (*bis*), 25:19, 25:20, 25:21, 25:23, 25:24, 25:26, 25:37, 25:44, 26:22, 27:10, 27:63. 28:6; **drihten** 7:21, 8:2, 8:6, 8:8, 8:21, 9:18, 9:28, 12:8, 13:27, 13:51, 14:28, 14:30, 15:22, 15:25, 15:27; *as.* ~ 9:38, 22:37, 22:43, 22:45; *gs.* **dryhtnes** 1:24, 4:7, 23:39, 25:21, 28:2; **dryht(nes)** 21:9, 25:23; **drihtnes** 1:20, 2:13, 2:19, 3:3, Mk1:3; ~ 25:18; *ds.* **dryhtne** 4:10, 18:31, 21:42, 22:31; **drihtne** 1:22, 2:15; **drihten** 5:33 [OED2 drightin | drighten | dright, *n.*]

drync *m.* 'drink, beverage' POTUS *as.* ~ 10:42 [OED2 drink, *n.*]

dumb *adj.* 'dumb, mute' MUTUS *mns.* ~ 12:22; *mns.* **dumbe** 9:33; *mas.* **dumb** 9:32 [n.]; *ap.* **dumbe** 15:30, 15:31 [OED2 dumb, *adj.* and *n.*]

dun *f.* 'mountain' MONS *as.* ~ 5:14; **dune** 5:1, 14:23, 15:29, 17:1,

26:30, 28:16; **þune** 4:8 [n.]; *ds.* **dune** 8:1, 17:9, 17:20, 21:1, 21:21, 24:3; *dp.* **dunum** 18:12 [n.], 24:16 [down, *n.1*]

durran (DOE dearr) *pret.pres.v.* 'dare' AUDERE *pt.3s.* **dyste** 22:46 [n.] || NL (TIMERE + *inf.*) *pt.3s.* (*ne*) **durste** 2:22 [n.] [dare, *v.1*]

duru *f.* 'door' IANUA *ns.* **dure** 25:10 [n.]; *ds.* **dure** 26:71; **dore** Mk1:33, Mk2:2; *dp.* **dorum** 24:33 || OSTIUM *as.* **dure** 6:6; *ds.* **dure** 27:60 || PORTA *np.* ~ 16:18 || [OED2 door, *n.*]

dust *n.* 'dust' PULVIS *as.* ~ 10:14 [OED2 dust, *n.1*]

dwola *m. wk* 'error, doubt' MAMMONA *ds.* **dwale** 6:24 [n.] [OED2 dwale, *n.1* (and *adj.*)]

gedwola *m. wk* 'error' ERROR *ns.* ~ 27:64; *as.* **gedwolan** 24:24 [see previous]

dwolian *v.2* 'go astray' ERRARE *ps.3p.* **dwaligað** 22:29 [OED2 dwele, *v.*]

gedwolian *v.2* 'go astray' ERRARE *pt.3s.* **gedwalade** 18:12; *pt.3p.* **gedwaladun** 18:13; *subj.ps.3s.* **gedwalige** 18:12 [see previous]

dypan *v.1* 'dip, baptize' BAPTIZARE *ps.1s.* **depu** 3:11 [n.]; *ps.3s.* **depið** 3:11; *pp.s.* **deped** 3:14; **depid** 3:13; *pp.p.* **depte** 3:6 (margin) [n.] || INTINGERE *ps.3s.* **depið** 26:23 [OED2 depe, *v.*]

gedypan *v.1* 'dip, baptize' BAPTIZARE *pp.s.* **gedeped** 3:16 [n.] [see previous]

dyppan *v.1* 'dip, baptize' BAPTIZARE *ps.1s.* **dyppe** 3:11 [n.]; *ps.3s.* **dyppeþ** 3:11; *ps.p. np.* **dyppende** 28:19 [OED2 dip, *v.*]

dyre *adj.* 'exellent, dear' PLUS *comp. mnp.* **diorre** 6:26 [OED2 dear, *adj.1*, *n.2*, and *int.*]

dyrwurþe *adj.* 'precious, valuable' PRETIOSUS *mas.* **diorwyrðe** 13:46; *fgs.* **deorwyrþe** 26:7 [OED2 dearworth | derworth, *adj.*]

dysig *adj.* 'foolish, stupid' FATUUS *mns.* ~ 5:22; *np.* **dysige** 25:2, 25:3; **dysege** 25:8 || STULTUS *mds.* **dysig** 7:26; *np.* ~ 23:17 [OED2 dizzy, *adj.*]

ea *f.* 'river, flood' FLUMEN *np.* **eae** 7:25, 7:27 [ea, *n.*]

eac *adv.* 'too, likewise' ET **ek** 5:39, 13:29, 15:3, 15:27, 18:33, 19:28, 20:4, 20:7, 20:14, 21:24 (*bis*), 21:27, 22:27, 23:26, 23:32, 24:33, 24:44, 26:13, 26:69, 26:71, 26:73, 27:41, 27:44; **ec** 6:12, 12:45, 25:11, 25:22, 26:73, 27:57, Mk1:38 || ETIAM **ec** 12:8; **ek** 11:9 || QUIDEM **ek** 23:28 || NL **ek** 13:26 (ET in WW), 20:10 (ET in WW), 24:37 (ET in WW), 24:39 (ET in WW), 25:24 (ET in WW), 25:41 (ET in WW); **æc** 24:27 (ET in WW); **ec** Mk2:13 [n.]

eac *prep.* 'in addition to, besides' EXCEPTUS **ek** 14:21 [OED2 eke, *adv.*]

eacen *adj.* 'pregnant' PRAEGNANS *dp.* **eknum** 24:19

eadig *adj.* 'fortunate, blessed' BEATUS *mns.* ~ 11:6, 16:17, 24:46; *mnp.* ~ 5:3, 5:11; *nnp.* **eadige** 13:16 [eady, *adj.* (and *n.*)]

eage *n. wk* 'eye' OCULUS *ns.* **ege** 5:29, 5:38, 6:22 (*bis*), 6:23; **eagan** 18:9 [n.]; **egan** 20:15; *as.* **ege** 5:38, 18:9; *ds.* **ege** 7:3 (*bis*), 7:4 (margin), 7:4, 7:5 (*bis*); *np.* **egan** 9:30; **ege** 13:16; **egna** 20:33; **eagun** 26:43; *ap.* **egan** 9:29, 17:8; **eagan** 18:9; **egu** 13:15; *dp.* **egum** 13:15, 20:34, 21:42 [eye, *n.1*]

eala *interj.* 'alas, o, oh' O ~ 17:17

eald *adj.* 'old' VETUS *nas.* **ald** 9:16; *mnp.* **ealde** 9:17; *map.* **alde** 9:17; *nap.* **ealde** 13:52

comp. (subst.) SENIOR 'ancestor, older one' *np.* **aeldra** 26:3; **eldre** 21:23; **eldran** 27:3; **ældru** 26:57; **ældre** 27:1; **ældran** 27:20; *gp.* **ældra** 15:2; *dp.* **ældrum** 16:21, 28:12; **eldrum** 27:41; **ældran** 26:47; **eldran** 27:12 || PRIMUS 'the elder' *mds.* **ældra** 21:28 [old, *adj.*]

ealdor *m.* 'chief, authority' PRINCEPS *ns.* **aldor** 12:24; *ds.* **aldre** 9:34

[alder, *n.2*]

ealdormann *m.* 'chief, leader, prince' PRINCEPS *ns.* **aldurmon** 9:18; *gs.* **aldormonnes** 9:23; *np.* **aldormenn** 20:25; *dp.* **aldurmonnum** 2:6 || MINISTER *ap.* **ealdormen** Jn18:3 [alderman, *n.*]

ealdorsacerd *m.* 'chief of the priests' PRINCEPS SACERDOTUM *ns.* **aldursacerd** 26:62; **aldur sacerdæs,** 26:65; **aldursacerdum** 27:20; *gs.* **aldorsacerdæs** 26:3, 26:58; **aldorsacerdos** 26:51; *ds.* **aldorsacerdos** 26:57; **aldorsacerd** Mk1:44; *np.* **aldorsacerdas** 21:23, 21:45; **aldursacerdos** 21:15; **aldursacerdas** 27:6; **aldor ... sacerdæs** 26:59 [n.]; **aldursacerdæs** 27:1; **aldursacerdun** 27:41; **alduras sacerdas** 26:3 [n.]; **alduras sacerdæs** 27:62; *ap.* **aldursacerdos** 2:4; *dp.* **aldorsacerdum** 16:21, 26:47; **aldursacerdum** 27:3, 27:12, 28:11; **aldursacerdæs** 26:14; **aldorsacerd** 20:18

eall *adj.* 'all' OMNIS *mns.* **eall** Mk2:13; *ns. (gender?)* **ealle** 3:5; **ealle** 2:3; *fns.* **all** 13:2; **alle** Mk1:33; *fds.* **alle** Mk1:39; *nns.* **eall** 3:5, 27:25; **all** 5:18 (or *p.?*); **ealle** 26:59; **alle** Mk1:5; *nas.* **all** 7:12, 23:3; **eall** 14:35, 18:25, 18:31, 28:11; *nds.* **allum** 6:29; *np.* **ealle** 10:30, 13:56, 19:11, 21:26, 25:5, 25:7, 25:31, 25:32, 26:27, 26:31, 26:33, 26:35, 26:52, 26:56, 27:1, 27:22, 27:41; **alle** 11:13, 11:28, 12:23, 14:20, 22:28, 23:8, 28:19, Mk1:27, Mk1:37, Mk2:12; **all** 6:33, 11:27, 13:56, 22:5, 24:30; **eall** 19:26, 23:36, 24:8, 24:34; *ap.* **all** 6:32, 8:33, 13:34, 13:41, 23:4, 24:47; **alle** 4:24, 8:16, 9:35, 14:35, 22:10, Mk1:32; **ealle** 2:4, 2:16, 12:15, 15:37, 18:32, 21:12, 24:39, 28:20; **eall** 4:8, 4:9, 13:51, 17:11, 18:26, 18:29, 19:20, 19:21, 19:27, 24:2, 24:33, 26:1, 28:20; *gp.* **ealra** 1:17 [n.], 22:27; **alra** 6:32, 13:32; *dp.* **allum** 2:16, 4:6, 5:15, 10:22, 23:20, 24:14, Mk2:12; **eallum** 21:13, 21:22, 24:9, 26:70; (case and number uncertain) **all** 5:42 [n.] || TOTUS *mns. mns.* **all** 5:29, 6:22, 13:33; **eall** 5:30, 6:23; *mas.* **ealne** 16:26, 20:6; *nns.* **eall** 1:22, 21:4, 26:56; *nas.* **all** 9:31; *nds.* **allum** 26:13; **alra** 22:37 [n.]; *as.* **alle** 4:23 (gender?); *fns.* **all** 8:32, 8:34; **ealle** 22:40; *f.?a/ds.* **alle** 4:24; *fds.* **alre** 22:37; **alra** 22:37 || UNIVERSUS *mas.* **alnę** 24:14; **ealne** 27:27; *ma/ds.* **ealle** 27:45 [n.]; *fns.* **eall** 21:10; *nas.* **all** 9:26; **eall** 13:46, 14:35; *nds.* **eallum** Mk1:28; *np.* **alle** Mk1:5; *ap.* **ealle** 18:34 [all, *adj.*, *pron.*, and *n.*, *adv.*, and *conj.*]

eallunga *adv.* 'altogetehr, (not) at all' OMNINO **allunga** 5:34 [alling, *adv.*]

ear *n.* 'ear (of grain)' SPICA *ap.* **æchir** 12:1 [n.] [ear, *n.2*; cf. OED2 icker, n.]

eardian *v.2* 'dwell, live' HABITARE *ps.3s.* **eardaþ** 23:21; *ps.3p.* **eardigaþ** 12:45; **eardigað** 13:32; *pt.3s.* **eardade** 2:23; [OED2 erde, *v.*]

geeardian *v.2* 'dwell, live' HABITARE *pt.3s.* **geeardade** 4:13 [see previous]

eare *n. wk* 'ear' AURIS *ds.* ~ 10:27; *np.* **earan** 13:16; *ap.* **earan** 11:15, 13:43; **eara** 13:9; *dp.* **earum** 13:15; **earan** 13:15 || AURICULA *as.* **eara** 26:51 [ear, *n.1*]

earfoþe *adj.* 'difficult, hard' ARTUS *mns.* **eorfeþe** 7:14

earn *m.* 'eagle' AQUILA *np.* **earnes** 24:28 [OED2 erne, *n.*]

earwunga *adv.* 'gratuitously' GRATIS **arwunga** 10:8; **arwunge** 10:8

eastan *adv.* 'from the east' AB ORIENTE ~ 2:1; (*from*) **eastan** 8:11 [easten, *adv.* (and *prep.*)]

eastdæl *m.* 'the East, eastern region' ORIENS *ds.* **eastdæle** 2:2, 2:9, 24:27 [eastdeal, *n.*]

eastre *f. wk* 'Easter, Eastertide' PASCHA *np.* **eastran** 26:2 [n.]; *ap.* **eastran** 26:19; **eastra** 26:17, 26:18 [Easter, *n.1*]

eaðe, **eþre**, see **ieþ**

eaþmod *adj.* 'humble' HUMILIS *mns.* **eadmod** 11:29 [OED2 edmod, *adj.*]

eaþmodian *v.2* 'humble' HUMILARE *ps.3s.* **eadmedaþ** 18:4 || OBOEDIRE *ps.3p.* **edmodað** Mk1:27 [see previous]

(†)**eawisfiren** *adj.* '(as subst.) publican, tax-collector' PUBLICANUS *mns.* **eawisfirina** 18:17 [n.]; *mnp.* **æwisfirine** 21:31; **ewisfirinæ** 21:32

†**eawisian** *v.2* 'manifest, reveal' MANIFESTUM FACERE *pt.3s.* **ewisade** 12:16 [n.]

[MK]**eawunga** *adv.* 'openly, publicly' MANIFESTE ~ Mk1:45

eaxl *f.* 'shoulder' UMERUS *ap.* **exlan** 23:4 [OED2 axle, *n.1*]

ece *adj.* 'eternal, perpetual' AETERNUS *nas.* ~ 25:41; **ecce** 18:8; **æce** 19:29, 25:46 (*bis*); *ngs.* **æce** 19:16 [n.] [OED2 eche, *adj.*]

eced *n.* or *m.* 'vinegar' ACETUM *gs.* **ecedes** 27:48

ecnes *f.* 'eternity, perpetuity' SEMPITERNUM *ds.* **eknisse** 21:19 [OED2 echeness, *n.*]

efenþeow *m.* 'fellow-servant' CONSERVUS *ns.* **efnþeuw** 18:29; *ds.* **ęfnðeuw** 18:33; *np.* **ęfnðeuwe** 18:31; *ap.* **efnþeu** 24:49; *gp.* **æfenþara** 18:28 [n.]

efenþrowian *v.2* 'sympathize, feel compassion' MISERERI *pt.3s.* **efnþrowade** 9:36

efne *adv.* 'even, only' TANTUM ~ 8:8, 9:21, 10:42; **æfne** 5:47; **efnæ** 21:19 [even, *adv.* and *prep.*]

[MK]**efnecuman** *v.IV* 'meet, assemble' CONVENIRE *pt.3p.* **efnecomon** Mk1:45, Mk2:2

eft *adv.* 'again' ITERUM ~ 5:33, 13:45, 13:47, 18:19, 20:5, 26:42; **æft** 4:8, 15:29, 19:24, 21:36, 22:4, 26:43, 26:44, 26:72, 27:50 || RURSUM **æft** 4:7 || RE- prefix ~ 2:8, 12:44, 24:18, 27:3; **æft** 21:18, 27:40 [OED2 eft, *adv.*]

eftacennes *f.* 'regeneration' GENERATIO *ds.* **æftakennisse** 19:28 [n.] (REGENERATIO in WW)

eftarisan *v.I* 'rise again, resurrect' RESURGERE *ps.1s.* **æftarise** 26:32, 27:63; *ps.3s.* **æftariseþ** 17:23; **eftariseþ** 20:19; *inf.* **æftarisan** 16:21 [n.]

egesa *m. wk* 'fear, terror' TIMOR *ds.* **ægsa** 14:26, 28:4; **egsa** 28:8 (or *a.*?)

ehtan *v.1* 'persecute' PERSEQUI *ps.2p.* **oehtaþ** 23:34; *ps.p. mnp.* **ehtende** 10:23; **hehtende** 5:11; **hoehtende** 5:12; *mdp.* **ehtendum** 5:44; **oihtende** 5:44

ehtan *v.1* 'estimate, consider' AESTIMARE *ps.1s.* **ehtu** 11:16

ehtnes *f.* 'persecution' PERSECUTIO *as.* **hoehtnisse** 5:10 [n.]; *ds.?* **oehtnisse** 13:21

elcor *adv.* 'otherwise, else' ALIOQUIN **elcur** 6:1 [n.], 9:17 [OED2 elchur, *adv.*]

ele *m.* 'oil' OLEUM *as.* **oele** 25:3, 25:4; *gs.* **oeles** 25:8 [n.] [OED ele, *n.*]

elebearu *m.* 'olive-grove' OLIVETUM *gs.* **oelebearwes** 21:1 [n.], 24:3, 26:30

elias *prop.n. ns.* ~ 11:14, 16:14, 17:10, 17:11, 17:12, 27:49; *as.* **eliam** 27:47

ell *adj.* 'other' RELIQUUS *np.* **elle** 22:6 [n.]

ellende *gender*? 'foreign country' PEREGRE *a/ds.* (*in*) **ellende** 21:33, (*on*) **ellende** 25:14

elles *adv.* 'otherwise, else' ALIOQUIN ~ 6:1, 9:17

eln *f.* 'ell' CUBITUM *as.* **elne** 6:27

elþeod *f.* 'foreign country' PEREGRE *a/ds.* (*in*) **elðiode** 21:33 [althede, *n.*]

elþeodig *adj.* 'foreign' PEREGRINUS *gp.* **elþeodigra** 27:7 [althedy, *adj.* and *n.*]

emtig, see **æmtig**

ende *m.* 'end' FINIS *ns.* ~ 24:6; *a/ds.* ~ 10:22, 24:13; *ds.* ~ 12:42 || CONSUMMATIO *a/ds.* ~ 28:20 [OED2 end, *n.*]

endian *v.2* 'end' FINIRE *ps.3s.* **endeþ** MtEXPLICIT (x3) [OED2 end, *v.1*]

geendian *v.2* 'end, finish' CONSUMMARE *ps.3p.* **geendigaþ** 10:23; *pt.3s.* **geendade** 11:1, 13:53, 19:1, 26:1; *pp.* (*hæfde*) **geendad** 7:28 [OED2 yend, *v.*]

endleofan *num.* 'eleven' UNDECIM *n.* **enlefan** 28:16 [OED2 eleven, *adj.* and *n.*]

endlyfta *ord. num.* 'eleventh' UNDECINUS *fds.* **ællefta** 20:6 [n.]; **elleftan** 20:9 [OED2 eleventh, *adj.* and *n.*]

endung *f.* 'ending, end' CONSUMMATIO *ns.* **endunge** 13:39, 24:14; *ds.* **endunge** 13:40, 13:49 || FINIS *as.* **endunge** 26:58 [OED2 ending, *n.*]

geendung *f.* 'end, limit' CONSUMMATIO *gs.* **geendunge** 24:3 [see previous]

engel *m.* 'angel' ANGELUS *ns.* ~ 1:20, 1:24, 2:13, 2:19, 28:5; **ængel** 28:2; *as.* ~ 11:10, Mk1:2; *np.* **englas** 4:11, 13:39, 13:49, 18:10, 22:30, 24:36, 25:31, Mk1:13; *ap.* **englas** 13:41, 24:31; *gp.* **ængla** 26:53; *dp.* **englum** 4:6 [n.]; **ænglum** 16:27; **englas** 25:41 [angel, *n.*]

eofulsian *v.2* 'blaspheme, reproach' BLASPHEMARE *ps.3s.* **hefalsaþ** 9:3 [n.]; **heofolsaþ** Mk2:7; *pt.3s.* **efalsade** 26:65; *pt.3p.* **hefalsadun** 27:39

eofulsung *f.* 'blasphemy' BLASPHEMIA *ns.* **efulsung** 12:31; **efalsung** 12:31 (margin); *as.* **efalsunge** 26:65; *np.* **hefalsunge** 15:19

eorcnanstan *m.* 'precious stone, pearl' MARGARITA *as.* **ercnastan** 13:46; *ap.* **ercnanstanas** 7:6 [n.], 13:45

eorre, eorsaþ see **ierre, iersian**

[MK]**eorþcrypel** *m.* 'paralytic' PARALYTICUS *ns.* **eorðcrypel** Mk2:4; *as.* **eorðcrypel** Mk2:3; *ds.* **eorðcrypele** Mk2:5; **eorðcryple** Mk2:9, Mk2:10

eorþe *f. wk* 'earth' TERRA *ns.* ~ 4:15, 5:18, 24:35, 27:51; **eorðu** 2:6, 4:15; *as.* **eorðe** 10:34, 13:5, 13:8, 13:23 (w. masculine adjective); **eorðæ** 5:35; **eorðu** 5:4; **eorþu** 2:21; **eorðan** 23:35; *gs.* **eorðu** 5:13, 17:25, 24:30; **eorðe** 11:25, 12:40, 12:42, 13:5; *ds.* **eorþu** 2:20; **eorþe** 6:10, 6:19, 25:18, 25:25, 28:18; **eorðe** 10:15, 11:24, 13:44, 18:18; **eorðan** 9:6, 16:19 (*bis*), 23:9; **eorþan** 10:29, 15:35, 18:19; **eordan** 18:18; **eorþa** Mk2:10 || ARIDA *as.* **eordu** 23:15 [earth, *n.1*]

eorþhrernes *f.* 'earthquake' MOTUS TERRAE *ns.* **eorþhreornisse** 24:7; *as.* **eorðhroernisse** 27:54

†**eorþstyrenes** *f.* 'earthquake' TERRAE MOTUS *ns.* **eorþstyrennis** 28:2

eosol *m.* 'donkey, ass' ASINA *as.* **ęosul** 21:2; **eosula** 21:7; *ds.* **eosule** 21:5 || ASINARIUS *gs.* **esules** 18:6 [n.]

eowan *v.1* 'show, appear' OSTENDERE *pt.3s.* **eaude** 16:1 (or *subj.*?); *subj.pt.3p.* **eawden** 24:1; *imp.p.* **eawaþ** 22:19; *inf.* **eawan** 16:21 || APPARERE *ps.3s.* **eaweþ** 24:27, 24:30; *ps.3p.* **eaweþ** 23:27

eowde *n.* 'flock, herd' GREX *gs.* **edæs** 26:31 [OED2 eowde, n.]

eowic ? QUIDEM 13:23 [n.]

erfe, erfeweard, see **yrfe-**

esne *m.* 'servant' SERVUS *ns.* ~ 10:24, 10:25, 18:26, 18:28, 18:32, 20:27, 24:45, 24:46, 24:48, 25:21, 25:23, 25:26; *as.* ~ 25:30, 26:51; *gs.* **esnes** 24:50; *ds.* ~ 8:9, 18:27; *np.* **esnas** 13:27, 13:28, 22:10; *ap.* **esnas** 18:23, 21:34, 21:35, 21:36, 22:3, 25:14; **ęsnas** 22:4, 22:6; *gp.* **esna** 25:19; *dp.* **æsnum** 22:8

essaias *prop.n. ns.* ~ 15:7; *as.* **esaiam** 1:22, 3:3, 8:17; **essaiam** 4:14, 21:4; **esaias** 12:17, 13:35; **esaia** Mk1:2; *gs.* ~ 13:14

etan *v.V* 'eat, consume' MANDUCARE *ps.3s.* **eteþ** 9:11; *ps.3p.* **etaþ** 15:32; **etað** 15:2; *pt.3p.* **etun** 14:20, 15:38; *subj.ps.2p.* **etan** 6:25; *imp.p.* **etæþ** 26:26; *inf.* ~ 14:16, 25:35, 25:42; **eton** 12:1 [n.]; **ete** 15:20; *ps.p. mns.* **etende** 11:18, 11:19; *gp.*

etendra 14:21 || COMEDERE *ps.2p.* **etaþ** 23:14; *pt.3s.* **et** 12:4; *pt.3p.* **etun** 15:37; *infl.inf.* **etanne** 12:4, 26:17; *ps.p. np.* **etende** 24:38 || EDERE *ps.3p.* **etaþ** 15:27; *ps.p. dp.* **etendum** 26:21 || DEMOLIRI *ps.3p.* **etaþ** 6:19 (or *3s.*?) || PASCERE *ps.p. fns.* **etende** 8:30 [OED2 eat, *v.*]

geetan *v.V* 'eat, consume' MANDUCARE *ps.1p.* **geetaþ** 6:31 [see previous]

eþa, eþþa, see **oþþe**

eþel *m.* 'homeland, home' PATRIA *as.* **oeþel** 13:54, 13:57 [ethel, *n.*]

ewyrdlu, see **æwyrdla**

faran *v.VI* 'go' IRE *imp.p.* **fęreþ** 11:3; *inf.* **færan** 2:22, 16:21 || TRANSIRE *inf.* ~ 8:28 || PROFICISCI *ps.p. mns.* **færende** 25:14 || VADERE *imp.s.* **fær** 2:20 (or forms of **feran**?) || EGREDI *ps.p. mns.* **færende** Mk1:5, Mk1:35, Mk2:13 || PRAETERIRE *ps.p. mns.* **færende** Mk1:16 [OED2 fare, *v.1*]

†**farennes** *f.* 'transmigration' TRANSMIGRATIO *a/ds.* **færennisse** 1:17 (*bis*)

farissea *prop.n. ns.* ~ 23:26; *np.* **fariseas** 7:29, 12:14, 12:24, 12:38, 15:1, 15:12, 16:1, 19:3, 22:15, 22:41, 23:2, 23:13, 23:14, 23:23, 27:62; **farisseas** 23:25; **farisei** 9:11, 9:14, 9:34; **farisaeos** 21:45, 22:34; **farissæis** 12:2; *ap.* **fariseos** Jn18:3; *gp.* **farisea** 3:7, 5:20, 16:11, 16:12; **farisseas** 16:6

farᛗ *prop.n. ns.* ~ MtCOLOPHON

fæc *n.* 'space of time' TEMPUS *ds.* **fæce** 25:19 [OED2 fec, *n.*]

fæder *m.* 'father' PATER *ns.* ~ 5:48, 6:4, 6:6 (margin), 6:8, 6:9, 6:14, 6:15, 6:18, 6:26, 6:32, 7:11, 10:21, 11:25, 11:26, 11:27, 15:13, 16:17, 18:35, 21:33, 23:9, 24:36, 25:41, 26:39, 26:42; *as.* ~ 3:9, 4:22, 6:1, 6:6, 10:25, 10:37, 11:27, 19:5, 19:19, 19:29, 23:9, 26:53, Mk1:20; *gs.* ~ 5:45, 7:21, 10:20, 12:50, 16:27, 18:10, 25:34, 26:29, 28:19; **fader** 13:43; **fæderes** 21:31; *a/ds.* ~ 2:22, 4:21, 5:16 (*d.*? see note), 10:29; **faeder** 10:35; *ds.* ~ 6:18, 8:21 [n.], 10:32, 11:27, 13:27, 13:52, 15:4 (*bis*), 15:5, 15:6, 18:14, 18:19, 20:1, 20:11, 20:23; **faeder** 10:33; *gp.* **fædra** 23:30; **fædera** 23:32 [father, *n.*]

fæger *adj.* 'beautiful' NL *mns.* ~ Jn18:1 [n.] [fair, *adj.* and *n.1*]

fæmne *f.* 'virgin' VIRGO *ns.* ~ 1:23; *np.* **femnan** 25:7, 25:11; *dp.* **femnan** 25:1

fær *n.* 'action of going, (specifically) transmigration' TRANSMIGRATIO *ds.* **fære** 1:11 [n.], 1:12 [fare, *n.1*]

fæs *n.* 'fringe, hem' FIMBRIA *as.* **fæss** 9:20, 14:36; *ap.* **fasu** 23:5 [OED2 fas, *n.*]

fæstan *v.1* 'fast' IEIUNARE *ps.1p.* **fæstaþ** 9:14; *ps.3p.* **fæstaþ** 9:14; *pt.3s.* **fæstę** 4:2; *subj.ps.2s.* **fæste** 6:17; *subj.ps.2p.* **faesten** 6:16; *subj.ps.3p.* **fæsten** 9:15; *ps.p. mns.* **fæstende** 6:18; *mnp.* **fæstende** 6:16; *map.* **fæstende** 15:32 [fast, *v.2*]

fæsten *n.* 'fast, fasting' IEIUNIUM *as.* ~ 17:21 [fasten, *n.*]

fæt *n.* 'vessel, container' VAS *ap.* **fatu** 12:29, 13:48, 25:4 [OED2 fat, *n.1*]

gefættian *v.2* 'fatten' INCRASSARE *pp.s.* **gefætted** 13:15

fæþ, see **don** and note to 5:32

gefea *m. wk* 'joy' GAUDIUM *as.* ~ 25:21, 25:23; *ds.* ~ 2:10, 13:44; *d/as.* ~ 13:21, 28:8

feald '-fold' (usually a suffix; apparently used as an independent word with *twæm*) part of DUPLUM *dp.* **fældum** 23:15 [n.] [cf. OED2 -fold, *suffix*]

feallan *v.VII* 'fall, collapse' CADERE *ps.3s.* **falleþ** 10:29, 17:15, 21:44; **fealleþ** 12:11; *ps.3p.* **falleþ** 15:27, 24:29; *pt.3p.* **feollan** 17:6; *subj.ps.3p.* **fallen** 15:14; *ps.p. mns.* **fallende** 4:9 || INRUERE *pt.3p.* **fellun** 7:25; **feollun** 7:27 || PROICERE *inf.*? **feallan** 15:30 (or *pt.3p.*, see note) [fall, *v.*]

gefeallan *v. VII* 'fall, collapse' CADERE *pt.3s.* **gefeoll** 7:25, 7:27; *pt.3p.* **gefeollun** 13:4; **gefeollon** 13:5 [yfall, *v.*]

fearr *m.* 'bull, ox' TAURUS *np.* **fearras** 22:4

feawe *adj. pl.* 'a few' PAUCUS *n.* ~ 7:14, 9:37, 20:16, 22:14; *d.* **fæawum** 25:21; **feawum** 25:23 [few, *adj.*, *pron.*, and *n.*]

fedan *v.1* 'feed' PASCERE *ps.3s.* **foedeþ** 6:26; *pt.1p.* **foeddan** 25:37

†**fedelfugel** *m.* 'fattened fowl' ALTILIS *np.* **foedelfuglas** 22:4 [n.] [cf. fedddle, *n.*]

[MK]†**feferdrifende** *adj.* 'having fever, in a fit of fever' *fns.* **feferdrifende** Mk1:30 [n.]

fela *adj.* (often as subst.) *indecl.* 'many' MULTUM *a.* **feola** 6:7, 13:3, 16:21, 27:19 [see also **hu fela**] [fele, *adv.* (and *n.*) and *adj.2*]

†**felaspræc** *f.* 'loquacity' MULTILOQUIUM *ds.* **feolasprece** 6:7 [n.]

fellen *adj.* 'made of skins' PELLICIUS *mas.* ~ 3:4; *mas.* **fellenne** Mk1:6

feogan *v.2* 'hate' ODIO HABERE *ps.3s.* **fiað** 6:24; *ps.3p.* **fiegaþ** 24:10 || ODISSE *subj.ps.3p.* **fiegę** 5:44

feoh *n.* 'money, cattle' PECUNIA *as.* ~ 10:9, 25:18, 25:27, 28:12; *ds.* **feo** 28:15 || part of CORBANA *as.* (*temples*) **feh** 27:6 [OED2 fee, *n.1*]

gefeoht *f.* 'fighting, war' PROELIUM *ap.* **gefæht** 24:6; *gp.* **gefæhta** 24:6 [cf. OED2 fight, *n.*]

gefeon *v. V* 'rejoice' GAUDERE *ps.3s.* **gefeaþ** 18:13; *pt.3p.* **gefegon** 2:10; *imp.p.* **gefeaþ** 5:12

feond *m.* 'fiend, enemy' INIMICUS *ns.* ~ 13:25; **fiond** 13:39; *as.* **fiond** 5:43 [n.]; *np.* **fiondas** 10:36; *ap.* **fiondas** 5:44; **feondas** 22:44 [fiend, *n.*]

feorh *n. or m.* 'life' ANIMA *ns.* **ferh** 6:25; *as.* **ferh** 2:20, 10:39 (*bis*), 16:26, 20:28; **feorh** 16:25 (*bis*); *gs.* **feorh** 16:26 [n.]; *ds.* **fere** 6:25

feormian *v.2* 'feed, welcome a guest' COLLIGERE *pt.2p.* **feormadun** 25:35, 25:43

gefeormian *v.2* 'feed, welcome a guest' COLLIGERE *pt.1p.* **gefeormadun** 25:38

feorr *adv.* 'far off' LONGE ~ 15:8 [OED2 far, *adv.*]

feorrane *adv.* 'from a distance, at a distance' A LONGE **feorran** 26:58, 27:55 || LONGE **feorranne** 23:14 [n.] [OED2 ferren, *adv.* and *adj.*]

feorþa *ord. num.* 'fourth' QUADRANS *mas.* **feorþan** 5:26 || QUARTUS *fas.* **feorðe** 14:25 [OED2 fourth, *adj.* and *n.*]

feoung *f.* 'hatred, hostility' ODIUM *ds.* **fiunge** 10:22, 24:9

feower *num.* 'four' QUATTUOR *g.* ~ 16:10 (margin); *d.* **feowre** 24:31; **feowrum** Mk2:3 [OED2 four, *adj.* and *n.*]

feowertig *num.* QUADRAGINTA 'forty' *a.?* ~ 4:2 (*bis*), Mk1:13 (*bis*) [OED2 forty, *adj.* and *n.*]

feowertyne *num.* 'fourteen' QUATTUORDECIM *n.* **feowertene** 1:17 (x3) [OED2 fourteen, *adj.* and *n.*]

fera *m. wk* 'companion, comrade' SOCIUS *np.* **foeran** 23:30 [OED2 fere, *n.1*]

feran *v.1* 'go' TRANSIRE *pt.3s.* **ferde** 8:34; **foerde** 9:9, 13:53, 15:29, 20:30 || IRE *inf.* ~ 8:18 || PROFICISCI *pt.3p.* **foerdon** 25:15 [n.] || EGREDI *pt.3s.* **foerde** Mk1:5, Mk1:35, Mk1:45; *pt.3p.* **foerde** Mk1:29 || DISCEDERE *pt.3s.* **foerde** Mk1:42 || PRAETERIRE *pt.3s.* **foerde** Mk2:14 || PROCEDERE *pt.3s.* **foerde** Mk1:28 || PROGREDI *pt.3s.* **foerde** Mk1:19 [OED2 fere, *v.1*]

geferan *v.1* 'go, depart, bring' PROFICISCI *pt.3s.* **gefoerde** 21:33; AFFERRE *pt.3p.* **gefoerdun** Mk1:32 [see previous]

ferian *v.1* 'carry, convey' NL *infl.inf.* **ferganne** 5:41 [n.] [ferry, *v.*]

(†)**gefetan** *v. V* 'fall' CADERE *pt.3p.* **gefetun** 13:7 [n.], 13:8

feþe *n.?* 'walking, going on foot'

on feþe 'on foot' PEDESTER **on**

foeðe 14:13
feþer *f.* 'feather' ALA *dp.* **feþran** 23:37 [OED2 feather, *n.*]
fic *m.* 'fig, fig-tree' FICUS *gs.* **fices** 21:19, 24:32; *ap.* **ficos** 7:16 [n.] || FICULNEA *ns.* ~ 21:19, 21:20; *ds.* **fice** 21:21 [OED2 fike, *n.1*]
fif *num.* 'five' QUINQUE *n.* ~ 14:21; **fife** 25:2 (*bis*), 25:3; *a.* ~ 14:17, 14:19, 25:15, 25:16, 25:20 (x3); **fife** 25:16, 25:20; *g.* ~ 16:9 (*bis*) [OED2 five, *adj.* and *n.*]
filippes, see **philippus**
findan *v.III* 'find' INVENIRE *ps.3s.* **findeð** 7:8; **findeþ** 13:44; *pt.3p.* **funden** 26:60; *subj.ps.3s.* **finde** 18:13 [find, *v.*]
finger *m.* 'finger' DIGITUS *ds.* **fringre** 23:4 [n.] [finger, *n.*]
firenfull *adj.* 'sinful, wicked' PECCATOR *gp.* **firenfullra** 11:19
firenian *v.2* 'sin' PECCARE *subj.ps.3s.* **firnige** 18:15 [n.]
gefirenian *v.2* 'sin' PECCARE *pt.1s.* **gefirinade** 27:4
fisc *m.* 'fish' PISCIS *as.* ~ 17:27; *gs.* **fiscæs** 7:10; *ap.* **fiscas** 14:17, 14:19, 15:36; *gp.* **fisca** 13:47 || PISCICULUS *ap.* **fiscas** 15:34 [OED2 fish, *n.1*]
fiscere *m.* 'fisher' PISCATOR *np.* **fisceras** 4:18; **fisceres** 4:19, Mk1:16, Mk1:17 [OED2 fisher, *n.1*]
fleam *m.* 'flight, fleeing' FUGA *ns.* ~ 24:20 [OED2 fleme, *n.1*]
fleax *n.* 'the plant flax, linen' LINUM *as.* **flæx** 12:20 [OED2 flax, *n.*]
fleoge *f.* or *m.* 'fly, gnat' CULEX *as.* **flega** 23:24 [OED2 fly, *n.1*]
fleon *v.II* 'flee' FUGERE *ps.2p.* **fleaþ** 23:33; *ps.3p.* **fleoþ** 24:16; *pt.3p.* **flugon** 8:33; **flugen** 26:56; *subj.pt.2p.* **flugan** 3:7; *imp.s.* **fleoh** 2:13; *imp.p.* **fleoþ** 10:23 [OED2 flee, *v.*]
flitan *v.I* 'contend, quarrel' CONTENDERE *ps.3s.* **fliteþ** 12:19 [OED2 flite | flyte, *v.*]
geflitan *v.I* 'contend, quarrel' CONTENDERE *inf.* ~ 5:40 [see previous]
flod *m.* 'flood' DILUVIUM *ns.* **flod** 24:39; *ap.* **flodes** 24:38 [n.] [flood, *n.*]
flownes *f.* 'flow, flux' FLUXUS *as.* **flownisse** 9:20
flyhte *m. or n.?* 'patch (of cloth)' PANNUS *gs.?* **flyhti** 9:16 [n.]
fola *m. wk* 'foal, young animal' PULLUS *as.* **folan** 21:2; ~ 21:7; *ds.* **folan** 21:5 [OED2 foal, *n.*]
folc *n.* 'folk, people' POPULUS *ns.* ~ 4:16, 15:8, 21:11, 27:25; *as.* ~ 1:21, 2:6, 14:5; *gs.* **folkes** 2:4, 13:15, 26:3; **folces** 26:47, 27:1, 27:3; **folcęs** 21:23; *ds.* **folce** 4:23, 9:35, 15:36, 26:5, 27:15, 27:20, 27:24; **folcę** 27:24 || PLEBES *ds.* **folce** 27:64 [OED2 folk, *n.*]
folgian *v.2* 'follow' SEQUI *ps.3s.* **fylgeþ** 10:38; *pt.3s.* **folgade** 9:19, 26:58; *pt.3p.* **folgadun** 4:22, 8:23, 12:15, 19:27, 20:29, 20:34; **folgedun** 4:20, 8:1, 14:13; **fylgdun** 9:27; **fylgadun** 19:2; **fylgendun** 4:25 [n.]; *subj.ps.3s.* **folge** 16:24; *inf.* ~ 8:19; *imp.s.* **fylge** 8:22, Mk2:14; **fylgæ** 9:9 [n]; **folga** 19:21; **folgam** Mk2:14 [n.]; *ps.p. dp.* **fylgendun** 8:10; *ps.p.* + *wesan* **fylgende** 19:28, 27:55, Mk1:18, Mk1:20, Mk1:36, Mk2:14; **fylgænde** 9:9 [follow, *v.*]
fon *v.VII* 'receive, seize take' ACCIPERE *pt.3s.* **feng** 1:24 [n.] || ADPRAEHENDERE *pt.3p.* **fengon** 21:35 || COMPRAEHENDERE *infl.inf.* **fone** 26:55 || DUCERE *subj.ps.3s.* **foe** 22:24 || INICERE *pt.3p.* **fengon** 26:50 || CAPERE *inf.* **foan** Mk2:2 [OED2 fang, *v.1*]
gefon *v.VII* 'receive, seize, take' ACCIPERE *pt.3s.* **gefeng** Jn18:3 || CAPERE *subj.pt.3p.* **gefenge** 22:1 || || COMPRAEHENDERE *pt.p. map.* **gefongnae** 4:24 [i-fang | i-fo, *v.*]
for *prep.* 'for' PROPTER ~ 5:11 (w.a.), 10:18, 10:22 (w.d.), 13:21 (w.d.), 13:58, 14:3 (w.a.), 14:9 (w.d.), 15:3, 15:6 (w.d.), 16:25, 17:20 (w.d.), 17:27 (w.a.), 19:5 (w.d.),

19:12, 19:29 (w.d.), 23:14 (w.i.), 24:9 (w.d.), 24:22 (w.d.), 27:19 (w.d.) || PRO 'for, in the place of' ~ 2:22, 5:38 (*bis*, w.a.), 5:44, 10:39 (w.a), 16:26 (w.a.), 20:28 (w.d.), 26:28 (w.d.), Mk1:44 (w.a.) || PRAE ~ 13:44, 14:26, 28:4, Mk2:4 || ANTE ~ 6:2, 11:10 || CORAM ~ 10:32 (w.d) || EX ~ 19:3 || NL ~ 5:44, 6:16 [OED2 for, *prep.* and *conj.*]

forbærnan *v.1* 'burn up' COMBURERE *ps.3s.* **forbęrneþ** 3:12; *pp.p.* **forberned** 13:40 || SUCCENDERE *pt.3s.* **forbernde** 22:7 [OED2 forburn, v.]

forbeodan *v.II* 'forbid, prohibit' COMMINARI *pt.3s.* **forbead** 9:30 || PROHIBERE *inf.* **forbeode** 19:14 [n.] [OED2 forbid, *v.*]

fordon *anom.v.* 'destroy' PERDERE *pt.3p.* **fordydun** 27:20; *inf.* **fordoan** 10:28 [OED2 fordo | foredo, *v.*]

[MK]**fordrifan** *v.I* 'drive out, expel' EICERE *pt.3s.* **fordraf** Mk1:34, Mk1:39 [OED2 fordrive, *v.*]

fore *prep.* 'before, in front of, for the sake of' CORAM ~ 5:16, 6:1 || PROPTER ~ 5:10 || NL ~ 19:9 [OED fore, *adv.* and *prep.*]

forebeacen *n.* 'foretoken, sign' PRODIGIUM *ap.* **forebecun** 24:24

forecuman *v.IV* 'prevent' PRAEVENIRE *pt.3s.* **forecuom** 17:25 [OED2 forecome, *v.*]

foregan *anom.v.* 'go before, precede' PRAECEDERE *ps.1s.* **forega** 26:32 || ANTECEDERE *pt.3s.* **foreeade** 2:9; [OED2 forego, *v.*]

foregearwian *v.2* 'prepare' PRAEPARARE *ps.3s.* **foregearweþ** 11:10; **foregearwað** Mk1:2

foreleoran *v.1* 'go forward' PRAETERIRE *ps.p. np.* **foreliorende** 27:39

[MK]**forelutan** *v.II* 'bend down' PROCUMBERE *ps.p. mns.* **forehlutende** Mk1:7 [n.]

foresecgan *v.3* 'foretell, predict' PRAEDICERE *pt.1s.* **foresægde** 28:7 [OED2 fore-say, *v.*]

foreþancol *adj.* 'provident' PRUDENS *dp.* **forðonclum** 11:25

[MK]**forgyfan** *v.V* 'forgive' DIMITTERE *pp.p.* **forgefen** Mk2:5, Mk2:9; *inf.* **forgeofan** Mk2:7 [OED2 forgive, *v.*]

[MK]**forgyfnes** *f.* 'forgiveness' DIMITTERE *gs.* **forgefnisse** Mk2:10 || REMISSIO *a/ds.* **forgefnisse** Mk1:4 [OED2 forgiveness, *n.*]

forgytan *v.V* 'forget' OBLIVISCI *pt.3p.* **forgetun** 16:5 [OED2 forget, *v.*]

forhtian *v.2* 'fear, be afraid' TIMERE *pt.3s.* **frohtade** 14:30; *pt.3p.* **frohtadun** 27:54; *subj.ps.2p.* **forhtige** 28:5; *imp.p.* **forhtigaþ** 10:31 [n.]; **forhtaþ** 14:27; *ps.p. mns.* **frohtende** 25:25

geforht *adj.* 'frightened, fearful' TIMIDUS *mnp.* **gefrohte** 8:26 [n.]

forhwon *interr.* 'why' QUARE ~ 9:11, 9:14, 13:10, 14:31, 15:2, 15:3, 16:11, 21:25, 27:46 (*bis*); **forwon** 17:19 || QUID ~ 6:28, 7:3, 8:26, 11:7, 11:8, 11:9, 26:10; **forwon** 22:18 || UT QUID ~ 9:4 [OED2 forwhy, *adv.* and *conj.*]

forlæran *v.1* 'lead astray, seduce' SEDUCERE *ps.3p.* **forlæræþ** 24:5; **forlæreþ** 24:11; *subj.ps.3s.* **forlære** 24:4 || SEDUCTOR *ps.p. mns.* **forlærd** 27:63 [n.] [OED2 forlere, *v.*]

forlætan *v.VII* 'leave, let' DIMITTERE 'dismiss' *ps.1s.* **forlete** 18:21; *ps.3s.* **forleteþ** 5:32 [n.], 6:14 [n.], 19:5, 19:9; **forleteð** 6:15, 21:3; *ps.2p.* **forleteð** 6:14; **forleteþ** 6:15; *pt.1s.* **forlet** 18:32; *pt.3s.* **forlet** 3:15, 8:15, 14:22, 14:23, 18:27, 27:26, Mk1:31; *subj.ps.1s.* **forlete** 27:17; *subj.ps.3s.* **forletae** 5:31; **forlete** 27:15 (or *pt.*?); *subj.pt.3s.* **forlete** 19:7; *imp.s.* **forlet** 5:40, 8:22, 14:15, 15:23; *inf.* **forletan** 19:3, 19:8, Mk2:7; **forleten** 1:19; **forlete** 15:32; *infl.inf.* **forletenne** 9:6; *pp.s.* **forleten** 12:31 (margin), 27:21; *pp.p.* **forletnae** 9:5; *pp.p. nas.* **forletne** 5:32; *ps.p. mns.* **forletende**

13:36, 15:39 || RELINQUERE *ps.3s.* **forleteþ** 18:12, 19:29; *pt.3s.* **forlet** 4:11, 4:13, Mk1:20; *pt.2p.* **forletun** 23:23; *pt.3p.* **forletun** 4:22; **forleten** 22:22, Mk1:18; **forleortun** 19:27; *imp.s.* **forlet** 5:24; *ps.p. mns.* **forletende** 16:4, 21:17, 26:44; *mnp.* **forletende** 26:56; **foletende** 4:20 [n.]; *pp.s.* **forleten** 23:38 24:40, 24:41 (bis) || REMITTERE *ps.2p.* **forletaþ** 18:35; *pt.3s.* **forlet** 18:27; *subj.ps.1p.* **forleten** 6:12; *imp.s.* **forlet** 6:12; *pp.s.* **forleten** 12:31, 12:32 (*bis*); *pp.p.* **forletne** 9:2; *ps.p. nns.* **forletendæ** 11:24; *comp. nns.* **forletendre** 11:22 || DERELINQUERE *ps.2s.* **forletes** 27:46 (*bis*) || SINERE *imp.p.* **forleteð** 15:14 || OMITTERE *inf.* **forletan** 23:23 [OED2 forlet, *v.1*]

forlætnes *f.* 'forgiveness, remission; abandonment, divorced woman (?)' REMISSIO *a/ds.* **forletnisse** 26:28 || DIMITTERE *as.* **forletnisse** 19:9

forlegennes *f.* 'fornication, adultery' FORNICATIO *gs.* **forlegennisse** 5:32; *np.* **forlaegennisse** 15:19 || part of MOECHARI *as.* **forlegenisse** 19:9; **forlægnisse** 19:9 || MERETRIX 'prostitute' *np.* **forlegnisse** 21:31 [n.]; **forlægenisse** 21:32

forlegernes *f.* 'fornication, adultery' FORNICATIO *ds.* **forlegernisse** 19:9

forleosan *v.II* 'lose' PERDERE *ps.3s.* **forleoseð** 10:39; **forleoseþ** 10:42, 16:25; *subj.ps.3s.* **forleose** 10:39, 16:25 || PERIRE *pp.p.* **forloren** 15:24 [OED2 forlese, *v.*]

forlicgan *v.V* 'fornicate, commit adultery' CONCUPISCERE *inf.* ~ 5:28 || ADULTER 'adulterous' *pt.p. fns.* **forlegene** 12:39, 16:4 [OED2 forlie, *v.*]

forlor *n.* 'loss, destruction' PERDITIO *ds.* **forlore** 7:13

forma *adj.* 'first' PRIMUS *mns.* ~ 20:27; *mas.* ~ 28:1; *mds.* **formæ** 26:17 [OED2 forme, *adj.1*]

forstellan *v.IV* 'steal' FURARI *ps.3p.* **forstelaþ** 6:19, 6:20; *subj.pt.3p.* **forstælan** 27:64; **forstælen** 28:13 [OED2 forsteal, *v.*]

fortynan *v.1* 'close, shut entirely' CLUDERE *pt.3p.* **fortyndon** 13:15

forþ *adv.* 'forth, forwards' PRAETER- **forð** 14:15 || AD- ~ 28:9; **forð** 26:73 || NL **forð** 13:35 (*bis*)
comp. 'further' AMPLIUS **forþor** 23:14 || part of PROGREDI **forþor** 26:39 [OED2 forth, *adv.*, *prep.*, and *n.*]

forþberan *v.IV* 'bring forth, produce' ADFERRE *ps.3s.* **forðbereþ** 13:23 || PROFERRE *ps.3s.* **forðbereð** 13:52 [OED2 forthbear, *v.*]

(†)**forþfeallan** *v.VII* 'fall down, fall prostrate' PROCIDERE *ps.p. mns.* **forþfællende** 18:26, 18:29; *mnp.* **forþfallende** 2:11

forþferan *v.1* 'go forth, depart' PRAECEDERE *inf.* **forðfere** 14:22 || TRANSIRE *pt.3s.* **forþfoerde** 9:27

forþgan *anom.v.* 'go forth' PROCEDERE *ps.3s.* **forþgaeþ** 4:4; **forðgæþ** 15:11 [OED2 forthgo, *v.*]

forþgangan *v.VII* 'go forth' PROCEDERE *ps.p. mns.* **forþgangande** 4:21 [OED2 forthgang, *v.*]

forþmest *adj. superl.* 'first, foremost' PRIMUS *ap.* **forþmestu** 23:6 [OED2 forthmost, *adj.* and *adv.*]

forþon *adv.* 'therefore' ENIM ~ 4:6, 4:10, 5:20, 5:46, 6:21, 6:34, 7:29, 9:13, 9:16, 9:21, 10:17, 10:19, 10:20, 10:26, 10:35, 11:10, 11:13, 11:18, 12:8, 12:34, 12:37, 12:40, 13:15, 14:3, 14:4, 16:2, 16:3, 18:7, 18:10, 18:11, 19:14, 20:16, 21:13, 21:26, 21:32, 22:14 (AUTEM in WW), 23:8, 23:9, 24:6, 24:7, 24:21, 24:26, 24:2, 24:38, 25:29, 26:9, 26:26, 26:28, 26:31, 26:52, 27:18, 28:2, 28:5, Mk1:16, Mk1:22, Mk1:38; **forþan** 27:19 || ERGO 5:19, 5:23, 5:48, 6:2, 6:8, 6:23, 6:31, 6:34, 7:12, 10:16, 10:26, 10:31, 10:32, 11:30, 13:18, 13:58, 27:64, 28:19 || IDEO ~ 6:25, 12:27, 12:31, 13:13, 13:52, 14:2,

21:43, 23:34, 24:44 || NAM - 15:4, 15:27; **forðon** 16:27 || ITAQUE - 12:12, 19:6 || AUTEM - 14:24 (ENIM in WW), 23:39 (ENIM in WW) || IGITUR - 7:20 || PROPTER HOC - 27:8 || NL - 18:4 (ERGO in WW), 19:12 (ENIM in WW)

forþon *conj.* 'because, that' QUIA - 7:13, 11:29, 13:17, 14:5, 16:2 (margin, see note), 16:7, 16:17, 17:15, 20:7, 23:10, 25:12, 25:21, 25:23, 26:29, Mk1:27, Mk1:37, Jn18:2; **forðon** 15:32 || QUONIAM - 5:3, 5:12, 23:14, 24:12, Mk1:15, Mk1:34

forþon þæt *conj.* QUIA **forþon ꝥ** 3:9, 16:8

forþon þe *adv./conj.* 'therefore, because' ENIM - 2:20, 3:2, 4:18, 5:12, 5:29, 5:30, 6:7, 6:8, 6:16, 6:24, 6:32 (*bis*), 16:25 [n.], 16:26, 17:22, 22:16, 22:28, 24:5, 24:24, 25:42, 26:43, 27:43, 28:6; **forðon þe** 4:17; **forþon the** 23:17; **forþon ðe** 2:13, 23:5 (separated), 24:27, 25:35; **forðon ðe** 3:15; **forþon þy 6:14** || QUIA (sometimes R reads QUI) - 2:18, 5:35, 5:36, 11:21, 12:41, 12:42, 13:5, 13:6, 13:11, 15:23, 20:15, 23:23 (separated), 24:42, 25:8, 25:13, 27:6; **forþon ðe** 5:34, 11:26, 23:25; **forðon þe** 11:23; **forþon þi** 5:35; **forþon de** 11:25 || QUONIAM - 5:4, 5:5, 5:6, 5:7, 5:9, 5:10, 19:8, 21:46; **forþon ðe** 18:32; **forþon the** 5:17 || NAM - 17:15, 26:11 || SIQUIDEM - 12:33 || IDEO **forþon ðe** 18:23 || AUTEM - 19:22 (ENIM in WW) || ERGO 22:30 (*þe … forþon*, ENIM in WW) || NL - 18:20 (ENIM in WW), 22:38 (ENIM in WW), 24:6 (ENIM in WW; AUTEM Xz), 25:14 (ENIM in WW)

[OED2 for-thon, *conj.*]

forþor, see **forþ**

forþsetennes *f.* 'offering' PROPOSITIO *gs.* **forðsetennisse** 12:4

[MK]**forweorpan** *v.III* 'throw away, cast out' EICERE *pt.3s.* **forwarp** Mk1:39 [OED2 forwerpe | forworpe, *v.*]

forweorþan *v.III* 'perish' PERIRE *ps.1p.* **forweorðað** 8:25; *ps.3p.* **forweorþað** 26:52; *pt.3s.* **forwearð** 18:11 [forworth, *v.*]

forwisnian *v.2* 'wither, waste' ARESCERE *pt.3p.* **forwisnadun** 13:6 || ARIDUS ESSE *pt.3s.* **forwisnade** 21:19

forwyrd *f.* 'death, destruction' PERDITIO *ns.* **forwyrd** 26:8; *ds.* **forwyrde** 7:13

fot *m.* 'foot' PES *np.* **foet** 18:8; *ap.* **foet** 18:8, 22:13, 28:9; *gp.* **fota** 5:35, 22:44; *dp.* **fotum** 4:6, 7:6, 10:14, 15:30 [foot, *n.* and *int.*]

fotsceamol *m.* 'footstool' SCABELLUM *ns.* **fotscamel** 5:35 [n.]

fox *m.* 'fox' VULPES *np.* **foxes** 8:20 [OED2 fox, *n.*]

fram *prep.* 'from, by' A/AB/ABS **from** 1:17, etc. || AD (AB in WW) **from** 1:17 (*bis*) [n.] || NL **from** 6:1 [n.], Mk1:31, Mk1:45 [OED2 from, *prep.*, *adv.*, and *conj.*]

frætwan *v.1* 'adorn' ORNARE *ps.2p.* **frętwæþ** 23:29; *inf.* **fretwan** 25:7

gefrætwan *v.1* 'adorn, ornament' ORNARE *pp. nas.* **gefrętwad** 12:44

fremman, -mian *v.1/2* 'do, perform, commit' FACERE *ps.3s.* **fremmað** 7:24; **fremmaþ** 7:26; *imp.s.* **fremme** 19:18 (*bis*); *ps.p. map.* **fremmende** 13:41 || part of MOECHARI *ps.3s.* **fremmaþ** 19:9 (*bis*) [OED2 freme, *v.*]

gefremman *v.1* 'render, make in a certain state' EFFICERE *ps.p. mnp.* **gefremmende** 18:3] [see previous]

fremde *adj.* 'foreign, strange' ALIENUS *mdp.* **fremðum** 17:25, 17:26 [OED2 fremd, *adj.*]

freo *adj.* 'free' LIBER *nnp.* **freo** 17:26 [free, *adj.*, *n.*, and *adv.*]

gefreogan *v.2* 'free, liberate' LIBERARE *subj.ps.3s.* **gefreoge** 27:43, 27:49 [OED2 yfree, *v.*]

freond *m.* 'friend, kindsman' AMICUS *ns.* - 11:19, 20:13, 22:12, 26:50 || PARENS *dp.* **freondum** 10:21 [n.]

[friend, *n.* and *adj.*]

fretan *v.V* 'devour, swallow' COMEDERE *pt.3p.* **frætun** 13:4 [OED2 fret, *v.1*]

frignan *v.III* 'ask' INTERROGARE *ps.2s.* **frægnast** 19:17; *pt.3s.* **frægn** 16:13, 27:11; *pt.3p.* **frugnun** 17:10; **frugan** 12:10; **frugon** 22:23 || CONQUIRERE *pt.3p.* **frugno** Mk1:27 [OED2 frayne | freyne, *v.*]

gefrignan *v.III* 'ask' INTERROGARE *pt.3s.* **gefrægn** 22:41 [see previous]

friþ *m.* (or *n.*?) 'peace' PAX *ns.* **frið** 10:12, 10:13 [n.]; *as.* **frið** 10:34 (*bis*) [OED2 frith, *n.1*]

†**friþsum** *adj.* 'peaceable' PACIFICUS *mnp.* **friðsume** 5:9

fruma *m. wk* 'beginning' INITIUM *ns.* **onfruma** Mk1:1; *ds.* **fruman** 19:4, 19:8, 24:21; *np.* **onfruma** 24:8 [n.] [OED2 forme, *adj.1*]

frumcenned *adj.* 'first-born' PRIMOGENITUS *mas.* **frumkendu** 1:25 [OED2 frumkenned, *adj.*]

fugel *m.* 'bird' VOLUCRIS *np.* **fuglas** 8:20, 13:4; **fluglas** 13:32 [n.] [OED2 fowl, n.]

full *adj.* 'full, filled' PLENUS *np.* **fulle** 23:25, 23:27, 23:28; *ap.* **fulle** 14:20, 15:37 || part of SATURARE *mnp.* **fulle** (*weorþan*) 5:6, 14:20 || NL *mas.* **fulne** 10:42 [n.]; *fas.* **fullę** 26:7 [full, *adj.*, *n.2*, and *adv.*]

fulluht *n.* 'baptizm' BAPTISMUM *ns.* **fullwiht** 21:25; *as.* **fullwiht** Mk1:4; *ds.* **fulluihte** 3:7 [fulloght, *n.*]

fulluhtan, -ian *v.1/2* 'baptize' BAPTIZARE *pp.s.* **fullwihted** 3:14

fulluhtere *m.* 'baptist' BAPTISTA *ns.* **fullwihtere** 11:7 [fulghtner, s.v. fulghten, *v.* under Derivatives]

[MK]**fullwian** *v.2* 'baptize' BAPTIZARE *pt.1s.* **fulwade** Mk1:8 [fullow, *v.*]

[MK]**gefullwian** *v.2* 'baptize' BAPTIZARE *ps.3s.* **gefulwað** Mk1:8; *pt.3s.* **gefulwade** Mk1:4; *pp.s.* **gefulwad** Mk1:9; *pp.p.* **gefullwade** Mk1:5 [see previous]

fultuman *v.1* 'help' ADIUVARE *imp.s.* **fultume** 15:25

fyllan *v.1* 'cause to fall, cause to stumble' SCANDALIZARE *ps.3p.* **fælleþ** 18:8; *subj.ps.3s.* **fælle** 5:29 [n.], 5:30 [fell, *v.*]

fyllan *v.1* 'fill, fulfill' SATURARE *pp.p.* **fylde** 15:37 [OED2 fill, *v.*]

gefyllan *v.1* 'fill, fulfll' (AD)INPLERE *ps.2p.* **gefyllaþ** 23:32; *pt.3s.* **gefylde** 27:48; *inf.* ~ 3:15; *infl.inf.* **gefyllenne** 5:17; *pp.s.* **gefylled** 1:22, 2:15, 2:17, 2:23, 4:14, 8:17, 12:17, 13:14, 13:35, 13:48, 21:4, 22:10, 27:9, Mk1:15; *pp.p.* **gefylled** 26:54, 26:56 || PERFECERE *pt.2s.* **gefylldęst** 21:16 [see previous]

fyllnes *f.* 'fullness, completeness' PLENITUDO *as.* **fyllnisse** 9:16 [fullness, *n.*]

†**fyllnes** *f.* 'scandal, offence' SCANDALUM *dp.* **fælnissum** 18:7 [n.]

fyr *n.* 'fire' IGNIS *as.* ~ 18:8, 25:41; *gs.* **fyres** 13:42, 13:50, 18:9; *ds.* **fyre** 3:10, 3:11, 3:12 (or *i.*), 7:19, 13:40, 17:15 [fire, *n.* and *int.*]

fylgan etc., see **folgian**

gegadrian *v.2* 'join together' CONIUNGERE *pt.3s.* **gegadrade** 19:6 [cf. OED2 gather, *v.*]

gafol *n.* 'tax, tribute' CENSUM *as.* **gæfel** 22:17; *gs.* **gæfles** 22:19 || TELONEUM *gs.* **gæflaes** (*monunge*) 9:9 || TRIBUTUM *ds.* **gæfle** 17:25 [OED2 gavel, *n.1*]

†**gafolmanung** *f.* 'toll-booth, custom-house' TELONEUM *ds.* **geafolmonunge** Mk2:14 [n.]

†**gafolrefa** *m.* 'tax-gatherer' PUBLICANUS *np.* **gæfelhroefe** 9:10

(†)**gafolgerefa** *m.* 'tax-gatherer' PUBLICANUS *ns.* **gæfelgeroefe** 10:3; *np.* **gæfelgeroefe** 5:46 [n.]; *gp.* **gæfelgeroefena** 11:19; *dp.* **gæfelgehrefum** 9:11

galdes, see **ceald**

galilea *prop.n. as.* ~ 4:12, 4:23, Mk1:14; *gs.* ~ 2:22, 4:15, 4:18, 15:29, 21:11, Mk1:16; **galilæę** Mk1:28; *ds.* ~ 3:13, 4:25, 17:22, 19:1, 26:32, 27:55, 28:7 (or *a.*?),

28:10 (or *a.*?), Mk1:9; **galile** Mk1:39

galileisc *adj.* 'Galilean, of Galilee' GALILAEUS *mas.* **galiliscu** 26:69

gan *anom.v.* 'go' IRE *ps.1s.* **gange** 21:29; *ps.2s.* **gæst** 8:19; *ps.3s.* **gæþ** 5:30; *ps.3p.* **gaþ** 25:46; *pt.3s.* **eode** 24:1; *pt.3p.* **eodun** 25:10; *subj.ps.1p.* **gæn** 13:28; **ga** Mk1:38; *imp.p.* **gæþ** 2:8, 11:4, 20:4, 25:9, 26:18, 27:65, 28:10, 28:19; **gaeð** 8:32; **gaþ** 10:6, 20:7, 22:9; **gað** 21:2 || ABIRE 'go away' *pt.1s.* **eode** 25:25; *pt.3s.* **eode** 4:24, 8:32, 12:1, 13:25, 13:46, 16:4, 18:30, 19:15, 19:22, 21:17, 21:30, 25:16, 25:18, 26:14, 26:42, 26:44, 27:60, Mk1:35, Mk2:12; **eade** 24:38; *pt.3p.* **eodun** 2:9, 8:32, 20:4, 22:5, 22:22, 28:11, 28:16; *subj.pt.3p.* **eoden** 11:7; *imp.p.* **gæþ** 10:5; *ps.p. mns.* **gangende** 27:5 || EXIRE 'go out' *ps.2s.* **gæs** 5:26; *ps.3s.* **gæþ** 2:6, 24:27; **gaeþ** 12:43, 15:19; *ps.3p.* **gæþ** 13:49; *pt.1s.* **eode** 12:44; *pt.3s.* **eode** 3:5, 8:34, 9:26, 13:3, 17:18, 20:1, 20:5, 20:6, 26:71; *pt.2p.* **eodun** 11:8; *pt.3p.* **eodun** 26:30, 28:8; *subj.ps.2p.* **gæn** 10:11; *subj.pt.2p.* **eoden** 11:7, 11:9; *subj.pt.3p.* **eoden** 25:1, 27:32; *imp.s.* **gaa** Mk1:25; *imp.p.* **gað** 10:14; **gæþ** 24:26, 25:6 || ACCEDERE *pt.3s.* **eode** 17:7, 17:14, 20:20, 21:29, 26:69, 27:58; *pt.3p.* **eodun** 5:1, 8:25, 9:14, 9:28, 13:36, 14:15, 15:1, 15:30, 16:1, 17:19, 17:24, 18:1, 21:14, 21:23, 22:23, 24:1, 24:3, 26:17, 26:73; **eoden** 26:50 || INTRARE *ps.3s.* **gæþ** 7:21, 19:23; **gaeþ** 7:21; *ps.2p.* **gæþ** 18:3, 23:13; *pt.2s.* **eodest** 22:12; *pt.3s.* **eode** 9:25, 12:4, 17:25, 21:12, 22:11; *subj.ps.2s.* **ga** 8:8; *imp.s.* **ga** 6:6, 25:23; *imp.p.* **gaþ** 5:20, 7:13; *inf.* **gæ** 18:9 || VADERE *ps.3s.* **gæþ** 8:9, 12:45, 13:44; **gæð** 26:24; **gað** 18:12; *imp.s.* **ga** 4:10, 5:41, 8:4, 8:9, 9:6, 19:21, 20:14, 21:28; **gae** 5:24; **gaa** Mk1:44, Mk2:11; *imp.p.* **gæþ** 9:13 || AMBULARE *ps.3s.* **gæþ** 12:43; *pt.3s.* **eode** 14:29; *imp.s.* **ga** 9:5; **gaa** Mk2:9 || EGREDI *pt.3s.* **eode** 20:3, Jn18:1; *pt.3p.* **eodun** 20:29 || INTROIRE *pt.3s.* **eode** 8:5, 21:10, Jn18:1 || FACERE *pt.3p.* **eodun** 27:1 (INIRE in WW) || INIRE *pt.3pt.* **eodun** 27:7 || PROCEDERE *pt.3p.* **gæð** 15:18 || VENIRE *subj.pt.2p.* **eoden** 26:55 (EXIRE in WW) || NL (part of OCCIDERE) *pt.3s.* **eode** Mk1:32 [go, *v.*]

[MK]**gang** *m.* 'way, path' SEMITA *ap.* **gongas** Mk1:3 [gang, *n.*]

gangan *v.VII* 'go' (EX/AB)IRE *ps.2s.* **ganges** 8:19; *subj.ps.3p.* ~ 28:10; *imp.p.* **gangaþ** 28:7; *inf.* ~ 2:22, 8:21, 26:46, Mk1:38; *infl.inf.* **gangenne** 14:16 (margin); *ps.p. mns.* **gangende** 13:1; **gangande** 14:14; *mnp.* **gangende** 8:28, 8:32, 9:31, 10:7, 12:14, 14:15, 21:6, 27:53, 27:66; **gangænde** 22:15 || EGREDI *ps.p. mns.* **gongende** 15:21; **gangende** 18:28, 26:75; **gangande** 24:1; *mnp.* **gangende** 22:10; *ps.p.* **gangende** 9:32; *pt.p. nns.* **gongen** 15:22 || ACCEDERE *ps.p. mns.* **gangende** 21:28, 21:30, 26:49; *mnp.* **gangende** 13:10 || AMBULARE *ps.3p.* **gangaþ** 11:5; *ps.p. mns.* **gangande** 4:18, 14:25; *mas.* **gangandne** 14:26; *np.* **gangande** 15:31 || VADERE *ps.1s.* **gange** 26:36; *ps.3s.* **gangeð** 15:17; *imp.s.* **gang** 8:13, 16:23, 17:27, 18:15 || INTRARE *subj.ps.2p.* **gangan** 10:12 [n.], 26:41; *imp.s.* **gang** 25:21; *inf.* **gangan** 12:29; *inf.inf.* **gangene** 19:24 || ORIRI *inf.* (*upp*) ~ 5:45 'rise' || PROCEDERE *ps.p. mns.* **gangende** 26:39 [gang, *v.1*]

gast *m.* 'spirit' SPIRITUS *ns.* ~ 10:20, 12:43, 26:41, Mk1:12, Mk1:25, Mk1:26; *gs.* **gastes** 12:31 (margin), 28:19; *as.* ~ 3:16, 12:18, 27:50, Mk2:8; **gastes** Mk1:10 (?) [n.]; *ds.* **gaste** 1:18, 1:20, 3:11, 4:1, 5:3, 12:28, 12:32, 22:43, Mk1:8 (margin), Mk1:23; *ap.* **gastas** 8:16; **gastes** 12:45; *gp.* **gastas** 10:1; *dp.*

gastum Mk1:27 [ghost, *n.* and *adj.*]

gærshoppa *m.* 'grasshopper, locust' LOCUSTA *ns.* **græshoppa** 3:4 [grasshop, *n.*]

ge *conj.* 'and, both' ET ~ 12:50, 13:12 || ETIAM ~ 12:8, 24:24 || NL **ge** (... ⁊ ...) 'both ... and ...' 10:28 [OED2 ye, *conj.* and *adv.*]

gea *adv.* 'yes' UTIQUE **gæ** 17:25 (ETIAM in WW) [yea, *adv.* and *n.*]

geara *adv.* 'long ago, formerly' OLIM **iara** 11:21 [OED2 yore, *adv.* (and *adj.*)]

geard *m.* 'hedge' SAEPES *ds.* **geard** 21:33 [n.] [OED2 yard, *n.1*]

gearu *adj.* 'ready' PARATUS *fns.* **iare** 22:8; *np.* **iara** 22:4; **gearwe** 24:44, 25:10 || PROMPTUS *mns.* **gearo** 26:41 [OED2 yare, *adj.*]

gearwian *v.2* 'prepare' PARARE *pt.3p.* **gearwadun** 26:19; *subj.ps.1p.* **iarwan** 26:17; *pp.s.* **iarward** 20:23 [n.]; *imp.p.* **gearwigað** 3:3, Mk1:3 || INDUERE *subj.ps.2p.* **gearwige** 6:25 || VESTIRE *ps.3s.* **gearwæþ** 6:30 || FACERE *pt.3s.* **iarwede** 26:12 [n.] [OED2 yare, *v.*]

gegearwian *v.2* 'prepare, dress' PARARE *pt.1s.* **geiarwad** 22:4; *pp.s.* **geiarwad** 25:34 || INDUERE *pt.3p.* **gegearwadun** 27:31 || PRAEPARARE *pp.s.* **geiarward** 25:41 [n.] || VESTIRE *pt.3p.* **gegearwade** 11:8 || NL *pp. mas.* **gegearwæd** 11:8 [n.] [see previous]

gearwung *f.* 'preparation' PARASCEVE *gs.* **gearwunga** (*dæge*) 27:62

geat *n.* 'gate' PORTA *ns.* **geatt** 7:13; **geate** 7:14; *as.* **geate** 7:13 (or *d.*?) || IANUA *ds.* **gete** Mk2:2; **geat** Mk1:33 (endingless?) [OED2 gate, *n.1*]

gella *m. wk* 'gall, bile' FEL *a/ds.* **gallan** 27:34 [OED2 gall, *n.1*]

gemung-, see **gyming**

gen *adv.* 'yet' ADHUC (*nu*) **gęn** 19:20

genesara *prop.n. gs.* ~ 14:34 (or *a.*?)

geoc *n.* 'yoke' IUGUM *ns.* **ioc** 11:30; *as.* **ioc** 11:29 [yoke, *n.*]

geoguþ *f.* 'youth' IUVENTUS *ds.* **iuguðe** 19:20 [OED2 youth, *n.*]

geomann *m.* ANTIQUUS '(used in plural) men of old' *dp.* **iumonnum** 5:21 [n.]; **gumonnum** 5:27, 5:33

geond *prep.* 'throughout' IN ~ 9:31, 24:14 || PER ~ 24:7 [OED2 yond, *prep.* and *adv.*]

geond *adv.* 'across, throughout' ILLIC ~ 24:23, 26:36 [see previous]

geondgan *anon.v.* 'pass through, traverse' CIRCUMIRE *pt.3s.* **geondeade** 4:23; **geondeode** 9:35

geong *adj.* 'young' ADOLESCENS *mns.* **iungæ** 19:20; **iunge** 19:22 [young, *adj.* and *n.1*]

georne *adv.* 'eagerly' DILIGENTER ~ 2:7, 2:8 [OED2 yerne, *adv.*]

geotan *v.II* 'pour' MITTERE *ps.3p.* **geotaþ** 9:17 || PONERE *ps.3p.* **geotaþ** 9:17 (MITTERE in WW) [n.] [yet, *v.*]

gerasing *m.* 'the tribe of Gerasa' GERASENUS *gp.* **gerasinga** 8:28 [n.]

gezemani *prop.n. ns.* ~ 26:36

gif *conj.* 'if' SI ~ 4:3, etc.; **gęf** 28:14 [if, *conj.* and *n.*]

gitsian *v.2* 'covet, long for' CONCUPISCERE *infl.inf.* **gitsanne** 5:28 [OED2 yisse, *v.*]

glendrian *v.2* 'devour, swallow' DEVORATOR *ps.p. mns.* **glendrende** 11:19 [n.] || DEGLUTIRE *ps.p. mnp.* **glendrende** 23:24

glesan *v1.* 'gloss, explain' NL *pt.3s.* **gleosede** MtCOLOPHON [cf. OED2 gloze *v.1*; gloss *v.1*]

god *m.* 'god' DEUS *ns.* ~ 1:23, 3:18, 6:30, 15:4, 19:4 (*bis*), 19:6, 19:17, 22:32 (x5), 27:46 (x4), Mk1:24, Mk2:7; *as.* ~ 5:8, 9:8, 15:31, 19:26, 22:37, 26:63, 27:43, Mk2:12; *gs.* **godes** 3:16, 4:3, 4:4, 4:6, 4:7, 5:9, 5:34, 6:33, 8:29, 12:28 (*bis*), 14:33, 15:3, 15:6, 16:16, 16:23, 21:12, 21:31, 21:43, 22:16, 22:21, 22:29, 22:30, 23:22, 24:13, 26:61, 26:63, 26:64, 27:40, 27:43, 27:54, Mk1:1, Mk1:14, Mk1:15; **gode** 12:4; *ds.* **gode** 4:10, 6:24, 22:21 || DOMINUS *dp.* **godum** 6:24 'lord, master' [god, *n.* and *int.*]

god *adj.* 'good' BONUS *mns.* ~ 12:35, 19:17, 20:15; **good** 19:16; *mns.* **goda** 25:21; **godu** 25:23; *mas.* **godne** 3:10, 7:17 [n.], 7:19, 12:33, 13:23 [n.]; *mds.* **godum** 12:35; *nns.* ~ 5:26, 7:17, 15:26, 17:4, 18:8, 18:9, 26:24; *nns.* **gode** 7:18, 13:38; *nas.* ~ 7:11 (*bis*), 7:12, 12:12, 12:33, 13:24, 13:27, 13:37, 26:10; *ngs.* **godes** 19:16; *nds.* **gode** 19:17; *fas.* **gode** 13:8; *map.* **gode** 5:45, 7:18, 13:45, 13:48, 22:10; *nap.* ~ 5:16, 12:34, 12:35, 19:21, 24:47, 25:14
comp. mns. **bettra** 12:12; *mnp.* **bettra** 10:31 [good, *adj.*, *n.*, *adv.*, and *int.*]

godspell *n.* or *m.*? 'gospel' EVANGELIUM *ns.* ~ Mt INCIPIT, 24:14; **godspel** 26:13; *gs.* **godspelles** 4:23 (or *ap.*?) [n.], 9:35 (or *ap.*?) [n.], Mk1:1, Mk1:14 (or *ap.*?); *ds.* ~ Mk1:15 || EVANGELIZARE *as.* ~ (*secgan*) 11:5 [OED2 gospel, *n.*]

gold *n.* 'gold' AURUM *ns.* ~ 23:17; *as.* ~ 2:11, 10:9, 23:17; *ds.* **golde** 23:16 [gold, *n.1* and *adj.*]

goldhord *m. or n.* 'treasure' THESAURUS *as/p.* ~ 2:11; *ds.* **goldhorde** 13:44; ~ 13:52 [gold hoard, *n.*]

golgoþa *prop.n. ns.* ~ 27:33

gomorring *m.* 'the people of Gomorrah' GOMORREUS *gp.* **gomorringa** 10:15

gorst *m.* 'gorse, thorn' TRIBULUS *dp.* **gorstum** 7:16 [n.] [OED2 gorse, *n.*]

græshoppa, see **gærshoppa**

grecisch *adj.* 'the Greek language' NL (*in*) **gc** 27:46 [n.] [OED2 Greekish, *adj.* and *n.*]

gretan *v.1* 'greet' COGNOSCERE 'have carnal relations with' (cf. DOE 1.c.) *pt.3s.* **groette** 1:25 [n.] [OED2 greet, *v.1*]

grimm *adj.* 'grim, fierce' SAEVUS *mnp.* **grimme** 8:28 [OED2 grim, *adj.* and *adv.*]

grindan *v.III* 'grind' MOLERE *ps.p. fnp.* **grindende** 24:41 [grind, *v.1*]

gegripan *v.I* 'grasp, clutch' ADPREHENDERE *pt.3s.* **gegrap** 14:31; *pt.3p.* **gegripan** 21:35; **gegripon** 21:39; *pp.s.* **gegripen** Mk1:31 [OED2 i-gripe, *v.*]

gristbatung *f.* 'gnashing, grinding of teeth' STRIDOR *ns.* ~ 8:12, 25:30; **gristbitung** 13:42, 13:50, 22:13, 24:51 [OED2 gristbiting, *n.*]

grornian *v.2* 'murmur, complain' MURMURARE *pt.3p.* **grornadun** 20:11 [n.]

grund *m.* 'bottom' PROFUNDUM *ds.* **grunde** 18:6 [OED2 ground, *n.*]

gyfan *v.V* 'give' REDDERE *imp.s.* **gef** 20:8 [OED2 give, *v.*]

gyfu *f.* 'gift' DONUM *ns.* **geofu** 23:19; *as.* **geofu** 23:19; *a/ds.* **geofu** 23:18 [OED2 give, n.1]

gyld *n.* 'payment' COMMERCIUM *as.* **geld** 16:26 [guild, *n.*]

gyldan *v.III* 'pay back, render' REDDERE *ps.3s.* **geldeþ** 6:4, 6:6, 6:18, 16:27 || SOLVERE *pt.3s.* **gald** 17:24 [OED2 yield, *v.*]

gyming *f.* or *n.*? 'marriage, wedding' NUPITAE *ns.* **gemung** 22:10; **gemunge** 22:8; *as.* **gemunge** 22:2 [n.]; *ds.* **gemunge** 22:3; **gemungæ** 22:4, 22:9, 25:10 [OED2 yeming, *n.*]

gyminglic *adj.* 'nupital' NUPITALIS *nas.* **gemunlic** 22:12; *nis.* **gemunglice** 22:11

gymnes *f.* 'care, concern' CURA *ns.* **gemnis** 22:16

gyrd *f.* 'stick, rod' VIRGA *as.* **ierde** 10:10 [yard, *n.2*]

gyrdels *m.* 'belt, girdle' ZONA *as.* ~ 3:4, Mk1:6; *dp.* ~ 10:9 [OED2 girdle, *n.1*]

gegyrela *m.* 'dress, garment' NL *dp.* **gegærelum** 27:28 [n.]

[MK]**gegyrelod** *adj.* 'clothed' VESTITUS *mns.* **gegerelad** Mk1:6 [n.]

gyrwan *v.1* 'prepare, strip?' EXUERE *ps.p. np.* **gærwende** 27:28 [n.]

gyt *adv.* 'yet' NUNDUM (w. negative) **get** 24:6 || ADHUC **get** 27:63 [yet, *adv.* and *adj.2*]

gyta *adv.* 'yet, (with *nu*, *þonne*) in addition, besides' ADHUC **geta** 15:16 (*nu* ~), 18:16 (*þonne* ~) || part of ETIAM? **geta** 24:24

habban *v.3* 'have' HABERE *ps.2s.* **hæfest** 19:21 (*bis*), 22:12; **hæfęþ** 25:25 [n.]; *ps.3s.* **hæfþ** 13:12; **hæfð** 1:23, 13:12, 13:27, 25:28 [n.]; **hæfþ** 13:12; **hæfeþ** 9:6, 13:21, 13:44; **hæfeð** Mk2:10; **hæfæþ** 11:18; *ps.1p.* **habbaþ** 3:9; *ps.2p.* **habbaþ** 5:46, 6:1, 8:20, 15:34, 16:8, 26:11, 27:65; **habbað** 17:20; **habbad** 26:11; *ps.3p.* **habbaþ** 21:26; *pt.3s.* **hæfde** 3:4, 13:46, 18:25, 19:22, 21:28, Mk1:22; *pt.2p.* **hæfdon** 21:21; **hæfdun** 21:32; *pt.3p.* **hæfdun** 4:24, 14:5, 21:46, 22:28, 27:16; **æfdon** 8:33 [n.]; **hęfde** 13:5; *subj.ps.1s.* **hæbbe** 19:16 (w. g.); *subj.ps.3s.* **hæbbe** 5:23, 11:15, 12:11, 13:9, 13:43, 25:29; *subj.pt.3s.* **hæfde** 22:24; *imp.s.* **hæfe** 18:26, 18:29; *imp.p.* **habbaþ** 14:27; *infl.inf.* **habanne** 14:4 (w. g.; see note); *ps.p. mns.* **hæbbende** 7:29, 8:9, 12:10; *mas.* **hæbbende** 9:32, 18:9, 18:9; *mds.* **hæbbende** 9:12 (or p.?), 18:8; *fns.* **hæbbende** 1:18; *nns.* **hæbbende** 26:7; *np.* **hæbbende** 8:28, 15:30, 24:10; *ap.* **hæbbende** 8:16 (*bis*), 14:35, Mk1:32; **hæbende** 4:24 [n.], Mk1:32; w. negative contraction *ps.3s.* **næfð** 8:20; **næfeþ** 25:29; *ps.1p.* **nabbaþ** 14:17; *ps.3p.* **nabbaþ** 14:16, 15:32; *pt.3s.* **næfde** 18:25, 22:25; *pt.3p.* **næfdon** 13:5; **nęfdun** 13:6 || DUCERE *pt.3s.* **hæfde** 22:25 || TOLLERE *imp.p.* **habbaþ** 11:29 [n.] || (with *pt.p.*) *pt.3s.* **hæfde** 7:28; *pt.3p.* **hæfdon** 14:34 || NL *subj.ps.3s.* **hæbbe** 18:12 [n.]; *subj.ps.1p.* **habbe** 21:38 (HABERE in WW) [n.] [have, *v.*]

had *m.* 'person' PERSONA *dp.* **hadum** 22:16 [OED2 had | hade | hod, *n.*]

hal *adj.* 'whole, sound' SALVUS *mns.* ~ 10:22, 19:25, 24:13; *fns.* ~ 9:21, 9:22; *fas.* **halne** 9:22 [n.]; *nns.* ~ 24:22; *nas.* ~ 16:25; *mnp.* **hale** 14:36 || HAVE(TE) *mns.* ~ 26:49, 27:29; *np.* **hale** 28:9 || VALENS *mdp.* **halum** 9:12 || NL *fas.* ~ Mk1:31 [n.] [hale, *adj.*, *n.4*, and *adv.*]

halettan *v.1* 'hail, salute' SALUTARE *ps.2p.* **halettaþ** 5:47; *imp.p.* **haleteþ** 10:12

halettung *f.* 'salutation, greeting' SALUTATIO *ap.* **hælettungæ** 23:7

halig *adj.* 'holy, (subst.) saint' SANCTUS *mns.* ~ Mk1:24; *mas.* **halga** Mk1:10 [n.]; *mgs.* **halgan** 28:19; *mds.* **halgum** 12:32, Mk1:8 (margin); *mds.* **halgan** 1:18, 1:20, 3:11; *fas.* **halgan** 4:5, 27:53; *fds.* **halig** 24:15; *ngs.* **halig** 7:6; *gp.* **haligra** 27:52 [OED2 holy, *adj.* and *n.*]

halgian *v.2* 'sanctify, hallow' SANCTIFICARE *ps.3s.* **halgaþ** 23:17, 23:19 [OED2 hallow, *v.1*]

gehalgian *v.2* 'sanctify, hallow' SANCTIFICARE *pp.s.* **gehalgad** 6:9 [see previous]

halsian *v.2* 'implore, entreat' ADIURARE *ps.1s.* **halsio** 26:63 [OED2 halse, *v.1*]

hana *m. wk* 'cock' GALLUS *ns.* **hona** 26:34, 26:74, 26:75

hand *f.* 'hand' MANUS *ns.* **hond** 5:30; *as.* **hond** 9:18, 9:25, 12:49, 14:31; **honda** 8:3, 8:15, 12:10, 12:13, 26:51, Mk1:41; **honde** 26:23; **hondæ** 12:13; *ds.* **hond** Mk1:31 (endingless or *n.*?); *ds.* **honda** 3:12; *np.* **honde** 18:8; *ap.* **honda** 15:2, 17:22, 18:8, 19:13, 19:15, 22:13, 26:45, 26:50, 27:24; *dp.* **hondum** 4:6, 10:10, 15:20 || COLAPHUS *dp.* **hondum** 26:67 || PALMA *ap.* (*brade*) **honde** 26:67 [n.] || NL *ns.* **hond** 6:3 [n.]; *as.* **hond** 27:29 [hand, *n.*]

hangian v.2 'hang' PENDERE *ps.3s.* **hongað** 22:40 [OED2 hang, *v.*]

hatan *v.VII* 'be called' DICERE *pt.3s.* **hatte** 13:55, 26:36, 27:33; *pp.s.* **haten** 26:3, 27:16 || NOMEN ('by name, called') *pp.s.* **haten** 9:9,

27:57 || VOCARE *pt.3s.* **hatte** 2:23 'command' || IUBERE *pt.3s.* **heht** 8:18, 14:9, 14:19, 14:22, 18:25, 27:58; *imp.s.* **hat** 14:28, 27:64 || PRAECIPERE *pt.3s.* **heht** Mk1:44 || IMPERARE *ps.3s.* **hataþ** Mk1:27 || NL *pt.3s.* **heht** 14:2 [n.] [hight, *v.1*]

gehatan *v.VII* 'promise, vow' POLLICERI *pt.3s.* **geheht** 14:7 [see previous]

hatian *v.2* 'become hot' AESTUARE *pt.3p.* **hatedun** 13:6 [hot, *v.*]

hatian *v.2* 'hate' ODISSE *ps.3p.* **hateþ** 5:44; *imp.* **hate** 5:43 || ODIO HABERE *ps.3s.* **hateþ** 6:24 [hate, *v.*]

hælan *v.1* 'heal' CURARE *subj.pt.3p.* **hælde** 10:1; *imp.p.* **hæleþ** 10:8; *inf.* **hælon** 12:10; *ps.p. mns.* **hælende** 9:35 || SANARE *ps.1s.* **hælo** 13:15; *pt.3s.* **hælde** 4:23 || SALVARE *imp.s.* **hæl** 8:25, 27:40 || SALVUM FACERE *pt.3s.* **hælde** 27:42; *imp.s.* **hæl** 14:30 [OED2 heal, *v.1*]

gehælan *v.1* 'heal' CURARE *ps.1s.* **gehæle** 8:7; *pt.3s.* **gehælde** 4:24, 8:16, 12:15, 12:22, 19:2; **gehelde** 14:14; **gehęlde** 15:30; *inf.* **gehælen** 17:16; *pp.s.* **gehæled** 17:18 || OSANNA *imp.s.* (as an interj.) **gehæl** 21:9 (*bis*), 21:15 || SANARE *pt.3s.* **gehælde** 21:14; *pp.s.* **gehæled** 8:8, 8:13 || SALVUM/SANUM FACERE *ps.3s.* **gehæleþ** 1:21; *inf.* **gehælun** 27:42; *pp.s.* **gehæled** 15:28 || SALVARE *infl.inf.* **gehęlanne** 18:11 [see previous]

gehæld *n.* 'watching, guard' CUSTODIA *as.* **gehæld** 27:65

hælend *m.* 'saviour' IESUS *ns.* ~ 1:16, etc.; **helend** 12:25, 13:57, 14:12, 14:13, 14:16, 14:25, 14:27, 14:31; **hęlend** 12:1; [ ]**lend** 18:2 (margin); *as.* ~ 1:21, 1:25, 9:10, 26:4, 26:59, 26:69, 27:17, 27:20, 27:26, 27:27, 27:54, 27:55, 28:5; **hæl(lend)** 26:50; *gs.* **hælendes** 1:1, 27:58, 27:59, Mk1:1; ~ 27:57; **hæl(lendes)** 26:75; *ds.* **helende** 14:29; ~ 17:4, 18:1, 26:71, 27:1; **hæl(lende)** 21:27, 26:49, 26:51, 27:22; ~ 8:34, 26:17 || ILLE *as.* ~ 17:3 [n.] || NL *ns.* 13:34 (IESUS in WW); **hælende** 16:20 [OED2 healend, *n.*]

hælu *f.* 'health' SANITAS *ds.* **hælo** 12:13 [OED2 heal | hele, *n.*]

hæman *v.1* 'marry' NUBERE *ps.3p.* **hæmeþ** 22:30; *subj.ps.3s.* **hęme** 19:10 [n.]; *ps.p. np.* **hemende** 24:38; *pp.p.* **hæmde** 22:30 (margin)

hæmed *n.* 'union, marriage' NUPTUS *ds.* **hęmde** 24:38

hær *n.* 'hair' PIL(L)IUS *dp.* **herum** 3:4, Mk1:6 [OED2 hair, *n.*]

hætu *f.* 'heat' AESTUS *as.* ~ 20:12 [OED2 heat, *n.*]

hæþen *adj.* 'heathen, pagan, a gentile (subst.)' ETHNICUS *mns.* **hæþenna** 18:17; *mnp.* **hæðne** 5:47; **hæðene** 6:7 || part of PROSELYTUS *mas.* **hæþne** 23:15 [OED2 heathen, *adj.* and *n.1*]

he *pron.* 'he' Latin equivalents: IS, ILLE, IPSE, QUI, SE (refl.), SUUS (refl. poss.), HIC (*mns.* ~ 9:34; *np.* **hiæ** 25:46; *gp.* **heora** 21:3)

Forms (citations are given only for relatively infrequent forms; instances that do not translate the Latin equivalents listed above are presented separately below): *mns.* **he**; *mas.* **hine**, **hinę** 5:41, 21:46, 27:38, 27:44, **hinae** 8:31, 22:15, 26:16, 27:54, 28:13; *mgs.* **his**, **is** 7:24, 24:46; *mds.* **him**, **heom** 19:21, 26:52, 26:64, 27:11; *nns.* **hit**; *nas.* **hit**; *ngs.* **his**; *nds.* **him**; *fns.* **hiu**, **hio**, **heo**, **hiæ**; *fas.* **hiae**, **hie** 1:19, **hio** 1:19, Mk1:31, **heo** 9:18, 9:22, **eo** 16:18; *fgs.* **hire**; *fds.* **hire**; *nap.* **hie**, **hię**, **hiæ**, **hiae**, **hye** 27:4, **heo** 27:17, 27:23, **hia** Mk1:20, Mk1:21, Mk1:22, **hi** 23:3, **he** (see below); *gp.* **heora**, **eora** 10:18, **hiora** 1:21, 4:21); *dp.* **heom**, **him** 2:7 (*bis*), 3:7, 4:21, 6:8, 15:30, 26:19, Mk2:2

NL *mns.* **he** 1:19, 1:21, 2:9, 2:16 (x3), 2:21, 2:23, 3:7, 3:13, 3:16 (*bis*), 4:1, 4:2, 4:6, 4:12, 4:18, 4:21, 4:24, 5:1 (*bis*), 5:15, 5:19, 5:21

(*bis*), 5:22 (x3), 5:32 (*bis*), 5:34, 6:24, 7:8 (*bis*), 7:9, 7:10 (*bis*), 7:24, 7:29, 8:1, 8:5, 8:9 (x3), 8:10, 8:17 (*bis*), 8:20, 8:28, 8:34, 9:7, 9:9, 9:16, 9:18, 9:19, 9:25, 9:28, 9:29, 9:36, 9:38, 10:25, 10:36 (*bis*), 10:39, 10:40, 10:41 (*bis*), 11:1, 11:18, 12:3, 12:9, 12:11, 12:13 (*bis*), 12:15, 12:18, 12:19, 12:22 (*bis*), 12:26, 12:43, 12:46, 13:2, 13:3, 13:4, 13:12, 13:34, 13:44, 13:46, 14:14, 14:23, 14:29, 16:1, 16:12, 16:20, 16:25 (*bis*), 16:26, 17:13, 17:14, 17:15, 17:20, 17:23, 17:25 (*bis*), 17:26, 18:6, 18:13 (*bis*), 18:16, 18:17 (*bis*), 18:24, 18:25 (x3), 18:30, 18:34, 19:8, 19:9, 19:13, 19:18, 19:22, 20:8, 20:23, 20:26, 20:27, 20:28, 21:10, 21:14, 21:23, 21:25, 21:27, 21:40, 21:44, 21:45, 22:7, 22:11, 22:34, 22:42, 22:45, 23:11, 23:12 (*bis*), 23:15, 23:20, 23:21, 24:2, 24:17, 24:18, 24:26, 24:33, 24:50 (*bis*), 25:29, 26:2, 26:16 (*bis*), 26:20, 26:24, 26:49, 26:53, 26:58, 26:65, 26:66, 26:74 (*bis*), 26:75, 27:3, 27:5, 27:12, 27:14, 27:15, 27:18, 27:19, 27:26 (*bis*), 27:31, 27:32, 27:34 (*bis*), 27:42 (*bis*), 27:43 (*bis*), 27:44, 27:60, 27:63, 27:64, 28:6 (x3), 28:7, Mk1:34, Mk2:4, Mk2:10, Jn18:1; **hæ** Mk1:22 [n.]; *mas.* **hine** 4:2, 7:9 [n.], 12:3, 16:22 (ILLE in WW), 24:51 (IS in WW), 26:15 [n.], 26:67; *mgs.* **his** 2:14, 5:25 [n.], 8:16 [n.], 10:22, 18:27, 20:20, 22:5 (SUUS in WW), 25:15 [n.], 25:23, 27:24, 27:50, 28:4; **is** 22:24 (IS in WW), 25:33 (SUUS in WW); *mds.* **him** 5:32, 6:1 (?) [n.], 7:8, 13:10, 13:25, 14:4 (ILLE in WW), 14:5, 14:23, 15:12, 19:9, 20:28 [n.], 22:23 (IS in WW), 24:1 [n.], 25:29, 26:50 (ILLE in WW), 27:24, 28:17; *fns.* **hio** 1:18 (*bis*), 1:21, 5:35 (*bis*), 9:24, 20:21, 22:13, 26:10; **hiu** 8:15, 14:7; **heo** 9:18, 9:21; **hiæ** 15:23; *fgs.* **hire** 1:18; *nns.* **hit** 1:25, 5:13 (*bis*), 5:37 (x4), 7:25 (*bis*), 7:27, 8:16, 13:27, 13:32, 13:48, 14:27, 20:8, 26:22, 26:25, 26:42, 26:48, 27:1; *np.* **he** 4:6 [n.], 7:16, 16:28, 18:19, 27:15, Mk1:34; **hiae** 1:18, 2:9, 5:16, 6:7; **hiæ** 6:16, 7:6, 10:23, 11:20, 11:23, 12:16, 13:16, 13:41, 14:32, 14:36, 15:2, 15:9, 21:31, 21:41, 22:22, 22:42, 23:5, 25:10, 26:47, 27:18, 27:20, 27:31, 27:32 (*bis*), 27:35, 27:39, 28:8, 28:12, 28:15; **hie** 1:23, 2:10, 2:18, 4:6, 5:9, 6:2 (*bis*), 6:5 (*bis*), 6:16, 6:28, 7:29, 8:20, 9:36, 10:17, 10:19, 10:25, 12:10 (*bis*), 12:14, 12:36, 13:5, 13:6, 13:13, 13:15, 13:25, 13:51 [n.], 13:54, 14:17, 14:34, 15:32 (*bis*), 15:35, 16:5, 16:12, 16:20, 17:12, 17:23, 20:7, 20:10, 21:1, 21:46 (*bis*), 22:21, 28:10, Mk1:27; **hię** 2:12, 4:18, 5:12, 6:16, 6:26, 9:24, 13:16, 14:15, 14:16, 15:32, 17:24, 20:22, 23:5; **hi** 20:31, 21:15, 21:25, 21:34, 22:10, 24:38, 28:10, 28:11, Mk2:4; **hy** 26:4, 26:5; **heo** 20:33; **hio** 21:37; **hia** Mk1:16, Mk2:12 [n.]; *ap.* **hie** 5:6 [n.]; **heo** 21:3 (R uobis; WW eos); **hiæ** 26:44; **hia** Mk2:13; *gp.* **heora** 6:2, 11:16, 20:8, 22:46, 23:5 (SUUS in WW), 23:6, 27:15; **heor** 27:30; *dp.* **him** 6:5, 21:46; **heom** 9:8, 17:6, 22:29 (ILLE in WW), 24:10, 27:17, 28:18; *?* **him** 6:7 (miscopy of a nominative plural form? See note.), 10:29 [he, *pron.*, *n.1*, and *adj.*]

heaf *m.* 'lamentation' FLETUS ~ *ns.* 24:51, 25:30 || ULULATUS *ns.* ~ 2:18

heafod *n.* 'head' CAPUT *ns.* **heafud** 14:11; *as.* ~ 6:17, 14:8, 21:42; **heafud** 5:36, 8:20, 26:7, 27:29, 27:30, 27:37; *gs.* ~ 10:30; *ap.* **heafud** 27:39 [head, *n.1*]

heafodpanne *f.* 'skull, brain-pan' CALVARIA *gs.* **heafodpanne** 27:33 [n.] [head pan, *n.*]

heah *adj.* 'high' EXCELSUS *fas.* **heh** 4:8; **hea** 17:1 [high, *adj.* and *n.2*]

heahsetl *n.* 'judgement seat, tribunal' TRIBUNAL *ds.* **hehsettle** 27:19

†**heahstow** *f.* 'high place, pinnacle'

PINNACULUM *ds.* **hehstowe** 4:5 [n.]

[MK]†**heahsunn** *adj.* 'publican, (subst.) tax-collector' PUBLICANUS *mns.* **hehsunne** Mk2:15 [n.]

heahsynn *f.* 'grievaous sin' CRIMEN *ds.* **hehsynne** 12:5

healdan *v.VII* 'hold, keep' SERVARE *pt.3p.* **heoldun** 27:36 *imp.s.* **hald** 19:17; *imp.p.* **haldeþ** 23:3 || CUSTODIRE *imp.p.* **haldeþ** 27:65; *ps.p. np.* **haldende** 27:54 || OBSERVARE *infl.inf.* **healdene** 28:20 [OED2 hold, *v.*]

gehealdan *v.VII* 'hold, guard' CUSTODIRE *pt.1s.* **geheold** 19:20; *subj.ps.3p.* **gehalden** 4:6; *inf.* **gehaldan** 27:64 || CONSERVARE *pp.p.* **gehalden** 9:17 || MUNIRE *pt.3p.* **geoldun** 27:66 [n.] [i-hald | i-hold, *v.*]

healf *f.* 'side, part' NL *as.* **healfe** 20:21 (*bis*), 25:33 (*bis*), 25:34; **halfe** 20:23, 22:44, 26:64; *ds.* **halfe** 25:41, Mk1:45 [OED2 half, *n.*]

healt *adj.* 'halt, lame' CLAUDUS *mns.* ~ 18:8; *np.* **halte** 11:5; **healte** 21:14; *ap.* **halte** 15:30; **healte** 15:31 [OED2 halt, *adj.*]

heanes *f.* 'height' ALTITUDO *as.* **heanisse** 13:5 ('depth') || EXCELSUM *dp.* **heanissum** 21:9 || EXCELSUS (*adj.*) *gs.*? **heanisse** 24:30 || RAMA 'the city of Ramah' *ds.* **heanisse** 2:18 [n.] || SUMMA *dp.* **heanissum** 24:31 [highness, *n.*]

heard *adj.* 'hard' DURUS *mns.* **eard** 25:24 [hard, *adj.* and *n.*]

heardnes *f.* 'hardness' DURITIA *a/ds.* **heardnisse** 19:8 [hardness, *n.*]

hearmcwedol *adj.* 'caluminious' CALMNIARI *mdp.* **hearmcwuidele** 5:44 (used as subst. 'one speaking ill of') [n.]

heawan *v.VII* 'hew, behead' ABSCINDERE *pt.3s.* **heow** 26:51 || DECOLLARE *inf.* ~ 14:2 [n.] [OED2 hew, *v.*]

geheawan *v.VII* 'hew' EXCIDERE *pt.3s.* **geheu** 27:60 [see previous]

hebban *v.VI* 'raise, lift up' LEVARE *ps.p. mnp.* **hebbende** 17:8 || TOLLERE *imp.s.* **hef** 21:21 [OED2 heave, *v.*]

hefalsaþ, see **eofulsian**

hefig *adj.* 'heavy' GRAVIS *ap.* **hæfige** 23:4; *comp. np.* **hæfigra** 23:23 [OED2 heavy, *adj.1* and *n.*]

hefiglice *adv.* 'heavily, sluggishly' GRAVITER ~ 13:15 [OED2 heavily, *adv.*]

hege *m.* 'hedge, fence' SAEPES *ds.* **heage** 21:33 [OED2 hedge, *n.*]

†**helan** *v.1* 'accuse falsely' CALMNIARI *ps.p. mdp.* **hoelende** 5:44

helle *f.* 'hell' GEHENNA *as.* **helle** 5:29, 5:30, 18:9; *a/ds.* **helle** 10:28; *gs.* **helle** 23:33; **helles** 23:15 || INFERNUS *as.* 11:23; *gs.* **helle** 16:18 [hell, *n.* and *int.*]

hellefyr *n.* 'hell-fire' IGNIS GEHENNAE **hellefyres** *gs.* 5:22 [n.] [hell-fire, *n.*, *adv.*, and *int.*]

helpan *v.III* 'help, be of use' PRODESSE *ps.3s.* **helpeð** 16:26 [OED2 help, *v.*]

henu, see **heonu**

henn *f.* 'hen' GALLINA *ns.* **henne** 23:37 [hen, *n.1*]

heofon *m.* 'heaven' CAELUM *ns.* **heofun** 5:18, 16:2 (margin), 16:2, 16:3, 24:35; *as.* **heofun** 5:34, 11:23, 14:19; *gs.* **heofunas** 8:20, 10:7, 11:12, 13:24, 13:31, 13:33, 13:44, 13:45, 13:47, 13:52, 18:3, 18:4, 18:23, 19:12, 19:14, 20:1, 22:2, 24:29, 24:30, 24:31 (*bis*), 25:1, 26:64; **heofunæs** 11:25; **heofun** 13:4, 13:32, 16:3; *ds.* **heofune** 3:17, 6:10, 16:1, 23:22, 24:29, 24:30, 28:18, Mk1:11; *np.* **heofunas** 3:16; *ap.* **heofunas** Mk1:10; *gp.* **heofuna** 3:2, 4:17, 5:3, 5:10, 5:19 (*bis*), 5:20, 7:21 (*bis*), 8:11, 11:11, 13:11, 16:19, 18:1, 19:23, 19:24; **heofona** 23:13; *dp.* **heofunum** 5:12, 5:16, 6:1, 6:9, 6:15, 6:20, 7:11, 7:21, 10:32, 10:33, 12:50, 16:17, 16:19 (*bis*), 18:10 (*bis*), 18:14, 18:18 (*bis*), 19:21, 21:25 (*bis*), 22:30, 23:9, 24:36, 28:2; **hefonum** 18:19;

heofon(um) 5:45 [heaven, *n.*]

heofonfugel *m.* 'bird of the air' VOLATILE CAELI *ap.* **heofunfuglas** 6:26 [n.]

heofonlic *adj.* 'heavenly' CAELESTIS *mns.* **heofunlica** 5:48, 6:14, 6:26, 15:13, 18:35 [heavenly, *adj.* and *n.*]

heonan *adv.* 'hence' HINC ~ 17:20 || RE- (RECEDERE) ~ 9:24 [hen, *adv.*]

heonu *interj.* 'lo' ECCE **henu** 1:20, 1:23, 2:1, 2:9, 2:13, 2:19, 3:16, 3:17, 4:11, 8:2, 8:24, 8:29, 8:32, 8:34, 9:2, 9:3, 9:10, 9:18, 9:20, 9:32, 10:16, 11:8, 11:10, 11:19, 12:2, 12:18, 12:41, 12:42, 12:46, 12:47, 12:49, 13:3, 15:22, 17:3, 17:5 (*bis*), 19:16, 20:18, 20:30, 21:5, 22:4, 24:26 (*bis*), 25:6, 25:20, 25:25, 26:45, 26:46, 26:47, 26:51, 26:65, 27:51, 28:2, 28:7 (*bis*), 28:9, 28:11, 28:20, Mk1:2 || NL **henu** 11:18 (ECCE in WW)

heorte *f. wk* 'heart' COR *ns.* ~ 13:15, 15:8; **eorta** 6:21; *gs.* **heorta** 12:34, 12:35 (*bis*); **heortan** 19:8; *ds.* **heortan** 5:8 (or *gs.*?), 22:37; ~ 5:28, 11:29, 12:40, 13:15, 13:19, 24:48; **heorta** 15:19; *dp.* **heortum** 9:4, Mk2:6 (*bis*) [n.], Mk2:8; **eortum** 18:35 [heart, *n.*, *int.*, and *adv.*]

her *adv.* 'here' HIC ~ 12:6, 12:41, 12:42, 14:17, 16:28, 17:4 (*bis*), 19:29, 20:6, 24:2, 24:23, 26:36, 26:38, 28:6 || NL ~ Mt INCIPIT, 14:8 (HIC in WW)

her is 'here is' (used *interj.*) ECCE 1:23 [n.] [OED2 here, *adv.* and *n.2*]

here *m.* 'army' EXERCITUS *ap.* **hergas** 22:7 || LEGIO *ap.* **herigæs** 26:53 [OED2 here, *n.1*]

herodes *prop.n. ns.* ~ 2:3, 2:7, 2:13, 2:16, 2:19, 14:1, 14:3; *gs.* ~ 2:15, 22:16; **erodes** 2:1; **herode** 14:6; *ds.* ~ 14:6; **herode** 2:12; **herodem** 2:22

herodiadi *prop.n. as.* ~ 14:3; *gs.* ~ **herodiade** 14:6

hete *m.* 'hatred, hate' NEQUITIA *as.* **hete** 22:18 [hete, *n.1*]

hider *adv.* 'hither' HUC ~ 8:29, 14:18, 17:17, 22:12 [OED2 hither, *adv.* and *adj.*]

hieremias *prop.n. ns.* ~ 16:14; *as.* **hieremiam** 2:17, 27:9

hiericho *prop.n. ds.* ~ 20:29

hierosolima *prop.n. ns.* ~ 2:3, 3:5; *as.* **hierosolimam** 2:1; **hierusalem** 5:35, 21:1, 21:10; *ds.* **hierosolimis** 4:25, 15:1; **hierusolimis** 20:17; **hierusalem** 16:21

hierosolimisc *adj.* 'of or from the city of Jerusalem' HIEROSOLOMITA *np.* **hierosolimisca** Mk1:5

hig *n.* 'hay' FAENUM *as.* **hoeg** 6:30, 14:19 [OED2 hay, *n.1*]

†**hinafæder** *m.* 'head of a household' PATER FAMILIAS *ns.* **hinefæder** 24:43 [n.]

hired *m.* 'household' FAMILIA *as.* **heorod** 24:45; *gs.* **heoredes** 13:27 [OED2 hird | hired, *n.*]

hiwan *m.p. wk* 'members of a household, family' DOMISTICI *n.* **hiwen** 10:36; **hine** 10:36; **higu** 10:36; *a.* **hiwæ** 10:25; **hine** 10:25 [n.] || FAMILIA *g.* **hina** 13:52, 20:1, 20:11, 21:33; **heora** 10:25 [n.] [OED2 hewe, *n.*]

hlaf *m.* 'bread, loaf' PANIS *as.* ~ 6:11, 7:9, 12:4 (or *p.*?, see note), 15:2, 15:26, 26:26; *ds.* **hlafe** 4:4, 16:11; *np.* **hlafes** 4:3; *ap.* **hlafas** 14:19, 15:33 [n.], 15:34, 15:36, 16:5, 16:7, 16:8, 16:10 (margin); **hlafes** 14:17, 14:19; *gp.* **hlafa** 16:9, 16:12 [OED2 loaf, *n.1*]

hlaford *m.* 'lord' DOMINUS *ns.* ~ 18:25, 18:26, 18:27, 20:8; **laford** 10:25; *as.* **hlaferd** 22:44 [n.] **laferd** 10:24; *gp.* **hlaferde** 15:27 [lord, *n.* and *int.*]

hlinian *v.2* 'recline, lie down' DISCUMBERE *pt.3s.* **hlionede** 9:10; **hleonede** 26:20; *pt.3p.* **hlionadun** 9:10; **hleonadun** Mk2:15 || RECUMBERE *ps.3p.* **hlionigaþ** 8:11; *pt.3p.* **hleonudun** 14:9; *ps.p. mgs.* **hlengendes** 26:7 [OED2 lean, *v.1*]

[MK]**gehlinian** *v.2* 'recline, lie down' ACCUMBERE *pt.3s.* **gehlionade**

Mk2:15 [see previous]

hlisa *m. wk* 'fame, reputation' FAMA *ns.* ~ 9:26; *as.* ~ 14:1 || OPINIO *ns.* ~ 4:24; *ap.* **hlisu** 24:6

†**hlynn** *f.* 'torrent' TORRENS *as.* **hlynne** Jn18:1 [n.] [OED2 linn, *n.1*]

gehnægan *v.1* 'cause to bow down, humble' HUMILIARE *ps.3s.* **genægeþ** 23:12; *pp.s.* **genægeþ** 23:12

hnesc *adj.* 'soft, delicate' MOLLIS *ndp.* **næscum** 11:8 (*bis*) [nesh, *adj.*, *n.*, and *adv.*]

hnutu *f.* 'nut' FICUS *ap.* **nyte** 7:16 [nut, *n.1* and *adj.2*]

†**gehnyscan** *v.1* 'grind?' CONTERERE *ps.3s.* **gehnyscet** 21:44 [n.]

hoc *m.* 'hook, fish-hook' HAMUS *as.* ~ 17:27 [OED2 hook, *n.1*]

hoehtnes-, see **ehtnes**

hol *n.* 'hole' FOVEA *ap.* **hole** 8:20 || APEX 'tip of a written character' *ns.* ~ (*stæfes*) 5:18 [n.] [OED2 hole, *n.*]

holunga *adv.* 'in vain' SINE CAUSA ~ 15:9 [n.]

hon *v.VII* 'hang, crucify' CRUCIFIGERE *ps.2p.* **hoaþ** 23:34; *infl.inf.* **hoanne** 20:19; *pp.s.* **hongen** 28:5 [OED2 hang, *v.*]

hord *m.* or *n.* 'hoard, treasure' THESAURUS *ns.* ~ 6:21; *as.* ~ 19:21; *ds.* **horde** 12:35 (*bis*) [n.]; *ap.* ~ 6:19, 6:20 [OED2 hoard, *n.1*]

hraþe *adv.* 'quickly' CONTINUO **hræþe** 4:20, 13:5; **hræðe** 26:74; **hraðe** 13:20, 13:21; **ræþe** 14:31|| STATIM **ræþe** 24:29, Mk1:28, Mk1:30; **hræþe** Mk1:42, Mk1:43 || CITO ~ 28:8; **hræþe** 5:25, 28:7 || CONFESTIM **hræþe** 3:16, 8:3 || ITERUM 'again?' **hræðe** Mk2:1 [rathe, *adv.*]

hrægl *n.* 'vestment' VESTIMENTUM *ns.* ~ 6:25; *gs.* **hrægles** 14:36; ~ 9:20; *as.* ~ 3:4, 9:16, 9:21; *ds.* **hræglę** 6:28; **hrægle** 9:16; *np.* ~ 17:2; **rægl** 28:3; *ap.* ~ 21:7, 21:8, 26:65, 27:35; *dp.* **hræglum** 11:8 || VESTIS *as.* ~ 22:12; *ds.* **hrægle** 22:11 [rail, *n.1*]

hreod *n.* 'reed' HARUNDO *as.* ~ 27:29, 27:30, 27:48; **read** 11:7; **hread** 12:20 [reed, *n.1*]

hreof *adj.* 'leprous, (subst.) leper' LEPROSUS *mns.* ~ 8:2; *mgs.* **hreofan** 26:6; *mnp.* **hreofe** 11:5; *map.* **hreofe** 10:8 [reof, *adj.*]

hreofl *f.* 'leprosy, scab' LEPRA *ns.* **hreoful** 8:3; **hriofal** Mk1:42

hreohnes *f.* 'turbulence, storm' TEMESTAS *ns.* **hreanis** 16:3 [see also **hrernes**]

hreordeþ, see **reordian**

hreowan *v.II* 'regret, repent' CONTEMNARE *subj.ps.3s.* **reuwe** 18:10 || MISERERI *ps.3s.* **hreoweþ** 15:32 [rue, *v.1*]

[MK]**hreowsian** *v.2* 'repent' PAENITERI *imp.p.* **hreowsiaþ** Mk1:15 [reusie, *v.*]

hreownis *f.* 'penitence' PENITENTIA *gs.* **hreunisse** 3:8 (or *d.*?); **hreownisse** Mk1:4; *as.* **hreunisse** 3:2, 12:41; **hrewnisse** 4:17; **hreuwnissę** 11:20; **hreuwnisse** 11:21, 21:32 [n.]; *a/ds.* **hreunisse** 3:11; **hreownisse** 21:30, 27:3 [rueness, *n.*]

hreran *v.1* 'move, stir' MOVERE *ps.p. np.* **hroerende** 27:39

gehreran *v.1* 'move, stir' COMMOVERE *pp.p.* **gehroered** 24:29

hrernes *f.* 'motion, disturbance' TEMPESTAS *ns.* **hreornis** 8:24 [see also **hreohnes**]

hrif *n.* 'womb' UTERUS *ds.* **hrife** 1:23, 19:12 [cf. midriff, *n.*; riff, *n.3*]

hrinan *v.I* 'touch' TANGERE *pt.3s.* **hran** 20:34, Mk1:41 [rine, *v.1*]

gehrinan *v.I* 'touch' TANGERE *ps.1s.* (*subj.*?) **gehrine** 9:21 [see previous]

†**hruxlian** *v.2* 'make a noise' TUMULTARI *ps.p. ap.* **ruxlende** 9:23 [n.] [cf. rustle, *v.*]

hryre *m.* 'collapse, destruction' RUINA *ns.* ~ 7:27 [rure, *n.*]

hu *interr.* 'how' QUAM ~ 7:14 || QUOMODO ~ 6:28, 7:4, 10:19, 12:4, 12:14, 12:26, 12:29, 12:34, 21:20, 22:12, 22:43, 22:45, 23:33, 26:54 || QUID ~ 6:25 || QUO ~ 6:31

|| QUOD ~ 18:21 [n.]
hu fela QUOT ~ 15:34
hu lange USQUE QUO ~ 17:17 (*bis*)
hu manig QUOT **hu monige** 16:9, 16:10 (margin)
hu micel QUANTUS ~ 6:23, 27:13
hu micle QUANTO ~ 10:25; **hu micele** 6:30; **hu miccele**, 7:11, 12:12
hu oft QUOTIENS ~ 18:21, 23:37 [OED2 how, *adv.* and *n.3*]

hulic *interr.* 'of what kind, what kind of' QUALIS ~ 8:27

hund *m.* 'dog' CANIS *dp.* **hundum** 7:6, 15:26 [ODE2 hound, *n.1*]

hundred *num.* 'hundred' CENTUM *a.* ~ 18:28 [OED2 hundred, *n.* and *adj.*]

hundnigontig *num.* 'ninety' NONAGINTA *a.* ~ 18:12; *d.* ~ 18:13 [cf. ninety, *adj.* and *n.*]

hundseofontig *num.* 'seventy' SEPTUAGIES **hundseofuntigum** *d.* 18:22 [cf. seventy, *adj.* and *n.*]

hundteontig *num.* 'hundred, hundredfold' CENTESIMUS *a.* ~ 13:8, 13:23 || CENTUM *a.* ~18:12

†**hundteonigfeald** *adv.* 'a hundredfold' CENTUPLUS **hundteantigfalde** 19:29

hungor *m.* 'hunger' FAMES *ns.* **hunger** 24:7 [OED2 hunger, *n.*]

hungrig *adj.* 'hungry' ESURIRE *mns.* ~ 21:18 [OED2 hungry, *adj.*]

hus *n.* 'house' DOMUS *ns.* ~ 10:13, 12:25, 21:13 (*bis*), 23:38; *as.* ~ 2:11, 7:24, 7:25, 7:26, 7:27, 9:6, 9:7, 9:23, 9:25, 9:28, 12:4, 12:29, 12:44, 13:57, 19:29, 24:43, Mk1:29, Mk2:4; **us** 17:25; *gs.* **huses** 10:6; **husęs** 15:24; *ds.* **huse** 8:6, 8:14, 9:10, 10:12 (*bis*), 10:14, 12:29, 13:1, 13:36, 24:17, 26:6, Mk2:1, Mk2:11, Mk2:15; **husae** 5:15; *ap.* ~ 23:14; *dp.* **husum** 11:8 [house, *n.1* and *int.*]

hwa, hwæt *interr.* 'who' QUIS *mns.* **hwa** 3:7, 10:11, 11:27, 16:24, 18:1, 19:25, 26:68, Mk2:7; **wa** 22:24; *mgs.* **hwæs** 21:23, 22:42; *mds.* **hwæm** 17:25; *nns.* **hwæt** 8:29, 9:13, 16:26, 17:25, 18:12, 19:20, 19:27, 21:10, 21:28, 22:42, 26:66, 27:4, Mk1:24 (*bis*), Mk2:9; *nas.* **hwæt** 5:47, 6:25, 6:31 (*bis*), 8:26, 10:19 (*bis*), 12:3, 12:7, 16:8, 16:15 (*bis*) [n.], 17:10, 19:7, 19:16, 19:17, 20:6, 20:21, 20:22, 20:32, 21:16, 21:40, 21:42, 26:15, 26:65, 26:70, 27:22, 27:23, Mk2:7, Mk2:8; **hwat** 6:3; **huat** 16:13; *ngs.* **hwæs** 6:8, 22:20; *nds.* **hwæm** 11:16, 12:27; *ni.* (*to*) **hwon** 26:50 || QUISNAM *nns.* **hwæt** Mk1:27 || QUOT *na.* **hwæt** 15:34 || UT QUID *ni.* (*to*) **hwon** 26:8 [OED2 who, *pron.* (and *n.*), etc.]

hwa *pron.* 'anyone' QUIS/ALIQUIS *mns.* ~ 5:39, 18:12 [n.], 21:3, 24:23

gehwa *pron.* 'each' OMNIS *nns.* **gehwæt** 15:17 || part of UNUSQUISQUE *mds.* **gehwæm** 16:27

hwamm *m.* 'corner' ANGULUS *gs.* **hwommes** 21:42; *dp.* **hwommum** 6:5

hwanon *interr.* 'whence, from where' UNDE **hwonan** 13:27, 13:54, 13:56, 18:25, 21:25; **hwonon** 15:33 [OED2 whenne | when, *adv.* and *conj.*]

hwæl *m.* 'whale' CETUS *gs.* **hwales** 12:40 [OED2 whale, *n.*]

hwær *interr.* 'where' UBI ~ 2:2; 2:4, 26:17; **wær** 8:20 [OED2 where, *adv.* and *conj.*]

hwæt *interj.* 'lo, behold' UTIQUE ~ 21:16, 23:31 || NL ~ 17:26 [n.], 25:27 [n.] [what, *pron.*, *adv.*, *int.*, *adj.1*, *conj.*, and *n.*]

hwæte *m.* 'wheat' TRITICUM *as.* ~ 3:12; **hwete** 13:29, 13:30; *gs.* **hwætes** 13:25; ~ 13:36 (or *gp.*?) [OED2 wheat, *n.*]

hwæthwega *pron.* 'something, anything' ALIQUID *nas.* **hwæthwugu** 5:23, 20:20

hwæþer *adj./interr.* 'which, whether' QUIS *mns.* **hweþer** 21:31; *mas.* ~ 27:17, 27:21; *nns.* ~ 23:19; **hweþer** 9:5; **hweþre** 23:17 || AN ~ 'whether' 27:49 [OED2 whether, *pron.*, *adj.* (and *n.*), and *conj.*]

hwæþere *adv.* 'however'
hwæþere þonne 'however' VERUMTAMEN **hweþre þonne** 18:7, 26:24, 26:39; **hwæþre þonne** 26:64; **hweðre þonne** 11:24 [OED2 whether, *adv.*]

hwelp *m.* 'whelp, young dog' CATULUS *np.* **welpas** 15:27 [OED2 whelp, *n.1*]

hwene *adv.* 'little, somewhat' PUSILLUM **hwæne** 26:39 [OED2 wheen, *adj.* and *n.*]

hweorfan *v.1* 'turn, change' REVERTERE *subj.ps.3s.* **weorfe** 10:13; *ps.p. mns.* **węrfende** 21:18 || CONVERTERE *pt.3s.* **werfde** 9:22 || DEMOLIRI *ps.3p.* **weorfaþ** 6:16 [OED2 wharve, *v.*]

gehweorfan *v.1* 'turn, change' CONVERTERE *ps.3p.* **gehwerfeþ** 7:6; *pp.p.* **gewerfe** 18:3; *pp. mns.* **gehwerfad** 16:23 || DEMOLIRI *ps.3s.* **gewyrfeþ** 6:19; **gewyrfeð** 6:20 [see previous]

hwider *adv.* 'whither' QUOCUMQUE **hwider** (*swa*) 'whithersoever' 8:19 [OED2 whither, *adv.* (and *n.2*)]

hwil *f.* 'time, hour' HORA *ns.* ~ 14:15, 26:45; *as.* **hwile** 25:13, 26:40; *ds.* **hwile** 8:13, 9:22, 10:19, 15:28 [n.], 18:1, 20:3, 20:5, 20:9, 24:36, 24:42, 24:43, 26:55, 27:45 (*bis*) || NL *ds.* **hwile** 26:73 [OED2 while, *n.*]

hwilc *adj./interr.* 'which, what, who' QUIS *mns.* ~ 6:27, 12:11; **hwælc** 7:9, 24:45; *mgs.* **hwylces** 22:28; *mds.* ~ 24:42; *nns.* ~ 22:36; **hwylc** 24:3; *nas.* **hwylce** 5:46; **hwælc** 16:26; *fns.* **hwelc** 12:48; ~ Mk1:27; *fds.* **hwilcę** 21:23; **wilce** 21:24; **hwilce** 21:27, 24:43, 24:44; ~ 24:42; *np.* **hwilce** 12:48; **hwælc** 19:18 [which, *adj.* and *pron.*]

gehwilc *adj.* 'each, every' OMNIS *nns.* ~ 18:16 || part of UNUSQUISQUE *nas.* **gehwylc** 18:35 [see above:

hwilen *adj.* 'temporary, transitory' TEMPORALIS *mns.* **wilen** 13:21 [n.]

hwit *adj.* 'white' ALBUS *nns.* ~ 17:2 (margin); *mas.* **hwitne** 5:36 || CANDIDUS *nnp.* **hwit** 28:3 [white, *adj.* (and *adv.*) and *n.*]

hwonne *interr.* 'when' QUANDO ~ 25:37, 25:39; **hwanne** 13:15, 24:3, 25:38, 25:44 [OED2 when, *adv.* (*conj.* and *n.*)]

hydan *v.1* 'hide, gather (treasure)' THESAURIZARE *imp.p.* **hydeþ** 6:19, 6:20 [OED2 hide, *v.1*]

gehydan *v.1* 'hide, conceal' ABSCONDERE *pt.3s.* **gehydde** 13:33; *pp. m/nds.* **gehyded** 13:44 [see previous]

hyhtan *v.1* 'hope' SPERARE *ps.3p.* **hyhtaþ** 12:21 [hight, *v.2*]

hyngran *v.1* 'hunger' ESURIRE *ps.3s.* **hyngriþ** 5:6 [n.]; *pt.3s.* **hyngrade** 4:2; **yngrade** 25:35; **hyngrede** 12:1 [n.], 12:3, 25:42; **hingrede** 21:18; *pp. mas.* **hyngrende** 25:37, 25:44 [OED2 hunger, *v.*]

hyran *v.1* 'hear, obey' AUDIRE *ps.2p.* **hoe[rað]** 13:17 (margin) [n.]; *inf.* **heran** 10:14; *pp.s.* **gehered** 2:18 || MINSTRARE *pt.3p.* **herdon** Mk1:13 [OED2 hear, *v.*]

gehyran *v.1* 'hear, obey' AUDIRE *ps.2s.* **geherest** 21:15; **gehoerest** 27:13; *ps.3s.* **gehereþ** 7:26, 13:20, 13:22, 18:15, 18:16; **gehereð** 7:24, 13:23; **geherað** 12:19, 18:17 (*bis*); *ps.2p.* **gehoerað** 10:27; **geherað** 13:14; *ps.3p.* **geheraþ** 11:5; **geherað** 13:16, 13:19; **gehoeraþ** 13:13; *pt.3s.* **geherde** 2:3, 14:13, 22:7; **geherdę** 4:12 (or *subj.*?); **gehoerde** 9:12, 12:22, 14:1; **gehyrde** 19:22; *pt.2p.* **geherdun** 5:21, 5:27, 5:33, 5:38, 5:43, 26:65; *pt.3p.* **geherdon** 2:9; **geh[erdon]** 13:17 (margin); **geherdun** 2:22 [n.], 11:4, 13:15, 20:30, 21:45, 22:34; **geherde** 15:12; **geyrdon** 19:25; *subj.ps.3s.* **gehere** 11:15, 13:9; **gehoęre** 13:43; *subj.ps.3p.* **geheran** 13:15; *imp.p.* **geherað** 13:18, 15:10, 17:5, 21:33; *inf.* **gehera[n]** 13:17 (margin) [n.]; *infl.inf.* **geheranne** 12:42; *ps.pp. mns.* **geherende** 8:10, 11:2; *np.* **gehoerende** 12:24;

geherende 13:13, 14:13, 17:6, 20:24, 22:22, 22:33, 24:6 (in periphrastic future), 27:47; *pp.s.* **gehoered** 28:14; **gehered** Mk2:1; *pp.p.* **gehered** 6:7 || OBOEDIRE *ps.3p.* **gehęraþ** 8:27 [n.] [OED2 yhere, *v.*]

hyrde *m.* 'herdsman, keeper' PASTOR *ns.* **hiorde** 25:32; *np.* **hiordes** 8:33; *as.* **heorde** 26:31 || CUSTOS *dp.* **heordum** 27:66 (*bis*) [OED2 herd, *n.2*]

hyrdeleas *adj.* 'without a sheperd' NON HABENS PASTOREM *nnp.* **heordeleas** 9:36 [n.] [OED2 herdless, *adj.*]

[MK]**hyrmann** *m.* 'hired servant' MERCENARIUS *dp.* **hyremonnum** Mk1:20 [n.] [OED2 hireman, *n.*]

hyrnes *f.* 'tribute, tax' CENSUM *ds.* **hernisse** 17:25 [n.]

gehyrnes *f.* 'hearing' AUDIENDUM *gs.* **gehernisse** 11:15, 13:43; **gehernesse** 13:9 || AUDITUS *a/ds.* **gehernisse** 13:14

hyrwan *v.1* 'feel contempt for, scorn' CONTEMPNERE *ps.3s.* **herweþ** 6:24

i *m.* 'the letter *i*, the Greek iota' IOTA *ns.* ~ 5:18 [I, *n.1*]

iacob *prop.n.* IACOB *gs.* **iacobes** 22:32; *as.* ~ 8:11

iacobus *prop.n.* IACOBUS 'James' *ns.* ~ 10:2, 10:3; **iacob** 13:55; *as.* ~ Mk1:19; **iacob** 4:21, Mk1:29; *gs.* **iacobes** 27:56

ic *pron.* 'I' Latin equivalents: EGO, NOS, (possessive) MEUS, NOSTER

Forms (citations are given only for relatively infrequent forms; instances that do not translate the Latin equivalents listed above are presented separately below):

ns. **ic;** *as.* **me, mec** 5:11, 8:2, 10:32, 10:39, 12:30 (*bis*), 14:28, 14:30, 15:8, 15:32, 17:27, 18:21, 23:34, 23:39, 25:35, 25:36, 25:43 (*bis*), 26:10, 26:11, 26:12, 26:23, 26:46, 26:55, Mk1:7; *gs.* **min** 22:18, 25:36, 25:43; *n. dual* **wit** (as listed under NL); *a. dual* **unc** 9:27 [n.], 20:30, 20:31; *np.* **we, wæ, wę** (as listed under NL); *ap.* **usic** 1:23, 8:25, 8:29, 8:31 (*bis*), 20:7, Mk1:24); **us** (6:13 (*bis*), 27:25; *dp.* **us**

Possessive forms: MEUS *mns.* **min;** *mas.* **minne, mine** 20:4, 20:7, **min** 21:37, 22:4, 26:53, Mk1:2; *mgs.* **mines;** *mds.* **minum, min** 17:15; *fns.* **min;** *fas.* **mine, min** 20:23 (*bis*); *fds.* **mine;** *nns.* **min;** *nas.* **min, mine** 13:30; *np.* **mine, min** 12:49, 24:35; *nap.* **min, minne** 8:8 [n.]; *gp.* **mine** 25:40; *dp.* **minum** || NOSTER *mns.* **ure** 6:9, 24:42; *mas.* **ure** 6:11; **userne** 6:11; *nns.* **uru** 21:38; *np.* **ure** 20:33, 25:8; *ap.* **ure** 6:12, 8:17, 27:25; *gp.* **ure** 23:30; *dp.* **urum** 8:17, 21:42

NL *ns.* ~ 2:13; 2:15, 3:9, 3:11, 4:9, 4:19, 5:17 (*bis*), 5:18, 5:20, 5:26, 6:2, 6:5, 6:16, 6:25, 6:29, 7:4, 7:23 (*bis*), 8:3, 8:8, 8:9 (*bis*), 8:10 (*bis*), 8:19, 9:13 (*bis*), 9:21 (x3), 9:28, 10:15, 10:23, 10:27, 10:34 (*bis*), 10:35, 10:42, 11:9, 11:11, 11:24, 11:25, 11:29, 12:6, 12:7, 12:18 (*bis*), 12:31, 12:36, 12:44 (*bis*), 13:13, 13:15, 13:17, 13:30, 13:35, 14:2, 15:24, 15:32, 16:11, 16:15, 16:18, 16:19, 16:28, 17:16, 17:20, 18:3, 18:10, 18:13, 18:18, 18:19, 18:21, 18:22, 18:26, 18:32, 18:33, 19:9, 19:16 (*bis*), 19:16 (*bis*), 19:20, 19:23, 19:24, 19:28, 20:4, 20:13, 20:14, 20:15, 20:18, 20:32, 21:21, 21:24, 21:27, 21:29, 21:30, 21:31, 22:44, 23:3, 23:36, 23:37, 23:39, 24:2, 24:25, 24:34, 24:47, 25:12 (*bis*) 25:20, 25:21, 25:22, 25:23, 25:24, 25:26 (x3), 25:35, 25:36 (*bis*), 25:40, 25:43, 25:45, 26:13, 26:18, 26:21, 26:29 (x3), 26:31, 26:32 (*bis*), 26:34 (margin), 26:35 (*bis*), 26:36, 26:42, 26:48, 26:53, 26:55, 26:61, 26:63, 26:64, 26:70, 26:72, 27:4, 27:17, 27:19, 27:22, 27:43, 27:63, 28:5, 28:7, 28:20, Mk1:2, Mk1:7, Mk1:11, Mk1:24, Mk1:38 (*bis*), Mk1:41, Mk2:11; *as.* **mec** 15:32,

25:35 (*bis*), 25:42 (*bis*); *a/d.s.* **me** 3:11, 26:36; *ds.* **me** (ME in WW) 19:21; *n. dual* **wit** 20:22; *np.* **we** 2:2, 3:9, 6:31, 7:22, 8:25, 11:3, 11:17, 12:38, 13:28, 14:17, 15:33, 16:7, 17:4, 17:27, 20:12, 20:17, 21:25, 21:26 (*bis*), 21:27, 21:38, 22:16, 23:30, 25:37 (x3), 25:33 (*bis*), 25:39 (*bis*), 25:44 (*bis*), 26:17, 27:42, Mk1:38; **wæ** 6:31 (*bis*), 26:65; **wę** 23:30; *a/d.p.* **us** 21:26; *dp.* **us** 21:38; (possessive) *mns.* **min** 26:41 [n.] [I, *pron.* and *n.2*]

geican *v.1* 'add' ADICERE *pp.p.* **geeced** 6:33 [cf. OED2 eche, *v.*]

idel *adj.* 'empty, fool' RACHA *mns.* **idla** 5:22 [OED2 idle, *adj.* and *n.*]

ieldan *v.1* 'delay, put off' MORAM FACERE *pt.3s.* **ælde** 25:5 [OED2 eld, *v.2*]

ielding *f.* 'delay' MORA *as.* **aeldingę** 24:48

ierde, see **gyrd**

ierre *n.* 'anger' IRA *ds.* **eorre** 3:7 [OED2 irre | erre, *n.*]

ierre *adj.* 'angry, in a rage' IRASCI *mns.* **eorre** 2:16, 22:7; **eorra** 18:34 [OED2 irre, *adj.*]

iersian *v.2* 'to be angry with, rage' IRASCI *ps.3s.* **eorsaþ** 5:22 || PECCARE *ps.3s.* **eorsaþ** 18:21

iesus *prop.n. ns.* ~ 4:7 [n.]

ieþ *adj.* 'easy' FACILIS *comp. nns.* **eþre** 9:5 [n.], 19:24, Mk2:9; **eaður** Mk2:9 || POSSIBILIS *nnp.* **eaðe** 19:26

ilca *adj.* 'same' IPSE *nas.* **ilce** 27:44; *ap.* ~ Mk1:19 || IDEM *nas.* **ilce** 26:44 || IS *fas.* ~ Mk1:31 [ilk, *adj.1*, *pron.*1, and *n.*]

in *prep.* 'in' IN ~ 1:11, etc. || AB ~ 25:32 [n.] || PER ~ 27:19 || NL ~ 1:18, 2:3, 5:3, 6:4, 7:14 [n.], 9:28, 10:22, 14:26, 21:10, 21:33 (*bis*), 23:31, 24:8, 24:33 (IN in WW), 24:36 [n.], 26:9, 27:1, 27:46 (*bis*), Mk1:8, Mk1:15; see also **innan** [in, *prep.*]

in *adv.* 'in, inwards' NL (corresponding to Latin *in-* prefix) **inn** 7:13, 22:11, 22:12, 23:13 [in, *adv.*]

inbyrnan *v.III* 'burn, kindle' ACCENDERE *ps.3p.* **inbeornað** 5:15 [n.]

geincfullian *v.2* 'scandalize, offend' SCANDALIZARE *subj.ps.1p.* **geincfulligæ** 17:27; *pp.s.* **geincfullad** 11:6 [n.]; *pp.p.* **geincfullad** 15:12

[MK]**inferan** *v.1* 'enter, go in' INGREDI *pt.3s.* **infoerde** Mk1:21; *pt.3p.* **infoerdun** Mk1:21 || INTRARE *pt.3s.* **infoerde** Mk2:1

ingan *anom.v.* 'go in, enter' INTRARE *ps.3s.* **ingæþ** 15:11; **ingæð** 15:17; *pt.3s.* **ineode** Mk2:1; *pt.3p.* **ineodun** 25:10; *subj.ps.2p.* **ingæn** 10:11; *subj.ps.3p.* ~ 7:13; *imp.p.* **iongaþ** 10:5 [n.] || INTROIRE *pt.3s.* **ineode** Mk1:45 || INGREDI *pt.3s.* **ineode** Mk1:21 || VENIRE *inf.* **innga** 19:17 (INGREDI in WW) || NL *pt.3p.* **ineoden** 28:12 [n.] [OED2 ingo, *v.*]

ingangan *anom.v.* 'go in, enter' INTRARE *inf.* **ingangen** 23:13; *ps.p. mnp.* **ingangende** 2:11, 12:45 || INTROIRE *inf.* ~ Mk1:45; *ps.p. ap.* **ingangende** 23:13 || INGREDI *ps.p. mns.* **ingangende** 26:58 [OED2 ingang | inyong, *n.*]

inginnan *v.III* 'begin' COEPISSE *pt.3s.* **ingann** 4:17; **ingon** 11:7, 14:30; **ingonn** 11:20, 16:21, 18:24; *pt.3p.* **ingunnun** 26:22 || INCIPERE *ps.p. mns.* **ingingende** 20:8 || NL *pt.3p.* **ingunnon** 25:7 [n.]

inhreran *v.1* 'move, stir up' COMMOVERE *pp.s.* **inhroered** 21:10 || MOVERE *pp. mns.* **inhroered** 21:30

inlihtan *v.1* 'grow light, dawn' LUCESCERE *pt.3s.* **inlihte** 28:1 [enlight, *v.*]

innan *adv.* 'inside' INTUS **innan** 23:28

in innan *adv.* INTRINSECUS 'inside' 7:15 || INTRA ~ 21:38 [inne, *adv.* and *prep.*]

innan *prep.* 'between, among' INTER

- 3:9 [n.] || INTRA - 9:3, 9:21 [see previous]

inne *adv.* 'inside' NL (*in*) **innæ** 24:26

innoþ *m.* 'womb' UTERUS **innoþe** *ds.* 1:18, 1:23 [OED2 inneth, *n.*]

†**instandendlice** *adj.* SUBSTANTIALIS *mas.?* **instondenlice** 6:11 [n.]

(†)**instyde** *adv.* 'immediately' CONTINUO - 21:19, 21:20, 27:48 || STATIM - Mk1:28, Mk2:11

intinga *m. wk* 'cause' CAUSA *ns.* **intinge** 19:10; *as.* **intinge** 27:37; *ds.* - 5:32; **intinge** 19:3

inwit *n.* 'malice, deceit' DOLUS *ds.* - 26:4

iohannes *prop.n. ns.* - 3:1, 3:14, 4:12, 10:2, 11:2, 13:55, 14:2, 16:14, Mk1:6, Mk1:14; **iohan(nes)** 11:18, 21:32; **ioh(anne)s** 14:4, Mk1:4; *as.* - 14:3, 14:10, Mk1:19, Mk1:29; **iohannem** 4:21, 11:13; **iohan(nem)** 21:26; *gs.* - 9:14, 11:12, 14:8; **iohan(nes)** 21:25; *ds.* - 11:4; **iohanne** 3:13, 11:7, 11:11, 17:13, Mk1:9

ionas *prop.n. - ns.* 12:41; **ione** 12:40; *gs.* - 12:39, 12:41; **iona** 16:4, 16:17

iongaþ, see **ingan**

iordanes *prop.n. gs.* - Mk1:5; *ds.* **iordane** 3:5, 3:13, 4:15, 4:25; **ior[ ]ne** 3:6 (margin); **iordanen** Mk1:9; **iordanen** 19:1

iosep *prop.n. ns.* - 1:20, 2:21, 27:59; **ioseph** 1:19, 27:57; *as.* **iosepe** 1:16; *gs.* - 2:13, 2:19, 13:55; *ds.* **iosefae** 1:18; **iosepep** 27:56

isaac *prop.n.. as.* - 8:11; *gs.* **isaces** 22:32

israhel *prop.n. as.* **israhæl** 2:6; *gs.* **israheles** 2:20, 2:21, 10:23, 15:24, 19:28, 27:9; - 15:31; **israhela** 10:6, 27:42; *ds.* **israhele** 8:10; - 9:33

iuda *prop.n. gs.* - 2:6

iudas *prop.n. ns.* - 10:4, 13:55, 26:14, 26:25, 26:47, 27:3, Jn18:2, Jn18:3

iudea *prop.n. ns.* - 3:5; *gs.* - 3:1; **iudeas** Mk1:5; *ds.* - 2:22, 4:25, 24:16

iudea *m.pl.* 'the Jews' IUDAEI *gp.* **iudeana** 2:1, 2:2, 2:5, 19:1, 27:11, 27:29, 27:37; *dp.* **iudeum** 28:15

iudisc *adj.* 'Jewish' part of PROSELYTUS *mas.* **iudiscne** 23:15 [n.] [Judeish, *adj.* and *n.*]

iumonn-, see **geomann**

k-, see **c-**

la *interj.* 'lo, indeed' UTIQUE - 9:28, 15:27 || ETIAM - 13:51 || O - 17:17 || NL - 15:28 (O in WW) [OED2 lo, *int.1*]

lac *n.* 'gift, offering' MUNUS *ns.* - 15:5; *as.* - 5:23, 5:24 (*bis*), 8:4; *as/p.* - 2:11, [OED2 lake, *n.1*]

[MK]**lacnian** *v.2* 'heal, cure' CURARE *pt.3s.* **lecnade** Mk1:34 [OED2 lechne, *v.*]

laf *f.* 'what is left, remnant' RELIQUIA *ap.* **hlafe** 14:20 [n.] || part of SUPERESSE *ds.* (*to*) **lafe** (*wesan*) 15:37 [OED2 lave, *n.1*]

lama *adj.* 'crippled, lame' PARALYTICUS *mns.* **loma** 8:6; *mas.* **loma** 9:2; *mds.* **loma** 9:2; **loman** 9:6; *map.* **loman** 4:24 [n.] [OED2 lame, *adj.*]

lamwyrhta *m. wk* 'potter' FIGULUS *gs.* **lamwyrhte** 27:7 [n.]; **lamwyrhtæ** 27:10

land *n.* 'land' AGER *ns.* **lond** 13:38, 27:8 (*bis*); *gs.* **londes** 6:28, 6:30, 13:36; *as.* **lond** 13:24, 13:27, 13:44, 27:7; *ds.* **londe** 13:31, 24:40, 27:10; **londæ** 24:18; *ap.* **lond** 19:29 || REGIO *ns.* **lond** 3:5; **londe** Mk1:5; *as.* **lond** 8:28, 14:35; *ds.* **londe** 2:12, 4:16 [n.], Mk1:28 || TERRA *as.* **lond** 9:26, 9:31, 14:34 || VICUS *ap.* **lond** Mk1:38 || NL *as.* - 13:5; *ds.* **londe** 4:25 [n.], 19:1; *ap.* - 13:20 [OED2 land, *n.1*]

lange *adv.* 'long' see also **hu lange** *comp.* 'further' ADHUC **leng** 26:65 [long, *adv.1*]

lar *f.* 'teaching, doctrine' DOCTRINA *ns.* - Mk1:27; *as.* **lare** 15:9; *a/ds.* **lare** 16:12; **lære** Mk1:22; *ds.* **lare** 7:28, 22:33 || LEX *as.* **lare** 5:17 || PRAEDICATIO *ds.* **lare** 12:41

[OED2 lore, *n.1*]

lareow *m.* 'teacher' MAGISTER *ns.* **laruw** 8:19, 10:25; **lareu** 12:38, 17:24, 22:16, 22:24, 22:36, 23:10, 26:18; **lareuw** 9:11, 19:16, 23:8; *as.* **laruw** 10:24; *np.* **lareu** 23:10 || RABBI *ns.* **lareu** 23:7, 26:25, 26:49; *np.* **larewas** 23:8 [OED2 larew, *n.*]

latteow *m.* 'leader' DUX *ns.* **latteuw** 2:6; *np.* **latewas** 23:16; **latuwas** 23:24; **lateuw** 15:14 [OED2 lattew, *n.*]

gelaþian *v.2* 'invite' INVITARE *pp.p.* **gelaþade** 22:8; *pp. mdp.* **gelaðadum** 22:3, 22:4

læce *m.* 'physician, doctor' MEDICUS *gs.* **læces** 9:12 [OED2 leech, *n.1*]

lædan *v.1* 'lead' DUCERE *ps.3s.* **lædeþ** 5:32, 7:13, 7:14, 15:14, 19:9; **lædaþ** 19:9; *pt.3s.* **lædde** 17:1; *pp.s.* **læded** 4:1; *pp. mns.* **lædde** 27:3 || ADDUCERE *pt.3p.* **læddon** 26:57; **læddun** 27:2; *imp.p.* **ledað** 21:2 || NL *infl.inf.* **lædenne** 5:41 [n.] [lead, *v.1*]

gelædan *v.1* 'lead' INDUCERE *pp.p.* **gelædde** 24:24; *inf.* **gelaede** 6:13 || DUCERE *pp.p.* **gelædde** 10:18 [see previous]

læfan *v.1* 'leave' RELINQUERE *pt.3s.* **læfde** 22:25; *pp.s.* **læfed** 24:2 [leave, *v.1*]

læran *v.1* 'teach' DOCERE *ps.2s.* **lærest** 22:16; *ps.3s.* **læreþ** 5:19 (*bis*); *pt.3s.* **lærde lærde** 5:2, 7:29, 11:1, Mk2:13; *imp.p.* **læreþ** 28:19; *ps.p. mns.* **lærende** 4:23, 9:35, 26:55, Mk1:22; *mnp.* **lærende** 15:9, 28:20 || PERSUADERE *pt.3p.* **lærdun** 27:20 || PRAEDICARE *inf.* ~ 4:17 [OED2 lere, *v.*]

gelæran *v.1* 'teach' DOCERE *pt.3s.* **gelærde** 13:54, Mk1:21; *pp.p.* **gelærde** 28:15; *pp. mns.* **gelæred** 13:52 [OED2 ylere, *v.*]

læt *adj.*
superl. **lætest** 'last' NOVISSIMUS *mns.* **lætest** 22:27 [late, *adj.1*]

lætan *v.VII* 'allow to remain, leave behind' SINERE *ps.2p.* **letaþ** 23:13; *pt.3s.* **let** Mk1:34; *imp.s.* **let** 3:15; *imp.p.* **leteþ** 13:30, 19:14; *inf.* **letan** 24:43 || PERMITTERE *pt.3s.* **let** 19:8; *imp.s.* **læt** 8:21 [OED2 let, *v.1*]

gelætan *v.VII* 'allow, let' PATI *imp.s.* **gelaet** 6:13 [see previous]

leaf *n.* 'leaf, foliage' FOLIUM *np.* ~ 24:32; *ap.* ~ 21:19 [leaf, *n.1*]

leafa *m. wk* 'belief' FIDES *as.* ~ 9:2 [OED2 leve, *n.*]

geleafa *m. wk* 'belief' FIDES *ns.* ~ 9:22, 15:28; *as.* ~ 8:10, 17:20, Mk2:5; **geleafu** 21:21, 23:23; *gs.* **geleafe** 6:30; ~ 8:26, 16:8; **gelefan** 14:31; *ds.* **geleafan** 9:29 [OED2 yleve, *n.*]

lean *n.* 'reward, gift' MERCES *ns.* ~ 5:12; *as.* ~ 5:46, 6:1, 6:2, 6:5, 6:16, 10:41 (*bis*), 10:42, 20:8 || NL *ds.* **leane** 20:7 [n.] [OED2 lean, *n.1*]

leas *adj.* 'false' FALSUS *map.* **lease** 7:15 || part of PSEUDOPROPHETA *np.* **lease** 24:11 [OED2 lease, *adj.* and *n.2*]

lecgan *v.1* 'lay, put' PROICERE *pt.3p.* **lægdun** 15:30 [OED2 lay, *v.1*]

lendenu *n.pl.* 'limbs' LUMBUS *ap.* ~ Mk1:6; **lendu** 3:4 [n.] [OED2 lend, *n.1*]

lengu *f.* 'length, height' STATURA *ds.* **lengo** 6:27 [OED2 lengh, *n.*]

leof *adj.* 'dear, beloved' DILECTUS *mns.* **leofa** 3:17, 12:18, 17:5, Mk1:11 [cf. OED2 yleof, *adj.* (and *n.*)]

leogan *v.II* 'lie' MENTIRI *ps.p. mnp.* **ligende** 5:11 [OED2 lie, *v.2*]

leoht *n.* 'light' LUX *ns.* ~ 5:14; **leht** 4:16; **liht** 5:16; ~ *as.* 4:16 || LUMEN *ns.* **leht** 6:23; *as.* ~ 24:29; *ds.* **lihte** 10:27 [light, *n.1*]

leoht *adj.* 'bright' LUCIDUS *mns.* **liht** 6:22; *nns.* **liht** 17:5 [light, *adj.2* and *n.3*]

leoht *adj.* 'light, not heavy' LEVIS *fns.* **liht** 11:30 [light, *adj.1* and *n.2*]

leohtfæt *n.* 'lantern, torch' LAMPAS *np.* **lehtfætu** 25:8; *ap.* **leohtfatu** 25:1, 25:3, 25:7; *dp.* **lehtfatum** 25:4 || LANTERA *ap.* **lehtfatu** Jn18:3

leoran *v.1* 'go, pass' TRANSIRE *ps.3s.*

liorað 17:20; *pt.3s.* **liorde** 9:27 [n.], 8:34, 20:30; **leorde** 11:1; *subj.ps.3s.* **leore** 26:39; *imp.s.* **leor** 17:20; *inf.* ~ 26:42; *infl.inf.* **lioranne** 19:24 || PRAETERIRE *ps.3p.* **leoraþ** 24:35

geleoran *v.1* 'go, depart' PRAETERIRE *ps.3s.* **geleoraþ** 24:34; **gelioreþ** 5:18 || TRANSIRE *ps.3s.* **geleoreþ** 5:18; *ps.3p.* **geleoraþ** 24:35 || SE TRANSFERRE *pt.3s.* **geleorde** 19:1

leornere *m.* 'disciple' DISCIPULUS *ns.* ~ 8:21 [n.], 10:24, 27:57; *gs.* ~ 10:42; *ds.* ~ 10:25; *np.* **leorneras** 8:23, 9:14 (*bis*), 9:19, 12:1, 13:10, 13:36, 14:12, 14:15, 14:19, 15:2, 15:12, 15:23, 15:33, 15:36, 16:5, 17:6, 17:10, 17:13, 17:19, 18:1, 19:10, 19:13, 19:25, 21:20, 24:1, 24:3, 26:8, 26:17, 26:19, 26:35, 26:56, 27:64; *ap.* **leorneras** 9:10, , 10:1, 11:1, 11:2, 14:22, 15:32, 16:13, 16:20 (*d.*? see below), 20:17, 21:1, 22:16,; *dp.* **leornerum** 9:11, 12:49, 17:16, 26:18; **leorneras** (often used after prep. *to*; see note to 9:37) 9:37, 14:19 (f. 24r, 6[1]), 15:36 (f. 26r, 11[1]), 16:21, 16:24, 19:23, 23:1, 26:1, 26:20 [OED2 learner, *n.*]

leornes *f.* 'going, departure, privy, latrine' SECESSUS *a/ds.* **leornisse** 15:17 [n.]

leornian *v.2* 'learn' DISCERE *imp.p.* **leorniað** 11:29; **leornaþ** 24:32 [OED2 learn, *v.*]

geleornian *v.2* 'learn' DISCERE *pt.3s.* **geliornade** 2:7; *imp.p.* **geleornigaþ** 9:13 [see previous]

libban, see lifian

lic *n.* 'body' CORPUS *ns.* ~ 24:28; *as.* ~ 26:12, 27:58 (*bis*), 27:59; *np.* ~ 27:52 || CARO *ns.* ~ 16:17, 19:6, 24:22, 26:41; *ds.* **lice** 19:5 [OED2 lich, *n.*]

lic *adj.* 'like, similar' ADSIMILARE *mns.* ~ 7:24 [like, *adj.*, *adv.*, *conj.*, and *prep.*]

gelic *adj.* 'like, similar' SIMILIS *mns.* ~ 7:26, 13:52; *nns.* ~ 13:24, 13:31, 13:33, 13:44, 13:45, 13:47, 22:39, 25:1; **gelice** 20:1, 22:2; *fns.* ~ 11:16; *fas.* **gelice** 11:16; *np.* **gelice** 23:27 || ADSIMILARE *mnp.* **gelice** 6:8 || PAR *ap.* **gelice** 20:12 [ylike, *adj.* and *n.*]

gelice *adv.* 'similarly' SIMILITER ~ 20:5, 21:30, 21:36, 22:26, 26:35 [see previous]

licettere *m.* 'hypocrite' HYPOCRITA *ns.* ~ 7:5; *gs.* **liceteras** 23:28; *np.* **liceteras** 6:2, 6:5, 16:3, 23:23, 23:25; **licetteras** 6:16, 22:18, 23:13, 23:15, 23:14; **licetheras** 15:7; *dp.* **liceterum** 24:51

licgan *v.V* 'lie' IACERE *ps.3s.* **legeþ** 8:6; *pt.3s.* **læg** Mk2:4; *ps.p. mas.* **licende** 9:2; *fas.* **licgende** 8:14; *np.* **liccende** 9:36; *ps.p.* **licgende** (*wæs*) Mk2:4 || MOECHARI (*dearninga licgan*) 'fornicate, commit adultery' *imp.s.* **lige** 5:27; *subj.ps.3s.* **licgę** 5:32 [lie, *v.1*]

gelicgan *v.V* 'lie' DECUMBERE *pp.s.* **gelegen** Mk1:30 [see previous]

lichama *m. wk* 'body' CORPUS *ns.* **lichoma** 5:29, 5:30, 6:22, 6:23, 6:25; **lichoman** 26:26; *as.* **lichoma** 10:28 (*bis*) [n.], 14:12; *gs.* **lichoma** 6:22; *ds.* **lichoma** 6:25 [OED2 licham, *n.*]

lician *v.2* 'please' PLACERE *pt.3s.* **licade** 14:6 || COMPLACERE *pt.1s.* (*wel*) **licade** Mk1:11 [like, *v.1*]

gelician *v.2* 'please' COMPLACERE *pt.3s.* **gelicade** 3:17, 12:18, 17:5 || PLACITUM ESSE *pt.3s.* **gelicade** 11:26 [ylike, *v.*]

gelicnes *f.* 'parable, image, likeness' PARABOLA *as.* **gelicnisse** 13:18, 13:24, 13:31, 13:33, 13:36, 15:15; *ap.* **gelicnisse** 13:53; *dp.* **gelicnissum** 13:3, 13:10, 13:13, 13:34 (*bis*), 13:35 || IMAGO *ns.* **gelicnis** 22:20 [ylikeness, *n.*]

[MK]**licþrowere** *m.* 'leper' LEPROSUS *ns.* **licþrowere** Mk1:40

[MK]**liesan** *v.1* 'loosen' SOLVERE *inf.* **leosan** Mk1:7 [OED2 leese, *v.2*]

geliesan *v.1* 'release, liberate' LIBERARE *imp.s.* **gelese** 6:13 [see previous]

lif *n.* 'life' VITA *as.* ~ 18:9, 19:29,

25:46; *gs.* **lifes** 19:16; *ds.* **life** 7:14, 18:8, 19:17 [life, *n.*]

lifian *v.2* 'live' VIVERE *ps.3s.* **leofaþ** 9:18; *ps.3p.* **lifgaþ** 4:4; *pt.3s.* **lifde** 27:63; *ps.p. gp.* **lifigendra** 22:32 || VIVUS *ps.p. mas.* **lifgende** 26:63: *mgs.* **lifigenda** 16:16; **lifgende** 26:63 [live, *v.1*]

liget *n.* or *m.* 'lightning' FULGOR *ns.* **læget** 24:27; **leget** 28:3 [OED2 lait, *n.1*]

lihtan *v.1* 'lighten, illuminate' LUCERE *pt.3s.* **lihte** 5:16 [light, *v.2*]

gelihtan *v.1* 'lighten, illuminate' LUCERE *pt.3s.* **gelihte** 5:15 [see previous]

lilie *f. wk* 'lily' LILIA *as.* **lilia** 6:28 [OED2 lily, *n.* and *adj.*]

lim *n.* 'limb, part of the body' MEMBRUM *gp.* **lioma** 5:29; **leoman** 5:30 [OED2 limb, *n.1*]

gelimpan *v.III* 'happen, occur' FIERI *pt.3s.* **gelamp** 11:1, 13:53, 19:1 || CONTINGERE *ps.3s.* **gelimpeþ** 18:13 [OED2 i-limp, *v.*]

lin *n.* 'flax, linen' LINUM *as.* **lin** 12:20 [OED2 line, *n.1*]

locc *m.* 'lock of hair, hair' CAPILLUS *as.* **loc** 5:36; *np.* **loccas** 10:30 [lock, *n.1*]

locian *v.2* 'see, behold, look' ASPICERE *ps.p. mns.* **locande** 14:19; **lokende** 19:26 || VIDERE *ps.2p.* **lokigæþ** 27:24; *imp.s.* **locæ** 27:4 || RESPICERE *ps.2s.* **locast** 22:16 [look, *v.*]

lof *n.* 'praise, glory' LAUS *as.* ~ 21:16 [lof, *n.*]

gelome *adv.* 'frequently' FREQUENTER ~ 9:14; Jn18:2 || CREBRO ~ 17:15 [OED2 ylome, *adv.*]

[MK]**loppestre** *f.* 'lobster, locust' LOCUSTA *gp.* **loppestra** Mk1:6 [OED2 lobster, *n.1*]

lor *n.* 'loss, destruction' PERIRE *ds.* (*to*) **lore** (*weorþan*) 5:29, 5:30 [n.], 9:17, 10:6 || part of PERDERE? **lorene** Mk1:24 [n.] [OED2 lore, *n.2*]

los *n.* 'loss, destruction' PERIRE *ds.* (*to*) **lose** (*weorþan*) 5:30 [n.], 18:14 [loss, *n.1*]

[MK]**losian** *v.2* 'destroy' PERDERE *infl.inf.* **losane** Mk1:24 [n.] [OED2 lose, *v.1*]

lucan *v.II* 'lock, close' CLAUDERE *ps.2p.* **lucaþ** 23:13 [n.] [louk, *v.1*]

lufian *v.2* 'love' DILIGERE *ps.3s.* **lufað** 6:24; *ps.2p.* **lufigaþ** 5:46; *ps.3p.* **lufigaþ** 5:46 (*bis*) [n.]; *imp.s.* **lufa** 5:43, 22:37, 22:39; **lufige** 19:19 (or *subj.*?); *imp.p.* **lufigaþ** 5:44 || AMARE *ps.3s.* **lufað** 10:37; **lufiaþ** 10:37; *ps.3p.* **lufigaþ** 6:5, 23:6 [love, *v.1*]

lufu *f.* 'love' CARITAS *ns.* ~ 24:12 [love, *n.1*]

lyfan *v.1* 'believe' CREDERE *imp.p.* **lefað** 24:26 [OED2 leve, *v.2*]

gelyfan *v.1* 'believe' CREDERE *ps.1p.* **gelefæþ** 27:42; *ps.2p.* **gelefaþ** 9:28; *ps.3p.* **gelefaþ** 18:6; *pt.2s.* **gelefdest** 8:13; *pt.2p.* **gelefdun** 21:32; **gelefdan** 21:25; *pt.3p* **gelefdun** 21:32; *subj.pt.2p.* **gelefde** 21:32; *imp.p.* **gelefaþ** 24:23, Mk1:15; *ps.p. mnp.* **gelæfende** 21:22 [OED2 yleve, *v.*]

gelyfan *v.1* 'allow' LICERE *pp.s.* **gelæfed** 12:4 [cf. OED2 leve, *v.1*]

lyge *adj.* 'lying, false' FALSUS *fas.* ~ 19:18, 26:59; *np.* ~ 15:19, 26:60 (*bis*); *ap.* ~ 7:15 || PSEUDO- *np.* ~ 24:11, 24:24 (*bis*) [OED2 lie, *adj.1*]

lygnes *n.* 'falseness, deceitfulness' FALLACIA *ns.* **lygnisse** 13:22

lytel *adj.* 'little' PUSILLUS *mgp.* **lytlera** 18:6; **lytra** 18:14; **lytilra** 18:10; *fds.* **lytle** (*hwile*) 26:73 || PARVULUS *dp.* **lytlum** 11:25

lytel hwon *adv.* PUSILLUM ~ Mk1:19

læssa *comp.* MINOR *mns.* **lessa** 11:11

læst *superl.* MINIMUS 'least' *mns.* **læsæst** 2:6; *mns.* **læsesta** 5:19; *mds.* or *gp.?* **læsest** 10:42; *nns.* **læsest** 13:32; *gp.* **læsesta** 25:40; **læsest** 5:19 [little, *adj.*, *pron.*, and *n.*, and *adv.*]

lytling *m. wk* 'little one, child' PARVULUS *ap.* **lytlingan** 19:14 [n.] [littling, n.1]

ma, see **micel** *adv.*

magan *pret.pres.v.* 'can, may' POSSE *ps.1s.* **mæg** 26:61; *ps.2s.* **mæht** 5:36, 8:2; **mæh** Mk1:40; *ps.3s.* **mæg** 3:18, 5:14, 6:24, 6:27, 7:18, 10:28, 12:29, 19:12, 19:25, 27:42, Mk2:7; *ps.1p.* **magun** 20:22; *ps.2p.* **magun** 6:24, 12:34, 16:3; **magon** 20:22; *ps.3p.* **magun** 9:15, 10:28; *pt.2s.* **mæhtest** 26:40; *pt.3s.* **mæhte** 8:28, 22:46, Mk2:2; *pt.1p.* **mæhton** 17:19; *pt.3p.* **mæhton** 17:16; **mæhtun** Mk2:4; *subj.ps.1s.* **mæge** 9:28, 26:53; *subj.ps.3s.* **mæge** 24:24, 26:42; *subj.pt.3s.* **mæhte** 26:9, Mk1:45 || VALERE *ps.3s.* **mæg** 5:13 || POSSIBILE ESSE *subj.ps.3s.* **mæge** 26:39 [may, *v.1*]

magdalenisc *adj.* 'Magdalene' MAGDALENA *fns.* **magdalenisca** 27:56, 27:61, 28:1

magedan *prop.n. gs.* ~ 15:39

man *n.* 'crime, wickedness' part of PERIURARE 'commit perjury' *as.* ~ 5:33 [man, *n.2*]

mand *f.* 'basket' COPHINUS *ap.* **monde** 14:20 [n.], 16:9 [maund, *n.1*]

manducat 24:49 Latin used as gloss? See note.

manian *v.2* 'claim (what is due)' (RATIONEM) PONERE *pt.3s.* (*rehtæs*) **monade** 25:19; *inf.* (*gerihtes*) **monige** 18:23 [n.], 18:24

gemanian *v.2* 'instruct, advise' PRAEMONERE *pp. fns.* **gemonade**14:8

manig *adj.* 'many' MULTUS *mnp.* **monige** 7:13, 7:22, 8:11, 9:10, 12:15, 13:17, 19:30, 20:16, 22:14, 24:10, 24:11, 26:60, Mk2:2, Mk2:15; **monig** 24:5; *map.* **monige** 3:7, 8:16, 15:30, 24:5, 24:11, Mk1:34, Mk1:34; *mgp.* **monegra** 24:12; **monigra** 24:24 [n.]; *fnp.* **monige** 4:25, 8:1, 15:30, 19:2; *fap.* **monige** 8:18, 19:22; *nnp.* **monig** 27:52; *nnp.* **monige** 27:55; *ngp.* **monegra** 8:30; *nap.* **monige** 7:22, 13:58; *mdp.* **mongum** 10:31, 20:28, 26:28; **monigvm** 27:53 [n.]; **monegu** 25:21, 25:23 || PLUS *mdp.* **mænigu** 21:36 [n.] (see also **hu manig**)
superl. nns. **mængistu** 11:20
[many, *adj.*, *pron.*, and *n.*, and *adv.*]

mann *m.* 'man' HOMO *ns.* **monn** 1:19, 7:9, 8:9, 11:19, 12:11, 12:12, 12:22, 12:35 (*bis*), 12:47, 13:28, 13:44, 16:26, 17:14, 19:3 (as indef. pron.?), 19:5, 19:6, 21:28, 21:33, 25:14, 25:24, 26:24, 27:57, Mk1:23; **mon** 12:10, 13:31; *as.* **monn** 26:72, 26:74, 27:32; *gs.* **monnes** 8:20, 9:6, 10:36, 11:19, 12:8, 12:32, 12:40, 12:45, 13:37, 13:41, 16:13, 16:27, 16:28, 17:9, 17:12, 17:22, 18:11, 19:28, 20:18, 20:28, 24:27, 24:30 (*bis*), 24:37, 24:39, 24:44, 25:31, 26:2, 26:24 (*bis*), 26:45, 26:64, Mk2:10; **monnæs** 10:23; *ds.* **menn** 12:13, 12:43, 13:24, 13:45, 13:52, 16:26, 18:7, 18:23, 19:10, 26:24, Mk1:25; **monn** 20:1 [n.], 22:2; *np.* **menn** 4:4 [n.], 5:15 [n.], 7:12, 8:27, 8:28, 12:36, 13:25, 16:13; *ap.* **menn** 5:19; *gp.* **monna** 4:19, 15:9, 16:9, 16:10 (margin), 16:23, 17:22, 22:16, 23:4; *dp.* **monnum** 5:13, 5:16, 6:1. 6:2, 6:5, 6:14, 6:15, 6:16, 9:8, 10:17, 10:22, 10:32, 10:33, 12:31, 19:12, 19:26, 21:25, 21:26, 23:5, 23:7, 23:13, 23:27, 23:28, Mk1:17 || VIR *gp.* **monna** 15:38 || NL *ns.* **mon** (*nænig* ~) 9:16, 9:30; **monn** (indef.) 12:10, 15:26, 19:7, 19:10, 23:23 (indef.), 27:6 (indef.), Jn18:1 (indef.); *as.* **monn** 27:16; *ds.* **menn** 26:18, Mk1:44; *np.* **menn** 6:30 [n.], 9:17 (indef.), 16:8 [man, *n.1* (and *int.*); man, *pron.*]

manna *m. wk* 'man' HOMO *as.* **monnu** 9:9 [n.], 9:32, 10:35, 11:8, 15:11 (*bis*), 22:11: **monnum** 15:20 (*bis*) [n.] [see previous]

manþwære *adj.* 'gentle, meek' MANSUETUS *mns.* **monnðwære** 21:5

manung *f.* 'place of toll' TELONIUM *ds.* (*gæflaes*) **monunge** 9:9

maria *prop.n. ns.* ~ 1:18, 13:55, 27:56 (*bis*), 27:61 (*bis*), 28:1 (*bis*); *as.* ~ 1:20, 2:11 (or *d.*?); *gs.* ~ 1:16

matheus *prop.n. ns.* ~ 10:3; *gs.*? ~ Mt INCIPT [n.]; *as.*? ~ 9:9 [n.]

gemæcca *m.* 'mate, companion' COAEQUALIS *dp.* **gemeccum** 11:16 [cf. match, *n.1*]

mægden *n.* 'maiden, girl' PUELLA *ns.* ~ 9:24, 9:25, 14:11; *ds.* ~ 14:11 [maiden, *n.* and *adj.*]

mægen *n.* 'might, virtue' VIRTUS *as.* ~ 22:29; *gs.* **mægænes** 26:64; *ds.* **mægene** 25:15; ~ 24:30; *np.* ~ 11:20, 11:21, 11:23, 13:54, 14:2, 24:29; *ap.* ~ 7:22, 13:58 || VIS *as.* ~ 11:12 || PONDUS 'burden' *as/p.* ~ 20:12 [main, *n.1*]

gemæne *adj.* 'common' NL *ngs.* **gemænes** 27:19 [n.] [i-mene, *adj.* and *adv.*]

gemæran *v.1* 'celebrate, spread about' DIFFAMARE *pt.3p.* **gemerdon** 9:31 || DIVULGARE *pp.s.* **gemæred** 28:15

mære *adj.* 'famous, notorious' INSIGNIS *mas.* **mernæ** 27:16 [mere, *adj.1*]

mære *f.* 'border' FINIS *ap.* **mæru** 15:39; **mære** 19:1 [mere, *n.2*]

gemære *f.* 'border' FINIS *dp.* **gemaerum** 4:13; **gemerum** 8:34; **gemoerum** 2:16 [n.]; **gemærum** 15:22 || TERMINUS *ap.* **gemęru** 24:31 [see previous]

[MK]**mærsian** *v.2* 'make famous, proclaim' DIFFAMARE *inf.* **mærsige** Mk1:45

[MK]**mærsung** *f.* 'fame, report' RUMOR *ns.* **mersung** Mk1:28

[MK]**mærþ** *f.* 'fame, glory' RUMOR *ns.* **mærðo** Mk1:28

mæssepreost *m.* 'mass-priest' SACERDOS *ds.* **messepreoste** 8:4 [mass-priest, *n.*]

gemearcian *v.2* 'mark, seal' SIGNARE *pt.3p.* **gemerkade** 27:66 [mark, *v.*]

meard *f.* 'reward' MERCES *ns.* ~ 5:12 [n.]; *as.* **mearde** 6:1, 10:41

mearu *adj.* 'tender, soft' TENDER *mns.* **merwe** 24:32 (gender?) [merrow, *adj.*]

medeme *adj.* 'worthy, perfect; middling, moderate' DIGNUS *mns.* **meoduma** 10:37 || MINOR *gp.* **meoduma** 25:45

medmicel *adj.* 'not great, small' MODICUS *mgs.* **medmiccles** 8:26, 14:31; **medmiclæs** 16:8
superl. MODICUS (or MINIMUS) *mgs.* **medmasta** 6:30

medtrumnes *f.* 'weakness, infirmity' AEGRITUDO *ap.* **metrymnisse** 8:17

melu *n.* 'meal, flour' FARINA *gs.* **melwæs** 13:33 [meal, *n.1*]

gemengan *v.1* 'mix' MISCERE *pp. nas.* **gemænged** 27:34 [cf. ming, *v.1*]

menigu *f.* 'multitude, host' TURBA *ns.* **mengu** 9:25, 13:2, 26:47; **mængu** 21:8; *as.* ~ 9:23 (or *p.*?); **mengu** 14:14, 14:19, 15:32 (?), 15:33, 15:39 (but with *þara*); **mængu** 21:26; *ds.* **mengu** 14:23; *a/ds.* **mengo** Mk2:4; *np.* ~ 9:8, 12:23; **mængu** 4:25, 19:2; **menga** 8:1; **mengu** 7:28, 9:33, 13:2, 14:13, 15:30, 15:31, 20:29, 20:31, 21:9, 22:33; *ap.* ~ 5:1; **mengu** 8:18, 9:36, 13:36, 14:15, 14:22; **mængu** 21:46; *dp.* **menigu** 11:7; **mengu** 14:19, 15:35, 17:14; **mengum** 12:46; **mængum** 13:34, 15:10, 26:55; **mongum** 23:1 [n.]

mennen *n.* or *f.* 'female servant, handmaiden' ANCILLA *ns.* **menen** 26:69

mennisc *n.* 'men, people' HOMO *np.* ~ 5:11 || NINEVITA *np.* **mennisce** 12:41 [n.] [mannish, *adj.* and *adv.*]

gemet *n.* 'measure' MENSURA *as.* ~ 23:32; *ds.* **gemete** 7:2

metan *v.V* 'measure' METIRI *ps.2p.* **metaþ** 7:2 || REMETIRI *pp.s.* **meten** 7:2

metan *v.1* 'find' INVENIRE *ps.2p.* **moeteþ** 21:2; *subj.ps.2p.* **moete** 22:9 [meet]

gemetan *v.1* 'find' INVENIRE *ps.2s.*

gemoetest 17:27; *ps.3s.* **gemoeteþ** 10:39, 12:43, 12:44, 16:25, 24:46; *ps.2p.* **gemoeteþ** 2:8, 11:29; **gemoetaþ** 7:7; *ps.3p.* **gemoetaþ** 7:14; *pt.1s.* **gemotte** 8:10; *pt.3s.* **gemoette** 18:28, 21:19; **gemette** 20:6, 26:40, 26:43; *pt.3p.* **gemoettun** 2:11, 27:32; **gemettun** 22:10; *subj.ps.3s.* **gemoete** 10:39; *ps.p. mns.* **gemoetend** 13:46; *pp.s.* **gemoeted** 1:18

mete *m.* 'food' ESCA *ns.* ~ 3:4, 6:25; *as.* ~ 14:15 || CIBUS *as.* ~ 24:45; *ds.* ~ 10:10 || part of AZYMA *gp.* **meta** 26:17 [meat]

micel *adj.* 'much, many, great' MAGNUS *mns.* ~ 5:19 [n.], 7:27, 15:28; *mas.* **micelne** 27:60; *mds.* **miccle** 2:10 (instr.?); *mgs.* **micclan** 5:35; *ma/ds.* ~ 28:8; *nns.* ~ 22:36; *nas.* ~ 4:16, 26:9 [n.]; *fns.* ~ 8:24, 8:26; **micelu** 24:21, 28:2; *fa/ds.* **micle** 24:31; *fds.* **miclæ** 27:46; **miccle** 27:50, Mk1:26; **micelre** Mk1:26; *ap.* **micel** 24:24 || MULTUS *mns.* ~ 2:18; *fns.* ~ 26:47; *fas.* **miccle** 13:5, 14:14; *nns.* ~ 9:37; *nds.* **micclum** 25:19; **miccle** 24:30 (instr.?); *np.* ~ 20:29 || TANTUM *mas.* (*swa*) **micel** 8:10, 9:21; *fas.* (*swa*) **miccle** 15:33; *np.* (*swa*) **micle** 18:25 (adv.?)

mara *comp.* 'more' MAIOR *mns.* **maræ** 11:11; **mare** 11:11, 18:1, 18:4, 20:26, 23:11; *nns.* **mara** 12:6, 13:32; **mare** 23:17, 23:19; *np.* **mare** 20:25 || PLUS *nns.* ~ 12:41, 12:42; *nns.* **mare** 6:25, 11:9; *nas.* **mare** 20:10 || AMPLIUS *nas.* **marae** 5:47

mæst *superl.* 'most, very large' PLURIMUS *fns.* **mæste** 21:8 || MAGNUS *nns.* **mæste** 22:38 (MAXIMUS in WW) [mickle, *adj.*, *pron.* (and *n.*), and *adv.*]

micle *adv.* QUANTO see **hu micle**

mare *comp.* 'more' MAGIS ~ 18:13 || part of DUPLUS ~ 23:15 [see previous]

ma *comp.* MAGIS **mae** 6:30, 7:11, 12:12; **mæ** 10:25 || POTIUS **mae** 10:6, 10:28; **mæ** 25:9 || PLUS **mæ** 5:20, 26:53 || AMPLIUS **mæ** 22:46 [mo, *adv.1*, *pron.1*, and *n.1*, and *adj.1*]

miclian *v.2* 'magnify, extol' MAGNIFICARE *ps.3p.* **micclaþ** 23:5; *pt.3p.* **micladun** 15:31 [mickle, *v.*]

mid *prep.* 'with' CUM ~ 1:23 (w.a.), 2:3 (w.a.), 2:11, 4:21, 5:25 (w.a.), 5:41 (w.a.), 8:11, 9:15 (w.d.), 12:3 (w.d.), 12:4 (w.d.), 12:30 (w.a.), 13:20, 15:30 (w.d.), 18:9 [n.], 18:23 (w.a.), 20:20, 21:2, 24:30, 24:31, 24:49 (w.d.), 25:3 (w.a.), 25:10 (w.a.), 25:27, 26:11, 26:18 (w.d.), 26:23, 26:29, 26:36 (w.d.), 26:38, 26:40, 27:38 (w.a.), 27:44 (w.a.), 27:54 (w.a.), 27:66 (*bis*, w.d.), Jn18:1 (w.d.), Jn18:3; **mið** 9:10 (w.a.), 9:11 (w.d.), 12:41 (w.a.), 12:42 (w.a.), 12:45 (w.d.), 13:29 (w.d.), 14:7 (w.d.), 14:9 (w.d.), 15:32 (w.a.), 16:27 (w.d.), 17:17 (postposed), 18:16 (w.a.), 19:26[1] (w.d.), 19:26[2] (w.a.), 22:16 (w.d.), 24:51 (w.d.), 25:4 (w.d.), 25:31 (w.a.), 26:20 (w.d.), 26:35, 26:47 (w.d.) (*bis*), 26:51, 26:55 (w.d.), 26:58 (w.d.), 26:69 (w.a.), 26:71 (w. a. and d.), 26:72 (w.d.), 27:41 (w.d.), 28:8 (*bis*), 28:12 (w.d.), 28:20, Mk1:13 (w.d.), Mk1:20 (w.d.), Mk1:29, Mk1:36 (w.d.), Jn18:2 (w.d.) || APUD ~ 6:1, 22:25, 26:55; **mið** 13:56, 26:18, 28:15 || EX **mið** 27:7 (w.d.) || IN **mið** Mk1:8 (margin) || NL **mid** 13:14, 21:30, 26:67 (*bis*), 27:3, Mk1:40; **mið** 20:7 (w.d.), Mk1:6 (w. a. and d.), Jn18:3 (w.d.)

mid þy *conj.* 'when' CUM **mid þy** 26:6; **mið þy** 25:31, Mk1:32, Mk1:37, Mk1:42, Mk2:4, Mk2:5, Mk2:14, Mk2:15; **mið ðy** Jn18:1 || NL **mið ðy** Mk1:18, Mk1:20; **mið þy** Mk1:31 [mid, *prep.1* and *adv.1*]

middangeard *m.* 'the word, earth' MUNDUS *ns.* ~ 13:38; *as.* **middengeard** 16:26; *gs.* **middangeardes** 4:8, 5:14, 13:35;

middang(eardes) 25:34; *ds.* **middang(earde)** 18:7 [n.] || ORBIS *ds.* **middang(earde)** 26:13 || SAECULUM *gs.* **middangeardes** 24:21 || TERRA *a/ds.* **middang(eard)** 27:45 [n.] [middenerd, *n.*]

midde *adj.* 'middle' MEDIUS *mds.* **middum** 14:24 [n.]; *fds.* **middere** 25:6 [mid, *adj.*, *n.1*, and *adv.2*]

midde *f.* 'middle' MEDIUM *ds.* (*in*) **midde** 10:16 [n.] [see previous]

middel *n.* 'middle, centre' MEDIUM *ds.* **midle** 13:25, 13:49, 14:6, 18:20; [ ]**idlæ** 18:2 (margin) [middle, *adj.* and *n.*]

miht *f.* 'might, power' POTESTAS *ns.* **mæht** 28:18; *as.* **mæht** 7:29, 21:23; **mæhte** 9:6, 9:8, 20:25, Mk1:22 [n.], Mk2:10; **mæhtae** 10:1; *a/ds.* **mæhti** 8:9; *ds.* **mæhte** 21:23, 21:24, 21:27, Mk1:27 [might, *n.1*]

mil *f.* 'mile' MILLE PASSUS *ns.* ~ 5:41 [mile, *n.1*]

milde *adj.* 'mild, meek' MITIS *mns.* ~ 11:29; *mnp.* ~ 5:4 [mild, *adj.*, *adv.*, and *n.1*]

mildheortness *f.* 'mercy, compassion' MISERCORDIA *as.* **mildheortnisse** 5:7, 9:13, 12:7, 23:23 || MISERCORS 'the merciful'? *np.* **mildheortnisse** 5:7 [n.] [cf. mildheartness, s.v. mild-heart, *adj.*]

miltsian *v.2* 'compassionate, show mercy' MISERERE *pt.1s.* **miltsade** 18:33; *pt.3s.* **milsade** 14:14; *subj.pt.2s.* **miltsade** 18:33; *imp.s.* **miltsa** 9:27, 15:22, 20:30; **miltse** 17:15; *ps.p. mns.* **miltsende** 18:27, 20:34, Mk1:41 [milce, *v.*]

gemiltsian *v.2* 'compassionate, show mercy' MISERERE *imp.s.* **gemiltsa** 20:31 [OED2 i-milce | i-milse, *v.*]

minte *f.* 'mint' MINTA *as.* **mintæ** 23:23 [mint, *n.1*]

mishweorfed *adj.* 'perverted' PERVERSUS *fns.* **miswerfde** 17:17

missenlic *adj.* 'various' VARIUS *dp.* **missenlicum** 4:24, Mk1:34

mitte *f.* 'bushel, measure' MODIUS *ds.* **mytte** 5:15 || SATUM *dp.* **mittum** 13:33 [mit, *n.*]

mod *n.* 'mind' MENS *ds.* **mode** 22:37 || NL *ds.* **mode** 2:3 [n.], 14:26, 26:37 [n.] [mood, n.1]

gemod *adj.* 'in agreement with' CONSENTIENS *ns.* ~ 5:25 [n.]

modor *f.* 'mother' MATER *ns.* **moder** 1:18, 12:46, 12:47, 12:48, 12:49, 12:50, 13:55, 20:20, 27:56 (*bis*); *as.* **moder** 2:13, 2:14, 2:20, 2:21, 10:37, 19:5, 19:19, 19:29; *gs.* **moder** 19:12; *ds.* **moder** 14:8, 14:11, 15:4 (*bis*), 15:5, 15:6; *a/ds.* **moder** 2:11, 10:35 [mother, *n.1* (and *int.*)]

mona *m.* 'moon' LUNA *ns.* ~ 24:29 [moon, *n.1*]

(†)**monseoc** *adj.* 'lunatic, insane' LUNATICUS *mns.* **monsek** 17:15; *map.* **monsekae** 4:24 [n.] [moonsick, *adj.*]

morgen *m.* 'morn, morning' CRAS *ds.* (*to*) **mærgen** 6:30; (*to*) **marne** 6:30 [n.]; (*an*) **mergenne** 16:2 || CRASTINUS *ns.* ~ 6:34; *as.* ~ 6:34 (or *d.*?) || MANE *ns.* ~ 27:1; *ds.* (*on*) **mærgne** 21:18 [morn, *n.*]

morðor *n.* 'murder' HOMICIDIUM *ns.* **morþur** 15:19; *as.* **murður** 19:18 [murder, *n.1* and *int.*]

gemot *n.* 'council, assembly' CONCILIUM *ns.* **gemot** 26:59; *ds.* **gemote** 5:22; *dp.* **gemotum** 10:17 || FORUM *ds.* **gemote** 23:7 || PRAETORIUM *ds.* **gemote** 27:27 [moot, *n.1*; OED2 gemot, *n.*]

motan *pret.pres.v.* 'be allowed' LICERE *ps.3s.* **mot** 12:10, 19:3, 27:6 || NL *pt.3p.* **mostun** 14:36 [mote, *v.1*; must, *v.1*]

moþþe *f.* 'moth' TINEA *ns.* **mohþa** 6:19, 6:20 [moth, *n.1*]

moyses *prop.n. ns.* ~ 8:4, 19:7, 19:8, 22:24, Mk1:44; *gs.* ~ 23:2

gemunan *pret.pres.v.* 'remember' RECORDARI *pt.3s.* **gemunde** 26:75 || REMEMORARI *ps.2s.* **gemynest** 27:63 (RECORDARI in WW) [OED2 i-mune | i-myne, *v.*]

muþ *m.* 'mouth' OS *ns.* **muð** 12:34;

as. ~ 5:2; **muð** 13:35, 17:27; *ds.* **muðe** 4:4, 15:11, 15:17, 15:18, 21:16; **muþe** 15:11, 18:16 [mouth, *n.*]

gemynd *f.* 'memorial, monument' MEMORIA *as.* **gemynd** 26:13 || MONUMENTUM *ap.* **gemynde** 23:29 [i-mind, *n.*]

myndgian *v.2* 'remember' MEMINISSE *ps.2p.* **myngað** 16:9 [cf. ming, *v.2*]

gemyndgian *v.2* 'warn, admonish' ADMONERE *pp. mns.?* **gemynga** 2:22 [n.] [see previous]

†**gemyne** *adj.* 'mindful' RECORDATUS *mns.* ~ 5:23

mynet *n.* 'coin' NUMISMA *as.* **mynet** 22:19 [mint, *n.1*]

mynetere *m.* 'money-changer' NUMMULARIUS *gp.* **mynetræ** 21:12; *dp.* **myneterum** 25:27 [minter, *n.1*]

myrra *m./f.?* 'myrrh' MURRA *as.* **murra** 2:11 (followed by *þ is smerennis*) [myrrh, *n.1*]

myrþra *m. wk* 'murderer' HOMICIDA *ap.* **myrðra** 22:7

na *adv.* 'not at all' NON **no** 7:25, 12:7, 21:27, Mk1:22 || NONNE **no** 13:27 [n.] [no, *adv.1*]

[MK]**genacian** *v.2* 'lay bare, strip' NUDARE *pt.3p.* **genacadun** Mk2:4 [cf. nake, *v.*]

nacod *adj.* 'naked' NUDUS *mns.* **nacud** 25:36, 25:43; *mas.* **nacudne** 25:38 [naked, *adj.* and *n.1*]

naht *n.* 'naught, nothing' NIHILUM *ns.* **nauwiht** 17:20, 23:18, 27:24; **nawiht** 27:19; **næht** 23:16; *nas.* **nauwiht** 21:19, 27:12; **nawiht** 26:62; *ds.* (*to*) **nohte** 5:13 [nought, *pron.*, *n.*, *adv.*, and *adj.*]

naht *adj.* 'useless, bad' NEQUAM *mns.* **nawiht** 18:32, 20:15 [see previous]

nama *m. wk* 'name' NOMEN *ns.* **noma** 6:9, 27:32; *as.* **noma** 1:21, 1:23, 1:25; *ds.* **noma** 7:22 (*bis*), 10:22, 18:5, 24:5, 24:9; **noman** 7:22, 10:41 (*bis*), 10:42, 12:21, 18:20, 19:29, 21:9, 23:39, 28:19; *np.* **noma** 10:2 [name, *n.* and *adj.*]

nan *pron./adj.* 'none' NEQUAM *ns.* ~ 6:23 [n.] || NL *ns.* (*eower*) **nan** 5:34 [n.]; 'no' *nas.* ~ 22:25 [none, *pron.*, *adj.*, and *adv.*]

nazarenisc *adj.* 'of/from Nazareth' NAZARENUS *mns.* ~ 2:23; *mns.* **nazarenisca** Mk1:24; *mas.* **nazarenisco** 26:71

nazareþ *prop.n. ns.* ~ 2:23; *as.* **nazaret** 4:13; *ds.* ~ 21:11; **nazareð** Mk1:9

nædl *f.* 'needle' ACUS *gs.* **nedle** 19:24 [needle, *n.*]

nædre *f. wk* 'viper, serpent' SERPENS *as.* **nedra** 7:10; *np.* **nedra** 10:16, 23:33 || VIPERA *gp.* **nedrana** 3:7, 12:34 [adder, *n.1*]

næfre *adv.* 'never' NUMQUAM /NUSQUAM ~ 9:33, 12:7, 21:19, Mk2:12; **næfræ** 7:23, 26:33 || NON ~ 21:16 [n.] (NUMQUAM in WW), 21:42 (NUMQUAM in WW), 24:35 [never, *adv.* and *int.*]

næglian *v.2* 'nail (on the cross)' part of CRUCIFIGERE *pp.s.* **nægled** (*on rode*) 27:23; (*on rode*) **nægled** 27:26 [nail, *v.*]

genæglian *v.2* 'nail (on the cross)' part of CRUCIFIGERE *pp.s.* (*on rode*) **genæglad** 27:22 [see previous]

nænig *pron.* 'no one' NEMO *mns.* ~ 8:28, 9:16 (w. *mann*), 11:27, 20:7, 22:46 (*bis*), 24:36; *mas.* **nænigne** 17:8; *mds.* **nængum** 8:4, 16:20; **nænegum** 17:9, Mk1:44 || NE QUIS ~ 9:30 (w. *mann*), 24:4 || ALIQUIS (+ negative) *mns.* **nænig** 12:19 || NEQUAM 'bad, useless?' *mnp.* **nænegu** 13:38 [n.]

nænig þinga *adv.* NEQUAQUAM 'not at all, by no means' 2:6 [nany, *adj.* and *pron.*]

ne *neg. particle* NON ~ 1:25, 2:18, 3:10, etc.; **næ** 26:53 || NE (w. subjunctive) ~ 3:9, 5:42, 6:13, 10:5, 10:28, 12:16, 18:10, 24:20, 26:41; **n** 10:5 [n.] || part of NELLE 1:19, 1:20, 2:18, etc. || NEC/NEQUE ~ 5:15, 5:34, 5:35

(*bis*), 5:36, 6:15, 6:20 (x3), 6:25, 6:26 (*bis*), 6:28, 7:6, 7:18, 9:17, 10:9 (*bis*), 10:10 (x3), 10:14, 10:24, 11:18 (*bis*), 11:27, 12:4, 12:19 (*bis*), 12:32 (*bis*), 13:13, 16:9, 21:32, 22:29, 22:30 (*bis*), 22:46, 23:10, 23:13, 24:21 (*bis*), 24:36, 25:13, 25:45 (*bis*), Mk2:2 || NONNE (with *ac*) ~ 5:46, 5:47, 6:26, 7:22, 10:29, 10:38, 12:11, 13:55, 13:56, 18:12, 18:33, 19:6 || NONDUM ~ 16:9 || part of NISI ~ 24:22 || NL (often translating such Latin verbs as NESCIRE, IGNORARE, etc.) ~ 2:12, 2:22 [n.], 6:1, 6:23 [n.], 6:24, 9:15, 12:19, 15:23 (NON in WW), 16:9 (*bis*) [n.], 19:18, 22:5, 22:29), 24:42, 24:44, 24:50, 25:12, 26:70, Mk2:12; **ni** 16:10 (margin) [n.] [ne, *adv.1* and *conj.1*]

neah *prep.* 'according to' IUXTA **neh** 16:27

neah *adj.* 'near, close' PROPE *mns.* **neh** 24:32; *fns.* **neh** 26:18

nearra *comp.* NOVISSIMUS *mns.* **nęrra** 21:31

niehst *superl.* NOVISSIMUS *mas.* **næhstu** 5:26 [n.]; *mds.* **næhsta** 20:14; *mnp.* **nęhstu** 19:30; **næhstu** 19:30, 20:12, 20:16 (*bis*); *dp.* **næhstum** 20:8 || PROXIMUS *mns.* **næhstu** 22:39; *map.* **nextan** 5:43; *nap.* **nehsto** Mk1:38; *dp.* **nehstum** 19:19 || NOVISSIME (*æt*) **nehsta** 21:37; (*æt*) **nihste** 25:11; (*æt*) **næhste** 26:60 [nigh, *adv.* (and *prep.*), *adj.*, and *n.*; near, *adj.* (and *n.*); next, *adj.* (and *prep.*), *adv.*, and *n.*]

nealles *adv.* 'not, not at all' NON **nalles** 4:4, 9:13, 15:11, 26:39; **nallæs** 7:21; **nallas** 7:29; **nælles** 21:21; **nællæs** 26:5

nealæcan *v.1* 'come near, approach' ADPROPINQUARE *ps.3s.* **neoliceþ** 3:2 [n.], 10:7; **neolicet** 4:17; *pt.3p.* **nealehctun** 21:1 [neighleche, *v.*]

genealæcan *v.1* 'come near, approach' ACCEDERE *pt.3s.* **geneolicte** 9:20; **geneolacede** Mk1:31; *ps.p. mns.* **geneleccende** 4:3 [OED2 i-nehleche, *v.*]

nearu *adj.* 'narrow' ANGUSTUS *nns.* **naru** 7:14; *nas.* **naarwe** 7:13 [narrow, *adj.* and *n.*]

nemnan *v.1* 'call, name' VOCARE *ps.2s.* **nemnest** 1:21; *ps.3s.* **nemneþ** 22:43, 22:45, Jn18:1; *ps.3p.* **nemnaþ** 1:23; *pt.3s.* **nemde** 1:25; *pt.3p.* **nemdun** 10:25; *imp.p.* **nemnaþ** 23:9; *inf.* ~ 23:10; *pp.s.* **nemned** 1:16, 2:23, 4:18, 5:19, 26:14; **næmned** 27:8; **nemneþ** 5:19; *pp.p.* **nemde** 23:7, 23:8 || DICERE *pp.s.* **nemned** 10:2 [nemn, *v.*]

genemnan *v.1* 'name, call' VOCARE *pp.s.* **genemned** 21:13; *pp.p.* **genemde** 5:9 || NOMINARE *pp.s.* **genæmned** 27:33 [see previous]

neosan *v.1* 'visit' VISITARE *pt.2p.* **neosadun** 25:36, 25:43

neptalimes *prop.n. gs.* ~ 4:15; **nepthales** 4:13

nese *adv.* 'no' NON ~ 25:9

nett *n.* 'net' RETE *as/p.* ~ 4:18, 4:21, 4:22 [n.], Mk1:16, Mk1:18; *as.* ~ 4:20, Mk1:19 || SAGENA *ds.* ~ 13:47 [net, *n.1*]

nic *adv.* 'no' NON ~ 13:29 [n.], 25:9

nied *f.* or *n.* 'need, necessity' NECESSE *ns.* **ned** 18:7 [need, *n.1*]

niedan *v.1* 'force, compel' ANGARI(Z)ARE *pt.3p.* **næddun** 27:32; *subj.ps.3s.* **nede** 5:41 [need, *v.1*]

nigon *num.* 'nine' NOVEM *a.* ~ 18:12; *d.* ~ 18:13 [nine, *adj.* and *n.*]

nigoþa *ord. num.* 'ninth' NONUS *fds.* **nigoþan** 20:5, 27:45 (or *a.*?), 27:46 (or *a.*?) [ninth, *adj.*, *n.*, and *adv.*]

niht *f.* 'night' NOX *a/ds.* **niht** 2:14; *ds.* **niht** 25:6, 26:34, 28:13; **næhte** 26:31; *gp.* **næhta** 4:2, Mk1:13; *ap.* **niht** 12:40; **nęht** 12:40 [night, *n.* and *int.*]

nihtes *adv.* 'at night' NOX **næhtes** 14:25 [nights, *adv.*]

niman *v.IV* 'take, receive' TOLLERE *imp.s.* **nim** Mk2:9, Mk2:11;

imp.p. **nimaþ** 11:29; *infl.inf.* **nimene** 24:18 || CAPERE *ps.3p.* **nimaþ** 19:11; *subj.ps.3s.* **nime** 19:12; *inf.* **nioman** 19:12, Mk2:2 || TENERE *pt.3p.* **noman** 26:55; *subj.pt.3p.* **noman** 26:4 || ACCIPERE *ps.3p.* **niomaþ** 26:52 || MUTUARI *inf.* (*on borg*) **nioma** 'take (something) on loan' 5:42 || NL *infl.inf.* **niomane** 15:33 [n.] [nim, *v.*]

geniman *v.IV* 'take, receive' ACCIPERE *ps.3s.* **genimaþ** 10:38; *pt.3s.* **genom** 2:14, 2:21, 14:19, 26:26, 26:27, 27:24, 27:48; *pt.1p.* **genoman** 16:7; *pt.2p.* **genoman** 16:10 (margin) (SUMERE in WW); *pt.3p.* **genoman** 25:4, 27:6, 27:9, 27:30, 27:59; *subj.pt.3p.* **genome** 16:5; *imp.s.* **genim** 2:13, 2:20; *ps.p. mns.* **genimende** 13:31, 15:36; *nns.* **genimende** 13:33; *np.* **genimende** 25:1; **genimænde** 25:3 || ADSUMERE *ps.3s.* **genimeþ** 12:45; *pt.3s.* **genom** 4:5, 4:8, 17:1, 20:17, 26:37; *pp.s.* **genumen** 24:40, 24:41 (*bis*); *ps.p. mns.* **genimende** 16:22 || TENERE *ps.3s.* **genimeþ** 12:11; *pt.3s.* **genom** 9:25, 14:3; *pt.3p.* **genoman** 22:6, 26:57; **genomen** 28:9; **genomun** 26:50; *subj.pt.3p.* **genoman** 21:46; *imp.p.* **genimeþ** 26:48; *ps.p. mns.* **genimende** 18:28 || TOLLERE *imp.s.* **genim** 9:6, 17:27, 20:14; *imp.p.* **genimað** 25:28; *inf.* **genioman** 5:40; *infl.inf.* **genimanne** 24:17 || SUMERE *pt.2p.* **genoman** 16:9; *pt.3p.* **genoman** 25:3; *subj.ps.3s.* **genime** 15:26; *imp.s.* **genim** 17:27 || FERRE *pt.3s.* **genom** 24:39; *pt.3p.* **genomun** 14:12; **genoman** 14:20; **genomen** 15:37 || ADHIBERE *imp.s.* **genim** 18:16 || SUSCIPERE *pt.3p.* **genoman** 27:27 [see previous]

niþer *adv.* 'down, below' DIS- ~ 7:25, 7:27; **niðer** 24:17; **nider** 11:23 || DEORSUM ~ 4:6 || SEORSUM **niðer** 17:1 [n.] [nether, *adv.1*]

niþerian *v.2* 'accuse, condemn' CONDEMNARE *ps.3s.* **niðrað** 12:42; *ps.3p.* **niðrigað** 12:41; *pt.2p.* **niðrade** 12:7; *pp.s.* **niðrad** 12:37 || DAMNARE *pp.s.* **niðrad** 27:3 [nither, *v.*]

niþerstigan *v.I* 'descend' DESCENDERE *ps.p. mas.* **niþerstigendne** 3:16; *mdp.* **niþerstigendum** 17:9

niþerweardes *adv.* 'downwards' PRAECEPS **niðerweardes** 8:32 [netherwards, *adv.*]

niþeweard *adj.* 'low, nethermost' DEORSUM *nds.* **neoþewearde** 27:51 [netherward, *adv.* and *adj.*]

niwe *adj.* 'new' NOVUS *fns.* **niowa** Mk1:27; *fgs.* **neowe** 26:28; *fds.* **neowe** 27:60; *nas.* **niowe** 9:17; **neowe** 9:17, 26:29; *map.* **neowe** 9:17, 13:52 || RUDIS *mas.* **neowenne** 9:16 [new, *adj.* and *n.*]

noe *prop.n. ns.* ~ 24:38; **noes** *gs.* 24:37

genog *adj.* 'enough, sufficient' SUFFICERE *mns.* **genoh** 6:34, 10:25 [enough, *adj.*, *pron.*, and *n.*, and *adv.*]

nu *adv.* 'now' NUNC ~ 5:5, 11:12, 26:65, 27:40, 27:42, 27:43, 28:19 || MODO ~ 3:15, 9:18, 24:21, 26:53 || IAM ~ 3:10 [n.], 15:32, 26:45 || ADHUC ~ (*geta, gen*) 15:16, 19:20 || ERGO ~ 22:9 || ITAQUE ~ 25:13

nu *conj.* 'now that, when' SI ~ 10:25 [n.] || CUM ~ 21:40 [n.]

nu nu *conj.* 'if' SI ~ 6:30 [n.], 7:11, 22:45 || CUM ~ 12:34 || NL ~ 18:1 [now, *adv.*, *conj.*, *n.1*, and *adj.*]

nydnima *f.* 'one who takes by force' VIOLENTUS *np.* **nedniomu** 11:12 [n.]

nydniman *v.III* 'take by force' RAPINA *ps.p. ngs.* **nednimende** 23:25

†**nyhtnes** *f.* 'abundance' ABUNDANTIA *ds.* **nyhtnisse** 12:34 [n.]

genyhtsum *adj.* 'abundant' AMPUS *nns.* **genyhtsume** 5:37 || COPIOSUS *nas.* **genyhtsum** 28:12

nyhtsumian *v.2* 'suffice, abound'

SUFFICERE *subj.ps.3s.* **nyhtsumigæ** 25:9
genyhtsumian *v.2* 'suffice, abound' ABUNDARE *ps.3s.* **genyhtsumaþ** 13:12, 24:12; **genyhtsumað** 25:29; *subj.ps.3s.* **genihtsumige** 5:20 || COPIOSUS ESSE *ps.3s.* **genihtsumað** 5:12 (or *pp.*?, see note)
nyle, see **willan**
nymþe *conj.* 'unless, except' NISI ~ 5:20, 11:27 (*bis*), 12:4 12:24, 12:29, 12:39, 13:57, 14:17, 15:24, 16:4, 17:8, 18:3, 21:19, 24:36, Mk2:7; **nymðe** 17:21, 19:9; NISI UT **nymþe** (*þæt*) 5:13 [n.], 26:42
nytan, nyte, niton, see **witan**

oele, see **ele**
oeþel, see **eþel**
of *prep.* 'of, from' DE ~ 1:3, 1:5, etc. || EX ~ 1:5, 1:6, etc. || A ~ 4:25, 6:13, 12:43, 15:22 || EXTRA ~ 21:17 || SUPER ~ 24:45 [n.] || IN ~ 22:37 (x3) || NL ~ 21:25 (E cancelled in R), 26:42, Mk2:8 [of, *prep.*]
of *adv.* 'off, away' NL ~ 18:9 [off, *adv.*, *prep.*, *n.*, and *adj.*]
[MK]**ofclipian** *v.2* 'cry out' EXCLAMARE *ps.p. mns.* **ofcliopande** Mk1:26
ofdon *anom.v.* 'put away' EICERE *ps.1s.* **ofdo** 7:4 (margin)
[MK]**ofdunestigan** *v.I* 'descend' DESCENDERE *fas.* **ofdunestigende** Mk1:10 [n.]
ofen *m.* 'furnace' CAMINUS *as.* **ofn** 13:50; *ds.* **ofne** 13:42 || CLIBANUS *ds.* **ofne** 6:30 [oven, *n.*]
ofer *prep.* 'over' SUPER/SUPRA ~ 3:16 (w.a.), 5:45 (*bis*, w.a.), 9:18 (w.a), 10:13 (w.a), 10:24 (*bis*, w.a.), 10:37, 11:29 (w.a), 12:18 (w.a.), 14:25 (w.a.), 14:26 (w.a.), 14:28 (w.a.), 14:29 (w.a.), 23:36 (w.a.), 24:2 (w.d.), 24:30 (w.a.), 24:47, 25:21 (w.d.), 25:21, 25:23 (w.d.), 25:23, 26:7 (w.a.), 27:25 (*bis*, w.a.), 27:37 (w.a.), 27:45, Mk1:22 || TRANS ~ 4:15, 8:18, 8:28, 14:22, 16:5, Jn18:1 || IN ~ 20:25 [over, *prep.* and *conj.*]
oferfaran *v.VI* 'go over, cross' TRANSFRETARE *pp.* (w. *habban*) **oferfæren** 14:34 [overfare, *v.*]
ofergan *anom.v.* 'transgress, come upon' TRANSGREDI *ps.2p.* **ofergæþ** 15:3; *ps.3p.* **ofergæþ** 15:2 || part of DORMIRE *pt.3s.* (*slep*) **ofereode** 25:5 [n.] [overgo, *v.*]
oferhiwian *v.2* 'transfigure' TRANSFIGURARE *pp.s.* **oferheowad** 17:2 [n.]
oferliþan *v.I* 'pass over, sail over' TRANSFRETARE *pt.3s.* **oferlaþ** (*þone sæe*) 9:1
ofersawan *v.VII* 'oversow' SUPERSEMINARE *pt.3s.* **oferseow** 13:25 [oversow, *v.*]
†**ofersceatt** *m.* 'interest, usury' USURA *ds.* **ofersceatta** 25:27 [n.]
†**oferscuwian** *v.2* 'overshadow' OBUMBRARE *pt.3s.* **oferscuade** 17:5
oferswiþrian *v.2* 'prevail, conquer' PRAEVALERE *ps.3p.* **oferswiðiaþ** 16:18 [n.]
[MK]**ofgan** *anom.v.* 'go out, go away' EXIRE *pt.3s.* **ofeode** Mk1:26 [ofgo, *v.*]
ofslean *v.VI* 'kill' OCCIDERE *ps.2p.* **ofslæþ** 23:34; *ps.3p.* **ofslægþ** 17:23; *pt.3s.* **ofslog** 2:16; *pt.2p.* **ofslogun** 23:35; *pt.3p.* **ofslogan** 21:35, 21:39; **ofslogun** 22:6; *subj.pt.3p.* **ofslogen** 26:4; *inf.* ~ 14:5; **ofslæan** 10:28; **ofslan** 21:38; *pp.s.* **ofslaegen** 16:21; *pp. np.* **ofslægene** 22:4 || PERDERE *inf.* ~ 12:14; *infl.inf.* **ofslæanne** 2:13 || DECOLLARE *pt.3s.* **ofslog** 14:10 [ofslay, *v.*]
oft *adv.* 'often' SAEPE ~ 17:15 || NL ~ Mk1:23 [n.] [see also **hu oft**] [oft, *adv.* and *adj.*]
†**ofwitan** *v.I* 'reproach?' REVERERI *pt.3p.* **ofwitun** 21:37 [n.]
[MK]**ofwundrian** *v.2* 'wonder, be amazed' MIRARI *pt.3p.* **ofwundradun** Mk2:12
olfend *m.* 'camel' CAMELUS *as.* **olbend** 19:24; **olbendu** 23:24; *gp.* **olbendena** 3:4 [n.] [olfend, *n.*]
om *m.* 'rust' ERUGO *ns.* ~ 6:19, 6:20

on *prep.* IN ~ 4:8, 5:1, etc. || SUPRA/SUPER ~ 4:5, 5:14, etc. || A ~ 25:33 (*bis*), 25:34, 25:41, 27:38 (*bis*) || IN- ~ 19:13 (postposed, see note), 19:15, 27:48 || AD 20:21 (*bis*), 20:23, 26:64 (A in WW) [n.] || EX ~ 8:13 || PER ~ 27:15 || PRO ~ 27:19 || NL ~ 2:14, 5:42, 12:1, 12:2, 12:5, 12:10, 12:11, 12:12, 14:6, 14:15, 20:1, 21:7 (SUPER in WW), 21:18, 24:20 (*bis*), 24:43, 25:14, 27:19, 27:22, 27:23, 27:26, 28:1, 28:13, Mk1:6, Mk1:35; **an** 16:2 [on, *prep.*]

onbæcling *adv.* 'backwards' RETRO **onbæclinc** 4:10 [n.]

†**onbrædan** *v.1* 'spread out' INPONERE *pt.3p.* **onbrędddon** 21:7 [n.]

ond-, see **and-**

ondrædan *v.VII* 'be afraid' TIMERE *ps.1p.* **ondredaþ** 21:26; *pt.3p.* **ondreordun** 17:6; *imp.s.* **ondred** 1:20; *imp.p.* **ondredaþ** 10:26, 10:28 (*bis*), 17:7; **ondredeþ** 28:10 [adread, *v.1*]

[MK]**onfindan** *v.III* 'find out' INVENIRE *pt.3p.* **onfundun** Mk1:37

onfon *v.VII* 'take, receive' ACCIPERE *ps.3s.* **onfoeþ** 7:8, 10:41 (*bis*); **onfoehþ** 13:20; **onfooþ** 19:29; *ps.2p.* **onfoeþ** 23:14 (w. g.); *ps.3p.* **andfoað** 17:25; *pt.3s.* **onfeng** 8:17, 25:17, 25:18, 25:20, 25:22, 25:24; **ondfeng** 25:16; *pt.3p.* **onfengon** 2:12, 10:8, 20:10, 20:11, 21:34, 28:12, 28:15 (w. d.); **ondfeongon** 17:24; **⁊fengon** 20:9; *subj.ps.2s.* **onfoiæ** 1:20 [n.]; *imp.s.* **onfoh** 1:20 [n.]; *imp.p.* **ondfoþ** 26:26; *inf.* **onfoon** 20:10; **onfo** 10:14 || RECIPERE *ps.3s.* **onfoeð** 10:40 (*bis*); **onfoeþ** 10:40 (*bis*), 10:41 (*bis*); *pt.3p.* **onfengun** 6:2, 6:5, 6:16; *subj.pt.1s.* **onfenge** 25:27 || SUSCIPERE *ps.3s.* **ondfoeþ** 18:5 [n.]; **andfoeþ** 18:5 || PERCIPERE *inf.* **andfoa** 11:14 [onfang, *v.*]

onfruma, see **fruma**

ongean *prep.* 'against, towards' OBVIAM **ongægn** 8:34, 25:1, 25:6; **ongæn** 27:32 || NL (part of OCCURRERE) **ongægn** 8:28, 28:9 [again, *adv.*, *prep.*, and *conj.*]

ongietan *v.V* 'perceive, understand' INTELLEGERE *ps3s.* **ongeteð** 13:23; *ps.2p.* **ongetaþ** 13:14, 13:51, 16:9, 16:11; **ongetað** 15:17; *ps.3p.* **ongeotað** 13:13; **ongetaþ** 13:19; *pt.3p.* **ongetun** 16:12; **ongeton** 17:13; *subj.ps.3s.* **⁊gete** 24:15 [n.]; *subj.ps.3p.* **ongeton** 13:15; *imp.p.* **ongeteþ** 15:10 || COGNOSCERE *ps.2p.* **ongetaþ** 7:16, 7:20; *pt.3s.* **onget** Mk2:8; *pt.3p.* **ongetun** 17:12, 21:45; **ongeotun** 24:39; *ps.p. mns.* **ongetende** 22:18; *mnp.* **ondgetende** 14:35 || AGNOSCERE *pp.s.* **ongeten** 12:33 [anyete, *v.*]

onginnan *v.III* 'begin' COEPISSE *ps.3s.* **onginnaþ** 24:49; *pt.3s.* **ongan** 16:22, 26:37, Mk1:45; **ongon** 26:74; *pt.3p.* **ongunnon** 12:1 || INCIPERE *ps.3s.* **onginneþ** Mt INCIPIT [ongin, *v.*]

onsacan *v.VI* 'deny, refuse' NEGARE *ps.1s.* **onsaece** 10:33; *ps.2s.* **onsæcest** 26:34; *ps.3s.* **onsaekeþ** 10:33; *pt.3s.* **onsoc** 26:70; **⁊soc** 26:72 [see also **andsacian**]

[MK]†**onstyde** *adv.* 'at once, immediately' STATIM **onstyde** Mk1:10 [n.]

ontynan *v.1* 'open' APERIRE *ps.1s.* **ontyno** 13:35; *pt.3s.* **ontynde** 5:2; *pt.3p.* **ontynden** 2:11; *pp.s.* **ontyned** 7:7, 7:8; *pp.p.* **ontynde** 3:16, 27:52; **ontyned** 9:30, 20:33; *imp.s.* **ontyn** 17:27, 25:11; *ps.p. map.* **ontynde** Mk1:10

onufan *adv.* 'above, upon' DESUPER ~ 21:7 [anoven, *adv.* and *prep.*]

onwreon *v.I* 'uncover, reveal' REVELARE *ps.3p.* **onwreoþ** 16:17; *pt.2s.* **onwrige** 11:25; *inf.* **onwrigan** 11:27

[MK]**openian** *v.2* 'open' PATEFACERE *pt.3p.* **openedon** Mk2:4; *ps.p. np.* **opnende** Mk2:4 [open, *v.*]

[MK]**openlice** *adv.* 'openly' part of PUBLICANUS ~ (*synnige*) Mk2:15

[openly, *adv.*]
georrettan *v.1* 'put to shame, disgrace' ADFLIGERE *pp. map.* **geonrettæ** 22:6 [n.]
orsorg *adj.* 'without care, anxiety' SECURUS *ap.* **orsorge** 28:14
oþ *prep.* USQUE (AD/IN) 'till' ~ 2:15, 10:22, 11:12 [n.], 11:13, 18:22 (*bis*), 24:13, 24:21, 24:38, 26:58, 27:64, 28:15; **oð** 11:23 (x3), 24:27, 26:29, 27:8
oþ to/þe *prep.* USQUE AD 'till' **oþ to** 1:17, 22:26, 23:35, 24:31, 26:38, 28:20; **oþ þe** 20:8
oþ þæt(te) *conj.* 'until' DONEC **oþ þæt** 1:25, 5:18, 10:11, 12:20, 13:33, 18:30; **oþ ꝥ** 14:22, 22:44, 26:36 || QUOAD USQUE **oþ þætte** 18:34 || USQUE DUM **oþ þætti** 2:9 [oth, *prep.* and *conj.*]
oþer *adj.* 'other, another' ALIUS *mns.* ~ 8:21; *mgs.* **oþres** 11:3; *mds.* **oþrum** 8:9, 25:15; ~ 2:12; *fns.* ~ 26:71; *fas.* ~ 13:24, 13:31, 13:33; **oþre** 10:23; *nas.* ~ 19:9; **oþre** 21:33; *np.* **oþere** 13:5; *ap.* **oþre** 4:21, 5:41, 12:45, 20:3, 20:6, 21:36, 22:4, 25:16, 25:17, 25:20 (*bis*), 25:22, 27:42; ~ 15:30; *dp.* **oþrum** 21:41 || UNUS *mns.* ~ 20:21, 24:40 (*bis*), 24:41, 27:38 (*bis*); **oþeru** 24:41 (or *fns.*? see note); *mas.* **oþerne** 6:24, 6:24 (margin); *fns.* **oþere** 24:41 (*bis*) || ALTER *mns.* ~ 25:22, 27:62; *mas.* **oþerne** 6:24, 6:24 (margin); *mds.* **oþrum** 21:30; *fns.* ~ 27:61, 28:1; **oþeru** 12:13; *nas.* ~ 5:39 || SECUNDUS *mns.* ~ 22:26; *mis.* **oþre** 26:42 || CETERUS *np.* **oþre** 27:49 || RELIQUUS *np.* **oþre** 25:11 || NL *mas.* **oþerne** 10:21 [n.] [other, *adj.*, *pron.*, and *n.*, and *adv.2*]
oþþe *conj.* 'or' AUT ~ 6:31 (*bis*), 7:10, 7:16, 10:11, 10:19, 10:37 (*bis*), 12:33 (*bis*), 16:14, 16:26, 19:29 (x6), 24:23, 25:37, 25:38, 25:44 (*bis*); **oþðe** 25:39 (*bis*), 25:44; **oþþa** 7:4, 7:9, 12:29; **eþþa** 5:17 [n.], 5:18; **oþþ** 12:5, 19:29; **eþa** 6:24 (margin); **þa** 6:24? [n.] || VEL ~ 5:36, 10:14, 14:36, 15:4, 15:5, 17:25, 18:8 (x3), 18:16 (*bis*), 18:20, 24:20, 24:42, 25:44; **oþþa** 12:25 || AN ~ 22:17, 23:19, 27:17; **oþþæ** 23:17; **oþðe** Mk2:9 || SED ~ 11:8 [n.], 11:9
oþþe *prep.* USQUE IN 'till' ~ 18:21, 27:45
oþþe to *prep.* USQUE AD 'till' 1:17 (*bis*), 13:30 [see also **oþ**]

parabside 26:23 Latin used as gloss? See note.
petrus *prop.n. ns.* ~ 4:18, 10:2, 14:28, 14:29, 15:15, 16:16, 16:18, 16:22, 26:35, 26:58, 26:69, 26:75, Mk1:16, Mk1:29, Mk1:30; **petre** 18:21, 26:33; *as.* ~ 26:37; *gs.* ~ 8:14; **petre** *ds.* 16:23, 17:24, 17:25, 26:40, 26:73
philippus *prop.n. ns.* ~ 10:3; *gs.* **philippes** 14:3; **filippes** 16:13
pilatus *prop.n. ns.* ~ 27:17, 27:22, 27:24, 27:65; **pilatos** 27:13; **pilatæ** 27:58; *ds.* ~ 27:58; **pylato** 27:2; **pilatu(m)** 27:62 [n.]
pipere *m.* 'piper' TUBICEN *ap.* **piperas** 9:23 [piper, *n.1*]
plegan *v.1* 'play, dance' SALTARE *pt.3s.* **pleagade** 14:6; *pt.2p.* **plagadun** 11:17 (margin) [play, *v.*]
pontisc *adj.* 'Pontius' PONTIUS *ds.* **pontiscan** 27:2
(†)**prodbor** *mn.*? 'marketplace?' FORUM *ds.* **prodbore** 11:16 [n.]; *ds.* **protbore** 20:3
pund *m.* 'pound (in money)' AS *ds.* **punde** 10:29 [n.] [pound, *n.1*]
pytt *m.* 'pit, hole' FOVEA *as.* ~ 12:11 [pit, *n.1*]

rachab *prop.n. ds.* ~ 1:5
rachel *prop.n. ns.* ~ 2:18
ræcan *v.1* 'reach, give' PORRIGERE *ps.3s.* **ræceþ** 7:9, 7:10 || 'govern, rule'? REGERE *ps.3s.* **ræccet** 2:6 (or form of *reccan* 'to rule'? see note) [reach, v.1]
geræcan *v.1* 'reach out' EXTENDERE *pt.3s.* **gerahte** Mk1:41 [see previous]

rædan *v.VII* 'read' LEGERE *subj.ps.3s.* **ręd ę** 24:15; *pt.2p.* **reordun** 21:42; **hreordun** 22:31 [see also **reordian**] [read, *v.*]

ræfnan *v.1* 'sustain' SUSTINERE *ps.3s.* **hræfneð** 6:24 (margin)

ræsan *v.1* 'rush, move violently' IMPETUS *pt.p. ds.*? **ræsed** 8:32 [rese, *v.2*]

read *adj.* 'red' RUBICUNDUS *nns.* ~ 16:2 (margin), 16:2 || COCCINEUS *nas.* **reade** 27:28 [red, *adj.* and *n.* (and *adv.*)]

readian *v.2* 'become read' RUTILARE *ps.3s.* **readaþ** 16:3 [red, *v.1*]

reccan *v.1* 'interpret' INTERPRETARI *pp.s.* **gerecht** 1:23 [rech, *v.*]

reccan *v.1* 'care for, desire' part of NEGLEGERE (with negative) *pt.3p.* **rohtun** 22:5 [reck, *v.*]

recels *n.* 'incense, frankincense' TUS *as.* **recils** 2:11 [rechels, *n.*]

[MK]**recene** *adv.* 'immediately' PROTINUS **recene** Mk1:29 [rekene, *adv.*]

[MK]**recenlice** *adv.* 'immediately' CONTINUO **ricenlice** Mk1:31 || PROTINUS **ricenlice** Mk1:18 [rekenly, *adv.*]

refa *m. wk* 'high official, reeve' referring to PILATUS *ns.* **roefa** 27:23 (PRAESES in WW) [reeve, *n.1*]

gerefa *m. wk* 'high official, reeve' PRAESES *ns.* **geroefa** 27:11, 27:14, 27:21; **geroefæ** 27:15; *gs.* **geroefe** 27:27; *ds.* **geroefe** 28:14; **geroefæ** 27:2; **gehreofa** 27:11; *dp.* **geroefum** 10:18 || PROCURATOR *ds.* **gereofa** 20:8 [OED2 gerefa, *n.*]

regn *m.* 'rain' PLUVIA *ns.* **rægn** 7:25, 7:27 [rain, *n.1*]

regnan *v.1* 'rain' PLUERE *ps.3s.* **regneþ** 5:45 [rain, *v.*]

reord *n.* (or *f.*?) 'speech, language' LOQUELLA *ns.* ~ 26:73 [reird, *n.*]

gereord *f.* 'food, sustenance' part pf RECUMBERE *dp.* **gereordum** 26:7

reordian *v.2* 'read' LEGERE *ps.2p.* **hreordeþ** 12:3 [n.]; *ps.2p.* **reordaþ** 12:5; *pt.2p.* **reordade** 19:4; **reordadun** 21:16 [see also **rædan**] [cf. reird, *v.* 'to speak, discourse']

gereordian *v.2* 'feed, refresh' REFICERE *ps.1s.* **gereorde** 11:28 || SATURARE *subj.ps.1p.* **gehreorde** 15:33

rest *f.* 'rest, repose' REQUIES *as.* **ræste** 11:29; **reste** 12:43 [rest, *n.1*]

restan *v.1* 'rest, repose' REQUIESCERE *ps.3p.* **restaþ** 8:20; *imp.p.* **restęþ** 26:45 [rest, *v.1*]

[MK]**gerestan** *v.1* 'rest, recline' DISCUMBERE *pt.3p.* **gereston** Mk2:15

restdæg *m.* 'Sabbath day' SABBATUM *gs.* **restedagas** 28:1; *ds.* **ræstedæge** 12:1, 12:5, 24:20; **restedæg** 28:1; *ap.* **restedagas** Mk1:21; *dp.* **restedagum** 12:2, 12:10, 12:12; **restedægum** 12:5, 12:11 [see previous]

gerestdæg *m.* 'Sabbath day' SABBATUM *gs.* **gerestedæges** 12:8 [cf. rest day, *n.*]

rice *n.* 'kingdom' REGNUM *ns.* ~ 3:2, 4:17, 5:3, 5:10, 6:10, 10:7, 11:12, 12:25, 12:26, 12:28, 13:24, 13:31, 13:33, 13:44, 13:45, 13:47, 18:23, 19:14, 20:1, 22:2, 21:43, 24:7, 25:1, Mk1:15; *as.* ~ 4:23 [n.], 6:33, 7:21 (*bis*), 18:3, 19:23, 19:24, 23:13, 24:7, 25:34; *gs.* ~ 8:12, 13:11, Mk1:14; **rices** 9:35, 13:19, 13:38, 16:19, 24:14; *ds.* ~ 5:19 (*bis*), 5:20, 8:11, 11:11, 13:41, 13:43, 13:52, 16:28, 18:1, 18:4, 19:12, 20:21, 21:31, 26:29; *ap.* ~ 4:8 (or singular?) [riche, n.]

ricsian *v.2* 'govern, rule, reign' REGNARE *pt.3s.* **ricsade** 2:22

[MK]**ridesoht** *f.* 'fever, fever-illness?' FEBRIS *ds.* **rideohte** Mk1:31 [n.]

rift *n.* 'cloak veil' CHLAMYS *as.* **ryfte** 27:28 [n.]; *is.* **ryhte** 27:31 [n.] || PALLIUM *as.* **hryft** 5:40 [n.] [rift, *n.1*]

riftre *m.* 'reaper' MESSOR *np.* **riftra** 13:39; *dp.* **riftrum** 13:30

riht *n.* 'account, reckoning, what is right' RATIO *as.* **reht** 12:36; *gs.* **rehtæs** 25:19 [right, *n.*]

riht *adj.* 'straight, just' RECTUS *map.* **rihte** 3:3; **rehte** Mk1:3 || IUSTUS *nns.* **reht** 20:4 [right, *adj.* and *int.*]
geriht *n.* 'what is due, right' RATIO *gs.* **gerihtes** 18:23, 18:24
geriman *v.1* 'count, number' NUMERARE *pp.p.* **gerimde** 10:30 [cf. rime, *v.1*]
rip *n.* 'reaping, harvest' MESSIS *ns.* ~ 9:37; *gs.* **ripes** 13:30; **hripes** 9:38; *ds.* **ripe** 13:30; **ripae** 9:38; *np.* ~ 13:39 [ripe, *n.1*]
ripan *v.I* 'reap' METERE *ps.1s.* **ripe** 25:26; *ps.2s.* **ripes** 25:24; *ps.3p.* **ripath** 6:26 || VELLERE *inf.* **hriopan** 12:1 [reap, *v.1*]
risan *v.I* 'rise' SURGERE *pt.3s.* **ras** 27:64 [rise, *v.*]
risan *v.I* 'seize' RAPAX *ps.p. mnp.* **risænde** 7:15 [n.]
gerisan *v.I* 'seize, take' RAPERE *ps.3s.* **geriseð** 13:19; *ps.3p.* **gerisaþ** 11:12
gerisan *v.I* 'behove, befit' OPORTERE *pt.3s.* **geras** 25:27 [OED2 i-rise, v.]
rocettan *v.1* 'eructate, belch forth' ERUCTARE *ps.1s.* **roketto** 13:35 [n.]
rod *f.* 'rood, cross' CRUX *as.* **rode** 10:38, 16:24, 27:32; *ds.* **rode** 27:40, 27:42 || part of CRUCIFIGERE *ds.* **rode** 27:22, 27:23, 27:26 [rood, *n.*]
rum *adj.* 'spacious' SPATIOSUS *mns.* ~ 7:13 [room, *adj.* (and *n.2*)]
ruð *prop.n. ds.* ~ 1:5
ruxlende, see **hruxlian**
geryne *n.* 'mystery' MYSTERIA *ap.* ~ 13:11

sacerd *m.* 'priest' SACERDOS *np.* **sacerdes** 12:5; *dp.* **sacerdum** 12:4
sadduceas *m. pl.* 'Sadducee' SADDUCAEUS *np.* ~ 16:1; **saduceas** 22:23; *gp.* **saducea** 3:7, 16:11; **sadducea** 16:6, 16:12; *dp.* ~ 22:34
salomon *prop.n. ns.* ~ 6:29; **salomonn** 12:42; **salomones** *gs.* 12:42
samaring *m.* 'the Samaritans' SAMARITANUS *gp.* **samaringa** 10:5
samnian *v.2* 'gather' CONGREGARE *ps.1s.* **somnige** 25:26; *ps.2s.* **somnast** 25:24; *ps.3s.* **somnaþ** 12:30 [n.], 23:37; *ps.3p.* **somniaþ** 6:26; **somnigað** 24:28; *pt.3p.* **somnadun** 22:10; *ps.p. nds.* **somnendum** 13:47 || COLLIGERE *ps.3p.* **somnigaþ** 7:16 [OED2 sam, *v.1*]
gesamnian *v.2* 'gather' CONGREGARE *ps.3s.* **gesomnaþ** 3:12; *ps.3p.* **gesomnaþ** 24:31; *pt.3s.* **gesomnade** 2:4, 28:12(?); *pt.3p.* **gesomnadun** 13:2, 22:34, 27:17, 27:27; **gesomnade** 18:20; *imp.p.* **gesomnigaþ** 13:30; *pp.s.* **gesomnad** Mk1:33; *pp.p.* **gesomnede** 25:32; **gesomnade** 22:41, 26:3; *inf.* **gesomnian** 23:37 || COLLIGERE *subj.ps.1p.* **gesomnige** 13:28; *pp.p.* **gesomnad** 13:40; *imp.p.* **gesomnigæþ** 13:30; *ps. p. mnp.* **gesomnende** 13:29 || CONVENIRE *pt.3p.* **gesomnadun** Mk1:45; *pp.p.* **gesomnade** 26:57 [see previous]
samnung *f.* 'union, congregation' SYNAGOGA *as.* **somnunge** 12:9; *ds.* **somnunge** 23:34 [n.]; **somnunga** Mk1:29; *dp.* **somnungum** 4:23, 6:2, 23:6, Mk1:21, Mk1:23, Mk1:39 [OED2 samening, *n.*]
gesamnung *f.* 'union, congregation' SYNAGOGA *ds.* **gesomnunge** 10:17; *dp.* **gesomnungum** 6:5, 9:35, 13:54 [see previous]
samod *adv.* 'simultaneously, together' SIMUL **somed** 13:29 [OED2 samed, *adv.*]
sand *n.* 'sand' ARENA *ds.* **sonde** 7:26 [OED2 sand, *n.2*]
sar *n.* 'pain, sickness' DOLOR *gs.* **sares** 24:8 [OED2 sore, *n.1*]
sawan *v.VII* 'sow' SEMINARE *ps.3s.* **sauweþ** 13:37; *pt.1s.* **seow** 25:26; *pt.2s.* **sewe** 25:24; *pt.3s.* **seow** 13:4, 13:24, 13:31, 13:39; *infl.inf.* **sawenne** 13:3; *pp.s.* **sawen** 13:19 (*bis*) || SERERE *ps.3p.* **saweð** 6:26 [OED2 sow, *v.1*]
gesawan *v.VII* 'sow' SEMINARE *pt.2s.* **geseowe** 13:27; *pp.s.* **gesauwen**

13:20, 13:22, 13:23 [see previous]
sawend *m.* 'sower' SEMINARE *ns.* ~ 13:3; *gs.* **sawendes** 13:18
sawol *f.* 'soul, life' ANIMA *ns.* ~ 26:38; *as.* **saule** 10:28 (*bis*), 10:39; *ds.* **saule** 12:18, 22:37; *dp.* **saulum** 11:29 [soul, *n.*]
sæ *m.* 'sea' MARIS *gs.* **saes** 4:15; **seæs** 18:6; *as.* ~ 23:15, 21:21 (or. *a.*?), Mk1:16; **sææ** 14:25; **sae** 14:26; *ds.* ~ 8:24, 16:5 (or *a.*?), 17:27, Mk1:16, Mk2:13; **sae** 4:18, 4:19, 8:26, 8:32, 13:47, 14:22, 14:24, 15:29; **sææ** 13:1; *np.* **sae** 8:27 (or *s.*?) || FRETUM *as.* **sae** 8:18, 8:28 || NL (part of TRANSFRETARE) *as.* **sææ** 9:1 [OED2 sea, *n.*]
sæceaster *f.* 'a maritime town' MARITIMUS *ds.* **sæcaestrae** 4:13 [n.]
sæd *n.* 'seed' SEMEN *ns.* **seęd** 13:38; *as.* **sed** 13:24, 13:27, 13:37, 22:24, 22:25; *gp.* **seda** 13:32 [seed, *n.*]
sæl *m.* or *f.* 'time, opportunity' OPPORTUNITAS *as.* **sel** 26:16 [OED2 sele, *n.*]
gesælan *v.1* 'bind, tie' ALLIGARE *pp. fas.* **gesælde** 21:2
scarioth *prop.n.* *ns.* ~ 26:14; *gs.* **scariothes** 10:4
scead *n.* 'shade, shadow' UMBRA *ds.* **scade** 4:16 [OED2 shade, *n.*]
sceadan *v.VII* 'divide, separate' SEPARARE *subj.ps.3s.* **sceade** 19:6; *infl.inf.* **sceadenne** 10:35 [shed, *v.1*]
gesceadan *v.VII* 'divide, separate' SEPARARE *ps.3s.* **gesceadiþ** 25:32 [see previous]
sceaf *m.* 'sheaf, bundle' FASCICULUS *dp.* **sceafum** 13:30 [OED2 sheaf, *n.1*]
sceap *n.* 'sheep' OVIS *ns.* **scep** 12:12; *as.* **scep** 12:11; *np.* **scep** 9:36, 26:31; *ap.* **scep** 10:16, 25:32; **scæp** 25:33; *gp.* **scepa** 7:15; **scipa** 18:12; *dp.* **sciopum** 10:6; **scepum** 15:24 [sheep, *n.*]
sceatt *m.* 'price' NL *as.* (*in*) **sceat** (*alecgan*) (DESPONSARE) 'betroth' 1:18 [n.] [OED2 sceat, *n.*]
sceaþa *m.* *wk* 'thief' LATRO *ds.* **scaþe** 26:55; *np.* **scaþe** 27:38; *gp.* **sceaþena** 21:13 [OED2 scathe, *n.*]
sceawian *v.2* 'look, gaze' CONSIDERARE *imp.p.* **sceawigaþ** 6:28 || VIDERE *infl.inf.* **sceawenne** 28:1 [show, *v.*]
gesceawian *v.2* 'look, gaze' VIDERE *ps.3p.* **gescawað** 5:8 [see previous]
scilling *m.* 'shilling'; ARGENTEUS *ap.* **scillingas** 27:5, 27:6; *gp.* **scillinga** 26:15, 27:9; **scyllinga** 27:3 || STATER *as.* ~ 17:27 [OED2 shilling, *n.*]
scinan *v.I* 'shine' FULGERE *ps.3p.* **scinaþ** 13:43 [n.]; RESPLENDERE *pt.3s.* **scan** 17:2 [OED2 shine, *v.*]
scinnlac *n.* 'magic, phantom' PHANTASMA *ns.* **scinlac** 14:26
scip *n.* 'ship' NAVICULA *ns.* ~ 8:24, 14:24; *as.* ~ 14:32; *ds.* **scipe** 8:23, 9:1, 13:2, 14:13, 14:22, 14:29, 14:33, 15:39 || NAVIS *ds.* **scipe** 4:21, Mk1:20; **scip** Mk1:19 [OED2 ship, *n.1*]
scoh *m.* 'shoe' CALCIAMENTUM *ap.* **scoas** 3:11, 10:10 [OED2 shoe, *n.*]
[MK]**gescoh** *m.* 'shoe' CALCIAMENTUM *ap.* **gescoas** Mk1:7 (or *g.*?) [see previous]
scort *adj.* 'short' part of BREVIARE *mnp.* **scorte** 24:22 [short, *adj.*, *n.*, and *adv.*]
gescræf *n.* 'hole, cave, den' SPELUNCA *ds.* **gescræfe** 21:13
scua *m.* 'shade, shadow' UMBRA *ds.* **scua** 4:16
sculan *pret.pres.v.* 'owe, shall, must' OPORTERE **sceal** 26:54; *ps.3p.* **sculon** 24:6; *pt.3s.* **scylde** 16:21; *subj.ps.1s.* **scyle** 26:35; *subj.ps.3.* **scyle** 17:10; || DEBERE *ps.1s.* **sceal** 3:14; *ps.2s.* **scealt** 18:28; *pt.3s.* **scalde** 18:24; **sculde** 18:28 || DECERE *ps.1p.* **sculon** 3:15 || part of NELLE *subj.ps.2p.* **scule** 6:7, 6:8; **sculon** 10:9 || NL *ps.3s.* **scalt** 11:3 [n.]; **scal** 11:14; *ps.2p.* **sculon** 23:10; *pt.3p.* **sculdon** 12:14, 20:10; *pt.3s.* **salde** 27:31 [shall, *v.*]
scyan *v.1* 'pursuade, prompt'

SUADERE *ps.1p.* **scyaþ** 28:14 [n.]

scyld *f.* 'sin, guilt, debt' DEBITUM *np.* **scylde** 18:25; *ap.* **scylde** 6:12, 18:32, 18:34; **scyld** 18:27, 18:30; || DELICTUM *ap.* **scyldæ** 6:14

scyldig *adj.* 'guilty' REUS *mns.* ~ 5:21 (*bis*), 5:22 (x3), 26:66 || DEBITOR *mns.* ~ 23:18; **scyldyg** 23:16 [OED2 shildy, *adj.*]

scyldigian *v.2* 'sin' DEBITOR *ps.3p.* **scyldigat** 6:12 [n.]

scyndan *v.1* 'hasten, shorten' BREVIARE *pp.p.* **scynde** 24:22 (*bis*)

scyte *f. wk* 'sheet, line cloth' SINDON *ds.* **scetan** 27:59 [shute, *n.1*]

se *dem.pron.* 'the, this, the same' Latin equivalents: HIC, ILLE, IPSE, IS, ISTE QUI, SUUS

Forms (citations are given only for relatively infrequent forms; instances that do not translate the Latin equivalents listed above are presented separately below): *mns.* **se**; *mas.* **þone, þæne** 7:13 [n.], 26:29, **þonne** 17:2, **þane** 7:14, 21:38, **þanne** 13:46 [n.]; *mgs.* **þæs, ðæs, þas** 26:27; *mds.* **þæm**; *nnas.* **þæt, ꝥ**; *ngs.* **þæs, ðæs**; *nds.* **þæm, ðæm, þęm, ðære** ?17:18 margin [n.]; *nis.* **þon** 23:14, **ðy**; *fns.* **seo, se, sio, siu, sie**; *fas.* **þa**; *fgs.* **þare, þara, þære**; *fds.* **þære, ðæm** 15:28; *nap.* **þa, ða**; *gp.* **þara**; *dp.* **þæm, ðæm**

NL *mns.* **se** 1:24, … 11:12 [n.], … 12:29 [n.], 27:17 (*a.* is expected), etc.; *mgs.* **þæs** 2:1, etc.; **ðæs** 1:1, 2:9; **þas** 2:20, 9:23, 13:27, 14:32; *mas.* **þone** 1:6, etc.; **þene** 25:30; **ðene** 20:22; **ðane** 21:33; **þæne** 21:39, 25:28; **þon** 27:66; **se** 26:4; *mds.* **þæm** 1:18 etc.; **þęm** 17:13; **ðæm** 3:11, 20:30, 21:33, Mk1:25, Mk1:44; **ðem** 2:8; **thæm** 7:9; *fns.* **seo** 5:30, 13:2; **se** 6:3 [n.], 25:10, 27:61; **sio** 6:3, 8:15, 16:4, 20:31, 21:8; **siu** 8:32, 9:25, 12:13, 27:56; **sie** 21:10; **þæt** 21:34 [n.]; *fas.* **þa** 2:7, 4:5, 8:12, 13:36, 14:1, 14:19, 20:21 (*bis*), 20:23 (*bis*), 22:44, 24:38, 25:13, 25:33 (*bis*), 25:34, 26:64, 27:29, 27:38 (*bis*), 27:53, 27:54, 27:64, 27:66, 28:1, 28:6, Mk2:4 (*bis*), Jn18:2; **ða** 23:19, Mk1:31, Mk1:45; **þah** Jn18:1; *fgs.* **þare** 1:1, 5:31; **þara** 14:6, 14:35, 23:23, 24:15, 26:28; **þære** 27:60; *fds.* **þęre** 2:23; **þære** 2:16, etc.; **þara** 14:23 [n.], 21:17, 21:43, 24:36, 27:61; **þæm** 20:5 (*bis*) [n.], 25:41; *nns.* **þæt** 3:5, 5:41, 6:23, 7:18, 9:24, 10:13, 12:7, 14:26, 26:39, 26:59; **ꝥ** 2:11, etc.; *nas.* **þæt** 5:24, 5:39, 8:4, 9:17, 12:20, 13:22, 13:27, 14:35, 19:22 [n.], 25:30, 26:25, 26:44, 27:58; **ðæt** 5:39; **ꝥ** 2:3, etc.; *ngs.* **þæs** 5:28, 9:38, 21:23, 21:34, 22:19, 23:16, 24:1, 26:3, 26:31, 26:47, 27:1, 27:3, 27:9, 27:51; *nds.* **þæm** 3:7, 3:16, 4:23, 8:10 [n.], 9:16, 10:14, 14:11, 14:29, 14:33, 15:36, 21:12, 21:14, 21:15, 22:39, 26:5, 27:15, 27:20, 27:24 (*bis*), 28:15; **ðæm** 7:2 (x3); **þęm** Mk1:28; *nis.* **þon** 4:2, 16:27; **ðy** 27:31; *np.* **þa** 5:3, etc.; **ða** 21:20, 25:3, 26:17, 28:16, Mk1:5; *ap.* **þa** 2:16, etc.; **ða** 15:31 (x3), 24:31, Mk1:38; *gp.* **þara** 4:15, 9:3, 10:2, 14:20, 14:21, 15:2, 15:37, 15:39, 16:9, 16:10 (margin), 16:14, 21:12, 22:28, 25:19, 26:14, 26:17, 27:21, 28:11; **ðara** 18:12; **þæræ** 16:28; **þære** 21:31, 26:47; *dp.* **þæm** 2:16 (*bis*), etc.; **þon** 19:5 [n.]; **þa** 21:12 [n.], 28:11 [n.]

þon in **ær þon, æfter þon** see under **ær, æfter** [the, *adj.*, *pron.2*, and *n.1*]

se *rel.pron.* 'who' QUI (sometimes with a preceding pronoun) (w. **þe**) *mns.* **se þe** 1:16, etc.; *mas.* **þone þe** 21:44, 26:36, 27:17, 28:5; **þane þe** 4:18; **þæne þe** 6:1; **þene þe** 27:15; *mgs.* **þæs þe** 7:21, 18:10, 23:35; *mds.* **þæm þe** 7:26, 11:10, 13:52, 18:14, 18:19, 18:23, 22:2, 25:28, 27:22, 28:1; **ðæm þe** 11:27, 13:24; **ðæm ðe** 20:1, 23:21; **þæm thi** 21:42; *nns.* **þætte** 4:16, 6:23, 13:35, 18:12, 21:4; **ꝥte** 9:20, 10:20 [n.], 13:19, 15:11 (*bis*), 15:37, 23:17, 23:19, 23:26, 25:34,

25:41, 26:13, 27:60 (referring to *f.* noun); **þ þe** 23:35, 28:11; **þ ðe** 18:31; *nas.* **þætte** 8:4, 18:25; (L. *quod* 'that which') **þætte** 1:20; 2:17, 5:37, 10:27, 20:4, 20:14; **þæt þe** 25:27; **þte** 2:15, 18:11, 19:6, 23:25, 23:26, 25:25, 27:9; *ngs.* **þæs þe** 15:17, 27:9; *nds.* **þæm þe** 4:4, 5:13 [n.], 5:40; **ðæm þe** 6:18; **þæm ðe** 10:33; *fas.* **þa þe** 15:13; *fds.* **ðære þe** Mk2:4; *np.* **þa þe** 2:16, 4:24, 5:6 [n.], 5:10, 6:5, 7:13, 7:14, 7:15, 11:8, 12:3, 14:33, 15:18, 15:20, 15:38, 16:28, 17:24, 18:31, 19:12 (x3), 20:9, 20:25, 21:9 (*bis*), 22:8, 22:21, 22:23, 23:27, 24:16, 25:10, 25:41, 26:52, 26:73, 27:54, 27:55, Mk1:34, Mk1:36; *ap.* **þa þe** 5:46 [n.], 12:4, 13:17, 13:17 (margin), 13:35, 23:23, 23:37, Mk1:44; *gp.* **þara þe** 3:10, 5:12, 5:28, 5:32, 7:21, 7:24, 10:32, 12:36, 13:19, 26:51; **þære ðe** 27:52; *dp.* **þæm þe** 5:44, 9:36, 11:16, 15:24, 21:41, 25:34, 26:62; **þæm ðe** 23:20; **ðæm þe** 14:9, 19:11; **ðæm ðe** 11:20; **ðęm ðe** 20:23 || QUOTQUOT *np.* **þa þe** 22:10 (QUOS in WW) || NL *mns.* **se þe** 5:42 [n.]; *mds.* **þæm ðe** 5:42 [n.]; *mdp.* **þæm þe** 6:12, 7:11

(w.o. **þe**) *mns.* **se** 10:20, 11:10, 16:23, 27:16, 27:57 (*bis*); *mas.* **þone** 24:46 [n.]; **þonne** 13:33; **þęne** 24:45; *mgs.* **þæs** 2:7 (or adverbial 'as'?), 3:12; **ðæs** Mk1:7; *mds.* **þæm** 12:18, 13:44 (or *neut.*), 27:32, Jn18:1; **ðæm** 3:17, 17:5; *fds.* **þære** 1:16; *nns.* **þ** 1:23, 8:17, 12:17, 25:29[1], 27:8; *nns.* **þæt** 1:22; 2:23, 4:14, 6:30, 10:26 (*bis*), 12:2, 13:32, 13:46, 26:28, 26:68 (*m.* is expected), 27:33; *nas.* **þ** 1:20, 10:27, 11:4 (*bis*), 13:44, 21:24; **þæt** 13:12, 13:31, 15:32, 18:28, 19:21, 20:15, 22:31; *nis.* **þon** Mk2:8; *np.* **þa** 2:9 (or *adv.*?), 11:23, 25:1, Mk2:13?; *gp.* **þara** 5:22, 7:19 [n.]; *dp.* **þæm** 27:56 [see previous]

sealt *n.* 'salt' SAL *ns.* **salt** 5:13 (*bis*) [OED2 salt, *n.1*]

sealtan *v.VII* 'salt' SALIRE *pp.s.* **salten** 5:13 [OED2 salt, *v.1*]

seaþ *m.* 'hole, pit' FOVEA *as.* ~ 12:11, 15:14 [OED2 seath, *n.*]

secan *v.1* 'seek' QUAERERE *ps.3s.* **soeceþ** 7:8, 16:4; **soecaþ** 2:13; **soecet** 12:39; *ps.3p.* **soecaþ** Mk1:37; *pt.3s.* **sohte** 13:45 [n.]; *pt.3p.* **sohtun** 2:20, 26:59; *imp.p.* **soecaþ** 6:33, 7:7; *inf.* **soece** 18:12; *ps.p. mns.* **soecende** 12:43; *mnp.* **soecende** 12:46, 12:47, 21:46 || INQUIRERE *ps.3p.* **soeceþ** 6:32 || DICERE *ps.p. mds.* **soecende** 12:48 [n.] [OED2 seek, *v.*]

gesecan *v.1* 'seek' QUAERERE *ps.2p.* **gesoecaþ** 28:5; *pt.3s.* **gesohte** 26:16 [see previous]

secgan *v.3* 'say' DICERE *ps.1s.* **sæcge** 2:13, etc.; **sæcga** 5:26; **sęcge** 24:47; **secge** 19:28; **sægce** 23:3; *ps.2s.* **sægest** 26:70; *ps.2p.* **sæcgaþ** 17:9 (or *imp.*?), 21:24; *ps.3p.* **sæcgaþ** 21:16, 23:3; **sægcaþ** 27:13; **sæcgað** 27:64; *pt.3s.* **sægde** 14:4, 17:13, 21:11, 21:45; *pt.3p.* **sægdun** 16:20; *subj.ps.2s.* **sæcge** 8:4, 26:63, Mk1:44; *subj.ps.3s.* **sæcge** 24:23; *subj.ps.3p.* **sæcge** 24:26; *imp.s.* **sæcge** 18:17, 19:18 (or *subj.*?); **sæg** 22:17; **sæge** 24:3; *imp.p.* **sęcgaþ** 11:3; **sæcgaþ** 21:3, 21:5, 21:24, 28:7, 28:13; **sæcgað** 22:4 || (AD)NUNTIARE *ps.3s.* **sægeþ** 12:18; *pt.3p.* **sægdun** 8:33, 14:12, 28:11; **sægdon** 18:31; *imp.p.* **sæcgaþ** 28:10; *inf.* ~ 28:8 || RENUNTIARE 'report' *imp.p.* **sæcgað** 2:8; **sæcgaþ** 11:4 || EVANGELIZARE *ps.3p.* (*godspell*) **secgaþ** 11:5 || NARRARE *pp.s.* **sægd** 26:13 || PROPONERE *pt.3s.* **sægde** 13:31 [say, *v.1* and *int.*]

gesecgan *v.3* 'say, relate' PONERE (PROPONERE in WW) *pt.3s.* **gesægde** 13:24 [n.] [see previous]

(†)**selescot** *n.* 'tabernacle, dwelling' TABERNACULUM *ap.* **selescota** 8:20 [n.]; **selescotu** 17:4

self *pron.* 'self' IPSE *mns.* (*he*) **selfe** 1:21; **sylf** 3:4, Jn18:1; **sylfe** 12:48;

selfa 6:34; *mas.* **seolfne** 19:19, 22:39, 27:40; **selfne** 27:42; *np.* **sylfe** 23:3; *dp.* **sylfum** 19:12; **seolfum** 23:31 || part of SE *mds.* (*him*) **seolfum** 12:26, 16:24; *nds.* (*him*) **seolfum** 12:25 (*bis*) [self, *pron.*, *adj.*, *n.*, and *adv.*]

sellan *v.1* 'give' DARE *ps.1s.* **selle** 4:9, 16:19 (*bis*) [n.], 20:4; *ps.3s.* **selleþ** 7:11, 25:29 [n.]; **seleþ** 10:42, 16:26, 24:29; *ps.3p.* **sellaþ** 24:24; *pt.3s.* **salde** 10:1, 14:11, 14:19, 15:36, 21:23, 25:15, 26:26, 26:27, 26:48, 27:48; *pt.1p.* **saldun** 25:37; *pt.2p.* **saldun** 25:35, 25:42 (*bis*); **salden** 25:35; *pt.3p.* **saldun** 13:8, 15:36, 27:10, 27:34, 28:12; *subj.ps.3s.* **selle** 5:31, 24:45; *subj.pt.3s.* **salde** 14:7, 19:7, 20:28; *imp.s.* **sel** 6:11; **selle** 14:8, 17:27, 19:21; *imp.p.* **sellaþ** 25:8; **sellað** 7:6, 25:28; **sella** 14:16; *inf.* ~ 7:11, 14:9, 20:14, 26:15; *infl.inf.* **sellanne** 20:23; **sellane** 22:17; **sellan** 20:15; *pp.s.* **sald** 7:7, 10:19, 12:39, 13:11 (bis), 13:12, 14:11, 16:4, 19:11, 26:9; **salde** 21:43 || TRADERE *ps.1s.* ~ 26:15 [n.]; *ps.3s.* **selleþ** 10:19; **sellað** 5:25, 26:46; **sellaþ** 10:21, 26:23; *ps.3p.* **sellaþ** 10:17, 20:19, 24:9, 24:10; *pt.2s.* **saldest** 25:20, 25:22; *pt.3s.* **salde** 10:4, 18:34, 25:14, 26:48, 27:3, 27:26; *pt.3p.* **saldun** 27:2, 27:18; *subj.ps.3s.* **selle** 5:25; *subj.pt.3s.* **salde**; *subj.pt.3p.* **salden** 27:1; **salde** 26:59; *inf.* (*to deaþe*) ~ Jn18:2; *pp.s.* **sald** 17:22, 20:18, 26:2, 26:24, 26:45; *pp.p.* **sald** 11:27; *ps.p. mns.* **sellende** 26:21, 26:25, 27:4; **sellend** 26:48; *np.* **sellende** 24:38 || IURARE (~ *aþ*) *ps.3s.* **sellaþ** 23:18; **selð** 23:20; *ps.2p.* **sellaþ** 5:34; *subj.ps.2s.* **selle** 5:36 || VENDERE 'sell' *ps.3s.* **sellaþ** 13:44; *pt.3s.* **salde** 13:46; *imp.s.* **sylle** 19:21; *ps.p. map.* **sellende** 21:12; *dp.* **sellendum** 21:12 [n.] || EXHIBERE *subj.ps.3s.* **selle** 26:53 || PRAEBERE *imp.s.* **sel** 5:39 || TRIBUERE *imp.s.* **sele** 5:42 (DARE in WW) [OED2 sell, *v.*]

gesellan *v.1* 'give' DARE *pt.3s.* **gesalde** 9:8; *imp.p.* **gesellaþ** 10:8; *pp.s.* **gesald** 28:18 || TRADERE *pp.s.* **gesald** Mk1:14 [see previous]

sendan *v.1* 'send' MITTERE *ps.1s.* **sende** 10:16, 11:10, Mk1:2; *ps.3s.* **sendeþ** 13:41, 13:42, 24:31; *ps.3p.* **sendaþ** 13:50; *pt.1s.* **sende** 23:34; *pt.2s.* **sendest** 25:27; *pt.3s.* **sende** 10:5, 10:40, 14:10, 18:30, 20:2, 21:1, 21:34, 21:36, 21:37, 22:3, 22:4, 22:7, 27:19; *pt.3p.* **sendun** 13:48, 14:35; **sendon** 22:16; *subj.ps.3s.* **sende** 9:38; *imp.s.* **send** 4:4, 8:31, 17:27; *imp.p.* **sendeþ** 22:13; *inf.* **sende** 27:6; *infl.inf.* **sendanne** 10:34 (*bis*); *pp.s.* **sended** 3:10, 5:25, 5:29, 6:30, 7:19, 18:8; *pp.p.* **sende** 23:37; *ps.p. mns.* **sendende** 2:8, 2:16; *nns.* **sendendu** 26:12 [n.]; *np.* **sendende** 27:35; *ap.* **sendende** Mk1:16 || SUBMITTERE *pt.3p.* (*adune*) **sendun** Mk2:4 [OED2 send, v.1]

gesendan *v.1* 'send' MITTERE *pt.3s.* **gesende** 11:2; *pp.s.* **gesended** 18:9 [n.] [OED2 i-send, *v.*]

senep *m.* 'mustard' SINAPIS *gs.* **senepes** 17:20; **sinapes** 13:31 [n.]

seofon *num.* 'seven' SEPTEM *n.* **siofun** 15:38, 22:25; *a.* **siofun** 12:45, 15:37, 16:10 (margin); **seofun** 15:34, 15:36; *g.* **seofuna** 22:28 || SEPTIES *d.* **seofun** 18:21, 18:22 [seven, *adj.* and *n.*]

seofoþa *ord. num.* 'seventh' SEPTIMUS *mds.* **siofund** 22:26 [seventh, *adj.*, *adv.*, and *n.*]

seolfor *n.* 'silver' ARGENTUM *as.* **sylfur** 10:9 [silver, *n.* and *adj.*]

seon *v.V* 'see, perceive' VIDERE *ps.2s.* **sis** 7:3; *ps.2p.* **seoþ** 13:17; *pt.3s.* **sæh** 21:19; *pt.1p.* **segun** 25:39; *pt.3p.* **segun** 11:4, 17:8; **segon** 15:31; *infl.inf.* **seenne** 11:9

sihþe *interj.* ECCE 'lo, look' 1:23, 2:9, 7:4, 19:16, 19:27, 23:38, 24:23, 24:25, 24:26, 25:22 (cf. BTS *seon* III. *add.*); see also **geseon** [see, *v.*]

geseon *v.V* 'see, perceive' VIDERE

ps.2s. **geseçs** 7:3; **gesihst** 7:5; (w. contracted subject) **gesihstu** 7:3; *ps3s.* **gesihþ** 5:28; **gesihð** 6:6 (margin); **gesið** 6:4; **geseoþ** 6:18; *ps.2p.* **geseaþ** 13:14; **geseoþ** 13:14, 23:39, 24:2, 24:15, 24:33, 26:64, 28:7; *ps.3p.* **geseoþ** 5:8, 13:13, 28:10; **geseoð** 13:16, 18:10; **geseeþ** 11:5; **geseaþ** 24:30; *pt.3s.* **gesæg** 3:16; **gesægh** 4:21; **gesæh** 3:7, 4:18, 8:14, 9:9, 9:23, 12:22, 14:14, 20:3, 22:11, 26:71, 27:24, Mk1:16, Mk1:19, Mk2:5, Mk2:14; **geseah** 2:16, 4:16, 9:22, 9:36, 14:30, 27:3; **geseh** Mk1:10; *pt.1p.* **gesegon** 2:2; **gesagun** 25:37, 25:44, 25:38; *pt.2p.* **gesegon** 21:32; *pt.3p.* **gesægon** 2:9, 15:31, 26:8; **gesægun** 27:55; **gesegon** 9:8, 9:11, 13:17, 21:15, 21:20; **gesegun** 14:26, 21:38, 27:54, Mk2:12 (or *1p.*?, see note); **gesęgun** 20:34; **gesęgon** 12:2; *subj.ps.3p.* ~ 5:16, 13:17 [n.]; **geseo** 13:15, 16:28; *subj.pt.3s.* **gesæge** 22:11, 26:58; *imp.s.* **gesech** 8:4; **gesih** Mk1:44; *imp.p.* **geseaeþ** 9:30, 24:4, 24:6; **geseoþ** 28:6; *inf.* ~ 12:38, 27:49; *infl.inf.* **geseene** 11:7; **geseonne** 11:8; *pps.s.* **gesene** 6:18; *pp.p.* **geseanę** 6:1; **gesęnæ** 6:5; **gesænę** 23:5; *ps.p. mns.* **geseende** 5:1, 9:2, 9:4; **geseonde** 8:18; *ns.* (gender not clear) **geseende** 8:34; *np.* **geseende** 13:13, 13:14; **geseænde** 2:10 [n.]; **geseonde** 18:31; **geseonde** 28:17 || PARERE *pp.p.* **geseanae** 6:16 || RESPICERE *imp.p.* **geseoþ** 6:26 [ysee, *v.*]

set *n.* 'setting (of the sun)' OCCASIO ~ 23:14 [n.] || part of OCCIDERE *ds.* **sete** Mk1:32 [OED2 set, *n.1*]

seten *f.* 'plantation' part of PLANTATIO *ns.* (*wæstma*) ~ 15:13 [n.]

setl *n.* 'seat, throne' CATHEDRA *ap.* **settlas** 21:12; **setulas** 23:6 [n.]; *ds.* **setule** 23:2 || SEDES *ds.* **sedle** 19:28, 25:31; *dp.* **sedlum** 19:28 || THRONUS *ns.* **seþel** 5:34; *ds.* **sedle** 23:22 || RECUBITUS *as.* **sætil** 23:6 [OED2 settle, *n.1*]

setnes *f.* 'foundation, creation, decree, tradition' CONSTITUTIO *ds.* **setnisse** 13:35 || ORIGO *ds.* **setnisse** 25:34 || TRADITIO *dp.* **settnisse** 15:6 [OED2 setness, *n.1*]

gesetnes *f.* 'tradition, decree' TRADITIO *as.* **gesettnisse** 15:2; *a/ds.* **gesettnisse** 15:3 [see previous]

settan *v.1* 'set' PONERE *ps.1s.* **sette** 12:18, 22:44; *ps.3s.* **seteþ** 24:51; *ps.3p.* **settaþ** 5:15; *pt.3s.* **sette** 14:3 || INPONERE *ps.3p.* **setteþ** 23:4; *pt.3s.* **sette** 27:48; *pt.3p.* **settun** 27:37; *subj.pt.3s.* **sette** 19:13 [n.], 19:15 || STATUERE *ps.3s.* **seteþ** 25:33; *pt.3s.* **sette** 4:5, 18:2 (margin) || PLANTARE *pt.3s.* **sette** 15:13, 21:33 || INMITTERE *ps.3s.* **setteþ** 9:16 || MITTERE *ps.p. map.* **settende** 4:18 || SUBMITTERE *pt.3p.* (*adune*) **settun** Mk2:4 [OED2 set, *v.1*]

gesettan *v.1* 'set' CONSTITUERE *ps.1s.* **gesette** 25:21; **gesete** 25:23; *ps.3s.* **gesetteþ** 24:47; *pt.3s.* **gesette** 24:45, 26:19 [n.], 27:10; **gesætte** 28:16; *pt.3p.* **gesettun** 26:15; *pp. mns.* **geseted** 8:9 || IMPONERE *pt.3s.* **gesettun** 22:34 [n.]; *pt.3p.* **gesettun** 27:29; *imp.s.* **gesette** 9:18 || LOCARE *ps.3s.* **geseteþ** 21:41; *pt.3s.* **gesette** 21:33 || COMPONERE *pt.3p.* **gesetton** Mk1:19 || PONERE *pt.3s.* **gesette** 13:24 [n.] (PROPONERE in WW) [OED2 i-set, *v.*]

sibb *f.* 'peace' PAX *ns.* ~ 10:12, 10:13; *as.* ~ 10:34 [sib, *n.1*]

sibsum *adj.* 'peace-loving, peaceable' PACIFICUS *mnp.* **sibsume** 5:9

sidone *prop.n. gs.* ~ 15:21; *ds.* 11:21, 11:22

siex *num.* 'six' SEX *d.* **sex** 17:1 [OED2 six, *adj.* and *n.*]

siexta *ord. num.* 'sixth' SEXTUS *fds.* **sextan** 20:5; **syxta** 27:45 [OED2 sixth, *adj.* and *n.*]

siextig *num.* 'sixty' SEXAGESIMUS *a.* **sextig** 13:8, 13:23 [OED2 sixty, *adj.* and *n.*]

sigor *m.* 'victory' VICTORIA *ds.* ~ 12:20 [n.]

gesihþ *f.* 'vision' VISIO *as.* **gesihþe** 17:9 || VISUM *ds.* **gesihþe** 27:19 [OED2 i-sight | i-siht, *n.*]

sihþe, see under **seon**

simon *prop.n. ns.* ~ 10:2, 10:4, 13:55, 16:16, 16:17, Mk1:36; **symon** 27:32; *as.* ~ 4:18; **simone(m)** Mk1:16; *gs.* **simonis** 26:6; *ds.* ~ 17:25

sincan *v.III* 'sink' MERGERE *inf.* ~ 14:30 [sink, *v.*]

singan *v.III* 'sing' CANERE *pt.1p.* **sungan** 11:17 [OED2 sing, *v.1*]

sion *prop.n. ds.* **sione** 21:5

sittan *v.V* 'sit' SEDERE *ps.3s.* **sitteþ** 19:28; **siteþ** 23:22; *ps.2p.* **sittaþ** 19:28; *pt.1s.* **sætt** 26:55; *pt.3s.* **sætt** 4:16, 26:69; **sæt** 24:3; **sett** 15:29, 27:19; *pt.3p.* **setun** 23:2; *subj.ps.3p.* **sittæ** 20:21; *imp.s.* **site** 22:44; *imp.p.* **sittaþ** 26:36; *inf.* **sitte** 20:23 (or *subj.*?); *ps.p. mns.* **sittende** 21:5; *mas.* **sittende** 9:9, 21:7, 26:64, Mk2:14; *np.* **sittende** 20:30, 27:36, 27:61, Mk2:6; *dp.* **sittendum** 4:16; **sittende** 11:16 || DISCUMBERE *ps.p. ap.* **sittendu** 22:11; *gp.* **sittendra** 22:10 [sit, *v.*]

gesittan *v.V* 'sit, possess' SEDERE *ps.3s.* **gesitæþ** 25:31; *pt.3s.* **gesæt** 13:1, 26:58; **gesett** 13:2, 28:2; *inf.* ~ 14:19; *ps.p. mnp.* **gesittende** 13:48; *pp.s.* (*wæs*) **gesett** 5:1 (or form of *settan*? see note) || DISCUMBERE *pt.3p.* **gesetun** 15:35 || 'possess' POSSIDERE *ps.3s.* **gesitteþ** 19:29; *ps.3p.* **gesittaþ** 5:4; *imp.p.* **gesittað** 25:34 [see previous]

siþ *m.* 'time, occasion' NL *is.* **siðe** 26:42, 26:44; *dp.* **siþum** 18:21; **siðum** 18:22 (*bis*)

siþ þæt *adv.* 'afterwards' AMODO **siðet** 26:29 [n.]; **sie þæt** 23:39 [n.] [sithe, *n.1*]

siþþan *adv.* 'since, afterwards' EXINDE **seoðþan** 4:17; **seoþþan** 26:16 || ULTRA **seoþþan** 5:13 [sithen, *adv.*, *conj.*, and *prep.*]

slæp *m.* 'sleep' SOMNUS *ds.* **slepe** 1:20, 1:24, 2:12, 2:19, 2:22 || part of DORMIRE *ns.* **slep** 25:5 [n.] [OED2 sleep, *n.*]

slæpan *v.VII* 'sleep' DORMIRE *ps.3s.* **slepeþ** 9:24; *pt.3s.* **slepte** 8:24; *pt.3p.* **sleptun** 13:25, 27:52; *imp.p.* **slepað** 26:45; *ps.p. ap.* **slepende** 26:40, 26:43; *dp.* **slepende** 28:13 || DORMITARE *pt.3p.* **slepade** 25:5 [OED2 sleep, *v.*]

slean *v.VI* 'slay, kill' OCCIDERE *ps.2s.* **slægst** 23:37; *ps.3s.* **slæþ** 5:21; **slæhþ** 10:28 [n.]; *ps.3p.* **slæhþ** 24:9; *pt.3p.* **slogun** 23:31; *imp.s.* **slag** 5:21 || PERCUTERE *ps.1s.* **slæ** 26:31; *pt.3s.* **slog** 26:51, 26:68; *pt.3p.* **slogun** 27:30; *subj.ps.3s.* **slae** 5:39; *inf.* **slan** 24:49 || PERDERE *pt.3p.* **slogan** 27:20; *inf.* **sla** 10:28 || CAEDERE *pt.3p.* **slogun** 26:67 || PALMAS DARE *pt.3p.* (*mid brade honde*) **slogun** 26:67 [OED2 slay, *v.1*]

slitan *v.I* 'slit, tear' SCINDERE *pt.3s.* **slat** 26:65 [OED2 slit, *v.*]

slite *m.* 'slit, tear' SCISSURA *ns.* ~ 9:16 [cf. OED2 slit, *n.*]

[MK]**smean** *v.1* 'think' COGITARE *pt.3p.* **smeadon** Mk2:8; *ps.p. np.* **smeande** Mk2:6

smican *v.1* 'smoke, fumigate' FUMIGARE *ps.p. nas.* **smikende** 12:20 [n.] [smeek, *v.*]

smierwan *v.1* 'smear, anoint' UNGERE *imp.s.* **smere** 6:17 [OED2 smear, v.]

smirenes *f.* 'ointment' UNGUENTUM *gs.* **smirenisse** 26:7; *ap.* **smerenisse** 26:12 || MURRA *ns.* **smerennis** 2:11 (as an explanatory gloss)

smitan *v.I* 'defile, polute' COINQUINARE *ps.3s.* **smiteþ** 15:11 [smite, *v.*]

smiþ *m.* 'smith' FABER *gs.* **smiðes** 13:55 [smith, *n.*]

smorian *v.2* 'choke, suffocate' SUFFOCARE *pt.3s.* **smorede** 18:28; *pt.3p.* **smoradun** 13:7 [n.] [OED2 smore, *v.*]

smylte *adj.* 'calm, peaceful' SERENUS

nns. ~ 16:2 [OED2 smolt, *adj.*]

smyltnes *f.* 'tranquillity, peace' TRANQUILLITAS *ns.* **smyltnisse** 8:26

snaw *m.* 'snow' NIX *ns.* **snau** 17:2, 28:3 [OED2 snow, *n.1*]

sniþan *v.I* 'cut, hew' CAEDERE *pt.3p.* **sneddun** 21:8 [OED2 snithe, *v.*]

snoru *f.* 'daughter-in-law' NURUS *as.* **snore** 10:35

snotor *adj.* 'wise, prudent' PRUDENS *mns.* **snotter** 24:45; *np.* **snottre** 25:2, 25:4, 25:9; *dp.* **snottrum** 25:8 || SAPIENS *mds.* **snottra** 7:24; *np.* **snottre** 10:16; *ap.* **snottre** 23:34; *dp.* **snottrum** 11:25 [OED2 snoter, *adj.*]

snyttru *f.* 'wisdom' SAPIENTIA *ns.* **snytru** 11:19; *as.* **snyttro** 12:42; *np.* **snottre** 13:54 [n.]

sodoming *m.* 'the people of Sodom' SODOMUS *gp.* **sodominga** 10:15, 11:24; *dp.* **sodomingum** 11:23

sona *adv.* 'soon, immediately' STATIM ~ 4:22, 14:22, 25:15, Mk1:12, Mk1:20, Mk1:21, Mk1:28, Mk2:8; **sonæ** 21:2 || CONFESTIM ~ 20:34; **sonæ** 21:3, 26:49 || CONTINUO ~ 14:27; **sonæ** 21:19 [OED2 soon, *adv.*]

sorgian *v.2* 'sorrow, grieve' SOLLICITUS ESSE *ps.3s.* **sorgaþ** 6:34 [n.]; *ps.2p.* **sorgiaþ** 6:28; *subj.ps.2p.* **sorgige** 6:25; *imp.p.* **sorgigaeþ** 6:31; **sorgigaþ** 6:34 [sorrow, *v.*]

soþ *adv.* 'indeed, therefore' AMEN ~ 5:18, 5:26, 6:2, 6:5, 6:16, 6:29, 8:10, 10:15, 10:23, 10:42, 11:11, 11:22, 13:17, 16:28, 18:3, 18:13, 18:18, 18:19, 19:28, 23:36, 24:2, 24:34, 24:47, 25:40, 25:45, 26:13, 26:21, 26:34, MtEXPLICIT; **soð** 17:20, 19:23, 21:21, 21:31 || AT **soð** Mk1:45 || ENIM ~ 3:9 || VERO ~ 8:24 [OED2 sooth, *adv.*]

soþfæst *adj.* 'just, faithful' IUSTUS *mns.* **soþfæst** 1:19; *mas.* **soþfest** 10:41; *mgs.* **soþfestes** 10:41; **soþfest** 10:41, 23:35; **soþfæste** 27:24; *mds.* **soþfæste** 27:19; *nns.* **soþfæst** 23:35; *nas.* **soþfæste** 27:4; *np.* **soþfeste** 13:17, 13:43, 25:37, 25:46; **soþfestę** 23:28; *ap.* **soþfeste** 5:45; *gp.* **soðfestra** 13:49, 23:29; *dp.* **soþfestum** 9:13 || VERAX *mns.* **soþfest** 22:16 [OED2 soothfast, *adj.* and *adv.*]

gesoþfæstian *v.2* 'justify' IUSTIFICARE *pp.s.* **gesoþfæsted** 12:37; **gesoþfęsted** 11:19

soþfæstnes *f.* 'truth, justice' IUSTITIA *ns.* **soþfæstnisse** 5:20; *as.* **soþfęstnisse** 3:15; **soþfestnisse** 6:1; **soþfæstnisse** 6:33; *a/ds.* **soþfæstnisse** 5:10; *gs.* **soþfæstnisse** 21:32; *oblique case* **soðfæstnisse** 5:6 [n.] || VERITAS *ds.* **soþfestnisse** 22:16

soþlice *adv.* 'indeed, however, therefore' AUTEM ~ 1:18, 1:19, 1:20, 1:21, 1:22, 1:24, 2:3, 2:10, 2:19, 2:21, 2:22, 3:1, 3:7, 13:25, 13:26, Jn18:2; **soðlice** 1:2 || ENIM ~ 1:20, 1:21, 2:2, 2:5, 2:6, 2:13, 2:20, 3:2, 3:3, 3:10, 4:7, 7:25, 18:7 (*om.* in WW), 23:19 || VERO ~ 16:14, 16:26, 20:6, 21:35, 25:15 **soðlice** 20:16; **soþlic** 27:20 || ERGO ~ 2:1, 3:8, 16:3, 23:3 || VERE ~ 14:33, 26:73, 27:54 || AMEN ~ MtEXPLICIT [OED2 soothly, *adv.* (and *conj.*)]

spatl *n.* 'spittle' NL *as.* **spaðl** 27:30 [n.] [OED2 spattle, *n.1*]

spearwa *m.* 'sparrow' PASSER *np.* **spearwas** 10:29, 10:31 [OED2 sparrow, *n.*]

spinnan *v.III* 'spin' NERE *ps.3p.* **spinnaþ** 6:28 [OED2 spin, *v.*]

spittan *v.1* 'spit' EXSPUERE *pt.3p.* **spittadun** 26:67; *ps.p.* *np.* **spittende** 27:30 [OED2 spit, *v.2*]

spowan *v.VII* 'profit, avail' PROFICERE *pt.3s.* **speou** 27:24

sprecan *v.V* 'speak' LOQUI *ps.1s.* **sprece** 13:13; *ps.2s.* **spreces** (*þu*) 13:10; *ps.3s.* **sprecaþ** 10:20, Mk2:7; **spreocaþ** 12:34; *pt.3s.* **spræc** 9:18, 23:1, 28:18; **sprec** 12:22, 13:3, 13:33, 13:34 (*bis*), 14:27; **spręc** 12:46; *pt.3p.* **sprecun** 26:47; *subj.ps.2p.* ~ 10:19; **sprece**

10:19; *subj.ps.3p.* **sprece** 12:46 [n.]; *inf.* ~ 12:34, Mk1:34; **spreocan** 6:7; *ps.p. mnp.* **sprecende** 17:3; *ap.* **sprecende** 15:31; **sprecende** (*wæs*) 9:33, Mk2:2 [OED2 speak, *v.*]

gesprecan *v.V* 'speak' LOQUI *pt.3s.* **gespræc** 17:5; *pp.* **gesprecan** (*beoþan*) 12:36 [n.] [see previous]

[MK]**springan** *v.III* 'jump, spring, spread' PROCEDERE *pt.3s.* **sprang** Mk1:28 [spring, *v.1*]

spynge *f.* 'sponge' SPONGIA *as.* **spynge** 27:48 [cf. sponge, *n.1*]

spyrte *f.* 'basket' SPORTA *ap.* **sperta** 15:37 [n.], 16:10 (margin)

stalu *f.* 'stealing, theft' FURTUM *as.* **stale** 19:18; *np.* **stale** 15:19 [OED2 stale, *n.1*]

stan *m.* 'stone' LAPIS *ns.* ~ 21:42, 24:2; *as.* ~ 7:9, 27:66, 28:2; *ds.* **stane** 4:6, 21:44, 24:2; *np.* **stanes** 4:3; *dp.* **stanum** 3:9; || PETRA *ds.* **stane** 7:24, 7:25, 16:18 [n.], 27:60; *np.* **stanes** 27:51 || SAXUM *as.* **stan** 27:60 [OED2 stone, *n.*]

standan *v.VI* 'stand' STARE *ps.3s.* **stondeþ** 12:25, 12:26; *ps.2p.* **stondeþ** 20:6; *ps.3p.* **stondaþ** 12:47; *pt.3s.* **stod** 13:2, 27:11; *pt.3p.* **stodan** 12:46; **stodun** 26:73; *subj.ps.3s.* **stonde** 18:16; *inf.* **stonde** 6:5 [n.]; *ps.p. mds.* **stondende** 24:15; *mnp.* **stondende** 6:5, 27:47; *map.* **standende** 20:3, 20:6; *mgp.* **stondendra** 16:28 [stand, *v.*]

gestandan *v.VI* 'stand' STARE *pt.3s.* **gestod** 2:9, 20:32 [i-stand, *v.*]

stanig *adj.* 'stony' PETROSUS *nas.* ~ 13:5; *nap.* **stanige** 13:20 [stony, *adj.*]

gestaþolian *v.2* 'fix, establish' FUNDARE *pp.s.* **gestaþulad** 7:25 [cf. stathel, *v.*]

stæf *m.* 'character, writing' NL *gs.* **stæfes** 5:18 [staff, *n.1*]

stænan *v.1* 'stone' LAPIDARE *ps.2s.* **stænęst** 23:37; *pt.3p.* **stædun** 21:35 [OED2 steen, *v.*]

stæne *f.* 'jug, pitcher' ALABASTRUM *as.* **stæna** 26:7 [n.] [OED2 stean, *n.*]

stæpe *m.* 'step, a measure of length' PASSUS *ap.* **steppan** 5:41 [OED2 step, *n.1*]

stæppan *v.VI* 'step, go' ACCEDERE *pt.3p.* **stopen** 28:9 [step, *v.*]

steall *m.* 'standing point' STARE *as.?* **stalle** 6:5 [n.]

stede *m.* 'place' LOCUS *ns.* **stede** 27:33 [n.]; *as.* **stede** Mk1:35 [OED2 stead, *n.*]

stefn, stemn *f.* 'voice' VOX *ns.* **stefu** 2:18; **stæfn** 17:5, Mk1:11; **stemn** 3:3, 3:17, Mk1:3; *as.* **stemn** 12:19; *a/ds.* **stæfne** 24:31; *ds.* **stæfnę** 27:46; **stæfne** 27:50, Mk1:26 [OED2 steven, *n.1*]

stencan *v.1* 'scatter' SPARGERE *ps.2s.* **stencæs** 25:24; *ps.3s.* **stenceþ** 12:30 [OED2 stench, *v.*]

steng *m.* 'stake, rod' FUSTIS *dp.* **stængum** 26:47, 26:55 [OED2 sting, *n.1*]

steorra *m. wk* 'star' STELLA *ns.* ~ 2:7, 2:9; *as.* ~ 2:2; **steorran** 2:10; *np.* **steorran** 24:29 [star, *n.1*]

stieran *v.1* 'restrain, rebuke, punish' INCREPARE *pt.3p.* **steordon** 19:13 [OED2 steer, *v.1*]

stig *m.* 'path' SEMITA *ap.* **stigas** 3:3; **stige** Mk1:3 [OED2 sty, *n.1*]

stigan *v.I* 'move, go up' ASCENDERE *pt.3s.* **stag** 8:23 || DESCENDERE *ps.3s.* **stigað** 24:17 (or *p.*?) [OED2 sty, *v.1*]

stillnes *f.* 'stillness, quiet' SILENTIUM *as.* **stillnesse** 22:34 [OED2 stillness, *n.*]

stow *f.* 'spot, place' LOCUS *ns.* **stowe** 14:15; *as.* **stouw** 27:33 [n.]; **stowe** 14:13, 26:52, 28:6, Mk1:35, Jn18:2; **stowę** 27:33; *gs.* **stowe** 14:35; *ds.* **stowe** 24:15, 26:52; *ap.* **stowe** 12:43; **stowa** 24:7; *dp.* **stowum** Mk1:45 [OED2 stow, *n.1*]

strang *adj.* 'strong' FORTIS *mns.* **stronge** 12:29 [n.]; *mgs.* **stronges** 12:29; *comp. mns.* **strængra** 3:11; **strongre** Mk1:7 [strong, *adj.*]

[MK]**stream** *m.* 'stream, river'

FLUMEN *ds.* **streame** Mk1:5 [OED2 stream, *n.*]

streaw *n.* 'straw, hay' FESTUCA *as.* **streu** 7:3, 7:4 (margin), 7:5 [straw, *n.1*]

stregdan *v.III* 'spread' STERNERE *pt.3p.* **strægdun** 21:8 (*bis*) || SPARGERE *pt.1s.* **strægde** 25:26

gestrienan *v.1* 'acquire, gain' LUCRARI *ps.2s.* **gestreonest** 18:15; *pt.3s.* **gestrionde** 25:16, 25:17; *subj.ps.3s.* **gestreone** 16:26 || part of SUPERLUCRARI *pt.1s.* **gestrionde** 25:20, 25:22 [cf. OED2 strene, *v.*]

[MK]**styltan** *v.1* 'be amazed, hesitate' STUPERE *pt.3p.* **stylton** Mk1:22

styrian *v.2* 'stir, move' MOVERE *pt.3p.* **styredun** 27:39; *inf.* **styrgan** 23:4; *pp.s.* **styred** 27:51 || AGITARE *pp. nas.* **styred** 11:7 [OED2 stir, *v.*]

sucan *v.II* 'suck' LACTARE *ps.p. gp.* **sukendra** 21:16 [OED2 suck, *v.*]

sum *adj.* 'a certain' QUIDAM *mns.* ~ 12:47, 21:28, 27:57; *mas.* **sumne** 8:2 (for nominative? see note), 12:38 [n.]; *mds.* **sumum** 26:18; *np.* **sume** 9:3, 13:4, 16:28, 27:47, 28:11, 28:17, Mk2:6 || ALIUS *mas.* **sume** 21:35 (x3, or *ap.*?; see note); *mds.* **sumum** 25:15; *nns. or p.?* **sume** 13:7, 13:8 (x4), 13:23 (x3); *np.* **sume** 16:14 (x3), 21:8, 26:67; **sum** 22:5 (*bis*) [OED2 some, *pron.*, *adj.1*, *adv.*, and *n.1*]

sumor *m.* 'summer' AESTAS *ns.* **sumer** 24:32 [summer, *n.1* and *adj*]

sundor *adv.* 'asunder, apart' SEORSUM ~ 14:13, 14:14 [n.]; **sundur** 17:1 [sunder, *adv.* and *adj.*]

sunne *f.* 'the sun' SOL *ns.* ~ 13:6, 13:43, 17:2, 24:29, Mk1:32; *as.* **sunne** 5:45 [sun, *n.1*]

sunor *f.* 'herd (of swine)' GREX *ns.* **suner** 8:30 [n.], 8:32; *as.* **sunrae** 8:31 [cf. sounder, *n.1*]

sunu *m.* 'son' FILIUS *ns.* ~ 1:20, 4:3, 4:6, 7:9, 8:20, 8:29, 9:2, 9:6, 9:27, 10:23, 11:27 (*bis*), 12:8, 12:23, 12:40, 13:37, 13:41, 13:55, 14:33, 15:22, 16:13, 17:5, 17:9, 17:22, 19:28, 20:18, 20:28, 20:30, 20:31, 21:28, 22:42, 22:45, 24:44, 26:2, 26:24 (*bis*), 26:63, Mk1:11, Mk2:5, Mk2:10; **sune** 3:17, 11:19, 16:16, 16:27, 17:12, 18:11, 25:31, 26:45, 27:40, 27:43, 27:54; *as.* ~ 1:21, 1:23, 1:25, 10:21, 10:37, 11:27, 16:28, 21:37 (*bis*), 21:38, 22:24, 23:15, 24:30, 26:64; *gs.* ~ 1:1, 23:35, 24:27, 28:19, Mk1:1; **sune** 1:1, 24:30, 24:37; **sunę** 24:39; *ds.* **sunę** 2:15; **sune** 17:15; ~ 21:5, 21:9, 21:15, 22:2; *a/d.s.* ~ 12:32; *np.* **suna** 10:21; **sunæ** 20:21; *ap.* ~ 18:25; **sunes** 21:28; **sunas** 26:37; *gp.* ~ 20:20; **sunena** 27:56 [n.]; *a/dp.* ~ 20:20 || NL ~ *ns.* 10:2, 10:3, 16:17; ~ *as.* 4:21, Mk1:19 [son, *n.1*]

suþan *adv.* 'from the south' AUSTER **suþan** 12:42 [southen, *adv.*]

swa *adv.* 'so' SIC ~ 2:5, etc.; **sua** 5:16; **swæ** 18:14, 18:35, 19:8, 26:40 || ITA ~ 7:12, etc. || TANTUM ~ (*micel*) 8:10, 9:21, 15:33, 18:25 || SIMILITER ~ 22:26, 26:35, 27:41 || QUIS ~ 21:23 (for *hwa*? see note) || VELUT ~ 28:4 || NL ~ 26:47

swa *conj.* 'as' SICUT ~ 1:24, etc. || QUASI ~ 26:55, Mk1:22 || CUM ~ 1:19 || UT ~ 17:20 (SICUT in WW) || QUAEMADMODUM ~ 23:37 || NL ~ 28:7 [n.]

swa swa 'as' SICUT ~ 6:10, 6:12, 6:16, 6:29, 7:29 (*bis*), 10:16 (x3), 10:25 (*bis*), 12:40, 13:43, 14:5

swa hwa/hwilc swa *pron.* QUICUMQUE *mns.* **swa hwa swa** 5:31, 5:41, 10:42, 12:50, 15:5, 19:9, 20:26, 23:16, 23:18; *mas.* **swa hwilc swa** 26:48; *mnp.* **swa hwælc swa** 12:32, 14:36; *nns.?* **swa hwilce swa** 10:14; *nas.* **swa hwęt swa** 7:12; **swa hwæt swa** 14:7, 16:19 (*bis*), 21:22, 23:3; **swa hwilc swa** 15:5; *ngs.* **swa hwæs swa** 18:19; *fds.* **swa hwilce ... swa** 10:11; *ap.* **swa hwælc swa** 17:12, 18:18; **swa hwylce swa** 18:18; **swa hwilce swa** 22:9; **swa hwæt swa** 28:20

swa hwa QUICUMQUE *mns.* ~ 18:4
swa hwær swa UBICUMQUE 24:28, 26:13
swa longe swa QUAMDIU 25:40, 25:45
hwider swa QUOCUMQUE 8:19 [n.] [OED2 so, *adv.* and *conj.*]

swær *adj.* 'dull, sluggish' PIGER *mns.* ~ 25:26 [OED2 sweer, *adj.*]

swefn *n.* 'sleep' SOMNUS *ds.* **swefne** 2:13 [OED2 sweven, *n.*]

sweger *f.* 'mother-in-law' SOCRUS *ns.* **swægre** Mk1:30; *as.* **swægre** 8:14; *a/ds.* **swegre** 10:35

swelgan *v.III* 'swallow' DEVORATOR *ps.p. mns.* **swelgande** 11:19 [OED2 swallow, *v.*]

sweltan *v.III* 'die' MORI *ps.3s.* **swælteþ** 15:4; *subj.pt.3s.* **swylte** 22:24; *inf.* **sweltan** 26:35 [OED2 swelt, *v.*]

swencan *v.1* 'trouble, distress, aflict' MOLESTUS *ps.p. mnp.* **swæncende** 26:10 [swench, *v.*]

geswencan *v.1* 'vex, distress' VEXARE *pp.p.* **geswæncte** Mk1:34 [see previous]

sweora *m. wk* 'neck' COLLUM *ds.* **swira** 18:6 [OED2 swire, *n.*]

sweord *n.* 'sword' GLADIUS *as.* ~ 10:34, 26:51, 26:52 (*bis*); *ds.* **sweorde** 26:52; *dp.* **sweordum** 26:47, 26:55 [OED2 sword, *n.*]

sweostor *f.* 'sister' SOROR *ns.* **swuster** 12:50; *np.* **swæster** 13:56; *ap.* **swuster** 19:29 [cf. sister, *n.*]

swerian *v.VI* 'swear' IURARE *ps.3s.* **sweræþ** 23:16; **sweraþ** 23:16, 23:20, 23:21 (*bis*), 23:22; **swerat** 23:22; **swæraþ** 23:18; *inf.* **swerige** 26:74; *subj.ps.2s.* **swergę** 5:36; *subj.ps.3s.* **swerge** 5:34 [n.] || PERIURARE *imp.* **swer** (*man*) 'commit perjury' 5:33 [OED2 swear, *v.*]

geswic *n.* 'offence' SCANDALUM *ap.* **geswicu** 13:41

swigian *v.2* 'be silent, keep silent' TACERE *pt.3s.* **swigade** 26:63; *pt.3p.* **swigadun** 20:31 || OBMUSTESCERE *imp.s.* **swiga** Mk1:25 || STUPERE *pt.3p.* **swigadun** Mk1:22 [OED2 swie, *v.*]

swilc *adj.* 'such' TALIS *mds.* **swælce** 18:5; *fas.* **swilce** 9:8; *nns.* **swilce** 19:14 (?) || QUALIS *fns.* **swilce** 24:21 [OED2 swilk, *adj.*, and *pron.*, and *adv.*]

swilce *adv.* 'too' ET ~ 2:8, 5:40 [n.], 6:10, 10:33, 18:18 (*bis*), 18:35, 20:7, 20:10, 20:14, 21:21, 25:44 || SIC **swilc** Mk2:12 || SIMILITER ~ 25:17 || NL ~ 5:48 [n.], 6:14 [n.]

swilce *conj.* 'just as' TAMQUAM ~ Mk1:10 || QUASI ~ Mk1:22 [see previous]

swin *n.* 'pig, swine' PORCUS *gp.* **swina** 8:30, 8:31; *dp.* **swinum** 7:6, 8:32 [swine, *n.*]

swincnes *f.* 'hardship, trial' TRIBULATIO *ds.?* **swincnisse** 13:21

swingan *v.III* 'beat, scourge, whip' FLAGELLARE *ps.2p.* **swingaþ** 23:34; *ps.3p.* **swingaþ** 10:17; *infl.inf.* **swinganne** 20:19 [OED2 swing, *v.1*]

geswingan *v.III* 'beat, scourge, whip' FLAGELLARE *pp. mas.* **geswunganne** 27:26 [see previous]

swiþ *adj.* 'strong' VALIDUS *mas.* **swiðne** 14:30
swiþra *comp.* DEXTER 'right (eye, hand, etc.)' *nns.* **swiþre** 5:29; *fns.* **swiþre** 5:30, 6:3; *nas.* **swiðran** 5:39; **swiðræ** 26:51; *fas.* **swiþran** 22:44, 25:34; **swiðran** 20:21, 20:23, 25:33, 26:64, 27:29, 27:38

swiþe *adv.* 'very much, greatly' VALDE ~ 2:10, 4:8, 19:25, 27:54; **swiðe** 2:16, 17:6, 18:31, 26:22, Mk1:35 || VEHIMENTER **swiðe** 17:23, 27:14 || NIMIS **swiðe** 8:28 || NL ~ 26:43 [n.]
swiþor *comp.* POTIUS **swiðor** 10:28 || PLUS **swiðor** 10:37 || MAGIS **swiðor** 12:12, 20:31, 27:23, 27:24 [OED2 swith, *adv.*]

symbel *n.* 'feast-day, festivitiy' SOLLEMNIS **symbel** 27:15 (possibly as the first element of **symbeldæg**, see note)

symbeldæg *m.* 'feast-day, festival'

DIES FESTUS *ds.* **symbeldæge** 26:5

synagoga 'synagogue' SYNAGOGA *dp.* **synagogum** 4:23 [n.] [cf. OED2 synagogue, *n.*]

syngian *v.2* 'sin, transgress' PECCARE *subj.ps.3s.* **syngige** 18:15 [OED2 sin, *v.*]

synn *f.* 'sin' PECCATUM *ns.* **synne** 12:31; *np.* **synne** 9:5, Mk2:5, Mk2:9; **synnae** 9:2; *ap.* **synne** 3:6, 6:15 (*bis*), 9:6, Mk1:5, Mk2:7; **synna** 6:14; *gp.* **synne** 26:28, Mk2:10; **synna** Mk1:4; *dp.* **synnum** 1:21 [OED2 sin, *n.*]

synnful adj. 'sinful' PECCATOR 'the sinful' *mnp.* **synnfulle** 9:10, Mk2:15; *mgp.* **synfulra** 26:45; *mdp.* **synnfullum** 9:11; **synfullum** 9:13 [OED2 sinful, *adj.* and *n.*]

[MK]**synnig** *adj.* 'guilty, sinful' part of PUBLICANUS *np.* (*openlice*) **synnige** Mk2:15 [OED2 sinny, *adj.*]

syria *prop.n. as.* ~ 4:24

tacen *n.* 'token, sign' SIGNUM *ns.* ~ 12:39, 16:4 (*bis*), 24:30; **taken** 12:39; **tacun** 24:3; *as.* ~ 12:38, 12:39, 16:4; **tacun** 26:48; **taken** 16:1; *ap.* ~ 16:3 (or *s.*?), 24:24 [OED2 token, *n.*]

taddeus *prop.n. ns.* ~ 10:3

tam *adj.* 'tame' SUBIUGALIS *fds.* **teoma** 21:5 [OED2 tame, *adj.*]

tan *m.* 'rod, twig (used in casting lots)' SORS *as.* **tan** 27:35

getæcan *v.1* 'teach' DEMONSTRARE *pt.3s.* **getahtæ** 3:7 || SUADERE *ps.1p.* **getæceþ** 28:14 [cf. OED2 teach, *v.*]

tægþigaþ, see **teogoþian**

getæl *n.* 'number, tribe' NUMERUS *np.* **getala** 14:21 || TRIBUS *np.* **getalu** 24:30 [OED2 i-tel, *n.*]

(†)**tæppelbred** *n.* 'footstool' SCABELLUM *ns.* ~ 5:35 [n.]; *as.* **tæppilbred** 22:44

telgra *m. wk* 'twig, branch' RAMUS *ns.* ~ 24:32; *ap.* **telgran** 21:8; *dp.* **telgrum** 13:32 [OED2 tiller, *n.3*]

tempel *n.* 'temple' TEMPLUM *ns.* ~ 23:17; *as.* ~ 21:12, 21:23, 23:16, 23:21 (or *d.*?), 23:35, 26:61 [n.], 27:40; **templ** 27:5; *gs.* **temples** 4:5, 23:16, 24:1, 27:51; *ds.* **temple** 21:12, 21:14, 24:1; **templæ** 26:55; **templ** 12:5 [n.], 12:6 (or *n.*?) || part of CORBANA *gs.* **temples** (*feh*) 27:6 [OED2 temple, *n.1*]

teogoþian *v.2* 'tithe' DECIMARE *ps.2p.* **tægþigaþ** 23:23 [tithe, *v.2*]

teoma, see **tam**

teon *v.II* 'pull, draw' DUCERE *ps.p. mnp.* **teonde** 13:48 [OED2 tee, *v.1*]

teona *m. wk* 'injury, wrong' INIURIA *as.* **teane** 20:13 [teen, *n.1*]

geteorian *v.2* 'fail, become weary, exhausted' DEFICERE *subj.ps.3p.* **geteorige** 15:32 [cf. OED2 tear, *v.1*]

tetrarcha *prop.n. ns.* ~ 14:1

ticcen *n.* 'kid' HAEDUS *ap.* ~ 25:33; *dp.* **ticnum** 25:32 OED2 [ticchen, *n.*]

tid *f.* 'time' HORA *ns.* ~ 14:15; *as.* **tide** 20:12; ~ 14:1, 24:42, 24:44, 26:40; *ds.* **tide** 8:13, 9:22, 20:5, 20:6, 20:9, 24:50; ~ 20:3, 27:45 (*bis*), 27:46 || TEMPUS *ns.* ~ 21:34, 26:18; *ns.* **tide** Mk1:15; *as.* ~ 2:7, 11:25 [n.], 12:1; *a/ds.* **tide** 2:16; *ds.* **tide** 8:29, 24:45; ~ 13:30; *ap.* **tide** 16:3; *dp.* **tidum** 21:41 [OED2 tide, *n.*]

tien *num.* 'ten' DECEM *n.* **tene** 20:24; *a.* **ten** 18:24, 25:28; *d.* **ten** 25:1 [OED2 ten, *adj.*, *n.*, and *adv.*]

tigelwyrhta *m. wk* 'brickmaker, potter' FIGULUS *gs.* **tiglewyrhte** 27:7 [n.]

timbrian *v.2* 'build' AEDIFICARE *ps.2p.* **timbraþ** 23:29; *pt.3s.* **timbrade** 7:26, 21:42 (for *pr.p.*? see note) [OED2 timber, *v.*]

getimbrian *v.2* 'build' AEDIFICARE *ps.1s.* **getimbre** 16:18, 26:61; *pt.3s.* **getimbrade** 7:24, 21:33 || REAEDIFICARE *ps.3s.* (*æft*) **getimbrað** 27:40 [see previous]

getimbru *f.* 'building' AEDIFICATIO *as.* ~ 24:1 [cf. OED2 timber, *n.1*]

tintreg *n.* 'torment, torture'

SUPPLICIUM *as.* **tintergu** 25:46 || TORMENTUS *dp.* **tintregum/ tintergum** 4:24 [n.] || part of TORTOR *gp.* **tinterga** 18:34 [OED2 tintregh, *n.*]

tintregian *v.2* 'torment' TORQUERE *inf.* **tinterga** 8:29 [cf. see previous]

to *prep.* 'to, as' AD ~ 2:12, etc. || AD + GERUND. (w. *infl.inf.*) ~ 2:13, 5:28, 15:33 [n.], 20:19 (x3), 26:12 || IN ~ 2:1, 2:8, 2:12, 2:20, 16:21, 24:16, 26:31, 26:34, Mk1:21, Mk2:11 || USQUE ~ 27:51 || AB ~ 27:60 (AD in WW) || NL (postposed instances are followed with P; see note to 15:33) ~ 2:2, 2:8, 2:11, 3:7. 3:15, 4:3, 4:6, 4:7, 4:9 (*bis*), 4:10 (x3), 4:19, 5:1P (separated), 5:29, 5:30, 5:34, 5:39, 5:44, 6:11, 6:25, 6:30 (*bis*), 7:21, 7:22, 8:4, 8:7, 8:8, 8:9 (*bis*), 8:10, 8:13, 8:19, 8:20, 8:21, 8:22, 8:26, 8:32, 9:2, 9:4, 9:6, 9:9, 9:15, 9:17, 9:18, 9:28 (*bis*), 9:37 (w.a.?) [n.], 10:6 (*bis*), 10:29, 11:3, 11:4, 12:2, 12:3, 12:11, 12:13, 12:25, 12:47, 12:48, 13:3, 13:10, 13:11, 13:27, 13:28, 13:29, 13:30, 13:33, 13:34, 13:52, 14:2, 14:16, 14:18, 14:27, 14:31, 14:35, 15:3, 15:5, 15:10, 15:12, 15:15, 15:24, 15:25, 15:28, 15:33P [n.], 15:34P, 16:6P, 16:11, 16:15P, 16:17, 16:23, 16:24, 17:7, 17:11, 17:19, 17:20 (*bis*), 17:22P, 17:24 (*bis*), 17:26, 18:14, 18:21 (*bis*), 18:22 (*bis*), 18:32, 19:4, 19:8, 19:10P, 19:14, 19:16P, 19:17P, 19:18, 19:20P, 19:21P, 19:23, 19:26, 19:27, 19:28, 20:4, 20:6, 20:7, 20:8, 20:17, 20:18, 20:21, 20:23, 20:28, 21:1, 21:2 (*bis*), 21:3 [n.], 21:13 (*bis*), 21:16 (*bis*), 21:19, 21:21 (margin), 21:21, 21:24, 21:25, 21:27, 21:31P, 21:42, 22:8, 22:12P, 22:13, 22:20, 22:21, 22:23P (AD in WW, separated), 22:24, 22:29, 22:31, 22:37P, 22:43P, 24:1P (separated, see note), 24:2P, 24:4P, 24:38, 25:8, 25:21P, 25:23P, 25:26P, 25:40, 25:41, 26:1, 26:8, 26:10P, 26:15, 26:18, 26:18P, 26:21P, 26:25P, 26:31, 26:33P, 26:34, 26:35P (separated), 26:36, 26:38, 26:40, 26:45P, 26:50P, 26:52P, 26:55, 26:62, 26:63, 26:64P, 26:71, 26:73, 27:1, 27:7, 27:11, 27:13P, 27:21P, 27:22P, 27:23P (separated), 27:65P, 28:5, 28:9, 28:10P, 28:17, 28:18, Mk1:9, Mk1:17P, Mk1:30, Mk1:32, Mk1:37, Mk1:38, Mk1:41, Mk1:44, Mk2:5, Mk2:8, Mk2:10, Mk2:14, Jn18:2 || NL w. *infl.inf.* ~ Mt INCIPIT, 2:2, 3:11, 5:17 (x3), 5:41 (*bis*), 9:5 (*bis*), 9:6, 9:13, 10:34 (*bis*), 10:35, 11:7, 11:8, 11:9, 11:16, 12:2, 12:4, 12:12, 12:42, 13:3, 13:30, 14:4, 14:16 (margin), 14:25, 15:37, 16:12, 18:11, 19:24 (*bis*), 20:15, 20:20, 20:23, 22:17, 24:17, 24:18, 24:48, 26:17, 26:55, 27:7, 28:1, 28:20, Mk1:24, Mk2:9; see also **oþ to** under **oþ** and **oþþe to** under **oþþe** *adv.* 'to, towards' (corresponding to Latin prefix AD-) ~ 6:10 [n.] [OED2 to, *prep.*, *conj.*, and *adv.*]

toberstan *v.III* 'burst apart' RUMPERE *ps.3p.* **tobersteþ** 9:17 || SCINDERE *pt.3s.* **toberst** 27:51 [OED2 to-burst, *v.*]

tobrecan *v.IV* 'break into pieces, scatter' CONFRINGERE *ps.3s.* **tobreceþ** 12:20 [OED2 to-break, *v.*]

tobregdan *v.III* 'tear in pieces' DIRIPERE *inf.* ~ 12:29 || ERIPERE *ps.3s.* **tobręgdeþ** 12:29

tobrengan *v.1* 'bring' ADDUCERE *pt.3p.* **tobrohtun** 21:7

tocyme *m.* 'coming, advent' ADVENTUS *ns.* ~ 24:37 [tocome, *n.1*]

togebiddan *v.V* 'pray, entreat' ADRARE *pt.3s.* **togebędde** 8:2

todæge *adv.* 'today' HODIE ~ 6:11, 6:30, 16:3 (MANE in R, but clearly reflecting HODIE), 21:28, 27:19 [today, *adv.*, *n.*, and *adj.*]

toeacan *prep.* 'besides' EXTRA **toekan** 15:38 [OED2 eke | teken, *adv.* and *prep.*]

toeacen *adv.* **'besides'** SUPER- **toeke** 25:20 [see previous]

[MK]**toferan** *v.1* 'carry, bring' FERRE *ps.p. np.* **toferende** Mk2:3 [OED2 to-fere, *v.*]

togangan *v.VII* 'go, approach' ACCEDERE *ps.p. mns.* **togangende** 28:2; *mnp.* **togangende** 15:12, 15:23, 28:18 [OED2 to-gang, *v.*]

togeanes *prep.* 'against, towards' CONTRA **togægnes** 27:61 [OED2 to-gains | to-gainst | to-yenst, *prep.* (and *conj.*)]

tolysan *v.1* 'dissolve, loosen' SOLVERE *ps.3s.* **tolesеþ** 5:19

tomas *prop.n. ns.* ~ 10:3

to(ge)nealæcan *v.1* 'come near, approach' ADPROPINQUARE *ps.3s.* **tonealiceþ** 26:45; **toneoliceþ** 26:46; *pt.3s.* **tonealehte** 21:34; **togenealacede** Mk1:15

†**torcul** *n.?* 'wine-press' TORCULAR *ds.* ~ 21:33 [n.] [cf. OED2 torcular, *n.*]

torr *m.* 'tower' TURRIS *as.* ~ 21:33 [OED2 tower, *n.1*]

†**tosaga** *ds.* 'story, narrative' NL **tosagan** Mt INCIPIT [n.]

toslitan *v.I* 'tear asunder, rend' DISRUMPERE *inf.* **toslite** 7:6 [n.] [OED2 to-slit, *v.*]

tosomne *adv.* 'together' CON-, COM- ~ 1:18, 10:1, 15:32 [OED2 to-same | to-samen, *adv.*]

tostencan *v.1* 'scatter, disperse' DISPERGERE *pp.p.* **tostænced** 26:31

toþ *m.* 'tooth' DENS *as.* ~ 5:38; **toð** 5:38; *gp.* **toþa** 8:12, 13:42, 13:50, 22:13, 25:30; **toða** 24:51 [OED2 tooth, *n.*]

toweard *adj.* 'approaching, future' FUTURUS *nds.* **towardan** 3:7; *fds.* **towarde** 12:32

toweard *adv.* FUTURUS **toward** 2:13, 17:22 [OED2 toward, *adj.* and *adv.*]

toweorpan *v.III* 'throw down, destroy' DESTRUERE *inf.* ~ 26:61; *pp.s.* **toworpen** 24:2 [OED2 to-warp, *v.*]

†**towyltan** *v.1* 'roll to' ADVOLVERE *pt.3s.* **towælede** 27:60 [n.]

tredan *v.V* 'tread' CONCULCARE *subj.ps.3p.* ~ 7:6; *pp.s.* **tredan** 5:13 [OED2 tread, *v.*]

treow *n.* 'tree' ARBOR *ns.* ~ 3:10, 7:17 (*bis*), 7:18 (*bis*), 7:19, 12:33, 13:32; *as.* ~ 12:33, 21:19; **treuw** 12:33; *gs.* **treowes** 3:10; *ds.* **treo** 24:32; *dp.* **treowum** 21:8 [OED2 tree, n.]

getreowan *v.1* 'believe, be confident' CONFIDERE *subj.ps.3s.* **getriowe** 27:43; *imp.s.* **getreowe** 9:2; **getreuwe** 9:22 [cf. OED2 trow, *v.*]

getreowe *adj.* 'true, faithful' FIDELIS *mns.* ~ 25:23; **getrewe** 24:45; **getreuwe** 25:21; **getreowa** 25:21, 25:23 [OED2 i-treowe, *adj.*]

tun *m.* 'village, town' VILLA *as.* ~ 26:36; *ds.* **tunę** 22:5 || VICUS *dp.* **tunum** 6:2 || NL *ds.* **tune** 26:6 [town, *n.*]

tunece *f. wk* 'tunic, under-garment' TUNICA *as.* **tonica** 5:40; **tunican** 24:18; *ap.* **tunica** 10:10 [OED2 tunic, *n.*]

tungolcræftiga *m.* MAGI 'magi' *np.* **tungulkræftgu** 2:1 [n.]; *dp.* **tungulkræftgum** 2:7, 2:16; **tungulkreftgum** 2:16

twegen *num.* 'two' DUO *mn.* ~ 8:28, 10:29, 18:19, 24:40, 24:41; **twægen** 19:5, 19:6, 20:21, 20:30, 26:60, 27:38; **twege** 18:20; **twa** 9:27 [n.], 9:28 [n.]; **tu** 9:28 [n.]; *ma.* ~ 4:18, 4:21, 5:41, 14:17, 18:16, 21:1; *a.* (gender?) **twegen** 25:15, 25:22; **twægen** 25:17 (*bis*), 25:22 (*bis*), 26:37; **twa** 18:8; **twægen** 11:2, 14:19, 21:28, 27:51; *fn.* **twa** 24:41; *fa.* **twa** 10:10, 18:8; *na.* **twa** 18:9; *g.* ~ 18:16; **twegra** 21:31, 27:21; *d.* **twæm** 6:24, 20:24, 22:40 || part of BIMATUS 'two (years)' *d.* **twæm** (*wintrum*) 2:16 || part of DUPLUM *d.* **twæm** 23:15 || part of AB INVICEM (*in*) **tu** 25:32 || part of BIDUUM *dp.* **twæm** 26:2 [OED2 two, *adj.*, *n.*, and *adv.*]

twelf *num.* 'twelve' DUODECIM *n.* **twælf** 10:1; *a.* ~ 9:20, 20:17; **twælf**

14:20, 26:53; **twelfe** 11:1, 19:28 (*bis*); **twælfe** 10:5; *g.* ~ 10:2; **twelfe** 26:47; **twælfe** 26:14; *d.* **twælf** 26:20 [OED2 twelve, *adj.* and *n.*]
tweon *v.1* 'doubt, hesitate' DUBITARE *pt.3p.* **tweodun** 28:17 || HAESITARE *ps.2p.* **twigaþ** 21:21 [OED2 tweon, *v.*]
getweon *v.2* 'doubt' DUBITARE *pt.2s.* **getwiodestu** 14:31 (w. subject contraction) [see previous]
tyre *prop.n.* ~ *gs.* 15:21; *ds.* **tyro** 11:21; **tiro** 11:22

þa *adv.* 'then' AUTEM ~ 3:15, ... 27:17 (ERGO in WW), etc. || TUNC ~ 2:7, etc.; **ða** 16:24, 25:1, 26:38, 27:9, 27:13 || VERO ~ 14:30, 25:19 || ERGO ~ 25:27 [n.] || PORRO ~ 8:27 || QUIDEM ~ 25:33 || AT ~ 27:21; **ða** 26:18 || IAM ~ 27:1 (AUTEM in WW) || AN ~ 20:15 [n.] || NL ~ 1:20, 1:24?, 2.3?, 2:5, 4:19 (poss. *pron.*?), 8:23, 9:22, 10:1, 12:22, 12:46 (or ADHUC?), 13:11, 13:37, 14:13, 14:18, 14:31, 14:32, 15:35, 15:39, 17:5, 17:7, 18:34, 20:6, 21:15, 22:19 (or AT?), 22:33, 25:20, 25:22 (AUTEM in WW), 26:7, 26:47 (or ADHUC?), 26:75 [n.], 27:25, 27:33, Mk2:12, Jn18:1; **ða** 8:13, 9:22 [n.], 16:8, 21:27, 22:10, 26:19, 27:46, 27:47, 28:11 (**þa** in 6:24, see **oþþe** and note)
þa *conj.* 'when' CUM ~ 2:1, etc.; **ða** 22:7 || DUM ~ 13:4 || QUANDO ~ 12:3 || NL ~ 2:19, 3:7 (or *adv.*?), 8:16, 9:12, 9:18, 9:22, 9:32, 11:7, 14:23, 20:11, 20:29, 21:39, 22:41, 24:4, 26:20[1], 26:27, 26:71, 27:1, 27:5, 27:6[2] (?), 27:7, 27:19, 27:24, 27:32, 27:59
  þa þe *conj.* 'when' CUM 1:18 [n.], 27:12 [OED2 tho, *adv.* (and *conj.*)]
geþafian *v.2* 'consent to, approve' CONSENTIRE *ps.3p.* **geþafigaþ** 18:19 [OED2 i-thave, *v.*]
ðamar *prop.n. ds.* ~ 1:3 [n.]
geþanc *m.* 'thought' COGITATIO *as.* ~ 16:8 [OED2 i-thank, *n.*]
þancian *v.2* 'thank' GRATIAS AGERE *pt.3s.* **þongade** 26:27 [OED2 thank, *v.*]
þancung *f.* 'thanking, thanks' GRATIA *ap.* **þongunge** 15:36 [OED2 thanking, *n.*]
þanon *adv.* 'thence' INDE **þonan** 4:21, 5:26, 9:9, 9:27, 12:9, 12:15, 14:13, 15:21, 15:29, Mk1:19; **ðonan** 11:1, 19:15 || AB- **þonan** 2:9, 11:7, 27:5 || TRANS- **þonan** 13:53 || PRAETER- **þonan** Mk2:14
  þanon þe *conj.* 'whence' UNDE **þonan þe** 12:44 [OED2 thenne | then, *adv.*]
ðariht, see **þærrihte**
þæc *n.* 'covering, roof' TECTUM *ds.* **þæce** 24:17; *ap.* **þacu** 8:8 [n.]; *dp.* **þacum** 10:27 [OED2 thack, *n.*]
þæcele *f.* 'lamp, torch' LAMPAS *ap.* **ðecele** 25:1
þær *adv.* 'there' IBI ~ 2:13, 2:15, 5:24, 6:21, 10:11, 13:5, 13:58, 15:29, 18:20, 19:2, 21:17, 26:71, 27:55, 27:61, 28:10; **ðær** 12:10, 17:27, 22:11, 28:7, Mk1:38; **þęr** 13:50; **ðęr** 5:23, 12:45, 14:23; **ðer** Mk1:35 || ILLIC ~ 13:42, 22:13, 24:51, 25:30, 27:47; **ðær** Mk2:6 || NL ~ 18:31 [n.], 28:11; **þęr** 27:54; **ðær** 18:31
þær *conj./rel.adv.* UBI 'where' ~ 6:19 (*bis*), 6:20 (*bis*), 6:21, 8:12, 18:20, 25:24 (*bis*), 25:26 (*bis*), 26:57 (as **þær þe**, see note), 28:6, 28:16, Mk2:4, Jn18:1; **þer** 8:20; **ðær** 2:9 || SI/NISI ~ 11:21 [n.], 11:23, 12:7, 23:30, 24:22, 24:24, 24:43, 26:24 || NL **þær** 9:10 [n.] [OED2 there, *adv.* (*adj.* and *n.*)]
[MK]**þærrihte** *adv.* 'immediately' STATIM **ðariht** Mk1:20 [n.] [OED2 thereright, *adv.*]
þærute *adv.* 'outside' FORIS ~ 26:69 [OED2 thereout, *adv.*]
þæt *conj.* 'that' UT ~ 4:1, 4:3, 5:13, 5:30, 5:45, 6:4, 7:12, 9:6, 9:38, 11:1, 12:10, 13:32, 13:35, 18:13, 20:21, 21:4, 22:24, 26:16, 26:56, 27:14, 27:20, Mk2:10; **ꝥ** 2:8, 5:15,

5:29, 6:1, 6:2, 6:5, 6:16, 8:8, 8:34, 10:1, 12:22, 13:2, 13:14, 13:54, 14:15, 14:29, 14:36, 15:31, 15:33, 15:35, 16:20, 18:6, 18:14, 18:16, 19:13, 19:16, 20:31, 20:32, 20:33, 21:32, 21:34, 22:11, 22:15, 23:5, 23:15, 23:34, 24:1, 24:24, 24:45, 26:2, 26:4, 26:42, 26:58, 26:59, 26:63, 27:1, 27:26, 27:31, 27:32, 28:10, Mk1:45 || QUIA ~ 4:6, 5:23, 5:28, 7:23, 11:24, 12:5, 12:6, 16:21, 17:12, 17:13, 18:13, 19:4, 19:23, 20:25, 21:3, 21:16, 21:43, 22:16, 24:33, 26:2, 26:34, 26:53, 27:24, 28:13; **ꝥ** 16:11, 16:18, 16:20, 18:10, 18:19, 19:9, 20:30, 21:13, 21:31, 23:31, 24:32, 24:34, 25:26, 26:21, 26:72, 27:3, 27:43, 28:7 || QUOD ~ 4:12, 6:7, 8:11, 15:32, 17:10, 19:28, 20:10, 21:45, 22:34, 27:63; **ꝥ** 27:18, 28:5 || QUONIAM ~ 12:36, 24:47; **ꝥ** 2:16, 6:16, 6:26, 6:29 || NE (w. negative) **ꝥ** 2:12, 6:1, 6:25 (*ne* wanting) [n.], 9:30, 12:16, 18:10, 24:4, 24:20, 26:41 || QUID **ꝥ** 6:32 (QUIA in WW) || CUM 'when' ~ 9:15 [n.] || QUIS ~ 22:17 || NL ~ 16:13, 24:2 [n.]; **ꝥ** 3:7, 3:11 [n.], 4:19 [n.], 5:32, 5:34, 5:39, 7:4 (margin), 8:4, 12:46, 13:17 [n.], 14:7, 16:5, 17:4, 19:7, 19:10, 20:28, 21:46, 25:24, $25{:}29^{2}$, 27:63, Mk1:17

þætte UT **ꝥte** 1:22, 2:13, 2:15, 2:23, 3:13, 4:6, 4:14, 5:16, 8:17, 8:24, 10:25, 12:17, 16:1, 17:22, Mk1:27, Mk1:38, Mk2:2, Mk2:12; ~ 8:28 || QUIA ~ 5:21, 5:22, 5:32, 5:33, 5:38, 10:7, 15:12, Mk2:10; **ꝥte** 5:27, 5:43, 15:17, 25:24, Mk2:12 || QUOD **ꝥte** 2:22, Mk2:1 || QUONIAM **ꝥte** 2:23; ~ 9:6 [that, *conj.*]

þe *adv.* NL 3:10 [n.]

þe *conj.* 'because, that' QUIA ~ 8:27, 9:28, 10:34, 11:20, 13:13, 13:16 (R QUI), 14:26, 23:15, 23:27, 24:44, 26:54; **ðe** 15:32 [n.]; **þi** 16:23 || QUONIAM ~ 5:8 (a variant of *þy*?) || CUM 'when' ~ 7:11 || QUI 13:16 [n.] || AUTEM ~ 25:17 [n.] || NL ~ 10:26 [n.] (part of *forþon þe*?), 11:13, 15:26 [n.], 23:23, 27:15 'or' AUT ~ 9:5 || AN ~ 11:3, 17:25; **ðe** 21:25

þe *def.art.?* (some of the examples under this heading may be better seen as variant spellings of the demonstrative *se*; expected gender, case, number are given in brackets; see Introduction III.2.2.3) NL **þe** 1:22 (*mas.*) [n.], 8:17 (*mas.*), 8:24 (*nns.*), 12:45 (*nns.*, w. superl.), 13:44 (*mns.*), 16:2 (*mns.*), 16:2 (margin) (*mns.*), 16:3 (*mns.*), 22:27 (*mns.*, w. superl.), 26:51 (*nas.*), Mk1:9 (*mns.*), Mk1:42 (*mns.*); **ðe** 24:39 (*mns.*; or part of *ær þon ðe*?), Mk1:12 (*mns.*), Mk1:26 (*mns.*), Mk2:1 (*fds.* or *a.*?); **ðæ** Mk1:24 (*mns.*)

þe *rel.pron.* (used by itself; see also use as particle under **se**) QUI ~ 1:6, 2:9, 2:16, 5:15, 5:45, 6:9, 7:2 (*bis*), 7:9, 7:13, 7:14, 7:23, 7:24, 7:26, 8:33, 9:8, 10:6, 11:21, 11:23, 11:28, 12:50, 18:7, 18:13, 19:28, 20:12, 21:2, 23:18, 23:37, 24:15, 25:29, 27:54; **ðe** 2:23, 5:16, 10:32, 12:4, 14:2, 16:23 (*bis*), 18:6, 19:29, 20:22, 21:15, 23:29, 24:38, 24:50 (*bis*), 26:24, 26:71, 27:44, Jn18:2 || HIC ~ 18:4 || NL **þe** 21:43, Jn18:1

þe þe *rel.pron.? ns.* **ðe þe** 17:27 (or *p.*?); *np.* ~ 2:20 [n.], 15:27

þeah *adv./conj.* 'though' NL **þæh** 15:20 [n.]

þeah þe 'though, if' SI ~ 24:23; **ðeah þe** 16:26; **þæh þe** 21:21 [n.], 24:26, 26:33, 26:35 [OED2 though, *adv.*, *conj.*, and *n.*]

þeahtung *f.* 'counsel' CONSILIUM *ds.* **þæhtunge** 27:1

geþeahtung *f.* 'counsel, consultation' CONSILIUM *as.* **geþehtunge** 12:14; **geþæhtungę** 22:15, 26:4; **geþæhtunge** 28:12; *ds.* **geþæhtunge** 27:7

þearf *f.* 'need' OPUS *ns.* **þærf** 9:12; **ðærf** 6:8 || NECESSE *as.* **þearfe** 14:16 [OED2 tharf, *n.*]

þearfa *m.* 'poor man, pauper' PAUPER *ap.* **þearfan** 26:11; *dp.* **ðearfum** 19:21; **þearfum** 26:9

þegn *m.* 'servant, disciple' DISCIPULUS *np.* **þægnas** 5:1, Jn18:1; *dp.* **þægnum** Jn18:1; **ðægnum** Jn18:2 || MINISTER *ns.* **þægn** 23:11; **ðægn** 20:26; *ds.* **dægne** 5:25 [n.]; *dp.* **þægnum** 22:13, 26:58 || PUER *dp.* **ðægnum** 14:2 || part of TORTOR *dp.* **þægnum** 18:34 || part of HERODIANUS *dp.* **þægnum** 22:16 [n.] [OED2 thegn, *n.*]

þegnian *v.2* 'serve, minister' MINISTRARE *pt.3s.* **ðægnade** 8:15, 20:28; *pt.1p.* **þegnnedun** 25:44; *pt.3p.* **ðęgnadun** 4:11; *pp.s.* **ðægnad** 20:28; *ps.p. np.* **þægnende** 27:55 [OED2 theine | theign, *v.*]

[MK]**geþegnian** *v.2* 'serve, minister' MINISTRARE *pt.3s.* **geþæignade** Mk1:31; *pt.3p.* **geþegnedon** Mk1:13 [see previous]

þencan *v.1* 'think' COGITARE *ps.2p.* **þencaþ** 9:4, 16:8, Mk2:8; *pt.3s.* **þohte** 1:20 (*bis*); *pt.3p.* **þohtun** 16:7, 21:25; **þohton** Mk2:8; *imp.p.* **þencaþ** 10:19; *ps.p. mns.* **þencende** 6:27; *np.* **ðencende** Mk2:6 || CONSENTIENS *ps.p.* **þencende** 5:24 [n.] [think, *v.2*]

þenden *conj.* 'while' QUAMDIU **þende** 9:15 || DUM **ðenden** 25:10 || CUM **þende** 26:6 [n.] || NL **ðendi** 1:20 [n.]; **þende** 12:46 [n.], 17:5, 26:26; **ðende** 17:22; ~ 26:47

þeod *f.* 'people, nation, gentile' GENS *ns.* ~ 24:7; *as.* **ðeode** 24:7; *gs.*? **þeode** 4:16 [n.]; *ds.* **ðiode** 21:43; *np.* **þeode** 6:32, 12:21, 25:32 **ðeode** 28:19; *gp.* **þeoda** 4:15; **ðeode** 10:5; **ðeoda** 20:25; *dp.* **þeodum** 10:18, 12:18, 24:9, 24:14; **ðeodum** 20:19, 21:13 [OED2 thede, *n.*]

þeof *m.* 'thief' FUR *ns.* ~ 24:43; *np.* **ðiofes** 6:19; ~ 6:20 || LATRO *gs.* **ðeofas** 21:13; *np.* **þeofes** 27:44 [OED2 thief, *n.*]

þeorf *adj.* 'unleavened' AZYMA *gp.* **ðefra** 26:17 [n.] [OED2 tharf, adj.]

þeostor *adj.* 'dark' TENEBROSUS *nns.* **ðeostru** 6:23 [OED2 thester, *adj.*]

þeostru *f.* or **þeostre** *n.* 'darkness' TENEBRAE *ns.* ~ 6:23; *ns.* **þeostre** 6:23 (neut.); *as.* **þiostre** 8:12; **ðiostre** 22:13 (neut.); **þeostra** 25:30 (neut.); *ds.* **þiostre** 4:16; **þeostre** 10:27 [OED2 thester, *n.*]

†**geþeostru** *f.* 'darkness' TENEBRA *np.* **geþriostra** 27:45 [see previous]

þeow *m.* 'servant' SERVUS *ds.* ~ 8:9 [n.] [OED2 theow | thew, *n.* and *adj.*]

þeowe *f.* 'female servant' ANCILLA *ns.* **þeowæ** 26:69 [see previous]

þeowian *v.2* 'serve' SERVIRE *subj.ps.2s.* **þewige** 4:10; *inf.* **ðeowigan** 6:24; **ðeowige** 6:24 [OED theow | thew, *v.*]

þes *dem.pron.* HIC 'this' *mns.* ~ 8:27, 12:24, 21:10, 26:61, 26:71; **þęs** 9:3, Mk2:7; **þis** 9:26? [n.]; **þeos** 26:42? [n.]; **ðeos** 27:47; *mas.* **þisne** 11:23; *mgs.* **þisses** 27:24; *mds.* **þissum** 8:9, 13:54, 13:56; **ðissum** 20:14; *nns.* **þis** 3:3, 3:17, 7:12, 11:10, 12:23, 13:55, 14:2, 15:8, 15:19, 17:5, 17:21, 21:11, 21:38, 22:38, 24:14, 26:12 [n.], 26:13, 26:26, 26:56, 27:37, Mk1:27; *nas.* **þis** 1:20, 8:9, 9:18, 15:12; *ngs.* **þisses** 13:15; *nds.* **þissum** 10:12, 26:29; *fns.* **þeos** 14:15, 24:34; **ðeos** 26:8; **þios** 18:7? [n.], 26:13; *fas.* **þas** 8:31, 11:16, 12:45, 15:32, 21:2, 21:23, 23:36; **ðas** 17:9; *fds.* **þisse** 17:20 [n.], 26:31; **ðisse** 12:32, 26:34, Mk1:38; **þissere** 21:21; *np.* **þas** 1:22, 6:33, 10:2, 20:12, 20:21, 21:16, 23:36, 24:6, 24:8, 27:37 [n.]; *ap.* **þas** 4:9, 6:32, 7:24, 7:26, 7:28, 8:5, 10:5, 11:1, 11:25, 13:34, 13:51, 19:1, 19:20, 21:23, 21:24, 21:27, 24:3, 24:33, 26:1, 26:12 [n.], 26:61 [n.]; *gp.* **þissa** 25:45; *dp.* **þissum** 22:40; **ðissum** 18:10 [n.] || ISTE *mns.* **þes** 26:39, 27:54; **þios** 18:4? [n.]; *nns.* **þis** 21:42, 26:9, 28:15; *fns.* **þios**

Mk1:27; *fas.* **þas** 10:23, 12:41, 12:42, 15:15; *fgs.* **þisse** 13:22; *fds.* **ðisse** 19:28; *np.* **þas** 4:3, 13:56, 26:62; **ðas** Mk1:27; *ap.* **þas** 13:53, 19:11, 24:2, Mk2:8; *gp.* **þisse** 5:19? [n.], 18:14; **þissa** 6:32, 18:6; **þissę** 10:42; *dp.* **þissum** 3:9; *ngs.* **þeos** 8:12? [n.] || HODIERNUS *mas.* **þeosne** 27:8; **þisne** (*ondwardan*) 28:15 || NL *mgs.* **þisses** 20:12; *fas.* **þas** 21:26, 26:23, MtCOLOPHON; *nns.* **þis** 9:37 [n.], 16:2, 24:21; *nas.* **þis** 9:30, 11:12; *np.* **þas** 10:31, 13:54 (HAEC in WW); *ap.* **þas** 14:15; *dp.* **þassum** 8:32 [n.] [OED2 this, *pron.* and *adj.*]

þider *adv.* ILLUC 'thither' ~ 2:22, 24:28 [n.], Jn18:2 [n.]; **þidera** Jn18:3 [OED2 thither, *adv.* and *adj.*]

þing *n.* 'thing, cause' RES *ds.* **þinge** 18:19 || CAUSA *ds.* **þinge** 5:32 || NL *dp.* **þingum** 19:5 [n.]
see also **nænig þinga** listed under **nænig** [thing, *n.1*]

geþingian *v.2* 'reconcile oneself (with), come to an agreement' CONVENIRE *pt.2s.* **geþingdest** 20:13 || CONVENTIONEM FACERE *pt.3p.* **geþingadun** 20:2 || RECONCILIARI *imp.s.* **geþinge** 5:24 [cf. thing, *v.1*]

geþo, see **gedon**

þoht *m.* 'thought' COGITATIO *ap.* **ðohtas** 9:4 [n.]; **þohtas** 12:25 [thought, *n.*]

geþoht *m.* 'thought' COGITATIO *np.* **geþohtas** 15:19 [see previous]

þonne *adv.* 'then' AUTEM ~ 3:11, etc.; **þanne** 3:4, 5:22, 7:15, 8:22, 13:43, 18:16, 19:9, 24:48, 26:32, 27:16; **þone** 3:12 || TUNC ~ 7:5, 7:23, 9:15 [n.], 12:29, 12:44, 12:45, 16:27, 24:9, 24:10, 24:14, 24:16, 24:21, 24:23, 24:30 (*bis*), 24:40, 25:31, 25:34, 25:37, 25:41, 25:44, 25:45; **þanne** 5:24 || ENIM ~ 9:16 (AUTEM in WW), 12:26 (*om.* in WW), 12:30 (*om.* in WW), 13:12, 23:4, 23:6 (AUTEM in WW), 23:8 (*bis*, AUTEM in WW); **þanne** 23:3 || ERGO ~ 6:9, 6:33 (AUTEM in WW), 7:11, 12:26, 13:27, 15:33, 17:26, 19:6, 19:25, 19:27, 22:17, 22:21, 22:31, 24:20 (AUTEM in WW), 24:37 (AUTEM in WW), 26:10, 26:54; **þanne** 9:38 || VERO ~ 8:24, 13:8, 13:23, 13:39, 23:3, 23:5, 25:18, 26:69, 27:49; **þanne** 21:44, 23:27 || IGITUR ~ 12:28; **þanne** 27:22 || QUIDEM ~ 13:23, 13:32 || part of QUOD SI ~ 5:13 [n.], 18:15; **þanne** 5:29 || ADHUC ~ 18:16 (~ *geta*) || NL ~ 12:27, 13:21 (AUTEM in WW), 13:49, 16:25 (AUTEM in WW), 18:14, 19:29, 20:10 (AUTEM in WW), 21:24, 23:13 (AUTEM in WW), 24:6 (part of NONDUM?), 24:8 (AUTEM in WW), 25:31 (AUTEM in WW)

þonne *conj.* 'when' CUM ~ 6:2, 6:5, 6:6, 6:16, 6:17, 10:18, 10:23, 12:43, 15:2, 19:28, 23:15, 24:15, 24:32, 26:60; **þanne** 2:8, 5:11, 24:33 || DUM **þanne** 5:25 || QUOD ~ 26:29
conj. 'than' QUAM ~ 5:20, 5:29, 5:30, 6:25 (*bis*), 10:15, 10:37, 11:9, 11:22, 11:24, 12:41, 12:42, 18:8, 18:9, 19:24, 23:15, 26:53 || NL ~ 6:26, 10:31, 12:12, 12:45 (*bis*); **þone** 27:64 [OED2 then, *adv.* (*conj.*, *adj.*, and *n.*)]

þorn *m.* 'thorn' SPINA *np.* **þornas** 13:7; *ap.* **þornas** 13:7; *dp.* **þornum** 7:16, 27:29; **ðornum** 13:22

þreagan *v.1* 'rebuke' INCREPARE *inf.* **ðreiga** 16:22 [OED2 threa, *v.*]

þreat *m.* 'troop' COHORS *as.* ~ 27:27; *ds.* **þreate** Jn18:3 || TURBA *ns.* **þreat** Mk2:13 [OED2 threat, *n.*]

þreatian *v.2* 'rebuke' INCREPARE *pt.3s.* **ðreatade** 17:18; *pt.3p.* (or *s.*?) **ðreattan** 20:31 [n.] || CORRIPERE *imp.s.* **þreata** 18:15 [OED2 threat, *v.*]

geþreatian *v.2* 'rebuke' INCREPARE *pt.3p.* **geþreatadun** 19:13 [see previous]

þridda *ord. num.* 'third' TERTIUS

(*form?*) **þridde** 16:21 [n.], 27:64; **ðridde** 17:23; *mns.* **þridde** 22:26; *mds.* **þridda** 20:19; *mis.* **ðridde** 26:44; *fds.* **ðridda** 20:3 [OED2 third, *adj.* (and *adv.*) and *n.*]

þrie *num.* 'three' TRES *ma.* **þreo** 12:40 (*bis*), 18:20; *fa.* **þreo** 12:40 (*bis*); *na.* **ðreo** 17:4; *g.* **þreo** 18:16; *d.* **ðrim** 13:33 || part of TRIDUUM *mn.* **þreo** 15:32; *d.* **ðrim** 26:61; **þrim** 27:40 || TERTIUS *d.* **þrim** 27:63 (TRES in WW) [OED2 three, *adj.* and *n.*]

þritig *num.* 'thirty, thirtyfold' TRIGENTA *a.* **ðritig** 26:15, 27:3; **ðrittig** 27:9 || TRICESIMUS *a.* ~ 13:8, 13:23 [OED2 thirty, *adj.* and *n.*]

þriwa *adv.* 'three times, thrice' TER **þriowa** 26:34 **þriuwa** 26:75 [OED2 thrie | thrye, *adv.*]

þrowian *v.2* 'suffer' PATI *ps.1s.* **ðrowa** 17:17; *ps.3s.* **þrowiaþ** 16:26; *ps.2p.* **þrowigaþ** 26:31; *ps.3p.* **þrowiaþ** 5:10, 11:12; *pt.1s.* **þrowade** 27:19; *pt.3s.* **þrowade** 9:20; *ps.p. mns.* **þrowende** 17:12 || part of SCANDALIZARE *ps.1s.* **þrowe** 26:33; *ps.3s.* **þrowað** 13:21; *pt.3p.* **þrowadun** 13:57; *subj.ps.3p.* **þrowige** 26:33 || CRUCIFIGERE *pp.s.* **þrowad** 27:44; *inf.* **þrowigan** 27:31 || TORQUERE *ps.3s.* **þrowað** 17:15 [throw, *v.2*]

geþrowian *v.2* 'suffer' PATI *inf.* **geþrowigan** 16:21 [see previous]

(†)**þrycnes** *f.* 'tribulation, afliction' TRIBULATIO *ns.* **ðrycnisse** 24:21; *as.* **ðricnisse** 24:9 [n.]; *dp.* **ðrycnissum** 24:29

þrymm *m.* 'majesty, glory' MAIESTAS *gs.* **ðrymmes** 19:28; **þrymmes** 25:31; *a/ds.* **ðrymme** 24:30; *ds.* **ðrymme** 25:31 [OED2 thrum, *n.1*]

þu *pron.* 'thou, you' Latin equivalents: TU, VOS, (possessive) TUUS, VESTER

Forms (citations are given only for relatively infrequent forms; instances that do not translate the Latin equivalents listed above are presented separately below):
ns. **þu, ðu**; *as.* **þe, ðe, þec** 4:6 (*bis*), 5:25, 5:29, 5:30 (*bis*), 9:22, 18:16, 22:39, 25:38, 27:40, **ðec** 5:39, 17:27, 18:8, 18:9, 18:15, **þæc** 19:19, 26:73, **ðæc** 21:21; *ds.* **þe, ðe**; *n. dual* **git** 4:19, 20:23 (*bis*); *a/d. dual* **inc** 21:2, 28:10; *d. dual* **inc** 9:28, 9:29, 20:23, 21:3; *np.* **ge**; *ap.* **eow, eowic** 3:11 (*bis*), 5:11, 5:44 (*bis*), 6:30, 7:6, 10:17 (*bis*), 10:19, 10:23, 11:29, 19:8, Mk1:8, Mk1:8 (margin), Mk1:17; *gp.* **eower** 5:11, 6:27, 7:9, 12:11, 18:19, 26:21; *dp.* **eow, heow** 6:14 [n.], **iu** 5:32 [n.], **eowic** 17:12 [n.], 18:10, 18:13

Possessive forms: TUUS *mns.* **þin** 5:29, 5:30, 6:4, 6:6 (margin), 6:10, 6:18, 6:21, 6:22, 6:23, 9:22, 15:28, 20:15, 21:5, 26:42; **ðin** 18:15; *mas.* **þinne** 11:10, 22:39; **þine** 5:43 [n.], 6:6, 6:17; *mas.* **þinne** 22:37; **þin** 6:6; **ðin** 17:27, 18:15, 19:19; *mgs.* **þines** 4:7, 7:5, 22:37? [n.], 24:3, 25:21; **ðines** 25:23; **þine** 7:3 [n.]; *mds.* **þinum** 4:10, 5:24, 5:25, 6:18, 7:4, 7:22 (x3), 11:10, 15:4, 18:33; **ðinum** 19:19; *nns.* **þin** 5:29, 6:10, 6:21, 6:22 (*bis*), 6:23, 20:14, 25:25, 26:73; **ðin** 18:9; **þinne** 5:40; *nas.* **þin** 5:23, 5:24 (*bis*), 5:36, 5:39, 6:17, 9:6 (*bis*), 13:27, 26:52; *nds.* **þinum** 1:20, 7:3, 7:4 (margin), 7:4, 7:5, 20:21, 22:37, Mk2:11; *fns.* **þin** 5:30, 6:3, 6:4, 12:47; *fas.* **þine** 6:6, 12:13, 20:21, 25:25 (gender?), Mk1:2, Mk1:44, Mk2:9, Mk2:11; **þin** 9:18, 20:21; **ðin** 19:19; *fds.* **þinre** 22:37, Mk1:2 (masc. is expected); **þin** 15:4; *np.* **þine** 9:2, 9:14, 12:2, 15:2, 18:8 (*bis*), Mk2:5, Mk2:9; **þin** 12:47; *ap.* **þine** 4:6, 5:33, 5:43, 22:44; **þin** 23:37; *gp.* **þinra** 22:44; *dp.* **þinum** 4:6, 12:37 (*bis*); **ðinum** 17:16; *gp.*(?) **þine** 5:29 [n.], 5:30 || VESTER *mns.* **eower** 5:48, 6:8, 6:14, 6:15, 6:26, 6:32, 9:11, 17:24, 20:26, 20:27, 23:8, 23:9, 23:10, 23:11 (*bis*),

24:20; **ewer** 7:11; *mgs.* **eowres** 5:45, 25:8; **eower** 10:20; *mas.* **eower** 6:1; *mds.* **eowrum** 5:16, 6:25, 17:20; **eower** 10:29; *nns.* **eower** 5:16 (*bis*), 5:37; **eowra** 23:38; *nds.* **eowrum** 6:25; *fns.* **eowra** 5:12, 10:13 (*bis*); **eower** 5:20; *fas.* **eowre** 6:1; *fgs.* **eowre** 19:8; *fd/as.* **eowre** 15:3; *fds.* **eowrum** 23:34; *np.* **eowre** 12:27 (*bis*); *nnp.* **eower** 13:16; **eowre** 13:16; *ap.* **eowre** 5:44, 5:47, 6:14, 7:6; **eowra** 6:15, 19:8; *gp.* **eowra** 23:32; *dp.* **eowrum** 7:11, 9:4, 10:9, 10:10, 10:14 (*bis*), 11:29, 15:6, 18:35, Mk2:8; (dual possessive) *ds.* **incrum** 9:29

NL *ns.* ~ 1:20, etc.; **þv** Mk1:24; **ðu** 4:6, 5:25, 5:26, 8:8, 8:31, 11:23, 15:28, 16:17, 16:23, 18:28, 18:33, 19:17 (*bis*), 20:13, 21:16, 21:23, 25:23, 25:24 (*bis*), 25:26, 25:27, 26:50, 26:73, 27:13, Mk1:40, Mk1:44; contracted with verbs **~tu** 7:3 (*gesihstu*), 7:4 (*cweþestu*), 13:28 (*wiltu*), 14:31 (*getwiodestu*), 20:21 (*wiltu*); *as.* **þe** 8:4 [n.]; **þec** 25:21, 25:23; *ds.* **þe** 1:20 (refl.), 18:33; **ðe** 18:10; *n. dual* **git** 9:28, 20:22, 20:32, 21:2, 28:5; *np.* **ge** 2:8, etc.; *gp.* **eower** 5:33; *ap.* **eowic** 6:25; **eow** 16:12; *a./d.p.* **eow** (refl. w. *biddan*) 6:5, 6:9, 10:26 (refl. w. *ondrædan*), 10:28 (refl. w. *ondrædan*), 17:7 (refl. w. *ondrædan*), 24:20 (refl. w. *gebiddan*), 26:41 (refl. w. *gebiddan*), 26:45 (refl. w. *restan*), 27:24 (refl. w. *locian*); (possessive) *fns.* **þin** 6:3 [thou, *pron.* and *n.1*]

þune, see **dun**

þurfan *pret.pres.v.* 'need' EGERE || *ps.1p.* **ðurfe** 26:65 || INDIGERE *ps.2p.* **ðurfun** 6:32 || OPUS HABERE *ps.3s.* **ðearf** 21:3 || PAUPER *ps.p. mnp.* **þurfende** 5:3; **þorfende** 11:5 [OED2 tharf | thar, *v.*]

þurh *prep.* 'through' PER ~ 1:22, 2:5, 2:12, 2:15, 2:17, 2:23, 3:3, 4:14, 5:34, 5:35 (*bis*), 5:36, 7:13 (*bis*), 8:17, 12:1, 12:17, 12:43, 13:35, 17:21, 18:7, 19:24, 21:4, 26:24, 26:63, 27:9, 27:18; **þyrh** 8:28 [n.] || IN ~ 23:16 (PER in WW) || NL ~ 8:16 (w.d., see note) [through, *prep.* and *adv.*]

†**þurhclænsian** *v.2* 'cleanse thoroughly' PERMUNDARE *ps.3s.* **þurhclęnsaþ** 3:12

þurhdelfan *v.III* 'dig through, pierce' PERFODERE *inf.* ~ 24:43

þurhwunian *v.2* 'remain, last' PERSEVERARE *ps.3s* **þurhwunaþ** 10:22, 24:13; *pt.3p.* **þurhwunadun** 15:32

þurstig *adj.* 'thirsty' SITIRE *mas.* **þyrstigne** 25:37, 25:44 [OED2 thirsty, *adj.*]

þus *adv.* 'thus' SIC ~ 1:18, 3:15, 6:9, 26:54, Mk2:12; **ðus** Mk2:7 || ITA ~ Mk1:27, Mk1:45, Mk2:2 || NL ~ 3:15, 5:18, MtCOLOPHON; **ðus** 24:34 [n.] [OED2 thus, *adv.*]

þusend *num.* 'thousand' MILLE *n.* ~ 15:38; *a.* ~ 5:41; *g.* **þusenda** 16:9, 16:10 (margin); *np.* **þusenð** 14:21; *ap.* **þusende** 18:24; **þusend** 26:53 [n.] [OED2 thousand, *n.* and *adj.*]

þwang *m.* 'thong' CORRIGIA *ap.* **þwongas** Mk1:7 [OED2 thong, *n.*]

þwang *f.?* 'phylactery' PHYLACTERIUM *ap.* **þwængae** 23:5 [n.]

þwean *v.VI* 'wash' LAVARE *ps.3p.* **thauð** 15:2 [n.]; *pt.3s.* **ðwog** 27:24; *imp.s.* **þwah** 6:17

þy *conj.*

þy læs *conj.* 'lest' NE FORTE **þy les** 4:6, 7:6, 13:29, 26:5, 27:64; **þy laes** 5:25; **ðy les** 25:9 || NE **þy les** 6:18, 13:15; **ðy les** 15:32 || UT NON **þy les** 7:1, 17:27 [thy, *adv.* and *pron.*]

geþyld *f.* or *n.* 'patience' PATIENTIA *as.* ~ 18:29; **geðyld** 18:26

þyncan *v.1* 'seem, appear' VIDERE (in passive) *ps.3s.* **ðynceþ** 17:25, 22:42, 26:66; **ðincaþ** 18:12: *subj.ps.3s.* **ðynce** 21:28; **ðyncę** 22:17 || NL *subj.ps.3s.* **þynce** 25:29 (VIDERE in WW) [think, *v.1*]

þyrel *n.* 'hole, opening' FORAMEN *as.* ~ 19:24 [OED2 thirl, *n.1*]
þyrstan *v.1* 'thirst' SITIRE *ps.3s.* **ðyrsteþ** 5:6 [n.]; *pt.3s.* **þyrste** 25:35; **ðyrste** 25:43 [OED2 thirst, *v.*]

ufanweard *adj.* 'highest, topmost' SUMMA *ds.* **ufawarde** 27:51
unadwæscendlic *adj.* 'unquenchable' INEXTINGUIBILIS *nis.* **unaduescendlice** 3:12
†**unandhefe** *adj.* 'unsupportable' INPORTABILIS *ap.* **un⁊hoife** 23:4 [n.]
unbindan *v.III* 'unbind, loosen' SOLVERE *ps.2s.* **unbindes** 16:19; *ps.2p.* **unbindaþ** 18:18; *pp.p.* **unbunde** 16:19; **unbunden** 18:18 [OED2 unbind, *v.*]
unbliþe *adj.* 'sad, sorrowful' MAESTUS *nds.* **unbliðum** 26:37 || TRISTIS *mns.* **unbliðe** 19:22 [OED2 unblithe, *adj.*]
unclæne *adj.* 'unclean' INMUNDUS *mns.* ~ Mk1:25, Mk1:26; **unklene** 12:43; *mds.* **unclænum** Mk1:23; *ap.* **unklene** 8:16; *gp.* **unclenra** 10:1; *gp.* **unclænum** Mk1:27 [unclean, *adj.*, *n.*, and *int.*]
unclænnes *f.* 'uncleanness, impurity' INMUNDITIA *gs.* **unclennisse** 23:25 [uncleanness, *n.*]
under *prep.* 'under' SUB ~ 5:15, 8:8, 8:9 (*bis*), 23:37 [OED2 under, *prep.*]
[MK]**underlutan** *v.II* 'raise, take up' SUFFERRE *pt.3s.* **underleat** Mk2:12
undernmete *m.* 'morning meal, breakfast' PRANDIUM *as.* ~ 22:4
[MK]**undon** *anom.v.* 'undo, loosen' SOLVERE *inf.* **undon** Mk1:7 [OED2 undo, *v.*]
uneaþe *adj.* 'not easy, difficult' IMPOSSIBILIS *nns.* **uneþe** 17:20; **uneaðe** 19:26 [OED2 uneath, *adj.*]
uneaþe *adv.* 'with difficulty' DIFFICILIS **uneaþe** 19:23 [OED2 uneath, *adv.*]
unfeor *adv.* 'not far, near' NON LONGE ~ 8:30
†**ungænge** *adj.* 'not valid, useless' IRRITUS *nas.* ~ 15:6 [n.]
†**ungegerad** *adj.* 'not clothed' NON VESTITUS *mas.* **ungegeradne** 22:11 [n.]
ungeleafa *m. wk* 'unbrief' INCREDULITAS *a/ds.* ~ 13:58; *ds.* **ungeleafa** 17:20
ungeleafful *adj.* 'unbelieving' INCREDULUS *fns.* **ungeleaffullæ** 17:17 [cf. unleveful, *adj.* (and *n.*)]
ungerec *n.* 'disorder, violence' TUMULTUS *ns.* ~ 26:5; **ungereo** 27:24 [n.] || IMPETUS *ds.* **ungerece** 8:32
ungeþwære *adj.* 'disagreeing, quarrelsome' AVERTARE *mns.* ~ 5:42
ungeþwære *n.* 'disturbance' TUMULTUS *ns.* ~ 26:5 [n.]
ungierwan *v.1* 'strip, divest' EXUERE *pt.3p.* **ungeredun** 27:31
unhold *adj.* 'disloyal, hostile' INIMICUS *mns.* ~ 13:28 [n.] [OED2 unhold, *adj.* (and *n.*)]
unmanig *adj.* 'not many, few' PAUCUS *map.* **unmonige** 15:34
unnyt *adj.* 'useless unprofitable' OTIOSUS *nas.* **unnytt** 12:36; *np.* **unnytte** 20:6; *ap.* **unnytte** 20:3 || INUTILIS *mas.* **unnytte** 25:30 [unnut, *adj.*]
unriht *n.* 'wrong, sin, injustice' INIQUITAS *ns.* **unreht** 24:12; *as.* **unreht** 13:41; *gs.* **unryhtæs** 23:28 [unright, *adj.* (and *n.2*)]
unrihthæman *v.1* 'commit adultery' *ps.3s.* **unrehthæmeþ** 5:32 [n.]
unrihthæmed *n.* 'fornication, aludtery' ADULTERIUM *np.* ~ 15:19 || part of ADULTARE *as.* ~ 19:18
unrihtnes *f.* 'injustice, wrong' INIQUITAS *as.* **unrihtnisse** 7:23 [unrightness, *n.*]
unrot *adj.* 'sad' TRISTIS *fns.* ~ 26:38; *mnp.* **unrote** 6:16 || part of CONTRISTARE *mns.* **unrot** 26:37
unrotlice *adv.* 'gloomily, sadly' TRISTE ~ 16:3
geunrotsian *v.2* 'be sad, make sad'

CONTRISTARE *pp.s.* **geunrotsed** 14:9; *pp.p.* **geunrotsad** 17:23, 18:31, 26:22

unsælan *v.1* 'untie, unfasten' SOLVERE *imp.p.* **unsæleþ** 21:2

unscæþþende *adj.* 'innocent' INNOCENS *ns.* **unsceþþende** 27:24; *ap.* **unsceþðende** 12:7

unsoþfæst *adj.* 'unjust, faithless' INIUSTUS *ap.* **unsoþfæste** 5:45 [OED2 unsoothfast, *adj.*]

unsyfernes *f.* 'impurity' SPURCITIA *gs.* **unsyfernissę** 23:27

untela *adv.* 'not well, badly' MALE **untale** 27:23

untrum *adj.* 'ill, infirm' INFIRMUS *mns.* ~ 25:36, 25:43; *mas.* **untymne** 25:39; ~ 25:44; *nns.* ~ 26:41 || LANGUIDUS *ap.* **untryme** 14:14 || MALE HABENS *dp.* **vntrymum** 9:12 [n.] [OED2 untrum, *adj.*]

untrumnes *f.* 'weakness, infirmity' INFIRMITAS *as.* **untymnisse** 4:23, 9:35, 10:1, 10:8; *dp.* **untrymnissum** 8:17 [OED2 untrumness, *n.*]

unþwægen *adj.* 'unwashed' NON LAVARE *dp.* **unðwegenum** 15:20

unwreon *v.I or II* 'uncover, reveal' NUDARE *pt.3p.* **unwreogon** Mk2:4 || REVELARE *pp.s.* **vnwrigan** 10:26 [n.] [OED2 unwry, *v.*]

up *adv.* 'up' NL **upp** 4:16, 5:45 [n.], 13:5, 13:6, 13:48, 17:27 [OED2 up, *adv.1*]

uparisnes *f.* 'resurrection' RESURRECTIO *ns.* **uparisnisse** 22:23 [n.]

urias *prop.n. as.* ~ 1:6 [n.]

ut *adv.* '(go) out, (throw) out… etc.' EX- prefix ~ 3:5, 5:26, 7:22, 8:16, 8:28, 8:31, 8:32, 8:34, 9:25 (or NL?), 9:31, 9:32, 9:33, 9:34, 10:1, 10:8, 10:11, 12:20, 12:26, 12:27, 12:28, 12:43, 12:44, 13:3, 14:14, 15:19, 15:22, 17:19, 17:21, 18:28, 20:3, 20:5, 20:6, 20:29, 21:12, 22:10, 24:1, 24:26, 24:27, 25:1, 25:6, 26:30, 26:71, 27:32 || FORAS ~ 5:13, 10:14, 13:48, 21:17 || FORIS ~ 26:75; **utæ** 12:46; **ute** 12:47 || NL ~ 12:14 (EX- in WW), 15:17 (E- in WW), 26:55 (EX- in WW) [out, *adv.*, *int.*, and *prep.*]

utan *adv.* 'from outside' DE/A FORIS ~ 23:25, 23:27, 23:28 [outen, *adv.*, *adj.*, and *prep.*]

utera *adj.* 'outer, exterior' EXTERIOR *fas.* **yterræ** 22:13; *fap.* **yterre** 25:30 [n.] [OED2 utter, *adj.*]

†**utgenga** *m.* *wk?* 'exit, passage?' EXITUS *dp.* **utgengum** 22:9 [n.] [cf. outgang, *n.*]

[MK]**uþwita** *m.* 'scholar, scribe' SCRIBA *np.* **uðwutu** Mk1:22; *dp.* **uþwutum** Mk2:6

vipere *f.? wk* VIPERA *gp.* **uiperana** 23:33 [n.] [cf. OED2 viper, *n.*]

wa *m.* 'woe, affliction' VAE (as *interj.*) ~ 11:21 (*bis*), 18:7 (*bis*), 23:13, 23:14, 23:16, 23:23, 23:25, 23:27, 24:19, 26:24; **wæ** 23:15 [woe, *int.*, *adv.*, *n.*, and *adj.*]

wacen *f.* 'vigil, watching' VIGILIA *ds.* **wacone** 14:25

wagian *v.2* 'move, shake' QUATERE *ps.p. nas.* **wagende** 12:20 [OED2 waw, *v.1*]

wagrift *n.* 'vail, curtain' VELUM *ns.* **wagryft** 27:51

wamb *f.* 'stomach, belly' VENTER *a/ds.* **wombe** 15:17; *ds.* **wombe** 12:40 [womb, *n.*]

wan *adj.* 'wanting, absent' part of ABESSE/DEESSE *nns.* **won** 16:22; **woen** 19:20 [OED2 wane, *adj.*]

wange *n.* 'cheek' MAXILLA *as.* **wonge** 5:39 [OED2 wang, *n.1*]

warnian *v.2* 'warn, caution' CAVERE *imp.p.* **warniaþ** 16:6; **warnaþ** 16:12 [OED2 warn, *v.1*]

warnian *v.2* 'deny, refuse' PROHIBERE *imp.p.* **wernað** 19:14 [OED2 warn, *v.2*]

waroþ *n.* 'shore, strand' LITUS *ds.* **waraþe** 13:2; **waraðe** 13:48 [OED2 warth, *n.*]

wæccan *v.1* 'watch' VIGILARE *imp.p.* **wæccaþ** 24:42, 26:38; **wæceþ**

25:13; **wæcceþ** 26:41; *ps.p. mns.* **wæcende** 24:43 [OED2 watch, *v.*]

wæcce, **wæcceþ** (glossing SUSCITARE), see **weccan**

wæd *f.* 'robe, garment' VESTIMENTAUM *ds.* **wede** 27:31; *np.* **wæda** 28:3 || VESTIS *as.* **wede** 22:12 [weed, *n.2*]

gewæd *f.* 'robe, dress' VESTIMENTUM *dp.* **gewedum** 7:15 [see previous]

[MK]**gewædian** *v.2* 'dress, clothe' VESTITUS *pp. mns.* **gewedad** Mk1:6

wælan *v.1* 'afflict, torment' TORQUERE *pp.s.* **wælid** 8:6 [n.] || VEXARE *pp.s.* **wæled** 15:22

gewælan *v.1* 'vex, afflict' VEXARE *pp.p.* **gewælde** 9:36

wæpen *n.* 'weapon' ARMA *ap.* **wepenu** Jn18:3 [OED2 weapon, *n.*]

wæpned *m.* 'male person' MASCULUS *as.* **wepned** 19:4

wærge, **wærgaþ**, see **wyrgan**

wæstm *m.n. or f.?* 'fruit' FRUCTUS *ns.* **wæstim** 21:19; *as.* **woestim** 3:10; **westęm** 7:19; **westem** 12:33 (*bis*), 13:23, 13:26; **wæstem** 13:8; **wæstim** 21:41, 21:43; *n/fas.* **westem** 3:8 [n.]; *ds.* **westem** 12:33; *ap.* **węstmas** 7:17; **westmas** 7:17, 7:18; **wæstmas** 7:18; *gp.* **wæstma** 21:34; *dp.* **wæstmum** 7:16, 7:20, 21:34 || part of PLANTATIO *gp.* **wæstma** 15:13 [n.] [OED2 wastum, *n.*]

wæstmleas *adj.* 'unfruitful' SINE FRUCTU *nns.* **westemleas** 13:22 [n.]

wæter *n.* 'water' AQUA *as.* ~ 14:28, 14:29 (margin), 27:24; *gs.* **wættres** 10:42; *ds.* **wættre** 3:11, 3:16, 17:15; **wætre** Mk1:8, Mk1:10; *dp.* **wættrum** 8:32 [water, *n.*]

wea *m.* 'misfortune, trouble' MALITIA *ns.* ~ 6:34

[MK]†**wealdstapa** *m.* 'grasshopper' LOCUSTA *gs.* **waldstapan** Mk1:6 [n.]

geweald *n.* 'power, control' part of DOMINARI *as.* **gewald** 20:25 [n.] [i-wald, *n.*]

weall *m.* 'wall' TURRIS *as.* **wall** 21:33 [OED2 wall, *n.1*]

weard *m.* 'guard' CUSTOS *np.* **weardas** 28:4; *gp.* **wearda** 28:11 [ward, *n.1*]

weaxan *v.VII* 'wax, grow' CRESCERE *ps.3s.* **wexeþ** 13:32; *ps.3p.* **waexaþ** 6:28; *pt.3s.* **weox** 13:26; *pt.3p.* **wexon** 13:7; *inf.* **wexan** 13:30 || NL *ps.3s.* **wæxeþ** Mk1:6 [OED2 wax, *v.1*]

weccan *v.1* 'awaken' SUSCITARE *subj.ps.3s.* **wæcce** 22:24; *pt.3p.* **wehton** 8:25; *imp.p.* **wæcceþ** 10:8 [OED2 wecche, *v.*]

wedan *v.1* 'become mad, rage' RAPAX *ps.p. mnp.* **woedende** 7:15 [n.] [OED2 wede, *v.*]

weg *m.* 'way' VIA *ns.* ~ 4:15, 7:13, 7:14; *as.* ~ 11:10; **wæg** 3:3, 10:5, 22:16; **weig** Mk1:3; *ds.* **wege** 2:12, 21:8; **wæge** 5:25, 8:28, 10:10, 13:4, 13:19, 15:32, 20:30, 21:8, 21:19; **wegæ** 21:32; **weg** Mk1:2 [n.]; *ap.* **weogas** 4:6 [n.], 22:9 [n.], 22:10 [way, *n.1* and *int.1*]

wel *adv.* 'well' BENE ~ 12:18, 15:7, 17:5 || EUGE ~ 25:21, 25:23 || part of BENEFACERE 'do well' (*don*) **wæl** 5:4 || part of COMPLACERE ~ Mk1:11 [well, *adv.* and *n.4*]

wela *m. wk* 'weal, riches' DIVITIAE *gp.* **weolan** 13:22 [OED2 weal, *n.1*]

weler *m.* or *f.* 'lip' LABIA *dp.* **welerum** 15:8

welig *adj.* 'rich' DIVES *mns.* **wælig** 27:57; *mns.* **weliga** 19:23; *mds.* **weligan** 19:24 [wealy, *adj.1*]

wemman *v.1* 'defile, profane' VIOLARE *ps.3p.* **wemmaþ** 12:5 [OED2 wem, *v.*]

gewemman *v.1* 'corrupt, pollute' MOECHARI *pp.s.* **gewemmed** 5:28 [n.]

wen *f.* 'expectation, belief' FORTE *ns.* ~ 11:23 [n.] [OED2 ween, *n.*]

wenan *v.1* 'imagine, expect' PUTARE *ps.2s.* **wenest** 18:1, 26:53; *ps.3p.* **woenaþ** 6:7; *imp.p.* **wenaþ** 5:17 || ARBITARI *pt.3p.* **wendon** 20:10; *imp.p.* **wenaþ** 10:3 || SPERARE *ps.3s.*

wenaþ 24:50 || NL *ps.2s.* **wenest** 24:45 (PUTARE in WW) [OED2 ween, *v.*]

wendan *v.1* 'turn, go' REVERTERE *inf.* (*eft*) ~ 12:44 [wend, *v.1*]

gewendan *v.1* 'turn' REVERTI 'return' *pt.3p.* **gewendun** 2:12 [see previous]

weod *n.* 'weed, injurious plant' ZIZANIA *as.* ~ 13:27; *np.* ~ 13:26, 13:38, 13:40; *ap.* ~ 13:25 (or *s.*?), 13:29, 13:30; *gp.* **weode** 13:36 [weed, *n.1*]

weofod *n.* 'altar' ALTARE *ns.* **wibed** 23:19; *as.* **weofud** 5:23, 5:24; **wibed** 5:24; **wibæd** 23:35; *ds.* **wibede** 5:23 [n.], 23:20; **wifode** 23:18 [OED2 weved, *n.*]

weorc *n.* 'work' OPUS *as.* ~ 5:16; **werc** 26:10; *is.* **weorcæ** 16:27; *ap.* **werc** 11:2; **wærc** 23:5; *dp.* **wærcum** 23:3 [work, *n.*]

weorpan *v.III* 'throw, cast' EICERE *ps.1s.* **wyrpe** 12:27; *ps.3s.* **weorpeþ** 12:26; **weorpeð** 9:34; *pt.3s.* **wearp** 9:33, 21:12; *pt.1p.* **wyrpon** 7:22; *pt.3p.* **wurpon** 21:39; *imp.p.* **weorpaþ** 10:8; **weorpað** 25:30 || MITTERE *ps.3s.* **weorpeþ** 15:26; *pp.s.* **worpen** 5:13; *imp.s.* **wearp** 21:21 (IACTARE in WW) || IACTARE *pp.s.* **worpen** 14:24 || PROICERE *pt.3s.* **wearp** 27:5; *imp.s.* **weorp** 18:8 [OED2 warp, *v.*]

geweorpan *v.III* 'throw' MITTERE *imp.p.* **gewearpaþ** 7:6 [see previous]

weorþ *adj.* 'worthy' DIGNUS *mns.* **wyrþe** 3:11, 10:11; **wyrðe** 8:8, 10:10, 10:13, 10:37 (*bis*), 10:38, Mk1:7; *nas.?* **wyrþe** 3:8 [n.]; *nns.* **wyrþe** 10:13; *np.* **wyrðe** 22:8 [worth, *adj.*]

weorþ *n.* 'worth, value' PRETIUM *ns.* ~ 27:9; **weorð** 27:6 [worth, *n.1*]

weorþan *v.III* 'become, happen' FIERI *ps.3s.* **werþeð** 9:16; **weorþaþ** 24:21; *ps.3p.* **weorðaþ** 12:45; *pt.3s.* **warð** 9:22; *pt.3p.* **wyrdun** 27:45; *subj.ps.3s.* **weorþe** 6:10; **werþe** 24:20; **wyrðe** 24:22; *inf.* ~ 24:6 || FACTUM ESSE *pt.3p.* **wurdon** 17:2, 19:12; **wvrdon** 14:36 [n.] || part of SATURARE *ps.3p.* (*fulle*) **weorþaþ** 5:6; *pt.3p.* (*fulle*) **wyrdun** 14:20 || part of PERIRE 'perish' *ps.3p.* **weorðaþ** 9:17 (*to lore*); *pt.3p.* **wyrðon** 10:6 (*to lore*); *subj.ps.3s.* **weorðe** 5:29 (*to lore*), 18:14 (*to lose*); **wearþe** 5:30 (*to lose*) [n.] || ESSE *pt.3s.* **wearð** 22:2 (FACTUM ESSE in WW) [worth, *v.1*]

geweorþan *v.III* 'become, happen' FIERI *ps.3s.* **geweorþað** 21:21; **gewyrð** 13:32; *ps.3p.* **geweorþað** 24:34; *pt.3s.* **gewarð** 7:28, 21:42 (*bis*), 26:56, 27:24, 28:2, Mk1:32; *pt.3p.* **gewurdun** 18:31, 27:54; *subj.ps.3s.* **geweorþe** 5:18, 18:19; **geweorðe** 8:13, 9:29, 15:28; **geweorþæ** 23:26; *subj.ps.3p.* **gewærþe** 4:3 [n.]; *subj.pt.3s.* **gewyrde** 26:5; *inf.* **geweorðan** 20:26; *pp. fds.?* **geworden** 13:21; *pp.* + *wesan* (FACTUM ESSE) **geworden** 1:22, 8:24, 8:26, 9:10, 17:1, 20:8, 21:4, 25:6, 26:1, 27:57, Mk1:11, Mk2:15; *pp.* (without *wesan*) **geworden** 14:15, 14:23, 16:2, 28:4 || EFFICERE *ps.3s.* **geweorðæd** 13:22 [yworth, *v.*]

weorþian *v.2* 'worship, honour' HONORIFICARE *pt.3p.* **worþadun** Mk2:12; *pp.p.* **weorþade** 6:2 || HONORARE *ps.3s.* **weorðaþ** 15:8 [worth, *v.2*]

wepan *v.VII* 'weep' LUGERE *inf.* ~ 9:15; *ps.p. mnp.* **wepende** 5:5 [n.] || PLANGERE *ps.3p.* **wepaþ** 24:30; *pt.2p.* **weopun** 11:17 || PLORARE *ps.p. fns.* **wepende** 2:18 || FLERE *pt.3s.* **weop** 26:75 [OED2 weep, *v.*]

wer *m.* 'man' VIR *ns.* ~ 1:19; *as.* **wær** 1:16; **were** 26:69; *ds.* **were** 7:24, 7:26; *np.* **weras** 12:41, 14:35; **weoras** 15:38; *gp.* **weora** 14:21 [OED2 were, *n.1*]

werian *v.2* 'forbid, prevent' PROHIBERE *pt.3s.* **werede** 3:14 [OED2 were, *v.*]

wesan *anom.v.* 'to be' ESSE (for other

Latin equivalents, see below) **Forms** (citations are given only for relatively infrequent forms): *ps.1s.* **eam**, **beom** 9:21, 17:17, 20:22; *ps.2s.* **eart**, **earð** 6:9, **bist** 5:23; *ps.3s.* **is**, **his** 3:3 [n.], 3:10, 5:3, 5:41, 17:4, 22:20, 23:18, 26:66, **biþ**, **bið**, **bid** 13:50, **beoþ** 6:23, 6:34 [n.]; *ps.p.* **sindun**, **sindon** 13:56, 15:20, **syndon** 12:5, 13:38, **sendon** 22:30, **sendun** 2:18, **sydun** 13:39, **sint** 1:17 (x3), 5:12, 6:23, 12:5, 24:16, **beoþ**, **beoð** 24:40, **bioþ** 24:6, 24:9, **beoþan** 4:19 [n.], 5:11, 18:18, 19:30, 25:41, **beoðan** 16:19; *ps.2p.* **arun** 19:28; *pt.1s.* **wæs**; *pt.2s.* **węre** 25:21, 25:23; *pt.3s.* **wæs**, **wæss** 2:18, **węs** Mk1:39; *pt.p.* **weron**, **wærun**, **wæron** 12:4, 23:30, **węron** 12:3; *subj.ps.1s.* **seo** 16:15; *subj.ps.2s.* **se** 5:25, **sie** 4:6, 5:25, 10:11, **siæ** 4:3, **się** 14:28, 16:13; **sy** 26:63; *subj.ps.3s.* **beon** 5:30?, **beo** 18:17, 20:26, 20:27, 23:11, 26:42, **sie** 5:37, 6:4, 6:8, 9:13, 10:25, 12:23, 18:1, **siae** 10:13 (*bis*), **seo** 22:23, **siæ** 24:17, 27:19, 27:40, **sy** 24:18, **się** 22:42, **syæ** 27:42; *subj.ps.1p.* **sie** 17:4, 24:45; *subj.ps.2p.* **sie** 5:44, **siæ** 16:22; *subj.ps.3p.* **beon** 4:3, 25:34; *subj.pt.3s.* **wære** 14:26, 16:20, 26:24, Mk1:45, Mk2:1; *imp.s.* **beo** 5:25, **wæs** 2:13, 5:25; *imp.p.* **beoþ** 5:48, 6:5, 24:44, **bioþ** 10:16, **wesaþ** 10:16; *inf.* **beon** 19:21, 19:25, 20:27, 24:24, 26:37, 26:39; with contraction with subject *ps.2s.* **arþu** 11:3; with negative contraction *ps.1s.* **næm** 3:11, **nam** 8:8, Mk1:7; *ps.3s.* **nis** 5:37 (x4), 6:25, 9:12, 9:24, 10:24, 10:26, 10:37 (*bis*), 10:38, 12:30, 13:55, 13:57, 15:26, 18:14, 20:23, 22:16, 22:17, 22:32, 23:16, 24:6, 28:6

Translating Latin verbs other than ESSE: FIERI *pt.3s.* **wæs** 8:16, 27:1; *imp.p.* **beoþ** 6:16; *inf.* **beon** 26:54 || HABERE *pt.3s.* **wæs** 12:22 [n.]; *pt.3p.* **werun** 8:33 [n.], 26:26 || part of DEESSE *ps.3s.* **is** 19:20 || NL (excluding those used in periphrastic verb phrases, e.g., passive) *ps.3s.* **is** 1:23, 2:11, 3:10 [n.], 5:35 [n.], 8:29, 9:18 [n.], 9:37 [n.], 12:24, 12:41, 12:42, 13:38 (ESSE in WW), 13:52 (ESSE in WW), 22:39 (ESSE in WW), 23:8 (ESSE in WW), 24:46, 26:8, 26:41, 27:4, Mk1:16, Mk1:29, Mk1:30; **biþ** 10:25, 16:3; *ps.2p.* **beoþan** Mk1:17; *imp.p.* **beoþ** 28:9; *ps.p.* **sindun** 1:1, 23:27 (ESSE in WW); *pt.3s.* **wæs** 2:19, 15:37 (part of SUPERESSE), Mk1:41; **węs** 27:32; *subj.ps.2p.* **seon** Mk1:17; *subj.ps.3p.* (*fulle*) **beon** 5:6 [n]; *imp.s.* **beo** 5:42 (partly corr. to *auertaris*); *inf.* (*gelice*) **beon** 6:8, 24:43 [be, *v.*]

westan *adv.* 'from the west' AB OCCIDENTE ~ 8:11 [westen, *adv.*]

westdæl *m.* 'western part' OCCIDENS *ds.* **westdæle** 24:27 [westdeal, *n.*]

westen *n.m.f.?* 'desert' DESERTUM *as.* ~ Mk1:12; **wæstenne** 11:7; *ds.* **wæstenne** 15:33; **westinne** 3:3; **woestenne** 3:1, 4:1 (or *as.*?); **węstene** 24:26; **westenne** Mk1:3, Mk1:4; **westen** Mk1:13

westen *adj.* 'deserted' DESERTUS *fas.* **woesten** 14:13 (or noun?)

westig *adj.* 'deserted' DESERTUS *fns.* **woestig** 14:15; *fas.* **westige** Mk1:35; *nns.* **woestig** 23:38; *dp.* **westigum** Mk1:45 [westy, *adj.1*]

wibed, **wibede**, see **weofod**

wid *adj.* 'wide' LATUS *nns.* ~ 7:13 [wide, *adj.*]

widuwana, see **wuduwe**

wif *n.* 'wife' MULIER *ns.* ~ 9:20, 9:22, 13:33, 15:22, 15:28, 22:27, 26:7; *as.* ~ 5:28; *ds.* **wife** 26:10; *np.* **wif** 27:55; *gp.* **wifa** 11:11; *dp.* **wifum** 14:21, 15:38, 28:5 || UXOR *ns.* ~ 22:28, 27:19; *as.* ~ 5:31, 5:32, 14:3, 18:25, 19:3, 19:9, 19:29, 22:25 (*bis*); *ds.* **wife** 19:5, 19:10, 22:24; *ap.* ~ 19:8 || CONIUX *ds.* **wife** 1:20; **wiue** 1:24 [n.] || FEMINA *as.* ~ 19:4 [wife, *n.*]

[MK]**wilddeor** *n.* 'wild animal, beast'

BESTIA *dp.* **wildedeorum** Mk1:13 [n.] [OED2 wild deer, *n.*]

willa *m. wk* 'will, desire' VOLUNTAS *ns.* ~ 6:10; **willæ** 26:42; **willan** 18:14; *as.* **willan** 12:50, 21:31; **wille** 7:21 || AMOR *ds.* **willan** 24:13 [n.] [will, *n.1*]

willan *anom.v.* 'will, wish' VELLE *ps.1s.* **wille** 8:3, 9:13, 12:7, 12:44, 20:14, 20:15, 26:39, Mk1:41; *ps.2s.* **wilt** 8:2, 19:17, 19:21, 26:39, Mk1:40; w. subject contraction **wiltu** 13:28, 20:21; **uuiltu** 26:17; *ps.3s.* **wille** 5:40, 5:42, 16:24, 20:26; **wile** 11:27, 16:25, 20:27, 27:43; *ps.1p.* **willaþ** 12:38; *ps.2p.* **willað** 7:12, 11:14, 26:15; **willaþ** 20:32, 27:17, 27:21; *pt.1s.* **wolde** 23:37; *pt.3s.* **wolde** 1:19, 14:5; **walde** 18:23, Jn18:2; *pt.3p.* **waldun** 17:12; *subj.ps.2s.* **wille** 15:28, 17:4; *subj.pt.3p.* **walden** 27:15; *imp.p.* **wellað** 3:9 [n.] || NELLE (with *ne*) *ps.1s.* **wille** 15:32; *pt.3s.* **walde** 1:19 [n.], 2:18; **wolde** 18:30; w. negative contraction *ps.1s.* **nyll** 21:30; *ps.3p.* **nylleþ** 23:4; *pt.3s.* **nolde** 27:34; *pt.2p.* **naldun** 23:37; *pt.3p.* **noldan** 22:3; *imp.p.* **nyllaþ** 23:8 || NL *ps.3s.* **wille** 8:19 [n.]; *pt.3s.* **walde** 24:43 (*bis*) [n.]; w. negative contraction *subj.ps.3s.* **nyle** 10:14 [will, *v.1*, *v.2*]

wilnian *v.2* 'wish, desire' CUPERE *pt.3p.* **wilnadun** 13:17 [OED2 will, *v.1*]

win *n.* 'wine' WINUM *ns.* ~ 9:17; *gs.* **wines** 11:19; *as.* ~ 9:17 (*bis*), 27:34 [OED2 will, *v.1*]

winbeger *n.?* 'wine-berry, grape' UVA *ap.* ~ 7:16 [n.] [OED2 wineberry, *n.*]

†**winbelg** *m.* 'leather bottle of wine' UTER *ap.* **winbeligas** 9:17 [n.]

wind *m.* 'wind' VENTUS *ns.* ~ 8:24, 14:24, 14:32; *as.* ~ 14:30; *ds.* ~ 8:26, 11:7; *np.* **windas** 7:25, 7:27; ~ 8:27 (or *s.*?); *dp.* **windum** 24:31 [OED2 wind, *n.1*]

windan *v.III* 'wind, plait' PLECTERE *ps.p. np.* **widende** 27:29 [n.] [OED2 wind, *v.1*]

†**windwigscofl** *f.* 'a winnowing-fan' VENTILABRUM *ns.* **winduiscoful** 3:12 [n.]

wingeard *m.* 'vineyard' VINEA *as.* ~ 20:1, 20:2, 20:4, 20:7, 21:30, 21:33, 21:39, 21:41; *gs.* **wingeardes** 20:8, 21:40; *ds.* ~ 21:28 [cf. OED2 vineyard, *n.*]

winnan *v.III* 'labour, toil' LABORARE *ps.2p.* **winnaþ** 11:28; *ps.3p.* **winnaþ** 6:28 [win, *v.1*]

winstre *adj.* 'left' SINISTER *fns.* **winstrae** 6:3; *fas.* **winstran** 20:21, 20:23, 25:33, 27:38; *fds.* **winstran** 25:41

winter *n.* 'year, winter' ANNUS *ap.* (adverbially) ~ 9:20 || part of BIMATUS 'two years' *dp.* (*twæm*) **wintrum** 2:16 || HIEMS *ds.* **wintre** 24:20 [winter, *n.1*]

wintreow *n.* 'vine' VINEA *gs.* **wintreowes** 21:34; **wintreos** 26:29 [OED2 wine-tree, *n.*]

wisfæst *adj.* 'wise, sagacious' PERFECTUS *comp. mns.* **wisfæstre** 19:21 [n.]

gewita *m.* 'witness' TESTIS *np.* **gewitu** 26:60 (*bis*) [cf. OED2 wite, *n.1*]

witan *pret.pres.v.* 'know' (NE)SCIRE *ps.1s.* **wat** 25:24, 26:70, 28:5, Mk1:24; *ps.2s.* **wast** 15:12; *ps.3s.* **wat** 6:32, 24:36 *ps.1p.* **wutan** 22:16; *ps.2p.* **witan** 24:44; **wutan** 26:2; *pt.3s.* **wiste** 12:15, 16:8, 27:18, Jn18:2; *pt.2p.* **wiston** 12:7; *pt.3p.* **wisten** Mk1:34; *subj.ps.3s.* **wite** 9:30; *subj.ps.2p.* **wite** 9:6; **witan** 24:32; *subj.pt.3s.* **wiste** 24:43; *imp.p.* **witaþ** 24:43, Mk2:10; **wite** 24:33; *pp.s.* **witen** 10:26; *ps.p. mns.* **witende** 12:25, 26:10; w. negative contraction **nytan** NESCIRE *ps.1p.* **niton** 21:27; *ps.2p.* **nytan** 20:22; *subj.ps.3s.* **nyte** 6:3 || part of IGNORARE *ps.3s.* (*ne*) **wat** 24:50 [OED2 wit, *v.1*]

witan *v.I* 'go, depart' NL *subj.ps.1p.* (w. inf. 'let us') **wutu** 21:38, 26:46, Mk1:38; **hwute** 27:49 [OED2 wite, *v.3*]

gewitan *v.I* 'go, depart' SECEDERE *pt.3s.* **gewat** 2:14 (RECEDERE in WW), 4:12, 12:15, 14:13, 15:21 || DISCEDERE *imp.p.* **gewitaþ** 7:23, 25:41 || RECEDERE *pt.3s.* **gewat** 27:5; *imp.p.* **gewitaþ** (~ *heonan*) 9:24 || TRANSIRE *ps.3s.* **gewitað** 17:20; *imp.s.* **gewit** 17:20 || PRAETERIRE *pt.3s.* **gewat** 14:15 || REGREDI 'return' *pp.p.* **gewitenę** 2:13 [OED2 i-wite, *v.2*]

wite *n.* 'punishment' CILICIUM *ds.* ~ 11:21 [or a form of *hwit*? see note] [OED2 wite | wyte, *n.2*]

witega *m.* 'prophet' PROPHETA *ns.* **witgu** 11:9; **witga** 12:39, 13:57, 16:4, 21:4, 21:11, 21:26 (or *a.*?); **wihtga** 21:46; *as.* **witgu** 1:22 [n.], 2:5, 2:15, 2:17, 3:3, 4:14, 8:17, 10:41, 11:9, 13:35, 14:5, Mk1:2; **witgan** 12:17, 27:9; *gs.* **witgu** 10:41 (*bis*); *ds.* **wihtga** 24:15; *np.* **witgu** 7:12, 11:13, 13:17; **witga** 22:40; *ap.* **witga** 5:17, 23:37; **witgu** 2:23, 7:15; **witgan** 23:31, 23:34; *gp.* **witgena** 5:12; **witgana** 16:14, 23:29, 26:56; **uitgana** 23:30 || part of PSEUDOPROPHETA *np.* **witga** 24:11; **witgu** 24:24 [OED2 witie, *n.*]

witegdom *m.* 'prophecy, prediction' PROPHETIA *ns.* **witigdom** 13:14

witegian *v.2* 'prophesy' PROPHETARE *pt.3s.* **witgade** 15:7; *pt.1p.* **witgadun** 7:22; *pt.3p.* **witgadun** 11:13 || PROPHETIZARE *imp.s.* **witga** 26:68 [OED2 witie, *v.1*]

gewitnes *f.* 'witness, knowledge' TESTIMONIUM *as.* **gewitnisse** 19:18, 26:59; *np.* **gewitnisse** 15:19 || TESTIS *ap.* **gewitnisse** 26:65; *gp.* **gewitnesse** 18:16 || TESTAMENTUM *gs.* **gewitnisse** 26:28 [OED2 i-witness, *n.*]

witodlice *adv.* 'truly, for' AUTEM **wiotudlice** 10:19, 16:3, 16:8, 16:14, 16:16 (*om.* in WW), 23:24; **wutudlice** Mk1:14, Mk1:30, Mk1:32, Mk2:6; **witudlice** Mk1:41; **witud** Mk2:10 [n.] || ENIM **weotudlice** 6:34 (*om.* in WW); **wiotudlice** 7:2 [n.], 7:8, 7:12, 17:22 || VERO **wiotudlice** 8:24, 13:38, Mk1:8 || NAM **wiotudlice** 8:9, 15:4 || ERGO **wiotudlice** Jn18:3 || IAM **wutudlice** Mk1:45 || NL **wiotudlice** 8:17 [n.]

wiþ *prep.* 'against, with' ADVERSUM/-US ~ 12:32; **wið** 5:11, 5:23, 10:35 (x3), 12:14, 12:26, 16:18, 20:11, 26:62, 27:1, 27:13 || CUM ~ 17:3; **wið** 5:40, 19:10, 20:2, 20:13, 27:34 || CONTRA **wið** 12:25 (*bis*), 12:30, 12:32, 26:59 || A/AB **wið** 7:15, 10:17, 16:6, 16:12 || NL ~ 5:24, 5:28; **wið** 6:12, 10:21, 12:46, 18:27 [OED2 with, *prep.*, *adv.*, and *conj.*]

wiþceosan *v.II* 'reject' REPROBARE *pt.3p.* **wiðcuron** 21:42

wiþerdune *adj.* 'uphill, steep' ANGUSTUS *nns.* ~ 7:14 [n.]

wiþermetan *v.V* 'compare' ADSIMILARE *pp.s.* **wiðermeten** 18:23 [n.]

wiþerweard *adj.* 'adverse, (subst.) adversary' SATANAS *mns.* **wiþerwearde** 4:10, 16:23; **wiþerwearð** 12:26; *mas.* **wiðerweard** 12:26; *mds.* **wiðerwearda** Mk1:13 || ADVERSARIUS *mns.* **wiðerwearde** 5:25 || CONTRARIUS *mns.* **wiðerweard** 8:24; **wiðerwear** 14:24 [OED2 witherward, *adj.*]

wiþerwearda *m.* 'adversary, enemy' ADVERSARIUS *ds.* **wiðerwearde** 5:25 [n.]

wiþstandan *v.VI* 'withstand, resist' RESISTERE *subj.ps.2p.* **wiðstonde** 5:39 [OED2 withstand, *v.*]

wlitig *adj.* 'radiant, beautiful' SPECIOSUS *np.* **wlitige** 23:27 [cf. wliti under OED2 wlite, *n.* Derivative]

wolcen *n.* or *m.* 'cloud' NUBES *ns.* **wolken** 17:5; *ds.* **wolcne** 17:5; *dp.* **wolcnum** 24:30, 26:64 [OED2 welkin, *n.*]

wop *m.* 'weeping, lamenting' FLETUS *ns.* ~ 8:12, 13:42, 13:50, 22:13 ||

PLORATUS *ns.* ~ 2:18 [OED2 wop, *n.1*]

word *n.* 'word' VERBUM *ns.* ~ 5:37, 12:36,18:16, 28:15; *as.* ~ 8:8 (or *p.*?), 12:32, 13:19 [n.], 13:20, 13:22 (*bis*), 13:23, 15:12, 19:22, 26:44, 26:75, Mk1:45, Mk2:2I; *ds.* **worde** 4:4, 8:16, 15:23, 22:46, 27:14; *ap.* ~ 7:24, 7:26, 7:28, 11:1, 19:1, 19:11, 26:1; *dp.* **wordum** 12:37 (*bis*), 13:21 || SERMO *gs.* **wordes** 21:24; *ds.* **worde** 22:15; *dp.* **wordum** 10:14 || NL *as.* ~ 2:9 [n.]; *dp.* **wordum** 5:37 [n.] [word, *n.* and *int.*]

woruld *f.* 'world, age' SAECULUM *gs.* **weorulde** 13:22, 13:39, 13:40, 24:3, 28:20; **weoruldes** 13:49 [n.], 24:14; *ds.* **weorlde** 12:32 [world, *n.*]

worþ *m.* (*wk*?) 'court, street' PLATEA *gp.* **worþana** 6:5 [n.]; *dp.* **worðum** 12:19 [worth, *n.2*]

wræd *f.* 'band, flock' GREX *ns.* **wræð** 8:32

gewregan *v.1* 'accuse' ACCUSARE *pp.s.* **gewroeged** 27:12 [cf. OED2 wray, *v.1*]

wreon *v.I or II* 'cover' COOPERIRE *pt.1p.* **wreogan** 25:38; *pt.2p.* **wriogan** 25:36; **wreogan** 25:43 [OED2 wry, *v.1*]

gewreon *v.I* 'cover' OPERIRE *pp.p.* **gewrigene** 6:31 [see previous]

gewrit *n.* 'scripture, inscription' SCRIPTURA *np.* **gewritu** 26:54; **gewriotu** 26:56; *ap.* **gewritu** 22:29; *dp.* **gewritum** 21:42 || SUPERSCRIPTIO *ns.* ~ 22:20 [i-writ, *n.*]

writan *v.I* 'write' SCRIBERE *pp.s.* **gewriten** 4:6 [write, *v.*]

[MK]**wudubinde** *f.* 'woodbine' NL *dp.* **wudebendum** Mk1:6 [n.] [OED2 woodbine, *n.*]

wuduhunig *n.* 'wild honey' MEL SILVESTRAE *gs.* or *ap.*? **wuduhuniges** 3:4 [n.], Mk1:6 [cf. wood-honey, under Compounds under OED2 wood, *n.1*]

wuduwe *f.* 'widow' VIDUA *gp.* **widuwana** 23:14 [widow, *n.*]

wuldor *n.* 'glory' GLORIA *as.* ~ 4:8, 16:27; *ds.* **wuldre** 6:29 [OED2 wulder, *n.*]

wuldrian *v.2* 'glorify, praise' GLORIFICARE *pt.3p.* **wuldradun** 9:8 || MAGNIFICARE *subj.ps.3p.* **wuldrigen** 5:16

wulf *m.* 'wulf' LUPUS *np.* **wulfas** 7:15; *dp.* **uulfum** 10:16 [OED2 wolf, *n.*]

wundor *n.* 'wonder, miracle' MIRABILIS *as.* **wundur** 21:15 [OED2 wonder, *n.*]

wundorlic *adj.* 'miraculous' MIRABILIS *nns.* **wundurlic** 21:42 [OED2 wonderly, *adj.*]

wundrian *v.2* 'wonder, be astonished' (AD)MIRARI *pt.3s.* **wundrade** 27:14; *pt.3p.* **wundradun** 7:28, 8:27, 9:33, 13:54, 15:31, 19:25, 21:20, 22:22, 22:33; *ps.p. s.* **wundriende** 8:10 [n.]; *ps.p. p.* **wundrende** Mk1:27 || STUPERE *pt.3p.* **wundradun** 12:23 [OED2 wonder, *v.*]

wunian *v.2* 'wait, remain' MANERE *pt.3p.* **wunade** 21:17; *subj.pt.3p.* **wunade** 11:23; *imp.p.* **wyngiaþ** 10:11; *ps.p. fas.* **wuniende** Mk1:10 [OED2 won | wone, *v.*]

gewunian *v.2* 'be accustomed, wont' CONSTITUERE *pt.3s.* **gewunede** 27:15 [OED2 i-wune | i-wone, *n.*]

wutu, see **witan** 'to go'

wynsum *adj.* 'pleasant, winsome' SUAVIS *nns.* ~ 11:30 [OED2 winsome, *adj.*]

wyrcan *v.1* 'work, do, make' FACERE *ps.1s.* **wyrce** 21:24, 21:27, 26:18; *ps.2s.* **wircest** 21:23; *ps.3s.* **wyrceþ** 5:19, 7:17, 7:21, 12:50, 13:23, 21:43; *ps.3p.* **wyrcaþ** 23:5; *pt.3s.* **worhte** 13:58, 19:4, 21:15, 21:31, 22:2; *pt.1p.* **worhton** 7:22; *pt.3p.* **worhtun** 20:12; *subj.ps.2s.* **wirce** 6:2; *imp.p.* **wircaþ** 3:3; **wyrceþ** 3:8, 12:33 (*bis*); **wyrcaþ** Mk1:3; *pp.p.* **worht** 11:21, 11:23 (*bis*); *ps.p. mds.* **wircendum** 6:3; (form uncertain) **wyrcende** 7:18 || OPERARI *ps.3p.* **wyrcaþ** 7:23; *pt.3s.* **worhtæ** 25:16;

worhte 26:10; *imp.s.* **wyrc** 21:28; *pp.p.* **worht** 14:2 [work, *v.*]

gewyrcan *v.1* 'work, make, do' FACERE *pt.3s.* **geworhte** 19:4; *subj.ps.1p.* **gewyrce** 17:4; *inf.* **gewirce** 5:36; *pp.p.* **geworhte** 11:20; **geworht** 11:21 [see previous]

wyrgan (see *wiergan* in CH; here the headword follows DOE's spelling of prefixed *a-wyrgan*) *v.1* 'curse, condemn' MALEDICERE *ps.3p.* **wærgaþ** 5:11; *subj.ps.3s.* **wærge** 15:4 || MALIGNUS *pp. mns.* **wærgad** 13:19 [OED2 wary, *v.*]

wyrhta *m. wk* 'worker, labourer' OPERARIUS *ns.* ~ 10:10; *np.* **wyrhtu** 9:37; *ap.* **wyrhte** 9:38; ~ 20:1; *dp.* **wyrhtum** 20:2, 20:8 [OED2 wright, *n.1*]

wyrse, **wyrresta**, see **yfel**

wyrt *f.* 'vegetable, herb' HOLUS *dp.* **wyrtum** 13:32 [wort, *n.1*]

wyrtrume *f.* 'root' RADIX *as.* **wytryme** 13:6; **wyrtruma** 13:21 (or *p.*?); *ap.* **wyrtruma** 3:10

gewyrtun *m.* 'garden' HORTUS *ns.* ~ Jn18:1

wyrþ, see **weorþ**

yfel *n.* 'evil, wickedness' MALUM *as.* ~ 5:11; *ds.* **yfle** 6:13, 17:18 (margin) [n.]; **yflę** 5:37; **yflæ** 5:39; *ap.* ~ 9:4 (or *s.*?) || MALE (HABENS) *as.* ~ 4:24; **yfle** 8:16, 9:12, 14:35, Mk1:32 [OED2 evil, *adj.* and *n.1*]

yfel *adj.* 'evil, ill' MALUS *mns.* ~ 12:35; **yfle** 24:48, 25:26; *mas.* **yfelne** 12:33; *m?ds.* **yfle** 12:35 [n.]; *fns.* ~ 12:39; **yfle** 16:4; *nns.* ~ 7:17; **yfle** 7:18; *nas.* ~ 12:33; *np.* **yfle** 7:11, 12:34 **yfele** 15:19; *ap.* **yfle** 5:45, 7:17, 7:18, 13:48, 13:49, 22:10; **yflu** 21:41; *nap.* **yfel** 12:35 (or noun?); *comp.* 'worse' PEIOR *mns.* **wyrse** 9:16, 12:45, 27:64 || NEQUIOR *map.* **wyrse** 12:45 [worse, *adj.* and *n.*]; *superl.* 'worst' PESSIMUS *fas.* **wyrresta** 12:45 (? see note) [worst, *adj.* and *n.*]

yfle *adv.* 'evilly, badly' MALE ~ 8:6, 15:22, 17:15, 21:41 [OED2 evil, *adv.*]

ymbe *prep.* 'around, after' CIRCA/-UM **ymb** 3:4, 3:5, 8:18, Mk1:6 || POST **ymb** 26:73 [OED2 umbe, *prep.* and *adv.*]

ymbgangan *anom.v.* 'go around, surround' CIRCUMIRE *ps.2p.* **ymbgangaþ** 23:15 [cf. umbegang under OED2 umbe-, *prefix*]

ymbhwyrft *m.* 'circuit, orbit' ORBIS TERRARUM *as.* ~ 24:14

ymbsellan *v.1* 'surround, clothe' CIRCUMDARE *pt.3p.* **ymbsaldun** 27:28

ymbtynan *v.1* 'hedge around' CIRCUMDARE *pt.3s.* **ymbtynde** 21:33

ymen *m.* 'hymn' HYMNUS *ds.* **ymne** 26:30 [OED2 hymn, *n.*]

yrfe *n.* 'heritage' HEREDITAS *ns.* **erfe** 21:38 [n.]

yrfeweard *m.* 'heir, son' HERES *ns.* **erfeweard** 21:38

yrnan *v.III* 'run, meet with' OCURRERE *pt.3s.* **arn** 27:48; *pt.3p.* **urnon** (*ongægn*) 8:28 || CURRERE *ps.p. np.* **eornende** 28:8 || OPERIRI *pp.s.* **urnen** 8:24 [run, *v.*]

ytemest *adj.* 'uttermost, extreme' EXTERIOR *fas.* **ytmæste** 8:12; **ytmæst** 22:13 || NOVISSIMUS *mns.* **ytmæste** 12:45 [n.] [OED2 utmost, *adj.* and *n.*]

yterræ, see **utera**

yþ *f.* 'wave' FLUCTUS *dp.* **yðum** 8:24; **yþum** 14:24 [ythe, *n.*]

zabulones *prop.n. gs.* ~ 4:13, 4:15

zacharias *prop.n. gs.* ~ 23:35

zebedeus *prop.n. gs.* **zabedeaes** 4:21; **zebedees** 10:2; **zebedeo** 26:37; **zebedes** 20:20, Mk1:19; **zebedeæs** 27:56; *as.* ~ Mk1:20

BIBLIOGRAPHY

Alexander, J. J. G. 1978. *Insular Manuscripts: 6th to the 9th Century*, A Survey of Manuscripts Illuminated in the British Isles, v. 1 (London: H. Miller)

Allen, Cynthia L. 1995. *Case Marking and Reanalysis: Grammatical Relations from Old and Early Modern English* (Oxford: Oxford University Press)

Assmann, B. (ed.) 1889. *Angelsächsische Homilien und Heiligenleben.* Bibliothek der angelsächsischen Prosa, 3. Bd. (Kassel: Georg H. Wigand; repr. with introduction by P. Clemoes, Darmstadt: Wissenschaftliche Buchgesellschaft, 1964)

Bains 1936, see Lindsay 1915

Bately, J. M. (ed.) 1986. *The Anglo-Saxon Chronicle: A Collaborative Edition.* Vol. 3: MS A (Cambridge: D. S. Brewer)

— 1988. 'Old English Prose before and during the Reign of Alfred', *Anglo-Saxon England*, 17: 93–138

Bennett, J. A. W. 1938. 'The History of Old English and Old Norse Studies in England from the Time of Francis Junius till the End of the Eighteenth Century' (Unpublished D.Phil. thesis, University of Oxford)

Berger, Samuel. 1893. *Histoire de la vulgate pendant les premiers siècles du moyen âge* (Paris: Hachette; repr. Hildesheim: Olms, 1976)

Bibire, Paul, and A. S. C. Ross. 1981. 'The Differences between Lindisfarne and Rushworth Two', *Notes and Queries*, 226: 98–116

Bischoff, Bernhard. 1954. 'La nomenclature des écritures livresques du IXe au XIIIe siècle' in *Nomenclature des écritures livresques du IXe au XVIe siècle*, ed. by B. Bischoff, G. I. Lieftinck, and G. Battelli (Paris: Centre national de la recherche scientifique), pp. 7–14

Bishop, T. A. M. 1964–68. 'An Early Example of the Square Minuscule', *Transactions of the Cambridge Bibliographical Society*, 4: 246–52

— 1971. *English Caroline Minuscule* (Oxford: Clarendon Press)

Bosworth, Joseph, and T. N. Toller with A. Campbell. 1898–1972. *Anglo-Saxon Dictionary* (Oxford: Oxford University Press, 1898; *Supplement* Oxford: Oxford University Press, 1921; *Enlarged Addenda and Corrigenda* Oxford: Clarendon Press, 1972)

Bouterwek, K. W. (ed.) 1857. *Die vier Evangelien in alt-nordhumbrischer Sprache. Aus der jetzt zum erstenmale vollständig gedruckten Interlinearglosse in St. Cûðbert's Evangelienbuche* (Gütersloh: C. Bertelsmann)

— (ed.) 1858. *Screadunga.* Anglosaxonica maximam partem inedita publicavit C. G. Bouterwek (Elberfeldae: Lucas)

Boyd, W. J. P. 1975. *Aldred's Marginalia: Explanatory Comments in the Lindisfarne Gospels* (Exeter: University of Exeter)

Breay, Claire, and Joanna Story. (eds) 2018. *Anglo-Saxon Kingdoms: Art, Word, War* (London: British Library)

Breeze, Andrew. 1996. 'The Provenance of the Rushworth Mercian Gloss', *Notes and Queries*, 241: 394–95

Brookes, Stewart. 2016. 'The Shape of Things to Come? Variation and Intervention in Aldred's Gloss to the Lindisfarne Gospels', in Fernández Cuesta and Pons-Sanz (2016), pp. 103–50

Brown, E. M. 1891. *Die Sprache der Rushworth Glossen zum Evangelium Matthäus und der mercische Dialekt (I. Vokale)* (Göttingen: Dieterich)

— 1892. *The Language of the Rushworth Gloss to the Gospel of Matthew and the Mercian Dialect Part II* (Göttingen: Dieterich)

Brown, M. P. 2003. *The Lindisfarne Gospels: Society, Spirituality and the Scribe* (Toronto: University of Toronto Press)

— 2012. 'Writing in the Insular World', in Gameson (2012), pp. 121–66

Brown, T. J. (ed.) with contributions by F. Wormald, A. S. C. Ross and E. G. Stanley. 1969. *The Durham Ritual*, EEMF Vol. 16 (Copenhagen: Rosenkilde and Bagger)

Brown, T. J. 1993. *A Palaeographer's View: The Selected Writings of Julian Brown*, ed. by Janet Bately, Michelle P. Brown and Jane Roberts; with a preface by Albinia C. de la Mare (London: Harvey Miller)

Brunner, Karl. 1965. *Altenglische Grammatik nach der Angelsächsischen Grammatik von Eduard Sievers*, 3rd edn (Tübingen: M. Niemeyer)

Burton, Philip. 2000. *The Old Latin Gospels: A Study of their Texts and Language* (Oxford: Oxford University Press)

Campbell, A. 1959. *Old English Grammar* (Oxford: Clarendon Press; repr. with corrections, 1968)

Carr, Charles T. 1939. *Nominal Compounds in Germanic* (London: Humphrey Milford)

Clark, Cecily. (ed.) 1970. *The Peterborough Chronicle 1070–1154*, 2nd edn (Oxford: Clarendon Press)

Clark Hall, J. R. 1960. *A Concise Anglo-Saxon Dictionary*, 4th edn with a Supplement by Herbert D. Meritt (Toronto, University of Toronto Press)

Coates, Richard. 1997. 'The Scriptorium of the Mercian Rushworth Gloss: A Bilingual Perspective', *Notes and Queries*, 242: 453–58

Cole, Marcelle. 2014. *Old Northumbrian Verbal Morphosyntax and the (Northern) Subject Rule*, *NOWELE* Supplement Series v. 25 (Amsterdam: John Benjamins)

— 2016. 'Identifying the Author(s) of the Lindisfarne Gloss: Linguistic Variation as a Diagnostic for Determining Authorship', in Fernández Cuesta and Pons-Sanz (2016), pp. 169–188

— 2019. 'Towards a Nuanced History of Early English Spelling: Old Northumbrian Witnesses and Northern Orthography', in *Revisiting the*

Medieval North of England: Interdisciplinary Approaches, ed. by Anita Auer (Cardiff: University of Wales Press), pp. 131–48

Colgrave, Bertram, and R. A. B. Mynors. (ed. and trans.) 1969. *Bede's Ecclesiastical History of the English People* (Oxford: Clarendon Press)

Cook, Albert S. 1894. *A Glossary of the Old Northumbrian Gospels (Lindisfarne Gospels or Durham Book)* (Halle: Niemeyer; repr. Darmstadt: Georg Olms, 1969)

— 1898. *Biblical Quotations in Old English Prose Writers edited with the Vulgate and Other Latin Originals, Introduction on Old English Biblical Versions, Index of Biblical Passages, and Index of Principal Words* (London: Macmillan; repr. Folcroft: Folcroft Library Editions, 1971)

— 1903. *Biblical Quotations in Old English Prose Writers. Second Series* (New York: Charles Scribner's Sons; repr. Folcroft: Folcroft Library Editions, 1974)

Cosijn, P. J. 1883–86. *Altwestsächsische Grammatik*, 2 vols (The Hague: Martinus Nijhoff)

Crawford, S. J. 1969. *The Old English Version of the Heptateuch: Ælfric's Treatise on the Old and New Testament, and His Preface to Genesis*, EETS o.s. 160, repr. with the text of two additional manuscripts transcribed by N.R. Ker (London: Oxford University Press)

Crowley, Joseph. 2000. 'Anglicized Word Order in Old English Continuous Interlinear Glosses in British Library, Royal 2.A.XX', *Anglo-Saxon England*, 29: 123–51

De Bruyne, Donatien. 1912. *Préfaces de la Bible latine* (Namur: [s.n.]; repr. as *Prefaces to the Latin Bible*, with new introductions by Pierre-Maurice Bogaert and Thomas O'Loughlin, Studia Traditionis Theologiae 19, Turnhout: Brepols, 2014)

— 1914. *Sommaires, divisions et rubriques de la Bible latine* (Namur: A. Godienne; repr. with new introductions by Pierre-Maurice Bogaert and Thomas O'Loughlin, Studia Traditionis Theologiae 18, Turnhout: Brepols, 2014)

De Smet, Gilbert A. R. 1987. 'Scandalum und Scandalizare in einigen altenglischen Übersetzungsdenkmalern', in *Studies in Honour of René Derolez*, ed. by A. M. Simon-Vandenbergen (Gent: Seminarie voor Engelse en Oud-Germaanse Taalkunde, Rijksuniversiteit Gent), pp. 122–31

Dekker, Kees. 2000. '"That Most Elaborate One of Fr. Junius": An Investigation of Francis Junius's Manuscript Old English Dictionary', in *The Recovery of Old English: Anglo-Saxon Studies in the Sixteenth and Seventeenth Centuries*, ed. by Timothy Graham (Kalamazoo: Medieval Institute Publications, Western Michigan University), pp. 301–43

— 2008. 'Reading the Anglo-Saxon Gospels in the Sixteenth and Seventeenth Centuries', in *Anglo-Saxon Books and their Readers: Essays in Celebration of Helmut Gneuss's Handlist of Anglo-Saxon Manuscripts*, ed. by Thomas N. Hall and Donald Scragg (Kalamazoo: Medieval Institute Publications, Western Michigan University), pp. 68–93

Doane, A. N. (ed.) 1991. *The Saxon Genesis: An Edition of the West Saxon* Genesis B *and the Old Saxon Vatican Genesis* (Madison, WI: University of Wisconsin Press)

Dobbie, Elliott van Kirk. (ed.) 1953. *Beowulf and Judith*, Anglo-Saxon Poetic Records 4 (New York: Columbia University Press)

DOE = *Dictionary of Old English: A to I online*, ed. by Angus Cameron, Ashley Crandell Amos, Antonette diPaolo Healey *et al.* (Toronto: Dictionary of Old English Project, 2018)

DOE Corpus = *Dictionary of Old English Web Corpus*, compiled by Antonette diPaolo Healey with John Price Wilkin and Xin Xiang (Toronto: Dictionary of Old English Project, 2009)

Doyle, Ian. 1984. 'The Library of Sir Thomas Tempest: Its Origins and Dispersal', in *Studies in Seventeenth-Century English Literature, History, and Bibliography: Festschrift for Professor T. A. Birrell on the Occasion of His Sixtieth Birthday*, ed. by G. A. M. Janssens and F. G. A. M. Aarts (Amsterdam: Rodopi), pp. 83–93

Dumville, David N. 1987. 'English Square Minuscule Script: The Background and Earliest Phases', *Anglo-Saxon England*, 16: 147–79

— 1993. *English Caroline Script and Monastic History: Studies in Benedictinism, A.D. 950–1030*, Studies in Anglo-Saxon History 6 (Boydell: Woodbridge)

— 1994. 'English Square Minuscule Script: The Mid-Century Phases', *Anglo-Saxon England*, 23: 133–64

Durkin, Philip. 2014. *Borrowed Words: A History of Loanwords in English* (Oxford: Oxford University Press)

Falluomini, Carla. 2010. '*Fullwiht* and the Baptismal Rite in Anglo-Saxon England', *Anglia*, 128: 391–403

Farr, Carol A. 2007. 'The Incipit Pages of the Macregol Gospels', in *Making and Meaning of Insular Art: Proceedings of the Fifth International Conference on Insular Art Held at Trinity College Dublin, 25-28 August 2005*, ed. by R. Moss (Dublin: Four Courts Press), pp. 275–87

— 2011. 'Irish Pocket Gospels in Anglo-Saxon England', in *Anglo-Saxon Traces*, ed. by Jane Roberts and Leslie Webster (Tempe: ACMRS Arizona Center for Medieval and Renaissance Studies), pp. 87–100

Fernández Cuesta, Julia, and Christopher Langmuir. 2019. 'Verbal Morphology in the Old English Gloss to the Durham Collectar', *NOWELE*, 72: 134–64

Fernández Cuesta, Julia, and Nieves Rodríguez Ledesma. 2020. 'Reduced Forms in the Nominal Morphology of the Lindisfarne Gospel Gloss. A Case of Accusative /Dative Syncretism?', *Folia Linguistica Historica*, 41: 37–65

Fernández Cuesta, Julia, and Sara M. Pons-Sanz. (eds) 2016. *The Old English Gloss to the Lindisfarne Gospels: Language, Author and Context* (Berlin: De Gruyter)

Fischer, Andreas. 1986. *Engagement, Wedding and Marriage in Old English* (Heidelberg: C. Winter)

Fischer, Bonifatius. 1988–91. *Die lateinischen Evangelien bis zum 10. Jahrhundert*, 4 vols (Freiburg: Herder)

— 2010. 'Die lateinischen Evangelien bis zum 10. Jahrhundert: Zwei Untersuchungen zum Text', *Zeitschrift für die neutestamentliche Wissenschaft und die Kunde der älteren Kirche*, 101: 119–44

Förster, Max. 1900. Review of A. S. Cook, *Biblical Quotations in Old English Prose Writers* (1898), *Englische Studien*, 28: 419–30

— 1908. 'Beiträge zur altenglischen Wortkunde aus ungedruckten volkskundlichen Texten', *Englische Studien*, 39: 321–55

Fulk, R. D. 2007. 'Old English Meter and Oral Tradition: Three Issues Bearing on Poetic Chronology', *JEGP*, 106: 305–24

— 2008. 'Anglian Dialect Features in Old English Anonymous Homiletic Literature: A Survey, with Preliminary Findings', in *Studies in the History of the English Language IV: Empirical and Analytical Advances in the Study of English Language Change*, ed. by Susan M. Fitzmaurice and Donka Minkova (Berlin: Mouton de Gruyter), pp. 81–100

Gameson, Richard. 2001. *The Scribe Speaks? Colophons in Early English Manuscripts*, H. M Chadwick Memorial Lectures 12 (Cambridge: Department of Anglo-Saxon, Norse and Celtic, University of Cambridge)

— (ed.) 2012. *The Cambridge History of the Book in Britain*, vol. 1 c.400–1100 (Cambridge: Cambridge University Press)

— 2013. *From Holy Island to Durham: The Contexts and Meanings of the Lindisfarne Gospels* (London: Third Millennium Publishing)

— (ed.) 2017. *The Lindisfarne Gospels: New Perspectives*, Library of the Written Word 57; The Manuscript World 9, (Leiden: Brill)

Ganz, David. 2001. 'The Annotations in Oxford, Bodleian Library, Auct. D. II. 14', in *Belief and Culture in the Middle Ages: Studies Presented to Henry Mayr-Harting*, ed. by Richard Gameson and Henrietta Leyser (Oxford: Oxford University Press), pp. 35–44

— 2012. 'Square Minuscule' in Gameson (2012), pp. 188–96

Ganz, David, and Jane Roberts with Richard Palmer. (eds) 2007. *Lambeth Palace Library and its Anglo-Saxon Manuscripts: Exhibition Mounted for the Biennial Conference of the International Society of Anglo-Saxonists. 3rd August, 2007* (London: Taderon Press)

Glauser, A., and Michelle P. Brown. 2002–3. *Das Buch von Lindisfarne* (Luzern: Faksimile Verlag)

Gneuss, Helmut. 1972. 'The Origin of Standard Old English and Æthelwold's School at Winchester', *Anglo-Saxon England*, 1: 65–83

— 1993. '*Anglicae linguae interpretatio*: Language Contact, Lexical Borrowing and Glossing in Anglo-Saxon England', *Proceedings of the British Academy*, 82: 107–48

Gneuss, Helmut, and Michael Lapidge. 2014. *Anglo-Saxon Manuscripts: A Bibliographical Handlist of Manuscripts and Manuscript Fragments*

Written or Owned in England up to 1100 (Toronto: University of Toronto Press)

Godden, Malcolm. 2000. *Ælfric's Catholic Homilies: Introduction, Commentary and Glossary*, EETS s.s. 18 (Oxford: Oxford University Press)

Godden, Malcolm and Susan Irvine. (eds) 2009. *The Old English Boethius: An Edition of the Old English Versions of Boethius's* De consolatione philosophiae (Oxford: Oxford University Press)

Grant, Raymond J. S. 1989. *The B Text of the Old English Bede: A Linguistic Commentary* (Amsterdam: Rodopi)

Gryson, Roger. 1999. *Altlateinische Handschriften/Manuscrits Vieux Latins 1–275*, Vetus Latina 1/2A (Freiburg: Herder)

— 2004. *Altlateinische Handschriften/Manuscrits Vieux Latins 300–485*, Vetus Latina 1/2B (Freiburg: Herder)

Hamper, William. 1827. *The Life, Diary, and Correspondence of Sir William Dugdale* (London: Harding, Lepard, and Co.)

Harris, Richard. (ed.) 1992. *A Chorus of Grammars: The Correspondence of George Hickes, and His Collaborators on the "Thesaurus linguarum septentrionalium"* (Toronto: Pontifical Institute of Mediaeval Studies)

Hertherington, M. S. 1975. 'Sir Simonds D'Ewes and Method in Old English Lexicography', *Texas Studies in Literature and Language*, 17: 75–92

— 1980. *The beginnings of Old English Lexicography* ([n.p.], privately printed)

Hickes, George. 1689. *Institutiones grammaticae Anglo-Saxonicae, et Moeso-Gothicae* (Oxford; repr. English Linguistics, 1500–1800: A Collection of Facsimile Reprints, 277, Menston: Scolar Press, 1971)

— 1703–5. *Linguarum vett. septentrionalium thesaurus grammatico-criticus et archaeologicus*, 2 vols (Oxford; repr. two volumes in one, Anglistica & Americana: A Series of Reprints Selected by Bernhard Fabian ... [et al.] 64, Hildesheim: G. Olms, 1970)

Hill, Joyce. (ed.) 2009. *Old English Minor Heroic Poems*, 3rd edn (Toronto: Pontifical Institute of Mediaeval Studies)

Hoad, T. F. (ed.) 1978. *A Second Anglo-Saxon Reader: Archaic and Dialectal*, (Oxford: Clarendon Press)

Hofmann, J. 1963. 'Altenglische und althochdeutsche Glossen aus Würzburg und dem weiteren angelsächsischen Missionsgebiet', *Beiträge zur Geschichte der deutschen Sprache und Literatur* (Halle), 85: 27–131

Hofstetter, Walter. 1987. *Winchester und der spätaltenglische Sprachgebrauch: Untersuchungen zur geographischen und zeitlichen Verbreitung altenglischer Synonyme* (München: W. Fink)

— 1988. 'Winchester and the Standardization of Old English Vocabulary', *Anglo-Saxon England*, 17: 139–61

Hogg, Richard M. 1992. *A Grammar of Old English*, Vol. 1: Phonology (Oxford: Blackwell)

— 2003. 'Regular Suppletion', in *Motives for Language Change*, ed. by Raymond Hickey (Cambridge: Cambridge University Press), pp. 71–81

— 2004. 'North Northumbrian and South Northumbrian: A Geographical Statement?', in *Methods and Data in English Historical Dialectology*, ed. by Marina Dossena and Roger Lass (Bern: Peter Lang), pp. 241–55

Hogg, Richard M., and R. D. Fulk. 2011. *A Grammar of Old English*, Vol. 2: Morphology (Oxford: Blackwell)

Holthausen, F. 1934. *Altenglisches etymologisches Wörterbuch* (Heidelberg: C. Winter)

Houghton, H. A. G. 2015. Review of Kenichi Tamoto (ed.), *The Macregol Gospels or The Rushworth Gospels. Edition of the Latin text with the Old English interlinear gloss transcribed from Oxford Bodleian Library, MS Auctarium D. 2. 19* (2013), *Novum Testamentum*, 57: 95–97

— 2016. *The Latin New Testament: A Guide to its Early History, Texts, and Manuscripts* (Oxford: Oxford University Press)

Huemer, Johann. 1891. *Gai Vetti Aqvilini Ivvenci Evangeliorvm libri qvattvor* (Vienna: F. Tempsky)

Irvine, Susan. (ed.) 1993. *Old English Homilies from MS Bodley 343*, EETS o.s. 302 (Oxford: Oxford University Press)

Johannesson, Nils-Lennart. 2000. 'On the Time-Depth of Variability: Orm and Farmon as h-droppers', in *Language Structure and Variation*, ed. by Magnus Ljung (Stockholm: Almqvist & Wiksell International), pp. 107–19

Jolly, Karen Louise. 2012. *The Community of St. Cuthbert in the Late Tenth Century: The Chester-le-Street Additions to Durham Cathedral Library A.IV.19* (Columbus: Ohio State University Press)

Jones, Charles. 1967. 'The Functional Motivation of Linguistic Change: A Study of the Development of the Grammatical Category of Gender in the Late Old English Period', *English Studies*, 48: 97–111

— 1988. *Grammatical Gender in English: 950 to 1250* (London: Croom Helm)

Jordan, Richard. 1906. *Eigentumlichkeiten des anglischen Wortschatzes: eine wortgeographische Untersuchung mit etymologischen Anmerkungen* (Heidelberg: C. Winter)

Jülicher, Adolf, Walter Matzkow, and Kurt Aland. (eds) 1972. *Itala: Das Neue Testament in altlateinische Überlieferung*, 1. Matthäus-Evangelium, 2nd edn (Berlin: De Gruyter)

Kendrick, T. D., T. J. Brown, R.L.S. Bruce-Mitford, H. Roosen-Runge, A. S. C. Ross, E. G. Stanley, and A. E. A. Werner. 1956–60. *Evangelium Quattuor Codex Lindisfarnensis*, 2 vols (Olten and Lausanne: Urs Graf)

Kenney, James F. 1968. *The Sources for the Early History of Ireland, Ecclesiastical: An Introduction and Guide* (Shannon: Irish University Press)

Ker, N. R. 1957. *Catalogue of Manuscripts Containing Anglo-Saxon* (Oxford: Clarendon Press; reissued with Supplement, Oxford: Clarendon Press, 1991)

— 1964. *Medieval Libraries of Great Britain: A List of Surviving Books*, 2nd edn (London: Office of the Royal Historical Society)

Kilpiö, Matti. 1989. *Passive Constructions in Old English Translations from Latin: With Special Reference to the OE Bede and the Pastoral Care*, Mémoires de la Société néophilologique de Helsinki 49 (Helsinki: Société Néophilologique)

Kimmens, Andrew C. (ed.) 1979. *The Stowe Psalter* (Toronto: University of Toronto Press)

Klaeber, Fr. 1902–4. 'Zur altenglischen Bedaübersetzung', *Anglia*, 25 (1902): 257–315, 27 (1904): 243–82, 399–435

Klaeber, Fr. 1905–6. 'Studies in the Textual Interpretation of "Beowulf"', *Modern Philology*, 3 (1905): 235–65, 4 (1906): 445–65

Koskenniemi, Inna. 1968. *Repetitive Word Pairs in Old and Early Middle English Prose: Expressions of the Type* Whole and Sound *and* Answered and Said, *and Other Parallel Constructions* (Turku: Turun YLIOPISTO)

Kotake, Tadashi. 2008. 'Differences in Element Order between *Lindisfarne* and *Rushworth Two*', in *Historical Englishes in Varieties of Texts and Contexts: The Global COE Program, International Conference 2007*, ed. by M. Amano, M. Ogura and M. Ohkado (Frankfurt am Main: Peter Lang), pp. 63–77

— 2010. 'Farman's Changing Syntax: A Linguistic and Palaeographical Survey', in *Aspects of the History of English Language and Literature*, Studies in English Medieval Language and Literature 25, ed. by Osamu Imahayashi, Yoshiyuki Nakao and Michiko Ogura (Frankfurt am Main: Peter Lang), pp. 241–55

— 2012a. 'Farman's Changing Orthography: With Special Reference to *e* and *æ*', in *Proceedings of the Second International Conference 'Language, Culture, and Society in Russian/English Studies' 25-26 July, 2011* (London: University of London), pp. 25–37

— 2012b. 'Lindisfarne and Rushworth One Reconsidered', *Notes and Queries*, 257: 14–19

— 2013. 'Gospel Glosses in Context: With Special Reference to Old English Scratched Glosses in London, BL, Additional 40000', in *Phases of the History of English: Selection of Papers Read at SHELL 2012*, Studies in English Medieval Language and Literature 42, ed. by Michio Hosaka, Michiko Ogura, Hironori Suzuki and Akinobu Tani (Frankfurt am Main: Peter Lang), pp. 111–25

— 2014. 'Aldred's Wanderings between Literal and Free Renderings: Some Manuscript Evidence', *Poetica: An International Journal of Linguistic-Literary Studies*, 81: 1–14

— 2016. 'Did Owun Really Copy from the Lindisfarne Gospels? Reconsideration of His Source Manuscript(s)', in Fernández Cuesta and Pons-Sanz (2016), pp. 377–95

— 2017. 'Binomials or not? A Study of Double Glosses in Farman's Glosses to the Rushworth Gospels', in *Binomials in the History of English: Fixed and Flexible*, ed. by Joanna Kopaczyk and Hans Sauer (Cambridge: Cambridge University Press), pp. 82–97

— 2021. 'Oxford, Bodleian Library, MS Broxbourne 90.28: A Fragment of an Old English Passion Narrative', *Notes and Queries*, 68: 25–35

— 2022. 'Word Order in Old English Interlinear Glosses: A Case Study on the Position of Inserted Pronominal Subjects', in *Medieval English Syntax: Studies in Honor of Michiko Ogura*, ed. by M. J. Toswell and Taro Ishiguro (Berlin: Peter Lang), pp. 191–204

Kuhn, Sherman M. 1945. '*E* and *Æ* in Farman's Mercian Glosses', *PMLA*, 60: 631–69

— (ed.) 1965. *The Vespasian Psalter* (Ann Arbor: University of Michigan Press)

— 1970. 'On the Consonantal Phonemes of Old English', in *Philological Essays: Studies in Old and Middle English Language and Literature in Honour of Herbert Dean Meritt*, ed. by James L. Rosier (The Hague: Mouton), pp. 16–49

Lapidge, Michael. 1982. 'The Study of Latin Texts in Late Anglo-Saxon England [1] The Evidence of Latin Glosses', in *Latin and Vernacular Languages in Early Medieval Britain*, ed. by Nicholas Brooks (Leicester: Leicester University Press), pp. 99–140

— 2006. 'An Aspect of Old English Poetic Diction: The Postpostioning of Prepositions', in *Inside Old English: Essays in Honour of Bruce Mitchell*, ed. by John Walmsley (Oxford: Blackwell), pp. 153–80

Lass, Roger and Margaret Laing. 2009. 'Databases, Dictionaries, and Dialectology. Dental Instability in Early Middle English: A Case Study', in *Studies in English and European Historical Dialectology*, Linguistic Insights: Studies in Language and Communication, v. 98, ed. by Mariana Dossena and Roger Lass (Bern: Peter Lang), pp. 91–133

Lendinara, Patrizia. 1993. 'The Old English Renderings of Latin tabernaculum and tentorium', in *Anglo-Saxonica: Beiträge zur Vor- und Frühgeschichte der englischen Sprache und zur altenglischen Literatur. Festschrift für Hans Schabram zum 65. Geburtstag*, ed. by Klaus R. Grinda and Claus-Dieter Wetzel (Munich: W. Fink), pp. 289–325

Lenker, Ursula. 1997. *Die westsächsische Evangelienversion und die Perikopenordnungen im angelsächsischen England* (Munich: W. Fink)

— 2018. 'Old English *þa* in Farman's Glosses to the Rushworth Gospels: Signal of Idiomatic Discourse Structuring in Old English?', in *Studies on Late Antique and Medieval Germanic Glossography and Lexicography in Honour of Patrizia Lendinara*, ed. by Claudia Di Sciacca, Concetta Giliberto, Carmela Rizzo, Loredana Teresi (Pisa: Edizioni Ets), pp. 489–501

Lewis, Charlton T., and Charles Short. 1879. *A Latin Dictionary* (Oxford: Clarendon Press, 1879)

Lindelöf, Uno. 1901. *Die südnorthumbrische Mundart des 10. Jahrhunderts: die Sprache der sog. Glosse Rushworth[2]* (Bonn: Hanstein)

Lindsay, W. M. 1915. *Notae Latinae: An Account of Abbreviation in Latin MSS. of the Early Minuscule Period (c.700–850)* (Cambridge: Cambridge University Press; repr. with Doris Bains, *A Supplement to Notae Latinae (Abbreviations in Latin MSS. of 850–1050 A.D.)* [Cambridge: Cambridge University Press, 1936], Hildesheim: Olms, 1964)

— 1923. 'Collectanea varia', in *Palaeographia Latina*, vol. 2, ed. by W. M. Lindsay (London: Oxford University Press)

Liuzza, R. M. (ed.) 1994–2000. *The Old English Version of the Gospels*, 2 vols, EETS o.s. 304, 314 (Oxford: Oxford University Press)

Liuzza, Roy M., and A. N. Doane. 1995. *Anglo-Saxon Manuscripts in Microfiche Facsimile. Vol. 3: Anglo-Saxon Gospels* (Binghamton: Medieval & Renaissance Texts & Studies)

Lockett, Leslie. 2011. *Anglo-Saxon Psychologies in the Vernacular and Latin Traditions* (Toronto: University of Toronto Press)

Los, Bettelou. 2005. *The Rise of the To-Infinitive* (Oxford: Oxford University Press)

Lowe, E. A. (ed.) 1935. *Codices latini antiquiores: A Palaeographical Guide to Latin Manuscripts Prior to the Ninth Century*, Part II Great Britain and Ireland (Oxford: Clarendon Press; 2nd edn, 1972)

Löweneck, Max. (ed.) 1896. *Peri didaxeon: Eine Sammlung von Rezepten in englischer Sprache aus dem 11./12. Jahrhundert. Nach einer Handschrift des Britischen Museums* (Erlangen: Junge; repr. Amsterdam: Rodopi, 1970)

Luick, Karl. 1914–40. *Historische Grammatik der englischen Sprache*, 2 vols. (Stuttgart: Bernhard Tauchnitz; repr. Oxford: Basil Blackwell, 1964)

Lutz, Angelika. 1998. 'The Study of the Anglo-Saxon Chronicle in the Seventeenth Century and the Establishment of Old English Studies in the Universities', in *The Recovery of Old English: Anglo-Saxon Studies in the Sixteenth and Seventeenth Centuries*, ed. by Timothy Graham (Kalamazoo: Medieval Institute Publications, Western Michigan University), pp. 1–82

Mac Airt, Seán, and Gearóid Mac Niocaill. (eds) 1983. *The Annals of Ulster (to A.D. 1131)* (Dublin: Dublin Institute for Advanced Studies)

McAllister, Douglas H. 1952. 'An Edition of the "Mercian" Portions of the Rushworth Manuscript' (Unpublished B.Litt. thesis, University of Oxford)

McGurk, Patrick. 1961. *Latin Gospel books from A.D.400 to A.D.800*, Les publications de scriptorium 5 (Paris: Éditions "Érasme")

— 1987. 'The Gospel Book in Celtic lands before AD 850: Contents and Arrangement', in *Irland und die Christenheit: Ireland and Christendom*, ed. by Próinséas Ní Chatháin and Michael Richter (Stuttgart: Klett-Cotta), pp. 165–89 [repr. in P. McGurk, *Gospel books and early Latin manuscripts*, Aldershot: Variorum, 1998]

McKee, Helen. 2012. 'The Circulation of Books between England and the Celtic Realms', in Gameson (2012), pp. 338–43

Madan, F., et al. 1895–1953. *A Summary Catalogue of Western Manuscripts in the Bodleian Library at Oxford* (Oxford: Clarendon Press)

Marckwardt, Albert H. (ed.) 1952. *Vocabularium saxonicum* (Ann Arbor: University of Michigan Press)

Marsden, Richard. 1999. 'The Gospels of St Augustine', in *St Augustine and the Conversion of England*, ed. by Richard Gameson (Stroud: Sutton), pp. 286–312

— (ed.) 2008. *The Old English Heptateuch and Ælfric's* Libellus de Veteri Testamento et Novo, EETS o.s. 330 (Oxford: Oxford University Press)

Mather, Frank Jewett, Jr. 1894. 'Anglo-Saxon *nemne* (*nymðe*) and the "Northumbrian" Theory', *Modern Language Notes*, 9: 152–56

Menner, R. J. 1934. 'Farman Vindicatus: The Linguistic Value of *Rushworth I*', *Anglia*, 58: 1–27

Merrit, Herbert D. 1954. *Fact and Lore about Old English Words* (Stanford: Stanford University Press)

Metzger, Bruce M. 1994. *A Textual Commentary on the Greek New Testament*, 2nd edn (Stuttgart: Deutsche Bibelgesellschaft)

Millar, Robert McColl. 2000. *System Collapse, System Rebirth: The Demonstrative Pronouns of English 900-1350 and the Birth of the Definite Article* (Bern: Peter Lang)

— 2016. 'At the Forefront of Linguistic Change: The Noun Phrase Morphology of the Lindisfarne Gospels', in Fernández Cuesta and Pons-Sanz (2016), pp. 153–67

Miller, T. (ed.) 1890–98. *The Old English Version of Bede's Ecclesiastical History of the English People*, 4 vols, EETS o.s. 95, 96, 110, 111 (London: N. Trübner; repr. London: Oxford University Press, 1959–63)

Mitchell, Bruce. 1978. 'Prepositions, Adverbs, Prepositional Adverbs, Postpositions, Separable Prefixes, or Inseparable Prefixes, in Old English?', *Neuphilologische Mitteilungen*, 79: 240–57

— 1985. *Old English Syntax*, 2 vols (Oxford: Clarendon Press)

— 1988. *On Old English: Selected Papers* (Oxford: Blackwell)

Morris, R. (ed.) 1874–80. *The Blickling Homilies with a Translation and Index of Words Together with The Blickling Glosses*, EETS o.s. 58, 63, 73 (London: N. Trübner; repr. London: Oxford University Press, 1967)

Muir, Bernard J. 2000. *The Exeter Anthology of Old English Poetry: An Edition of Exeter Dean and Chapter MS 3501*, rev. 2nd edn (Exeter: University of Exeter Press)

Murray, J. A. H. 1874. '*Correspondence*: The Rushworth Glosses', *The Academy*, Nov. 21, 1874: 561–62

— 1875. 'The Anglo-Saxon Gospels', *The Athenæum*, Apr. 3, 1875: 451–53

Mustanoja, Tauno F. 1960. *A Middle English Syntax*, Part I: Parts of Speech (Helsinki: Société Néophilologique)

Napier, Arthur. S. (ed.) 1900. *Old English Glosses: Chiefly Unpublished.* (Oxford: Clarendon Press; repr. Hildesheim: Olms, 1969)

Nees, Lawrence. 2003. 'Reading Aldred's Colophon for the Lindisfarne Gospels', *Speculum*, 78: 333–77

O'Conor, C. 1814. *Rerum hibernicarum scriptores veteres* (Buckingham: J. Seeley)

Ó Cróinín, Dáibhí. 1988. *Evangeliarium Epternacense (Universitätsbibliothek Augsburg, Cod. I 2 4° 2); Evangelistarium (Erzbischöfliches Priesterseminar St. Peter, Cod. ms. 25) Colour Microfiche Edition*, Codices illuminati medii aevi 9 (Munich: H. Lengenfelder)

O'Neill, Patrick P. (ed. and trans.) 2016. *Old English Psalms*, Dumbarton Oaks Medieval Library 42 (Cambridge, MA: Harvard University Press)

O'Neill, Timothy. 2014. *The Irish Hand: Scribes and Their Manuscripts from the Earliest Times* (Cork: Cork University Press)

OED Online (Oxford, Oxford University Press, 2021)

Ogura, Michiko. 1983. 'OE *þa hwile (þe)* and its Equivalents', *Studies in English Literature* (Tokyo), English Number, 1983: 221–43

— 1984. '*Cwyst þu* as an OE Interrogative Equivalent', in *Studies in English Philology and Linguistics in Honour of Dr. Tamotsu Matsunami* (Tokyo: Shubun International), pp. 14–33

— 1988. '*Ne ondræd þu* and *nelle þu ondrædan* for *noli timere*', *Studies in English Literature* (Tokyo), English Number, 1988: 87–101

— 2008. 'Old English Verbs of Tasting with Accusative/Genitive/*Of*-Phrase', *Neophilologus*, 92: 517–22

Owen-Crocker, Gale R. (2004) *Dress in Anglo-Saxon England* (Woodbridge: Boydell)

Pächt, Otto, and Jonathan Alexander. 1973. *Illuminated Manuscripts in the Bodleian Library, Oxford*, vol. 3, British, Irish and Icelandic Schools with Addenda to Volumes 1 and 2 (Oxford: Clarendon Press)

Page, R. I. 1958. 'Northumbrian *æfter* (= in memory of) + accusative', *Studia Neophilologica*, 30: 145–52

Parkes, Malcolm B. 1976 'The Palaeography of the Parker Manuscript of the Chronicle, Laws and Sedulius, and Historiography at Winchester in the Late Ninth and Tenth Centuries', *Anglo-Saxon England*, 5: 149–71

Pheifer, J. D. 1974. *Old-English Glosses in the Épinal-Erfurt Glossary* (Oxford: Clarendon Press)

Plater, W. E., and H. J. White. 1926. *A Grammar of the Vulgate Being an Introduction to the Study of the Latinity of the Vulgate Bible* (Oxford: Clarendon Press)

Pope, J. C. (ed.) 1967–68. *Homilies of Ælfric: A Supplementary Collection*, 2 vols, EETS o.s. 259, 260 (London: Oxford University Press)

Ranke, Ernst. 1968. *Codex Fuldensis. Novum Testamentum Latine interprete Hieronymo ex manuscripto Victoris Capuani* (Marburg: Elwert)

Rauh, Hildegard. 1936. *Wortschatz der altenglischen Uebersetzungen des Matthaeus-Evangeliums* (Diss., Berlin)

Roberts, Jane. 1970. 'Traces of Unhistorical Gender Congruence in a Late Old English Manuscript', *English Studies*, 51: 30–37

— (ed.) 1979. *The Guthlac Poems of the Exeter Book* (Oxford: Clarendon Press)

— 2005. *Guide to Scripts Used in English Writings up to 1500* (London: British Library; repr. with corrections, Liverpool: Liverpool University Press, 2015)

— 2006. 'Some Thoughts on the Expression of "Crippled" in Old English', in *Essays for Joyce Hill on Her Sixtieth Birthday*, ed. by Mary Swan, Leeds Studies in English, n.s. 37, (Leeds: Univ. of Leeds, School of English), pp. 365–78

— 2009. 'On Multi-Using Materials from the Dictionary of Old English Project, with Particular Reference to the hapax legomena in the Old English Translation of Felix's *Vita Guthlaci*', *Florilegium*, 26: 175–205

Robinson, Fred C. 1994. 'Latin for Old English in Anglo-Saxon Manuscripts', in his *The Editing of Old English* (Oxford: Blackwell), pp. 160–63

Rodríguez Ledesma, Nieves. 2022. 'Changes in Progress in Late Northumbrian: The Extension of *-s* as Genitive and Plural Marker', *English Language and Linguistics*, 26: 697–722

Roeder, Fritz. 1907a 'Die "Schloss-" oder "Kniesetzung", eine angelsächsische Verlobungszeremonie', in *Nachrichten von der Gesellschaft der Wissenschaften zu Göttingen: Philologisch-historische Klasse* (Berlin: Weidmanndsche Buchhandlung), pp. 300–14

— (1907b) 'Der "Schatzwurf", ein Formalakt bei der angelsächsischen Verlobung', in *Nachrichten von der Gesellschaft der Wissenschaften zu Göttingen: Philologisch-historische Klasse* (Berlin: Weidmanndsche Buchhandlung), pp. 373–83

Ross, A. S. C. 1932. 'The Errors in the Old English Gloss to the Lindisfarne Gospels', *Review of English Studies*, 8: 385–94

— 1933. 'The Accusative and Dative of the Pronouns of the First and Second Persons in Germanic', *JEGP*, 32: 481–82

— 1936. 'Sex and Gender in the Lindisfarne Gospels', *JEGP*, 35: 321–30

— 1937. *Studies in the Accidence of the Lindisfarne Gospels*, Leeds School of English Language Texts and Monographs 2 (Kendal: Titus Wilson)

— 1967. '"This" in the Lindisfarne Gospels and the Durham Ritual', *Notes and Queries*, 212: 284–88

— 1976. 'Notes on the Accidence of Rushworth 1', *Neuphilologische Mitteilungen*, 77: 492–509

— 1977. 'Notes on the Accidence of Rushworth 2', *Neuphilologische Mitteilungen*, 78: 300–308

— 1979a. 'Lindisfarne and Rushworth One', *Notes and Queries*, 224: 194–98

— 1979b. 'The Rare Words of Rushworth One', *Notes and Queries*, 224: 495–98

Ross, A. S. C., and Ann Squires. 1980. 'The Multiple, Altered and Alternative Glosses of the Lindisfarne and the Durham Ritual', *Notes and Queries*, 225: 489–95

Rushforth, Rebecca. 2012. 'English Caroline Minuscule' in Gameson (2012), pp. 197–210

Samuels, M. L. 1952. 'The Study of Old English Phonology', *Transactions of the Philological Society*, 51: 15–47

Schabram, Hans. 1965. *Superbia. Studien zum altenglischen Wortschatz* (München: Wilhelm Fink)

Scheck, Thomas P. (trans.) 2008. *St. Jerome: Commentary on Matthew* (Washington D.C.: Catholic University of America Press)

Schreiber, Carolin. 2003. *King Alfred's Old English Translation of Pope Gregory the Great's* Regula pastoralis *and its Cultural Context: A Study and Partial Edition According to All Surviving Manuscripts Based on Cambridge, Corpus Christi College 12* (Frankfurt am Main: Peter Lang)

Schulte, Ernst. 1903. *Untersuchung der Beziehung der altenglischen Matthäusglosse in Rushworth-Manuskript zu lateinischen Text der Handschrift* (Bonn: Carl Georgi)

— 1904. *Glossar zu Farmans Anteil an der Rushworth-Glosse (Rushworth I)* (Bonn: Carl Georgi)

Scragg, D. G. 1970. 'Initial *h* in Old English', *Anglia*, 88: 165–96

— (ed.) 1992. *The Vercelli Homilies and Related Texts*, EETS o.s. 300. (Oxford: Oxford University Press)

— 2012. 'Sin and Laughter in Late Anglo-Saxon England: The Case of Old English *(h)leahtor*', in *Saints and Scholars: New Perspectives on Anglo-Saxon Literature and Culture in Honour of Hugh Magennis*, ed. by Stuart McWilliams (Cambridge: D. S. Brewer), pp. 213–23

Sievers, Eduard. 1892. *Tatian. Lateinisch und altdeutsch mit ausführlichem Glossar* (Münster: Paderborn)

Sievers, Eduard, ed. and trans. by Albert S. Cook. 1903. *An Old English Grammar*, 3rd edn (Boston: Ginn and Company)

Sisam, Kenneth. 1953. 'Humfrey Wanley', in his *Studies in the History of Old English Literature* (Oxford: Clarendon Press), pp. 259–277

Skeat, Walter W. (ed.) 1871–87. *The Holy Gospels in Anglo-Saxon, Northumbrian, and Old Mercian Versions, Synoptically Arranged, with Collations Exhibiting All the Readings of All the MSS.; together with the Early Latin Version as Contained in the Lindisfarne MS., Collated with the Latin Version in the Rushworth MS.* (Cambridge: The University Press; repr. in two volumes, Darmstadt: Wissenschaftliche Buchgesellschaft,

1970; originally published Mark in 1871, Luke in 1874, John in 1878, Matthew in 1887)

— (ed.) 1881–1900. *Ælfric's Lives of Saints*, EETS o.s. 76, 82, 94, 114 (London: Trübner; repr. in 2 vols, London: Oxford University Press, 1966)

Smith, A. H. (ed.) 1933. *Three Northumbrian Poems* (London: Methuen; revised version with a new bibliography by M. J. Swanton, Exeter: University of Exeter Press, 1978)

— 1956. *English Place-Name Elements*, 2 vols, English Place-Name Society 25–26 (Cambridge: Cambridge University Press)

Smith, Jeremy. 1996. *An Historical Study of English: Function, Form and Change* (London: Routledge)

Sparks, Nicholas A. 2013. 'An Insular Fragment of Bede's *Historia ecclesiastica*', *Anglo-Saxon England*, 42: 27–50

Sprockel, C. 1965–73. *The Language of the Parker Chronicle*, 2 vols (Hague: M. Nijhof)

Squires, Ann. (ed.) 1988. *The Old English Physiologus*, Durham Medieval Texts 5 (Durham: Durham Medieval Texts)

Stanley, E. G. 1952–53. 'The Chronology of *R*-Metathesis in Old English', *English and Germanic Studies*, 5: 103–15

— 1969. 'Spellings of the *Waldend* Group', in *Studies in Language, Literature, and Culture of the Middle Ages and Later*, ed. by E. Bagby Atwood and Archibald A. Hill (Austin: University of Texas), pp. 38–69

— 1998. 'The Sources of Junius's Learning as Revealed in the Junius Manuscripts in the Bodleian Library', in *Franciscus Junius F.F. and His Circle*, ed. by Rolf H, Bremmer Jr (Amsterdam: Rodopi), pp. 159–76

Stanton, Robert. 2002. *The Culture of Translation in Anglo-Saxon England* (Cambridge: D. S. Brewer)

Stevenson, J., and G. Waring. 1854–65. *The Lindisfarne and Rushworth Gospels: Now First Printed from the Original Manuscripts in the British Museum and the Bodleian Library*, 4 vols, Publications of Surtees Society nos. 28, 39, 43, 48 (Durham: George Andrews)

Stokes, Peter A. 2014. *English Vernacular Minuscule from Æthelred to Cnut, circa 990 – circa 1035* (Cambridge: D. S. Brewer)

Sundaram, Mark S. 2003. 'The Conceptualisation of Futurity in Old English', (unpublished Ph.D. dissertation, University of Toronto)

Svensson, Jacob V. 1883. *Om Språket i den förra (Merciska) delen af Rushworth-Handskriften: I. Ljudlära* (Göteborg: D. F. Bonniers Boktryckeri)

Tamoto, Kenichi. 2010. 'Palaeographical Facts and Conjectures about the Rushworth Gospels (Oxford, Bodleian Library, MS Auct. D. 2. 19', in *Multiple Perspectives on English Philology and History of Linguistics*, ed. by Tetsuji Oda and Hiroyuki Eto (Frankfurt am Main: Peter Lang), pp. 28–53

— (ed.) 2013. *The Macregol Gospels or The Rushworth Gospels: Edition of the Latin text with the Old English Interlinear Gloss Transcribed from Oxford Bodleian Library, MS Auctarium D. 2. 19* (Amsterdam: John Benjamins)

Terasawa, Jun. 2010. 'The Weak Man in Old English Poetry', *JEGP*, 109: 22–32

Tilghman, Benjamin C. 2011. 'Writing in Tongues: Mixed Scripts and Style in Insular Art', in *Insular & Anglo-Saxon Art and Thought in the Early Medieval Period*, ed. by Colum Hourihane (University Park, PA: Pennsylvania State University Press), pp. 93–108

Timmer, B. J. 1957. 'Junius' Stay in Friesland', *Neophilologus*, 41: 141–44

Tite, Colin G. 1997. 'Sir Robert Cotton, Sir Thomas Tempest and an Anglo-Saxon Gospel Book: A Cottonian paper in the Harleian library', in *Books and Collectors 1200–1700: Essays presented to Andrew Watson*, ed. by Colin G. Tite and James P. Carley (London: The British Library), pp. 429–39

Toon, T. E. 1992 'Old English Dialects', in *The Cambridge History of the English Language*, vol. 1: The Beginning to 1066, ed. by Richard M. Hogg (Cambridge: Cambridge University Press), pp. 409–51

Tupper, Frederick, Jr. (ed.) 1910. *The Riddles of the Exeter Book* (Boston: Ginn and Company)

van Romburgh, Sophie. 2001. 'Why Francis Junius (1591–1677) Became an Anglo-Saxonist, or, the Study of Old English for the Elevation of Dutch' in *Appropriating the Middle Ages Scholarship, Politics, Fraud*, ed. by Tom Shippey with Martin Arnold (Cambridge: D. S. Brewer), pp. 5–36

— (ed.) 2004 *'For my worthy freind [sic] Mr Franciscus Junius': An Edition of the Complete Correspondence of Francis Junius F.F. (1591–1677)*, 2 vols (Leiden: Brill)

Vleeskruyer, R. (ed.) 1953. *The Life of St. Chad: An Old English Homily* (Amsterdam: North-Holland Pub. Co.)

Waite, G. G. 1984. 'The Vocabulary of the Old English Version of Bede's Historia Ecclesiastica', 2 vols (Unpublished Ph.D. Thesis, University of Toronto)

Watson, Andrew G. 1966. *The Library of Sir Simonds D'Ewes* (London: Trustees of the British Museum)

— 1984. *Catalogue of Dated and Datable Manuscripts c. 435–1600 in Oxford Libraries* (Oxford: Clarendon Press)

Weber, R, R. Gryson et al. (eds) 2007. *Biblia Sacra iuxta Vulgatam versionem*, 5th edn (Stuttgart: Deutsche Bibelgesellschaft)

Wenisch, F. 1979. *Spezifisch anglisches Wortgut in der nordumbrischen interlinear Glossierungen des Lukasevangeliums*, Anglistische Forschungen 132 (Heidelberg: C. Winter)

Wiley, R. A. 1979. 'Anglo-Saxon Kemble: The Life and Works of John Mitchell Kemble 1807–1857, Philologist, Historian, Archaeologist', *Anglo-Saxon Studies in Archaeology and History*, 1: 165–273

Williamson, Craig. (ed.) 1977. *The Old English Riddles of the Exeter Book.* (Chapel Hill: University of North Carolina Press)

Wordsworth, John, and H. I. White. (eds) 1889–98. *Nouum testamentum domini nostri Iesu Christi Latine: secundum editionem Sancti Hieronymi. Pars Prior: Quattuor Euangelia* (Oxford: Clarendon Press)

Wright, C. E. 1972. *Fontes Harleiani: A Study of the Sources of the Harleian Collection of Manuscripts Preserved in the Department of Manuscripts in the British Museum* (London: British Museum)

Yamamoto, Tomonori. 2013. 'The Semantic and Syntactic Study of Periphrastic "Modal Verb + Infinitive" Constructions in OE: Comparing the Versions of the OE Gospels', in *Phases of the History of English: Selection of Papers Read at SHELL 2012*, Studies in English Medieval Language and Literature 42, ed. by Michio Hosaka, Michiko Ogura, Hironori Suzuki and Akinobu Tani (Frankfurt am Main: Peter Lang), pp. 127–39

Young, Karl. 1910. 'Observations on the Origin of the Mediæval Passion-Play', *PMLA*, 25: 309–54

— 1933. *The Drama of the Medieval Church*, 2 vols (Oxford: Clarendon Press)

Zupitza, Julius. 2003. *Aelfrics Grammatik und Glossar: Text und Varianten*, 4th edn with an introduction by Helmut Gneuss (Hildesheim: Weidmann)

Appendices

The following appendices list Farman's (Appendix I, designated 'R^{Fa}' in the textual apparatus of the present edition) and possibly another Anglo-Saxon corrector's (Appendix II, 'R^{c}') corrections to the Latin text of the Rushworth Gospels (R), as discussed in Introduction III.1.3.2 and relevant notes in the Commentary. When these corrections differ from the reading adopted by WW, the manuscripts that share the corrected reading are noted by using WW's sigla (special ligatures used in it are represented by simplified forms in brackets, e.g., (EP) for the Echternach Gospels). The Gospels portions of WW are now in the public domain and freely available online. For details of relevant Vulgate manuscripts, see also Houghton (2016).

Appendix 1: Latin corrections attributable to Farman's hand

	Verse (fol.)	**R**	**R^{Fa}**	**WW (or MSS agreeing with R^{Fa})**
1	2:10 (3v, 8)	uidens	uidentes	uidentes
2	2:16 (4r, 5)	regionibus	+ ł finibus	finibus
3	2:23 (4r, 20)	galileae	+ et	+ et
4	4:6 (5v, 5)	scriptum	+ (est)	+ est
5	5:15 (7r, 5)	neque	+ homines	WW=R* [R^{Fa} *unique*]
6	5:22 (7v, 3)	patri	fratri	fratri
7	5:23 (7v, 5)	tum	tuum	tuum
8	6:4 (9r, 2)	tua	+ in abscondito	+ in abscondito
9	6:6 (9r, 8)	tuum	+ et pater tuus qui uidet	+ et pater tuus qui uidet
10	6:24 (9v, 21)	alterum	+ diligit aut unu(m) sustinebit et alterum	+ diliget [diligit FLZ*] aut unum sustinebit et alterum
11	7:4 (10v, 5)	tuo	+ frat(er) sine eiciam festucam de oculo tuo	+ fratri tuo sine eiciam festucam de oculo tuo
12	7:25 (11v, 6)	su	sup(er)	supra [super D(EP)JLQ]
13	8:3 (11v, 18)	extendens	et extendens	et extendens
14	9:28 (14v, 7)	facere	+ uos	+ uobis [+ uos *unique*]

	Verse (fol.)	R	R^{Fa}	**WW (or MSS agreeing with R^{Fa})**
15	10:14 (15v, 11)	uestris	+ [ ]n testimonio(m) [ ]llorum	WW=R* [+ in testimonium eorum ABFHMQXY; illorum *unique*]
16	10:15 (15v, 12)	illi	illa	WW=R* [R^{Fa} *unique*]
17	11:18 (17v, 10)	dicunt	+ ecce	WW=R* [R^{Fa} *unique*]
18	11:21 (17v, 17)	et	+ ue tibi	(*om.* et) + uae tibi
19	11:30 (18r, 15)	leue	+ (est)	+ est
20	12:31 (19v, 5)	hominibus	+ sp(iritu)s blasfemia non dimittetur	+ spiritus autem blasphemia non remittetur [dimittetur *unique*]
21	12:34 (19v, 12)	mali	+ estis	WW=R* [R^{Fa} *unique*]
22	13:2 (20v, 6)	et[1]	ad	ad
23	13:3 (20v, 9)	paruulis	parbolis	parabolis
24	13:17 (21r, 14)	uiderunt	+ et audir[ ] que audi[ ] et n(on) audi[ ]	et audire quae auditis et non audierunt
25	13:35 (22r, 15)	absconsa	qui absconsa erant	abscondita [R^{Fa} *unique*]
26	13:51 (23r, 2)	dicunt	+ ei	+ ei
27	14:1 (23r, 17)	tetracha	tetrarcha	tetrarcha
28	14:5 (23v, 2)	profetam	+ eum	+ eum
29	14:16 (24r, 1)	necessire	+ adeuntes	necesse ire [R^{Fa} *unique*]
30	14:27 (24r, 19)	continuo quae	et continuo quae	statimque [R^{Fa} *unique*]
31	14:28 (24r, 22)	dixit	et dixit	dixit [R^{Fa} *unique*]
32	14:29 (24v, 2)	super	+ aquam	+ aquam
33	14:30 (24v, 2)	uentum	+ ualidu(m)	+ ualidum
34	16:2 (26r, 19)	respondens ait	respondens illis ait	respondens ait eis [illis E]
35	16:2 (26r, 20)	erit	+ quia rubicundus (est) celum	rubicundum est enim caelum [quia *unique*]

	Verse (fol.)	R	R^{Fa}	WW (or MSS agreeing with R^{Fa})
36	16:10 (26v, 12)	sumpsistis	+ et de uii panes iiii milia hominum ⁊ q(u̲o)t sporte accipistis	neque septem panum quattuor milia hominum et quot sportas sumsistis [R^{Fa} *unique*]
37	16:24 (27r, 19)	sequar	sequatur	sequatur
38	17:2 (27v, 11)	sunt	+ alba	+ alba
39	17:3 (27v, 12)	et[1]	+ ecce	+ ecce
40	17:4 (27v, 14)	faciamus	+ hic	+ hic
41	17:5 (27v, 17)	et	+ ecce	ecce
42	17:6 (27v, 19)	ciciderunt	ceciderunt	ceciderunt
43	17:18 (28r, 17)	puer	+ de illa ma[ ]	+ ex illa hora [R^{Fa} *unique*]
44	17:26 (28v, 11)	illi	+ iesus	+ iesus
45	18:2 (28v, 17)	cælorum	+ et ad uocans [ ]s paruulos [ ]tatuit in medio eorum	et aduocans iesus paruulum statuit eum in medio eorum
46	18:3 (28v, 18)	intrabis	intrabitis	non intrabitis
47	18:4 (28v, 20)	hic	+ est	+ est
48	18:6 (29r, 1)	expedit	+ ei	+ ei
49	18:9 (29r, 10)	bonum est tibi unum oculum habentem in uitam intrare	bonum est tibi cum unum oculum habentem in uitam intrare	bonum tibi est uno oculum in uitam intrare [cum unum oculum Z*; cum uno oculo E^c(EP)JK(MT)OVXZ^c]
50	18:10 (29r, 14)	oculi	angeli	angeli
51	18:10 (29r, 14)	eorum	+ in celis	+ in caelis
52	18:10 (29r, 15)	uestri	mei	mei
53	18:14 (29r, 22)	uestrum	meum	WW=R* [R^{Fa} *unique*]
54	19:1 (30v, 2)	iodanen	iordanen	iordanen
55	19:9 (30v, 17)	diserit	dimiserit	dimiserit

	Verse (fol.)	R	R^{Fa}	WW (or MSS agreeing with R^{Fa})
56	19:26 (31v, 13)	deum	+ autem	+ autem
57	19:29 (31v, 21)	reliquerit	relinquerit	reliquit [R^{Fa} *unique*]
58	20:06 (32r, 14)	uidit	inuenit	inuenit
59	20:21 (33r, 1)	illi	+ dic	+ dic
60	20:21 (33r, 2)	filii	+ mei	+ mei
61	20:21 (33r, 2)	et^2	ad	ad
62	20:23 (33r, 7)	dexteram	+ meam	+ meam
63	20:24 (33r, 10)	dubus	duobus	duobus
64	21:1 (33v, 7)	adpropinquassent	+ hierosolimis ⁊ uenissent	+ hierosolymis et uenissent
65	21:1 (33v, 8)	misit	+ duos	+ duos
66	21:2 (33v, 9)	dicens	+ illis	+ eis [R^{Fa} *unique*]
67	21:4 (33v, 14)	adinplere	adinpleretur	impleretur
68	21:5 (33v, 16)	pullum	+ filium	+ filium
69	21:21 (34v, 7)	iesus	+ ait illis	+ ait eis [R^{Fa} *unique*]
70	21:25 (34v, 19)	e	de	WW=R* [de EH*W(cel.)X*]
71	21:26 (34v, 22)	sunt	sicut	sicut
72	21:28 (35r, 4)	uade	+ hodie	+ hodie
73	21:28 (35r, 5)	uiam	uineam	uinea
74	21:31 (35r, 9)	dicunt	+ ei	WW=R* [+ ei BDE(EP^{mg})KM (MT)V]
75	21:35 (35r, 22)	cederunt	ceciderunt	ceciderunt [cederunt Y]
76	21:39 (35v, 7)	adpraeso	adpraehenso eo	adprehensum
77	21:45 (35v, 18)	uenissent	audissent	audissent
78	21:46 (35v, 20)	uolentes	querentes	quaerentes
79	22:6 (36r, 10)	adflictos	adfectos	adfectos

	Verse (fol.)	R	R^{Fa}	WW (or MSS agreeing with R^{Fa})
80	22:9 (36r, 15)	et[1]	ad	ad
81	22:13 (36r, 22)	dixit	+ rex	+ rex
82	22:14 (36v, 3)	enim	+ sunt	autem sunt
83	22:14 (36v, 3)	uoci	uocati	uocati
84	22:24 (36v, 20)	hens	habens	habens
85	22:24 (36v, 21)	sen	semen	semen
86	22:35 (37r, 16)	temptans	+ eum	temptans eum
87	22:46 (37v, 8)	quis fuerat	quisquam fuerat	fuit quisquam
88	23:2 (37v, 11)	sedent	sederunt	sederunt
89	23:2 (37v, 12)	farissæi	+ dicentes	WW=R* (pharisaei) [R^{Fa} *unique*]
90	23:8 (38r, 1)	fratres	+ estis	+ estis
91	23:9 (38r, 2)	nolite	+ uocare	+ uobis
92	23:9 (38r, 2)	est autem	est enim	enim est
93	23:24 (38v, 11)	culicem exspuentes	+ et	excolantes culicem [R^{Fa} *unique*]
94	24:1 (39v, 3)	egressus	+ iesus	+ iesus
95	24:3 (39v, 10)	saeci	saeculi	saeculi
96	24:38 (41r, 4)	bibentes	+ et nubentes	+ nubentes [et DLOQ]
97	24:48 (41r, 22)	ille seruus	ille seruus male	malus seruus ille [male *unique*]
98	25:20 (42r, 16)	tradidisti mihi	+ ecce	mihi tradidisti et ecce [et *om.* DEHΘLKQT VWX*Z]
99	25:31 (42r, 18)	sedet	sedebit	sedebit
100	26:6 (43v, 13)	esset	+ iesus	+ iesus
101	26:34 (44v, 19)	iesus	+ amen dico tibi	+ amen dico tibi
102	26:35 (44v, 21)	oportuerit	+ me	+ me

	Verse (fol.)	R	R^{Fa}	WW (or MSS agreeing with R^{Fa})
103	26:39 (45r, 7)	pater	+ mi	WW=R* [pater mi B(EP)HJK (MT)OQVX^{c}Z]
104	26:51 (45v, 9)	gladium	+ suum	+ suum
105	26:53 (45v, 14)	exibit	exibebit	exhibebit
106	26:53 (45v, 14)	mihi	+ modo	+ modo
107	26:56 (45v, 22)	eius	omnes	omnes
108	26:64 (46r, 17)	hominis	+ sedentem	+ sedentem
109	26.72. (46v, 10)	dicens	quia	quia
110	27:5 (47r, 5)	argenteis	+ in	+ in
111	27:7 (47r, 9)	agrum	+ figuli	+ figuli
112	27:31 (48r, 12)	exuerunt	+ eum	+ eum
113	27:44 (48v, 15)	inproperant	inproperabant	inproperabant
114	27:50 (49r, 6)	exclans	exclamans	clamans
115	28:7 (50r, 11)	dixi	predixi	praedixi
116	Mk1:5 (52v, 10)	pecca	peccata	peccata
117	Mk1:8 (52v, 17)	babtizabit	+ uos in sp(irit)u s(an)c(t)o	uos spiritu sancto [uos + in DE(EP^{mg})G (MT)OQ]
118	Mk1:10 (53r, 1)	spiritum	+ s(an)c(tu)m	WW=R* [+ sanctum H^{c}ΘOZ]
119	Mk1:10 (53r, 2)	discendentem	descendentem	Descendentem
120	Mk1:14 (53r, 8)	Postquam	+ autem	+ autem
121	Mk1:16 (53r, 14)	mittens	mittentens	mittentes
122	Mk1:17 (53r, 15)	dixit	+ eis	+ eis
123	Mk1:19 (53r, 19)	in	inde	inde
124	?Mk1:24 (53v, 10)	sis	es	WW=R* [AB(EP*)HOXY]
125	Mk1:43 (54r, 29)	est	+ ei	ei (*om.* est)

	Verse (fol.)	R	R^{Fa}	WW (or MSS agreeing with R^{Fa})
126	Mk2:5 (54v, 14)	peccata	+ tua	WW=R* [+ tua BDEGLO]
127	Mk2:13 (55r, 7)	rursus	rursum	WW=R* [rursum G]
128	Mk2:14 (55r, 9)	telonum	theloneum	teloneum [theloneum BCGWX]

Appendix 2: Latin corrections in Matthew Passion by another A-S hand

	Verse (fol.)	R	R^c	WW (or MSS agreeing with R^c)
1	26:1 (43v, 7)	dixit	+ iesus discipulis suis	+ discipulis suis
2	26:5 (43v, 12)	enim	+ ł autem	autem
3	26:7 (43v, 16)	infudit	effudit	effudit
4	26:7 (43v, 16)	recumbente ipso	recumbentis	recumbentis
5	26:8 (43v, 17)	dicipuli	discipuli	discipuli
6	26:8 (43v, 18)	per haec	perdictio haec	perditio haec
7	26:10 (43v, 20)	estis	+ huic	WW=R* [huic $BEH^c\Theta K(MT)O^{gl}$ VWZ^3]
8	26:10 (43v, 20)	mulieri	+ opus enim	+ opus [enim VZ^3]
9	26:19 (44r, 14)	praecipit	+ ł constituit	constituit
10	26:24 (44r, 21)	eo	illo	illo
11	26:24 (44v, 1)	non nasci ille homo	ei si natus non fuisset homo ille	ei si natus non fuisset homo ille
12	26:25 (44v, 2)	eum	+ dixit	+ dixit
13	26:26 (44v, 3)	cannantibus	cænnantibus	cennantibus
14	26:30 (44v, 13)	olieti	olivueti	olivueti
15	26:31 (44v, 13)	omnes	omnis	omnes [R^c unique]
16	26:32 (44v, 16)	praecidam	praecedam	praecedam
17	26:36 (45r, 1)	ait	et dixit	et dixit
18	26:39 (45r, 8)	sed tamen	ueruntamen	uerumtamen

	Verse (fol.)	R	R^{c}	WW (or MSS agreeing with R^{c})
19	?26:40 (45r, 10)	posuisti	potuisti	posuistis [potuisti Q]
20	26:43 (45r, 16)	ocli	oculi	oculi
21	26:51 (45v, 9)	eximit	exemit	exemit
22	26:52 (45v, 12)	omnes	omnis	omnes [omnis JO]
23	26:52 (45v, 13)	in gaudio	gladio	gladio
24	26:53 (45v, 15)	xii	+ milia	duodecim [milia BJOXZ]
25	26:62 (46r, 11)	exsurgens	et exsurgens	et surgens
26	26:64 (46r, 18)	uirtutis	+ dei	WW=R* [+ dei FT, from Lk?]
27	26:67 (46v, 1)	colophis	colaphis	colaphis
28	26:69 (46v, 5)	dicens	+ et	+ et
29	27:6 (47r, 8)	mitti	mittere	mittere
30	27:6 (47r, 8)	corban	corbanan	corbanan
31	27:9 (47r, 15)	adpraetiauerunt	+ a	+ a
32	27:11 (47r, 18)	praesis	+ dicens	+ dicens
33	27:19 (47v, 9)	eo	eum	illo
34	27:19 (47v, 11)	illum	illo	eo
35	27:23 (47v, 18)	mali	male	mali [male E*H*M*]
36	27:25 (48r, 1)	populus	+ dicens	+ dixit [dicens *unique*]
37	27:29 (48r, 9)	dexteram	+ eius	+ eius
38	27:31 (48r, 12)	calamidem	clamidem	clamyde
39	27:37 (48v, 1)	hæc	hic	*om.*
40	27:52 (49r, 11)	dormientium	qui dormierunt	qui dormierant [dormierunt ELO^{gl}W*]
41	27:55 (49r, 19)	illi	ei	ei
42	27:60 (49v, 6)	et	ab	ad [ab *unique*]

	Verse (fol.)	R	R[c]	WW (or MSS agreeing with R[c])
43	27:65 (49v, 15)	dicent	dicant	dicant
44	27:65 (49v, 16)	milites	custodia	custodiam [custodia *unique*]
45	27:66 (49v, 19)	et discessserunt	cum custodibus	cum custodibus

www.ingramcontent.com/pod-product-compliance
Lightning Source LLC
LaVergne TN
LVHW050954080826
845145LV00006B/1494

* 9 7 8 1 9 1 1 6 9 4 1 5 1 *